LIFT

TAKE YOUR STUDYING TO THE NEXT LEVEL.

This book comes with 1-year digital access to the
Examples & Explanations for this course.

Step 1: Go to **www.CasebookConnect.com/LIFT** and redeem your access code to get started.

Access Code:

Step 2: Go to your BOOKSHELF and select your online *Examples & Explanations* to start reading, highlighting, and taking notes in the margins of your e-book.

Step 3: Select the STUDY tab in your toolbar to access the questions from your book in interactive format, designed to give you extra practice and help you master the course material.

Is this a used casebook? Access code already scratched off?

You can purchase the online *Examples & Explanations* and still access all of the powerful tools listed above. Please visit CasebookConnect.com/Catalog to learn more about Connected Study Aids.

PLEASE NOTE: Each access code provides 12 month access and can only be used once. This code will also expire one year after the discontinuation of the corresponding print title and must be redeemed before then. CCH reserves the right to discontinue this program at any time for any business reason. For further details, please see the Casebook Connect End User Agreement.

PIN: 9111149618

02488

D0023212

PROBLEMS AND MATERIALS ON PAYMENT LAW

ASPEN CASEBOOK SERIES

PROBLEMS AND MATERIALS ON PAYMENT LAW

TENTH EDITION

DOUGLAS J. WHALEY
PROFESSOR EMERITUS
MORITZ COLLEGE OF LAW
THE OHIO STATE UNIVERSITY

STEPHEN M. MCJOHN
PROFESSOR OF LAW
SUFFOLK UNIVERSITY LAW SCHOOL

 Wolters Kluwer

Published by Wolters Kluwer in New York.

Wolters Kluwer serves customers worldwide with CCH, Aspen Publishers, and Kluwer Law International products. (www.wolterskluwerlb.com)

To contact Customer Service, e-mail customer.service@wolterskluwer.com, call 1-800-234-1660, fax 1-800-901-9075, or mail correspondence to:

Wolters Kluwer
Attn: Order Department
PO Box 990
Frederick, MD 21705

Printed in the United States of America.

2 3 4 5 6 7 8 9 0

ISBN 978-1-4548-6332-8

Library of Congress Cataloging-in-Publication Data

Whaley, Douglas J., author.
  Problems and materials on payment law / Douglas J. Whaley, Professor Emeritus, Moritz College of Law, The Ohio State University; Stephen M. McJohn, Professor of Law, Suffolk University Law School. — Tenth edition.
    pages cm — (Aspen casebook series)
  ISBN 978-1-4548-6332-8
1. Negotiable instruments — United States. 2. Payment — United States. I. McJohn, Stephen M., 1959- author. II. Title.
  KF957.W47 2016
  346.73'096 — dc23
                                                                                    2015033640

About Wolters Kluwer Law & Business

Wolters Kluwer Law & Business is a leading global provider of intelligent information and digital solutions for legal and business professionals in key specialty areas, and respected educational resources for professors and law students. Wolters Kluwer Law & Business connects legal and business professionals as well as those in the education market with timely, specialized authoritative content and information-enabled solutions to support success through productivity, accuracy and mobility.

Serving customers worldwide, Wolters Kluwer Law & Business products include those under the Aspen Publishers, CCH, Kluwer Law International, Loislaw, ftwilliam.com and MediRegs family of products.

CCH products have been a trusted resource since 1913, and are highly regarded resources for legal, securities, antitrust and trade regulation, government contracting, banking, pension, payroll, employment and labor, and healthcare reimbursement and compliance professionals.

Aspen Publishers products provide essential information to attorneys, business professionals and law students. Written by preeminent authorities, the product line offers analytical and practical information in a range of specialty practice areas from securities law and intellectual property to mergers and acquisitions and pension/benefits. Aspen's trusted legal education resources provide professors and students with high-quality, up-to-date and effective resources for successful instruction and study in all areas of the law.

Kluwer Law International products provide the global business community with reliable international legal information in English. Legal practitioners, corporate counsel and business executives around the world rely on Kluwer Law journals, looseleafs, books, and electronic products for comprehensive information in many areas of international legal practice.

Loislaw is a comprehensive online legal research product providing legal content to law firm practitioners of various specializations. Loislaw provides attorneys with the ability to quickly and efficiently find the necessary legal information they need, when and where they need it, by facilitating access to primary law as well as state-specific law, records, forms and treatises.

ftwilliam.com offers employee benefits professionals the highest quality plan documents (retirement, welfare and non-qualified) and government forms (5500/PBGC, 1099 and IRS) software at highly competitive prices.

MediRegs products provide integrated health care compliance content and software solutions for professionals in healthcare, higher education and life sciences, including professionals in accounting, law and consulting.

Wolters Kluwer Law & Business, a division of Wolters Kluwer, is headquartered in New York. Wolters Kluwer is a market-leading global information services company focused on professionals.

For My Parents, Robert and Lenore Whaley

DJW

For Lorie and Ian

SMM

SUMMARY OF CONTENTS

Contents

In many areas, paper-based payment systems are giving way to electronic transfers of funds. In the future, it may be that electronic payment will be the norm, and paper transfers increasingly rare, although at present, promissory notes and checks still play important roles in commercial transactions. Given that, it makes little sense to call casebooks on point "Negotiable Instruments Law" or "Commercial Paper" and a number of recent books have opted for a title such as "Payment and Credit Systems Law." We have chosen to call this work "Problems and Materials on Payment Law." The omission of a reference to "credit" is deliberate. Of course, promissory notes and credit cards are used to acquire credit (as are checks when the drawer is attempting to ride the float period during their collection), but the law covered by the casebooks doesn't focus on the credit function. If it did, it would have to cover all the credit issues better left to a course in consumer law (qualifying for credit, granting credit, the disclosing of credit information, etc.). Instead, even with promissory notes and credit cards, the legal issues we are concerned with deal with payment problems: Who owes what to whom? Consequently, the umbrella term "payment law" seems to us the best shorthand reference to our subject.

This book explores the law of payment primarily through focusing on a series of Problems designed to encourage the student to concentrate on the exact statutory language in the Uniform Commercial Code, the Electronic Fund Transfer Act, and the Expedited Funds Availability Act. While we have included illustrative cases to demonstrate the reactions of the courts to these issues, we have used only those we felt were very important; most UCC court decisions are too imposing, either factually or legally, to make good pedagogical tools.

Unfortunately, students reared on the case method sometimes have trouble concentrating on Problem after Problem. Such an attitude here can be academically fatal. As a guide to the degree of concentration required, we have used a hierarchy of signals. When the Problem states "Read §3-406," we mean "Put down this book, pick up the Uniform Commercial Code, and study §3-406 carefully." When the instruction is "See §3-406," the reader need look at the cited section only if unsure of the answer. "Cf. §3-406," or simply "§3-406," is a lesser reference included as a guide for the curious.

We have heard it said that law students cannot follow legal Problems having more than two characters. If true, payment law would be unteachable, as its issues almost always involve three or more parties. To help the reader keep them straight, we have given the characters in our Problems distinctive names and, we hope, have created interesting factual patterns, all designed to keep the mind alive.

We have edited the footnotes out of most cases; the ones that remain have been stripped of their original numbering and have been consecutively numbered with our own footnotes. Unless clearly indicated otherwise, all footnotes in the cases are the court's own. We have also taken the liberty to change most statutory citations in cases to their simple Uniform Commercial Code form.

Whaley wishes to acknowledge the debt he owes to the late Professor R. Bruce Townsend, formerly of the faculty of the Indiana University, Indianapolis Law School, one of the drafters of the Uniform Commercial Code and Whaley's mentor in his early days of teaching this subject. Professor John J. Slain, New York University School of Law, also deserves thanks for helping Whaley organize his initial exploration of the world of investment securities. As always, Whaley is indebted to the fine people at Aspen Publishers, who have taken good care of him through seven casebooks. McJohn adds his thanks to our friends at Aspen and his colleagues at Suffolk. Finally, our grateful thanks go to our many students, who through the years have taught us as much about the law as we taught them.

Douglas J. Whaley
Stephen M. McJohn

December 2015

PROBLEMS AND MATERIALS
ON PAYMENT LAW

CHAPTER 1

INTRODUCTION TO THE UNIFORM COMMERCIAL CODE AND PAYMENT LAW

I. *A BIT OF HISTORY*

During medieval times, commercial law varied widely from place to place throughout the trading world, and the statutes of the various countries either didn't address the relevant issues that traders cared about or reached results that were at odds with what those traders thought either realistic or fair. During much of English history, for example, the common law courts were lumbered by such arcane rules of procedure that justice was either unavailable or so slow as to come far too late.

To solve this dilemma the traders developed their own legal system, the so-called law merchant (or "lex mercatoria" in Latin). By agreement they created their own courts, chose their own judges, and developed those mercantile understandings that made trade efficient and fair (in their own eyes). At some point the real courts became aware that they were being bypassed and began to incorporate the law merchant into their own rules. During the time of the American Revolution the English court system had as its Chief Justice the great jurist Lord Mansfield. He believed in pragmatism in his courtroom, and during his tenure the law merchant was given much influence in English decisions. Lord Mansfield would call merchants into court to testify as to what mercantile understandings were about the matter before the court, and was not above putting merchants on the jury and then asking them questions as cases proceeded. Mansfield was the father of many of the concepts we will study in this course, most particularly the "holder in due course" doctrine (Chapter 4).

LORD MANSFIELD.

In 1881, the British Parliament adopted the Negotiable Instruments Act to govern that portion of commercial law that we will study in this course: the law of checks (more formally called "drafts" or "bills of exchange") and promissory notes. Originating in India, that statute is still in effect in the United Kingdom, and was the statutory forerunner of those that followed in the United States, where the first statute that gained wide popularity by being enacted in all states was called simply the Negotiable Instruments Law.

II. THE CREATION OF THE UNIFORM COMMERCIAL CODE

Starting in the 1940s, two private bodies, the American Law Institute (ALI) and the National Conference of Commissioners on Uniform State Law (NCCUSL), decided it was time to modernize the state laws on commercial matters. Over the coming years they gathered together the greatest commercial experts in the country to draft a new giant statute that would supersede existing ones for the areas that were covered. Chief draftsman was Professor Karl N. Llewellyn, the leading voice for the "legal realism" school of jurisprudence (very much in Lord Mansfield's tradition), and he led a drafting team that by 1952 produced the first version of what was called the "Uniform Commercial Code."

Karl Llewellyn

The Uniform Commercial Code went through various versions from that day to this. The UCC (or, in this course, simply "the Code") is divided into "Articles" covering different aspects of commercial law. The chief Articles we will study are Article 3 (Negotiable Instruments), Article 4 (Bank Deposits and Collections), Article 4A (Fund Transfers), and Article 8 (Investment Securities), though references will be made to other parts of the Code, particularly Article 1, which deals with general provisions applicable throughout the rest of the giant statute.

It is important to appreciate that the UCC is not federal law. Instead, the two drafting bodies submitted it for adoption to the states, and it had to be individually enacted into law state by state. The idea was that if commercial law were uniform throughout the country, commerce would be more certain and efficient (the same goals animating the law merchant centuries before). Most states did adopt the Code with few changes (though some have sneaked in through the years, and you, budding lawyer, should always check your own state's enactment to make sure some evil alteration hasn't muddled what you've learned in this course). By the end of the last quarter of the twentieth century, all states and most U.S. territories had adopted the UCC completely (though Louisiana, with its French law, Napoleonic Code, tradition did not enact Article 2 on the Sale of Goods, but has its own civil law version thereof).

III. FEDERAL LAW

The federal government, of course, has a great interest in commercial matters, and thus has enacted a wide number of statutes that exist alongside the states' UCC mandates. Federal law supersedes inconsistent state laws, and in this book we will explore these collisions as they occur. Particularly for check collection is the Federal Reserve involved, but, as we'll see, happily the "Fed" (as it's known) has arranged things so that federal and state laws by and large are the same in this area. Importantly, credit card and debit card law is almost entirely regulated by federal statutes and regulations, which we will explore in a later chapter.

IV. ARTICLE 1 OF THE CODE

The first Article of the UCC covers "General Provisions," and it applies to all UCC matters unless a more specific section elsewhere in the Code says otherwise. Article 1's most recent rewrite occurred in 2001, and that version, now adopted by most of the states, is the one referred to in this book.

Look at §1-103 and let's highlight some of what it says. Subsection 1-103(a)(1) tells us that the UCC shall be "liberally construed." This is not a political statement, but instead is meant to combat the old presumption that the common law (meaning the law as created by precedent with no statutory guidance) was thought so wise that a rule of statutory construction arose stating that "statutes in derogation of the common law are to be *strictly* construed" so as to change the common law result as little as possible. Karl Llewellyn was having none of that: the UCC is to be read broadly, the common law be damned.

Subsection 1-103(a)(3) commands the courts of the various states to work to make the law "uniform" throughout the country. This gives the attorney finding a favorable ruling in one state a strong argument that it's a good precedent in another—a valuable thing to remember.

Finally, §1-103(b) preserves all of the common law rules (including the rules of equity and even the law merchant) to the extent that they do not contradict the statutory rules contained in the UCC. If the UCC doesn't speak to an issue, then attorneys must look to other laws to find the desired result.

One of the most important sections in the Code is §1-201, which is a huge definition section containing definitions for 43 different words. You will consult it often when exploring the matters we'll discuss in later chapters. Section 1-202 has complicated definitions of "notice" and "knowledge" that answer important questions such as what the two terms mean and at what moment a notice is effective (when sent? when received?). Section 1-204 defines "value" and §1-205 explores the issues of "reasonable time" and "seasonable."

There's a choice of law provision in §1-301 that generally applies the law of the enacting state if "appropriate," but allows the parties by agreement to choose the law of any state having a "reasonable relation" to the transaction.

Another important section, often referred to in this book and the case law, is §1-303, which explains what are sometimes called "construction" terms: the items that make up the understanding of the parties as to what the contract means. Section 1-303(c) explains that a "usage of trade" is a *custom* within the industry (sort of a throwback to the law merchant) and this custom binds all of those who should know about it, sometimes including even consumers. Ask yourself this: is it the "usage of trade" that car dealers can lie about the attributes of the vehicle being sold and therefore get away with that? (Of course not—a usage of trade can't violate the law, and such lies would be fraud.) "Course of dealing" in §1-303(b) refers to what the parties did in their *past* contacts with one another. If the parties have dealt with each other in prior dealings, that history creates an expectation of what will happen in this contract, and the Code thusly recognizes it. Finally, "course of performance" in §1-303(a) means what the parties do in performing this one particular contract, especially important where the contract goes on over a period of time and creates its own history and expectations. The common law called "course of performance" by the term "practical construction" and found it gave great guidance to the true boundaries of the contract. Then, in §1-303(e), there is a hierarchy of importance of these construction terms, with the more relevant ones beating out the less relevant. Under this idea, express terms control course of performance, but course of performance is more important than both course of dealing or usage of trade, and course of dealing beats out an inconsistent usage of trade. One caveat to this little list: §1-303(f) explains that an express term in a contract ("deliveries must be made on time or the contract is breached") can be *waived* by course of performance (accepting late deliveries without protest means one cannot suddenly call a breach for this reason—a result codified by §2-209 for the sale of goods).

Section 1-304 provides that "[e]very contract or duty within the Uniform Commercial Code imposes an obligation of good faith in its performance and enforcement." The definition of "good faith" is "honesty in fact and the observance of reasonable commercial standards of fair dealing," §1-201(b)(20). So good faith has a subjective component (honesty in fact) and an objective component (observance of reasonable commercial standards of fair dealing). This standard has changed over time. Some states have kept to the old definition of good faith, which required only "honesty in fact." Failure to act in good faith, by itself, "does not support an independent cause of action." Official Comment to §1-304; see, e.g., Brooklyn Bagel Boys, Inc. v. Earthgrains Refrigerated Dough Products, Inc., 212 F.3d 373 (7th Cir. 2000). However, a party who has performed in bad faith may be unable to assert rights under the Code. In one case, for example, a creditor who behaved in a blatantly evil manner had the usual Article 9 priorities reversed and ended up losing its collateral; see Ninth Dist. Prod. Credit Assn. v. Ed Duggan, Inc., 821 P.2d 788 (Colo. 1991).

V. *THE OFFICIAL COMMENTS*

All of the sections of the Code are followed by the Official Comments (like the one quoted in the previous paragraph), which explain how the drafters wanted the sections to be interpreted. These Comments, the courts have said clearly, are not the law, but they are important to understanding the meaning of the relevant section and are to be studied in that light. If in a future case you have an Official Comment in your favor you will of course call it to the court's attention and remind the court that this Comment was written by the very experts who wrote the statute and therefore it should be given great weight. If the relevant Comment hurts your case and has, annoyingly, been raised by the other side, remind the court that the Comments are not the law, and that sometimes these Comments have the look of "Oops, we meant to say this, but knew we couldn't get it through the legislature so we're trying to amend the law through a more devious channel."

CHAPTER 2
NEGOTIABILITY

I. INTRODUCTION

We begin our exploration of payment law with Article 3 of the Uniform Commercial Code, titled "Negotiable Instruments." It should be noted that Article 3 was rewritten in 2002 and that is the version that is likely to be in your statute book. But that version is only the law in the following jurisdictions: Arkansas, District of Columbia, Indiana, Kentucky, Michigan, Minnesota, Mississippi, New Mexico, Nevada, Oklahoma, South Carolina, and Texas. (Massachusetts was considering its enactment as this book went to press in 2015.) The 2002 revision only made slight changes from the version in effect in the other states, and the important ones will be noted as they arise.

Let's start with the question of why our ancestors created negotiable instruments in the first place. There is not, of course, enough money to go around, and what money is available is frequently too physically awkward to be moved easily. Human civilization has been able to create additional sources of money in the form of transferable contractual debt. Thus one can borrow money and give the lender a written promise to repay it (a promissory note) and in this way realize early expected future prosperity. We solved the problem of the awkwardness of the physical transfer of money, and the concomitant possibility of its theft while in transit, by putting the money in the hands of a guarded depository (typically a bank) and then issuing written orders (drafts) for the money's transfer to various people.

In time, complicated things began to happen to these pieces of paper. For one thing, they were transferred (negotiated) through many hands before being presented for payment. If payment was then refused for some reason (the goods proved defective, the maker was financially embarrassed, the bank failed to open its doors one morning), rules had to be invented to straighten out who owed what to whom and to establish which defenses would be good against the person demanding payment and which would not. Similarly, if the instrument was stolen or forged, rules had to be established to put the risk of loss on somebody. Article 3 (Negotiable Instruments) and Article 4 (Bank Deposits and Collections) of the Uniform Commercial Code are designed to supply these rules.

II. TYPES OF NEGOTIABLE INSTRUMENTS

There are many types of negotiable instruments in the world. *Money* itself is technically an instrument. A dollar *bill* is a *bill of exchange*—that is, a *draft* (defined below) drawn on the United States Treasury. The Code deals with investment securities (stocks and bonds) in Article 8, and with wire transfers in Article 4A, these matters being specifically excluded from the coverage of Article 3 by §3-102(a).

The types of negotiable instruments that Article 3 does cover can be divided into two basic categories: *notes* and *drafts*.

A *note* is a written promise to pay money. If the note is created by a *bank*, it is called a *certificate of deposit* (or CD for short). Read §3-104(j). Investors buy CDs because they pay higher rates of interest than a normal savings account, but CDs have the disadvantage that the investor is not able to reclaim the money until the CD *matures* (comes due).[1] The typical note is not made by a bank but is the promissory note signed by those who borrow money or make credit purchases, most commonly when buying a home via a bank loan.

A *draft* is a written order by one person (the *drawer*—see §3-103(a)(5)) to another (the *drawee*, §3-103(a)(4)), directing the latter to pay money to a third person (the *payee*). The most common situation involving drafts arises

---

1. If a certificate of deposit states that it is non-negotiable, then Article 3 would not apply (though Article 8 on Investment Securities might). In re Isaacson, 508 So. 2d 1131 (Miss. 1987).

when someone deposits money in a checking account and then writes checks ("drafts") addressed to the bank, ordering it to pay out the account money to those nominated. In this situation, the bank's customer is the *drawer*, the bank is the *drawee*, and the nominee (the electric company, the book club, the IRS, etc.) is the *payee*. A draft written on a bank and payable on demand is called a *check*; read §3-104(f). If the check is drawn by the bank on itself (the bank is both the drawer and the drawee), the instrument is called a *cashier's check*; see §3-104(g). If one bank draws a draft on another or makes the draft "payable through" another bank, the instrument is called a *teller's check*; see §3-104(h).[2]

PROBLEM 1

When law student Portia Moot went to buy a used car from a man who sold it through the newspaper, the seller told her he refused to take her personal check, demanding instead a cashier's check payable to his order. Portia went to Octopus National Bank and paid the bank the amount required, and the bank then issued the cashier's check, with Portia's car seller being named as payee. The bank gave the check to Portia, and she in turn handed it over to the payee. What is the name that the Code gives to Portia in this situation? See §3-103(a)(15).

If the drawee on a draft is *not* a bank, Article 3 still applies, but the instrument no longer meets the technical definition of a check (which requires that the drawee be a bank). The most common situation in which non-bank drafts are written occurs in the sale of goods. Seller in Boston contracts to sell 100 boxes of goods to buyer in San Francisco, buyer agreeing to pay $5,000 one month after receipt of the goods. Seller ships the goods, but decides that it would be nice to get the money now, before, for instance, going bankrupt. Seller sits down and draws up a $5,000 draft with *buyer as drawee*, leaving the payee line blank. Seller then goes down to a bank and asks the bank if it would be willing to buy the draft at a discount—say, $4,750. The bank investigates buyer's credit rating and, finding it good, buys the draft from seller for $4,750, having seller fill in the payee line with the bank's name. At the end of one month, the bank presents the draft to buyer for payment and receives $5,000, thus making a $250 profit on the deal. Buyer doesn't care who gets the payment as long as the debt to seller is discharged; seller, getting the money early, doesn't mind losing $250. Everybody is happy (unless

---

2. Section 3-104 also contains a definition of a *traveler's check* in §3-104(i) and a *money order* in §3-104(f), and their legal significance is described in Official Comment 4 to that section.

buyer discovers the goods are defective and refuses to pay the draft when the bank represents it; more on that later).[3]

Thus a negotiable instrument containing a *promise* to pay money is a note and one containing an *order* to pay money is a draft. Read §3-104(e).

III.   THE NEGOTIABILITY CONCEPT

Whenever the word *negotiable* is applied to any type of paper, the concept always means this: if the paper is technically *negotiable* (which refers to its form), it is technically *negotiated* (which refers to the transfer process) and reaches the hands of a purchaser for value who has no knowledge of problems with the transactions giving rise to the paper's creation (such a person is called a *holder in due course*); then the later purchaser becomes *super-plaintiff*[4] and can sue the parties to the instrument who are not (with

3. Drafts, then called *bills of exchange*, originated in Europe in the Middle Ages and were used to transfer money during travels. Merchants wishing to journey from City A to City B in the year 1220 faced the very real possibility of robbery en route. They solved this problem by going to a banking company in City A and there exchanging their money for a letter addressed to a corresponding banking company in City B, telling it to give a like amount of money to the merchants on arrival. In an era of rampant illiteracy, this bill of exchange was a lot easier to slip past the brigands than were coins of the realm. Here is a bill of exchange from the nineteenth century:

4. The designation "super-plaintiff" to describe a holder in due course is taken from J. White & R. Summers, Uniform Commercial Code 14-1 (5d ed. 2000); for a more specialized treatise, see B. Clark, The Law of Bank Deposits, Collections, and Credit Cards (revised edition, updated quarterly).

certain exceptions) permitted to defend the lawsuit; the defendants simply lose and pay up.

Before the rules of Article 3 apply to an instrument, regardless of whether it is a note or a draft, the instrument must be technically *negotiable* within the rigid definitional requirements of §3-104(a). Every element specified therein must be met or the instrument is non-negotiable, and Article 3 does not apply, except by analogy; see §3-104(b). Read §3-104(a) carefully; it is almost (but not quite) worth memorizing, since the first issue an attorney should explore when dealing with a problem involving commercial paper is this: "Is the instrument technically *negotiable?*"

The question is also important because negotiable instruments pass more freely in commerce than do non-negotiable ones. The transferee of negotiable paper, if qualifying as a holder in due course, has the protection of the rule mentioned above, and the original maker and all other parties to the paper will have to pay it at maturity even if they have defenses arising from the transactions in which they signed the paper. This rule promotes the desirability of buying *negotiable* instruments. If the paper is non-negotiable, its transfer is nothing more than the assignment of a contract right, and, as is the basic rule of contracts law, later holders (assignees) of a contract take subject to *all* defenses arising from the underlying transaction. As Lord Mansfield, when developing the concept of holding in due course, said in Peacock v. Rhodes, 2 Douglas 633, 99 Eng. Rep. 402 (K.B. 1781):

> The holder of a bill of exchange, or promissory note, is not to be considered in the light of an assignee of the payee. An assignee must take the thing assigned, subject to all the equity to which the original party was subject. If this rule applied to bills and promissory notes, it would stop their currency. The law is settled, that a holder, coming fairly by a bill or note, has nothing to do with the transaction between the original parties; unless, perhaps, in the single case, (which is a hard one, but has been determined) of a note for money won at play.[5]

It follows then that it is important for everyone to know without question whether or not any given instrument is negotiable as soon as it is examined. In situations in which the deviation from the Code's requirements for negotiability is small, pleas are sometimes made to extend Article 3 by analogy to permit the non-complying instruments to be deemed negotiable. The courts are usually deaf to such entreaties:

---

5. This last statement refers to instruments that arise from gambling. More on that issue later when we discuss holders in due course in Chapter 4.

Because the prerequisites to negotiability are formal, it is both simple and necessary to comply with them. To hold that [the notes in question] are negotiable would certainly preserve the integrity of these notes and in that limited sense serve the interests of commerce; however, it would reward shoddy drafting and introduce unnecessary doubt into the formalities of negotiability. The reason for employing formalities in legal rules is to preclude the kinds of arguments that the banks offer to circumvent them here. It will not do to argue that the goal of promoting the expansion of commerce with predictably negotiable paper is served by artful reconstruction of the formalities set up initially to serve that same goal.

In re Boardwalk Marketplace Sec. Litig., 668 F. Supp. 115, 122 (D. Conn. 1987).

Each element of the negotiability requirements listed in §3-104(a) and related sections is discussed below.

A. *"Writing"*

A negotiable instrument cannot be oral (how could it be transferred around?), and the definitions of both *promise* and *order* in §3-103(a) require a "written" instruction or undertaking. However, there is no requirement that the writing be on a piece of paper. See Sir Alan Herbert's article, The Negotiable Cow, reprinted in A.P. Herbert, More Misleading Cases 117 (1930). Banks must sometimes cope with instruments written on odd surfaces (and frequently balk at doing so). The IRS is sometimes the payee of a negotiable shirt.

No one could be the holder of an oral promise to pay. But the law now provides that someone may be the holder of an electronic promissory note, as the next case discusses.

Good v. Wells Fargo Bank, N.A.

Court of Appeals of Indiana, 2014
18 N.E.3d 618

BARNES, Judge.

. . .

FACTS

On March 14, 2008, Good purchased real estate in Elkhart. Good executed an electronic promissory note ("the Note") in favor of Synergy Mortgage Group, Inc. ("Synergy"). The Note included the following term:

11. Issuance of Transferable Record; Identification of Note Holder; Conversion from Electronic Note to Paper-Based Note

* * *

(B) Except as indicated in Sections 11(D) and (E) below, the identity of the Note Holder and any person to whom this Electronic Note is later transferred will be recorded in a registry maintained by *MERS CORP, Inc., a Delaware corporation* or in another registry to which the records are later transferred (the "Note Holder Registry"). The authoritative copy of this Electronic Note will be the copy identified by the Note Holder after loan closing but prior to registration in the Note Holder Registry. If this Electronic Note has been registered in the Note Holder Registry, then the authoritative copy will be the copy identified by the Note Holder of record in the Note Holder Registry or the Loan Servicer (as defined in the Security Instrument) acting at the direction of the Note Holder, as the authoritative copy. The current identity of the Note Holder and the location of the authoritative copy, as reflected in the Note Holder Registry, will be available from the Note Holder or Loan Servicer, as applicable. *The only copy of this Electric Note that is the authoritative copy is the copy that is within the control of the person identified as the Note Holder in the Note Holder Registry (or that person's designee). No other copy of this Electronic Note may be the authoritative copy.* . . .

Appellee's App. p. 29 (emphasis added). The loan was secured by a mortgage. The mortgage identified Synergy as the lender and Mortgage Electronic Registration Systems, Inc. ("MERS") as a nominee for the lender.

In 2011, Good stopped making payments on the loan. On November 9, 2011, MERS, as nominee for Synergy, assigned the mortgage to Wells Fargo. This assignment was recorded on November 14, 2011.

On November 7, 2012, Wells Fargo filed a complaint to foreclose the mortgage. Good, acting pro-se, filed an answer alleging that Wells Fargo was not a holder in due course of the Note and that it lacked standing.

On April 5, 2013, Wells Fargo moved for summary judgment. In support of its motion, Wells Fargo designated an Affidavit in Support of Judgment ("the Affidavit") in which Shemeka Moye, Wells Fargo's Vice President of Loan Documentation, stated Wells Fargo "directly or through an agent, has possession of the Promissory Note at issue in the plaintiff's cause of action. Wells Fargo Bank, N.A., is either the original payee of the Promissory Note or the Promissory Note has been duly indorsed [sic]." *Id.* at 95. Good responded, arguing that Wells Fargo held only a photocopy of the Note without any endorsements and, without more, did not establish that it was entitled to enforce the Note.

Wells Fargo replied claiming Good failed to designate evidence that creates a genuine issue[] of material fact for trial. Wells Fargo also asserted that it controlled the electronic note and was entitled to enforce it as the holder pursuant to 15 U.S.C.A. §7021(d). In support of this argument, Wells Fargo relied on a Certificate of Authentication ("the Certificate") in which Assistant Vice President of Wells Fargo, Theresa Russell, stated:

> 1. . . . The Bank acts as a servicer for the Federal National Mortgage Association ("Fannie Mae") with respect to the residential mortgage loan executed on the [sic] 3/14/2008 by BRYAN GOOD ("Borrowers"). . . . The promissory note evidencing the Borrowers' obligation to repay the Loan is an electronic record, as authorized by the federal ESIGN Act, 15 USC §7001 et seq., and in particular 15 USC §7021.
>
> 2. As part of its function as servicer, the Bank maintains a copy of the Borrowers' electronic promissory note on behalf of Fannie Mae. I am responsibilities [sic] for overseeing the process by which the Bank maintains the electronic promissory notes evidencing residential mortgage loans. ("Electronic Records").
>
> 3. Each Electronic Record is received in accordance with established procedures and processes for reliable receipt, storage and management of Electronic Records (the "Electronic Record Procedures"). The Electronic Record Procedures provide controls to assure that each Electronic Record is accurately received as originally executed and transmitted, and indexed appropriately for later identification and retrieval. Each Electronic Record is protected against undetected alteration by industry-standard encryption techniques and system controls. The Electronic Record is an official record of the Bank and is readily accessible for later reference.
>
> 4. Each Electronic Record is maintained and stored by the Bank in the ordinary course of business. The Electronic Records are maintained and stored by the Bank continuously from the time of receipt.
>
> 5. The paper copy of the Electronic Record attached . . . is a true and correct copy of the Borrowers' promissory note described above, as maintained and stored by the Bank in accordance with the procedures in Paragraphs 3 and 4 of this Certificate.

Id. at 130.

After a hearing, the trial court concluded that Wells Fargo had standing to enforce the Note and mortgage and partially granted Wells Fargo's motion for summary judgment as to that issue. The trial court also concluded that there were genuine issues of material fact regarding the validity of Good's electronic signature on the Note and the amount due and owing on the Note. Both parties filed motions to reconsider, which were discussed at the September 16, 2013 bench trial on the unresolved issues. After the trial, the trial court reaffirmed its initial ruling on the motion for summary judgment and concluded in part:

> 11. Plaintiff Wells Fargo Bank presented attached to the copy of the Promissory Note in its control a Certificate of Authentication which affirms that the Promissory Note was accurately received as it was originally executed

and transmitted electronically. Plaintiff also affirmed that the record was protected against undetected alteration by industry standard encryption techniques and system controls. In this respect, the court concludes that Plaintiff maintained control of the subject Promissory Note which was originally signed by the Defendant, Bryan Good. Further endorsement of an electronic promissory note is not required and the promissory note is self-authenticating pursuant to Ind. Rule of Evidence 902. Accordingly, Defendant is liable on the Promissory Note and related Mortgage.

Appellant's App. P. 134. The trial court determined the payoff amount and entered judgment for Wells Fargo in that amount. The trial court then issued a judgment of foreclosure. Good now appeals.

Analysis

Among other things, Good appeals the trial court's entry of partial summary judgment on the issue of whether Wells Fargo was entitled to enforce the Note. "We review an appeal of a trial court's ruling on a motion for summary judgment using the same standard applicable to the trial court." Perdue v. Gargano, 964 N.E.2d 825, 831 (Ind. 2012). "Therefore, summary judgment is appropriate only if the designated evidence reveals 'no genuine issue as to any material fact and that the moving party is entitled to a judgment as a matter of law.'" *Id.* (quoting Ind. Trial Rule 56(C)). Our review of summary judgment is limited to evidence designated to the trial court. *Id.* (citing T.R. 56(H)). All facts and reasonable inferences drawn from the evidence designated by the parties is construed in a light most favorable to the non-moving party, and we do not defer to the trial court's legal determinations. *Id.*

There is no dispute that the mortgage was assigned from Synergy to Wells Fargo in 2011. The issue is whether Wells Fargo was entitled to enforce the Note. Regarding traditional paper notes, "Indiana has adopted Article 3 of the Uniform Commercial Code (UCC), which governs negotiable instruments, and it is well-established that a promissory note secured by a mortgage is a negotiable instrument." Lunsford v. Deutsche Bank Trust Co. Americas as Tr., 996 N.E.2d 815, 821 (Ind. Ct. App. 2013). According to the UCC, a negotiable instrument may be enforced by "the holder of the instrument." Ind. Code §26-1-3.1-301(1). The term "holder" means "the person in possession of a negotiable instrument that is payable either to bearer or to an identified person if the identified person is in possession of the instrument[.]" I.C. §26-1-1-201(20). In this context, "bearer" means the person in possession of a negotiable instrument "payable to bearer or endorsed in blank." I.C. §26-1-1-201(5).

Wells Fargo initially asserted that it had possession of the Note and was either the original payee or the Note had been duly endorsed. Good responded, challenging Wells Fargo's status as holder because the Note designated by Wells Fargo was not endorsed. In its reply, Wells Fargo asserted that, because the Note was an electronic note, "delivery, possession, and endorsement of an electronic promissory note are not required pursuant to federal statute." Appellee's App. p. 91. Wells Fargo claimed it controlled the Note and was entitled to enforce it pursuant to 15 U.S.C. §7021, which provides:

(a) Definitions

For purposes of this section:

(1) Transferable record

The term "transferable record" means an electronic record that—

(A) would be a note under Article 3 of the Uniform Commercial Code if the electronic record were in writing;

(B) the issuer of the electronic record expressly has agreed is a transferable record; and

(C) relates to a loan secured by real property.

A transferable record may be executed using an electronic signature.

(2) Other definitions

The terms "electronic record," "electronic signature," and "person" have the same meanings provided in section 7006 of this title.

(b) Control

A person has control of a transferable record if a system employed for evidencing the transfer of interests in the transferable record reliably establishes that person as the person to which the transferable record was issued or transferred.

(c) Conditions

A system satisfies subsection (b) of this section, and a person is deemed to have control of a transferable record, if the transferable record is created, stored, and assigned in such a manner that—

(1) a single authoritative copy of the transferable record exists which is unique, identifiable, and, except as otherwise provided in paragraphs (4), (5), and (6), unalterable;

(2) the authoritative copy identifies the person asserting control as—

(A) the person to which the transferable record was issued; or

(B) if the authoritative copy indicates that the transferable record has been transferred, the person to which the transferable record was most recently transferred;

(3) the authoritative copy is communicated to and maintained by the person asserting control or its designated custodian;

(4) copies or revisions that add or change an identified assignee of the authoritative copy can be made only with the consent of the person asserting control;

(5) each copy of the authoritative copy and any copy of a copy is readily identifiable as a copy that is not the authoritative copy; and

(6) any revision of the authoritative copy is readily identifiable as authorized or unauthorized.

(d) Status as holder

Except as otherwise agreed, a person having control of a transferable record is the holder, as defined in section 1-201(20) of the Uniform Commercial Code, of the transferable record and has the same rights and defenses as a holder of an equivalent record or writing under the Uniform Commercial Code, including, if the applicable statutory requirements under section 3-302(a), 9-308, or revised section 9-330 of the Uniform Commercial Code are satisfied, the rights and defenses of a holder in due course or a purchaser, respectively. *Delivery, possession, and endorsement are not required to obtain or exercise any of the rights under this subsection.*

(e) Obligor rights

Except as otherwise agreed, an obligor under a transferable record has the same rights and defenses as an equivalent obligor under equivalent records or writings under the Uniform Commercial Code.

(f) Proof of control

If requested by a person against which enforcement is sought, the person seeking to enforce the transferable record shall provide reasonable proof that the person is in control of the transferable record. Proof may include access to the authoritative copy of the transferable record and related business records sufficient to review the terms of the transferable record and to establish the identity of the person having control of the transferable record.

(g) UCC references

For purposes of this subsection, all references to the Uniform Commercial Code are to the Uniform Commercial Code as in effect in the jurisdiction the law of which governs the transferable record.

15 U.S.C. §7021 (emphases added).

Wells Fargo is correct that, pursuant to §7021(d), a person having control of a transferable record, which includes the Note, is the holder for purposes of the UCC and that delivery, possession, and endorsement are not required. According to §7021(b), to show it controlled the note, Wells Fargo was required to designate evidence that a system employed for evidencing the transfer of interests in the Note reliably established Wells Fargo as the person to whom the Note was transferred. A system that satisfies the control requirement is described in §7021(c). Wells Fargo contends that its "possession of the Note and the recitation of its electronic record keeping procedures in the Certificate evidences Well Fargo's control of the Note. . . ." Appellee's Br. p. 15. We disagree.

Regarding possession, the Affidavit, which does not mention an electronic note, provides only that Wells Fargo, directly or through an agent, "has possession of the Promissory Note at issue in the plaintiff's cause of action." Appellee's App. p. 95. When considering Wells Fargo's assertion that the note in its possession was endorsed and its argument that the endorsement of an electronic note is not required pursuant to §7021(d), it is not clear from the Affidavit whether Wells Fargo was claiming to have possession of an endorsed paper copy or the electronic note.

Even if the Affidavit established that Wells Fargo possessed the electronic note, control, not possession, is the relevant consideration under §7021, and the Certificate does not establish that Wells Fargo controlled the Note. The Certificate does establish that Wells Fargo, as servicer of Good's mortgage loan for Fannie Mae, "maintains a copy of [Good's] promissory note on behalf of Fannie Mae." *Id.* at 26. The Certificate also establishes that Wells Fargo's electronic records are received, stored, and managed in a secure manner with controls to assure they are accurately received as originally executed and protected against alteration. However, the Certificate does not suggest that Wells Fargo maintains the single authoritative copy of the Note as described in §7021(c)(1). Even if we were to assume that the copy of the Note maintained by Wells Fargo is the authoritative copy, it does not indicate that the Note has been transferred or identify either Wells Fargo or Fannie Mae as the person to whom the Note was most recently transferred. *See* 15 U.S.C. §7021(c)(2)(B).

Such a record of transfer is described in the Note, which calls for the recording of any transfer of the Note in a note holder registry. The Note also specifies, "The only copy of this Electric Note that is the authoritative copy is the copy that is within the control of the person identified as the Note Holder in the Note Holder Registry (or that person's designee). No other copy of this Electronic Note may be the authoritative copy." *Id.* at 29. Wells Fargo has not designated any evidence of a note holder registry, let alone evidence showing that Wells Fargo, or even Fannie Mae, is identified as the note holder in the note holder registry.

Pursuant to statute, upon Good's request, Wells Fargo was required to provide "reasonable proof" that it was in control of the Note. 15 U.S.C. §7021(f). "Proof may include access to the authoritative copy of the transferable record and related business records sufficient to review the terms of the transferable record and to establish the identity of the person having control of the transferable record." *Id.* Although Good repeatedly requested such proof, Wells Fargo did not provide any evidence documenting the transfer or assignment of the Note from Synergy to either Wells Fargo or Fannie Mae. Thus, Wells Fargo did not demonstrate it controlled the Note by showing that a system employed for evidencing the transfer of interests in the Note reliably established that the Note had been transferred to Wells Fargo. *See* 15 U.S.C. §7021(b).

Because Wells Fargo did not establish that it controlled the Note as described in §7021, it did not establish that it was the person entitled to enforce the Note as the holder for purposes of the UCC. *See* 15 U.S.C. §7021(d); I.C. §26-1-3.1-301(1). Thus, partial summary judgment for Wells Fargo on this issue was improper.

Wells Fargo goes on to argue that, irrespective of the trial court's summary judgment ruling, it presented uncontroverted evidence at the bench trial that it controlled the Note. Procedurally, however, the issue of Wells Fargo's right to enforce the Note was not before the trial court during the bench trial because it had been resolved, albeit improperly, in the summary judgment proceedings. It would be inappropriate for us to use evidence from the subsequent trial to justify the judgment when Good did not have notice that this issue would be relitigated. Regardless, we are not convinced that the trial testimony establishes that Wells Fargo controlled the Note for purposes of §7021.

Wells Fargo relies on the testimony of Donna Mouzon, a loan verification analyst for Wells Fargo, who testified at trial that Wells Fargo "acquired" the loan on August 1, 2008. Tr. pp. 17-18. Mouzon was also questioned as follows:

> Q. Thank you. Is [Wells Fargo] presently in control of the electronic note?
> A. Yes.
> Q. Does [Wells Fargo] currently maintain the electronic note?
> A. Yes.
> Q. Does [Wells Fargo] also service the loan?
> A. Yes.
>
> * * *
>
> Q. Who's the owner of the note?
> A. Fanny Mae.
> Q. Who's the holder of the note?
> A. Wells Fargo.

Id. at 18.

Given the lack of evidence regarding a transfer or assignment from Synergy to Wells Fargo or Fannie Mae, Mouzon's conclusory testimony was not sufficient to establish that it controlled the Note as defined in §7021. Thus, Mouzon's trial testimony did not establish that Wells Fargo is entitled to enforce the note as the holder, and is not a basis for affirming the judgment of foreclosure.

CONCLUSION

Wells Fargo has not shown that it controls the Note for purposes of §7021(b) and, accordingly, has not established its status as holder for purposes of the UCC. Because Wells Fargo has not established that it was entitled to enforce the Note as its holder, the trial court's grant of summary judgment was improper and the resulting judgment must be set aside. We reverse and remand.

Reversed and remanded.

B.   "Signed"

Section 3-103(a)'s definitions of both "promise" and "order" require that the instrument be "signed." This is an obvious requirement, but it has interesting wrinkles.

PROBLEM 2

Texas millionaire Howard Chaps signs all of his checks with a small branding iron that prints a fancy "X" on the signature line. Are his checks negotiable? See §1-201(b)(37); cf. Official Comment 39.

PROBLEM 3

Walter Capitalist is the sole proprietor of the Capitalist Company. He signs all of the store's checks by writing "Capitalist Company" on the drawer's line, but the checks are drawn on his personal checking account at the Octopus National Bank. Can the bank treat the check as if Walter had signed his own name? See §3-401(b).

C.   "Unconditional Promise or Order"

A promissory note must contain an unconditional *promise* to pay; a draft must contain an unconditional *order* to the drawee requiring payment. See §3-104(a). The rule that the promise or order be *unconditional* is obviously a necessity if negotiable paper is to circulate without question. If conditional paper were negotiable, prospective holders of the paper would not feel safe in taking it until they had checked to see if the condition had occurred. See First State Bank v. Clark, 91 N.M. 117, 570 P.2d 1144 (1977); Annot., What Constitutes an Unconditional Promise, 88 A.L.R.3d 1100. To prevent this kind of worry, the Code requires that the promise or order be unconditional, or the paper will be technically non-negotiable. Nonetheless, certain conditions are permitted in the instrument without destroying negotiability. Read §3-106 carefully. (The plan of the §§3-100s, which deal generally with negotiability, is to set out all of the requirements in §3-104(a), and then, section by section, to elaborate on them. Section 3-106 is the first elaboration.)

1.   Implied Conditions

The fact that it is possible to think up things that *might* happen to destroy the maker's liability on the instrument does not destroy negotiability unless the instrument makes itself *expressly* conditional as to these matters. For example, if Joanie Singer leases a theater from Music Hall, Inc., and gives the lessor the following signed note, "(Date), I have this day rented a theater from Music Hall, Inc., and I promise to pay $800 to the order of Music Hall, Inc.," the possibility that the theater may burn down prior to Joanie's use of it does not make the note conditional (and therefore non-negotiable); this condition is only implied. On the other hand, if the note had said, "I promise to pay $800 to the order of Music Hall, Inc., *only if* the theater does not burn down before I use it," the note would have been non-negotiable, since it would then be subject to an *express* condition. See §3-106(a)(i).

Triffin v. Dillabough

Supreme Court of Pennsylvania, 1998
552 Pa. 550, 716 A.2d 605

NEWMAN, Justice.

Appellant American Express Travel Related Services Company, Inc. (American Express) asks this Court to decide whether certain of its money orders are negotiable instruments pursuant to the Pennsylvania version of the Uniform Commercial Code, 13 Pa. C.S. §1101, et seq. (Commercial Code), and if they are, whether appellee Robert J. Triffin (Triffin) has the rights of a holder in due course who may recover the face value of those money orders from American Express. We hold that the money orders in question are negotiable instruments and Triffin has the rights of a holder in due course, entitling him to recover the value of the money orders from American Express.

FACTS AND PROCEDURAL HISTORY

American Express, among other endeavors, sells money orders through its authorized agents. In a typical transaction, an agent collects an amount of cash from the purchaser, also known as the sender, equal to the face value of the money order plus a small fee. The sender receives a partially completed money order embossed with the amount of the money order and blank spaces for the sender to fill in his or her own name and address, the name of the payee and the date.

On an unknown date, three American Express money orders were stolen from the premises of one of its agents, Chase Savings Bank. In an apparently unrelated incident, one hundred American Express money orders were stolen while being shipped to another agent, I.W. Levin & Company. When they were stolen, all of the money orders contained the pre-printed signature of Louis Gerstner, then Chairman of American Express, but they were blank as to amount, sender, payee and date.

On December 11, 1990, Stacey Anne Dillabough (Dillabough) presented two American Express money orders for payment at Chuckie Enterprises, Inc. (Chuckie's), a check cashing operation in Philadelphia. The money orders were in the amounts of $550.00 and $650.00, respectively, and listed Dillabough as the payee and David W. (last name indecipherable) of 436 E. Allegheny Avenue as the sender. On February 25, 1991, Robert Lynn (Lynn) presented one American Express money order at Chuckie's in the amount of $200.00, which listed himself as payee and Michael C. Pepe as the sender. In each instance, Charles Giunta (Giunta), the owner of Chuckie's, recognized Dillabough and Lynn from their previous visits to Chuckie's. Dillabough and Lynn provided photographic identification to Giunta and properly endorsed their money orders. Giunta paid the face amounts of the money orders to Dillabough and Lynn, less his standard 2 percent fee.

Giunta was unaware the American Express money orders that he cashed had been stolen. The two Dillabough money orders were stolen from the premises of Chase Savings Bank and the Lynn money order was stolen from the shipment to I.W. Levin and Company. After being cashed at Chuckie's, the money orders traveled the regular bank collection routes and were presented for payment at the United Bank of Grand Junction, Colorado. Because American Express had noted on its "fraud log" that the money orders were stolen, they were returned to Chuckie's bearing the stamp "reported lost or stolen. do not redeposit." American Express refused to pay Chuckie's the face amounts of the money orders. Chuckie's then sold the Dillabough and Lynn money orders to Triffin, a commercial discounter.[6] Pursuant to written agreements, Chuckie's assigned all of its right, title and interest in the money orders to Triffin.

Triffin filed separate complaints in the Court of Common Pleas of Philadelphia County (trial court) against Dillabough and American Express in July 16, 1992, and against Lynn and American Express on August 20, 1992, seeking payment of the money orders. The trial court consolidated the two actions. Triffin obtained default judgments against Dillabough and Lynn and proceeded to a non-jury trial with American Express. The trial court found that the money orders were not negotiable instruments and entered a verdict in favor of American Express. On appeal, the Superior Court reversed and trial court and held that the money orders were negotiable instruments and Triffin had the status of a holder in due course, entitling him to recover the face amount of the money orders from American

---

6. Triffin testified that he regularly purchases various types of choses in action from members of the check cashing industry. Although a law school graduate, Triffin is not a member of the Pennsylvania Bar and he is proceeding *pro se* in this appeal.

Express. We granted American Express' Petition for Allowance of Appeal from the Order of the Superior Court, and we now affirm. . . .

1. NEGOTIABILITY

The Superior Court has described the purpose of negotiable instruments and the Commercial Code as follows:

> A negotiable instrument is an instrument capable of transfer by endorsement or delivery. Negotiability provides a means of passing on to the transferee the rights of the holder, including the right to sue in his or her own name, and the right to take free of equities as against the assignor/payee. [Citations omitted.] The purpose of the Commercial Code is to enhance the marketability of negotiable instruments and to allow bankers, brokers, and the general public to trade in confidence. [Citations omitted.] As a matter of sound economic policy, the Commercial Code encourages the free transfer and negotiability of commercial paper to stimulate financial interdependence.

Manor Bldg. Corp. v. Manor Complex Assocs., 435 Pa. Super. 246, 252-53, 645 A.2d 843, 846 (1994) (en banc). With these principles in mind, we turn to a discussion of the American Express money orders at issue here.

The threshold question is whether the money orders qualify as negotiable instruments under Division Three of the Commercial Code, 13 Pa. C.S. §3101, et seq., which governs negotiability. Both parties agree that if the money orders are not negotiable instruments then Triffin's claims against American Express must fail. Initially, we note that the Commercial Code does not specifically define the term "money order," nor does it provide a descriptive list of financial documents that automatically qualify as negotiable instruments. Instead, 13 Pa. C.S. 3104(a) sets forth the following four part test to determine if a particular document qualifies as a negotiable instrument:

> (A) Requisites to negotiability—Any writing to be a negotiable instrument within this division must: (1) be signed by the maker or drawer; (2) contain an unconditional promise or order to pay a sum certain in money and no other promise, order, obligation or power given by the maker or drawer except as authorized by this division; (3) be payable on demand or at a definite time; and (4) be payable to order or to bearer.

13 Pa. C.S. §3104(a).

The Superior Court described the face of the money orders in question as follows:

> Prior to being stolen[,] the American Express money orders read: "AMERICAN EXPRESS MONEY ORDER . . . CHASE SAVINGS BANK . . . DATE (blank). PAY THE SUM OF (blank), NOT GOOD OVER $1,000, TO THE ORDER OF (blank). Louis V. Gerstner, Chairman. SENDER'S NAME

AND ADDRESS (blank). Issued by American Express Travel Related Services Company, Inc., Englewood, Colorado. Payable at United Bank of Grand Junction, Downtown, Grand Junction, Colorado." The two Dillabough instruments were in this form. The third Lynn instrument was identical, except it did not bear an authorized agent's name, e.g., Chase Savings Bank, and was not good for over $200.

Triffin v. Dillabough, 448 Pa. Super. 72, 82, 670 A.2d 684, 689 (1996). When presented at Chuckie's, the sections for date, amount, payee and sender had been completed.

The first requisite of negotiability, a signature by the drawer or maker, "includes any symbol executed or adopted by a party with present intention to authenticate a writing." 13 Pa. C.S. §1201. "Authentication may be printed, stamped or written; it may be by initials or by thumbprint. . . . The question always is whether the symbol was executed or adopted by the party with present intention to authenticate the writing." 13 Pa. C.S. §1201, Comment 39. Additionally, section 3307(a)(2) states that when the effectiveness of a signature is challenged, it is presumed to be genuine or authorized unless the signer has died or become incompetent. 13 Pa. C.S. §3307(a)(2). Here, the drawer, American Express, affixed the pre-printed signature of Louis Gerstner, its then Chairman, to the money orders in question before forwarding them to its agents. American Express does not argue that Gerstner's signature was affixed to the money orders for any reason other than to authenticate them. Accordingly, the money orders satisfy the first requisite for negotiability.

The second requisite, American Express argues, is lacking because the money orders do not contain an unconditional promise or order to pay. Specifically, American Express claims that a legend it placed on the back of the money orders qualifies an otherwise unconditional order on the front directing the drawee to "PAY THE SUM OF" a specified amount "TO THE ORDER OF" the payee. The legend provides as follows:

IMPORTANT
DO NOT CASH FOR STRANGERS

THIS MONEY ORDER WILL NOT BE PAID IF IT HAS BEEN ALTERED OR STOLEN OR IF AN ENDORSEMENT IS MISSING OR FORGED. BE SURE YOU HAVE EFFECTIVE RECOURSE AGAINST YOUR CUSTOMER.

_____
PAYEE'S ENDORSEMENT

According to American Express, this legend renders the order to pay conditional on the money order not being altered, stolen, unendorsed or forged and destroys the negotiability of the instrument.

We disagree. In a factually similar case, the Louisiana Court of Appeal construed a legend on the bank of an American Express money order similar to the one at issue here. Hong Kong Importers, Inc. v. American Express Co., 301 So. 2d 707 (La. App. 1974). The legend there stated "cash only if recourse from endorser IS AVAILABLE. IF THIS MONEY ORDER HAS NOT BEEN VALIDLY ISSUED OR HAS BEEN FRADULENTLY NEGOTIATED, IT WILL BE RETURNED." Id. at 708. The money order also had the following language printed on its face: "know your endorser cash only if recourse is available." Id. The Louisiana Court held that the legend on the back and the language on the front did not convert the money order into a conditional promise to pay, but merely operated as a warning to the party cashing the money order to protect himself against fraud. Although *Hong Kong* was decided before Louisiana adopted the Uniform Commercial Code, we find its rationale to be persuasive and applicable to 13 Pa. C.S. §3104.

American Express attempts to distinguish *Hong Kong* by asserting that the legend in this case is more specific because it explicitly conditions payment on the money orders not being altered, stolen, unendorsed or forged. This argument misses the point. "Any writing which meets the requirements of subsection [(a)] and is not excluded under Section [3103] is a negotiable instrument, and all sections of this [Division] apply to it, *even though it may contain additional language beyond that contemplated by this section.*" 13 Pa. C.S. §3104, Comment 4 (emphasis added). An otherwise unconditional order to pay that meets the section 3104 requirements is not made conditional by including implied or constructive conditions in the instrument. 13 Pa. C.S. §3105(a)(1). Moreover, purported conditions on an otherwise negotiable instrument, that merely reflect other provisions of the law, do not vitiate negotiability. State v. Phelps, 125 Ariz. 114, 608 P.2d 51 (App. 1979); see also Falk's Food Basket, Inc. v. Selected Risks Ins. Co., 214 Pa. Super. 522, 257 A.2d 359 (1969); 4 William D. Hawkland & Larry Lawrence, Uniform Commercial Code Series §3-105:03 (Clark Boardman Callaghan) (1994). Here, the alleged conditions on the back of the money orders are nothing more than a restatement of American Express's statutory defenses against payment because of alteration, 13 Pa. C.S. §3407, theft, 13 Pa. C.S. §3306(4), absence of signature, 13 Pa. C.S. §3401, and forgery, 13 Pa. C.S. §3404. Contrary to American Express's claims, expressing those statutory defenses in a legend with the conditional phrase "this money order will not be paid if . . ." does not elevate the legend to a condition for the purposes of 13 Pa. C.S. §3104(a) because it is merely a restatement of the defenses present in the Commercial Code. See 13 Pa. C.S. §3104, Comment 4; Phelps. The legend is simply a warning that American Express has reserved its statutory defenses. Whether these defenses are effective against Triffin is a separate question to be answered after resolving the issue of negotiability. See 13 Pa. C.S. §3104, Comment 4. We hold, therefore, that the money orders contain an unconditional order to pay, and satisfy the second requisite of negotiability.

The third requisite, that the writing be payable on demand or at a definite time, and the fourth requisite, that the writing be payable to order or bearer, are clear from the face of the money orders and are not disputed by the parties. Thus, the American Express money orders qualify as negotiable instruments pursuant to 13 Pa. C.S. §3104. . . .

[The court then found that Triffin had the rights of a holder in due course, so as to be free of American Express's defense of non-issue. As to this, see §3-105 of the Revision, and its Official Comment 2.]

As previously discussed, the legend on the back of the money orders is merely a warning that restates American Express's defenses against persons other than holders in due course in the event of alteration, theft, lack of endorsement or forgery. These defenses are ineffective against a holder in due course. 13 Pa. C.S. §3305; 13 Pa. C.S. §3407(c). Because Triffin has attained holder in due course status through the assignment of the money orders from Chuckie's, American Express cannot enforce the defenses against him. Accordingly, American Express is liable to Triffin for the face value of the money orders.

The Order of the Superior Court is affirmed and this matter is remanded to the trial court for the entry of an order consistent with this Opinion.

CASTILLE, Justice, dissents.

The majority concludes that appellee Robert J. Triffin ("appellee") is entitled to recover the value of the money orders at issue because the money orders were negotiable instruments and because appellee was a holder in due course of those negotiable instruments. However, since the money orders at issue contained express conditional language which precluded negotiability under the relevant statute, I must respectfully dissent from the majority's conclusion. . . .

At issue here is the second of the four statutory prerequisites to negotiability, the requirement of an "unconditional" promise or order. Regarding this prerequisite, section §3105 provides:

(A) Unconditional promise or order.—A promise or order otherwise unconditional is not made conditional by the fact that the instrument: (1) is subject to implied or constructive conditions; . . .

The comment to section 3105 states:

1. . . . Nothing in [paragraph (a) subsection (1)] is intended to imply that language may not be fairly construed to mean what it says, but implications, whether the law or fact, are not to be considered in determining negotiability.

Thus, the statute clearly distinguishes between language which creates an implied condition and language which creates an express condition. The latter renders a promise or order non-negotiable while the former does not. This conclusion derives further support from the revised §3106(a), which provides that ". . . a promise or order is unconditional unless it states (1) an express condition to payment. . . ."

Here, the operative language in the money orders at issue clearly created an "express" condition and thereby rendered the money orders non-negotiable. [Reprints language on the money order.]

This language explicitly conditions payments on the money orders' not being altered or stolen and the endorsements' not being missing or forged. The use of the word "if" renders the condition an express one, since "if" by definition means "on *condition* that; in case that; supposing that." Webster's New World Dict., 2d College ed. (Emphasis added.)

Furthermore, the official comment to revised section 3106 explains what the code intends by drawing the distinction between implied and express conditions: If the promise or order states an express condition to payment, the promise or order is not an instrument. For example, a promise states, "I promise to pay $100,000 to the order of John Doe if he conveys title to Blackacre to me." The promise is not an instrument because there is an express condition to payment. However, suppose a promise states, "In consideration of John Doe's promise to convey title of Blackacre I promise to pay $100,000 to the order of John Doe." That promise can be an instrument *if* [section 3104] is otherwise satisfied. 13 Pa. C.S. §3106 (1992 amended version) (emphasis added). Accordingly, the use of the word "if" creates an express condition which otherwise might be lacking, and thereby precludes a money order from being a negotiable instrument under the statute. The language at issue in this case created the same type of express condition which is embodied in the Comment; consequently, the language precludes the money orders from being negotiable instruments.[7]

The reasons proffered by the majority to justify its departure from this seemingly inescapable statutory logic are strained. First, the majority cites a case, decided by the Louisiana Court of Appeal in 1974, in which a condition incorporating the word "if was construed not to bar negotiability. In that case, the Louisiana Court did not evaluate the significance of the word "if" or the significance of the condition which that word introduced. Moreover, in 1974, Louisiana had not yet adopted Article III of the Uniform Commercial Code ("UCC"). Hence, it appears that the Louisiana decision

---

7. Additionally, I note that if there was any doubt about this conclusion, the doubt would be resolved against negotiability. See United States v. Gonzalez, 797 F.2d 1109, 1113 (1st Cir. 1986) ("when a writing is ambiguous with respect to negotiability, the conclusion to be reached is that it is *not negotiable*") (emphasis added) (other citations omitted).

was decided against the backdrop of the Code of Napoleon. See 9 to 5 Fashions, Inc. v. Petr L. Spurney, 538 So. 2d 228, 233 (La. 1989) (discussing roots of Louisiana's civil code in the Napoleonic code). Pennsylvania, on the other hand, has adopted Article III of the UCC, which speaks directly to the issue presented in this case, as explained supra. A decision by an intermediate Louisiana appellate court interpreting French legal principles should not override the explicit statutory guidance furnished by the Pennsylvania legislature on an issue of Pennsylvania law.

The majority also seizes on Comment 4 to 13 Pa. C.S. §3104, which states that "any writing which meets the requirements of subsection [(a)] and is not excluded under Section [3103] is a negotiable instrument, and all sections of this [Division] apply to it, *even though it may contain additional language beyond that contemplated by this section*" (emphasis added by majority). Since, as explained supra, the money orders contained language which precluded them from satisfying subsection (a), the quoted language from Comment 4 does not further the majority's argument.

Finally, the majority attempts to support its conclusion by referring to the principle that "purported conditions on an otherwise negotiable instrument, that merely reflect other provisions of the law, do not vitiate negotiability." Op. at 609 (citations omitted). The majority contends that the language at issue amounts merely to a restatement of appellant's statutory defenses against payment where there has been alteration (13 Pa. C.S. §3407), theft (3306(4)), absence of signature (3401) and forgery (3404). The majority overlooks the fact that all of these statutory defenses are, by their own terms, ineffective against holders in due course. On the other hand, the language at issue here—which categorically states that the money order will not be paid if it was stolen—is operative even against holders who have taken in due course. As noted in the Comment to section 3105(a)(1), conditional language may be fairly construed to mean what it says. By its plain terms, the language at issue here sweeps beyond the scope of appellant's statutory defenses, and therefore does more than simply "reflect other provisions of the law." In sum, the statute at issue in this case is devoid of ambiguity, and the application of that statute to these facts compels a conclusion contrary to that reached by the majority. Consequently, I respectfully dissent.

CAPPY, J., joins this dissenting opinion.

This case has been cited with approval by the Montana Supreme Court in Smith v. Farmers Union Mut. Ins. Co., 361 Mont. 516, 260 P.3d 163 (2011).

It is generally accepted that federally guaranteed student loan notes are not negotiable instruments, because they are discharged upon death or disability, thus creating a condition on time of payment; Trent v. North Carolina, 2014 WL 2773579 (W.D.N.C. 2014).

2. Consideration Stated

In the example before the last reprinted case, the note mentioned that it was given in return for the leasing of the theater—that is, it stated exactly what the consideration was that caused the note to be written. Section 3-106 permits the instrument to mention the details of the underlying contract without destroying negotiability as long as payment of the note is not made "subject to" the performance of that contract. Section 3-106(a)'s last sentence clearly permits a *reference* to the underlying contract, though an incorporation of the terms of that contract (without restating them in the note itself) would be fatal to negotiability. The reason is that the prospective holder should never be required to investigate whether all is well with the original agreement; if the instrument requires the current holder to check on this, it is non-negotiable. Gem Global Yield Fund, Ltd. v. Surgilight, Inc., 2006 WL 2389345 (S.D.N.Y. 2006). Another reason is that the separate agreement might contain terms placing a condition on payment; the requisites of *negotiability* will not even entertain such a possibility. The holder must be able to determine the negotiability of an instrument from within its own four corners alone. Mary Margaret Bibler v. Arcata Investments 2, LLC, 2005 WL 3304127 (Mich. App. 2005).

PROBLEM 4

Are the following notes negotiable?

(a) "(Date), I promise to pay bearer $500, subject to the contract I signed with Honest John today, (Signature)." See Official Comment 1, second paragraph, to §3-106; Jackson v. Luellen Farms, Inc., 877 N.E.2d 848 (Ind. App. 2007).

(b) "(Date), I promise to pay bearer $500 as per contract I signed today with Honest John, (Signature)." Cf. §3-117, which says that a separate agreement affects only the parties thereto and not a subsequent holder in due course.

(c) "(Date), I promise to pay bearer $500 on January 1, 2018. For rights as to prepayment and acceleration, see the contract signed September 25, 2018, between the maker and the payee. (Signature)." See §3-106(b)(i).

PROBLEM 5

Whenever it mails out a check, the Adhesion Insurance Company marks it "Void After 90 Days." Is such an instrument technically negotiable?

PROBLEM 6

The promissory note contained this clause: "The collateral for this note is a security interest in the maker's art collection; for rights and duties on default, see the security agreement signed this day creating the security interest." Does this clause destroy negotiability? See §3-106(b)(i) and its Official Comment 1, third paragraph.

D.   "Fixed Amount of Money"

It is elementary that an instrument will be non-negotiable if one cannot look at it and readily calculate the amount that the maker or drawer has promised to pay.

PROBLEM 7

The promissory note stated that the rate of interest was "2% above the prime rate as of the date of maturity." The prime rate is the interest charged by banks to their best customer and can be ascertained by reference to financial publications. Does the fact that the holder of the note has to consult sources outside of the instrument in order to calculate the interest due destroy negotiability? See §3-112.

"I promise to pay 100 bales of cotton to bearer" is a non-negotiable promise; a negotiable instrument must promise or order payment in *money*. This requirement then raises this amusing question: what is money? If in Borneo a note is made payable with "50 boar's teeth," is the note negotiable? Section 1-201(b)(24) defines *money* as the "medium of exchange authorized or adopted by a domestic or foreign government as a part of its currency." The Official Comment to that section states that the "test adopted is that of the sanction of government . . . which recognizes the circulating medium as a part of the official currency of that government."

Note that *money* does not mean only U.S. currency. According to §3-107 an instrument payable in foreign currency is presumed to be payable in either that currency or the U.S. dollar equivalent on the date due *unless the instrument limits payment to the foreign currency.* As a test in statutory reading, read §3-107 and answer this question: If an instrument states that it is payable only with French francs, is it or is it not negotiable? See §3-107's Official Comment.

Heritage Bank v. Bruha

Supreme Court of Nebraska, 2012
283 Neb. 263, 812 N.W.2d 260

CONNOLLY, J.

Heritage Bank (Heritage) sued Jerome J. Bruha on promissory notes that it had purchased from the Federal Deposit Insurance Corporation (FDIC). The FDIC had obtained the notes after it became a receiver for the failed bank that had initially lent the money to Bruha. The notes secured lines of credit for Bruha's benefit. The district court granted summary judgment to Heritage and awarded it $61,384.67 on one of the notes. Bruha appeals. The primary issues are whether either the holder-in-due-course rule of Nebraska's Uniform Commercial Code or federal banking law bars Bruha's defenses to the enforcement of the note. We conclude that federal law bars Bruha's defenses, and thus, we affirm in part. But because of a minor error in the court's calculation of interest, we reverse in part, and remand for correction.

I.   BACKGROUND

1.   PROMISSORY NOTES

On four different occasions in 2008, Bruha signed promissory notes with Sherman County Bank. Although the district court ultimately granted summary judgment to Heritage on all four notes, Bruha's arguments relate only to the fourth and final note. So we will limit our discussion to the facts regarding this note. We will, however, provide some background to put the note in context.

The notes secured lines of credit under which Bruha could borrow money from Sherman County Bank. Bruha then apparently invested the money in accounts with a trading company, which allegedly shared management with Sherman County Bank. In brief, Bruha claims that Sherman County Bank misled him into borrowing money that, in turn, he invested with a trading company that generated trade commissions through risky and speculative commodity trading.

In an affidavit, Bruha claimed that representatives of Sherman County Bank repeatedly advised him against taking money out of his trading account, stating that he would lose more money if he did so than he would by leaving it in. Bruha claimed that the representatives often understated the potential losses he would suffer by staying in the account. Also, Bruha claims he was told that the existing collateral would cover the credit he later took. Further, although he admittedly knew he was increasing his debt burden, he thought it was under one note as opposed to four. The record, however, contains no internal records or documents of Sherman County Bank evidencing any of the representations regarding his account that Bruha claims Sherman County Bank made.

Bruha signed the fourth note, No. 1723, on December 16, 2008. The note evidenced a promise to pay "the principal amount of Seventy-five Thousand & 00/100 ($75,000.00) or so much as may be outstanding, together with interest on the unpaid outstanding principal balance of each advance." The note stated that it "evidence[d] a revolving line of credit."

The note contained a variable interest rate. The rate was subject to change every month and calculated on an index maintained by Sherman County Bank. The interest rate on Bruha's note was 1 percentage point under the percentage on the index at any given time. The initial rate was 7.25 percent, and was later adjusted to 6.75 percent. On default, this interest rate would increase by 5 percentage points. . . .

On note No. 1723, Bruha received the following advancements: He received $10,000 on December 16, 2008; $40,000 on December 17; and $1,000 on January 30, 2009. This totaled $51,000. There is no dispute that Bruha received all of this money.

An affidavit also established the interest rate on the notes. It shows that the initial rate was 7.25 percent. This rate was adjusted to 6.75 percent on February 1, 2009. Then, on August 2, after Bruha defaulted, the rate increased to 11.75 percent.

Sherman County Bank eventually failed, and the FDIC was appointed as receiver. The FDIC then sold and assigned some of Sherman County Bank's assets to Heritage. These assets included the notes signed by Bruha.

Heritage sued Bruha to enforce the notes. The complaint alleged that Bruha owed Heritage on the four notes and that Heritage had received the notes from the FDIC after Sherman County Bank had been placed into receivership. But as mentioned, only note No. 1723 is the subject of this appeal. As to note No. 1723, Heritage claimed that the principal was $75,000 and that the initial interest rate was 8.25 percent. Heritage also alleged that the interest rate was to jump 5 percentage points upon default. Heritage alleged that it was a holder in due course and entitled to enforce the note.

In his amended answer, Bruha admitted that he signed note No. 1723 but claims that he did not do it voluntarily. He claimed that Sherman County Bank had procured his signature "by fraud and/or misrepresentation." Bruha admitted that he had not paid the note but denied that he was obligated to do so.

[The District Court found that the bank was a holder in due course and took free of Bruha's defense of fraud.]

IV. ANALYSIS

1.   BECAUSE NOTE NO. 1723 WAS NOT NEGOTIABLE, HERITAGE IS NOT A HOLDER
IN DUE COURSE

Bruha argues that Heritage is not a holder in due course. Similarly, he argues that the FDIC was not a holder in due course when it held the note. A holder in due course is, with some exceptions, "immune to defenses, claims in recoupment, and claims of title that prior parties to commercial paper might assert. The holder in due course always enjoys certain pleading and proof advantages."[8] So if Heritage were a holder in due course, it would enjoy an advantageous position in litigation with Bruha.

We conclude, however, that Heritage is not a holder in due course because the note was not "negotiable" and article 3 of the Uniform Commercial Code does not apply to this case.

Neb. U.C.C. §3-104(a) (Cum. Supp. 2010) provides: "Except as provided in subsections (c) and (d), 'negotiable instrument' means an unconditional promise or order to pay *a fixed amount of money,* with or without interest or other charges described in the promise or order. . . ." (Emphasis supplied.) Here, the note fails to meet the definition of a "negotiable instrument" because it was not a promise "to pay a fixed amount of money."

Although the Uniform Commercial Code allows notes to have a variable interest rate,[9] under §3-104(a), the principal amount must be fixed.[10] "A fixed amount is an absolute requisite to negotiability."[11] This is because unless a purchaser can determine how much it will be paid under the instrument, it will be unable to determine a fair price to pay for it, which defeats the basic purpose for negotiable instruments.[12]

We applied this principle in Rodehorst v. Gartner,[13] in which we stated that "[a] guaranty is not an agreement to pay a fixed amount and is therefore not a negotiable instrument subject to article 3 of the Nebraska Uniform Commercial Code." To meet the fixed amount requirement, the fixed amount generally must be determinable by reference to the instrument itself without any reference to any outside source.[14] If reference to a

8. 2 James J. White & Robert S. Summers, Uniform Commercial Code §17-1 at 168-69 (5th ed. 2008).

9. See Neb. U.C.C. §3-112 (Reissue 2001).

10. See *id.,* comment 1. See, also, 6 William D. Hawkland & Lary Lawrence, Uniform Commercial Code Series §3-104:7 (rev. 1999).

11. 6 Hawkland & Lawrence, *supra* note [10] at 3-45.

12. *Id.*

13. Rodehorst v. Gartner, 266 Neb. 842, 848, 669 N.W.2d 679, 684 (2003).

14. 4 William D. Hawkland & Lary Lawrence, Uniform Commercial Code Series §3-106:2 (rev. 1999).

separate instrument or extrinsic facts is needed to ascertain the principal due, the sum is not " 'certain' " or fixed.[15]

Here, the text of the note states that Bruha "promises to pay . . . the principal amount of Seventy-five Thousand & 00/100 Dollars ($75,000.00) *or so much as may be outstanding. . . .*" (Emphasis supplied.) Further, the note states that it "evidences a revolving line of credit" and that Bruha could request advances under the obligation up to $75,000. This fails the "fixed amount of money" requirement of §3-104(a); one looking at the instrument itself cannot tell how much Bruha has been advanced at any given time. So, the note is not negotiable. Stated simply, "[a] note given to secure a line of credit under which the amount of the obligation varies, depending on the extent to which the line of credit is used, is not negotiable. . . ."[16]

For a person to be a holder in due course, the instrument must be negotiable.[17] Because the note was not a negotiable instrument, neither the FDIC nor Heritage could ever become a holder in due course of it under Nebraska law. And further, because this note is not a negotiable instrument, article 3 does not apply.[18]

[The court, however still ruled in favor of the bank as an assignee from the FDIC, and that portion of the case will be studied in Chapter 4, when we get to the issue of holding in due course.]

E. *"Courier Without Luggage" Requirement*

Pennsylvania's Chief Justice John Gibson once said that a negotiable instrument must be a "courier without luggage." Overton v. Tyler, 3 Pa. 346, 347 (1846). This oft-repeated description means that the instrument must not be burdened with anything other than the simple and clean unconditional promise or order; it cannot be made to truck around other legal obligations. If the maker of a note adds any *additional* promises to it, the note becomes non-negotiable because the prospective holder is then given notice that the note is or may be conditioned on the performance of the other promise. Section 3-104(a)(3) specifies the few additional items that may be mentioned in an instrument without destroying its negotiable character; read it and then do Problem 8.

---

15. See *id.* at 3-100. See, also, Resolution Trust v. Oaks Apts. Joint Venture, 966 F.2d 995 (5th Cir. 1992); Branch Banking and Trust Co. v. Creasy, 301 N.C. 44, 269 S.E.2d 117 (1980).

16. 11 Am. Jur. 2d *Bills and Notes* §84 at 463-64 (2009). See, also, Yin v. Society National Bank Indiana, 665 N.E.2d 58 (Ind. App. 1996); Farmers Production Credit Assoc. v. Arena, 145 Vt. 20, 481 A.2d 1064 (1984).

17. See Neb. U.C.C. §3-302 (Reissue 2001).

18. See Neb. U.C.C. §3-102 (Reissue 2001).

PROBLEM 8

Do the following clauses in an otherwise negotiable promissory note destroy negotiability?

(a) "Maker agrees that signing this note also indicates acceptance of the contract of sale for which it is given."

(b) "Maker agrees and promises that if the holder of this note deems himself insecure at any time, he may so inform the maker, who will then supply additional collateral in an amount and kind to be specified by the holder."

(c) "Maker agrees to let the holder select an attorney for the maker; at any time the holder directs, said attorney is hereby given the authority to confess judgment against the maker in any appropriate court."

(d) The promissory note contained the following clause:

I have the right to make payments of Principal at any time before they are due. A payment of Principal only is known as a "Prepayment." When I make a Prepayment, I will tell the Note Holder in writing that I am doing so. I may not designate a payment as a Prepayment if I have not made all the monthly payments due under this Note.

Does it destroy negotiability? See HSBC Bank USA, Natl. Assn. v. Gouda, 2010 WL 5128666 (N.J. Super. 2010).

(e) "Maker hereby grants the payee a security interest in the collateral described below."

The following case was decided before the effective date of the 1990 version of Articles 3 and 4 of the Uniform Commercial Code, but the rule of law it states has not changed. The court cites the original numbering of Article 3; you need look only at the new version of §3-104(a).

Woodworth v. The Richmond Indiana Venture

Ohio Court of Common Pleas, 1990
1990 WL 293436

Johnson, J.

This matter is before the court on plaintiff's motion for partial summary judgment and defendant Signet Bank's motion for summary judgment. On December 18, 1987, plaintiff executed a promissory note in which he promised to pay to the order of The Richmond Indiana Venture, A Limited Partnership or holder the sum of $655,625.00. The promissory note was given to pay part of the deferred portion of plaintiff's investment in the partnership. The promissory note was subsequently assigned or negotiated to defendant, Signet Bank. Plaintiff is in default on the promissory note having failed to make payments that fell due on July 1, 1989 and July 1, 1990. Plaintiff filed this action on November 2, 1989.

The standard for granting summary judgment is clear. On a motion for summary judgment, the moving party bears the burden of demonstrating that no genuine issue of material fact exists and that it is entitled to judgment as a matter of law. Adickes v. S.H. Kress and Co. (1970), 398 U.S. 144; Harless v. Willis Day Warehousing Co. (1978), 54 Ohio St. 2d 64, 66. The court will construe the evidence most strongly in favor of the party against whom the motion for summary judgment is made. *Harless*, 54 Ohio St. 2d at 66.

In order to be negotiable, a promissory note must be a signed, unconditional promise to pay a sum certain in money which is payable on demand or at a definite, stated time. The note must be payable to order or bearer and contain no other promise, order, obligation, or power given by the maker except as authorized by §§3-101 to 3-805, inclusive, of the Revised Code. UCC §3-104.

The policy under pre-Code law was that instruments should be as concise as possible and free from collateral engagements. Akron Auto Finance Co. v. Stonebraker (1941), 66 Ohio App. 507. As noted above, the Code continues this policy by mandating that the unconditional promise to pay not be cluttered by other promises, orders, obligations, or powers unless otherwise authorized.

The promissory note at issue contains the following term:

> The undersigned agrees that, in the event any payment due pursuant to the terms of this note be not timely made, at the option of the Partnership, the undersigned shall retroactively lose any interest in the Partnership from the date hereof and the Partnership shall have no obligation to account for any payments theretofore made by the undersigned, and that this remedy is in addition to other remedies afforded by the Partnership Agreement.

This term is clearly a promise by the maker resulting in a forfeiture of his partnership interest and payments in the event of default. The term is more than a mere reference to the partnership agreement, a recitation of security, or an agreement to protect collateral; it is a forfeiture provision in addition to other remedies under the referenced partnership agreement.

In Pacific Finance Loans v. Goodwin (1974), 41 Ohio App. 2d 141, the court held that the requirement of an unconditional promise to pay is contravened by a term providing for the repossession of collateral by a seller without judicial process. The case sub judice is analogous since the term at issue is a forfeiture without resort to judicial process.

Nothing in R.C. §3-104 or §3-112 authorizes the forfeiture term at issue. Based on the above analysis, the court finds that the negotiability of this promissory note is doubtful. Where there is doubt, the decision should be against negotiability. Official Code Comment 5 to UCC §3-104. Since the promissory note is not negotiable, defendant Signet Bank cannot claim the status of a holder in due course and is subject to ordinary contract defenses that plaintiff may assert.

Having considered the pleadings and memoranda filed herein, the court finds that plaintiff has fulfilled his burden. Accordingly, plaintiff's motion is sustained. Defendant's motion is denied. Counsel for plaintiff shall prepare an appropriate entry. . . .

MOTION FOR RECONSIDERATION

This matter is before the court on defendant's motion for reconsideration. Upon consideration of the memoranda filed herein, the court affirms its decision of September 19, 1990.

The court finds persuasive the fact that the forfeiture provision may be exercised at the option of the *partnership*, not the holder of the instrument. The provision does not require that the holder must declare a default before the partnership may exercise its option. Instead, the partnership may declare a forfeiture if payments are not timely made. A situation could develop, by mistake or otherwise, wherein the partnership exercises its option before the holder declares a default. In such case, the maker might well decline to cure an overdue payment or to make future payments because of the forfeiture. This exemplifies the reason why negotiable instruments may contain no other promise, order, obligation, or power except as authorized by statute.

The forfeiture provision at issue is not, as defendant suggests, analogous to collateral. It is a basic maxim of law that collateral follows the debt; here the option to declare a forfeiture remains with the partnership and the benefit of its exercise flows to the partnership, not the holder of the instrument.

This case is distinguishable from Standard Premium Plan Corp. v. Hirschorn (N.Y. Sup. Ct., 1968), 5 U.C.C. Rep. Serv. 163. In *Hirschorn*, the payee or assignee, in the event of default, could cancel an underlying insurance policy and apply returned premiums against the unpaid balance. Here the forfeiture flows to the partnership, not the holder and the forfeited interest is not applied to the unpaid balance on the instrument.

Any deleterious effects upon the flow of commercial instruments can be avoided by confining forfeiture provisions such as this one to the partnership agreement. Including such provision in the instrument clutters the unconditional promise to pay and thereby makes the commercial viability of this instrument less certain. . . .

. . . Counsel for plaintiff shall prepare an appropriate entry.

F.   "Payable on Demand or at a Definite Time"

A holder of an instrument must be able to tell when it comes due, or the instrument is non-negotiable; however, there is no requirement that the instrument be dated. An undated instrument that specifies no time of payment is treated as an instrument payable on demand by the holder. Read §§3-108 and 3-113.

PROBLEM 9

Do the following clauses in a promissory note destroy negotiability?

(a) "Payable 30 days after sight."

(b) "Payable in eleven successive monthly installments of $2,414.92 each and in a final payment of $2,415.03 thereafter. The first installment being payable on the _____ day of _____ 20___, and the remaining installments on the same date of each month thereafter until paid." The blanks were not filled in. See Barclays Bank PLC v. Johnson, 129 N.C. App. 370, 499 S.E.2d 768 (1998).

(c) "Payable on November 8, 2018, but the holder may demand payment at any time prior thereto if he deems himself insecure." Cf. §1-309 (Option to Accelerate at Will).

(d) "Payable when the sun comes up tomorrow."

(e) "Payable on November 8, 2018, but if my potato crop fails that year, payment shall be extended until November 8 of the following year."

(f) "Payable on November 8, 2018, but the maker hereby reserves the option to extend the time of payment until he can pay without serious financial hardship." See Smith v. Vaughn, 174 Ohio App. 3d 473, 882 N.E.2d 941 (2007).

(g) "Payable 120 days after my rich uncle Al dies." Such notes are called *post-obituary* notes.

(h) "Payable 100 years from the date of this note, but if my rich uncle Al dies before this note is due, it shall become payable 10 days after his death." See Smith v. Gentilotti, 371 Mass. 839, 359 N.E.2d 953(1977).

(i) "Payable on my next birthday."

PROBLEM 10

A paragraph in a promissory note required the maker to give written notice to the holder of the note in the event that the maker wanted to make a prepayment of the principal amount before the scheduled date of maturity of the loan. Is this note payable at a definite time, in your opinion? Consider whether such an obligation makes the payment of the note less certain, and note §3-108(b). See In re Steinberg, 498 B.R. 391 (B.A.P. 10th Cir. 2013).

G. *"Payable to Bearer or to Order"*

The early English common law courts would not permit a subsequent holder of a contract to sue one of the original parties to it; the courts said that there was no *privity* (connection) between the plaintiff and the defendant. These cases were frustrating to the merchants of the day because they recognized the desirability of permitting a direct suit by a remote transferee against the original promisor. These merchants and their attorneys devised two clever ways of establishing privity between the original creator of the paper and the later holder.

The first way was to make the original promise or order payable to *bearer*—that is, payable to the holder of the paper and not to any specific person. In this way, privity passed with the physical delivery of the instrument. The only problem with bearer paper, which is still with us, is that it is too negotiable; it is a little bit too much like money for safety. In Miller v. Race, 1 Burr. 452, 97 Eng. Rep. 398 (K.B. 1758), Lord Mansfield was faced with the problem of a bearer note that had been stolen from the mails and negotiated to plaintiff by one "who had the appearance of a gentleman." Lord Mansfield held that title to bearer paper passes with the instrument since negotiable paper is to be "treated as money, as cash." Plaintiff, a holder in due course, took free of the defense of theft, and defendant had to pay the note.

The second means of establishing privity was to have the creator of the instrument make it payable to a specified person or to whomever that person further ordered the paper paid; thus, notes were made payable to "John Smith or Order" or "John Smith or his assigns." This means the person to whom Doe ordered payment acquired privity, since the original promise ran directly to the assignee. This order paper today simply says "Pay to the order of John Smith," meaning that the instrument will be paid to John Smith or to whomever he orders as his nominee. Until John Smith makes some sort of *order*, the instrument cannot be validly transferred. He usually does this by writing his order on the back of the instrument and then signing his own name.

Section 3-104(a)(1) of the Code continues this ancient requirement that the maker or drawer use either bearer or order language (*words of negotiability*) on an instrument before it is technically negotiable. These special words have become so associated with negotiable instruments that they now serve as one means of easily identifying contracts that are meant to be negotiable, and thus warn people that they may be creating paper having the legal consequences of negotiable transfer (loss of defenses on the underlying contract). Read §3-109.

PROBLEM 11

Do the following clauses in a promissory note create bearer paper?

(a) "Pay to John Smith." See Sunrizon Homes, Inc. v. American Guar. Inv. Corp., 782 P.2d 103 (Okla. 1988).

(b) "Pay to the order of John Smith or bearer." See Official Comment 2 to §3-109.

(c) "Pay to bearer."

(d) "Pay to the order of Cash."

(e) "Pay to a Merry Christmas."

PROBLEM 12

Do the following clauses create order or bearer paper, or do they make the instrument non-negotiable for failure to create either?

(a) "Pay to the order of (blank)." See §3-115 and Official Comment 2.

(b) A promissory note with this language: "Pay to John Doe's estate." See §3-110(c)(2)(i); Sirius LC v. Erickson, 144 Idaho 38, 156 P.3d 539 (2007).

(c) "Pay to the order of the President of the United States." See §3-110(c)(2)(iv).

(d) The drawer of a check drew a line through the words "the order of" that were printed on the check prior to the space for the payee's name. Is the check, as altered, negotiable? See §3-104(c). If the drawer of a check or the maker of a promissory note wants to destroy negotiability, what should be done? See §3-104(d). Why would this ever be desirable?

H.   Consumer Notes

Because the creation of a negotiable instrument deprives a maker of the usual contract defenses, most commentators have argued that it is unwise to permit consumers to sign promissory notes. Many state consumer statutes forbid a seller or a lessor to take a negotiable instrument (other than a check) as part of a consumer sale or lease. These statutes do not typically destroy the negotiability of such an instrument, however, and if a consumer note were to get into the hands of a holder in due course, the consumer would still be unable to assert contract defenses when the holder in due course demanded payment. See Circle v. Jim Walter Homes, Inc., 535 F.2d 583 (10th Cir. 1976); see also Jefferson v. Mitchell Select Furniture Co., 56 Ala. App. 259, 321 So. 2d 216 (1975) ("Of course, it is difficult to conceive how one could be a holder of a negotiable instrument which showed that it was taken in the credit sale of consumer merchandise with retention of title and a purchase money security interest, without knowledge that it arose from [a violation of the statute]."). The Uniform Consumer Credit Code §3.404(1) (1974 text) does preserve a consumer's defenses even if the instrument is owned by a holder in due course.

The Federal Trade Commission has promulgated a regulation, 16 C.F.R. part 433, requiring that all promissory notes and contracts taken in consumer sales or *purchase money loans* (defined as loans made to purchase goods or services from a seller who refers the consumer to the lender or who is affiliated with the lender by common control, contract, or business arrangement) contain the following language:

NOTICE

ANY HOLDER OF THIS CONSUMER CREDIT CONTRACT IS SUBJECT TO ALL CLAIMS AND DEFENSES WHICH THE DEBTOR COULD ASSERT AGAINST THE SELLER OF GOODS OR SERVICES OBTAINED PURSUANT HERETO OR WITH THE PROCEEDS HEREOF. RECOVERY HEREUNDER BY THE DEBTOR SHALL NOT EXCEED AMOUNTS PAID BY THE DEBTOR HEREUNDER.

The regulation applies to all such notes or contracts signed after May 14, 1976; see J. White & R. Summers, Uniform Commercial Code (6th ed. 2010) [hereinafter White & Summers, a leading treatise on the meaning of the UCC] §15-9. Failure to include the required statement violates §5 of the Federal Trade Commission Act (forbidding Unfair and Deceptive Practices), and §3-305(e) in the 2002 Revision of Article 3 of the Uniform Commercial Code automatically adds the missing statement to all consumer transactions that should carry it.

QUESTION

Does the required FTC language destroy negotiability? See §3-106(d).

PROBLEM 13

Sonata, about to take music lessons, purchased a violin on credit from Barenboim Music, which negotiated the note to Titolare Finance Co. The note bore the above FTC legend. When the note came due, Sonata refused to pay Titolare Finance because the violin fell apart after three lessons. Can Titolare Finance claim it is a holder in due course and thus entitled to enforce the note in spite of her defense? See §3-305(e). Is this true even if the note had failed to contain the FTC notice? See also §§9-403(d) and 9-404(d). Would we reach the same result if Sonata were a professional musician?

CHAPTER 2   ASSESSMENT

Multiple Choice Questions

1. Djuna purchased a 3D printer from Joyce for $19,390. As part of the trans-action, Djuna signed a piece of paper promising to pay $19,390. What difference does it make if that piece of paper is a negotiable instrument?
   a. If it is a negotiable instrument, Djuna would have to pay $19,390 to a holder in due course of the paper, even if Joyce delivered a defective printer or no printer at all.
   b. If it is not a negotiable instrument, Djuna would have to pay only if she was obliged to pay under contract law. If Joyce does not deliver as promised, that would reduce or excuse Djuna's obligation to pay.
   c. If it is a negotiable instrument, UCC Article 3 would govern most issues that would arise: how to transfer rights in the paper to someone else, who is liable if the paper is stolen, how to present the paper for payment, what effect it would have if there were a mistake in the numbers on the paper, etc.
   d. All of the above.

2. The paper that Djuna signed contains this provision: "Djuna is obliged to pay if Joyce delivers the 3D printer as promised." Can the paper be a negotiable instrument?
   a. Yes. She has made an unconditional promise to pay once the printer is delivered.
   b. Yes, but she only has to pay if Joyce delivers the 3D printer as promised.
   c. No. It is conditional and so not a negotiable instrument.
   d. No. Negotiable instruments are used only in loan transactions, not sales.

3. Shaun got a loan from Isobel for $50,000. He signed a mortgage, putting up his house as collateral for the loan. The parties then realized they had forgotten to prepare a promissory note. Shaun copied the text of a negotiable promissory note into an email message, edited it to be payable to the order of Isobel for the amount of $50,000, typed his name at the bottom, and sent it to Isobel. Could someone be a holder in due course of that electronic promissory note?
   a. Yes, if the text meets all the requirements of Article 3.
   b. No. It is neither a writing nor made effective by UETA, because there is no "single authoritative copy of the transferable record."
   c. Yes. Shaun will be bound by his promise to pay, without regard to formalities.
   d. No. Only paper documents can be negotiable instruments.

4. Shem Bank loaned $45,000 to Issy. Issy signed a promissory note payable to the order of Shem Bank, which contains this clause: "Issy hereby promises Shem Bank to have right of first refusal, should she need to borrow money in the future." Can the promissory note be negotiable?

   a. No, because it has an undertaking in addition to the promise to pay the money.

   b. No, because the clause did not read "Issy hereby promises *to the order of* Shem Bank."

   c. Yes. Issy has promised to pay the money without any conditions. The extra promise does not detract from that.

   d. Yes. Otherwise Issy would not have to repay the loan which would defeat the purpose of the transaction.

5. Which of the following could be on a negotiable check?

   a. Pay to the order of Freddie.

   b. Pay to bearer.

   c. Pay to Freddie.

   d. Pay to Freddie or bearer.

   e. All of the above.

Answers

1. D is the best answer. This fact pattern illustrates the role of negotiability. UCC Article 3 applies to negotiable instruments. If the piece of paper is a negotiable instrument, then it will be governed by Article 3, so C is correct. One of the rules in Article 3 is the holder in due course doctrine. Later chapters cover that doctrine in detail, but basically a holder in due course can recover from anyone who signed the instrument, even if that person has a defense to payment. A holder in due course could recover from Djuna if Joyce delivered a defective printer. So A is also correct. The holder in due course doctrine only applies to negotiable instruments. So if the piece of paper is not a negotiable instrument, that promise would be governed by contract law. As you learned in contracts, if Joyce breached, then Djuna's promise to pay would be reduced or excused — even if the contract had been assigned. B is correct as well, so the best answer is D. All of the above.

   Note that, as the last section in this chapter explains, the holder in due course doctrine does not apply to notes in consumer credit sales, but such notes may still be negotiable, and so governed by the other rules in Article 3.

2. C is the best answer. The provision states an express condition to payment, so the promise to pay is conditional, making the promissory note non-negotiable. The fact pattern shows the reason for the rule. The

promissory note says, right on its face, that Djuna is obliged only if Joyce performs as promised. It would not make sense to apply Article 3's holder in due course doctrine, under which Djuna would have to pay a holder in due course even if Joyce did not perform as promised (i.e., Djuna could not raise any defense to payment against a holder in due course).

The condition (like all conditions) may be fulfilled. The question is whether there is an express condition to payment. So B and C are both wrong. D is incorrect. Negotiable instruments may be used in loans, sales, or any other type of transactions — or even as gifts.

3. B is the best answer. As discussed in Good v. Wells Fargo Bank, the UETA provides that an electronic promissory note for a mortgage loan may be treated as a negotiable instrument, so D is wrong. But, to be effective as a negotiable instrument, the record must meet all the conditions in the UETA. The key requirement is that there be a "single authoritative copy of the transferable record." Negotiable instrument law assumes that there is only one copy of the instrument, and so only one holder of the instrument entitled to payment. If there were multiple copies, then there could be multiple holders entitled to payment. The UETA accommodates this policy, by providing that for electronic promissory notes, there must be the equivalent, just one authoritative copy. An email can be freely copied and forwarded, so the email would not qualify. A is incorrect, because negotiability does not depend only on the text. C has it backward. Article 3 and the UETA use formalities to ensure that Article 3 only applies to the sort of promises it was intended to apply to. Contract law has flexibility to deal with other promises.

4. A is the best answer. The clause is an additional undertaking, making the promissory note non-negotiable, under §3-104(a)(3). B simply misleads, referring to a different and irrelevant rule. To be negotiable, an instrument must be unconditional *and* must not have extra undertakings, so C is incorrect.

If a promissory note is non-negotiable, that does not mean that the promise is not enforceable. Rather, it simply means that the promise is not governed by UCC Article 3, but is governed by some other body of law, usually contract law. A promise to pay money may be enforced under contract law. D is incorrect.

5. E is the best answer. Someone who signs a negotiable promissory note is really promising to pay. Even if the person does not get what was promised, or the person has some other defense to payment, the person will nevertheless have to pay, if the note ends up in the hands of a holder in due course. To limit the rule to notes that the signer should expect to be presented by such strangers, a negotiable note must be payable to order ("I'll pay whomever payee orders me to pay") or bearer ("I'll pay whomever

shows up with this note"). A promise to pay Freddie (as opposed to "pay to the order of Freddie"), by contrast, is a personal obligation to pay Freddie, and if Freddie is not entitled to payment, should not be enforceable. If this were a promissory note, only A, B, and D could be negotiable. But that rule does not apply here, because the facts involve a check, not a promissory note.

Some promissory notes are negotiable, some are not. But everyone expect checks to be passed on. So the rule requiring order or bearer language is not required on checks. Any of the possibilities is permitted on a negotiable check, so the best answer is E. All of the above.

CHAPTER 3
NEGOTIATION

The movement of negotiable instruments from one person to another can be as involuntary as a theft or as deliberate as a sale. It is the lawyer's job to make sure that clients observe the formalities so that transfers are valid and clients won't be thinking ugly thoughts about malpractice.

I. SOME TECHNICAL TERMS

A. Parties

Those whose names appear on a negotiable instrument are given definite labels with specific legal consequences varying according to the label affixed.

A promissory note in its most pristine state is a two-party instrument. The person who issues the instrument and promises to pay is called the *maker*. According to §3-412, the legal duty of the issuer of a promissory note is to "pay the instrument (i) according to its terms at the time it was issued ... (ii) if the issuer signed an incomplete instrument, according to its terms when completed."[1] The person to whom the note is made payable is the *payee*. If the note is made payable to *bearer*, there is no specific payee, and whoever has possession of the paper is presumptively entitled to payment by the maker.

A draft (or check) is always a three-party instrument. The person who creates the draft and orders the drawee to pay is called the *drawer*. Though the courts, and others who should know better, frequently do so, be careful that you do not confuse a *drawer* with a *maker*; there are important differences between their legal responsibilities. A *drawer* creates a *draft*, a *maker* creates a *note*. According to §3-414(b), by drawing a draft, the drawer engages that upon dishonor of the draft by the drawee the drawer will pay the amount of the draft. The *drawee* is the person to whom the drawer addresses the order of payment. On a check, the drawee is the bank at which the drawer has an account.[2] The *payee* of a draft is the person specified by the drawer as entitled to receive payment. As with notes, if the draft is payable to bearer, there is no specific payee, and any holder is entitled to payment from the drawee. If a check is drawn payable to the order of a specific person, that person is the *payee* and may further transfer (*negotiate*) the check in the manner described below.

B. Negotiability vs. Negotiation

Be careful not to confuse these two very similar terms. The question "Is an instrument negotiable?" asks if the instrument is in the proper form to meet the technical requirements of negotiability found in §3-104(a). The question "Has the instrument been negotiated?" asks about the legal validity of the attempted transfer of the instrument. Thus, negotiability refers to *form*, negotiation to *transfer*.

II.   TRANSFER AND NEGOTIATION

A negotiable instrument goes through three stages in its life. The first stage is called *issuance*. Read §3-105. Skipping for a moment the middle stage, the final stage in the existence of a negotiable instrument is its *presentment* for payment. Read §3-501(a). We will consider the legal ramifications

---

1. The issuer of a cashier's check assumes the same liability according to §3-412.

2. As we shall see when we get to bank collection, in Article 4 of the Code the drawee is referred to there as the *payor bank*. See §4-105(3).

of both issuance and presentment elsewhere. For now, we focus on the middle stage: the *transfer* of the instrument, meaning every legally significant movement of the paper between issuance and presentment.

It was a basic rule at common law and is now a statutory rule, §3-203(b), that the physical transfer of an instrument, if intended to give the recipient rights to the instrument (whether or not a technical *negotiation*), vests in the transferee whatever rights the transferor had in the instrument. This is the called the "shelter rule" because the transferee takes shelter in the rights of the transferor. We will consider the shelter rule in detail in Chapter 4 when it is used to even pass holder in due course rights to parties who themselves do not qualify as HIDCs. For now just write the words "shelter rule" next to §3-203(b).

Under the Code, if the physical transfer is done in such a manner as to make the transferee a technical *holder* of the instrument, then the transfer is called a *negotiation*.[3] This is important because no one can become a *holder in due course* unless that person is first a holder, and becoming a holder is tied up with proper negotiation. Carefully read §1-201(b)(21), defining *holder*, and §3-201, discussing *negotiation*. Think of it this way: a proper negotiation confers holder status on the transferee, with all the benefits holder status carries (including the possibility of becoming a holder in due course). Without a valid negotiation, the transferee is not a holder and has much more limited rights.

The negotiation of order paper is accomplished by (a) the indorsement by the proper person (who thereby becomes an *indorser*) and (b) the delivery of the instrument to the transferee (who thereupon qualifies as a *holder*). An *indorsement* is a signature placed on an instrument by the payee or any later transferees. The negotiation of bearer paper needs no indorsement; delivery to the transferee is all that is required for the transferee to qualify as a holder. Read all of §3-201.

III. SPECIAL AND BLANK INDORSEMENT

If the instrument is made payable to the order of a specific payee, that payee will be required to indorse the instrument to transfer it to another. A drawee bank, as a matter of course, will require the payee's indorsement

---

3. The issuance of the instrument to the first taker also creates *holder* status in that person without a negotiation having occurred. A named payee becomes a holder on getting possession of the instrument, and if the instrument is payable to bearer, anyone in possession of it is automatically a holder.

before it makes payment ("Please sign the back of the check here" the teller will say if you present the check across the counter); see §3-501(b)(2)(iii). As we shall see in Chapter 5 when we get to check collection, the bank in which checks are deposited into the payee's own account need not get its customer's signature as payee, but can pass the checks on to other banks unendorsed, while at the same time making a warranty that the check went into the payee's account at the depositary bank. The idea here was to speed up check collection by eliminating unneeded indorsements for items deposited in the correct accounts.

There are two different ways the payee can indorse any instrument. The payee can simply sign the back of the instrument. Such a signature is called a *blank indorsement* and has the legal effect of converting the instrument into bearer paper. If the payee wishes to preserve the *order* character of the instrument, the original payee may specify a new payee by writing "Pay (name of new payee)" above the indorsement. Such an indorsement is called a *special indorsement* and has the legal effect of making the instrument the sole property of the new payee, who becomes a *holder* as soon as the instrument is delivered. Further, the common law always provided that, until that moment, the original payee can strike out the special indorsement and do anything with the instrument—after all, until delivered to someone else it still belongs to the original payee.

No further "order" language is necessary as part of the special indorsement; the negotiability of an instrument is not affected by language written on the instrument during the course of negotiation. An indorsement that reads "Pay to Jane Doe" is legally the same as one that says "Pay to the order of Jane Doe." Read §3-205.

PROBLEM 14

David Hansen banked with the Mechanical National Bank. Hansen owed $50 to William Egger and decided to pay him by writing out a check for $50, using one of the checks Mechanical furnished him when he opened his account. He gave the check to Egger, who wrote his name on the back of the check. Egger gave the check to his wife, Cynthia, who took it down to the Cornucopia Grocery and asked the manager to cash it. The manager paid Cynthia $50 and then took the check and wrote "Pay to the Cornucopia Grocery" just above William Egger's signature. When Billy Speed, the Check Collection Service's messenger, came by, the manager gave the check to him for delivery to the Octopus National Bank, where the grocery had an account. Speed delivered the check to Octopus National Bank, where the bank's check processing machine merely stamped the words "Octopus National Bank" on the back of the check. Octopus National Bank then forwarded the check to the Mechanical National Bank. Answer the following questions:

(a) To which parties should these labels be attached: drawer, drawee, payee, or depositary bank (defined in §4-105(2))?

(b) Did the following people qualify as *holders*: David Hansen, William Egger, Cynthia Egger, the manager of Cornucopia Grocery, Cornucopia Grocery, Billy Speed, Octopus National Bank, and Mechanical National Bank?

(c) If William Egger had failed to indorse the check, but simply deposited it in his account with Octopus National Bank, would the bank have been a *holder*? See §4-205.

(d) What was the legal effect of the language written on the check by the grocery store manager?

(e) Which of the parties are properly called *indorsers*? See §3-204.

PROBLEM 15

A check was made payable to "Mary and Donald Colpitts." Must both payees indorse it in order to negotiate the instrument? What if the check were payable to "Mary or Donald Colpitts"? Must both payees indorse now? Finally, what if it simply is payable to "Mary Colpitts, Donald Colpitts" with no connecting word? Are two indorsements needed here? To answer all these questions, see §3-110(d) and its Official Comment 4. What result where the payees names are "stacked" like this:

Mary Colpitts
Donald Colpitts
Pay to the order of <u>Facade Motor Company</u>

See Pelican National Bank v. Provident National Bank of Maryland, 381 Md. 327, 849 A.2d 475 (2004). If a check payable to multiple payees is indorsed by only one of them, is that a proper negotiation? See McAllen Hospitals, L.P. v. State Farm County Mut. Ins. Co. of Texas, 57 Tex. Sup. Ct. J. 579 (Tex. 2014).

PROBLEM 16

When Portia Moot received her first paycheck from the law firm that recently hired her, she was annoyed to discover that it was made out to "Portia Mort." When she took the check to her bank to cash it, she mentioned the problem to the bank clerk, who promptly called you, the bank's attorney. What steps would you suggest the bank follow in this situation? See §3-204(d) and its Official Comment 3.

In the original version of Article 3, only a *holder* has the right to sue on an instrument to enforce payment, but §3-301 in the revised version would allow owners who are non-holders to sue in some circumstances, replacing the original word *holder* with the more inclusive *person entitled to enforce the instrument.* This term generally means a holder, but it also includes certain parties to whom other sections of the Code give similar rights (matters we will explore later). Read §3-301. To qualify as a holder under §1-201(b)(21), a person must meet two requirements: (a) possession of the instrument and, for non-bearer instruments, (b) be the *person identified* in the instrument (either as payee or special indorsee). Failure to establish *holder* status because of defects in negotiation can be legally fatal.

Sometimes the indorsement is not made on the promissory note, but on a separate piece of paper, called an "allonge," which is formally defined as a piece of paper attached to the original note for purposes of indorsement.[4] An allonge has an interesting history, traceable to the days in which instruments circulated for long periods before being presented for payment. Consider, for example, the early period in United States history before it was even a country. People living in the Americas frequently had their banks back in Great Britain. If they drew up drafts ("checks") on these banks and gave them to another American, that person was unlikely to immediately send it across the Atlantic to the mother country. Instead, the payee would simply indorse it over to one of the payee's creditors, who would do the same. In those days drafts would circulate, more or less like money, for extended periods of time. But the drafts quickly ran out of room on which to place indorsements, so a separate piece of paper, called an "allonge," was glued to the original draft and the new indorsements were placed on the allonge. There are cases from Great Britain where the allonge had over a hundred indorsements before finally being presented to the drawee for payment.

The Uniform Commercial Code still allows the use of an allonge, and given the large number of transfers that some mortgage promissory notes have had in the last few years, there are many new cases dealing with the allonge. These cases frequently reveal problems with negotiation that give the current holder of the instrument difficulties in trying to establish "holder" status.

PROBLEM 17

Desert Paradise, Inc., initiated a scam in which hundreds of middle-class people signed promissory notes in order to invest in the supposed development of a retirement community to be built in the Southwest. Desert Paradise, the payee on all these notes, sold them in bulk to Octopus National Bank

---

4. See Official Comment 1 (last paragraph) to §3-204.

(ONB). Rather than indorsing its name hundreds of times on each of the notes, Desert Paradise had its indorsement printed on a separate sheet of paper, which it then folded into each promissory note, not connecting it in any way other than the fold. Desert Paradise's officials then absconded with the money and left the desert land untouched. Octopus National Bank demanded payment from the makers of the notes, and when they tried to raise defenses of breach of contract and fraud, ONB claimed to be a holder in due course, so as to take free of these defenses. Is ONB even a holder? See §3-204(a) and the last paragraph in its Official Comment 1. For a case with somewhat similar facts, see Adams v. Madison Realty & Dev., Inc., 853 F.2d 163 (3d Cir. 1988) ($19.5 million involved). The last sentence of §3-204(a) says that an allonge must be affixed to the instrument. What does "affixed" mean? Would a paper clip do the trick? A staple? See Lamson v. Commercial Credit Corp., 187 Colo. 382, 531 P.2d 966 (1975) ("Stapling is the modern equivalent of gluing or pasting. Certainly as a physical matter it is just as easy to cut by scissors a document pasted or glued to another as it is to detach the two by unstapling."). One court has blessed the used of an Acco fastener; Federal Home Loan Mortg. Corp. v. Madison, 2011 WL 2690617 (D. Ariz. 2011). Do you think a paper clip affixes the allonge to the instrument?

IV. FORGERY OF THE PAYEE'S NAME

Understanding the following rule is crucial to an appreciation of many of the issues we will study in this course.

If an instrument is payable to the *order* of a named payee, only that payee can become a *holder,* and even this status is not conferred until the payee gets possession of the instrument. Thereafter no one can qualify as a *holder* until the payee indorses the instrument; without the payee's valid indorsement, no later transferees will have taken by a valid *negotiation* of the instrument, which remains the payee's property. An unauthorized signature (i.e., a forgery or a signature by a non-agent) is *not* effective to negotiate the instrument, so following a forgery of the payee's name, no later transferee (no matter how innocent, no matter how good the forgery, no matter how far down the line the taker is, etc.) can qualify as a holder.

PROBLEM 18

When Laura Lawyer's briefcase was stolen, it contained her monthly paycheck from the law firm for which she worked, made payable to her order.

She had not indorsed it. The thief who stole the briefcase forged her name to the back of the paycheck and transferred it to an innocent party, Cornucopia Grocery. When the latter tried to cash the check at the drawee bank, the bank alerted Laura, and she arrived at the bank immediately. Can she retrieve the check from Cornucopia Grocery? See §3-306.

PROBLEM 19

Assume that on receiving her paycheck, Laura Lawyer (from the last Problem) had signed her name to the back of the instrument, which then was blown out a window and landed at the feet of a criminal, Harry Thief. Harry took the check down to Cornucopia Grocery and told the manager that he (Harry) was Lance Lawyer, Laura's father, and asked the manager to cash it for him. The manager made Harry indorse the instrument (reason: to make Harry contractually liable thereon (§3-415(a)), so Harry wrote "Lance Lawyer" under Laura's indorsement. Is Cornucopia Grocery a holder?

PROBLEM 20

Assume that Laura (from the above Problems) wanted to indorse the instrument over to her mother, so on the back she wrote "Pay to Lilly Lawyer" and then signed her own name. Thus indorsed, the instrument was blown out a window, and Harry Thief found it. He indorsed "Lilly Lawyer" under Laura's name and transferred the check to Cornucopia Grocery. Is Cornucopia Grocery now a holder? See §3-205(a).

The important rule to understand here is that any unauthorized indorsement of the payee's name or any special indorsee's name is *not* a valid negotiation and gives subsequent transferees no legal rights in the instrument, no matter how innocent they are or how far removed from the forgery. The same rule applies to missing indorsements of the payee or special indorsee; later possessors of the instrument do not qualify as holders. BUT once an instrument becomes bearer paper, anyone in possession of it is a holder. Subsequent unauthorized signatures have no effect on the holder status of later takers of bearer paper, or, phrased another way, valid indorsements are not required to negotiate bearer paper (§3-201(b)), mere transfer of possession is enough.

PROBLEM 21

Laura (again from the above Problems) never had a course in commercial paper, so when she received her paycheck, she simply wrote her name on the back and mailed the check to her mother. Her mother (who had had a commercial paper course) needed for some reason to hold onto the check for a week before cashing it, so she wrote "Pay to Lilly Lawyer" *above* Laura's indorsement. Has the check now become order paper requiring the mother's indorsement for further negotiation? See §3-205(c).

CHAPTER 3   ASSESSMENT

Multiple Choice Questions

1. Micawaber borrowed money from Wickfield, signed a negotiable promissory note payable to the order of Wickfield, and handed it to Wickfield. What term applies to that transfer of possession?
   a. Transfer.
   b. Issuance.
   c. Negotiation.
   d. All of the above.

2. Wickfield sold the note and delivered it to Trotwood. Wickfield neglected to indorse the note. What term applies to that transfer of possession?
   a. Transfer.
   b. Issuance.
   c. Negotiation.
   d. None of the above, because the note was not properly indorsed.

3. Spenlow issued a check to his employee, Copperfield. Murdstone stole the check. After much practice, Murdstone wrote a perfect copy of Copperfield's signature on a piece of paper, wrote "Pay to Gummidge" over the forged signature, stapled the paper to the check, and sold it to Gummidge. Is Gummidge a holder?
   a. Yes, if she took the check for value, in good faith, and with no notice of the theft and forgery.
   b. No, because the check was not indorsed by Copperfield.
   c. Yes, because an indorsement on an allonge is effective and the indorsement looked perfectly genuine.
   d. No, because Murdstone did not write "Pay to the order of Gummidge."

4. Traddles stopped by his bank one evening to deposit his paycheck. Just after Traddles signed his name on the back of the check, Little Em'ly appeared with a revolver and relieved him of the instrument. Was Little Em'ly a holder?

    a. Yes. She is in possession of bearer paper.
    b. No. She stole the check, which still belongs to Traddles.
    c. No. Traddles indorsed the check in blank, not specifically to Little Em'ly.
    d. No. Traddles is still the holder.

Answers

1. B is the best answer. The first time the instrument is delivered is the issuance. An issuance is not a transfer or a negotiation (even if it makes the payee a holder). That means (as we will see in later chapters) that the issuer has different rights and liabilities than a transferor. For example, a transferor makes a transfer warranty, that there are not legal problems with the instrument.

2. A is the best answer. Any time an instrument is physically transferred with intent to give the recipient the right to enforce the instrument, that is a transfer. A transfer that makes the recipient a holder is a negotiation. But Wickfield did not indorse the note, so Trotwood is not a holder. The transfer was not a negotiation, so C is incorrect. A transfer that does not make the recipient a holder is still a transfer, so D is incorrect. That will be important for several reasons. For example, a transfer conveys all the rights of the transferor to the transferee. Only the first delivery is an issuance, so B is not correct.

3. B is the best answer. As stated earlier in this chapter: "To qualify as a holder under §1-201(b)(21), a person must meet two requirements: (a) possession of the instrument and, for non-bearer instruments, (b) be the person identified in the instrument (either as payee or special indorsee)." Gummidge is in possession. But the instrument was payable to Copperfield and he has not made it payable to anyone else. It is not payable to Gummidge, so she is not a holder. B is correct. The forged indorsement does not count as Copperfield's indorsement, no matter how skillfully done, so C is incorrect. D gives the wrong reason. Order language is not required on an indorsement, but the indorsement fails here because it is not authorized. Answer A likewise looks to irrelevant matters. We mention them here, because good faith, notice, and value do become relevant in later chapters, when we ask if a holder is a holder in due course—or a mere holder.

4. A is the best answer. Traddles indorsed the check in blank, making it bearer paper. Little Em'ly is in possession of bearer paper, so she is a holder. The check still belongs to Traddles, but that is a different question, so B is incorrect. Little Em'ly would be a holder either if in possession of an instrument made specifically payable to her or (as here) in possession of bearer paper, which is payable to whoever is in possession. C misstates the rule. Traddles is not in possession, so he is not a holder, contrary to D.

Traddles need not give up hope! As we will see, just because Little Em'ly is a holder does not mean she is entitled to payment or even has the right to keep the check. Rather, *holder* is a key term we will meet in later chapters, just like *issuer, indorser, transfer, negotiation,* and the other terms we learned in this chapter.

CHAPTER 4

HOLDERS IN DUE COURSE

I. *ACQUIRING HOLDER IN DUE COURSE STATUS*

A. *Some History of the Doctrine*

Let it be clear at the outset that most contracts are assignable but they travel with their defenses into the hands of the assignee; Restatement of Contracts (Second) §336. For example, if the owner of land hires a contractor to build a building on it and promises to pay the contractor a set amount of money, the contractor could sell the contractual right to this money to someone else. The terminology of the law would call the contractor the assignor, the entity buying the contract would be the assignee, and the owner of the land would be the obligor (the one who owes the money). The assignee gets the right to collect the money from the owner of the land (the obligor), but if the original contractor failed to construct the building according to the contract, the obligor could subtract whatever damages this caused from the amount being paid to the assignee. It is against this background that we study the contrary rule that has developed through the centuries for negotiable instruments.

Lord Mansfield was responsible for popularizing the idea that a holder in due course takes free of most of the defenses the parties to the original transaction have against one another, a doctrine that makes it easy to see why it is important to determine if the person currently possessing the instrument qualifies as a holder in due course. The basic definition is found in §3-302(a), which you should read carefully. The doctrine was thought necessary in a historical era where notes and drafts would often circulate from one person to another, or one business to another, for months, sometimes even years before being presented for payment. This was particularly true in an age when people were living far from their homes (in foreign countries, for example) and great distances from the cities where the banks on which drafts were drawn were located or the makers of promissory notes were living, and rapid communications between these locales was impossible. Many innocent holders of these instruments took them as sort of a private form of money, exchanging them back and forth by indorsements, and if defenses from the original transactions were good against these people financial chaos would reign. Thus there arose the rule that if these innocents qualified as a "holders in due course" they could force payment from the creators of the instruments even if those creators could have avoided paying their original transferee (who knew of the defense and was still subject to it) were it still in that person's hands. The creator, having paid, could then press the original transferee for reimbursement, using breach of contract as the cause of action. Once everyone understood this system, it didn't seem unfair to protect holders in due course and let them take free of defenses. As you read the cases that follow, ask if this doctrine still makes sense in the twenty-first century, when most people have never heard of it, but still sign mortgage notes when buying a house, wrongly thinking that if the seller gyps them they surely won't have to pay the note no matter who owns it now.

B.   The Payee as Holder in Due Course

Official Comment 4 to §3-302 makes it clear that the *payee* can qualify as a holder in due course in some rare situations. Normally, the payee is so involved in the underlying transaction that he or she has notice of problems affecting payment obligations, and thus cannot be a holder in due course. But the examples given in Official Comment 4 describe fact patterns where the payee is innocent of such knowledge and can therefore qualify for the protection given to holders in due course. See also Eldon's Super Fresh Stores, Inc. v. Merrill Lynch, Pierce, Fenner & Smith, Inc., 296 Minn. 130, 207 N.W.2d 282 (1973), for an example of the payee as a holder in due course.

Subsection (c) gives a list of extraordinary transactions—creditors seizing instruments by judicial process, the sale of an inventoried business (a "bulk transaction"), or the appointment of the administrator of an estate containing negotiable instruments—in which the transferee is statutorily denied holder in due course status.

In spite of §3-302(c), which would seem to reach the opposite result, the federal courts have held that federal agencies such as the Federal Deposit Insurance Corporation, when taking over failed financial institutions, acquire holder in due course status as a matter of federal law. The following case is a continuation of a case that we first looked at in Chapter 2, when the court explored whether a promissory note was negotiable when no fixed amount of money was to be lent. The court decided no. The part of the opinion below continues with the issue of holding in due course under federal law.

Heritage Bank v. Bruha

Supreme Court of Nebraska, 2012
283 Neb. 263, 812 N.W.2d 260

[Part I of the opinion can be found in Chapter 2 at page 33.

In this case, Mr. Bruha alleged that the Sherman County Bank, which was the payee on the note he signed, committed fraud by exposing him to investment risks about which the bank lied in recommending. The note was taken over by the Federal Deposit Insurance Company when Sherman County Bank failed, and the FDIC then sold the note to Heritage Bank. In Part I of the opinion, the Nebraska Supreme Court held that the note was not negotiable due to lack of a fixed amount to be paid, and thus under the Uniform Commercial Code, the defense of holding in due course was not available to anyone possessing a non-negotiable note. The court then turned to other arguments in the case.]

2. DEFENSES . . .

(b) Allegations of Fraud

Bruha's brief also makes glancing, undeveloped references to fraud. Bruha's fraud allegations are sketchy at best.

We begin by noting that there are potentially two different types of fraud at issue: fraud in the execution and fraud in the inducement.

Fraud in the execution goes to the very existence of the contract, such as where a [contract] is misread to the [party] or where one paper is surreptitiously substituted for another, or where a party is tricked into signing an instrument he or she did not mean to execute. . . . Fraud in the inducement, by contrast, goes to the means used to induce a party to enter into a contract. In such cases, the party knows the character of the instrument and intends to execute it, but the contract may be voidable if the party's consent was obtained by false representations. . . .[1]

In liberally construing his complaint, it appears that Bruha has alleged fraud in the inducement. Bruha submitted his own affidavit. The gist of the affidavit is that officials at Sherman County Bank repeatedly told Bruha he would be better off if he maintained his trading account rather than closing it. They allegedly induced Bruha into taking additional loans by misrepresenting the profitability of the trading accounts. But nowhere does Bruha claim that he was unaware that he was incurring additional debt in his negotiations with the bank, although he might have thought it was under one note instead of four notes. In sum, Bruha knew the character of the transactions he was entering, although he might have been led there by false pretenses. This sounds in fraud in the inducement, not fraud in the execution.

3. §1823(e) BARS BRUHA'S FRAUD IN THE INDUCEMENT DEFENSE

Having concluded that if Bruha has stated any defense, he has stated a defense of fraud in the inducement, we move on to Bruha's next argument. For this purpose, we assume, but do not decide, that Bruha could prove the elements of his fraud-in-the-inducement defense.

Bruha argues that the district court erred in applying the *D'Oench* doctrine and its codification at 12 U.S.C. §1823(e). We begin our discussion of this issue with the U.S. Supreme Court case that gave rise to these rules.

In D'Oench, Duhme & Co. v. F.D.I.C.,[2] the U.S. Supreme Court recognized a common-law rule that barred the invocation of secret agreements to defeat a claim of the FDIC. The case involved the FDIC's efforts to enforce notes it had acquired from a failed bank. The signer of the notes and the bank, however, had secretly agreed that the bank would never seek to enforce the notes; the bank had taken the notes to make it appear in better financial shape than it actually was. The FDIC did not learn of this secret agreement until after it had demanded payment on the notes. When the FDIC sought to enforce one of the notes, the defendant pointed to the secret agreement, arguing that the parties had never intended the notes to be enforced and that the notes lacked consideration. Citing "a federal policy to protect [the FDIC], and the public funds which it administers, against misrepresentations as to the securities or other assets in the portfolios of the

---

1. Gonzalez v. Union Pacific R.R. Co., 282 Neb. 47, 66, 803 N.W.2d 424, 442 (2011).
2. [315 U.S. 447 (1942)].

banks [that the FDIC] insures or to which it makes loans," the Court ruled that the defendant could not rely on the secret agreements in its defense.

The *D'Oench* doctrine generally applies to bar defenses or claims against federal regulators in those instances where a financial institution enters into an oral or secret agreement that alters the terms of an existing unqualified obligation. The doctrine provides well-reasoned, unchallengeable finality to the lender's books and records when used by regulatory agencies to assess the lending institution's solvency. We stress that this doctrine is separate from the doctrine of holder in due course, so whether the document is negotiable is irrelevant.[3]

The *D'Oench* doctrine is codified at 12 U.S.C. §1823(e), which provides in relevant part:

> No agreement which tends to diminish or defeat the interest of the Corporation in any asset acquired by it under this section or section 1821 of this title, either as security for a loan or by purchase or as receiver of any insured depository institution, shall be valid against the Corporation unless such agreement—
> (A) is in writing,
> (B) was executed by the depository institution and any person claiming an adverse interest thereunder, including the obligor, contemporaneously with the acquisition of the asset by the depository institution,
> (C) was approved by the board of directors of the depository institution or its loan committee, which approval shall be reflected in the minutes of said board or committee, and
> (D) has been, continuously, from the time of its execution, an official record of the depository institution.

Section 1823(e)'s most obvious purpose "is to allow federal and state bank examiners to rely on a bank's records in evaluating the worth of the bank's assets."[4] These evaluations, which sometimes "must be made 'with great speed,'"[5] would be virtually impossible if "bank records contained seemingly unqualified notes that [were] in fact subject to undisclosed conditions."[6]

---

3. See, e.g., Resolution Trust Corp. v. Kennelly, 57 F.3d 819 (9th Cir. 1995); Randolph v. Resolution Trust Corp., 995 F.2d 611 (5th Cir. 1993); Adams v. Madison Realty & Development, Inc., 937 F.2d 845 (3d Cir. 1991); Federal Deposit Ins. Corp. v. P.L.M. Intern., Inc., 834 F.2d 248 (1st Cir. 1987).

4. Langley v. F.D.I.C., 484 U.S. 86, 91, 108 S. Ct. 396, 98 L. Ed. 2d 340 (1987).

5. *Id.*, quoting Gunter v. Hutcheson, 674 F.2d 862 (11th Cir. 1982).

6. *Id.*, 484 U.S. at 92, 108 S. Ct. 396.

All courts agree that §1823(e) is a codification of the *D'Oench* doctrine.[7] Further, courts agree this doctrine also protects assignees of the FDIC.[8] We note that there is an "open question whether the judicially created doctrine and its statutory counterpart are coterminous."[9] There is also a dispute whether subsequent U.S. Supreme Court case law[10] has effectively disapproved of the common-law rule.[11] But we need not decide these issues because §1823(e) bars Bruha's defense; so deciding whether a common-law rule would provide greater protection for Heritage is unnecessary.

As mentioned, the only defense that Bruha has alleged is a defense of fraud in the inducement. We now consider whether under §1823(e), Bruha may assert this defense against Heritage. Our starting point in this analysis is Langley v. F.D.I.C.,[12] the seminal case interpreting §1823(e).

In *Langley*, a bank (later received by the FDIC) sued the defendants to collect on promissory notes that the defendants had signed in order to receive money to purchase land. The defendants argued that the bank had procured their signatures by misrepresentation. They claimed that the bank had misrepresented the size of the tract of land, the amount of mineral deposits on the land, and the lack of existing mineral leases on the land. The bank records, the minutes of the board of directors, and the minutes of the bank's loan committee, however, contained no evidence of such misrepresentations.

The Court held that §1823(e) barred the misrepresentation defense, which the Court characterized as fraud in the inducement. The Court reasoned that generally, the truthfulness of a warranty was a condition of a contract, and that the word "agreement" in §1823(e) encompassed such warranties, even if such warranties were made fraudulently. So the terms of the agreement were subject to §1823(e). And fraud in the inducement would not be a defense unless such fraud met the requirements of §1823(e).

---

7. See, e.g., Young v. F.D.I.C., 103 F.3d 1180 (4th Cir. 1997); DiVall Insured Income v. Boatmen's First Nat. Bank, 69 F.3d 1398 (8th Cir. 1995); Vasapolli v. Rostoff, 39 F.3d 27 (1st Cir. 1994); *Adams, supra* note [5].

8. See, e.g., Beal Bank, SSB v. Pittorino, 177 F.3d 65 (1st Cir. 1999); Caires v. JP Morgan Chase Bank, 745 F. Supp. 2d 40 (D. Conn. 2010) (collecting cases); AAI Recoveries, Inc. v. Pijuan, 13 F. Supp. 2d 448 (S.D.N.Y. 1998); Santopadre v. Pelican Homestead and Sav. Ass'n, 782 F. Supp. 1138 (E.D. La. 1992); OCI Mortg. Corp. v. Marchese, 255 Conn. 448, 774 A.2d 940 (2001); AGI v. Pacific Southwest Bank, F.S.B., 972 S.W.2d 866 (Tex. App. 1998).

9. *Vasapolli, supra* note [9], 39 F.3d at 33 n.3.

10. See, Atherton v. F.D.I.C., 519 U.S. 213, 117 S. Ct. 666, 136 L. Ed. 2d 656 (1997); O'Melveny & Myers v. F.D.I.C., 512 U.S. 79, 114 S. Ct. 2048, 129 L. Ed. 2d 67 (1994).

11. Compare, e.g., *DiVall Insured Income, supra* note [9], with Motorcity of Jacksonville v. Southeast Bank N.A., 120 F.3d 1140 (11th Cir. 1997).

12. *Langley, supra* note [6].

Thus, *Langley* holds that §1823(e) bars the defense of fraud in the inducement unless the defense meets the requirements of the statute. In this case, Bruha has failed to show that his defense does so.

To assert his defense of fraud in the inducement, Bruha must show that the agreement, including the allegedly fraudulent assertions made by Sherman County Bank regarding the profitability of the accounts, has met §1823(e)'s requirements as follows: The agreement is in writing; was executed by the depository institution and any person claiming an adverse interest thereunder, including the obligor, contemporaneously with the acquisition of the asset by the depository institution; was approved by the board of directors of the depository institution or its loan committee, with such approval reflected in the minutes of said board or committee; and has been, continuously, from the time of its execution, an official record of the depository institution.

Bruha does not point to anything regarding the fraud in any writing. Nor does he explain how the alleged fraudulent misrepresentations satisfy any of the other requirements of §1823(e). Summed up, his defense does not meet the requirements §1823(e). . . .

V. Conclusion

We agree with the district court that §1823(e) bars Bruha's defense. Because the court erred in applying an initial interest rate of 7.75 percent instead of 7.25 percent, we reverse in part, and remand to the district court to recalculate the interest on the judgment.

Affirmed in part, and in part reversed and remanded.

We now turn to the elements of holding in due course under the Uniform Commercial Code.

C. *"Holder"*

Note, first of all, that in order to be a holder in due course, the possessor of the instrument must qualify as a *holder*. This means that the instrument must be technically *negotiable* and must have been technically *negotiated* into the hands of its current possessor (however, the named payee becomes a holder on issuance of the instrument without the necessity of a negotiation, as does anyone to whom a bearer instrument is issued). No one can be a holder in due course of a non-negotiable instrument, nor even of a negotiable instrument if there is some defect in the transfer (negotiation) process.

Further, the holder must have *possession* of the instrument; §§1-201(b)(21), 3-301. Obviously, you can't be "holder" unless you hold. The Code nowhere defines the word "possession," leaving attorneys who must do so looking at property cases, some of which were decided many centuries ago.

One technical point: the drawee bank on which a check is drawn, taking the check for payment, does not qualify as a "holder." The reason is that an instrument must be *negotiated* to a holder, and the process by which the drawee bank acquires the instrument is not a "negotiation," it is a mere surrender for payment (a "presentment"). Thus the drawee bank is not a holder, and consequently cannot be a holder in due course.

D.   "Value" Stop here for next Class

It is important to emphasize that whether or not someone qualifies as a holder in due course is measured at the moment he or she gave value for the instrument (assuming there has been a valid negotiation so as to create holder status). Things that happen after value is given (such as receiving notice of problems with the instrument) do not destroy holder in due course status once achieved.

What is "value"?

First of all, the *gift* of an instrument will never create holder in due course status in the donee (though the donee may get similar rights under the *shelter* rule, discussed below). The confusing part of the value requirement is that giving value is not the same thing as giving *consideration*. Read §3-303's Official Comment 1, first paragraph. The drafters of the Code decided that one gives value only to the extent that the holder has performed the consideration or made some irrevocable commitment in connection with it. If all that has been exchanged for the instrument is an unexecuted promise and then a problem arises, the holder has the self-help remedy of refusing to perform and does not need the extraordinary status of holding in due course; thus the holder has not given *value* under the Code. This is true even though the promise would be sufficient consideration at common law. Read §3-303 and its Official Comment and then resolve the Problems that follow.

PROBLEM 22

Joe Lunchpail arrived home one day to find a note from his wife stating that she was divorcing him and that he should get a lawyer. Since he had just been paid that day, he took his paycheck down to the law office of Nathan Novice and indorsed it over to Nathan in return for the latter's promise to represent Joe in his divorce. Later that evening, Joe's wife sent the sheriff to seize his paycheck. Joe laughingly referred the sheriff to his attorney. Can the sheriff succeed in wresting the check from Nathan's hands? See §§3-306, 3-303; Carter & Grimsley v. Omni Trading, Inc., 306 Ill. App. 3d 1127, 716 N.E.2d 320 (1999).

PROBLEM 23

Zach Taylor bought a car for his business from Fillmore Motors, signing a promissory note for $23,000 payable to Fillmore. Fillmore sold the note to the Pierce Finance Company for $22,800, a $200 discount. The car fell apart, and Zach refused to pay. Is the finance company (assuming good faith and lack of notice) a holder in due course for $23,000 or $22,800? See Bankers Guar. Title & Trust Co. v. Fisher, 2 Ohio Misc. 18, 204 N.E.2d 103 (C.P. 1964). If Millard Fillmore, the owner of Fillmore Motors, owed his mother $21,000 and gave her the note with the understanding that the extra $2,000 was a Mother's Day gift, would the mother be a holder in due course for the full amount? See §3-303.

PROBLEM 24

Tom Winker tricked old Mrs. Nodding into writing a check payable to Tom (she thought he was the agent for a local charity). The check for $1,000 was drawn on her bank, the First County Bank. Tom took the check to his bank, the Last National Bank, and, after indorsing it, put it in his checking account. Last National Bank sent the check to the First County Bank for payment, but by the time it got there Mrs. Nodding had stopped payment so that the check was dishonored and returned to Last National. Is Last National Bank a holder in due course? This question will be important if Tom has skipped town and Last National decides to sue Mrs. Nodding under §3-414.

The bank's major problem in situations like Problem 24 is in proving that it *paid* value for the check. Is the bank out of pocket anything? If so, the Code will permit the bank to recover. Thus, if the bank had permitted Tom to get the money *before* the check cleared through the drawee bank, the Last National Bank would be a holder in due course. Article 4 of the UCC (which deals with bank collection) sets out special rules for this kind of value. Section 4-211 provides that for purposes of determining its holder in due course status, a bank gives *value* whenever it has a security interest in the instrument. The situations in which this occurs are spelled out in §4-210(a). Read these sections, and consider the following case.

Falls Church Bank v. Wesley Heights Realty, Inc.

District of Columbia Court of Appeals, 1969
256 A.2d 915

Hood, J.

The sole issue on this appeal is whether and under what circumstances, may a depositary bank achieve the status of holder in due course of negotiable paper deposited with it by a customer. The facts are undisputed.

The appellees drew a check for $1,400.00, payable to the order of a customer of appellant bank. The customer deposited this check in his account with the bank and was given a provisional credit of this amount. The customer was permitted to withdraw $140.00 from this account prior to the bank's discovering that appellees had stopped payment on the $1,400.00 check. When the check was returned to the bank dishonored, the bank's customer had "skipped," leaving no credits in his account on which to charge the $140.00. The bank, thereupon, made demand on appellees for that amount and when appellees refused, this action was brought.

At trial appellees moved for, and were granted, judgment on grounds that the bank "was an agent for collection only and did not have a security interest and was not a holder in due course for value."

We reverse. The Uniform Commercial Code, which controls in this case, expressly provides that a bank acquires a security interest in items deposited with it to the extent that the provisional credit given the customer on the item is withdrawn. UCC §4-208 [§4-210 in the revised version of Article 4—Eds.]. It further provides that, for purposes of achieving the status of holder in due course, the depositary bank gives value to the extent that it acquires a security interest in the item in question. UCC §4-209 [§4-211 in the Revision—Eds.].

We agree that appellant bank is deemed by the Uniform Commercial Code to be an agent of its customers (§4-201) but under the scheme of the Code, a "bank may be a holder in due course while acting as a collecting agent for its customer." Citizens Bank of Booneville v. National Bank of Commerce, 334 F.2d 257, 261 (10th Cir. 1964). See also cases collected at 18 A.L.R.3d 1388-1391.

As a holder in due course as to $140.00, appellant's claim cannot be defeated except by those defenses set out in UCC §3-305(2), none of which are herein alleged. The judgment below is accordingly reversed with instructions to enter judgment for appellant.

PROBLEM 25

Same situation as the last Problem except that when Tom deposits the $1,000 check in his account, the account contains $500. Later that afternoon he withdraws $500. Is the bank a holder in due course for any amount? See §4-210(b) (the FIFO rule: First In, First Out). What result if he withdraws $750?

E.   *"Good Faith" and "Notice"*

To become a holder in due course the owner of the instrument must be, in effect, a bona fide purchaser—that is, the owner must have given value for the instrument in *good faith,* defined in §1-201(b)(20)[13] as "honesty in fact and the observance of reasonable commercial standards of fair dealing," thus making the test one that is both subjective and objective. Read Official Comment 20 to §1-201(b). The holder must also be without *notice* that there are problems with the instrument. These two concepts—good faith and notice—are inevitably intertwined: if, at the time value is given for the instrument, a person has *notice* of a defense the maker of a note has against the payee, the holder cannot be said to take the note with the good faith expectation that it should be paid in spite of the defense. See Annot., 36 A.L.R.4th 212. In the cases that follow, you should note how often the court fails to separate these two issues.

In re Dixon-Ford

United State Bankruptcy Court, District of New Jersey, 2011
2011 WL 6749083

Donald H. Steckroth, Bankruptcy Judge.

On June 17, 2010, the Debtor filed a single-count adversary complaint alleging claims for fraud at common law and under New Jersey's Consumer Fraud Act, N.J.S.A. 56:8-1 *et seq.* ("CFA"), against each of the defendants in this adversary proceeding. Before the Court is a pair of summary judgment motions filed against the Plaintiff-Debtor, Mary L. Dixon-Ford ("Debtor"), by the Movant-Defendant U.S. Bank National Association, as Trustee for CMLTI 2007-10 ("US Bank") and Movants-Defendants Weichert Co., d/b/a Weichert Realtors ("Weichert Realtors") and Mortgage Access Corp. d/b/a Weichert Financial Services ("WFS") (together, "Weichert") (collectively, the "Defendants"). . . .

---

13. As discussed in Chapter 1, some states still have a version of §1-201(b)(20) that requires only "honesty in fact." The present version of Article 3 recommends that such states adopt, for the purposes of Article 3, the definition of good faith requiring both "honesty in fact and the observance of reasonable commercial standards of fair dealing." Legislative Note to §3-103. This is a reminder that, as always, in an actual UCC case, you should go by the UCC as in effect in your jurisdiction.

FACTS AND PROCEDURAL HISTORY

I. MOVANTS' FACTS

A. *Property Taxes*

In 2006, the Debtor engaged Weichert as her real estate representative for the purpose of locating a multi-family home. (Weichert's 56.1 Stmt. of Material Facts, ¶1) ("Weichert's Stmt. of Facts") On February 19, 2007, the Debtor executed a sale contract in which she offered to purchase a residence located in Hillside, New Jersey. (*Id.* at ¶10) The Debtor was represented by attorney John B. D'Alessandro in the transaction. (*Id.* at ¶15) Mr. D'Alessandro has testified that he discussed post-closing property taxes with the Debtor and further instructed that "she and the realtor . . . should really go to town hall to check it out." (Decl. of Michael Millar, Ex. H at 20:10-21:10) ("Millar Decl.") One of the Debtor's real estate agents, Lillian PeloteHodges, testified that they did not have information regarding property taxes. (Weichert's Reply Br. in Further Supp., p. 6) Lastly, Weichert alleges that prior to closing, the Debtor had no communication with her real estate agents. (Weichert's Stmt. of Facts, ¶19)

B. *The Mortgage*

The Debtor sought to finance the purchase of real property with a mortgage loan from WFS. At all times relevant to this transaction, the Debtor was employed by the Social Security Administration ("SSA") as a "telephone service representative" earning approximately $45,000 annually. (Weichert's Stmt. of Facts, ¶¶20-1; Millar Decl., Ex. B at 10:7-16, 21:16-20) The Debtor contracted with WFS to obtain a "stated income" mortgage loan. (*Id.* at ¶29) In a stated income loan program, the borrower applies for financing based on her income as stated in her loan application. (*Id.* at ¶30) The lender then performs a Verification of Employment ("VOE") directly with the borrower's employer to confirm the borrower's stated income. (*Id.* at ¶31) On February 24, 2007, the Debtor executed a loan application indicating she was employed as the "Vice President" of the SSA earning $11,900 monthly ($142,800 annually). (Weichert's Stmt. of Facts, ¶22)

On April 9, 2007, the Debtor accepted a mortgage loan commitment with WFS. (*Id.* at ¶28) Also on April 9, and again on April 10, WFS submitted a VOE form to the SSA. (Weichert's Br. in Supp. of Mot. for Summ. J., pp. 5-6) ("Weichert's Br.") Weichert alleges that on or about April 10, 2007, someone at the SSA provided a VOE form to the Debtor together with a handwritten note to the Debtor's attention, arguably, before it was returned to WFS. (*Id.* at ¶35; Millar Decl., Ex. P) On April 18, 2007, the Debtor closed on the property and executed a second loan application which also misstated her employment and income information. (Weichert's Stmt. of Facts,

¶¶36-7) Post-closing review revealed the existence of two VOEs. One correctly stated the Debtor's employment as a "Telephone Service Rep[resentative]" while the other incorrectly stated she was the "Vice President" of the SSA. (Weichert's Stmt. of Facts, ¶¶46-7) The incorrect VOE was supplied to the WFS underwriter. (Weichert's Stmt. of Facts, ¶48)

The Debtor occupied the property with several family members, some of whom contributed to household expenses, including the mortgage. (*Id.* at ¶¶42-3) The Debtor defaulted on her mortgage when one of the contributing family members relocated. (*Id.* at ¶45)

C. Assignment of the Debtor's Mortgage

On October 31 2007, Citigroup Mortgage Loan Trust Inc. ("Buyer") and Citigroup Markets Realty Corp. ("Seller") executed a Mortgage Loan Purchase Agreement ("MLPA") as part of a mortgage-backed securities transaction. (U.S. Bank's 56.1 Statement of Facts, ¶21-23) ("US Bank's Stmt. of Facts") The details of the transaction are set forth in a Pooling and Servicing Agreement ("PSA") that provides for the "selling, purchase, [and] deposit . . . of a series of residential mortgage loans . . . in trust CMLTI 2007-10," with U.S. Bank as trustee. (*Id.* at ¶23) The mortgage loan schedule attached to the MLPA and the PSA indicate that the Debtor's mortgage was included in the transaction and deposited in the trust. (*Id.* at ¶24) U.S. Bank did not conduct an independent review of the individual mortgages because the Seller warranted that the mortgages were enforceable and underwritten in accordance with its guidelines at the time of their originations. (*Id.* at ¶28)

Pursuant to the PSA, U.S. Bank received the Debtor's mortgage note and the original recorded mortgage. (*Id.* at ¶32) There are no indicia of fraud, alteration, or invalidity on the face of the Debtor's mortgage or note. (*Id.* at ¶35-36) Further, neither Weichert nor the Debtor alerted U.S. Bank to any alleged misrepresentations or other flaw in the origination of the mortgage. (*Id.* at ¶18-20)

II. PLAINTIFF'S ADDITIONAL AND DISPUTED FACTS

The Debtor asserts that pursuant to WFS's loan officer's request, she provided documentation that accurately described her employment and overall financial position. (*Id.* at p. 6; Ex. B at 15:20-25, 16:1-9, 17:24-25, 18:1-6) The Debtor provided the following documentation: (1) pay stubs; (2) tax returns; (3) a bank statement for the period between February 14, 2007 and March 16, 2007, which includes an entry for the direct deposit of the Debtor's wages in the amount of $782.60; and (4) a credit report, indicating the Debtor's employment as "Teller Service." (*Id.* at p. 6-7) Nevertheless, the WFS loan officer prepared the loan application containing the incorrect employment information. (Pl.'s Br. in Opp'n, p. 6)

In addition, during post-closing review, the WFS Vice President of Processing, Laura Williamson, spoke with the Debtor's supervisor at the SSA, John Elder, regarding the VOE. (*Id.* at p. 7; Williamson Dep. 25:12-13) Mr. Elder confirmed that he completed a VOE accurately stating the Debtor's employment as a telephone service representative. (*Id.* at 7-8; Williamson Dep. 30:1-10) Importantly, Ms. Williamson testified that the VOE containing incorrect information appeared to have been altered. (*Id.* at p. 8; Williamson Dep. 35:13-18) Lastly, Ms. Williamson stated that the altered VOE was faxed to Weichert from a number with a 908 area code. (*Id.* at p. 7; Williamson Dep. 25:1-3) The office where the loan application was allegedly completed is located in Union, New Jersey and has an area code of 908. (*Id.* at p. 8) Accordingly, the Debtor opines that the WFS loan officer altered the VOE in order to qualify the Debtor for a larger loan.

DISCUSSION

* * *

III. US BANK'S MOTION FOR SUMMARY JUDGMENT: HOLDER IN DUE
       COURSE

The Debtor brings claims for fraud against U.S. Bank, arguing that U.S. Bank knew or should have known of the alleged misrepresentations made in connection with the origination of the Debtor's mortgage. In its defense, U.S. Bank asserts holder in due course status. Where a defense exists against the payee, the party "claiming the rights of a holder in due course has the burden of establishing that he is . . . such a holder." Gen. Inv. Corp. v. Angelini, 58 N.J. 396, 403-404, 278 A.2d 193 (1971). The Uniform Commercial Code, as adopted in New Jersey, provides that a holder of an instrument becomes a holder in due course when he takes the instrument "for value, in good faith, and without notice of any defense or claim against it." Carnegie Bank v. Shalleck, 256 N.J. Super. 23, 33, 606 A.2d 389 (App. Div. 1992); N.J. Stat. Ann. §12A:3-302(a)(2). Additionally, it is required that "the instrument when . . . negotiated to the holder does not bear such apparent evidence of forgery or alteration or is not otherwise so irregular or incomplete as to call into question its authenticity." N.J. Stat. Ann. §12A:3-302(a)(1). A holder in due course takes an instrument free of any personal defenses the maker may assert against the payee. Bancredit Inc. v. Bethea, 65 N.J. Super. 538, 544, 168 A.2d 250 (App. Div. 1961).

That U.S. Bank took the mortgage instrument for value is undisputed. Instead, the Debtor alleges that U.S. Bank "knew or should have known of the misrepresentations made by [WFS] and [Weichert Realtors]. . . ." (Pl.'s Compl., ¶32) Such allegations implicate the holder's good faith. Good faith is defined by statute in N.J.S.A. 12A:3-103(a)(4) as "honesty in fact and the observance of reasonable commercial standards of fair dealing." Good faith then, concerns both the subjective actions of the holder and the objective elements of the transaction. Wawel Savings Bank v. Jersey Tractor Trailer Training Inc. (In re Jersey Tractor Trailer Training Inc.), 580 F.3d 147, 157 (3d Cir. 2009) (citing Trifin v. Pomerantz Staffing Services, L.L.C., 370 N.J. Super. 301, 308, 851 A.2d 100 (App. Div. 2004)). Often, the critical issue is whether "[a] party [ ] fails to make an inquiry[ ] reasonably required by the circumstances. . . ." Trifin v. Pomerantz Staffing, 370 N.J. Super. at 309, 851 A.2d 100. As the court in *Carnegie Bank* observed,

> [o]rdinarily where the note appears to be negotiable in form and regular on its face, the holder is under no duty to inquire as to possible defenses . . . unless the circumstances of which he has knowledge rise to the level that the failure to inquire reveals a deliberate desire on his part to evade knowledge because of a belief or fear that investigation would disclose a defense from the transaction.

Carnegie Bank, 256 N.J. Super. at 35, 606 A.2d 389 (quoting *Gen. Inv. Corp.*, 58 N.J. at 403-404, 278 A.2d 193).

The above derives from the oft quoted rule laid down in Rice v. Barrington, 71 N.J.L. 806 (E. & A. 1968): "[b]ad faith, i.e. fraud, not merely suspicious circumstances, must be brought home to a holder . . . in order to defeat his recovery on a[ ] note upon the ground of fraud in its inception or between the parties to it." *Rice*, 71 N.J.L. at 807, 60 A. 1134; *see* HSBC Bank USA, N.A. v. Gouda, 2010 N.J. Super. Unpub. Lexis 3029 at *11, 2010 WL 5128666 (App. Div. Dec. 17, 2010). In the present matter, the note has been supplied to the Court for evaluation. (Standing Certif., [ECF Doc. 48], Oct. 19, 2011) The note is facially free from any irregularity that could have alerted U.S. Bank to the existence of a potential fraud. While U.S. Bank does possess the mortgage file containing the allegedly altered VOE, it was under "no duty to inquire" under the circumstances. *Carnegie Bank*, 256 N.J. Super. at 35, 606 A.2d 389; *see* Triffin v. Somerset Valley Bank, 343 N.J. Super. 73, 85, 777 A.2d 993 (App. Div. 2001) ("to preclude liability from a holder in due course under [N.J.S.A. 12A:3-302], it must be apparent on the face of the instrument that it is fraudulent"). Failure to investigate inconsistencies in the mortgage file regarding the Debtor's income, without more, does not evidence bad faith sufficient to prevent U.S. Bank from a holder in due course status. *See* HSBC Bank USA, N.A. v. Gouda, 2010 N.J. Super. Unpub. Lexis 3029, 2010 WL 5128666 (that loan documents indicated the material terms of a loan changed shortly before closing did not implicate the holder's good faith); *see also* Ocwen Loan Servicing, LLC v. Branaman, 554 F. Supp. 2d 645, 649 (N.D. Miss. 2008) ("while the [d]efendants have alleged a potential forgery in the loan documents, no specific evidence has been presented which casts doubt on the authenticity of the promissory note").

Certainly, fraud is one explanation in the array of possibilities, however, constructive notice requires "circumstances [ ] so strong that if ignored they will be deemed to establish bad faith on the part of the transferee." *Provident Sav. Bank v. Pinnacle Mortg. Inv. Corp. (In re Pinnacle Mortg. Inv. Corp.)*, 1998 U.S. Dist. Lexis 23289 at *32 (D.N.J. Dec. 9, 1998) (simultaneously construing holder in due course status under Pennsylvania and New Jersey law as the law of the two states "[was] largely consistent on the issues," raised therein).

Moreover, the undisputed facts show that U.S. Bank did not participate in the origination of the mortgage, nor is there evidence of collusion or communication between Weichert and U.S. Bank regarding the Debtor's mortgage. *See* Davis v. Clark, 85 N.J.L. 696, 699, 90 A. 303 (E. & A. 1914) (there was no showing that the holder in due course had any knowledge of fraud perpetrated upon a debtor in the original transaction); *see also* Driscoll v. Burlington-Bristol Bridge Co., 8 N.J. 433, 480, 86 A.2d 201 (1952) (the subsequent holder "must have had actual knowledge of such facts that his action in taking the instrument amounted to bad faith") *accord* Westfield Inv. Co. v. Fellers, 74 N.J. Super. 575, 583, 181 A.2d 809 (Law Div. 1962). On the record, there are simply no facts which tend to apprise U.S. Bank of potential defenses at the time of taking and impair good faith. Thus, U.S. Bank holds the Debtor's mortgage in due course and is entitled to the benefits of its status.

The instant case involves alleged fraudulent inducement in connection with the origination of the Debtor's mortgage, that is, "the [Debtor] was led by deception to execute what [s]he knew to be a negotiable instrument. . . ." *New Jersey Mortg. & Inv. Co. v. Dorsey*, 60 N.J. Super. 299, 302, 158 A.2d 712 (App. Div. 1960). Under New Jersey law, fraud in the inducement is a personal defense against "transferees who have been parties to any fraud or illegality affecting the instrument or transferees who were prior holders with notice of the defenses or claims and not against holders in due course." *Carnegie Bank*, 256 N.J. Super. at 43, 606 A.2d 389; *see Bancredit*, 65 N.J. Super. at 544, 168 A.2d 250 ("a holder in due course plaintiff is, of course, immune to all personal defenses of the maker against the payee, including that of fraud in the inducement"); *see also New Jersey Mortg.*, 60 N.J. Super. at 302, 158 A.2d 712 (fraudulent inducement is a personal defense not available against a holder in due course). Thus, U.S. Bank is immune to the Debtor's claims and the Court will grant U.S. Bank's motion for summary judgment against the Debtor.

CONCLUSION

Summary judgment is granted in favor of U.S. Bank and Weichert Realtors against Plaintiff. The Plaintiff's common law and statutory fraud claims survive as to WFS because material questions of fact remain in connection with the Debtor's mortgage application.

─────────────

As we saw at the end of Chapter 2, the Federal Trade Commission has promulgated a regulation abolishing the holder in due course doctrine, where a consumer gives a promissory note to a seller or lender when purchasing goods or services. But that rule does not apply to checks or to promissory notes in real property purchases, perhaps where consumers like Mary Dixon-Ford in this case need it most. Is the application of the doctrine here fair? Why would the FTC have created such a gap, do you suppose?

PROBLEM 26

Dubious Mortgage Lender convinced a 91-year old widower to refinance his home by granting him an adjustable rate mortgage, along with bountiful fees, after making fraudulent promises galore to him about the benefits of the new mortgage. Dubious kept the promissory note in a safe deposit box down at its own bank, where it remains to this day. Shortly after the mortgage was given and the mortgage deed recorded in the mortgage records, Dubious sold the note and the mortgage contract to Investment National Bank, which paid good value but did not bother to take possession of the note. When the widower learned he had been defrauded, he stopped making payments on the note and Investment National Bank filed a foreclosure action against him. Is the bank a holder in due course?

PROBLEM 27

The corporate treasurer of the Business Corporation was having major troubles paying his personal bills, so finally he decided to embark on a life of crime. He used a corporate check to pay his American Express bill, making the check out to "Amerex Corp., 770 Broadway, N.Y., N.Y. 10003" (the actual address of American Express). On the corporate check requisition form he wrote a phony explanation that this check represented shipping expenses. This caused no suspicions at Business Corporation and, thus encouraged, he did it every month for two years. When Business Corporation finally figured out what had happened, it sued American Express in quasi-contract for all the money it had received in this fashion. American Express replied that it was a holder in due course of these checks and, as such, was not amenable to this suit. Business Corporation pointed to the suspicious circumstances and to UCC

§§3-302(a) and 3-307 (arguing that the corporate treasurer was a fiduciary). How should this be resolved? See Hartford Accident & Indem. Co. v. American Express Co., 74 N.Y.2d 153, 542 N.E.2d 1090, 544 N.Y.S.2d 573 (1989); Grand Rapids Auto Sales, Inc. v. MBNA American Bank, 227 F. Supp. 2d 721 (W.D. Mich. 2002).

Any Kind Checks Cashed, Inc. v. Talcott ~~SKIP~~

District Court of Appeal of Florida, 2002
830 So. 2d 160

GROSS, J.

The issue in this case is whether a check cashing store qualifies as a holder in due course so that it can collect on a $10,000 check written by an elderly man who was fraudulently induced to issue the check by the person who cashed it.

We hold that the check cashing store was not a holder in due course, because the procedures it followed with the $10,000 check did not comport with reasonable commercial standards of fair dealing.

The case is the story of John G. Talcott, Jr., a ninety-three-year-old Massachusetts resident, D.J. Rivera, a "financial advisor" to Talcott, and Salvatore Guarino, a cohort of Rivera. In the mid-1990's, Rivera sold Talcott an investment for "somewhere in the amount of $75,000." The investment produced no returns.

On December 7, 1999, Guarino established check cashing privileges at Any Kind Checks Cashed, Inc. ("Any Kind") by filling out a customer card. The card included his social security number and identification by driver's license. On the card, Guarino listed himself as a broker. That day, he cashed a $450 check without incident.

On January 10, 2000, Rivera telephoned Talcott and talked him into sending him a check for $10,000 made out to Guarino, which was to be used for travel expenses to obtain a return on the original $75,000 investment. Talcott understood that Guarino was Rivera's partner. Rivera received the check on January 11.

Talcott spoke to Rivera on the morning of January 11. Rivera indicated that $10,000 was more than what was needed for travel. He said that $5,700 would meet the travel costs. Talcott called his bank and stopped payment on the $10,000 check.

In spite of what Rivera told Talcott, Guarino appeared at Any Kind's Stuart, Florida office on January 11 and presented the $10,000 check to Nancy Michael. She was a supervisor with the company with the authority to approve checks over $2,000. Guarino showed Michael his driver's license and the Federal Express envelope from Talcott in which he received the check. She asked him the purpose of the check. Consistent with the information on the customer card, he told her that he was a broker and that the maker of the check had sent it as an investment. She was unable to contact the maker of the check by telephone. Based on her experience, Michael believed the check was good; the Federal Express envelope was "very crucial" to her decision, because it indicated that the maker of the check had sent it to the payee trying to cash the check. After deducting the 5 percent check cashing fee, Michael cashed the check and gave Guarino $9,500. The next day she deposited the check in the company's bank.

On January 15, 2000, Rivera called Talcott and asked about the $5,700, again promising to send him a return on his investment. The same day, Talcott sent a check for $5,700. He assumed that Rivera knew that he had stopped payment on the $10,000 check.

On January 17, 2000, Guarino went into the Stuart Any Kind store and presented the $5,700 check to the teller, Joanne Kochakian. He showed her the Federal Express envelope in which the check had come. Company policy required a supervisor to approve a check over $2,000. Kochakian noticed that Michael had previously approved the $10,000 check. She called Michael, who was working at another location, and told her about Guarino's check.

Any Kind had no written procedures that a supervisor was required to follow in deciding which checks over $2,000 to cash. Michael had the discretionary "decision-making power as a supervisor to decide whether or not the check [was] any good." She relied on "instinct and judgment" in deciding what inquiry to make before cashing a check. In the brief non-jury trial, there was no evidence concerning the general practice of the check cashing industry.

Michael instructed the cashier not to cash the check until she contacted the maker, Talcott, to obtain approval. On her first attempt, Kochakian received no answer, using the number on the back of Guarino's check cashing card. When she told Guarino that she would not cash his check, he gave her another number to call, which was the same as the first number except that two numbers were reversed. On the second call, a woman answered the phone. Kochakian identified herself and asked for Talcott. Talcott approved cashing the $5,700 check. There was no discussion of the $10,000 check. Any Kind cashed the second check for Guarino, from which it deducted a 3 percent fee.

On January 19, Rivera called Talcott to warn him that Guarino was a cheat and a thief. Talcott immediately called his bank and stopped payment on the $5,700 check. Talcott's daughter called Any Kind and told it of the stop payment on the $5,700 check. There was no dispute at trial that Guarino and Rivera had pulled a scam on Talcott to get him to issue the checks. Any Kind filed a two-count complaint against Guarino and Talcott, claiming that it was a holder in due course. Talcott's defense was that Any Kind was not a holder in due course and that his obligation on the checks was nullified because of Guarino's illegal acts.

The trial court entered final judgment in favor of Any Kind for only the $5,700 check. On the $10,000 check, the judge found for Talcott. The court found that the circumstances surrounding the cashing of the $10,000 check

> were sufficient to put [Any Kind] on notice of potential defenses and/or infirmities. The best evidence of this is that the plaintiff attempted to contact the maker but was unable to do so on the first check, and did so on the second. The circumstances of a person describing himself as a broker, receiving funds in the amount of $10,000 and negotiating the check for those funds at a $500 discount are sufficient to put [Any Kind] on inquiry notice that some confirmation or explanation should be obtained.

Using the terminology of the Uniform Commercial Code, Talcott was the maker or "drawer" of the check, the person who signed the draft "as a person ordering payment." §3-103(a)(3). By Federal Expressing the check to Guarino, Talcott issued the check to him. See §3-105(a) (defining "issue" as "the first delivery of an instrument by the maker or drawer . . . for the purpose of giving rights on the instrument to any person"). Guarino indorsed the check and cashed it with Any Kind. See §3-204(a) (defining "indorsement"). Any Kind immediately made the funds available to Guarino, less its fee. Talcott stopped payment on the check with his bank, so the check was returned to Any Kind. See §4-403 (regarding a customer's right to stop payment).

When Guarino negotiated the check with Any Kind, it became a holder of the check, making it a "person entitled to enforce" the instrument. See §§1-201(20), 3-301. As the drawer of the check dishonored by his bank, Talcott's obligation was to pay the draft to a person entitled to enforce the draft "[a]ccording to its terms at the time it was issued. . . ." §3-414(b).

Unless Any Kind is a holder in due course, its right to enforce Talcott's obligation to pay the draft is subject to (1) all defenses Talcott could raise "if the person entitled to enforce the instrument were enforcing a right to payment under a simple contract," and (2) a claim of "ecoupment" Talcott could raise against Guarino. §3-305(a)(2) and (3). Because Talcott was fraudulently induced to issue the checks, this case turns on Any Kind's entitlement to holder in due course status.

A "holder in due course" is a holder who takes an instrument without "apparent evidence of forgery or alteration" for value, in good faith, and without notice of certain claims and defenses. See §3-302(a). As the party claiming that it was a holder in due course, Any Kind had the burden to prove that status by a preponderance of the evidence. See §3-308(b); Seinfeld v. Commercial Bank & Trust Co., 405 So. 2d 1039, 1041 (Fla. 3d DCA 1981).

The question for this court is whether the trial court erred in finding that Any Kind was not a holder in due course of the $10,000 check based on the findings of fact made at trial, keeping in mind that Any Kind bore the burden of proof. That question turns on whether Any Kind acted "[i]n good faith" within the meaning of §3-302(a).

The good faith requirement of the holder in due course doctrine "has been the source of an ancient and continuing dispute." White & Summers, Uniform Commercial Code §17-6 (4th ed. 1995). On the one hand,

> [s]hould the courts apply a so-called objective test, and ask whether a reasonably prudent person, behaving the way the alleged holder in due course behaved, would have been acting in good faith? Or should the courts instead apply a subjective test and examine the person's actual behavior, however stupid and irrespective of the reaction a reasonably prudent person would have had in the same circumstance? The legal establishment has steered a crooked course through this debate.

Id.; see Patricia L. Heatherman, Comment, Good Faith in Revised Article 3 of the Uniform Commercial Code: Any Change? Should There Be?, 29 Willamette L. Rev. 567 (1993).

Prior to 1992, section §1-201(19) defined "good faith" as "honesty in fact in the conduct of the transaction concerned." Florida courts interpreted this definition as creating a subjective test. See Cash-A-Check of S. Fla., Inc. v. Sunshine Elec. Contractors, Inc., 26 Fla. Supp. 2d 17, 19 (Fla. Palm Beach County Ct. 1987). For example, we wrote in Barnett Bank of Palm Beach County v. Regency Highland Condo. Ass'n, 452 So. 2d 587, 590 (Fla. 4th DCA 1984), that "good faith" under the holder in due course doctrine did "not include due care; rather lack of good faith must be the result of actual, not constructive, knowledge of the wrongdoing tantamount to dishonesty or bad faith." In another case, Judge Schwartz wrote that the "Florida version of the holder in due course provision of the U.C.C. does seem to protect the objectively stupid so long as he is subjectively pure of heart." *Seinfeld*, 405 So. 2d at 1042.

Application of *Barnett Bank*'s "honesty in fact" standard to Any Kind's conduct in this case would clothe it with holder in due course status. It is undisputed that Any Kind's employees were pure of heart, that they acted without knowledge of Guarino's wrongdoing.

However, in 1992, the legislature adopted a new definition of "good faith" that applies to the §3-302's definition of a holder in due course: "'[g]ood faith' means honesty in fact and the observance of reasonable commercial standards of fair dealing." Ch. 92-82, §2, at 759, Laws of Fla.—U.C.C. §3-103(a)(4). To the old, subjective good faith, "honesty in fact" standard, the legislature added an objective component—the "pure heart of the holder must now be accompanied by reasoning that assures

conduct comporting with reasonable commercial standards of fair dealing."
Maine Family Fed. Credit Union v. Sun Life Assurance Co. of Canada, 727
A.2d 335, 342 (Me. 1999). No longer may a holder of an instrument act
with "a pure heart and an empty head and still obtain holder in due course
status." Id.

Comment 4 to §3-103 attempts to shed light on how to interpret the
new standard:

> Although fair dealing is a broad term that must be defined in context, it is
> clear that it is concerned with the fairness of conduct rather than the care
> with which an act is performed. Failure to exercise ordinary care in conduct-
> ing a transaction is an entirely different concept than failure to deal fairly in
> conducting the transaction.

The Code does not define the term "fair dealing." As the Maine Supreme
Court has observed, the "most obvious question arising from the use of the
term fair is: fairness to whom?" *Maine Family*, 727 A.2d at 343.

Application of holder in due course status is the law's value judgment
that certain holders are worthy of protection from certain types of claims. For
example, it has been argued that application of the old subjective standard
facilitated the transfer of checks in the stream of commerce; arguably one
would be "more willing to accept the checks if . . . she knows . . . she can be a
holder in due course of that instrument and take it free of defenses that might
have existed between the buyer and the seller in the underlying transaction."
White & Summers, §17-1. In applying the new standard, "fairness" should be
measured by taking a global view of the underlying transaction and all of its
participants. A holder "must act in a way that is fair according to commercial
standards that are themselves reasonable." *Maine Family*, 727 A.2d at 343.

To apply the law requiring "good faith" under §3-302(a), we adopt the
analysis set forth by the Supreme Court of Maine:

> The factfinder must . . . determine, first, whether the conduct of the holder
> comported with industry or "commercial" standards applicable to the trans-
> action and, second, whether those standards were reasonable standards
> intended to result in fair dealing. Each of those determinations must be
> made in the context of the specific transaction at hand. If the factfinder's
> conclusion on each point is "yes," the holder will be determined to have acted
> in good faith even if, in the individual transaction at issue, the result appears
> unreasonable. Thus a holder may be accorded holder in due course status
> where it acts pursuant to those reasonable commercial standards of fair deal-
> ing—even if it is negligent—but may lose that status, even where it complies
> with commercial standards, if those standards are not reasonably related to
> achieving fair dealing.

Id.

There was no evidence at trial concerning the check cashing industry's commercial standards. Even assuming that Any Kind's procedures for checks over $2,000 met the industry's gold standard, we hold that in this case the procedures followed were not reasonably related to achieve fair dealing with respect to the $10,000 check, taking into consideration all of the participants in the transaction, Talcott, Guarino, and Any Kind.

Check cashing businesses are regulated by Chapter 560, Florida Statutes (2001), the Money Transmitters' Code. See §560.101, Fla. Stat. (2001). Among the purposes of Chapter 560 are to provide for and promote:

> (b) The maintenance of public confidence in the money transmitter industry.
> (c) The protection of the interests of the public in the money transmitter system . . . .
> (e) The opportunity for money transmitters to be and remain competitive with each other and with other business organizations. . . .
> (f) The opportunity for money transmitters to effectively serve the convenience and needs of their customers and the public. . . .
> (g) The opportunity for the management of money transmitter businesses to exercise its business judgment within the framework of the code.

§560.102(2). Nothing in Chapter 560 purports to alter or amend any of the provisions of Chapter 673, leading to a conclusion that the legislature did not intend to bend the holder in due course provision of the Uniform Commercial Code—Negotiable Instruments to specially accommodate check cashing businesses.

Check cashing businesses occupy a special niche in the financial industry. They are part of the "alternative financial services"[14] or "fringe banking"[15] sector, a part of the market that "has become a major source of traditional banking services for low-income and working poor consumers, residents of minority neighborhoods, and people with blemished credit histories." Lynn Drysdale & Kathleen E. Keest, The Two-Tiered Consumer Financial Services Marketplace: The Fringe Banking System and its Challenge to Current Thinking About the Role of Usury Laws in Today's Society, 51 S.C. L. Rev. 589, 591 (2000). Check cashing involves "charging a service fee for providing instant cash to unbanked customers." Joseph R. Falasco, Who's Getting Used in Arkansas: An Analysis of Usury, Check Cashing, and the Arkansas Check-Cashers Act, 55 Ark. L. Rev. 149, 156 (2002); see Drysdale & Keest, at

---

14. See, e.g., John Burton et al., The Alternative Financial Sector: Policy Implications for Poor Households, 42 Consumer Interests Ann. 279, 279 (1996).

15. See John P. Caskey, Fringe Banking: Check Cashing Outlets, Pawnshops, and the Poor (1994).

626. Check cashing customers "generally have limited resources available to access immediate cash." Falasco, at 155.

Check cashing stores are often in locations where traditional banks fear to tread. Drysdale and Keest report the research that demonstrates that check cashing outlets are usually located in lower income neighborhoods:

> For example, the Federal Reserve Bank of Boston looked at multi-census tract areas in cities in New England where check cashers were most densely clustered—Boston, Hartford, and Providence. The Boston study found that the cities with high [check cashing outlet] clusters tended "to have high percentages of low- and moderate-income census tracts and households," high percentages of households below the poverty level, and higher shares of households on fixed incomes (either public assistance or social security). More dramatic is the Woodstock Institute's study of the relative distribution of banks and [check cashing outlets and currency exchanges] in Chicago, which examines specific census tracts. This study found that the currency exchanges are predominately located in lower income, minority communities. The currency exchange to bank ratio in five predominately minority communities with median household incomes below $22,000 exceeded ten to one. The lowest income communities, with median incomes of $7908 and $12,570, each had twelve check cashers for every one or two banks.[16]

Drysdale & Keest, at 629 (footnotes omitted). In such areas, the typical check presented for cashing is not a large one—a paycheck, child support, social security, or public assistance check. Section 560.309(4)(b) contemplates that such checks will be presented at check cashing outlets; it limits the fee charged for the payment of "any kind of state public assistance or federal social security benefits payable to the bearer."

Attractions of check cashing outlets are convenience and speed. As the amicus points out, many check cashing businesses are open twenty-four hours a day, seven days a week. Unlike banks, check cashing stores cannot place a hold on a check before releasing funds. The Florida Administrative Code requires payment to be made "immediately in currency for every payment instrument received by a person engaging in the activities of a check casher." Fla. Admin. Code R. 3C-560.804(1). The statute and administrative rules also contemplate that a check cashing business will engage in various types of "verification" of a check. §560.309. Rule 3C 560.801 of the Florida Administrative Code permits a check casher to collect the "direct costs associated with verifying a payment instrument holder's identity, residence, employment, credit history, account status, or other necessary information."

16. The two studies referred to in this paragraph are Lesly Jean Paul & Luxman Nathan, Check Cashers: Moving from the Fringe to the Financial Mainstream, Communities & Banking (Federal Reserve Bank of Boston) 5, 8 (1999), and Woodstock Inst., Reinvestment Alert: Currency Exchanges Add to Poverty Surcharge for Low Income Residents (1997).

(Italics supplied). "Other necessary information" could include long distance or telephone charges incurred to contact the drawer of a check.

Against this backdrop, we cannot say that the trial court erred in finding that the $10,000 check was a red flag. The $10,000 personal check was not the typical check cashed at a check cashing outlet. The size of the check, in the context of the check cashing business, was a proper factor to consider under the objective standard of good faith in deciding whether Any Kind was a holder in due course. See *Maine Family*, 727 A.2d at 344.

Guarino was not the typical customer of a check cashing outlet. As the trial judge observed, because of the 5 percent fee charged, it is unusual for a small businessman such as a broker to conduct business through a check cashing store instead of through a traditional bank. Guarino did not have a history with Any Kind of cashing checks of similar size without incident. The need for speed in a business transaction is usually less acute than for someone cashing a paycheck or welfare check to pay for life's necessities. The need for speed in cashing a large business check is consistent with a drawer who, for whatever reason, might stop payment. Fair dealing in this case required that the $10,000 check be approached with a degree of caution.

If a drawer has a right to stop payment of a check, and a traditional bank usually places a hold on uncollected funds after a payee deposits a check into an account, then the legal dispute after a stop payment will usually be between the drawer of the check and the payee, the two parties that had the dealings leading to the payment. Thus, where a check is cashed at a bank or savings and loan, the law will often place the loss on the wrongdoer in the underlying transaction. This is a desirable goal.

Where a check cashing store releases funds immediately, the holder in due course doctrine steps in, frequently putting the loss on a wronged maker, in furtherance of the policy that facilitating the transfer of checks benefits the economy. In this case, the policy reasons behind easy negotiability do not outweigh the reasons for caution. Very loose application of the objective component of "good faith" would make check cashing outlets the easy refuge of scam artists who want to take the money and run. The concept of "fair dealing" includes not being an easy, safe harbor for the dishonest.

To affirm the trial court is not to wreak havoc with the check cashing industry. Verification with the maker of a check will not be necessary to preserve holder in due course status in the vast majority of cases arising from check cashing outlets. This was neither the typical customer, nor the typical transaction of a check cashing outlet.

We disagree with the amicus, who worries that requirement of verification by the maker in this case "would inhibit the long standing policy of the free negotiation of instruments." Again, this is not the usual case. Also, as White and Summers have written, "there has been debate about the importance of the holder in due course doctrine in facilitating" check transactions. The Federal Trade Commission's abolition of the holder in due course doctrine in most consumer credit transactions has "not had the cata-strophic impact upon the consumer market that some predicted. Indeed, twenty years from now we may conclude that it caused barely a ripple on the consumer credit pond." White & Summers, §17-1.

The legislature's addition of an objective standard of conduct may well have the effect of "slowing the 'wheels of commerce'" in some transactions. *Maine Family*, 727 A.2d at 344. However, by adopting changes to the "good faith" standard in the holder in due course doctrine, the legislature "necessarily must have concluded that the addition of the objective requirement to the definition of 'good faith' serves an important goal. The paramount necessity of unquestioned negotiability has given way, at least in part to the desire for reasonable commercial fairness in negotiable transactions." Id. In this case, reasonable commercial fairness required Any Kind to approach the $10,000 check with some caution and to verify it with the maker if it wanted to preserve its holder in due course status.

Affirmed.

QUESTION

Would a check cashing business be in good faith if it acquired a post-dated check before the date of the check? Compare RR Maloan Investments, Inc. v. New HE, Inc., 428 S.W.3d 355 (Tex. App. 2014) (yes), with Buckeye Check Cashing, Inc. v. Camp, 159 Ohio App. 3d 784, 825 N.E.2d 644 (2005) (no). In State Sec. Check Cashing, Inc. v. American General Financial, 409 Md. 81, 972 A.2d 882 (2009), the court found a check-cashing company that took a $10,000 check from a stranger to be a holder in due course; the decision quoted White and Summer's leading UCC treatise, §17-6, as saying:

> [C]ourts . . . are quick to deny holder in due course status to check cashing facilities. We wonder how these courts would have handled these cases had the plaintiffs been banks and not check cashing facilities. In effect the courts are asking check cashers to adhere to a higher standard than might be required of a bank. Given the clientele of check cashing facilities, the courts' skepticism might be justified, but we would like to see a little more evidence that check-cashing facilities are a home for persons engaged in fraudulent behavior before we would subject them to higher standards than might be applied to a bank.

Winter & Hirsch, Inc. v. Passarelli   SKIP

Illinois Appellate Court, 1970
122 Ill. App. 2d 372, 259 N.E.2d 312

McCormick, J.

This appeal is taken from an order denying a motion to vacate a judgment by confession. The judgment was entered against the defendants,

Dominic and Antoinette Passarelli, on behalf of the plaintiff, Winter & Hirsch, Inc. Defendants made a motion before the trial court to vacate the judgment; the motion was denied, and from that order of the trial court this appeal is taken. The questions before this court are: 1) whether the loan entered into between the parties provided for a usurious rate of interest, and 2) whether the plaintiff was a holder in due course of the note evidencing the loan in question.

The defendants first contacted the Equitable Mortgage & Investment Corporation (hereinafter referred to as Equitable), attempting to secure a loan. Equitable is a brokerage firm which makes its profit by selling loan contracts to finance companies at a discount. In this case Equitable was to lend the defendants $10,000. Of the several provisions in the note, we will consider the following: 1) a provision whereby the defendants agreed "for value received" to repay a total of $16,260 over a period of 60 monthly payments of $271 each; and 2) a confession of judgment clause. The promissory note signed by the defendants provided for payment to the bearer and was secured by a trust deed.

The maximum legal rate of interest which could have been charged the defendants was exceeded by Equitable, and it is uncontested that Equitable charged a usurious rate of interest. The question to be resolved by this court, however, is whether the defense of usury is available for use against the plaintiff, who claims to be holder in due course of the promissory note and therefore claims to have taken it free from the defense of usury. In the trial court the defense of usury was rejected and judgment was entered against the defendants based on the court's conclusion that the plaintiff was a holder in due course of the promissory note.

In this appeal the defendants pray that the trial court's order be reversed and that the loan be held to be usurious. Defendants further ask that the trial court be directed to enter an order allowing them twice the rate of interest, plus attorney's fees and court costs. They seek this relief based on Ill. Rev. Stat. 1965, c.74, 6. At the time of the original transaction that section allowed one aggrieved by the imposition of a usurious rate of interest to be freed of the obligation to pay any interest at all, but an amendment to the statute, in effect at the time of trial, granted one the right to a penalty in the amount of double the usurious interest charged, plus attorney's fees and court costs.

Defendants defaulted on the note and the plaintiff obtained a judgment by confession. At the trial the defendants attempted to show that before the plaintiff purchased the note it knew of the usurious interest being charged, and consequently could not have become a holder in due course. Defendants point out that the loan application which the defendants filled out on January 7, 1963, has on it the name of the plaintiff. They also call attention to the testimony of Dominic Passarelli that he had been told by an agent of Equitable that Winter & Hirsch might give them $10,000. By the terms of the promissory note the monthly payments were to be made at the office of Ralph E. Brown, an attorney for plaintiff.

The most compelling fact presented to the court is that plaintiff issued a check to Equitable for $11,000 on February 18, 1963, with the notation on the stub that the funds were for "the Passarelli deal," but the defendants did not receive the $10,000 until February 28, 1963, ten days later. In other words, the plaintiff had extended the money to Equitable for the Passarelli loan prior to the time the defendants executed the note which plaintiff claims to have bought from Equitable. This fact renders inapposite an entire series of cases upon which plaintiff relies. Those cases hold that a loan may be discounted at more than the usury rate if the purchaser is without knowledge that the note was originally tainted with usury. Stevenson v. Unkefer, 14 Ill. 103; Sherman v. Blackman, 24 Ill. 345; Colehour v. State Sav. Institution, 90 Ill. 152. The critical factual distinction between those cases and the one before us is that the plaintiff in the instant case provided the money for the usurious loan before the loan was actually made, whereas in the cited cases the party claiming to be the innocent holder of the usurious note had purchased it subsequent to its execution.

On oral argument counsel for plaintiff argued that there must have been a clerical error in the dates, and that no loan company would have given out money without the loan contract in its possession. The insurmountable difficulty with counsel's argument is that the date of the check issued to Equitable (February 18) and the date of the note executed by the defendants (February 28) are clearly established through the admission into evidence, without objection, of the check issued to Equitable and the note signed by the defendants. This court must accept those dates as accurate.

From these dates it appears that the plaintiff was a co-originator of the note since it advanced the funds for the usurious loan before the loan was formalized. As a co-originator it is charged with the knowledge of the terms of the loan, and that knowledge includes information regarding anticipated return on its investment. Such information should have made it clear that a usurious rate of interest was being charged the defendants; nevertheless, the plaintiff still elected to consummate the transaction, and it must now accept the consequences.

We note, however, that the plaintiff has argued that it did not give the $11,000 to Equitable until after it saw the loan contract; in other words, that it was a purchaser of the note after it had already been executed. Although the facts do not sustain this contention because of the respective dates on which the check to Equitable was issued and the note signed by the defendants, even if that version were correct, we would hold for the defendants.

If the note was seen, as alleged by plaintiff, prior to its giving Equitable $11,000, then the plaintiff also saw that the defendants had signed a note promising to repay $16,260. From the face of the note one cannot ascertain the principal amount the defendants had received; it can only be known that "for value received" the defendants agreed to repay $16,260. We feel, however, that as reasonable businessmen, assuming arguendo that plaintiff did not know the truth, it should have raised the question of why Equitable was willing to sell a $16,260 note for $11,000. The difference between what the plaintiff was paying Equitable and the amount of the note was a charge beyond that permitted under the usury statute, and plaintiff should, therefore, have inquired how much money the defendants were receiving. We cannot permit parties to intentionally keep themselves in ignorance of facts which, if known, would defeat their unlawful purpose. The Uniform Commercial Code (Ill. Rev. Stat. 1965, c.26, §3-304(1)) provides that when an instrument is so incomplete as to call its validity into question, a purchaser of that instrument is on notice of the possibility of a claim against it [in the Revision, see §3-302(a)(1) — Eds.]. In this case we feel that the instrument, without the information as to the principal sum of the loan extended to the defendants, was "so incomplete" as to call its validity into question after plaintiff learned that it was able to buy it for only $11,000.

In Springer v. Mack, 222 Ill. App. 72, the court said at p. 75:

> The question of usury was discussed exhaustively and the authorities reviewed in the case of Clemens v. Crane, 234 Ill. 215, where it was held in substance, that in determining whether the essential elements of usury are present in a particular case, the intention of the parties, as the same appears from the facts and circumstances of the case, may be considered in connection with other evidence.

The court also said, p. 230:

> The form of the contract is not conclusive of the question. The desire of lenders to exact more than the law permits and the willingness of borrowers to concede whatever may be demanded to obtain temporary relief from financial embarrassment have resulted in a variety of shifts and cunning devices designed to evade the law. The character of a transaction is not to be judged by the mere verbal raiment in which the parties have clothed it, but by its true character as disclosed by the whole evidence. If, when so judged, it appears to be a loan or forbearance of money for a greater rate of interest than that allowed by law, the statute is violated and its penalties incurred, no matter what device the parties may have employed to conceal the real character of their dealings.

By failing to include the principal amount loaned to the borrower on the face of the loan contract or note, a subsequent purchaser of that contract is able to say "I had no idea that usury was involved. I simply bought the paper because it was a good buy." If the principal amount were shown, however, all subsequent purchasers would be put on notice if usury were involved, and they could not avoid their own involvement in the charging of a usurious rate by the purchase of such paper.

We feel we are justified in saying that where it appears from the facts and circumstances of the particular transaction under review that a reasonably prudent businessman would have found the purchase suspicious, he should inquire as to the truth. One should become suspicious when, as here, he is himself able to purchase paper at a price which is in itself so far below the amount to be repaid from the borrower that because of that differential the contract would have been usurious had it been the original transaction. The suspicion should be all the more compelling when the paper is bought from a broker or other company that is in the business of selling such paper. Since brokers are in the business of selling loan contracts for a profit, they are likely to have loaned out less than the amount for which they are willing to sell the contract to another. Thus, if one is able to buy a loan contract from a broker for $11,000, it is more than likely that the broker had loaned some figure less than the $11,000, and the broker's profit then becomes the difference between the amount he actually loaned and that for which he sold the contract. It would then appear likely that when this difference is itself usurious, the original transaction was also. Stevenson v. Unkefer, 14 Ill. 103, and similar cases do not dictate a contrary result. . . .

Under the circumstances, if the plaintiff was a purchaser, as it claims to be, it was on notice of a defense, since section 3-304 [in the Revision, §3-302(a)(1) — Eds.], chapter 26 of Ill. Rev. Stat. 1965 provides:

> (1) The purchaser has notice of a claim or defense if
> (a) the instrument is so incomplete, bears such visible evidence of forgery or alteration, or is otherwise so irregular as to call into question its validity, terms or ownership or to create an ambiguity as to the party to pay. . . .

This code provision is consistent with the earlier definition of "notice" found in section 1-201(25), chapter 26, providing:

> A person has "notice" of a fact when . . .
> (c) from all the facts and circumstances known to him at the time in question he has reason to know that it exists.

The intendment of these provisions would seem to be an attempt to prevent those dealing in the commercial world from obtaining various rights when, from a reasonable inquiry into the true facts that person would have discovered that a fact existed which prevented him from obtaining the rights which he was seeking. Under the circumstances in the present case, it is fair to say that the plaintiff had "reason to know" there was a good defense against the note in question. Even the earlier cases point out that notice of usury destroyed one's rights in the note. . . .

The judgment of the Circuit Court is reversed, and the cause is remanded with directions to enter a judgment for defendants and for further proceedings in conformity with this opinion.

Reversed and remanded with directions.

LYONS, J. concurs. [The dissenting opinion of Burke, J., is omitted.]

QUESTION

Would the Federal Trade Commission holder in due course rule (see page 43) apply to the promissory note signed in this case if the transaction had taken place after May 14, 1976 (the effective date of that rule)?

PROBLEM 28

Fred wrote a check on January 5, 2018, but mistakenly put down "2017" as the year. He saw his error, crossed out the last digit, and wrote "8" above it. Can anyone become a holder in due course of this instrument?

PROBLEM 29

Ace Finance Company was the payee on a promissory note signed by John Maker. On its face, the note calls for John to make 12 monthly interest payments before the note matures. Ace sold the note at a discount to Big Town Bank (BTB). If the note has written on it, in big letters, a penciled notation, "Missed Paying First Installment," can BTB ever qualify as a holder in due course? See §3-304(b) and (c) and its Official Comment 2.

PROBLEM 30

Dan Drawer wrote a check dated April 30 to Dr. Paine, his dentist, for $80, in payment for services rendered. Dr. Paine was not aware that the check fell to the floor behind his desk, where it lay until the end of August, when the janitor found it. Dr. Paine then deposited the check in his bank on August 31, and it bounced on September 3, when the drawee bank informed the depositary bank that Dan had stopped payment because the dental work had been done badly. Is the depositary bank a holder in due course? See §3-304(a)(2).

Dawda, Mann, Mulcahy & Sadler, P.L.C. v. Bank of America, N.A.

United States District Court, Eastern District of Michigan, 2014
2014 WL 6669277

Read

TERRENCE G. BERG, District Judge.

This matter is before the Court on Defendant Bank of America, N.A.'s ("Defendant's") motion to dismiss under Federal Rule of Civil Procedure 12(b)(6). (Dkt. 10.) This motion was fully briefed and the parties presented oral argument on June 9, 2014. For the reasons set out below, Defendant's motion to dismiss is DENIED.

I. INTRODUCTION

This is a negligence case. Plaintiff, the law firm of Dawda, Mann, Mulcahy & Sadler, P.L.C. ("Plaintiff"), alleges that it suffered significant monetary losses because of Defendant Bank of America, N.A.'s negligence in accepting over $500,000 in diverted trust account checks. As part of a fraudulent scheme, a former partner of Plaintiff caused Plaintiff to write a number of checks made payable to Defendant from Plaintiff's IOLTA account.[17] The partner, an account holder and customer of Defendant, presented these checks to Defendant, and Defendant deposited the funds into the partner's personal account maintained by Defendant. Though Plaintiff did not owe Defendant any money and did not have a business relationship with Defendant, it is alleged that Defendant made no inquiry regarding the checks before depositing them. As a result, Plaintiff alleges that Defendant violated the common law "duty of inquiry." Defendant counters that it did not owe Plaintiff any duty and that it held the checks as a holder in due course under the Uniform Commercial Code ("UCC"), free from any claims on the checks. For the reasons that follow, Defendant's motion to dismiss is DENIED.

II. FACTUAL AND PROCEDURAL BACKGROUND

Plaintiff is a law firm located in Bloomfield Hills, Michigan. (Second Amended Complaint, Dkt. 9, at ¶1.) Beginning on or about November 15, 2010, Plaintiff's former partner Kenneth Flaska ("Flaska") defrauded Plaintiff by laundering funds through Defendant.[18] (*Id.* at ¶6.) Flaska's fraud consisted of presenting and depositing checks drawn on Plaintiff's IOLTA

17. An IOLTA ("Interest on Lawyer's Trust Account") account is an interest-bearing account maintained by an attorney or law firm to pool funds being held in trust for a client or clients, as required under Michigan Rule of Professional Responsibility 1.15(d).

18. Flaska pled guilty to bank fraud and money laundering for this scheme, and was sentenced to 64 months in prison. *See* E.D. Mich. Case No. 14-20131.

account into Flaska's personal bank account maintained by Defendant. (*Id.*) From November 2010 until March 2013, Defendant received and credited nine of these checks into Flaska's account, totaling $529,676.50. (*Id.* at ¶7.) All of the checks were drawn from Plaintiff's IOLTA account and were payable on their face to "Bank of America," the Defendant. (*Id.* at ¶¶6-7, Exs. A-I.) Despite the fact that Plaintiff was not one of Defendant's customers and was not indebted to Defendant, Defendant allegedly never inquired into these checks before crediting them to Flaska's account. (Second Amended Complaint, Dkt. 9 at ¶¶9, 13.)

On November 15, 2013, Plaintiff sued Defendant in Oakland County Circuit Court.[19] (Dkt. 1, Ex. 1.) Plaintiff amended its state court complaint on February 5, 2014, alleging four counts against Defendant, including: (1) breach of the common law duty of inquiry; (2) common law conversion; (3) statutory conversion; and (4) negligence. (*Id.*) Defendant removed the case to this Court on February 11, 2014. (Dkt. 1.) Plaintiff subsequently amended its complaint, eliminating Counts 2 and 3 and proceeding solely on Counts 1 and 4. (*Id.*)

III.   ANALYSIS

* * *

1.   THE COMMON LAW DUTY OF INQUIRY

Plaintiff alleges that Defendant was negligent because it breached its common law "duty of inquiry." In diversity jurisdiction actions, federal courts must "appl[y] the substantive law of the forum state—in this case, Michigan." Conlin v. Mortg. Elec. Registration Sys., Inc., 714 F.3d 355, 358 (6th Cir. 2013). The Michigan Court of Appeals first recognized a common law duty of inquiry in Allis Chalmers Leasing Servs. Corp. v. Byron Ctr. State Bank, 129 Mich. App. 602, 341 N.W.2d 837 (1983). In *Allis Chalmers*, the plaintiff wrote a check payable to the defendant, Byron Center State Bank, as part of a purchase and leaseback agreement that the plaintiff had entered into with Gary Deneen, a customer of the defendant. *Id.* at 839. Deneen presented the check to the defendant as part of a fraudulent scheme Deneen

---

19. The Uniform Law Commissioners first promulgated the Uniform Negotiable Instruments Law ("N.I.L.") in 1896 as way to organize the law of negotiable instruments. A revised version of the N.I.L. makes up the current version of Article 3 of the UCC. *See* Uniform Law Commission, UCC Article 3, Negotiable Instruments (1990) Summary, *available at* http://www.uniformlaws.org/ActSummary.aspx?title=UCC% 20Article% 203,% 20Negotiable% 20Instruments%20(1990) ("The old NIL in either its independent form or as part of the UCC has governed negotiable instruments in the United States for about 80 years, as its first major revisions are prepared for promulgation by the ULC in the year 1989. Another 80 or so years of service is expected for the revisions.").

devised to defraud the plaintiff. *Id.* The defendant's employee distributed the proceeds according to Deneen's instructions without making any inquiry into how the funds should be used. *Id.*

Seeking to recover its losses, the plaintiff brought a negligence action against the defendant bank for the amount of the check. The plaintiff alleged that the defendant bank was negligent in disbursing the check to Deneen without first inquiring into how the funds should be disbursed. *Id.* On appeal, the Michigan Court of Appeals affirmed the trial court's grant of summary judgment in favor of the plaintiff, citing the general rule that "[w]here a check is drawn to the order of a bank to which the drawer is not indebted, the bank is authorized to pay the proceeds only to persons specified by the drawer; it takes the risk in treating such a check as payable to bearer and is placed on inquiry as to the authority of the drawer's agent to receive payment." *Id.* (internal citation omitted).

In addition, the Michigan Court of Appeals, adopting a California Supreme Court decision, held that plaintiff's negligence action was not abrogated by the UCC's "holder in due course" doctrine. The defendant in *Allis Chalmers* argued that it was a holder in due course under the UCC and not liable under the common law duty of inquiry. A holder in due course then, and now, takes an instrument free of any claims on the instrument. *See* Mich. Comp. Laws §440.3306. The Michigan Court of Appeals rejected the defendant's argument and instead adopted the California Supreme Court's holding in Sun 'n Sand, Inc. v. United Cal. Bank, 21 Cal. 3d 671, 148 Cal. Rptr. 329, 582 P.2d 920 (1978). *Id.* at 840.

In *Sun'n Sand*, the California Supreme Court recognized that banks have a duty of inquiry that is "activated only when checks, not insignificant in amount, are drawn payable to the order of a bank and are presented to the payee bank by a third party seeking to negotiate the checks for his own benefit." 148 Cal. Rptr. 329, 582 P.2d at 937. *Sun'n Sand* explained that the duty of inquiry is narrow in scope, stating

"[T]he bank's obligation is minimal. We hold simply that the bank may not ignore the danger signals inherent in such an attempted negotiation. There must be objective indicia from which the bank could reasonably conclude that the party presenting the check is authorized to transact in the manner proposed. In the absence of such indicia the bank pays at its peril." *Id.* Since the bank was under the duty of inquiry, *Sun'n Sand* held that the UCC's holder in due course doctrine was not a defense to the common law duty of inquiry because banks were on notice "so as to preclude UCB from holder in due course status[.]" *Id.*, 148 Cal. Rptr. 329, 582 P.2d at 933.

2. THE 1993 REVISION TO THE UCC

In response, Defendant argues that *Allis Chalmers* is old law, and that Michigan's 1993 revision to the UCC abrogated the common law duty of inquiry. Defendant cites no case law in support of its position that the duty of inquiry was preempted or overturned in Michigan as a result of the 1993 UCC revisions, and the Court finds little precedential support for this assertion.

Indeed, contrary to Defendant's position, there is case law holding that the duty of inquiry recognized in *Allis Chalmers* remains in force in Michigan and may preclude a party from taking as a holder in due course under the UCC. In Grand Rapids Auto Sales, Inc. v. MBNA Am. Bank, 227 F. Supp. 2d 721, 725-726 (W.D. Mich. 2002), citing *Allis Chalmers*, the court held that there is a duty of inquiry that "arises only in circumstances where the check is physically presented to the bank for negotiation by the dishonest employee and the bank, through its agent, has the opportunity to inspect the check for irregularities that should alert the bank that fraud is amiss." *Grand Rapids* involved an employee of a Michigan company who defrauded the company by taking company checks made payable to defendant MBNA bank and having MBNA apply the checks to her husband's credit card. *Id.* at 723. The bank accepted the checks through automatic electronic processing. *Id.* The company, who did not have a relationship with MBNA, sued MBNA alleging that MBNA violated its common law duty of inquiry. *Id.* at 722.

Although the court rejected the company's argument and held that MBNA was a holder in due course, it did so because it ruled that the duty of inquiry did not *extend* to automatic credit card payments, not because the duty of inquiry did not *exist*. *Id. at 726.* And the court explicitly distinguished its holding from *Allis Chalmers* based on the factual circumstances of the case, "[t]he key distinction between this case and *Sun'n Sand* and *Allis Chalmers* is that the banks in those cases actually inspected the checks and should have been alerted by the circumstances—a check drawn payable to the order of the bank by a drawer not indebted to the bank and presented by a third party seeking to negotiate the check for his own benefit—that the employee's conduct may have been improper." *Id.* at 726-27 (internal citations omitted). The factual scenario offered by the court as an example of the situation where the duty of inquiry should still apply is exactly what Plaintiff alleges happened in the case at bar. . . .

3. *SUN 'N SAND*'S HOLDING THAT A PARTY UNDER A DUTY OF INQUIRY TAKES WITH NOTICE AND IS NOT A HOLDER IN DUE COURSE REMAINS GOOD LAW

Defendant next attempts a collateral attack on *Allis Chalmers* by arguing that *Sun'n Sand*, the basis for *Allis Chalmers*, is no longer good law. This argument is not well taken. . . .

Defendant's second point fares no better. Defendant argues that the 1993 revision of the UCC abrogated *Sun'n Sand*'s holding that defendant had notice and as such was not a holder in due course. . . .

Additionally, Mich. Comp. Laws §440.3302(1)(a), the current section that defines a holder in due course, retains the language concerning irregularity on the instrument that the *Sun 'n Sand* court interpreted. Mich. Comp. Laws §440.3302(1)(a) states that a party is a "holder in due course" if both of the following apply:

> (a) The instrument when issued or negotiated to the holder does not bear such apparent evidence of forgery or alteration *or is not otherwise so irregular or incomplete as to call into question its authenticity.*
>
> (b) The holder took the instrument (*i*) for value, (*ii*) in good faith, (*iii*) without notice that the instrument is overdue or has been dishonored or that there is an incurred default with respect to payment of another instrument issued as part of the same series, (*iv*) without notice that the instrument contains an unauthorized signature or has been altered, (*v*) without notice of any claim to the instrument described in section 3306, and (*vi*) without notice that any party has a defense or claim in recoupment described in section 3305(1).

(emphasis added). A check written to a bank as a payee by a non-customer who does not owe it any money is likely an irregularity under Mich. Comp. Laws §440.3302. This is consistent with the position of the court in *Grand Rapids* where the court held that banks that physically inspect a suspect check are in a position to be placed on notice. 227 F. Supp. 2d at 726 ("the banks in those cases actually inspected the checks and should have been alerted by the circumstances . . .").

Defendant counters that under Mich. Comp. Laws §440.3302, the irregularity must be on the face of an instrument and not merely based on the circumstances of a transaction. In support of this argument, Defendant points to Comment One of Mich. Comp. Laws §440.3302(a)(1), which states in relevant part:

> Subsection (a)(1) is a return to the N.I.L. rule that the taker of an irregular or incomplete instrument is not a person the law should protect against defenses of the obligor or claims of prior owners. This reflects a policy choice against extending the holder in due course doctrine to an instrument that is so incomplete or irregular "as to call into question its authenticity." The term "authenticity" is used to make it clear that the irregularity or incompleteness must indicate that the instrument may not be what it purports to be. Persons who purchase or pay such instruments should do so at their own risk. Under subsection (1) of former Section 3-304, irregularity or incompleteness gave a purchaser notice of a claim or defense. But it was not clear from that provision whether the claim or defense had to be related to the irregularity or incomplete aspect of the instrument. This ambiguity is not present in subsection (a)(1).

Defendant's reading of Comment One to say that any irregularity must be on the face of an instrument is not supported by the language of the Comment itself. A more accurate reading of this Comment is that where the irregularity *is* present on the face of the instrument, so that a doubt is created that the instrument is what it purports to be, the taker of an instrument with such an irregularity is not protected as a holder in due course. The Comment does not preclude a finding that the actual language of Mich. Comp. Laws §440.3302(a)(1) contemplated the possibility of irregularities arising both on the face of the instrument and in the circumstances of its negotiation. That language speaks not only of the face of the instrument but also of its negotiation when it states: "[t]he instrument when issued *or negotiated* to the holder does not bear such apparent evidence of forgery or alteration *or is not otherwise so irregular or incomplete as to call into question its authenticity.*" (*Id.*) (emphasis added). An instrument that has no marks of forgery or alteration on its face may nevertheless have its authenticity called into question by the surrounding circumstances of its negotiation. Further, had the drafters of the UCC intended to change the holder in due course section to require that an irregularity must be on the face of an instrument, they would have so stated. Indeed, the drafters were clear in their express rejection of *Sun 'n Sand*'s warranty holding. This Court does not find support in the statutory text to hold that an irregularity must be on the face of the check. . . .

5. MICH. COMP. LAWS §440.3307

Defendant also seeks refuge in another section of the UCC, claiming that Mich. Comp. Laws §440.3307 [U.C.C. §3-307] effectively abrogates the common law duty of inquiry. Mich. Comp. Laws §440.3307 defines when a taker of a negotiable instrument has notice of a breach of fiduciary duty and thus does not take as a holder in due course. Mich. Comp. Laws §440.3307(2) provides:

> If (*i*) an instrument is taken from a fiduciary for payment or collection or for value, (*ii*) the taker has knowledge of the fiduciary status of the fiduciary, and (*iii*) the represented person makes a claim to the instrument or its proceeds on the basis that the transaction of the fiduciary is a breach of fiduciary duty, the following rules apply:
>
> (a) Notice of breach of fiduciary duty by the fiduciary is notice of the claim of the represented person.
>
>   * * *
>
> (d) If an instrument is issued by the represented person or the fiduciary as such, to the taker as payee, the taker has notice of the breach of fiduciary duty if the instrument is (*i*) taken in payment of or as security for a debt known by the taker to be the personal debt of the fiduciary, (*ii*) taken in a transaction known by the taker to be for the personal benefit of

the fiduciary, or (*iii*) deposited to an account other than an account of the fiduciary, as such, or an account of the represented person. . . .

The Court begins with a plain reading of Mich. Comp. Laws §440.3307. Comment Two of Mich. Comp. Laws §440.3307 states that the section applies where a "fiduciary in effect embezzles money of the represented person by applying the proceeds of an instrument that belongs to the represented person to the personal use of the fiduciary." Mich. Comp. Laws §440.3307(1)(a) defines "fiduciary" narrowly, as an "an agent, trustee, partner, corporate officer or director, or other representative *owing a fiduciary duty with respect to an instrument.*" (emphasis added). So, even if a party is a fiduciary of an organization, Mich. Comp. Laws §440.3307 is inapplicable if the party is not a fiduciary with respect to the check itself. This is what the Seventh Circuit held in *Elizabeth State Bank.* There, the Seventh Circuit found that a controller for a company who managed the company's books and accounts was not a fiduciary under Illinois' version of Mich. Comp. Laws §440.3307 because he had "no authority to direct the proceeds" of checks on the company's account at issue. 265 F.3d at 622. As such, the Seventh Circuit held that the controller "may have been a fiduciary for some purposes, but he did not qualify as a fiduciary with respect to checks drawn on the operating account and made payable to the bank's order." *Id.* Because this section applies only where a fiduciary (as to a particular check) is involved, it is narrowly drawn and does not cover every situation where a third-party attempts to divert the proceeds of a check by presenting a check made payable to a taker. It follows that the scope of Mich. Comp. Laws §440.3307, like its Illinois counterpart, does not encompass every situation where the common law duty of inquiry applies.

The Court must also consider that the UCC by its own terms provides for supplementation by other sources of law, such as the common law duty of inquiry. Mich. Comp. Laws §440.1103 provides that "[u]nless displaced by the particular provisions of this act, the principles of law and equity . . . shall supplement its provisions." As discussed above, Mich. Comp. Laws §440.3307 only applies where a fiduciary with respect to a certain instrument presents that instrument to a taker as payee. Because the duty of inquiry applies more broadly to situations that do not involve a fiduciary, the common law duty of inquiry is not displaced by a particular provision of the UCC.

Similarly, the holder in due course section specifically provides for supplementation by other sources of law. Mich. Comp. Laws §440.3302(7) provides that "[t]his section is subject to any law limiting status as a holder in due course in particular classes of transactions." As evidenced by the considerable body of case law discussed above, numerous jurisdictions deny banks holder in due course status when they are "presented with a check made out to it by someone who owes it no money, for deposit in the presenter's account." *Travelers*, 374 F.3d at 527-28. Consequently, the duty of inquiry limits the holder in due course section.

Finally, the UCC's underlying purpose of promoting uniformity among jurisdictions weighs against a finding that Mich. Comp. Laws §440.3307 has abrogated the common law duty of inquiry. Mich. Comp. Laws §440.1103 provides:

> (1) This act must be liberally construed and applied to promote the following underlying purposes and policies:
>> (a) To simplify, clarify, and modernize the law governing commercial transactions.
>>> * * *
>> (c) To make uniform the law among the various jurisdictions.

Various jurisdictions have upheld the common law duty of inquiry both before and after the enactment of the UCC. This Court has found no case abrogating the common law duty of inquiry in any jurisdiction. Hence, the interest of uniformity militates against abrogating the common law duty of inquiry.

For the foregoing reasons, this Court holds that the Mich. Comp. Laws §440.3307 does not abrogate the common law duty of inquiry.

6. PLAINTIFF HAS RAISED A PLAUSIBLE CLAIM THAT DEFENDANT HAD A DUTY OF INQUIRY

Having found that the common law duty of inquiry remains viable as a legal claim, we must now analyze whether Plaintiff's facts present a plausible claim that Defendant had a duty of inquiry in this case. *Sun 'n Sand* held that the duty is "activated only when checks, not insignificant in amount, are drawn payable to the order of a bank and are presented to the payee bank by a third party seeking to negotiate the checks for his own benefit." 148 Cal. Rptr. 329, 582 P.2d at 937. Here, Plaintiff's checks were payable to Defendant. These checks were for a significant amount; together the nine checks totaled $529,676.50. And Flaska, a third-party, presented the checks to Defendant for his own benefit. Under these circumstances, a "bank may not ignore the danger signals inherent in such an attempted negotiation." *Id.* Based on these allegations, Plaintiff has raised a plausible claim that Defendant had a duty of inquiry. . . .

IV. CONCLUSION

For the foregoing reasons, Plaintiff has stated a plausible claim for relief and Defendant's motion to dismiss is DENIED.
SO ORDERED.

PROBLEM 31

When Ellen Brown found out that the computer she had purchased didn't work, she was furious and decided not to pay the promissory note she had signed. The note stated that it was "payable at Busy State Bank" (which in this case means that the bank would pay the note when presented and then expect reimbursement from the maker; cf. §4-106(b)). Harold Slow, the head cashier at the bank, took Ellen's phone call and promised not to pay the note when it was presented. Four months went by, and, on one hectic afternoon, the bank paid the note by accident. Slow said he had forgotten the request not to pay. The bank now demands payment, claiming to be a holder in due course. Is it?

The last Problem involves the *forgotten notice doctrine,* which under the NIL permitted a holder to *forget* notice and thus become a holder in due course if sufficient time passed between the notice and the acquisition of the instrument. See First Natl. Bank of Odessa v. Fazzari, 10 N.Y.2d 394, 179 N.E.2d 493, 233 N.Y.S.2d 483 (1961) ("[W]e think that the doctrine should be applied with great caution in the case where a simple promissory note is involved. A lapse of memory is too easily pleaded and too difficult to controvert to permit the doctrine to be applied automatically irrespective of the circumstances surrounding each transaction and the relationship of the parties."). The UCC has no position on the *forgotten notice doctrine;* see §1-202's Official Comment; McCook County Natl. Bank v. Compton, 558 F.2d 871 (8th Cir. 1977).

PROBLEM 32

Giant Earthmovers bought some machinery from Tractors, Inc., and in payment executed a promissory note payable to the order of Tractors for $2,000. Tractors sold the note without indorsement to the Friendly Finance Company for $1,500. The maker of the note refused to pay the note when it matured, stating that the machinery did not operate properly. Friendly decided to sue Giant Earthmovers, and the day before the lawsuit was filed, Friendly's lawyer noticed that the note had never been indorsed by Tractors, Inc. He had Tractors' president specially indorse the note over to Friendly right away, and then the suit was filed. Is Friendly a holder in due course? See §3-203(c) and its Official Comment 3, and Case #4 in Official Comment 4; Ballengee v. New Mexico Fed. Sav. & Loan Assn., 109 N.M. 423, 786 P.2d 37 (N.M. 1990).

Jones v. Approved Bancredit Corp.

Delaware Supreme Court, 1969
256 A.2d 739

HERRMANN, J.

The dispositive question in this appeal is whether the plaintiff finance company is a holder in due course of the defendant's note. We hold that the finance company was not a holder in due course under the party-to-the-transaction rule.

I

The relevant facts are undisputed for present purposes.

The defendant, Myrtle V. Jones, owned a lot of land in Delaware and wished to have a house built on it. She responded to a newspaper advertisement by Albee Dell Homes, Inc. (hereinafter "Dell"), a sales agency for pre-cut homes in Elkton, Maryland. After selecting a type of house from various plans presented, Mrs. Jones signed a purchase order contract and credit application and made a deposit. Several weeks later, Dell's representative presented to Mrs. Jones for signature a series of documents evidencing an obligation of $3,250,[20] to be paid by Mrs. Jones in monthly installments over a period of years for the house. The documents evidencing the obligation included the following papers: a mortgage; a judgment bond and warrant; a promissory note; a construction contract; a request for insurance; an affidavit that the masonry work and foundation were completed and paid for (when in fact none of the work had been commenced); and an affidavit that no materials were delivered or work started as of the date of the mortgage.

Mrs. Jones demurred to the signing of the mass of documents thus placed before her and stated that she would like to consult her attorney before signing because she did not understand the documents. Dell's representative objected, stating that it was not necessary for Mrs. Jones to have an attorney; that it would be a waste of money to do so; that he would advise her. Although Mrs. Jones reiterated her wish for an attorney several times, Dell's representative insisted upon her signing the papers then and there, stating that it was necessary to do so if the work was to start seasonably. He assured her that Dell would take care of the entire situation to her satisfaction. Mrs. Jones finally acquiesced and signed all the documents. Immediately thereafter, the paper was endorsed and assigned by Dell to the plaintiff Approved Bancredit Corp. (hereinafter "Bancredit") which paid Dell $2,250.00 for the $3,250.00 note.

_____

20. The principal amount of the obligation was $2,500. The balance consisted of "charges."

During the construction, an employee of the builder drove a bulldozer into the side of the partially completed house and knocked it off its foundations. Thereafter, the builder refused to go forward with the work. Dell disclaimed responsibility on the ground that the damage to the structure was a result of a "cave-in" and was "a work of God." The structure was left in a dangerous condition with the water-filled basement constituting an attractive nuisance to children. The County authorities demanded that this unsafe condition be rectified. Mrs. Jones consulted an attorney who notified Dell and Bancredit that Mrs. Jones would be obliged to remove the remnants of the building and fill the basement, in order to make the area safe, unless another satisfactory course of action was suggested. There was no reply and the demolition was accomplished at Mrs. Jones' expense. Later, Dell closed its office and terminated its business except for the servicing of certain contracts through a representative in Delaware.

Thereafter, Bancredit brought this action against Mrs. Jones, seeking foreclosure on the mortgage and collection of an unpaid balance of $2,560.23, with interest. Mrs. Jones interposed several defenses, mainly that of fraud by Dell. During pretrial proceedings, the action developed into a suit upon the promissory note, which Bancredit contended was secured by the mortgage and was negotiable in its hands as a holder in due course by assignment of Dell. Thereupon, Bancredit moved for summary judgment on the ground that the defenses claimed against Dell were not available against it as a holder in due course. The Superior Court denied summary judgment, stating that Mrs. Jones should have the opportunity to "demonstrate the precise relationship" between Dell and Bancredit. Thereafter, depositions were taken and the following facts, inter alia, appeared regarding that relationship:

Dell and Bancredit were both wholly owned subsidiaries of Albee Homes, Inc. (hereinafter "Homes"). The business of the parent corporation was to process pre-cut lumber and sell pre-cut homes. It had between 50 and 70 sales agencies in 19 states. Dell was its Maryland sales agency. Ninety-nine percent of Bancredit's business came from Dell and the other wholly owned sales agency subsidiaries of Homes; it was organized for this purpose. Bancredit examined into the laws of the various states in which the sales agencies operated and prescribed the forms of contracts and financing documents to be used by each agency, including Dell, in concluding a transaction. Homes and Bancredit had the same officers and directors; Homes named the directors and officers of Dell. Checks of Bancredit, issued to consummate a financing transaction like that entered into by Mrs. Jones and Dell, were countersigned by Homes. During the construction of a house, Bancredit routinely requested and received progress reports. Specifically, the manager of Bancredit testified on deposition that Bancredit was a "finance department" of Homes; that each transaction of Dell, like the transactions of each of the other sales agencies, was approved in advance by Bancredit; that the first paper received was the application of the purchaser for extension of credit which was reviewed and passed upon in advance by Bancredit, with directions back to Dell as to any special condition to be imposed upon the purchaser in connection with the loan under consideration. Bancredit had the exclusive power of approval, condition, or rejection of a transaction tendered by the sales agency.

As the result of a pretrial conference, the trial judge stated that with a full understanding of the evidence to be adduced by each side at trial, he had concluded that a directed verdict in favor of Bancredit must necessarily result because, in his opinion, Bancredit was a holder in due course and the defenses sought to be interposed by Mrs. Jones were not available to it. Each of the parties then made a detailed offer of proof on the record and, thereupon, the Superior Court entered judgment for Bancredit on the ground that it was a holder in due course. Mrs. Jones appeals.

II

The question before us has not been heretofore answered by this court. It is a difficult question, as to which the authorities are in sharp conflict.

In dealing with the holder in due course status, a basic problem has been recognized by the courts in cases involving the financing of installment sales, especially of consumer goods and household improvements. The problem arises from the increasingly apparent need for a balancing of the interest of the commercial community in the unrestricted negotiability of commercial papers, on the one hand, against the interest of the installment buyers of the community, on the other hand, in the preservation of their normal remedy of withholding payment whenever there has been misrepresentation, failure of consideration, or other valid reason for refusal to pay. This problem and this need have given rise to this concept: The more the holder knows about the underlying transaction which is the source of the paper, the more he controls or participates in it, the less he fits the role of good faith purchaser for value, and the less justification there is for according to him the protected status of holder in due course considered necessary for the free flow of paper in the commercial world.

The rule, balancing the needs of the installment-buying community and the commercial community, has evolved in various ways. Many courts have solved the problem by denying holder in due course status to the finance company where it maintains a close business relationship with the dealer whose paper it buys; where the financier is closely connected with the particular credit transaction under scrutiny; or where the financier prescribes to the dealer the forms of the papers, the buyer signs the purchase agreement and the note concurrently, and the dealer endorses the note and assigns the contract immediately thereafter. In such situations, many courts look upon the transaction as a species of tri-partite transaction; and the tenor of the cases is that the finance company, in such situation, should not be permitted to hide behind "the fictional fence" of the UNIL or the UCC and thereby achieve an unfair advantage over the purchaser. See Unico v. Owen, 50 N.J. 101, 232 A.2d 405 (1967); Buffalo Industrial Bank v. DeMarzio, 162 Misc. 742, 296 N.Y.S. 738 (1937).

The rule of balance thus evolved is exemplified by Mutual Finance Co. v. Martin, 63 So. 2d 649 (Fla. 1953). There a finance company was held not to be a holder in due course where it appeared that the finance company furnished to the payee electrical appliance dealer the form of conditional sales contract and promissory note with its name imprinted thereon; that before the sales transaction occurred the finance company had investigated the purchaser's credit standing, had approved the proposed terms and agreed to purchase the contract and note in the event the transaction was consummated; that over a period of years immediately prior to the transaction, the finance company had provided much financing for the dealer in other transactions. In holding that, under those circumstances, the finance company was sufficiently a party to the transaction to deprive it of holder in due course status, the Supreme Court of Florida stated:

> . . . It may be that our holding here will require some changes in business methods and will impose a greater burden on the finance companies. We think the buyer—Mr. & Mrs. General Public—should have some protection somewhere along the line. We believe the finance company is better able to bear the risk of the dealer's insolvency than the buyer and in a far better position to protect his interests against unscrupulous and insolvent dealers. . . .
>
> If this opinion imposes great burdens on finance companies it is a potent argument in favor of a rule which will afford protection to the general buying public against unscrupulous dealers in personal property. . . .

Another leading case supporting the rule of balance is Commercial Credit Co. v. Childs, 199 Ark. 1073, 137 S.W.2d 260 (1940), wherein the automobile sales contract, note, and assignment forms were attached together, were furnished by the finance company, and were all executed on the same day. The Supreme Court of Arkansas there stated:

> We think appellant was so closely connected with the entire transaction or with the deal that it can not be heard to say that it, in good faith, was an innocent purchaser of the instrument for value before maturity. . . . Rather than being a purchaser of the instrument after its execution it was to all intents and purposes a party to the agreement and instrument from the beginning. . . .

See also Commercial Credit Corporation v. Orange County Machine Works, 34 Cal. 2d 766, 214 P.2d 819 (1950), where the Supreme Court of California held:

> When a finance company actively participates in a transaction . . . from its inception, counseling and aiding the future vendor-payee, it cannot be regarded as a holder in due course. . . .

And in Unico v. Owen, 50 N.J. 101, 232 A.2d 405 (1967), wherein the finance company was formed expressly to handle the financing of sales by the dealer exclusively, the Supreme Court of New Jersey summarized its position on the question before us as follows:

> For purposes of consumer goods transactions, we hold that where the seller's performance is executory in character and when it appears from the totality of the arrangements between dealer and financier that the financier has had a substantial voice in setting standards for the underlying transaction, or has approved the standards established by the dealer, and has agreed to take all or a predetermined or substantial quantity of the negotiable paper which is backed by such standards, the financier should be considered a participant in the original transaction and therefore not entitled to holder in due course status. . . .

The factual situation in the *Unico* case is especially analogous to the instant case.

The divergent line of cases, reflecting an underlying conflict in policy considerations, accords determinative importance to the maintenance of a free flow of credit. These cases protect the finance company from purchaser defenses on the ground that this is an overriding consideration in order to assure easy negotiability of commercial paper and the resultant availability of the rapid financing methods required by our present-day economy. The cases of both lines of authority are collected at Annots., 128 A.L.R. 729 (1940), 44 A.L.R.2d 8, 134-157 (1955), 4 A.L.R.2d Later Case Serv. 929 (1965). See also Swanson v. Commercial Acceptance Corporation (9th Cir.), 381 F.2d 296 (1967); 39 S. Cal. L. Rev. 48, 68-74 (1966); 10 Vill. L. Rev. 309 (1965); 65 Colum. L. Rev. 733 (1965); 53 Harv. L. Rev. 1200 (1940); 1958 Wash. U. L.Q. 177; 35 U. Chi. L. Rev. 739 (1968); 939 Minn. L. Rev. 775 (1954).

Under the totality of facts and circumstances of this case, we hold that the rule of balance should be adopted and applied; that it should operate in favor of the installment buyer for the reason that, in our opinion, Bancredit was so involved in the transaction that it may not be treated as a subsequent purchaser for value. By reason of its sister corporation relationship to Dell and the established course of dealing between them, Bancredit was more nearly an original party to the transaction than a subsequent purchaser of the paper; and, for the reasons of fairness and balance stated in the foregoing authorities, Bancredit should be denied the protected status of holder in due course which would prevent Mrs. Jones from having her day in court on the defenses she would have otherwise had against Dell.

The rule we here adopt must be applied carefully because of the delicate balance of the interests of the installment buying community and the commercial community. But the need for special care in application should not foreclose the adoption of the rule and its application in a proper case. In this day of demonstrated need for emphasis upon consumer protection and truth in lending, special consideration must be given to preventing the misuse of negotiable instruments to deprive installment purchasers of legitimate defenses. In a proper case, such as the one before us, this becomes the controlling consideration.

For the reasons stated, we conclude that the Superior Court erred in holding that Bancredit was a holder in due course. Accordingly, the judgment below is reversed and the cause remanded for further proceedings consistent herewith.

This decision is typical of a large number of cases in which the courts have held that the buyer-transferee of the paper is too "closely connected" with the seller-transferor to be permitted to obtain holder in due course status. The doctrine has been chiefly of benefit to consumers, but it has been applied in purely commercial settings. See, e.g., St. James v. Diversified Commercial Fin. Corp., 102 Nev. 23, 714 P.2d 179 (1986). Following are some of the tests the courts use to assess the connection.

(1) Is the buyer-transferee the alter ego of the seller-transferor? Do they have the same officers, same personnel, same location?
(2) Who drafted the original promissory note?
(3) Is the buyer-transferee mentioned in the note?
(4) Does the seller-transferor sell paper to other buyers, or is the buyer-transferee the only market?
(5) Did the buyer-transferee get involved in the transaction by which the note was created? Did it, for instance, conduct a credit investigation of the maker?
(6) Did the buyer-transferee have some knowledge of the seller-transferor's poor past performance of similar contracts?

If the court concludes that the buyer-transferee is too *closely connected* to the seller-transferor, the court has a variety of ways to deny holder in due course status to the plaintiff. It can say that the plaintiff was not acting in *good faith*, that the plaintiff had notice of underlying defenses, or that the plaintiff is the same entity as the seller-transferor and can stand in no better situation.

In light of this problem, what would you advise Bancredit to do in the future to become a holder in due course of notes that pass through the hands of payees like Dell?

Lest you get the idea that in promissory note lawsuits the finance company always loses (which is not even vaguely true), read the following case. It makes the important point that knowledge of the underlying transaction is not the same thing as notice of a claim or a defense arising out of that transaction.

Sullivan v. United Dealers Corp.

Kentucky Court of Appeals, 1972
486 S.W.2d 699

REED, J.

The sole issue presented is whether appellee, United Dealers Corporation, a finance company, was a holder in due course of a promissory note executed and delivered by appellants, James Earl Sullivan and Norma Jean Sullivan, his wife, in payment for building materials and labor furnished by Memory Swift Homes, Inc., the payee of the note.

Memory Swift Homes, Inc., contracted with the Sullivans to construct a prefabricated dwelling house for them. The contract was dated March 26, 1963, and on April 9, 1963, the Sullivans executed and delivered to Memory Swift, the contractor, their promissory negotiable note in the sum of $18,224.64 secured by a mortgage on the real property and the improvement to be located thereon. On the same day, the contractor negotiated the note and assigned the mortgage to the finance company.

On June 25, 1963, the finance company negotiated the note to a bank which took the instrument with right of recourse. After the negotiation of the note to the finance company but prior to its negotiation by the finance company to the bank, the Sullivans delivered written statements to the finance company that the foundation of the house had been properly installed and also certified that all framing members in the house were properly and sufficiently nailed to make it a sound and sturdy structure and that all work had been performed in a workmanlike manner.

Beginning in August 1963, the Sullivans made several monthly payments according to the terms of the note but then defaulted. The last monthly payment was made in April 1966, but this covered the monthly installment due in August 1965. On April 25, 1966, the bank transferred the note back to the finance company, for value, without recourse. The finance company then instituted action against the Sullivans for collection of the note and foreclosure of the mortgage. The Sullivans pleaded that the finance company was not a holder in due course of the note and that the contractor had constructed the house in an unworkmanlike manner by reason of which they had been damaged; they sought to assert their claim against the contractor as a defense against the finance company. The parties to the action failed to demand a jury trial and, with their consent, the factual issues were tried by the court without a jury.

The trial court found from the evidence that the finance company was a holder in due course of the note; therefore, the defenses arising from the alleged breaches of contract by the contractor and payee of the note were held nonassertable against the finance company. Judgment was entered for the unpaid balance of the note and foreclosure of the mortgage was ordered. The Sullivans appeal and argue the single proposition that the finance company did not become a holder in due course at the time the note was transferred and negotiated to it by the payee. We affirm the judgment of the circuit court.

The entire case for the Sullivans may be summarized by the following quotation from the brief filed on their behalf:

> The testimony shows that the appellee [the finance company] was cognizant and knew about this contract. The appellee [the finance company] had done around $500,000 with Memory Swift Homes, Inc., over a period of a number of years beginning in 1951. The appellee also knew at the time they purchased this note and mortgage that no work had been performed on the construction of the house. The appellee [the finance company] knowing about this contract, they were put on notice that there *might be* a defense on the note because of the faulty construction of the dwelling house and is, therefore, not a holder in due course and did not take the instrument in good faith — that is the note and mortgage. [Parenthetical expressions and emphasis supplied.]

Notice, in order to prevent one from being a bona fide holder under the law merchant, or a holder in due course under the NIL or the Commercial Code, means notice at the time of the taking or at the time the instrument is negotiated, and not notice arising subsequently. The time when value is given for the instrument is decisive. The moment value is given without notice the status as a holder in due course generally is definitely and irrevocably fixed. The Commercial Code, which has been adopted in Kentucky, provides that to be effective notice to a purchaser must be received at such time and in such manner as to give a reasonable opportunity to act on it. K.R.S. §3-304(6) [in the Revision, see §3-302(f) — Eds.]. See 11 Am. Jur. 2d, Bills and Notes, §428, pp. 458, 459.

Where a close business association between the payee and one who purchases an instrument from him implies the knowledge of such facts as to show bad faith or renders himself a participant in the transaction between the payee and the maker, a finding that such purchaser is not a holder in due course has been regarded as supportable. See 44 A.L.R.2d 154. In Massey-Ferguson v. Utley, Ky., 439 S.W.2d 57 (1969), we discussed several aspects of the basic problem. Therein we expressed the thought that the policy of the Commercial Code was to encourage the supplying of credit for the buying of goods by insulating the lender from lawsuits over the quality of the goods. The insulation provided, however, appears intended primarily for finance institutions acting independently to supply credit, rather than to protect a manufacturer who finances his own sales either in his own name or by a dominated and controlled agency.

In the case before us, there is no allegation of fraud involving the payee of the note and the finance company. There is no claim any fact existed that the finance company could have discovered at the time of the transfer of the instrument and that would have indicated any deficiency or defect. The maker of the note represented that the state of facts at that time was one of compliance by the contractor with the duties imposed by the contract. The evidence failed to demonstrate any direct connection between the contractor and the finance company except a frequent course of dealing between them. In short, the evidence failed to demonstrate any bad faith on the part of the finance company at the time of the negotiation and transfer of the note to it. All of the evidence demonstrated a complete lack of notice to the finance company that would justify a finding that it failed to acquire the status of a holder in due course.

The judgment is affirmed.

All concur.

F.   The Shelter Rule

It has always been a basic rule of the common law that the unqualified transfer of a chose in action places the transferee in the transferor's shoes and gives the transferee all the rights of the transferor. This rule is codified in §3-203(b), where it is made clear that even holder in due course rights can pass to a person not otherwise entitled to them. Because the transferee of a holder in due course takes "shelter" in the status of the transferor, §3-203(b) is called the *shelter rule*. Read §3-203(b) and its Official Comments, paying particular attention to Comment 4 and the examples therein. (Similar shelter rules abound throughout the UCC: for sales of goods, see §2-403(1); for documents of title, see §7-504(a); and for investment securities, see §8-302(a).)

PROBLEM 33

Happy Jack, the used car salesman, sold Manny a lemon car for his business, taking in payment a promissory note for $2,000 made payable to the order of Happy Jack. Jack discounted the note with Alfred, a local licensed money broker, who paid him $1,700 and took the note without knowledge of the underlying transaction. Alfred's daughter Jessica had a birthday shortly thereafter, so Alfred indorsed the note in blank and gave it to her as a present. When the note matured, Manny refused to pay it to Jessica — the car had fallen apart, and he felt that he shouldn't have to pay for a pile of junk. Is Jessica a holder in due course?

PROBLEM 34

If in the above Problem Jessica had thereafter made a gift of the note to her husband, Lorenzo, would Lorenzo have holder in due course rights? Does it matter if Lorenzo, prior to the gift, knows of Manny's problems with the car? If Manny won't pay, is Alfred liable to Lorenzo? See §§3-305(a)(2) and 3-303.

PROBLEM 35

After Lorenzo (from the last Problem) acquired the note, he sold it for $1,800 to Portia, a local attorney. She had no notice of problems with the instrument. When she presented it to Manny for payment, he refused to pay and instead filed for bankruptcy. May she recover from Alfred? See §3-305(b). If she does and prevails, Alfred will reacquire the instrument. Does the shelter rule give him Portia's holder in due course rights? Does Alfred reacquire his *original* holder in due course status when he gets the instrument back? Could he sue Jessica or Lorenzo? See the following discussion.

Reacquisition of an Instrument. If Alfred is forced to pay Portia, he will get the instrument back into his possession. In such a case, §121 of the now-repealed NIL provided that on reacquisition a holder "is remitted to his former rights as regards all prior parties." See Chafee, The Reacquisition of a Negotiable Instrument by a Prior Party, 21 Colum. L. Rev. 538 (1921).[21] Thus, if Alfred used to be a holder in due course, on reacquiring the instrument he would get that status back vis-à-vis parties prior to his first holding. Although the UCC never expressly states the same rule, the idea is implicit

---

21. Section 3-207 discusses reacquisition, but the rules therein are not relevant to the issues raised by the preceding Problems.

Read through here! For next week: Start here

throughout the Code, and the NIL rule is therefore still the law. As to the issue of whether Alfred can sue Jessica and Lorenzo, we will explore the liability of an indorser in the next chapter.

Section 3-207 provides that when a previous holder reacquires the instrument, he or she has the power to strike the intervening indorsements. As one court explained:

> Intervening indorsements simply vanish from the chain of title when called by a reacquirer. That concept is the obvious product of the principle that permits the current holder of a negotiable instrument to sue its predecessor in the indorsement chain, in which event that party can in turn look to its own predecessor. If those lawsuits up the chain would ultimately lead back to the current holder, that pointless circular process is best avoided by the cancellation of the intervening indorsements and the discharge of those intermediate parties from liability.

Resolution Trust Corp. v. Juergens, 965 F.2d 149, 154 (7th Cir. 1992).

Triffin v. Somerset Valley Bank

New Jersey Superior Court, Appellate Division, 2001
343 N.J. Super. 73, 777 A.2d 993

CUFF, J.A.D.

This case concerns the enforceability of dishonored checks against the issuer of the checks under Article 3 of the Uniform Commercial Code (UCC), as implemented in New Jersey in N.J.S.A. 12A:3-101 to 3-605. Plaintiff purchased, through assignment agreements with check cashing companies, eighteen dishonored checks, issued by defendant Hauser Contracting Company (Hauser Co.). Plaintiff then filed suit in the Special Civil Part to enforce Hauser Co.'s liability on the checks. The trial court granted plaintiff's motion for summary judgment. Hauser Co. appeals the grant of summary judgment. It also argues, for the first time, that plaintiff lacked standing to file suit against Hauser Co. We affirm.

In October 1998, Alfred M. Hauser, president of Hauser Co., was notified by Edwards Food Store in Raritan and the Somerset Valley Bank (the Bank), that several individuals were cashing what appeared to be Hauser Co. payroll checks. Mr. Hauser reviewed the checks, ascertained that the checks were counterfeits and contacted the Raritan Borough and Hillsborough Police Departments. Mr. Hauser concluded that the checks were counterfeits because none of the payees were employees of Hauser Co., and because he did not write the checks or authorize anyone to sign those checks on his behalf. At that time, Hauser Co. employed Automatic Data Processing, Inc.

(ADP) to provide payroll services and a facsimile signature was utilized on all Hauser Co. payroll checks.

Mr. Hauser executed affidavits of stolen and forged checks at the Bank, stopping payment on the checks at issue. Subsequently, the Bank received more than eighty similar checks valued at $25,000 all drawn on Hauser Co.'s account.

Plaintiff is in the business of purchasing dishonored negotiable instruments. In February and March 1999, plaintiff purchased eighteen dishonored checks from four different check cashing agencies, specifying Hauser Co. as the drawer. The checks totaled $8,826.42. Pursuant to assignment agreements executed by plaintiff, each agency stated that it cashed the checks for value, in good faith, without notice of any claims or defenses to the checks, without knowledge that any of the signatures were unauthorized or forged, and with the expectation that the checks would be paid upon presentment to the bank upon which the checks were drawn. All eighteen checks bore a red and green facsimile drawer's signature stamp in the name of Alfred M. Hauser. All eighteen checks were marked by the Bank as "stolen check" and stamped with the warning, "do not present again." Each of the nine payees on the eighteen checks are named defendants in this case.

Plaintiff then filed this action against the Bank, Hauser Co., and each of the nine individual payees. Plaintiff contended that Hauser Co. was negligent in failing to safeguard both its payroll checks and its authorized drawer's facsimile stamp, and was liable for payment of the checks.

The trial court granted plaintiff's summary judgment motion, concluding that no genuine issue of fact existed as to the authenticity of the eighteen checks at issue. Judge Hoens concluded that because the check cashing companies took the checks in good faith, plaintiff was a holder in due course as assignee. Judge Hoens also found that because the checks appeared to be genuine, Hauser Co. was required, but had failed, to show that plaintiff's assignor had any notice that the checks were not validly drawn. . . .

As to the merits of the appeal, Hauser Co. argues that summary judgment was improperly granted because the court failed to properly address Hauser Co.'s defense that the checks at issue were invalid negotiable instruments and therefore erred in finding plaintiff was a holder in due course. . . .

As a threshold matter, it is evident that the eighteen checks meet the definition of a negotiable instrument. N.J.S.A. 12A:3-104. Each check is payable to a bearer for a fixed amount, on demand, and does not state any other undertaking by the person promising payment, aside from the payment of money. In addition, each check appears to have been signed by Mr. Hauser, through the use of a facsimile stamp, permitted by the UCC to take the place of a manual signature. N.J.S.A. 12A:3-401(b) provides that a "signature may be made manually or by means of a device or machine . . . with present intention to authenticate a writing." It is uncontroverted by Hauser Co. that the facsimile signature stamp on the checks is identical to Hauser Co.'s authorized stamp.

Hauser Co., however, contends that the checks are not negotiable instruments because Mr. Hauser did not sign the checks, did not authorize their signing, and its payroll service, ADP, did not produce the checks. Lack of authorization, however, is a separate issue from whether the checks are negotiable instruments. Consequently, given that the checks are negotiable instruments, the next issue is whether the checks are unenforceable by a holder in due course, because the signature on the checks was forged or unauthorized.

N.J.S.A. 12A:3-203 and N.J.S.A. 12A:3-302 discuss the rights of a holder in due course and the rights of a transferee of a holder in due course. Section 3-302 establishes that a person is a holder in due course if:

> (1) the instrument when issued or negotiated to the holder does not bear such apparent evidence of forgery or alteration or is not otherwise so irregular or incomplete as to call into question its authenticity; and
>
> (2) the holder took the instrument for value, in good faith, without notice that the instrument is overdue or has been dishonored or that there is an uncured default with respect to payment of another instrument issued as part of the same series, without notice that the instrument contains an unauthorized signature or has been altered, without notice of any claim to the instrument described in 12A:3-306, and without notice that any party has a defense or claim in recoupment described in subsection a. of 12A:3-305.

Section 3-203 deals with transfer of instruments and provides:

> a. An instrument is transferred when it is delivered by a person other than its issuer for the purpose of giving to the person receiving delivery the right to enforce the instrument.
>
> b. Transfer of an instrument, whether or not the transfer is a negotiation, vests in the transferee any right of the transferor to enforce the instrument, including any right as a holder in due course, but the transferee cannot acquire rights of a holder in due course by a transfer, directly or indirectly, from a holder in due course if the transferee engaged in fraud or illegality affecting the instrument.

The official comment to N.J.S.A. 12A:3-203 adds that in situations where a transferee does not take the instrument by indorsement (as in this case), the transferee still assumes the rights of the transferor, so long as the transferee can show that the transferor had valid rights to the instrument, and that the transferee acquired the instrument in accordance with section 3-203's requirements. Specifically, Comment 2 reads:

Subsection (b) states that transfer vests in the transferee any right of the transferor to enforce the instrument "including any right as a holder in due course." *If the transferee is not a holder because the transferor did not indorse, the transferee is nevertheless a person entitled to enforce the instrument under Section 3-301 if the transferor was a holder at the time of transfer. Although the transferee is not a holder, under subsection (b) the transferee obtained the rights of the transferor as holder. Because the transferee's rights are derivative of the transferor's rights, those rights must be proved.* Because the transferee is not a holder, there is no presumption under Section 3-308 that the transferee, by producing the instrument, is entitled to payment. The instrument, by its terms, is not payable to the transferee and the transferee must account for possession of the unindorsed instrument by proving the transaction through which the transferee acquired it. Proof of a transfer to the transferee by a holder is proof that the transferee has acquired the rights of a holder. At that point the transferee is entitled to the presumption under Section 3-308.

Under subsection (b) a holder in due course that transfers an instrument transfers those rights as a holder in due course to the purchaser. The policy is to assure the holder in due course a free market for the instrument.

[N.J.S.A. 12A:3-203, Comment 2 (emphasis added).]

The record indicates that plaintiff has complied with the requirements of both sections 3-302 and 3-203. Each of the check cashing companies from whom plaintiff purchased the dishonored checks were holders in due course. In support of his summary judgment motion, plaintiff submitted an affidavit from each company; each company swore that it cashed the checks for value, in good faith, without notice of any claims or defenses by any party, without knowledge that any of the signatures on the checks were unauthorized or fraudulent, and with the expectation that the checks would be paid upon their presentment to the bank upon which the checks were drawn. Hauser Co. does not dispute any of the facts sworn to by the check cashing companies.

The checks were then transferred to plaintiff in accordance with section 3-203, vesting plaintiff with holder in due course status. Each company swore that it assigned the checks to plaintiff in exchange for consideration received from plaintiff. Plaintiff thus acquired the check cashing companies' holder in due course status when the checks were assigned to plaintiff. See N.J.S.A. 12A:3-203, Comment 2. Moreover, pursuant to section 3-203 (a)'s requirement that the transfer must have been made for the purpose of giving the transferee the right to enforce the instrument, the assignment agreements expressly provided plaintiff with that right, stating that "all payments [assignor] may receive from any of the referenced Debtors . . . shall be the exclusive property of [assignee]." Again, Hauser Co. does not dispute any facts relating to the assignment of the checks to plaintiff.

Hauser Co. contends, instead, that the checks are per se invalid because they were fraudulent and unauthorized. Presumably, this argument is predicated on section 3-302. This section states a person is not a holder in due course if the instrument bears "apparent evidence of forgery or alteration" or is otherwise "so irregular or incomplete as to call into question its authenticity." N.J.S.A. 12A:3-302(a)(1).

In order to preclude liability from a holder in due course under section 3-302, it must be apparent on the face of the instrument that it is fraudulent. The trial court specifically found that Hauser Co. had provided no such evidence, stating that Hauser Co. had failed to show that there was anything about the appearance of the checks to place the check cashing company on notice that any check was not valid. Specifically, with respect to Hauser Co.'s facsimile signature on the checks, the court stated that the signature was identical to Hauser Co.'s authorized facsimile signature. Moreover, each of the check cashing companies certified that they had no knowledge that the signatures on the checks were fraudulent or that there were any claims or defenses to enforcement of the checks. Hence, the trial court's conclusion that there was no apparent evidence of invalidity was not an abuse of discretion and was based on a reasonable reading of the record.

To be sure, section 3-308 (a) does shift the burden of establishing the validity of the signature to the plaintiff, but only if the defendant specifically denies the signature's validity in the pleadings. The section states:

> In an action with respect to an instrument, *the authenticity of, and authority to make, each signature on the instrument is admitted unless specifically denied in the pleadings.* If the validity of a signature is denied in the pleadings, the burden of establishing validity is on the person claiming validity, but the signature is presumed to be authentic and authorized unless the action is to enforce the liability of the purported signer and the signer is dead or incompetent at the time of trial of the issue of validity of the signature.

[N.J.S.A. 12A:3-308(a) (emphasis added).]

Comment 1 explains that a specific denial is required

> to give the plaintiff notice of the defendant's claim of forgery or lack of authority as to the particular signature, and to afford the plaintiff an opportunity to investigate and obtain evidence. . . . In the absence of such specific denial the signature stands admitted, and is not in issue. Nothing in this section is intended, however, to prevent amendment of the pleading in a proper case.

[N.J.S.A. 12A:3-308, Comment 1.]

Examination of the pleadings reveals that Hauser Co. did not specifically deny the factual assertions in plaintiff's complaint.

Even if Hauser Co.'s general denial was sufficient, the presumption that the signature is valid still remains, unless Hauser Co. satisfies the evidentiary requirements of N.J.S.A. 12A:3-308. Comment 1 to that section explains that even when the defendant has specifically denied the authenticity of a signature, the signature is still presumed to be authentic, absent evidence of forgery or lack of authorization. Comment 1 states:

> The burden is on the party claiming under the signature, *but the signature is presumed to be authentic and authorized* except as stated in the second sentence of subsection (a). *"Presumed" is defined in Section 1-201 and means that until some evidence is introduced which would support a finding that the signature is forged or unauthorized, the plaintiff is not required to prove that it is valid.* The presumption rests upon the fact that in ordinary experience forged or unauthorized signatures are very uncommon, and normally any evidence is within the control of, or more accessible to, the defendant. *The defendant is therefore required to make some sufficient showing of the grounds for the denial before the plaintiff is required to introduce evidence.* The defendant's evidence need not be sufficient to require a directed verdict, but it must be enough to support the denial by permitting a finding in the defendant's favor. Until introduction of such evidence the presumption requires a finding for the plaintiff.

[N.J.S.A. 12A:3-308, Comment 1 (emphasis added).]

Here, Hauser Co. has not provided any evidence of the invalidity of the signature. Hauser Co.'s reliance on conclusory statements does not constitute such a "sufficient showing." See Coupounas v. Madden, 401 Mass. 125, 514 N.E.2d 1316, 1320 (1987) (defendant disputing validity of notes "had to do more than 'call into question' the 'integrity' of the notes").

In addition, as a matter of summary judgment, Hauser Co.'s reliance on its answer, amended answer and Mr. Hauser's affidavit as material, disputed facts is inadequate. In order to defeat a motion for summary judgment, a party must show that there are genuine issues of material fact. *Brill,* supra, 142 N.J. at 540, 666 A.2d 146. "Bare conclusions in the pleadings, without factual support in tendered affidavits, will not defeat a meritorious application for summary judgment." United States Pipe and Foundry Co. v. American Arbitration Ass'n, 67 N.J. Super. 384, 399-400, 170 A.2d 505 (App. Div. 1961); see also Brae Asset Fund v. Newman, 327 N.J. Super. 129, 134, 742 A.2d 986 (App. Div. 1999). Hauser Co. provided no factual evidence tending to disprove the authenticity of the signature, relying instead on self-interested and conclusory statements. Consequently, the trial court did not err in finding that Hauser Co. had failed to provide any evidence of the invalidity of the checks.

In conclusion, we hold that Judge Hoens properly granted summary judgment. There was no issue of material fact as to: (1) the status of the checks as negotiable instruments; (2) the status of the check cashing companies as holders in due course; (3) the status of plaintiff as a holder in due course; and (4) the lack of apparent evidence on the face of the checks that they were forged, altered or otherwise irregular. Moreover, Hauser Co.'s failure to submit some factual evidence indicating that the facsimile signature was forged or otherwise unauthorized left unchallenged the UCC's rebuttable presumption that a signature on an instrument is valid. Consequently, the trial court properly held, as a matter of law, that plaintiff was a holder in due course and entitled to enforce the checks.

Affirmed.

———————————

It may seem unfair to use the shelter rule to give holder in due course status to non-purchasers and those who take with notice of defenses, but on reflection the unfairness disappears. If the rule were otherwise, the current holder would simply pass the instrument back up the chain until it reached a former holder in due course, who would then reacquire that status, sue the instrument's creator, and prevail. The shelter rule accomplishes the same result without all these maneuvers and has the further benefit of promoting commercial confidence in the soundness of the instrument once it has floated through the hands of multiple purchasers.

II.   REAL AND PERSONAL DEFENSES/CLAIMS

A.   Defenses Against a Holder in Due Course

Holder in due course status has as its primary attribute the ability to enforce the instrument free from the usual legal excuses that could be raised in an ordinary contracts action. The key Uniform Commercial Code section reaching this extraordinary result is §3-305, to which we now turn.

Section 3-305 is difficult to read, primarily because a number of the concepts therein are complicated to sort out. Let's take it a point at a time.

First of all, the *obligor* mentioned throughout §3-305 is the party to the instrument who is being sued by the holder of the instrument. Thus the obligor could be the drawer of a draft, the maker of a note, or someone who indorsed the instrument. In the next chapter, we shall discuss the nature of the obligations these parties incur by virtue of having signed the instrument in one of the above capacities.

A "defense," of course, is the legal excuse the obligor may have to avoid paying the obligation. Subsection (b) tells us that a holder in due course takes subject to the defenses listed in subsection (a)(1), meaning that these defenses, if true, defeat the right of the holder in due course to enforce the instrument. Defenses that are good against a holder in due course are commonly called *real defenses*, a label you might wish to write next to §3-305(a)(1). Subsection (b) tells us that a holder in due course is not subject to the defenses raised in subsection (a)(2), the so-called *personal defenses*.

Subsection (b) also states that a holder in due course holds free of "claims in recoupment" per §3-305(a)(3), but what does that mean? Recoupment is the legal ability to *subtract* from any payment due the amount the person trying to collect the debt (or that person's predecessor) happens to owe the debtor. For example, if I owe you $500 pursuant to our contract, and, as a result of your breach of that same contract, you have caused me $200 worth of damages, my claim in recoupment permits me to subtract those damages and only pay you $300. A claim in recoupment is so similar to a defense that the original version of Article 3 seemed to lump it in with the other personal defenses, but the revised version of Article 3 gives it its own special treatment (leading to awkward references throughout to a "defense or claim in recoupment"). Read Official Comment 3 to §3-305.

PROBLEM 36

Stephen Maturin bought a sailboat from Jack Aubrey, paying $500 down and signing a $1,000 promissory note for the balance due. Maturin loved everything about the boat except its color, and he promptly repainted it his favorite color, black. Prior to the sale Aubrey had told Maturin that the boat was constructed so that it wouldn't sink even in the roughest weather. This proved to be untrue when the sailboat went down in the first storm that came along, and it cost Maturin $300 to have it dredged from the bottom and restored. In the meantime, Aubrey had given the promissory note to his father as a birthday gift, and the father presented it to Maturin for payment at maturity. May Maturin assert his damages against the father's demand for payment? Same result if the boat never sank, but Aubrey's dog bit Maturin on the leg one week after the delivery of the sailboat, and Maturin incurred $100 in medical bills as a consequence? See Zener v. Velde, 135 Idaho 352, 17 P.3d 296 (Idaho App. 2000).

Federal Deposit Insurance Corp. v. Culver

United States District Court, District of Kansas, 1986
640 F. Supp. 725

O'CONNOR, J.

This matter comes before the court on defendant's motion to dismiss for lack of personal jurisdiction, on plaintiff's motion for summary judgment, and on defendant's motion for leave to file a demand for jury trial out of time. After reciting the material facts (construed most favorably to defendant), we will address these pending motions.

In 1984, defendant entered into a business arrangement with a Mr. Nasib Ed Kalliel. Kalliel was to assume control over the financial aspects of defendant's farm, while defendant was to manage the farming operation—receiving both a salary and a share of the profits. In July or August of that year, defendant informed Kalliel that he urgently needed money in order to stave off foreclosure. One week later, $30,000.00 was wire-transferred from the Rexford State Bank in Rexford, Kansas, to defendant's bank in King City, Missouri. Although defendant knew that the money had come from the Rexford State Bank, he thought that Kalliel would be responsible for its repayment.

About one week later, defendant was approached by a Mr. Jerry Gilbert, whom defendant believed was working for Kalliel. Gilbert told defendant that "Rexford State Bank wanted to know where the $30,000.00 went, . . . for their records." Gilbert presented defendant with a document and asked defendant to sign it. Apparently, Gilbert either told defendant, or at least led him to believe, that the document was merely a receipt for the $30,000.00 he had received. In any event, defendant signed the document without thereby intending to commit himself to the repayment of any money.

The document defendant signed was a preprinted promissory note form. As might be expected, the form contained a number of blanks into which the parties were expected to insert terms specific to their own transaction. At the time defendant signed the document, none of those blanks had been completed. Thus, the note contained no execution date, no maturity date, no principal amount, and no interest rate. The name of the payee, "THE REXFORD STATE BANK, Rexford, Kansas," *was* printed on the note at that time. Moreover, the note did provide that the principal and accrued interest were to be paid to the payee "at its offices."

Although defendant assumed that the figure $30,000.00 would eventually be written on the document, some unknown individual completed the note as follows:

(1)   The principal amount was shown as $50,000.00;
(2)   the execution date was shown as August 2, 1984;
(3)   the maturity date was shown as February 2, 1985; and
(4)   the interest rate was shown as 14 percent per annum until maturity, and 18½ percent per annum thereafter.

Although defendant received only $30,000.00, the Rexford State Bank did deposit the full $50,000.00 in an account controlled by Kalliel. The $30,000.00 apparently came from that account.

Eventually, the note was returned to the Rexford State Bank. When that bank became insolvent, the Federal Deposit Insurance Corporation ["FDIC"] was appointed as its receiver. In its *corporate* capacity, the FDIC then purchased a number of the bank's assets from the receiver—including the note at issue here. At that time, the FDIC had no actual knowledge of the events that had transpired prior to its purchase of the note. As of yet, defendant has made no payment of either principal or interest.

Other than receiving the $30,000.00 wire-transfer from the Rexford State Bank, and then signing the note naming the bank as payee, defendant has had no other relevant contact with the state of Kansas. . . .

II. Plaintiff's Motion for Summary Judgment

. . . Recognizing that "[t]here is no doubt that state and federal law provide the Federal Deposit Insurance Corporation with holder in due course status in the instant litigation" (Defendant's Brief of May 2, 1986, at 11), defendant concedes that the "personal" defenses of fraud in the inducement, estoppel, and failure of consideration would be ineffective against plaintiff's claim. See F.D.I.C. v. Vestering, 620 F. Supp. 1271 (D. Kan. 1985). Accordingly, defendant seeks to assert the "real" defense of fraud in the factum. See K.S.A. 84-3-305(2)(c) [in the Revision, see §3-305(a)(1)(iii)—Eds.]. Plaintiff denies that the facts as alleged by defendant constitute fraud in the factum. Alternatively, even assuming that defendant can establish the elements of fraud in the factum, plaintiff contends that such a defense is ineffective against the FDIC because of the doctrine enunciated in D'Oench, Duhme & Co. v. F.D.I.C., 315 U.S. 447 (1942), and codified at 12 U.S.C. §1823(e). Because we conclude that defendant cannot demonstrate fraud in the factum, we do not reach plaintiff's arguments regarding *d'Oench, Duhme* and section 1823(e).

The "fraud in the factum" defense is codified at K.S.A. 84-3-305(2)(c) [in the Revision, see 3-305(a)(1)(iii)—Eds.], which provides as follows:

> Rights of a holder in due course. To the extent that a holder is a holder in due course he takes the instrument free from . . .
>> (2) all defenses of any party to the instrument with whom the holder has not dealt *except* . . .
>>> (c) such misrepresentation as has induced the party to sign the instrument with neither knowledge nor reasonable opportunity to obtain knowledge of its *character* or its *essential terms.*

(Emphasis added.) As suggested by our factual summary, defendant contends that he signed the note under the misapprehension that it was merely a receipt. He thus denies having knowledge of the document's "character" at the time he signed it. Moreover, because the note's execution date, maturity date, principal amount and interest rate were all blank at the time he signed it, defendant contends that he had neither knowledge nor reasonable opportunity to obtain knowledge as to the note's "essential terms."

To determine whether these facts fit the definition of fraud in the factum, we look elsewhere in the Kansas Uniform Commercial Code. For instance, Official UCC Comment 7 to §3-305 provides this advice:

> Paragraph (c) of subsection (2) is new. It follows the great majority of the decisions under the original Act in recognizing the defense of "real" or "essential" fraud, sometimes called fraud in the essence or fraud in the factum, as effective against a holder in due course. The common illustration is that of the maker who is tricked into signing a note in the belief that it is merely a receipt or some other document. The theory of the defense is that his signature on the instrument is ineffective because he did not intend to sign such an instrument at all. Under this provision the defense extends to an instrument signed with knowledge that it is a negotiable instrument, but without knowledge of its essential terms.
>
> *The test of the defense here stated is that of excusable ignorance of the contents of the writing signed.* The party must not only have been in ignorance, but must also have had no reasonable opportunity to obtain knowledge.

(Emphasis added.) A portion of the 1983 Kansas Comment to this same section offers guidance as to the proper construction of the term "excusable ignorance." The Comment provides as follows:

> Kansas decisional law would seem to be in accord on the possibility of fraud in the factum as a real defense, the decision in Ort v. Fowler, 31 Kan. 478, 2 P. 580 (1884), being a good example of facts not satisfying the defense because of the failure of the maker to satisfy a standard of conduct comparable to that required by this subsection.

Given this Kansas Comment's reference to *Ort*, an examination of the facts and the holding in that case should be useful in determining whether defendant showed "excusable ignorance" in mistaking the note at issue here for a receipt.

In *Ort*, a farmer was working alone in his field. A stranger came up to him and represented himself to be the state agent for a manufacturer of iron posts and wire fence. After some conversation, the stranger persuaded the farmer to accept a township-wide agency for the same manufacturer. The stranger then completed two documents which he represented to be identical versions of an agency contract. Because the farmer did not have his glasses with him and, in any event, "could not read without spelling out every word," 31 Kan. at 480, the stranger purported to read the document to the farmer. No mention was made of any note. Both men signed each document, with the farmer not intending to sign anything but a contract of agency. Ultimately, it was established that at least one of those documents was a promissory note. A bona fide purchaser of that note brought suit against the farmer, and the farmer attempted to defend the action on the basis of fraud in the factum. After the trial court rejected that defense, the farmer appealed.

The Kansas Supreme Court, in an opinion by Justice David Brewer (later a United States Supreme Court Associate Justice), phrased the issue on appeal as follows: "A party is betrayed into signing a bill or note by the assurance that it is an instrument of a different kind. Under what circumstances ought he to be liable thereon?" 31 Kan. at 482. Three alternative answers were then suggested:

> One view entertained is, that as he never intended to execute a bill or note, it cannot be considered his act, and he should not be held liable thereon any more than if his name had been forged to such an instrument. A second view is, that it is always a question of fact for the jury whether under the circumstances the party was guilty of negligence. A third is the view adopted by the trial court, that as [a] matter of law, one must be adjudged guilty of such negligence as to render him liable who, possessed of all his faculties and able to read, signs a bill or note, relying upon the assurance or the reading of a stranger that it is a different instrument.

Id. Defendant herein would obviously prefer either the first or second alternative. The court, however, made its preference clear:

> *We approve of the latter doctrine.* It presents a case, of course, of which one of two innocent parties must suffer; but the bona fide holder is not only innocent, but free from all negligence. He has done only that which a prudent, careful man might properly do, while on the other hand the maker of the note has omitted ordinary care and prudence. A party cannot guard against forgery; but if in possession of his faculties and able to read, he can know the character of every instrument to which he puts his signature; and it is a duty which he owes to any party who may be subsequently affected by his act, to know what it is which he signs. By his signature he invites the credence of the world to every statement and promise which is in the instrument he has subscribed; and he is guilty of negligence if he omits to use the ordinary means of ascertaining what those provisions and statements are. If he has eyes and can see, he ought to examine; if he can read, he ought to read; and he has no right to send his signature out into the world affixed to an instrument of whose contents he is ignorant. If he relies upon the word of a stranger, he makes that stranger his agent. He adopts his reading as his own knowledge. What his agent knows, he knows; and he cannot disaffirm the acts of that agent done within the scope of the authority he has intrusted to him.

Id., 31 Kan. at 482-483 (emphasis added). Although *Ort is* of rather ancient vintage, this aspect of the decision has been cited with approval as recently as 1966. See Mid Kansas Federal Savings & Loan Assn. v. Binter, 197 Kan. 106, 110, 415 P.2d 278, 282 (1966).

It is obvious from reading defendant's deposition that he is able to read and understand the English language. Thus, under the rule announced in *Ort*, defendant was negligent in relying on Gilbert's assurance that the note was only a receipt. Given the 1983 Kansas Comment referring to the *Ort* absence-of-negligence standard as "comparable to that required by [K.S.A. 84-3-305(2)(c)]," we must also conclude that defendant has failed to show the "excusable ignorance" necessary to establish fraud in the factum. In the words of the statute, we conclude as a matter of law that defendant had a "reasonable opportunity to obtain knowledge of [the document's] character" before he signed it.

Defendant's second argument, assuming that we reject his contention that he neither knew nor had reasonable opportunity to know the "character" of the document he signed, is that he had no such opportunity to learn of the note's "essential terms." Because the note's execution date, maturity date, principal amount and interest rate were all blank when defendant signed the note, he asserts that he had no (let alone a reasonable) opportunity to learn of those terms. On its face, this argument has great appeal; but defendant's reliance thereon is foreclosed by other Code provisions.

Questions arising from incomplete instruments and material alterations are governed by K.S.A. 84-3-115 and -407, respectively. The former provides as follows:

> (1) When a paper whose contents at the time of signing show that it is intended to become an instrument is signed while still incomplete in any necessary respect it cannot be enforced until completed, but when it is completed in accordance with authority given it is effective as completed.
>
> (2) *If the completion is unauthorized the rules as to material alteration apply (section 84-3-407).*

K.S.A. 84-3-115 (emphasis added). Because defendant claims not to have authorized anyone to complete the note as it now reads, we are referred by part (2) of this section to K.S.A. 84-3-407. The latter statute provides, in part, as follows:

> (3) A subsequent holder in due course may in all cases enforce the instrument according to its original tenor, *and when an incomplete instrument has been completed, he may enforce it as completed.*

K.S.A. 84-3-407(3) (emphasis added). As a holder in due course, plaintiff is thus entitled to enforce this note as it was eventually completed—and not merely as defendant would have authorized it to be completed.

The fraud allegedly committed by Gilbert does not affect this conclusion. We learn from Official UCC Comment 4 to K.S.A. 84-3-407 that "this result is intended even though the instrument was stolen from the maker or drawer and completed after the theft." In other words, one who signs an instrument before all essential terms have been completed creates a "blank Check" that may be enforced by a subsequent holder in due course according to any terms that are completed by an intervening holder. See K.S.A. 84-3-305, Kansas Comment 1983. That was precisely what happened here. Defendant executed the note in blank; an intervening holder completed the note as it reads today; and plaintiff, as a holder in due course, is entitled to enforce the note according to its present terms. Defendant's only legal recourse is against the intervening holder who actually completed the note without defendant's authorization. As between the parties now before the court, we must grant plaintiff's motion for summary judgment. . . .

PROBLEM 37

When Ronald Rube, newly rich, moved to New York City, he was impressed by the Brooklyn Bridge when first he saw it. Simon Mustache, a con man, told Rube that he was the owner of the bridge (a lie, of course), and offered to sell it to Rube for $2,000,000 (described as "a bargain"). Rube paid $20,000 cash as a down-payment and signed a promissory note, payable to the order of Mustache, for the rest. Mustache negotiated the note to a finance company, which claimed to be a holder in due course. When Rube discovered that Mustache lacked title to the bridge, he refused to pay the note. Does he have a real defense of fraud here? See Brown v. Carlson, 26 Mass. L. Rptr. 61, 2009 WL 2914191 (Mass. Super. 2009).

PROBLEM 38

A child prodigy, Thomas Minor, had been playing the piano since he was three and making professional tours of the world since he was 12. He looked much older than his 17 years. He signed a promissory note for $800 payable to the order of Merry Music Company as payment for a piano, planning to tour with it. The company was unaware of Minor's age. The payee indorsed the note over to the Big National Bank for $725. When the first payment came due, Minor refused to pay. He told the bank to come pick up the piano—he was disaffirming the sale. Who wins?

PROBLEM 39

Childe Harold, also age 17, received a check for $1,000 from his employer and decided to use it to buy a car from Byron Auto Sales, a used car dealership. He picked out the car he wanted, indorsed the check in blank, and handed it over to the salesman. Byron Auto Sales indorsed the check on the back and cashed it at its own bank, the Crusaders National Bank. Before this bank could present the check to the drawee bank, Childe Harold decided to buy a horse instead of an automobile, so he returned the car to the dealer and asked for the check back. Informed that the bank had it, Childe Harold called up the bank and informed it of his rescission of the contract. When the bank refused to return the check to Childe Harold, he filed suit, asking the court to restrain the bank from presenting the check to the drawee and to order replevin of the check. How should the court rule? It is clear that a holder in due course takes subject to the defense of infancy, but does he take subject to a claim to the instrument based on infancy? See §§3-202, 3-305(a) and (b), and 3-306.

Mental Incapacity. Notes signed by those who are mentally incompetent are *void* or *voidable* depending on the equities of the situation (i.e., the knowledge of the person dealing with the incompetent, the benefit received by the incompetent, the degree of incompetency, etc.). If someone has been judicially declared incompetent, his or her instruments are more likely to be declared void (hence a nullity) than if no adjudication has taken place. See Annot., Insanity as Defense Against Holder in Due Course, 24 A.L.R.2d 1380.

Sea Air Support, Inc. v. Herrmann   SKIP

Nevada Supreme Court, 1980
613 P.2d 413

PER CURIAM.

Ralph Herrmann wrote a check for $10,000 payable to the Ormsby House, a hotel-casino located in Carson City, Nevada, and exchanged it for three counter checks he had written earlier that evening to acquire gaming chips. The Ormsby House was unable to collect the proceeds from the check because Herrmann had insufficient funds in his account. The debt evidenced by the check was assigned to Sea Air Support, Inc., dba Automated Accounts Associates, for collection. Sea Air also was unsuccessful in its attempts to collect and, therefore, filed this action against Herrmann to recover $10,567.

The district judge dismissed the action on the ground that Sea Air's claim is barred by the Statute of Anne. Sea Air appeals the dismissal. We are asked to reconsider the long line of Nevada cases refusing to enforce gambling debts. We refuse to do so, and affirm the dismissal.

Nevada law incorporates the common law of gambling as altered by the Statute of 9 Anne, c.14, 1, absent conflicting statutory or constitutional provisions. N.R.S. 1.030; West Indies v. First National Bank, 67 Nev. 13, 214 P.2d 144 (1950); Burke v. Buck, 31 Nev. 74, 99 P. 1078 (1909). The Statute provides that all notes drawn for the purpose of reimbursing or repaying any money knowingly lent or advanced for gaming are "utterly void, frustrate, and of none effect." Despite the fact that gambling, where licensed, is legal in Nevada, this court has long held that debts incurred, and checks drawn, for gambling purposes are void and unenforceable. Corbin v. O'Keefe, 87 Nev. 189, 484 P.2d 565 (1971); Wolpert v. Knight, 74 Nev. 322, 330 P.2d 1023 (1958); Weisbrod v. Fremont Hotel, 74 Nev. 227, 326 P.2d 1104 (1958); *West Indies*, 67 Nev. at 31; *Burke*, 31 Nev. at 80; Evans v. Cooke, 11 Nev. 69 (1876); Scott v. Courtney, 7 Nev. 419 (1872).

In this case, Herrmann's $10,000 check clearly was drawn for the purpose of repaying money knowingly advanced for gaming. See Craig v. Harrah, 66 Nev. 1, 201 P.2d 1081 (1949). The check is void and unenforceable in this state. If the law is to change, it must be done by legislative action.

Sea Air seeks to avoid the defense that the check is void and unenforceable because of gaming purpose by claiming to be a holder in due course, immune to most defenses. N.R.S. 3-305. "A holder in due course is a holder who takes the [negotiable] instrument (a) For value; and (b) In good faith; and (c) Without notice that it is overdue or has been dishonored or of any defense against or claim to it on the part of any person." N.R.S. 3-302(1). Sea Air promised to take "such legal action as may be necessary to enforce collection" of the $10,000. The promise to perform services in the future does not constitute taking for value under N.R.S. 3-303. Anderson, 2 Uniform Commercial Code (2d ed.) §3303:3. In addition, Sea Air had at least constructive notice of a defense against collection because the check was payable to a casino, and Sea Air knew the check had been dishonored. Consequently, Sea Air is not a holder in due course. The action was properly dismissed.

Affirmed.

QUESTION

If Sea Air had been a holder in due course, would it have been able to enforce the check? See §3-305(a); Casanova Club v. Bisharat, 189 Conn. 591, 458 A.2d 1 (1983). It should be noted that following the decision in *Sea Air Support*, the Nevada legislature amended its gaming laws to permit casinos to sue on credit instruments received in payment of gambling debts. Nev. Rev. Stat. 463.368.

Kedzie & 103rd Currency Exchange, Inc. v. Hodge

Illinois Supreme Court, 1993
156 Ill. 2d 112, 619 N.E.2d 732

FREEMAN, J.

We consider here whether a holder in due course of a check is precluded from payment as against the drawer where the check was given in exchange for contract services for which the provider was required to be, but was not, a licensed plumber. We conclude such a claim is not precluded.

BACKGROUND

Pursuant to a written "work order," Fred Fentress agreed to install a "flood control system" at the home of Eric and Beulah Hodge of Chicago for $900. In partial payment for the work, Beulah Hodge drafted a personal check payable to "Fred Fentress—A-OK Plumbing" for $500 from the Hodges' joint account at Citicorp Savings.

The system's components were not delivered to the Hodges' home as scheduled. And, when Fentress failed to appear on the date set for installation, Eric Hodge telephoned him to announce the contract "cancelled." Hodge also told Fentress that he would order Citicorp Savings not to pay the check Fentress had been given.

Records of Citicorp Savings confirm acknowledgment of a stop-payment order entered the same day.

Nevertheless, Fentress presented the check at the Kedzie & 103rd Street Currency Exchange (Currency Exchange), endorsing it as "sole owner" of A-OK Plumbing, and obtained payment. However, when the Currency Exchange later presented the check for payment at Citicorp Savings, payment was refused in accordance with the stop-payment order.

The Currency Exchange, alleging it was a holder in due course (see Ill. Rev. Stat. 1989, ch. 26, par. 3-302), then sued Beulah Hodge, as drawer of the check, and Fentress for the amount stated. Hodge, in turn, filed a counterclaim against Fentress. Hodge also moved to dismiss the Currency Exchange's action against her (see Ill. Rev. Stat. 1989, ch. 110, par. 2-619). The disposition of Hodge's motion gives rise to this appeal.

Hodge asserted a defense provided by 3-305 of the Uniform Commercial Code (UCC) (Ill. Rev. Stat. 1989, ch. 26, par. 3-305). Under that section, the claim of a holder in due course of a negotiable instrument may be barred based on "illegality of the transaction." (Ill. Rev. Stat. 1989, ch. 26, par. 3-305(2)(b).)[22] Hodge contended Fentress was not a licensed plumber as was required under the Illinois Plumbing License Law (see Ill. Rev. Stat.

22. [Now §3-305(a)(1)(ii)—EDS.]

1989, ch. 111, pars. 1101 through 1140). The director of licensing and registration of the Chicago department of buildings and the keeper of plumbing licensing records of the Illinois Department of Public Health provided affidavits supporting that contention. Hodge asserted that, because Fentress was in violation of the Illinois Plumbing License Law, his promised performance under the contract gave rise to the requisite "illegality" to bar the Currency Exchange's claim for payment.

The circuit court granted the motion and dismissed the Currency Exchange's action against Hodge. The appellate court, with one justice dissenting, affirmed. (234 Ill. App. 3d 1017.) Pursuant to Supreme Court Rule 315(a) (134 Ill. 2d R. 315(a)), we allowed the Currency Exchange's petition for leave to appeal.

DISCUSSION

. . . The Illinois Plumbing License Law requires that all plumbing, including "installation . . . or extension" of "drains," be performed by plumbers licensed under the Act. (Ill. Rev. Stat. 1989, ch. 111, pars. 1102(5), (8), 1103.) The affidavits establish that Fentress was not licensed either by the City of Chicago or the State of Illinois. That failure is a violation of the Illinois Plumbing License Law and is punishable as a misdemeanor. Ill. Rev. Stat. 1989, ch. 111, pars. 1103, 1128. . . .

. . . The concern is whether noncompliance by Fentress with the Illinois Plumbing License Law gives rise to "illegality of the transaction" with respect to the contract for plumbing services so as to bar the claim of the Currency Exchange, a holder in due course of the check initially given Fentress.

The issue of "illegality" arises "under a variety of statutes." (Ill. Ann. Stat., ch. 26, par. 3-305, Uniform Commercial Code Comment, at 66 (Smith-Hurd Supp. 1992).) In view of the diverse constructions to which statutory enactments are given, "illegality" is, accordingly, a matter "left to the local law." (Ill. Ann. Stat., ch. 26, par. 3-305, Uniform Commercial Code Comment, at 66 (Smith-Hurd Supp. 1992).) Even so, it is only when an obligation is made "entirely null and void" under "local law" that "illegality" exists as one of the "real defenses" under 3-305 to defeat a claim of a holder in due course. (Ill. Ann. Stat., ch. 26, par. 3-305, Uniform Commercial Code Comment, at 66 (Smith-Hurd Supp. 1992).) In effect, the obligation must be no obligation at all. If it is "merely voidable" at the election of the obligor, the defense is unavailable. Ill. Ann. Stat., ch. 26, par. 3-305, Uniform Commercial Code Comment, at 66 (Smith-Hurd Supp. 1992).

Historically, this court has recognized "illegality" to arise only in view of legislative declaration affecting both the underlying contract or transaction and the instrument exchanged upon it. (Pope v. Hanke (1894), 155 Ill. 617, 628-30; Town of Eagle v. Kohn (1876), 84 Ill. 292, 295-96.) A contract or transaction which is void must certainly negate the obligation to pay arising from it as between the contracting parties. (*Pope*, 155 Ill. at 626; *Kohn*, 84 Ill. at 296.) But, unless an instrument memorializing the obligation is also made void, an innocent third party who has no knowledge of the circumstances of the initial contract or transaction may yet claim payment of it against the drawer or maker. *Pope*, 155 Ill. at 626; *Kohn*, 84 Ill. at 296.

Thus, "illegality" has been held to defeat the claims of holders in due course in cases involving contracts of a gaming nature or for retirement of gambling debts. [Citations omitted.] Owing to a deep-seated hostility toward nongovernmental-sanctioned gambling, our legislature has declared that any instrument associated with such activity is void, independent of the status of who may possess it. [Citations omitted.] The absence of similar legislative declaration as for an instrument given upon a usurious contract must account, in part, for the conclusion that usury has not been held to give rise to "illegality" as a defense against a holder in due course. [Citations omitted.]

That the existence or absence of legislative declaration controls the issue was recognized by our appellate court in McGregor v. Lamont (1922), 225 Ill. App. 451, a case involving circumstances similar to those here. John T. Lamont was the maker of a note used to pay for shares of stock issued by the Corn Belt Farmers' Cooperative Association (Association). Lamont's note subsequently came into the possession of Robert Roy McGregor, a holder in due course. When Lamont failed to pay on the note, McGregor filed suit and obtained a judgment against him.

Lamont moved to vacate the judgment. Lamont asserted that the purchase of the shares of stock was void under the Illinois Securities Law because the Association had not complied with its requirements. Because the transaction was void, Lamont concluded, the note given in payment must also be void despite McGregor's status as a holder in due course.

The appellate court noted that the Illinois Securities Law did, indeed, make transactions for the sale of shares of stock void based on noncompliance with the Law's requirements. (*McGregor*, 225 Ill. App. at 453-454, 455.) But the court noted that only the "sale and contract of sale" of shares of stock were expressly made void, not instruments exchanged upon such contracts. (*McGregor*, 225 Ill. App. at 455.) Absent legislative declaration making such instruments void, the court declined to recognize a defense to McGregor's action for payment on the note. *McGregor*, 225 Ill. App. at 455.

The same rule obtains in New Jersey. In New Jersey Mortgage & Investment Corp. v. Berenyi (App. Div. 1976), 140 N.J. Super. 406, 356 A.2d 421, a holder in due course of a note was permitted to maintain a claim for its payment even though the note had been initially obtained by a corporation in a transaction which violated an injunctive order. No statute rendered the note void, and the holder in due course had no knowledge or notice of the injunction. (*Berenyi*, 140 N.J. Super. at 408, 356 A.2d at 423.) But in Westervelt v. Gateway Financial Service (Ch. Div. 1983), 190 N.J. Super. 615, 464 A.2d 1203, the "illegality" defense was held to bar the claim of a holder in due course of a secondary mortgage and note because New Jersey's Secondary Mortgage and Loan Act specifically made void "[a]ny obligation on the part of the borrower arising out of a secondary mortgage loan." (*Westervelt*, 190 N.J. Super. at 620, 464 A.2d at 1205.) *Westervelt* involved what *Berenyi* did not: applicability of a direct statutory expression that an instrument, itself, arising from a particular contract or transaction was void. *Westervelt*, 190 N.J. Super. at 623, 464 A.2d at 1207.

Several other jurisdictions also find reason to draw a distinction between the voidness of a negotiable instrument and the underlying contract or transaction upon which it is exchanged. (See Annot., 80 A.L.R.2d 465, 472-476 (1961) (summarizing several state decisions in which holders in due course were permitted to claim payment of instruments executed in favor of foreign corporations doing business in states without complying with local licensing requirements).) Although recognition of that distinction is not universal (see Columbus Checkcashiers v. Stiles (1990), 56 Ohio App. 3d 159, 565 N.E.2d 883; Wilson v. Steele (1989), 211 Cal. App. 3d 1053, 259 Cal. Rptr. 851 (holding that "illegality" need only be present in the underlying contract between an unlicensed contractor and the drafter of a negotiable instrument to bar the claim of a holder in due course)), we are convinced it remains the better rule.

A plaintiff is precluded from recovering on a suit involving an illegal contract because the plaintiff is a wrongdoer. (See Bankers Trust Co. v. Litton Systems, Inc. (2d Cir. 1979), 599 F.2d 488, 492 (citing the Restatement of Contracts and Restatement (Second) of Contracts).) Enforcement of the illegal contract makes the court an indirect participant in the wrongful conduct. See *Litton*, 599 F.2d at 493.

But a holder in due course is an innocent third party. (*Litton*, 599 F.2d at 492-493.) Such a holder is without knowledge of the circumstances of the contract upon which the instrument was initially exchanged. (Ill. Rev. Stat. 1989, ch. 26, par. 3-302(1)(c) (defining a holder in due course, in part, as a holder who is "without notice . . . of any defense against or claim to [the instrument] on the part of any person").) The same rationale that precludes recovery by a wrongdoing plaintiff is inapplicable in determining such a holder's right to claim payment. (*Litton*, 599 F.2d at 492-493.) Enforcement of that claim does not sully the court. *Litton*, 599 F.2d at 492-493.

The holder in due course concept is intended to facilitate commercial transactions by eliminating the need for "elaborate investigation" of the nature of the circumstances for which an instrument is initially exchanged or of its drafting. (*Litton*, 599 F.2d at 494.) If "illegality" means simply negation of the initial obligation to pay, a holder in due course enjoys no more protection than a party to the original contract or transaction. The "real" defense of "illegality" is reduced to a "personal" one. See Vedder v. Spellman (1971), 78 Wash. 2d 834, 839-840, 480 P.2d 207, 210 (Neill, J., concurring).

It is, therefore, not enough simply to conclude that the initial obligation to pay arising from a void contract or transaction is void. Negation of that obligation as between the contracting parties has little bearing on whether a holder in due course of an instrument arising from the contract or transaction should nevertheless be permitted to make a claim for payment.

The "local law" (Ill. Ann. Stat., ch. 26, par. 3-305, Uniform Commercial Code Comment, at 66 (Smith-Hurd Supp. 1992)) of this state has been formulated upon this court's recognition, in cases predating the UCC, of legislative prerogative regarding negotiable instruments. In adopting the UCC and, in particular, 3-305, our legislature chose to confer upon a holder in due course of a negotiable instrument considerable protection against claims by persons to it. Our legislature also continues to declare certain obligations void because of the circumstances of the agreements from which they arise and without regard to the status of who may claim ownership. (Ill. Rev. Stat. 1989, ch. 38, par. 28-7(b) (subjecting "[a]ny obligation" made void by reason of gambling to be "set aside and vacated" by any court).) The selective negation of obligations reflects a legislative aim to declare what will and will not give rise to "illegality" in cases now governed by the UCC. As legislative direction indicates which obligations are always void, legislative silence indicates when the protection afforded a holder in due course must be honored.

We therefore reaffirm, today, the view this court has consistently recognized in cases predating the UCC. Unless the instrument arising from a contract or transaction is, itself, made void by statute, the "illegality" defense under §3-305 is not available to bar the claim of a holder in due course.

CONCLUSION

To determine whether Hodge is entitled to a judgment of dismissal, we need not engage in an analysis aimed at characterizing the contract between Fentress and the Hodges. Whether the underlying contract should be considered void because Fentress was not licensed as required by the Illinois Plumbing License Law is not dispositive of the Currency Exchange's right, as a holder in due course, to claim payment of the check. It is relevant only to determine whether the Illinois Plumbing License Law provides that any obligation arising from a contract for plumbing services made in violation of its requirements is void. It does not.

For the reasons stated, the judgments of the appellate and circuit courts are reversed, and the cause is remanded to the circuit court for further proceeding. Judgments reversed; cause remanded.

BILANDIC, J., dissenting. . . .

The plain language of §3-305 and the comments to §3-305 make it clear that where the illegality of a transaction renders the obligation of the maker of an instrument a nullity, the illegality of the transaction can be raised as a defense by the maker of the instrument, even against a holder in due course. Section 3-305 does not state that illegality is a defense only where the instrument arising from a contract or transaction has been expressly declared void by the legislature due to the illegality of the transaction. Had the legislature intended for illegality to be a defense only where it had expressly declared an instrument void due to the illegality of the underlying transaction, it could easily have said so in §3-305. It did not say so, however.

The only inquiry necessary to resolve the issue presented in this case, then, is whether the contract between Hodge and Fentress is void on the grounds of illegality. The comments to the UCC instruct that one must look to Illinois statutory and case law to determine whether the underlying contract was illegal and, as a result of that illegality, void. (Ill. Ann. Stat., ch. 26, par. 3-305. Uniform Commercial Code Comment, at 66 (Smith-Hurd Supp. 1992).) An examination of the statute providing for the licensing of plumbers, the public policy behind that statute, and Illinois case law concerning the illegality of contracts made in contravention of professional licensing laws establishes that the contract between Hodge and Fentress is illegal and void.

The Illinois Plumbing License Law (Ill. Rev. Stat. 1989, ch. 111, par. 1101 et seq.) specifically prohibits the performance of plumbing work by nonlicensed plumbers. Pursuant to the Act, "all plumbing shall be performed only by plumbers licensed under the provisions of this Act." (Ill. Rev. Stat. 1989, ch. 111, par. 1103(1).) The Act imposes criminal penalties on anyone performing plumbing services without a license. (Ill. Rev. Stat. 1989, ch. 111, par. 1128.) The rationale behind the prohibition of plumbing work by nonlicensed plumbers is set forth in the Plumbing License Law. The portion of the Law setting forth its purpose and underlying policy states:

> It has been established by scientific evidence that improper plumbing can adversely affect the health of the public. . . . Faulty plumbing is potentially lethal and can cause widespread disease and an epidemic of disastrous consequences.
>
> To protect the health of the public it is essential that plumbing be installed by persons who have proven their knowledge of the sciences of pneumatics and hydraulics and their skill in installing plumbing.
>
> Consistent with its duty to safeguard the health of the people of this State, the General Assembly therefore declares that individuals who plan, inspect, install, alter, extend, repair and maintain plumbing systems shall be individuals of proven skill. . . . [T]his Act is therefore declared to be essential to the public interest. (Ill. Rev. Stat. 1989, ch. 111, par. 1101.)

end here for next week— March 5 & 7

Here, the contract between Hodge and Fentress presents the kinds of dangers the Illinois Plumbing License Law was intended to guard against. Affidavits attached to Hodge's 2-619 motion to dismiss, which were not contradicted by the plaintiff, establish that Fentress was not a licensed plumber. The affidavits also establish that Hodge and her husband, Eric, believed that Fentress was a licensed plumber at the time they contracted with him for plumbing services. Had Fentress performed the work required of him pursuant to the contract with Hodge, it is likely that his work would not have conformed to acceptable plumbing standards and would have posed the kinds of dangers which the Plumbing License Law was intended to prevent. . . .

The majority asserts that to bar recovery by the Currency Exchange in this case would be unfair because the Currency Exchange is an innocent third party which had no knowledge of the circumstances of the contract between Hodge and Fentress. However, section 3-305 clearly provides that the general policy favoring free negotiability is not absolute. There is a competing policy disfavoring certain transactions, such as those involving infancy, duress, illegality or misrepresentation as to the true nature of an instrument (i.e., fraud in the factum). (Ill. Rev. Stat. 1989, ch. 26, par. 3-305.) Pursuant to §3-305, the Currency Exchange takes a check subject to these and certain other real defenses. The Illinois legislature has provided that, by definition, a holder in due course is one who does not have notice of any of the real defenses listed in §3-305. (See Ill. Rev. Stat. 1989, ch. 26, par. 3-302(1)(c).) By statute, the innocence of the holder in due course cannot defeat *any* of the real defenses listed in §3-305, including illegality. Accordingly, the argument that the Currency Exchange could not have known that the underlying transaction was illegal is simply misplaced. Such reasoning would lead to the conclusion that all of the defenses listed in §3-305 should be unavailable to defeat the claim of a holder in due course, a conclusion obviously contrary to the provisions of §3-305.

For the above reasons, I dissent. I would affirm the judgment of the appellate court which affirmed the circuit court's dismissal of the Currency Exchange's action against Hodge.

PROBLEM 40

When she heard her creditors fighting over priorities on her doorstep, Elsie Maynard knew that she had no choice but bankruptcy. Among the debts that she reported to the bankruptcy court was the loan she had taken from Point National Bank, which was evidenced by a promissory note she had signed. In due course the bankruptcy proceeding culminated in the judge's ordering that Elsie be discharged from all her scheduled debts. Two years later, the promissory note surfaced in the possession of Shadbolt State Bank, which claimed quite convincingly to be a holder in due course. Must Elsie pay? See §3-305(a)(1) and (b).

A Little Lecture on Discharge as a Real Defense

Subsection (b) to §3-302 tells us that:

> Notice of discharge of a party, other than discharge in an insolvency proceeding, is not notice of a defense under subsection (a), but discharge is effective against a person who becomes a holder in due course with notice of the discharge. . . .

What does this mean? Well, first of all, as the above Problem illustrates, discharge in bankruptcy *is always a real defense*, regardless of what the subsequent holder knows or doesn't know at the time of acquisition of the instrument. Any other discharge that the Code or common law creates is not effective against a holder in due course *unless* that holder, at the time of acquisition, knew of the discharge, in which case the discharge is, in effect, a real defense and assertable against the holder in due course. For example, suppose that there are four sureties who have signed their names as indorsers on a promissory note. The current holder of the note decides to excuse one of them from future liability, and so draws a line through that surety's name, thus discharging that person from all liability (see §3-601 and its Official Comment). Even a later holder in due course of the note, seeing the line drawn through the former surety's name, would know that that surety is no longer liable on the note, and therefore could only enforce it against the other obligors.

PROBLEM 41

Malvolio, a traveling salesman, bought a new car from Valentine Auto Sales, signing a note for $18,000. The payee discounted the note for $16,800 to the Orsino Finance Company, which notified Malvolio that he should make all future payments to them. Malvolio immediately sent them a check for the outstanding balance (he had come into some money when his aunt died). He asked for the note back, but Orsino was evasive. A week later Malvolio received a note from the Olivia Finance Company saying that his note had been assigned to them and that he should direct his payments to their office. When Malvolio protested, they made holder in due course noises and became quite nasty. Malvolio, worried, comes to you for advice. What should he do? See §3-501(b)(2); read §§3-601 and 3-602. For the result in the 2002 version of Article 3, see §3-602(b). Does Malvolio have remedies outside the Code? Think back to your course in Contracts.

B.   A Special Note on Forgery

Forgery creates very complicated problems under the Code, and these will be dealt with later. The important issue for now is whether forgery is a real defense under the Code, so that it can be raised against a holder in due course, or a personal defense, so that it cannot. The answer to this question lies in §3-401(a): "A person is not liable on an instrument unless (i) the person signed the instrument . . ." and in §3-403(a):

> Unless otherwise provided in this Article or Article 4, an unauthorized signature is ineffective except as the signature of the unauthorized signer in favor of a person who in good faith pays the instrument or takes it for value. . . .

Consider the following Problem.

PROBLEM 42

Jimmy Slick, an expert con man, went into John's Jewelers and told John, the owner, that he was Milton Money, the richest man in town. John was too awed to ask for identification. Slick then picked out several very expensive pieces of jewelry and signed Money's name to a promissory note to pay for them. Slick skipped town with the jewelry. When the note matured, the Tenth National Bank (a holder in due course to whom John has negotiated the paper) presented it to Milton Money for payment. May Money refuse to pay a holder in due course?

The answer to this Problem is obviously that Money is not liable, but as an attorney how do you get away from the all-encompassing language of §3-305(a) and (b)? Read §3-305(a) and (b) again and see if you can determine how Money's forgery defense fits into the statute; see State Bank v. Smith, 2014 WL 6088513 (Mich. Ct. App. 2014).

Additionally, if the forgery is of a name necessary to a valid negotiation, there can be no holder in due course following the forgery because no later transferee will qualify as a *holder*. See the discussion supra at pages 55-57. *— does not apply here — if you look @ those pages. it discusses forgery of the Payee's name — not the makers name*

PROBLEM 43

When Barbara Shipek was off to Las Vegas for a fun weekend, she bought a traveler's check for $3,000 from Octopus National Bank (ONB). The payee line on the traveler's check was blank, but the bank had her sign a line on the check indicating the name of the remitter (see §3-103(a)(11)). The check contained another blank for a countersignature, under which was printed a statement that the bank would pay the traveler's check only if the remitter re-signed the check on this blank at the time of negotiation to the payee. On Ms. Shipek's first night in Las Vegas a thief stole her purse, getting the traveler's check as part of the booty. The thief apparently forged Ms. Shipek's name on the countersignature line and negotiated the check to Vegas Check-Cashing City, an entity listed as payee when the check was presented by Vegas Check-Cashing City to ONB for payment, by which time Ms. Shipek had phoned the bank and told them what had happened. You are the attorney for the bank. Should it pay the traveler's check to Vegas Check-Cashing City? See §§3-104(i) and 3-106(c) with its Official Comment 2.

C. Procedural Issues

One does not have to be a holder in due course in order to sue on the instrument; a "person entitled to enforce the instrument," a phrase defined in §3-301, may do so. Generally a "person entitled to enforce the instrument" means the *holder* of the instrument (someone in possession pursuant to a valid negotiation), though the phrase does include some non-holders—namely, someone who gets holder rights under the shelter rule (or a depositary bank per §4-205), the rightful owner of a lost instrument (§3-309), or the defendant in a successful restitution action (§3-418(d), yet to be discussed). Only if a defense or claim to the instrument arises will the holder's due course status become relevant, at which time the holder has the burden of establishing the position as a holder in due course. Read §3-308(b).

As mentioned above, and elaborated on later in the forgery discussion, a holder must take through a chain of indorsements that is free of forgeries affecting the title. When the genuineness of signatures becomes an issue, §3-308(a) allocates the procedural burdens. Read it.

Virginia National Bank v. Holt

Virginia Supreme Court, 1975
216 Va. 500, 219 S.E.2d 881

COMPTON, J.

. . . In May 1974, the plaintiff, Virginia National Bank, filed a motion for judgment against the defendants, Edgar M. Holt and Gustava H. Holt, his wife, jointly and severally, seeking recovery of the face amount of a "Homestead Waiving Promissory Note," plus interest and attorney's fees. The instrument, payable to the order of the Bank and allegedly made by the

Holts to evidence an indebtedness, was dated December 12, 1973, was due 90 days after date, and was in the amount of $6,000.

Edgar M. Holt was duly served with process, but failed to appear on file pleadings in response. A default judgment in the amount sued for was entered against him in August 1974.

In her pleadings, Gustava H. Holt generally denied liability and specifically denied that the instrument was signed by her. On November 20, 1974, judgment was entered on a jury verdict in her favor and we granted the Bank a writ of error.

The dispositive issue is whether the evidence relating to the genuineness of Mrs. Holt's signature on the instrument presented a question of fact to be decided by the jury. We hold that it did not and reverse.

We will summarize only the evidence pertinent to the issue we decide. Testifying for the Bank was one of its commercial loan officers, who did not handle the Holt transaction but through whom the instrument in question was introduced into evidence, and two other witnesses, one of whom was an expert in handwriting analysis, whose statements supported the Bank's position that the signature on the note was in fact the defendant's.

Mrs. Holt did not appear at the trial, but her attorney endeavored to show that his client did not execute the instrument. During cross-examination, the loan officer, over the Bank's objection based on the hearsay rule, was required to answer whether he was present during the taking of Mrs. Holt's discovery deposition in July 1974 when she "denied that she signed the note." The record shows that the witness responded, "Yes, I was. Somewhat surprised." No other statement was elicited by defendant's counsel from any of the Bank's witnesses which would support the defendant's claim that she did not sign the writing.

The only evidence offered in the defendant's behalf was a set of answers previously filed by the Bank to six interrogatories propounded by her attorney. Those responses indicated that the Bank did not know of any witness who saw the defendant sign the note or who heard her admit that she signed it. They further indicated that the Bank had no information that she ever authorized her husband to sign her name to any promissory note or that she ever ratified any act of his in signing her name to such a writing.

By a motion to strike at the conclusion of the evidence, and again by a motion to set aside after the verdict, the Bank moved for judgment in its favor contending, as it does on appeal, that the foregoing hearsay testimony on cross-examination was erroneously admitted and, in the alternative, that even if such evidence was properly received, the defendant had failed, as a matter of law, to overcome the presumption established by §3-307 [§3-308 in the Revision — Eds.] that her signature was genuine and authorized. The trial court, in refusing to sustain the motion to strike and in overruling the motion to set aside, ruled that the question of whether the signature was genuine was for the jury. This was error.

Section 3-307, inter alia, sets out the burden of proof in an action which seeks recovery upon an "instrument" and deals with issues arising, in such a suit, from a challenge of the genuineness or authorization of signatures. 2 R. Anderson, Uniform Commercial Code §3-307:3 (2d ed. 1971). Under that section, each signature on an instrument is admitted unless, as in this case, the "effectiveness" of the signature is put in issue by a specific denial. The burden of establishing the genuineness of the signature is then upon the party claiming under the signature and relying on its "effectiveness," but such party is aided by a presumption that it is genuine or authorized. In this context, "presumption" means that "the trier of fact must find the existence of the fact presumed unless and until evidence is introduced which would support a finding of its nonexistence." Code §1-201(31).

The effect of the presumption is to eliminate any requirement that the plaintiff prove the signature is authentic until some evidence is introduced which would support a finding that the signature is forged or unauthorized. §3-307, Official Comment 1. It is based upon the fact that in the normal course of events forged or unauthorized signatures are very uncommon, and that evidence of such is usually within the defendant's control or more accessible to him. Id. Therefore, under §3-307, the party denying a signature must make some sufficient showing of the grounds for the denial before the plaintiff is put to his proof. The evidence need not be sufficient to require entry of summary judgment in the defendant's favor, "but it must be enough to support his denial by permitting a finding in his favor." Id. "Until the party denying the signature introduces such sufficient evidence, the presumption requires a finding for the party relying on the effectiveness of the signature." §3-307, Virginia Comment. See 2 F. Hart & W. Willier, Commercial Paper Under the Uniform Commercial Code §2.07(2) (1975).

An application of the foregoing analysis of the statute to the facts of this case demonstrates that the Bank was entitled to entry of summary judgment in its favor at the conclusion of all the evidence, since no material issue of fact requiring resolution by a jury was presented. Rule 3:18.

The defendant's specific denial put the genuineness of the defendant's signature in issue. Because of the foregoing presumption, the signature, which appeared to be that of Gustava H. Holt, was presumed to be genuine and the defendant was thus required to present "sufficient evidence" in support of the denial of genuineness. This she failed to do. We will assume, but not decide, that the disputed answer during cross-examination was properly admitted in evidence. Nonetheless, we conclude that this bit of testimony is insufficient to sustain a finding that the signature was forged or unauthorized. Furthermore, the answers to interrogatories furnish no support to the defendant's claimed defense. A forgery or an unauthorized signature may not be shown by merely demonstrating the plaintiff's apparent lack of evidence on that issue.

We hold, therefore, that the defendant has failed, as a matter of law, to make a sufficient showing to support a finding that she, or her authorized representative, did not in fact write her name on the instrument. The presumption then requires a finding that the signature on the instrument is genuine and effective. Accordingly, production of the instrument entitled the Bank to recover, because the defendant established no defense, 3-307(2), and it was error to submit the case to the jury. For these reasons, the judgment in favor of Gustava H. Holt will be reversed and final judgment will be entered here in favor of the Bank.

Reversed and final judgment.

QUESTION

Would it have been sufficient to overcome the presumption if Mrs. Holt had taken the stand and denied the signature? See Metropolitan Mortgage Fund v. Basiliko, 407 A.2d 773 (Md. App. 1979); Freeman Check Cashing, Inc. v. State, 97 Misc. 2d 819, 412 N.Y.S.2d 963 (Ct. Cl. 1979); Bates & Springer, Inc. v. Stallworth, 56 Ohio App. 2d 223, 382 N.E.2d 1179 (1978).

D.   Defenses Against a Non-Holder in Due Course

Read §§3-305(a) and (b) and 3-306 carefully. Note the legal result: all *claims* and both real and personal *defenses* may be asserted against anyone who does not qualify as a holder in due course.[23] The most common personal defenses are *want of consideration* (no consideration) and *failure of consideration* (breach of contract, called a *claim in recoupment* in the Revision).

Herzog Contracting Corp. v. McGowen Corp.

United States Court of Appeals, Seventh Circuit, 1992
976 F.2d 1062

POSNER, Circuit Judge.

The district judge granted summary judgment in favor of Herzog Contracting Corporation in its diversity suit to enforce two promissory notes, aggregating $400,000, against the issuer, McGowen Corporation. The

---

23. The only claim a non-holder in due course takes free of is a perfected security interest in non-negotiable instruments, and then only if they are purchased for value in the ordinary course of business without notice of the security interest (§9-330). This is an Article 9 matter, and at this point don't worry what it means.

appeal raises a tangle of jurisdictional and substantive questions, the latter governed, the parties agree, by Indiana Law. . . .

The next jurisdictional issue requires us to delve into the facts. In 1989 Herzog, the plaintiff, bought the assets of Tru-Flex Metal Hose Corporation from McGowen, the defendant, and formed a wholly owned subsidiary of Herzog (also called Tru-Flex) to hold them, to which Herzog assigned the asset purchase agreement. The agreement called for annual payments from Tru-Flex to McGowen of $500,000 for five years. The two promissory notes, both demand notes, were issued by McGowen to Tru-Flex later in 1989. The parties have radically different positions on the purpose of the notes. Herzog claims that it loaned McGowen $400,000 and the notes are McGowen's promises to repay the loan. McGowen acknowledges having received the $400,000 but denies that it was a loan, contending instead that it was partial prepayment of the next year's installment due under the asset purchase agreement and that the only purpose of the notes that it gave Tru-Flex was to enable it (that is, McGowen) to postpone the realization of taxable income to the following year by making the $400,000 payment look like a loan.

The parties soon fell to squabbling and Herzog refused to make further payments under the asset purchase agreement, precipitating a suit by McGowen against Herzog in an Indiana state court for breach of contract that remains pending. At about the same time that the state court suit was brought, Tru-Flex assigned McGowen's promissory notes to Herzog, which shortly afterward brought this suit to enforce them. . . .

We come to the merits. The case was decided on summary judgment and there has been no determination of the truth of McGowen's claim that the promissory notes were never intended to be presented for payment. So we must assume that the claim is true. The question is whether, as the district judge held, solely on the basis that the notes are "clear and unambiguous," they are enforceable regardless of what the parties actually intended.

They would be if enforcement were being sought by a holder in due course, UCC §3-305, Ind. Code §26-1-3-305, but Herzog concedes that it is not that. It places its case on the parol evidence rule. The promissory notes are unambiguous—they promise Herzog a specified sum of money on demand—and their terms cannot be varied by extrinsic evidence. At first glance Herzog's argument seems a complete nonstarter. A holder of a promissory note who is not a holder in due course takes the note subject to "all defenses of any party which would be available in an action on a simple contract," UCC §3-306(b) [§3-305(b) in the Revision—Ed.], and one of those defenses, notwithstanding the parol evidence rule, is that the parties did not intend to create an enforceable contract. 2 E. Allan Farnsworth, Farnsworth on Contracts §7.4, at p. 212 (1990); James J. White & Robert S. Summers, Handbook of the Law under the Uniform Commercial Code §2-10, at p. 78 (1980). "It is well settled that whatever the formal documentary evidence, the parties to a legal transaction may always show that they understood a purported contract not to bind them; it may, for example, be a joke, or a disguise to deceive others." In re H. Hicks & Son, Inc., 82 F.2d 277, 279 (2d Cir. 1936) (L. Hand, J.); see also Nice Ball Bearing Co. v. Bearing Jobbers, Inc., 205 F.2d 841, 845 (7th Cir. 1953). The deceived others may, of course, be able to object to the attempt to prove the contract a sham, as in Central States, Southeast & Southwest Areas Pension Fund v. Gerber Truck Service, Inc., 870 F.2d 1148 (7th Cir. 1989) (en banc), and FDIC v. O'Neil, 809 F.2d 350 (7th Cir. 1987), but that is not a factor here. More to the point, a minority of jurisdictions "have refused to admit such evidence [i.e., that the purported contract was a joke, a disguise, in short, a sham of some sort] where the purpose of the sham agreement was offensive to public policy." 2 Farnsworth, supra, §7.4, at p. 212 n.4; see Annot., "Admissibility of Oral Evidence to Show That a Writing Was a Sham Agreement Not Intended to Create Legal Relations," 71 A.L.R.2d 382, 393-397 (1960); 67 A.L.R.2d Later Case Service 555 (1984), and for an illustrative case Kergil v. Central Oregon Fir Supply Co., 213 Or. 186, 323 P.2d 947 (1958).

We prefer the majority rule, illustrated by our decision in Nice Ball Bearing Co. v. Bearing Jobbers, Inc., supra, so will apply it here in default of any Indiana cases on the question. Apart from the fact that the minority rule rewards a party to the sham agreement and imposes a punishment that may be disproportionate to the promisor's misconduct, it invites a collateral inquiry into the character of the alleged "sham." Here the party accused of shamming by his fellow shammer was angling for a tax advantage. Did that make the transaction a "sham"? Despite the doctrine of tax law that substance prevails over form, Gregory v. Helvering, 293 U.S. 465 (1935); Yosha v. Commissioner, 861 F.2d 494 (7th Cir. 1988), many transactions that would strike a nonspecialist as contrived purely to avoid taxes are entirely lawful. Must we therefore, to resolve this case, decide whether McGowen's effort to postpone its tax liability for the sale of Tru-Flex was one of them? We trust not.

But we are not done. In the face of the principle that any defenses to a contract are available in a suit on a promissory note unless the plaintiff is a holder in due course, some courts enforce the parol evidence rule more broadly in such suits than in suits to enforce ordinary contracts. Annot., "Admissibility of Parol Evidence to Show That a Bill or Note Was Conditional, or Given for a Special Purpose," 54 A.L.R. 702, 717-718 (1928). In Perez-Lizano v. Ayers, 695 P.2d 467, 469 (Mont. 1985), for example, the court refused to allow the admission of parol evidence to show that the note was a sham. One of the cases in this line is an Indiana case, Highfield v. Lang, 394 N.E.2d 204, 206 (Ind. App. 1979). But it is readily distinguishable from our case; and we have found two recent cases from other jurisdictions in which courts admitted parol evidence to show that a promissory note was not intended to be enforceable. American Underwriting Corp. v. Rhode Island Hospital Trust Co., 303 A.2d 121, 125 (R.I. 1973); Simpson v. Milne, 677 P.2d 365, 368 (Colo. App. 1983). The second was a case of a sham; the parol evidence was that the notes in suit "were executed as a fiction to satisfy plaintiff's wife, who was near death, and who strongly felt that [the defendant and his wife] still owed [the plaintiff and his wife] money from prior business transactions." Id.

Despite these last two cases and despite UCC §3-306(b), the parties have tacitly agreed that the applicability of the parol evidence rule to this case is governed not by general contract law but by a special doctrine that allows parol evidence to show, against a plaintiff who is not a holder in due course, that the delivery of the negotiable instrument that he is suing to collect was "for a special purpose." Brames v. Crates, 399 N.E.2d 437, 441 (Ind. App. 1980); UCC §3-306(c); Ind. Code §26-1-3-306(c). This approach is understandable though not inevitable. While §3-306(b) subjects the nonholder in due course to "all defenses" that the original promisor would have had, implicitly including the defense that the promise was not intended to create enforceable rights, §3-306(c) deals with some of these defenses in greater detail. This could be taken to imply that the defense that no enforceable rights were intended to be created is to be analyzed in accordance with the "special purpose" doctrine that predates the Code, though a likelier inference is that the draftsmen wanted simply to make sure that no defense was overlooked.

However this may be, Herzog argues that the special-purpose doctrine is limited to allowing the promisor (McGowen here) to defend by showing that his obligation to make good on the note was subject to a condition precedent, which is not the case here. For it is McGowen's contention not that something had to happen before Herzog could demand payment, but that Herzog could never demand payment. Parol evidence is always admissible to prove a fraud, Franklin v. White, 493 N.E.2d 161, 165 (Ind. 1986); In re Estate of Fanning, 333 N.E.2d 80, 85 (Ind. 1975); Kruse Classic Auction Co. v. Aetna Casualty & Surety Co., 511 N.E.2d 326, 330 (Ind. App. 1987), but McGowen does not contend that when Herzog agreed to the scheme for making the prepayment of the purchase installment look like a loan it intended to double-cross McGowen by demanding payment of the notes. If there was a fraud, it was against the Internal Revenue Service, though no one is arguing this. With fraud out of the picture and the scope of the parol evidence rule applicable to promissory notes conceded by McGowen to be governed by §3-306(c) rather than §3-306(b), McGowen is left with the special-purpose doctrine and Herzog concludes that a sham case is outside that doctrine, which, as we have noted, he believes to be limited to conditions precedent.

There are cases, none from Indiana, on both sides of the question whether "delivery for a special purpose" is limited to conditions precedent, although the majority view is that it is not. Compare Perez-Lizano v. Ayers, supra, 695 P.2d at 469-470, with American Underwriting Corp. v. Rhode Island Hospital Trust Co., supra, 303 A.2d at 125. Text and history can help us choose between these positions, though history more than text. Section 3-306(c) expressly recognizes a defense of "nonperformance of any condition precedent," making the "special purpose" defense redundant on Herzog's construal of it. But redundancy is built into §3-306(c), as we have seen, and maybe this is another example of it. So let us turn to history.

Until sometime after the middle of the nineteenth century, courts were highly reluctant to admit parol evidence, in suits on promissory notes, for any purpose other than to prove fraud or mistake. John Barnard Byles, A Treatise on the Law of Bills of Exchange 169 note I (4th Am. ed. 1856). A little later, they were allowing such evidence in three additional types of cases: delivery of the note together with a mortgage deed, with the note as additional security for payment of the mortgage; delivery of the note to escrow; and delivery contingent on the satisfaction of a condition precedent. Id. at 112-113 (14th ed. 1885). Some courts also allowed the admission of parol evidence "to show that a contract signed and delivered was never intended to be the real contract between the parties." Id. at 113 note o. One case—oddly enough it is factually similar to ours—used the term "special purpose" to describe the defense in a "no obligation" or "sham" case. Juilliard v. Chaffee, 92 N.Y. 529, 534 (1883). And when the English codified their law of negotiable instruments in 1882, they expressly allowed evidence (other than against a holder in due course) that delivery had been "conditional or for a special purpose only, *and not for the purpose of transferring the property in the bill.*" James W. Eaton & Frank B. Gilbert, A Treatise on Commercial Paper and the Negotiable Instruments Law 697 (1903). The meaning brought out by the words that we have italicized seems unmistakable: the "special purpose" defense encompassed all cases in which the negotiable instrument had not been intended to create an enforceable obligation. Byles, supra, at 122 (17th ed. 1911).

The American Negotiable Instruments Law—the first statute drafted by the National Conference of Commissioners on Uniform State Laws—copied the English provision word for word. Joseph Doddrige Brannan, The Negotiable Instruments Law Annotated 129 (4th ed. 1926); see also id. at 135-41. Later, however, darkness descended, and we find some authorities distinguishing among condition cases, no-obligation cases, and special-purpose cases. Annot., "Admissibility of Parol Evidence to Show That a Bill or Note Was Conditional, or Given for a Special Purpose," 20 A.L.R. 421, 490, 498-502 (1922); 4 William D. Hawkland & Lary Lawrence, Uniform

Commercial Code Series 3-306:07, at p. 481 (1990). This proliferation of unhelpful distinctions was abetted by the fact that the Uniform Commercial Code, in recodifying negotiable instruments law, dropped the explanatory phrase "and not for the purpose of transferring the property in the bill" from the formulation of the special purpose defense. But this was done without any intention of changing the meaning of the defense as it had appeared in the Negotiable Instruments Law. "Notes and Comments to Tent. Draft No. 2—Art. III," 3 Uniform Commercial Code: Drafts 186-187 (Elizabeth Slusser Kelly ed. 1984). Certainly nothing in the history of the Uniform Commercial Code suggests a purpose of abolishing the "no obligation" defense and returning to the law as it existed before the Civil War. The tendency of our law for almost a century has been to relax strict rules, perhaps because of growing (though possibly misguided and even sentimental) confidence in the ability of judges and juries to resolve factual questions (such as, What was the purpose of McGowen's notes?), with reasonable accuracy and at reasonable cost, by sifting testimony. The legal realists who, led by Karl Llewellyn, drafted the Uniform Commercial Code were leaders in the movement to soften the contours of strict common law rules. See, e.g., UCC §§2-103(1)(b), 2-204, 2-205.

It hardly matters whether the no-obligation cases are subsumed under the special-purpose defense or set off by themselves or, as seems simplest and therefore — no other values being at stake so far as we can see — preferable, assimilated to the general contract doctrine that allows parol evidence to show that a contractual-looking document was not intended to be binding. The office of the parol evidence rule is to prevent parties to a written contract from seeking to vary its terms by reference to side agreements, or tentative agreements reached in preliminary negotiations. 2 Farnsworth, supra, §7.2, at p. 197. In the case of a condition precedent the promisor is not trying to vary the terms, but to deny the enforceability of the promise by pointing to some condition that has not been fulfilled. The distinction may seem fine-spun and even arbitrary, but it has been deemed consistent with the policy behind the parol evidence rule, or at least a tolerable qualification of it. 2 id., §7.4, at pp. 211-215. Two points can be made on behalf of the distinction. The weaker, as it seems to us, is that without such an exception the rule would work dramatic forfeitures, by preventing a party from showing not merely that the terms were somewhat different from what they appeared to be but that he had never agreed to do or pay anything. The stronger point is that the parol evidence rule, properly understood, is not a rule imposed on contracting parties from without but merely an inference, drawn from the language of the document, that the parties intended it to be the complete statement of their agreement, extinguishing any agreements that might have emerged from the preliminary negotiations. Patton v. Mid-Continent

Systems, Inc., 841 F.2d 742, 745 (7th Cir. 1988); 2 Farnsworth, supra, §§7.2, 7.3, at pp. 197-198. The document is unlikely to reveal whether the parties intended it to be taken seriously, and if it does not, there is no basis for applying the rule. In re H. Hicks & Son, Inc., supra, 82 F.2d at 279.

At all events, to allow parol evidence to expose a sham case such as this is alleged to be would make no greater inroads into the parol evidence rule than the cases on conditions precedent do. McGowen is not trying to change the terms in the promissory notes, but to show that the notes were not in fact intended to create a legally enforceable obligation. They were, not to put too fine a point on it, intended to fool the Internal Revenue Service. Herzog, perhaps fearing that it will be found to have been a party to this little deception, does not argue that McGowen's unclean hands should forfeit its right to make a sham-transaction defense, if there is such a defense, and we think there should be because we can think of no principled distinction between it and the condition-precedent defense that Herzog concedes is valid.

The policy of the law is to facilitate negotiability by allowing assignees of negotiable instruments to take free of defenses not obvious on the fact of the note. Northwestern National Ins. Co. v. Maggie, No. 92-1037 (7th Cir. Sept. 23, 1992). But that policy is expressed in the doctrine of holders in due course. Id. Herzog made no effort to discount the notes to one who would have been such a holder and therefore could have enforced the notes against McGowen regardless of the oral agreement not to enforce them on which McGowen relies in this suit.

The judgment is reversed and the case remanded for further proceedings consistent with this opinion.

QUESTION

How would this case be decided under the current version of Article 3? See §§3-117 and 3-105(b), plus the latter's Official Comment 2.

E.   Jus Tertii

It is a basic rule of law that litigants must succeed or fail on the basis of their *own* rights and not the rights of others. The rights of another, called *jus tertii*, are available to other litigants only in special circumstances. Sureties, called "accommodation parties" in the Code, are permitted, with some exceptions, to raise the defenses of their principals (called "accommodated parties"); see §3-305(d). And, as we shall see when we get to the issue of restrictive indorsements, §3-206(f) permits an obligor to refuse payment if doing so would violate the terms of a restrictive indorsement.

The Code's general prohibition against using jus tertii is found in §3-305(c), which you should now read. Note two important things about it. The first is that the claims of another may always be asserted if that person joins the lawsuit. The second is that §3-305(c)'s last sentence permits one jus tertii to be asserted against a non-holder in due course: the instrument has been lost or stolen so that the current possessor is not the true owner. If this latter jus tertii could not be raised, then the obligor would be exposed to the possibility of double payment when the true owner showed up.

PROBLEM 44

Craig Covey was the maker of the following promissory note, which he signed in order to buy a computer:

> I, Craig Covey, promise to pay to bearer the sum of $5,000, on demand. I also promise to buy the bearer lunch on the date of presentment.

The note was given to his uncle, who had loaned him the money for the purchase. The uncle sold the note to the Stonewall Finance Company in return for a check for $4,500. Stonewall Finance Company's check bounced, and the uncle was very angry. He went down to the finance company's office and found that there was a sign on the door saying "GONE OUT OF BUSINESS." The next day the note was stolen from the office of the Stonewall Finance Company and later surfaced in the hands of Jane Eleanor, an innocent purchaser for value, who presented it to Craig for payment. In the meantime both his uncle and the Stonewall Finance Company had contacted Craig and asked him to refrain from paying the instrument, the uncle pointing to the bounced check and Stonewall to the fact that the note had been stolen from it. Is Jane a holder in due course? If not, can Craig raise the suggested jus tertii against her? If Craig wants to pay Jane, can his uncle stop him? See §3-602.

F. Conclusion

Reference has already been made to special statutes and rules (such as the FTC regulation) that restrict the holder in due course doctrine in consumer transactions. But these statutes do not cover the whole consumer field; for example, a couple signing a promissory note to a bank for a home improvement loan can still lose a lawsuit to a holder in due course, as we have seen. Should the doctrine be wiped out completely in consumer transactions? We've already seen the havoc it can raise in cases in which a home owner buys a home due to fraudulent inducements but cannot assert this defense against a subsequent holder in due course of the promissory note signed at the closing. What about abolishing HIDC status in commercial ventures?

Professor Grant Gilmore, one of the original drafters of the Uniform Commercial Code, has commented:

> The "holder in due course" concept was worked out by Lord Mansfield and his successors in the late eighteenth and early nineteenth centuries against a business background in which bills of exchange and promissory notes did in fact circulate and could be expected to pass through a number of hands before being retired. As the modern banking system developed, instruments gradually ceased to circulate. In this century nothing is rarer than a true negotiation to a third party purchaser for value — the use of negotiable notes which pass from dealer to finance company in the attempt to carry out consumer frauds is hardly a "true negotiation." The whole "holder in due course" concept could usefully have been abolished when negotiable instruments law was codified at the end of the nineteenth century. In fact it was preserved like a fly in amber both in the N.I.L. and in its successor, Article 3 of the Uniform Commercial Code. Indeed our codifications typically preserve once vital but now obsolete concepts in much the same way that our museums preserve the ancient artifacts of bygone civilizations.

G. Gilmore, The Death of Contract 108 n.18 (1974). Professor Gilmore developed this idea more fully in a fascinating article: Gilmore, Formalism and the Law of Negotiable Instruments, 13 Creighton L. Rev. 441 (1979). A leading article containing the same theme is Rosenthal, Negotiability — Who Needs It?, 71 Colum. L. Rev. 375 (1971).

In a recent book, The End of Negotiable Instruments (2012), Professor James Rogers has gone even further. He advocates the complete repeal of Article 3 of the Code! What would be the result if that extraordinary event occurred? The common law and contractual arrangements, supplemented by federal enactments (such as various banking and check regulations) would then control. Physical checks (which are decreasing in number as the twenty-first century progresses) would be controlled by the rules of Article 4 of Bank Deposits and Collections (which itself is being supplanted by federal law or organizational agreements). Promissory notes would be replaced by contractual agreements to pay debts. Thus a home mortgage's payment arrangement would be dictated by the mortgage contract, and the assignment of that contract would be all that is necessary to transfer rights to enforce the mortgage debt. The holder in due course doctrine would disappear since at common law contracts travel *with* their defenses when assigned to new owners; see Restatement (Second) of Contracts §336. Should homeowners have a defense of fraud, as did the woman in the second case in this chapter, the foreclosing entity couldn't foreclose, but would have to pass the contract back to its assignor, and so on until it was returned to the entity committing the fraud. Surely that is a happier result than allowing the fraudster to escape liability while the defrauded homeowner ends up sitting on the curb. Whether Professor Rodger's arguments will prevail is uncertain, but repealing Article 3 is an interesting idea (though it would put your authors out of work).

CHAPTER 4   ASSESSMENT

Multiple Choice Questions

1. Rahel signed a negotiable promissory note payable to Ammu Gallery, to buy a painting for her law firm. Ammu Gallery indorsed the note to Holly Bank, who bought the note honestly, in a transaction typical for the industry. Rahel proudly displayed the painting in the firm's conference room until a discerning client alerted her that it was a forgery. Will Rahel be obliged to pay, if Holly Bank seeks payment on the note?
   a. No. Rahel could be liable only to Ammu Gallery, the person she promised to pay.
   b. No. Rahel was defrauded, a defense that can be raised even against a holder in due course.
   c. No. The painting was forged, so the seller breached warranties to Rahel, the buyer.
   d. Yes. Rahel has no defense she can raise against a holder in due course.

2. What would be the result in the previous question if Rahel had bought the painting to hang in the living room of her home?
   a. The same, because application of the holder in due course doctrine depends on Holly Bank's status, not Rahel's.
   b. Rahel could raise any defense she had against any one seeking payment on the note.
   c. The same — fraud can always be raised as a defense, in consumer or business cases.
   d. The holder in due course doctrine applies only to loans, not sales.

3. Chacko wrote a check payable to Baba, to buy furniture for Chacko's home. Baba did not deliver the furniture as promised the next day. Baba deposited the check, without indorsing it, in his account at Valor Bank and withdrew the money. Meanwhile, Chacko stopped payment on the check, so the check was not paid when Valor Bank presented it to Chacko's Bank. Valor Bank sued Chacko. Can Chacko raise the defense of breach of contract?

a. Yes. The holder in due course doctrine does not apply to consumer transactions.

b. Yes. Valor Bank is not a holder in due course. Baba did not indorse the check, so Valor is not a holder.

c. Valor Bank is not a holder in due course, because it did not give value.

d. No. As a holder in due course, Valor Bank is not subject to the defense of breach of contract.

4. Triffin is in the business of purchasing checks that have been dishonored, paying cents on the dollar. Triffin purchases the checks from banks and check-cashers that were holders in due course. Triffin itself is not a holder in due course, because Triffin buys the checks with notice they were dishonored. One might also argue that Triffin does not act in good faith, because Triffin's purchases are atypical for checks, Triffin pays little for the checks, and Triffin knows that at least some of the drawers may have good reason not to pay. If Triffin sues the issuer of a check, can the drawer raise defenses, such as breach of contract or unconscionability, to payment?

a. No, because that defense was against the payee, not Triffin.

b. No, because Triffin has the rights of a holder in due course.

c. Yes, because Triffin is not a holder in due course.

d. Yes. One who has promised to pay can always raise any reason that the promise should not be enforceable, such as breach of contract or unconscionability.

5. Roy is the holder in due course of a promissory note signed by Velutha. If Roy sues Velutha on the note, which defenses could Velutha raise?

a. Velutha was defrauded, because the payee promised to loan Velutha money but never delivered the funds.

b. Breach of contract, because the promissory note was given for some business equipment that was completely defective.

c. Unconscionability.

d. Velutha signed the note at a time that he was too young to make a binding legal obligation.

Answers

1. D is the best answer. Holly Bank is a holder in due course. It is a holder because Ammu Gallery indorsed the note and delivered it to Holly Bank. It took for value, in good faith, and with no notice of Rahel's defenses. So Holly Bank would be subject to only the "real defenses," none of which applies here. A is wrong. The whole point of negotiability is that the signer promises to pay whomever becomes the holder of the instrument.

B is incorrect because the only sort of fraud that can be raised against a HIDC is "real fraud" (signing an instrument, but reasonably not knowing what it is), not fraud in the inducement, as here. Mere breach of contract likewise is not a real defense, so C is incorrect.

2. B is the best answer. This question reminds us that the holder in due course doctrine does not apply to promissory notes signed in consumer credit sale transactions, so Rahel can raise any defense she has. C and D cite fictitious rules.

3. D is the best answer. This question illustrates several key points. Contrary to A, not all consumer transactions are immune to the holder in due course doctrine. The FTC rule makes the holder in due course doctrine inapplicable to promissory notes signed for a sale or lease of goods or services to consumers (consumer credit sales). But that leaves other consumer transactions subject to the holder in due course doctrine: transactions involving checks (as opposed to promissory notes); notes signed for loans of money (as opposed to sales of goods or services); and mortgage notes (signed for sales of real estate, not goods). So consumers often have the pleasure of learning about the holder in due course doctrine.

    The question also illustrates rules we have seen that ensure depositary banks may get holder in due course status. Valor Bank is a holder, even with no indorsement, because a depositary bank automatically becomes holder of a check deposited by a holder, contrary to B. Valor Bank also gave value, by allowing withdrawal of funds.

4. B is the best answer. Triffin is indeed not a holder in due course. But Triffin has the rights of a holder in due course, under the shelter rule. When an instrument is transferred, the transferee gets the rights of the transferor, including any HIDC rights (unless the transferee was actually involved in an underlying fraud). If Triffin buys a check from a HIDC, Triffin gets the rights of a HIDC. A and D respectively understate and overstate the right of a signer to raise defenses.

5. D is the best answer. This question illustrates how someone that signs an instrument generally gives up her right to raise defenses against a HIDC. By signing a negotiable promissory note, Velutha effectively says, "I will pay this, even if I do not get what was promised, or I am being deceived, or I am being taken advantage of. . . ." Only the real defenses may be raised against a HIDC, including infancy, making D correct.

THE NATURE OF LIABILITY

It may seem odd to a lawyer to talk about defenses to a lawsuit, as the last chapter did, before talking about the various causes of action that can be brought giving rise to those defenses. We did this strange thing because holder in due course law is the primary factor that distinguishes negotiable instruments proceedings from all others, and those proceedings cannot be understood without first appreciating a concept that overarches the whole field. Now that that key issue is out of the way, we can turn to the various negotiable instrument-related legal theories that lawyers must know when clients come to them with questions triggering Article 3 of the Uniform Commercial Code.

Once a negotiable instrument is created and enters commerce, the parties thereto are automatically locked into relationships that may lead to legal liability. When a problem arises in connection with one of these instruments, the knowledgeable lawyer (and the wise student facing an exam question) asks four preliminary questions:

(1) What negotiable instrument labels(*drawer, payee, drawee, maker, indorser, guarantor,* etc.) do the parties bear?
(2) What causes of action (contractual obligation, warranty, conversion, suits "off the instrument") are available to each party?

(3) What defenses are possible?
(4) Can liability be passed to someone else?

The basic labels applied to the original parties to notes and drafts have been discussed. You will recall that a promissory note is initially a two-party instrument involving a *maker* and a *payee*. If the payee signs the instrument, whether a blank or special indorsement, he/she becomes an *indorser*. Anyone who thereafter signs his/her name to the instrument is also presumed to be an indorser (§3-204(a)). A draft always begins as a three-party instrument. A *drawer* orders the *drawee* to make payment to the order of the *payee*. If the draft is a check drawn by Carl Consumer on the Big Bank to the order of the Gas Company, the parties are, respectively, the drawer, the drawee, and the payee. If the Gas Company places its name on the back of the check, it will become an indorser, as will anyone else who signs the back of the check prior to its payment by the drawee. The labels that can be applied to other parties to the instrument(*acceptor, accommodation party, guarantor*) will be explained as they come up below.

The remainder of this segment of the book will discuss the different causes of action (legal theories) that one party can bring against another. Negotiable instruments law draws on the basic fields of contract (§§3-412 to 3-415, 4-401), property (that is, warranty rights, §§3-416, 3-417, 4-207, 4-208), and tort (primarily, conversion, §3-420) to provide the three possible legal theories on which parties can sue under the Code. In addition, of course, the parties frequently have rights against each other that arise outside of the scope of Articles 3 and 4. There is no way to catalogue all the possible non-commercial paper suits here, but the discussion immediately below introduces the most obvious one.

I. THE UNDERLYING OBLIGATION

The most common lawsuit connected with negotiable instruments, but not created by Articles 3 and 4, is a suit on the *underlying obligation* that generated the instrument. If a corporation mails a dividend check to one of its stockholders and the check is lost in the mail, the stockholder can sue on the underlying obligation (in this case, the agreement to pay the dividend) and ignore whatever rights negotiable instruments law would give.

Does this mean that in addition to the negotiable instruments suits described below, a party may always bring suit on the underlying obligation? The answer has to be "No," and the following Problem illustrates why.

PROBLEM 45

Aunt Fran was unable to pay the annual rent on her hat shop, so she asked the landlord, Simon Mustache, to accept instead a promissory note from her to him for the amount of the rent, the note to be due three months in the future. Simon took the note and immediately discounted it with a local bank. A week later (and before the note matured), Simon brought suit against Aunt Fran for nonpayment of the rent (the underlying obligation being the lease agreement). Can she defend by saying that the note somehow suspended his right to sue on the underlying obligation?

The answer is "Yes." The common law doctrine of *merger* stated that once an instrument was offered and accepted in satisfaction of an underlying obligation, the obligation merged with the instrument, and until the instrument was dishonored, the underlying obligation was suspended (unavailable as a cause of action). This doctrine is codified in §3-310(b), which you should read carefully. Note that under §3-310(b)(1) and (2) actual payment of a check or a note discharges the underlying obligation, but until then that obligation is suspended. Once the instrument is dishonored, subsection (b)(3) divorces the underlying contract from the instrument and separate causes of action then exist for each.

PROBLEM 46

Suppose in the last Problem Aunt Fran had paid her rent by giving a cashier's check to Simon. The check was drawn by Octopus National Bank (ONB) on itself (the very definition of a cashier's check—see §3-104(g)). Simon took the check down to ONB and was dismayed to discover that the bank had failed and was now closed. He returned to Aunt Fran and demanded the rent money. What should she tell him? See §3-310(a).

Gray1 CPB, LLC v. SCC Acquisitions, Inc.

California Court of Appeals, 2014
169 Cal. Rptr. 3d 906

Moore, J.

You cross continents and spend years trying to collect a judgment for your client. Late one Friday afternoon, the debtor's lawyer walks into your office and hands you a cashier's check for almost $13 million, covering the entire judgment and all accumulated interest. Do you accept the check or say, "no thank you, I need to make a motion for attorney fees first?" Put another way, is a bird in the hand worth two in the bush?

Gray1 CPB, LLC (Gray1), obtained a judgment against SCC Acquisitions and Bruce Elieff (collectively defendants). Almost two years later, defendants paid the amount of the outstanding judgment and accrued interest with a cashier's check. In the interim, Gray1 allegedly incurred more than $3 million in attorney fees in an effort to enforce its judgment. The fees were largely incurred in litigating a separate action against Elieff in an effort to untangle what Gray1 asserts were a number of fraudulent transactions resulting in the placement of fraudulent liens on Elieff's real property as part of a scheme to insulate Elieff's properties from the judgment.

According to Gray1, it was only when it appeared the separate action was imminently headed toward resolution in Gray1's favor that defendants gave Gray1 the cashier's check to pay the judgment. Gray1 did not immediately cash the check. It held onto the check long enough for its attorneys to file a motion for postjudgment costs, including attorney fees. Once deposited, the issuing bank honored the check.

Judgment creditors who have prevailed on a contract authorizing the award of attorney fees are entitled to postjudgment attorney fees. (Code of Civ. Proc., §§685.040, 685.070, subd. (a)(6); all statutory references are to the Code of Civil Procedure unless otherwise stated.) However, a motion for postjudgment costs must "be made before the judgment is satisfied in full." (§685.080, subd. (a).) The trial court denied Gray1's motion for postjudgment costs, finding the motion was made after the judgment had been fully satisfied. Gray1 appealed. In this appeal we are called upon to determine when a judgment paid with a cashier's check is deemed satisfied.

In addition to opposing Gray1's motion, defendants filed a motion of their own. They sought a determination that Gray1 unjustly failed to file a timely acknowledgment of full satisfaction of judgment. (§724.050, subd. (e).) The trial court denied defendants' motion, finding defendants failed to prove damages, and concluding Gray1's failure to file a timely full satisfaction of judgment was not without just cause. Defendants appealed from that order.

I. FACTS

In August 2010, Gray1 obtained a judgment in excess of $9.1 million, plus interest, against defendants as a result of the defendants' failure to make good on their guaranties of a loan made to a limited liability company owned by Elieff. . . . The written guaranties contained provisions providing for the award of attorney fees. . . . The judgment provided Gray1 was entitled to attorney fees and costs to be established by a cost bill or motion. By interlineation, the court amended the judgment to reflect the award of over $1.5 million in attorney fees and more than $44,000 in costs.

Defendants made no payments on the judgment until June 8, 2012. On that date, defendants' attorney hand delivered to Gray1's attorneys a cashier's check in the amount of $12,918,654.46 and a letter. According to the letter, the cashier's check covered the amount of the judgment, including accumulated interest, and the judgment was now fully satisfied. The letter also demanded Gray1 immediately file a full satisfaction of judgment. Additionally, the letter contained a notice in the language of section 724.050, subdivision (b): " 'Important warning. If this judgment has been satisfied, the law requires that you comply with this demand not later than 15 days after you receive it. If a court proceeding is necessary to compel you to comply with this demand, you will be required to pay my reasonable attorney's fees in the proceeding if the court determines that the judgment has been satisfied and that you failed to comply with the demand. In addition, if the court determines that you failed without just cause to comply with this demand within the 15 days allowed, you will be liable for all damages I sustain by reason of such failure and will also forfeit one hundred dollars to me.' "

Twelve days after receiving the cashier's check, on June 20, 2012, Gray1 filed a motion for postjudgment costs, including attorney fees incurred in attempting to enforce the judgment. Gray1 alleged that in the two years following the judgment, it had incurred more than $3.1 million in attorney fees in efforts to collect on its judgment. On June 22, 2012, Gray1 filed an acknowledgment of partial satisfaction of judgment. Gray1 contended it was entitled costs (including attorney fees) incurred in attempting to enforce its judgment, and therefore, the amount paid by defendants was not in full satisfaction of the judgment.

Gray1 deposited the cashier's check on June 21, 2012, the day after it filed the motion for postjudgment costs. The bank "fund[ed]" the check on June 25, 2012.

Fifteen days after hand delivering the cashier's check and letter, defendants filed a motion to compel Gray1 to file an acknowledgement of full satisfaction of judgment on June 27, 2012. (§724.050, subd. (d).) The motion alleged defendants not only paid the judgment in full, but overpaid by more than $281,000, based on a miscalculation as to the date postjudgment interest started accumulating and "numerous collections and levies that Gray1 has evidently already made."

The court heard the parties' respective motions on September 12, 2012. Defendants argued Gray1's motion for postjudgment attorney fees was untimely because section 685.080 requires a motion for costs, including attorney fees permitted by section 685.040, to be filed before the judgment has been fully satisfied (§§685.070, subd. (b), 685.080, subd (a)). Defendants further asserted the judgment was fully satisfied when the cashier's check was delivered to Gray1 and accepted on June 8, 2012, almost two weeks before Gray1 filed its motion for postjudgment costs. Gray1 conceded that had defense counsel walked into Gray1's attorney's office and paid off the outstanding judgment with a briefcase full of cash, instead of with a cashier's check, the judgment would have been fully satisfied that same day and Gray1 would have been prohibited from thereafter filing a motion for postjudgment costs. Gray1 argued, however, its motion was not untimely because a judgment paid by check is not satisfied until the check is ultimately honored by the issuing bank, citing section 724.010.

In a five-page ruling, the court denied as untimely Gray1's motion for postjudgment costs. The court also denied defendants' motion for damages and sanctions (§724.050, subd. (e)), finding defendants failed to present any evidence of costs, attorney fees, or other damages and that Gray1's failure to file a timely acknowledgment of full satisfaction of judgment was not without just cause.

II. Discussion

A. GRAY1'S APPEAL

Gray1 appeals, contending the trial court erred in finding its motion for postjudgment costs untimely. As we are not faced with disputed facts and this matter involves statutory interpretation, our review is de novo. (Jaffe v. Pacelli (2008) 165 Cal. App. 4th 927, 934, 82 Cal. Rptr. 3d 423.)

Under the "American rule," followed in California, "each party to a lawsuit ordinarily must pay his or her own attorney fees. [Citations.]" (Musaelian v. Adams (2009) 45 Cal. 4th 512, 516, 87 Cal. Rptr. 3d 475, 198 P.3d 560.) An exception to this rule exists where the parties have agreed to "the measure and mode of compensation of attorneys." (§1021.) For example, a contract may contain a provision providing for attorney fees in enforcing the contract. Where a contract contains such a provision, the court must fix reasonable attorney fees as an element of the costs of the lawsuit. (Civ. Code, §1717, subd. (a); §1033.5, subd. (a)(10)(A).) In this instance, the written guarantees signed by the defendants provided for "reasonable attorneys' fees," including "attorneys' fees and related costs of enforcement of" a judgment. . . .

There does not appear to be any dispute concerning Gray1's right to timely seek reasonable attorney fees as costs in efforts to enforce its judgment. That having been said, any motion for such costs must be timely made. To be timely, the motion must be made *before* the underlying judgment has been fully satisfied and within two years of the fees being incurred. (§685.080, subd. (a); Lucky United Properties Investment, Inc. v. Lee (2010) 185 Cal. App. 4th 125, 141, 110 Cal. Rptr. 3d 159; Carnes v. Zamani (9th Cir. 2007) 488 F.3d 1057, 1060; cf. §685.070, subd. (b) [memorandum of costs].) "[T]he statutory purpose of requiring that the motion for enforcement costs be brought 'before the judgment is satisfied in full' (§685.080, subd. (a)) is to avoid a situation where a judgment debtor has paid off the entirety of what he believes to be his obligation in the entire case, only to be confronted later with a motion for yet more fees. [Citation.]" (Lucky United Properties Investment, Inc. v. Lee, *supra,* 185 Cal. App. 4th at p. 144, 110 Cal. Rptr. 3d 159.) That is the present situation. . . .

"'Performance of an obligation for the delivery of money only, is called payment.' [Citation.] Payment to a judgment creditor is governed by the cases and statutes which govern commercial transactions. [Citation.]" (Long v. Cuttle Construction Co., *supra,* 60 Cal. App. 4th at p. 837, 70 Cal. Rptr. 2d 698.) In the present case, that means California Uniform Commercial Code section 3310. "Unless otherwise agreed, if a certified check, cashier's check, or teller's check is taken for an obligation, the obligation is discharged to the same extent discharge would result if an amount of money equal to the amount of the instrument were taken in payment of the obligation." (Cal. U. Com. Code, §3310, subd. (a).) . . .

The rule we announce today does no disservice to judgment creditors who have incurred postjudgment costs they wish to add to the judgment. Like Gray1, if they have not yet filed a motion for postjudgment costs at the time the judgment debtor tenders a cashier's check in full payment of the outstanding judgment, they are free to reject the payment and to file a motion for postjudgment costs. In fact, for purposes of filing a timely motion for postjudgment costs, postjudgment creditors who are provided a cashier's check may be in a better situation than those who are paid in cash. A judgment creditor must accept cash, but may reject a cashier's check and instead file a motion for postjudgment costs, including attorney fees.

This is not to say Gray1's argument is not without sympathetic appeal. If Gray1 is to be believed, Elieff's slippery efforts to evade paying the judgment against him required Gray1 to follow a tortuous paper (or rather, electronic) trail—with discovery battles in foreign jurisdictions—to prove the liens on Elieff's properties were fraudulent and put in place by a company run by a close associate of Elieff's based on phony loans. That being said, Gray1 could have made a motion or motions for postjudgment costs, including attorney fees, prior to defendants fully satisfying the judgment nearly two years after entry of the judgment. And as stated earlier, Gray1 could have refused the cashier's check and prepared its motion for postjudgment costs. Having accepted the cashier's check, the judgment against defendants was fully satisfied to the same extent it would have been had Gray1 been paid in cash.

Contrary to Gray1's contention, the trial court did not "allow[ ] Elieff to escape his obligation to pay for" postjudgment costs, including attorney fees. The court applied the plain language of the applicable statutes. If Elieff escaped, it is not because the trial court "allowed" it, but rather because Gray1 did not file its motion *before* the outstanding judgment was fully satisfied, as required by law. (§§685.070, subd. (b), 685.080, subd. (a).) Accordingly, we find defendants fully satisfied the judgment on June 8, 2012, when defendants delivered and Gray1 accepted a cashier's check in an amount sufficient to cover the judgment plus accumulated interest. Gray1's motion for postjudgment costs was untimely when made 12 days later. . . .

III. Disposition

The orders of the trial court are affirmed. In the interests of justice, the parties shall each bear their own costs on appeal.

PROBLEM 47

When Aunt Fran (from the last Problem) told Simon that she was not liable for the rent as long as the note was outstanding, he got it back from the bank and tore it up. May he now sue her for the rent even though the note has not yet matured? See §§3-604, 3-310(b)(4), 3-309; Peterson v. Crown Fin. Corp., 661 F.2d 287(3d Cir. 1981) (creditor's subjective intent irrelevant). See also Annot., 59 A.L.R.4th 617. If the cancellation had been a clerical error, what result? See Gloor v. BancorpSouth Bank, 925 So. 2d 984 (Ala. App. 2005).

Ward v. Federal Kemper Insurance Co.

Maryland Court of Appeals, 1985
62 Md. App. 351, 489 A.2d 91

Adkins, J.

The issue posed to us by appellant, Aaron Ward, is whether appellee, Federal Kemper Insurance Company, properly cancelled an insurance policy for nonpayment of a premium. The question is whether Ward owed the premium at the time of cancellation. The answer to this seemingly simple question is complicated by a problem in the law of negotiable instruments: in whose hands are the funds represented by a check that the drawer (Federal Kemper) has mailed to the payee (Ward) but that is never paid by the drawee bank because never negotiated by the payee? The facts are undisputed.

On May 19, 1981, Federal Kemper issued an automobile liability policy to Ward and his then wife (hereinafter "Ward"). Ward paid the premium in full. By its terms, the policy was to expire on November 17, 1981. On August 4, because of a change of vehicles owned by Ward, Federal Kemper sent him a check (payable to him) in the amount of $12.00, and drawn on The

Citizens National Bank of Decatur, Illinois. This represented a refund of overpaid premium. Ward received the check but never negotiated it.

Soon after sending the check, Federal Kemper discovered that the proper refund should have been $4.50, rather than $12.00. On August 18, it billed Ward the difference of $7.50. Ward did not recall receiving the bill. In any event Ward never paid the $7.50, and pursuant to provisions of the policy, Federal Kemper mailed Ward a notice of cancellation effective October 11. On November 15 Ward was involved in an accident while driving the insured vehicle. The accident resulted in personal injury and property damage to him, his vehicle, and to the persons and properties of others involved in the accident. Federal Kemper declined to provide coverage.

Ward sued the insurance company in the Circuit Court for Baltimore City, seeking a declaratory judgment as to coverage. There were cross-motions for summary judgment. Because he believed that summary judgment is inappropriate in a declaratory judgment action, the hearing judge treated the proceedings as a hearing on the merits. No one objected. The judge concluded that "at the time the bill was sent . . . in the amount of $7.50, that amount was not due Kemper." He thought that "until the negotiable instrument is negotiated and paid by the drawee back [bank] Kemper has suffered no debit." Nevertheless, he went on to opine:

> I . . . conclude that Kemper proceeded properly on an assumption that its bill was being ignored in moving for cancellation. As a matter of fact, the negotiable instrument which it had issued to Mr. Ward was still outstanding and perfectly valid on its face for a period of six months by its very terms. It is not required under the statutory provisions dealing with cancellation to wait for the expiration of the six month period of the draft before seeking its set off amount due. I conclude from the stipulated facts that cancellation was proper on October 11, 1981. That being so, there was no insurance coverage . . . by Kemper . . . at the time of the accident on November 15. . . .

He granted judgment in favor of Federal Kemper.

In this court Ward contends that unless a premium is actually due and unpaid, an insurer may not cancel a policy for its nonpayment, citing Art. 48, §234A(a) to the effect that "[n]o insurer . . . shall cancel . . . a particular insurance risk . . . for any arbitrary, capricious, or unfairly discriminatory reason." Whatever the precise reach of §234A(a), Lumbermen's Mutual Casualty Co. v. Insurance Commissioner,_Md._,_A.2d_,_, No. 161, September Term, 1982 (filed February 11, 1985), we agree that an insurer may not cancel a policy for nonpayment of premium unless the premium is in fact due. See Government Employees Co. v. Insurance Commissioner, 273 Md. 467, 483, 330 A.2d 653 (1975). To put this self-evident point more directly:

Where the propriety of the cancellation of a policy depends upon the nonpayment of a premium it necessarily follows that there is no effective cancellation when in fact the premium has been paid. For if a premium has been paid, the insurer cannot cancel for nonpayment of such premium [citations omitted].

M. Rhodes, Couch Cyclopedia of Insurance Law §67.74 (rev. 2d ed. 1983).

Federal Kemper does not dispute these propositions. The parties agree that the real issue is who had the $7.50 premium due balance that was included in the unnegotiated $12.00 check. If this money was Ward's by virtue of his possession of the check and his ability to negotiate it, then Ward owed Federal Kemper the $7.50 and the cancellation was proper. If, on the other hand, the $7.50 was still under Federal Kemper's control, because the check has not been negotiated when the policy was cancelled, the cancellation was improper. To resolve this question we must turn to the Uniform Commercial Code rather than to Art. 48A.

Ward points to §3-409(1) of the Commercial Law Article (§3-409(1) of the UCC [§3-408 in the Revision—Eds.]) which provides that:

A check or draft does not of itself operate as an assignment of any funds in the hands of the drawee available for its payment, and the drawee is not liable on the instrument until he accepts it.

Because of this rule, he argues, his mere possession of the $12.00 check did not have the effect of transferring the $12.00 to him. Federal Kemper could have stopped payment or, for that matter, closed its account at the drawee bank prior to presentment of the check. In either of these events, he would have had nothing more than a claim against Federal Kemper for the $4.50 in fact due him; the $7.50 overpayment would at all times have remained under the insurer's control, as it in fact did. He cites Malloy v. Smith, 265 Md. 460, 290 A.2d 486 (1972), in which the Court of Appeals, by way of dictum, observed that a personal check cannot be the subject of a gift causa mortis. Referring to §3-409(1), the court explained:

The point is, of course, that when the donor uses his own check to make the gift, there is no assignment of funds because he does not relinquish control of the sum which the check represents. A consequence of this is that a valid delivery alone will not complete the gift. To perfect the gift the check must be presented by the donee and accepted by the drawee, because the donor could stop payment, withdraw from his account the very funds which the check represents, or die before payment is made, any one of which would revoke the gift. 265 Md. at 463.

Federal Kemper counters that by virtue of §3-413 [§3-414 in the Revision—Eds.] the drawer of a check "engages that he will pay the

PROBLEM 52

Charlie Brown wanted to borrow $10,000 from the Peanuts National Bank, but the bank told him that it would not loan him the money unless his note was indorsed by four responsible people. Charlie explained his problem to his friend Lucy, and she signed her name to the back of the instrument. Charlie then took the note to another friend, Schroeder, who not only signed, but also persuaded his friend Pig Pen to add his name below Schroeder's. Finally, Charlie Brown had Peppermint Patty sign her name, at which point he took the note back to the bank, and it loaned him the money. When the note came due, the bank made a presentment of it to Charlie Brown and demanded payment. He had used the money in a business venture that, predictably enough, was a moral but not a financial success, and so he was unable to pay the note (a dishonor). The Peanuts National Bank gave notice of dishonor to all four indorsers, but demanded payment of Peppermint Patty alone. She resisted, claiming she was liable at most for only one-fourth of the amount ($2,500). Look at §3-415 and decide:

(a) Is she right?

(b) If she pays $10,000, can she sue Pig Pen for the entire amount or only for part? Once again look at §§3-116, 3-205(d).

(c) If she is sued, can she bring the other indorsers into the lawsuit? See §3-119 (explaining the so-called vouching in notice).

(d) If Charlie Brown comes back into the chips, can she sue him? On what theory?

Co-Suretyship vs. Sub-Suretyship. The common law presumed, unless the sureties agreed otherwise, that those signing later in time could get complete reimbursement from those signing prior in time, and this was called the presumption of *sub-suretyship*. If the sureties have agreed, expressly or impliedly, to share the liability, then they are *co-sureties* and have a right of partial contribution from each other. Where the parties have made what §3-205(d) calls an *anomalous* indorsement (one made by a non-holder — i.e., a surety), §3-116 changes the common law and now presumes that the parties are co-sureties, and hence must share the liability among themselves proportionately. See Official Comment 5 to §3-415.

Indorsers and Sureties. Whether the indorser intends it or not, the imposition of a §3-415 obligation makes the indorser an unintentional surety for the parties who have signed the instrument prior to the indorser, and the Code generally gives indorsers all the rights it gives to voluntary sureties, whom it calls *accommodation parties*.

Qualified Indorsements. How can the indorser avoid incurring the §3-415 obligation? The answer is by writing the words "without recourse" next to his or her name, preferably above it. In this manner the indorsement (technically called a *qualified* indorsement) operates to negotiate the instrument, but does not create any contractual liability. See §3-415(b).

PROBLEM 53

Marian Melody, a professional pianist, bought a piano from the Ivory Keys Music Company, signing a promissory note payable to the company for $3,000. The day after the piano was delivered, the music company discounted the note to the Friendly Loan Company for $2,700, indorsing it on the back, "Pay to the Friendly Loan Company, *Ivory Keys Music Company (Without Recourse)*." The piano fell apart, and Melody refused to pay the note when it came due. Friendly Finance sued both Melody and the Ivory Keys Music Company. What is its cause of action against each? What defenses can each defendant raise?

Practical Note. When a lawsuit is settled, the losing side will frequently send the victorious attorney a check on which the attorney and the attorney's client are joint payees. This is done to protect the attorney's lien and to help the attorney get payment from the client. When the attorney indorses such a check, the indorsement should be "without recourse." This makes it clear that the indorsement is made only to negotiate the check and that the attorney assumes no §3-415 obligation. There is no reason why the attorney (or the client for that matter) should make an unqualified indorsement and become, in effect, a surety for the drawer of the check, already known to be a loser.

C. The Surety's Obligation

This section must of necessity be a long one, not because the concepts herein are particularly complex, but because there is a great deal of suretyship law that one must gulp down and digest before the Code's suretyship provisions look friendlier.[3] In a negotiable instruments setting, suretyship problems come up whenever, as in the Charlie Brown Problem above, the maker must get others to "lend their names" to the maker's basic obligation. Suretyship matters can arise even in connection with checks. If you are the payee on a check drawn on Bank *A*, just see how easy it is to cash the check at Bank *B* if you do not have an account there. Bank *B* will probably not take

---

3. The following brief outline of some of the basic rules of the suretyship can and should be supplemented by the two leading treatises: Stearns, Suretyship (4th ed. 1951), and Simpson, Suretyship (1950). See also the Restatement (Third) of Suretyship and Guaranty.

instrument according to its tenor . . ." and further "engages that upon dishonor [as through a stop payment order] and any necessary notice of dishonor or protest he will pay the amount of the draft to the holder. . . ." According to Federal Kemper, a stop payment order may be effective to prevent payment of a check by the drawee, but that does not affect the drawer's liability to a holder in due course. Section 3-305. Had Ward negotiated the $12.00 to a holder in due course, thereby receiving value for it, Federal Kemper would have been liable to the holder in due course despite any stop payment order. First National Bank of Trinity, Texas v. McKay, 521 S.W.2d 661 (Tex. Civ. App. 1975). When Federal Kemper billed Ward for the $7.50 and when it issued the cancellation notice, it had no way of knowing whether a holder in due course had entered the picture. Thus, the argument continues, by issuing the check to Ward, Federal Kemper obligated itself to pay $12.00. And since the obligation was $7.50 more than its actual premium refund debt to Ward, Ward was obligated to pay Federal Kemper the difference. Therefore, Ward owed Federal Kemper a premium of $7.50, a sum that has never been paid.

We think Federal Kemper misapprehends the nature of a check and the relationships of the parties to it. A check is a draft or bill of exchange—an order by a drawer (Federal Kemper) to a drawee (Citizens National Bank of Decatur) to pay money to a payee (Ward). Section 3-104. B. Clark, The Law of Bank Deposits, Collections and Credit Cards Par 1.1[1] (rev. ed. 1981) (hereinafter "Clark"). As between drawer and drawee, the relationship is one of creditor and debtor. The drawer does not "own" the funds it has on deposit with the drawee. Its balance on the drawee's books represents a debt owed the drawer by the drawee. The funds are "owned" by the drawee. Id. par 2.1.

When the drawer draws a check on the drawee and delivers the check to the payee, the check ordinarily is regarded as only a conditional payment of the underlying obligation. Merriman v. Sandeen, 267 N.W.2d 714, 717 (Minn. 1978). H. Bailey, Brady on Bank Checks §1.8, 4.5 (5th ed. 1979 & 1984 Cum. Supp.) (hereinafter "Bailey"). See also Moore v. Travelers Indemnity Ins. Co., 408 A.2d 298 (Del. Super. 1979). The conditions are that the check be presented and honored. Until those conditions are met, no one is directly liable on the check itself; Clark, par 1.3. The underlying obligation represented by the check is similarly suspended until those conditions are met; §3-802(1)(b). If they are not met (if, for example, the check is dishonored), an "action may be maintained either on the [check] or the obligation. . . ." Id.

The point is that the drawer is only secondarily liable on the check when he issues it. Stewart v. Citizens and Southern Natl. Bank, 225 S.E.2d 761 (Ga. App. 1976); Clark, par 1.3; §§3-122(3) and 3-413(2). As Ward correctly asserts, the delivery of Federal Kemper's check did not operate as an assignment to him of any funds in the hands of the drawee; §3-409(1). Clark, par 3.1[1]. Ward, when he received the check acquired no proprietary interest in the fund on deposit. Bailey §4.1.

The $12.00 check involved in this case was, of course, never dishonored. Thus, Federal Kemper never became liable directly on the check, nor was its underlying obligation (to refund $4.50 to Ward) ever actually discharged. The check was never presented to the drawee and, therefore, never paid, so the funds it represented were never transferred to Ward. In point of fact, those funds remained (and so far as we know, still remain) in the Citizens National Bank of Decatur, subject to Federal Kemper's control. Under these circumstances, we do not think that Ward owed any premium to Federal Kemper. See Owl Electric Co. v. United States Fidelity and Guaranty Co., 268 N.E. 493 (Ill. App. 1971). See also Klein v. Tabatchnik, 459 F. Supp. 707, 715-716 (S.D.N.Y. 1978), *aff'd* (as to relevant issue), 610 F.2d 1043, 1049 (2d Cir. 1979) and In re Sportsco, 12 B.R. 34 (Bkr. Ct., D. Ariz. 1981).

It is perfectly true that when Federal Kemper billed Ward, and when it sent the cancellation notice, there might have been a holder in due course lurking in the wings. That is a business risk Federal Kemper took when it proceeded as it did. The policies underlying the protections given a holder in due course, Lawrence & Minan, The Effect of Abrogating the Holder in Due Course Doctrine on the Commercialization of Innovative Consumer Products, 64 B.U. L. Rev. 325, 327-330 (1984), do not affect the underlying relationships between Ward and Federal Kemper, especially when, as here, there was no holder in due course. When Federal Kemper attempted to cancel the policy the entire premium was in its bank account; Ward owed it nothing at that time.

Accordingly, we hold that the Circuit Court for Baltimore City correctly concluded that "at the date the [premium due] bill was sent in the amount of $7.50 on August 18, 1981, it was not due." That being so, Federal Kemper could not lawfully have cancelled Ward's policy for nonpayment of that premium. Ward is entitled to a declaratory judgment to the effect that his Federal Kemper policy was in full force and effect when the accident occurred. See Jennings v. Government Employees Ins. Co., _ Md. _ , _ A.2d _ , No. 27, Sept. Term, 1983 (filed February 22, 1985).

Judgment reversed.

Case remanded for entry of declaratory judgment consistent with this opinion. Appellee to pay the costs.

Payment in Full Checks. One issue that's often litigated concerns a "payment in full check" sent by one party to a dispute to the other with the offer of settlement. If the other party to the dispute, the payee, cashes the check, is the dispute over? Your course in Contracts probably covered this issue in the chapter on offer and acceptance, but here is a brief précis of the rules.

The underlying policy at work reflects the legal adage that "the law favors a compromise."

The common law provided that an offer of settlement was called "accord" and the other side's agreement to settle the dispute by taking the accord was a "satisfaction." If the accord is a check, the law is now governed by §3-311, which you should read. Use it to resolve the issues in the next Problem.

PROBLEM 48

Cassandra Troy was annoyed when she saw the sloppy work that Apollo Construction Company had done when it finished building her new front porch, so she subtracted $1,000 from the amount still due on the contract and sent a check clearly marked "Payment In Full" both on the front of the check and on the back where Apollo would have to indorse it, along with a cover letter expressing her disappointment at the work and explaining this was her offer to settle the dispute. Godfrey Apollo, president of the company, was outraged when he saw the check, believing that construction of the porch was first rate.

a. If he cashes the check, is the dispute over? What if he crosses off the language about "payment in full" and writes "cashed under protest, all rights reserved"? See §1-308 and its Official Comment 3; Glassman Corp. v. Champion Bldrs., L.L.C., 83 2014 WL 2226920 (Kan. App. 2014).

b. If Apollo can prove that Cassandra Troy is lying and had told neighbors she was delighted with the work, will cashing the check work an accord and satisfaction? See §3-311(a) and its Official Comment 4.

c. If Apollo's bookkeeper cashes the check and then Apollo learns that it contained "payment in full" language, can he do anything to avoid the accord and satisfaction? See §3-311(c)(2).

d. If you are the attorney for Apollo Construction Company and Godfrey calls you for advice as to what he should do with the check, what should you tell him?

One of your authors has a blog post entitled "The Payment-In-Full Check: A Powerful Legal Maneuver," covering these issues in more detail; if you are interested, see http://douglaswhaley.blogspot.com/2011/04/payment-in-full-check-powerful-legal.html.

II.   *LIABILITY ON THE INSTRUMENT*

As soon as someone places a signature on a negotiable instrument, an *implied contractual obligation* is automatically made promising to pay the instrument when it matures (unless in the meantime a defense, real or personal, develops). The original version of Article 3 actually called these obligations "contracts," but the name was misleading because the legal responsibility imposed thereby did not depend on the intention of the relevant party. The so-called *contract* was imposed as a matter of law whether or not the contracting party understood the fact or extent of liability.

In the current language of Article 3 these promises are called *obligations* and not *contracts*, but the basic idea is the same. Putting one's signature on a negotiable instrument in anything other than an innocuous capacity ("witness," for example) leads to a promise *implied in law* (actual intent being irrelevant) to pay the instrument under certain circumstances. This obligation is sometimes described as liability *on the instrument*—that is, as a result of signing the instrument, and the person who could enforce that liability was the current holder of the instrument.

Before the nature of this liability in contract is explored further, let me emphasize the basic rule found in §3-401(a): "A person is not liable on an instrument unless (i) the person signed the instrument. . . ." This means that no contractual liability arises on a negotiable instrument until and unless a signature is placed thereon. What is a signature? Read the definition of *signed* in §1-201(b)(37) and the description of signatures in §3-401(b). If you now review Problems 2 and 3, you should have this concept well under control.[1]

A. *The Maker's Obligation*

The maker of a promissory note is absolutely liable on the instrument; a maker's liability has no technical implied conditions to it. The same thing is true of a bank that issues a cashier's check. This "primary" liability is codified in §3-412 (where both the maker of a promissory note and the bank issuing a cashier's check are lumped together as *issuers*).[2] If there is more than one maker, those who sign are presumed to be jointly and severally liable to the rest of the world (meaning that they can be sued individually or as a group), but they have a right to contribution from their co-makers if they are forced to pay more than their share.

---

1. If a forger places your name on a check, does the forgery operate as your signature? The answer is found in §3-403(a), which states that an unauthorized signature is "ineffective" as that of the person whose name is signed, but it does operate as if the forger had signed his or her real name. We will come back to this issue in the section on forgery.

2. Section 3-105(c): "Issuer" means a maker or drawer of an instrument.

PROBLEM 49

Winkin, Blinkin, and Nod signed the following promissory note:

Oct. 1, 2018 $3,000

On or after six months from date, we promise to pay to the order of *Grimms National Bank, the sum of three thousand dollars ($3,000).* We, along with all sureties and subsequent indorsers, waive all rights to presentment, notice of dishonor, and protest, and all parties hereto agree to any extension of time granted by the holder to the makers.

Wilber Winkin
Barney Blinkin
Harry Nod

Grimms National Bank indorsed the note in blank and discounted it to Andersen Finance Co. When the note matured, Andersen sued only Winkin, demanding the entire amount. May he defend on the basis that Andersen should have sued all three of them, since the note contains the words "we promise to pay"? If Andersen wins, can Winkin sue Blinkin for $2,000? $1,000? See §3-116; Ghitter v. Edge, 118 Ga. App. 750, 165 S.E.2d 598 (1968).

PROBLEM 50

In an actual case, the Tips Family Trust signed a promissory note in favor of Patriot Bank secured by a mortgage on real property the family owned. The note, the security agreement, and the guaranty agreement all described the principal amount of the loan as follows:

ONE MILLION SEVEN THOUSAND AND NO/100 ($1,700,000.00) DOLLARS

This language appears five times in the three documents, in exactly the same form each time, and no other language in the documents describes the amount of the loan. Before the note matured, the trust made payments totaling $595,586, and then defaulted and the bank sold the property for $874,125. The bank then sued the trust for the deficiency, and the trust countered with the argument that the bank had been overpaid and must remit the excess to the trust. How should this come out? Read §3-114; see Charles R. Tips Family Trust v. PB Commercial LLC, 2015 WL 730481 (Tex. Ct. App. 2014).

B. *The Indorser's Obligation*

Once the payee signs the back of the instrument, the payee automatically incurs the obligation the law imposes on an *indorser*. In fact, per §3-204(a), *anyone who* signs an instrument in an ambiguous capacity is conclusively presumed to assume this liability. This obligation is described in §3-415, which you should read carefully. Note that unlike the obligation of a maker, the indorser's obligation is *secondary*, in that there are certain technical conditions that must be met before the indorser can be sued on the §3-415 obligation: the instrument must have first been *presented* to the maker (if it is a note) or to the drawee (if it is a draft), there must have been a *dishonor* (by the maker or drawee), and in certain circumstances §3-503 requires that the indorser be given *notice of dishonor*.

These three rights (presentment, dishonor, and notice of dishonor) are discussed ad nauseam in the 3-500 sections of the Code. It is unfortunate, but unavoidable, that we must explore these sections at some time, but let's postpone that until after we've established the drawer's liability on a draft. For now it is sufficient if you remember that an indorser is not liable until the person primarily liable has dishonored the instrument and the indorser has been so notified. Section 3-415 settles other problems, too, as illustrated by the following Problems.

PROBLEM 51

Billy Bigelow wrote out a check payable to the order of Enoch Snow to pay for some carnival equipment. Snow cashed the check at Bascombe Check Cashing Store, indorsing his name on the back. Bascombe Store then indorsed the check and deposited it in its account at Jordan State Bank. This bank also indorsed the check and then presented it to the drawee bank, Rodgers National Bank, which dishonored it because Bigelow had no money in his account, marking it "NSF" ("Not Sufficient Funds"). The check was returned to Jordan State Bank. You are the bank's attorney, and it calls you with three questions:

(1) Bascombe Check Cashing Store, has suddenly gone out of business and there is no money in its account. Can Jordan State Bank sue Enoch Snow and, if so, on what theory? Read §3-415(a) carefully.

(2) If Jordan State Bank sues Snow, may he raise his defenses (say, that Bascombe Check Cashing Store, had failed to pay him any money when he indorsed it over to them), or is the indorser liability found in §3-415 strict liability?

(3) If the bank does recover from Snow, will he have to pay the whole amount or do the indorsers divide up the indorsement liability and share it proportionately? Cf. §§3-116, 3-205(d).

the check unless one of its customer-depositors is willing to sign (become a surety) along with you.

It is an awesome thing to become surety for someone else, but people nonetheless do it, often with very little thought about the consequences, thus becoming the so-called fool with a pen (the Bible has a similar thought: "A man void of understanding . . . becometh surety in the presence of his friend"—Proverbs 17:18). In the desire to help out a friend or relative who is temporarily financially embarrassed (and who often assures the prospective surety "I guarantee you that you really won't have to pay"), the surety co-signs and, like it or not, understand it or not, takes on liability for the debt. To alert potential sureties to the nature of their undertaking, both the Federal Trade Commission and the Federal Reserve Board have issued regulations requiring consumer debts to carry a notice to co-signers (defined for these purposes as natural persons who are uncompensated) in the following manner:

> *Notice to Co-Signer*
>
> You are being asked to guarantee this debt. Think carefully before you do. If the borrower doesn't pay the debt, you will have to. Be sure you can afford to pay if you have to, and that you want to accept this responsibility.
>
> You may have to pay up to the full amount of the debt if the borrower does not pay. You may also have to pay late fees or collection costs, which increase this amount. The creditor can collect this debt from you without first trying to collect from the borrower.
>
> The creditor can use the same collection methods against you that can be used against the borrower, such as suing you, garnishing your wages, etc. If this debt is ever in default, that fact may become a part of your credit record.
>
> This notice is not the contract that makes you liable for the debt.

See F.T.C. Trade Regulation Rule Concerning Credit Practices, 16 C.F.R. part 444.3, effective March 1, 1985, and F.R.B. Reg. AA, 12 C.F.R. part 227, effective January 1, 1986.

In any true surety setting, there are three basic contracts involved. The first contract is the underlying obligation between the principal and the creditor. The second contract is the promise of the surety to back up the underlying obligation and see that the creditor loses nothing as a result of accepting the principal's promise on the first contract. The third contract is the promise of the principal to *reimburse* the surety if the surety is forced to pay off on the surety's promise to the creditor.[4] The contract of reimbursement is frequently implied, as where a sister co-signs for her brother and expects to lose no money from the transaction; when a professional surety's

---

4. This contract of reimbursement is one of the theories for Peppermint Patty's suit against Charlie Brown in Problem 52.

liability is obtained, the contract of reimbursement will be spelled out in a multi-page, fine-print document.

PROBLEM 54

Frank Family wanted to move out of his apartment and into his dream house. He hired Quickie Contractor to build the house on land Family had purchased, requiring Quickie to get a performance and payment bond guaranteeing that Quickie would do the work and pay its laborers and suppliers. Quickie got Big Bank to issue the bond guaranteeing these matters. Quickie went bankrupt halfway through the job, and Family called on Big Bank to finish the work. Which of these parties is the surety? Which the principal? Which the creditor? Identify the three contracts.

Sureties have several remedial rights in addition to the right of reimbursement. These include the rights of exoneration, subrogation, and contribution and the principle of *strictissimi juris*.

1. Exoneration

This is an equitable right by which the surety, at maturity, can compel the principal to perform instead of the surety. That is, by a bill in equity, the surety can prevent the need for a later suit for reimbursement. The basis for this right is said to be the implied duty that every principal owes to the surety to perform at the earliest moment and exonerate the surety from liability.

2. Subrogation

If the surety is forced to pay off the creditor, the surety is subrogated to whatever rights the creditor had. Put another way, the surety steps into the shoes of the creditor and is said to take an "equitable assignment" of the creditor's rights. This may be important if the creditor possesses rights the surety can take advantage of — for instance, a lien, a security interest in collateral, a priority in bankruptcy, a power to confess judgment, etc. In effect, by paying off on the second contract, the surety's right of subrogation permits the surety to become a party to the first contract and enforce it *as if the surety were the creditor.*

3. Contribution

This is a right of partial reimbursement that co-sureties have against each other for proportionate shares of the debt. If *X*, *Y*, and *Z* each sign *M*'s note for $9,000 agreeing to be co-sureties, the payee may enforce the entire obligation against any one of the three, and the right of contribution will then permit that one to sue the other two for their shares.

4. *Strictissimi Juris*

The following is a discussion of the common law rules only; as we shall see, the revision of Article 3 has drastically changed the rules.

A surety, particularly an uncompensated surety, is a *favorite of the law*, so that at common law the surety's obligation is to be construed *strictissimi juris* (of the *strictest law*), and thus the surety prevails if possible. Since the surety has agreed to back up only the first contract, the courts have held that an agreement between the creditor and the principal that changes that contract *in any detail* operates to discharge and release the non-consenting surety from further liability. Restatement of Security 128 (1941). Why? Because the modification of the first contract converts it into a new contract to which the surety did not consent. The courts even go so far as to say that a surety is discharged by a modification of the first contract that *benefits* the surety by lessening the principal's obligation. See Merchants Natl. Bank v. Blass, 282 Ark. 497, 669 S.W.2d 195 (1984) (new note given by maker containing a higher interest rate discharged surety on original note); First Natl. City Bank v. Carbonaro 1971 WL 17894 (N.Y. Civ. Ct. 1971) (surety who agreed to back loan of $4,176 discharged when promissory note filled in with only $1,656 as the amount).

Moreover, if the creditor agreed by a binding commitment to excuse the principal from liability or to give the principal extra time to pay the first contract, the Restatement (Third) of Suretyship and Guaranty would hold that a non-consenting surety is discharged unless the creditor warns the principal that this agreement works a "preservation of recourse" by the surety against the principal, meaning that the agreement in no way affects the rights of the surety against the principal.

There are theoretical reasons for these rules. By extending the time without the surety's consent, the creditor is thought to prejudice the surety's right of subrogation, but if the creditor expressly states that the surety's right of recourse is unimpaired, supposedly no prejudice occurs to the subrogation rights because the principal debtor is then alerted to the fact that the creditor's promise is conditional on the surety's rights (including subrogation) being preserved intact. The surety who dislikes this modified agreement can ignore it and exercise the usual rights, including exoneration, reimbursement, and even subrogation to the creditor's premodification position. For our purposes it is easier to memorize this black letter rule:

If the creditor releases the principal debtor from liability on the first contract or gives the debtor a binding extension of time in which to pay, the surety is discharged *unless* (1) the surety consents, or (2) the creditor informs the principal of the preservation of the surety's rights against the principal.

Notice that the non-consenting surety is discharged only by a *binding* extension of time. There is all the (legal) difference in the world between the following two hypotheticals:

(1) The note comes due, and the principal does not pay it; the creditor waits a month before suing.
(2) The note comes due, and the creditor and principal *agree* to wait a month to enforce it, with the principal agreeing to pay an extra month's worth of interest.

In the first hypothetical the surety is not discharged even if thereby an extra month's worth of interest is added to the obligation.[5] The creditor and the principal have not *agreed* to change the original contract, and surely the surety cannot object if the creditor does not declare an immediate forfeiture. But in the second hypothetical, the surety is discharged by the new agreement unless the surety consents or the creditor adds to the agreement the *preservation of secondary obligator's recourse clause.* The Restatement (Third) of Suretyship and Guaranty, which calls the creditor the "obligee," the principal the "principal obligor," and the surety the "secondary obligor," puts it this way:

§129. *Preservation of Secondary Obligor's Recourse.*

(1) When an obligee releases the principal obligor from, or agrees to extend the time for performance of, a duty to pay money pursuant to the underlying obligation, the release or extension effect a "preservation of the secondary obligor's recourse" with respect to that duty if the express terms of the release or extension provide that:
    (a) the obligee retains the right to seek performance of the secondary obligation by the secondary obligor; and
    (b) the rights of the secondary obligor to recourse against the principal obligor (§§21-31) continue as though the release or extension had not been granted.
(2) When the obligee effects a preservation of the secondary obligor's recourse in conjunction with a release or extension, the principal obligor's duties of performance and reimbursement and the secondary obligor's rights of restitution and subrogation continue as though the release or extension did not occur.

5. However, if the surety is also an indorser, a delay in presentment (discussed later in the book) may result in a discharge under §3-415(e).

There are other important rules of suretyship (for instance, a surety's promise—the second contract—must be in writing to be enforceable under the Statute of Frauds), but these rules play little part in negotiable instruments law. Section 3-419(b), for instance, completely does away with the Statute of Frauds defense as far as negotiable instruments are concerned. Instead, our study will focus on how the above rules have been varied in the law of negotiable instruments.

5. The Accommodation Party

The Uniform Commercial Code in §3-419 reserves special suretyship rights for those who deliberately lend their names to an instrument to accommodate another. These sections spell out the obligation incurred by the Code's sureties. Section 3-419 applies to an *accommodation party*, defined in subsection (a) as a party who "signs the instrument for the purpose of incurring liability on the instrument without being a direct beneficiary of the value given for the instrument." Read Official Comment 1 to §3-419. Subsection (b) informs us that the accommodation party may sign in any capacity (as maker, drawer, acceptor, or indorser), but is "obligated to pay the instrument in the capacity in which the accommodation party signs." This means that the surety (accommodation party) has the same liability as a maker if the surety signs as a maker, but the surety signing as an indorser is liable only in that capacity (and has the rights of an indorser: presentment, notice of dishonor, etc.); in addition, of course, the surety gets both statutory and common law suretyship rights.

PROBLEM 55

Consider the following promissory note:

FRONT: December 23, 2018

I, *Mary Maker*, promise to pay *$4,000* to the order of *Paul Payee* on December 25, 2018, with interest at 8 percent per annum from date.

/s/ George Generous
/s/ Mary Maker

BACK:

Pay to *Ace Finance* /s/ *Paul Payee*

Ace Finance comes to you early in 2019 and tells you that the note is in default, but that it failed to give notice of dishonor—a right that indorsers have but makers do not—to George Generous.

(a) May George Generous establish his status as surety against a holder in due course? See §3-419(c) with its Official Comment 3, §§3-205(d), 3-605(h).

(b) May George defend on the basis that he received no consideration for his undertaking? See §3-419(b) and its Official Comment 2.

(c) Is George an accommodation maker or an accommodation indorser? See §§3-116(a), 3-204(a); cf. Philadelphia Bond & Mortgage Co. v. Highland Crest Homes, Inc., 221 Pa. Super. 89, 288 A.2d 916 (1972) ("Thus by long established practice judicially noted or otherwise established, a signature in the lower right hand corner of an instrument indicates an intent to sign as the maker of a note or the drawer of a draft.").

It should be emphasized that Article 3's rules apply only to accommodation parties who *sign the instrument*. If the accommodation party signs a *separate* suretyship agreement but not the note itself, common law rules, not the Code, govern the result. See Official Comment 3, last paragraph, to §3-419; Uniwest Mortgage Co. v. Dadecor Condominiums, Inc., 877 F.2d 431 (5th Cir. 1989).

a. Guarantors.   A *guarantor* is a surety who adds words of guaranty to his or her signature ("I hereby guarantee this instrument," for example), but words of guaranty add nothing to the suretyship obligation unless the surety has specifically guaranteed *collection* only, in which case the guarantor is given the extra protections described in §3-419(d), which you should now read.

PROBLEM 56

Suppose in the prior Problem George Generous had written the word *Guarantor* after his name. Would Ace Finance have had to sue Mary Maker first or not? See §3-419(d).

Floor v. Melvin

Illinois Appellate Court, 1972
5 Ill. App. 3d 463, 283 N.E.2d 303

Alloy, J.

The action in the present case was instituted by Majorie Irene Floor in the Circuit Court of LaSalle County to recover money alleged to be due on a promissory note. On motion of defendant Mildred B. Melvin, executrix of the estate of Charles W. Melvin, deceased, an order was entered dismissing the claim for failure to state a cause of action. Claimant, Majorie Irene

Floor, seeks reversal of the order on the theory that the deceased Charles W. Melvin was a guarantor of payment.

On April 14, 1959, Melco, Inc., an Illinois corporation, acting through its president, Charles W. Melvin, made and issued its negotiable promissory note in the principal amount of $12,000.00, payable to the order of Majorie Irene Floor. On the back of the note the following language appears: "For and in consideration of funds advanced herein to Melco, Inc., we irrevocably guarantee Majorie Irene Floor against loss by reason of nonpayment of this note." The signature of Charles W. Melvin, as well as others, appeared below such statement.

The complaint of plaintiff in this case does not allege prosecution of her claim to judgment as against the principal obligor on the note and it, also, does not allege the insolvency of the obligor, Melco, Inc. The only issue, therefore, before the court is whether, with respect to the undertaking on the back of the note, plaintiff is required to prosecute her claim against the maker of the note as a pre-condition to making a valid claim as against the estate of Charles W. Melvin.

[The court quoted §3-416, the precursor to §3-419(d)—Eds.] The quoted subsection in the portion marked as "(1)" codifies the rule of several Illinois cases including Beebe v. Kirkpatrick, 321 Ill. 612, 152 N.E. 539, and Weger v. Robinson Nash Motor Co., 340 Ill. 81, 172 N.E. 7. In the *Weger* case referred to, the guaranty contract that had been executed read (at page 85, 172 N.E. at page 9):

> We, the undersigned directors and stockholders of the Robinson Nash Motor Company, do hereby guarantee the *payment of notes* of said company given the Robinson State Bank of Robinson, Illinois, and hereby agree to be personally liable therefore and to all the conditions and requirements written in said notes . . . [emphasis ours].

The court in construing said language said, at page 90, 172 N.E. at page 11:

> A contract guaranteeing the payment of a note is an absolute contract, and by it the guarantor undertakes for a valuable consideration, to pay the debt at maturity if the principal debtor fails to do so, and upon it, if the debt is not paid at maturity, the guarantor may be sued at once. Guarantors must be regarded as original promisors, who bound themselves to pay the notes when they matured, and their duty was, on their maturity, to go to the holder and take them up, and their liability was not to depend upon the prosecution of suit against the maker.

In Beebe v. Kirkpatrick, 321 Ill. 612, 152 N.E. 539, the question was with respect to construction of the words "I hereby guarantee this loan." In support of its holding that the cited language was absolute in nature, the Supreme Court stated (at page 616, 152 N.E. at pages 540-541):

> In this state contracts of guaranty of negotiable instruments are of two kinds: Contracts guaranteeing the collection of the notes, and contracts guaranteeing the payment of the notes. A contract guaranteeing the collection of a note or debt is conditional in its character, and the guarantor thereby undertakes to pay the debt upon condition that the owner thereof shall make use of the ordinary legal means to collect it from the debtor with diligence but without avail. A contract guaranteeing the payment of a note or a debt is an absolute contract, and by it the guarantor undertakes, for a valuable consideration, to pay the debt at maturity if the principal debtor fails to do so, and upon it, if the debt is not paid at maturity, the guarantor may be sued at once.

Other cases, such as Dillman v. Nadelhoffer, 160 Ill. 121, 43 N.E. 378, treat the language of subsection (2) referring to "collection guaranteed." In the *Dillman* case the language before the court was "for a valuable consideration, we do hereby guarantee the collection of the within note at its maturity . . ." (at page 124, 43 N.E. at page 378). In construing this language, the Supreme Court stated that "the guaranty is not a guaranty of the payment of the note, but a guaranty of the collection of the note." The court stated (at page 125, 43 N.E. at page 379) that a contract guaranteeing the collection of a note or debt is conditional in its character and the guarantor thereby undertakes to pay the debt, "upon condition that the owner thereof shall make use of the ordinary legal means to collect it from the principal debtor with diligence, and without avail."

In the cause before us, the primary contention made by plaintiff is that the language of defendant's guarantee presents an absolute undertaking and is, therefore, a guarantee of payment within purview of subsection (1) of the statute in question. In support of that contention, Beebe v. Kirkpatrick, 321 Ill. 612, 152 N.E. 539, Hance v. Miller, 21 Ill. 636, and Empire Sec. Co. v. Berry, 211 Ill. App. 278, are cited as authority. We have indicated that in the *Beebe* case, the court found that the language "I hereby guarantee this loan" presented a guarantee of payment and not collection. The *Hance* case involved construction of language which read "For value received I guarantee payment of the within note at maturity." Consistently, the court had no difficulty in construing that language to be a guarantee of payment. In the *Berry* case, the guarantor had agreed to pay the note if the maker did not "retire" it at maturity. The court found that the word "retire" as used in the context meant "pay" and, therefore, that the guarantee was of payment and not of collection.

The language involved in each of the cases referred to by plaintiff is clearly in conformity with the law in Illinois regarding guaranty contracts.

We believe, however, that plaintiff draws an erroneous analogy between guarantees appearing in those cases and that which we have under consideration in the cause before us. In our opinion, the terms of the guarantee in the instant case are made conditional upon collection of the note. While it is true that the word "collection" has not been used, in our view the guarantee as against "loss" is in effect a guarantee of collection rather than payment. At least one case of another jurisdiction, Michelin Tire Co. v. Cutter, 116 Or. 217, 240 P. 895 (1925), involved language similar to that in the instant case. There the defendant agreed to indemnify plaintiff against "any loss on account of any monies" which a certain party may owe from time to time. The court had no difficulty in concluding that the guarantee involved was of collection and not of payment in that case. . . .

A final contention made by plaintiff is that subsection "(3)" of the Illinois statute quoted earlier in our opinion to the effect that where words of guaranty do not otherwise specify, the guarantee [is] of payment could be controlling in such case. We cannot agree with such analysis since it is apparent that the use of subsection "(3)" is limited to instances where no conditional language of the type we find in the present case has been used.

We, therefore, conclude that it is apparent that the instant guarantee is one of collection and not of payment. Since plaintiff does not allege that her claim was prosecuted to judgment and execution thereon returned unsatisfied or that the maker was insolvent, she has not complied with Section 3-416(2) of the Uniform Commercial Code (Illinois Revised Statutes, Ch. 26). The trial court's dismissal of the action was, therefore, proper, and should be affirmed.

Affirmed.

Strouder, J., and Dixon, J., concur.

———————————

To recap: the Uniform Commercial Code's *accommodation maker, accommodation indorser,* and *guarantor*—known to non-lawyers as *co-signers*—are nothing more than common law sureties dressed up with new labels, their rights partially codified. The common law rights of subrogation and reimbursement are codified in §3-419(f), which states that an "accommodation party who pays the instrument is entitled to enforce the instrument against the accommodated party. An accommodated party who pays the instrument has no right of recourse against, and is not entitled to contribution from, an accommodation party."

b. Who Is the Surety?   In most cases, the form of the transaction or the language of the promissory note makes it clear which party signed for accommodation. Section 3-419(a) has a basic definition, which you should read, noting particularly the "direct benefit" test therein. Situations can arise, as the Problem below illustrates, in which the usual presumptions are turned on their head, and the issue becomes more complicated.

PROBLEM 57

When Portia Moot graduated from law school, she moved to a new city and needed to borrow money but discovered that her credit rating was so bad no one would lend her the money. She appealed to her mother, Margaret Moot, a successful doctor, and Margaret agreed to help her out. Margaret borrowed $5,000 from Octopus National Bank (ONB), signing a promissory note as maker with the bank as payee. Margaret had Portia indorse the note on the back before it was handed over to ONB in return for the money.

(a) If Margaret Moot is forced to pay this note when it matures, can she sue Portia, the indorser? Normally, the maker of the note has no cause of action against indorsers, whose §3-415(a) obligation runs to "a person entitled to enforce the instrument," defined in §3-301 as the holder (itself defined in §1-201(b)(21) as the person identified in the instrument as the person to whom it is payable, which would not include the maker).

(b) If ONB recovers its money from Portia at maturity, can Portia sue her mother, whose maker's obligation, §3-412, does run to indorsers such as Portia?

In the above Problem, Portia has made what is called an *anomalous indorsement*, §3-205(d), one that is put on the instrument by a non-holder, and that can only mean that she signed for accommodation. Anyone looking at this note should know that Portia is a surety; she is not named as the payee, but is the first person to indorse the note and must therefore have signed for some reason other than negotiation. This means that (if it had been relevant) in the above Problem the bank is conclusively presumed to know that Portia is entitled to be treated as a surety. The mere fact that the bank is presumed to know of Portia's accommodation status does not, however, keep the bank from becoming a holder in due course. A surety may prove accommodation status against a knowledgeable holder in due course or against a non-holder in due course, but if a holder in due course has no reason to know that a party is a surety, the holder in due course will take free of the suretyship defenses. See §3-605(h).

6. Tender of Payment

Read the "tender of payment" rule (§3-603), which has meaning beyond suretyship problems; indeed, you may skip the last sentence of §3-603(c), which deals with an issue to be considered later. For an excellent article on point, see Comment, Tender of Payment Under UCC §3-604: A Forgotten Defense?, 39 Ohio St. L.J. 833 (1978). Use §3-603 to solve the following Problem.

PROBLEM 58

When Saul Panzer needed to borrow money, his friend Rex Stout agreed to loan him $10,000 if Saul could get a co-signer. Saul talked Orrie Cather into signing Saul's promissory note as co-maker. The note was payable to the order of Rex Stout, who loaned Saul the $10,000 and took the note in return for the money. Stout indorsed the note and sold it at a discount to Archie Goodwin.

(a) On the date the note matured, knowing that Saul Panzer, the maker, was in financial trouble and, wanting to stop the running of interest,[6] Orrie Cather, the co-signer, went to Archie Goodwin, the current holder, and offered to pay the note, planning to seek reimbursement from Saul. Goodwin replied, "Let's give poor Saul a chance to pay it off himself." A month later, Saul went bankrupt, and Goodwin demanded that Cather pay the initial amount due plus interest for the extra month. Cather refused, and Goodwin sued, adding a claim for attorney's fees. To what is he entitled, if anything? See §3-603(c)'s first sentence; Kennedy v. Boles Investments, Inc., 53 So. 3d 60 (Ala. 2010).

(b) On the due date Saul went to Goodwin and offered to pay, but Goodwin said, "Look, I know you need the money for your other bills—pay me next month." A month later Saul went bankrupt. Can Goodwin now recover from Cather? From Stout, the payee/indorser? See §3-603(b).

(c) Instead of the above, assume that on the maturity date Orrie Cather went to Goodwin and offered to pay the debt, to which Goodwin made the same reply. A month later, Saul went bankrupt, and Orrie Cather filed for bankruptcy at the same time. Is Stout, the payee/indorser, liable to Goodwin? Cf. §3-415(a).

7. Section 3-605 — *Strictissimi Juris* Again

Sureties are the beneficiaries of a number of common law maxims, among them that a "surety is a favorite of the law" and that "security follows the debt." The former you must remember to quote to the court should your client be a surety. The latter refers to the collateral (*security*) given to the creditor by the principal and means that on paying off the creditor

---

6. Section §3-112 requires the instrument to specify an interest rate or it has none.

and thereby acquiring the negotiable instrument (*debt*), the surety is also entitled to that collateral.

It follows that the surety has an interest in the creditor's handling of the collateral. Both at common law and under §3-605(e), (f), and (g) [§3-605(d) in the 2002 revision of this section] the non-consenting surety is discharged, up to the value of the collateral, if the creditor (holder) fails to protect the collateral and if it is thereby unavailable to pay the debt.

PROBLEM 59

When Butch Byrd borrowed $10,000 from Octopus National Bank, the bank not only made him get a surety, but also demanded that the inventory of Butch's feed store stand as collateral. Butch talked his brother Arnold into signing the promissory note as a guarantor and signed the necessary papers for the bank to get an Article 9 security interest in the inventory. Unfortunately, the bank failed to file the Article 9 financing statement in the correct place, so when Butch had financial difficulties, other creditors prevailed over the bank's attempt to claim the inventory. The inventory was worth $6,000. What is the effect of the bank's Article 9 difficulties on Arnold's liability? See §3-605(e) and (g) [§3-605(d) in the 2002 revision of this section]; Cliff Findlay Automotive, LLC v. Olson, 228 Ariz. 115, 263 P.3d 664 (Ariz. App. 2011).

Chemical Bank v. Pic Motors Corp.

New York Supreme Court, Appellate Division, 1982
87 A.D.2d 447, 452 N.Y.S.2d 41,
aff'd on the opinion below, 58 N.Y.2d 1023, 448 N.E.2d 1349,
462 N.Y.S.2d 438

Fein, J.

Pic, an established car dealership, entered into an inventory financing agreement with plaintiff Bank, pursuant to which the Bank agreed to lend funds to Pic periodically under an established line of credit on the security of Pic's inventory of automobiles as collateral. Under this form of agreement, known as floor plan financing, the borrower draws upon the line of credit for the purpose of financing the purchase of automobiles for sale. The Bank extends loans within the credit limit based on the value of the vehicles purchased by the borrower. Upon the sale of any vehicle, the borrower pays back the portion of the loan that was granted based on the value of that vehicle. Thus, the bank loan always remains secured. Sales to purchasers in the ordinary course of business are made free of the Bank's lien. As a matter of practice, the Bank conducted periodic inspections of Pic's inventory to determine whether the financed vehicles were owned by Pic and whether the loan was reduced by an appropriate payment upon sale of a financed vehicle. The Bank also followed a curtailment policy under which any loan was proportionately reduced and finally paid in full for inventory remaining unsold over specified periods of time.

Siegel had been director, president and principal stockholder of Pic for many years and had personally guaranteed the loans in writing. In 1978 Siegel sold his interest in the company to defendant Manfred Robl and resigned as an officer and director of Pic. However, it is undisputed that his guaranty continued, as agreed, during all the relevant periods of time. The guaranty reads, in pertinent part, as follows:

> NOW, THEREFORE, in consideration of the premises and of other good and valuable consideration and in order to induce the Bank from time to time, in its discretion, to extend or continue credit to the Borrower, *the undersigned hereby guarantees, absolutely and unconditionally*, to the Bank *the payment of all liabilities of the Borrower to the Bank of whatever nature, whether now existing or hereafter incurred*, whether created directly or acquired by the Bank by assignment or otherwise, whether matured or unmatured and whether absolute or contingent (all of which are hereinafter collectively referred to as the "Liabilities of the Borrower"). . . .
>
> The undersigned hereby consents that from time to time, before or after any default by the Borrower or any notice of termination hereof, *with or without further notice to or assent from the undersigned, any security* at any time held by or available to the Bank for any obligation of the Borrower, or any security at any time held by or available to the Bank for any obligation of any other person secondarily or otherwise liable for any of the Liabilities of the Borrower, *may be exchanged, surrendered or released* and any obligation of the Borrower, or of any such other person, *may be changed, altered, renewed, extended, continued, surrendered, compromised, waived or released in whole or in part*, . . . and *the Bank . . . may extend further credit in any manner whatsoever to the Borrower*, and generally deal with the Borrower or any such security or other person as the Bank may see fit; *and the undersigned shall remain bound under this guaranty notwithstanding any such exchange, surrender, release, change, alteration, renewal, extension, continuance, compromise, waiver, inaction, extension of further credit or other dealing*.
>
> The undersigned thereby waives (a) notice of acceptance of this guaranty and of extensions of credit by the Bank to the Borrower; (b) presentment and demand for payment of any of the Liabilities of the Borrower; (c) protest and notice of dishonor or default to the undersigned or to any other party with respect to any of the Liabilities of the Borrower; (d) all other notices to which the undersigned might otherwise be entitled; and (e) any demand for payment under this guaranty.
>
> This is a guaranty of payment and not of collection. . . .
>
> . . . [N]or in the event shall any modification or waiver of the provisions of this guaranty be effective unless in writing nor shall any such waiver be applicable except in the specific instance for which given. [Emphases added.]

In July 1979 the Bank informed Siegel that Pic was "out of trust." More than 50 percent of the inventory was unaccounted for. Pursuant to an understanding with the Bank, Siegel arranged for the sale of the remaining inventory and partial repayment was made. Following demand, the Bank instituted suit for the balance against Pic and the individual guarantors, including Siegel. Siegel appeals from the summary judgment granted against him as guarantor.

By way of defense, Siegel asserts that the deficiency was caused by the failure of the Bank to conduct regular inspections and to enforce its curtailment policy. He further alleges that two of the Bank's employees, either negligently or in complicity with Robl, submitted incorrect or false inventory reports and approved loans on nonexistent automobiles. Siegel asserts that he was assured, as a condition of his continuing guaranty upon his sale to Robl, that regular inspections and enforcement of the curtailment policy would continue. He asserts that the activities of the Bank and its employees impaired the value of the collateral, thus relieving him from liability.

Siegel argues there is a triable issue as to whether the Bank was obligated to conduct regular inspections and enforce the curtailment program, and whether the dishonesty or negligence of the Bank's employees operated to impair the collateral and thus discharge his obligation as guarantor.

It is undisputed that there is no provision in the inventory financing agreement or in the guaranty obligating the Bank to conduct inspections or to maintain the curtailment policy. The guaranty is a fully integrated unambiguous contract which by its terms could not be modified or varied by parol or by an alleged course of conduct. The guaranty expressly provides, in pertinent part:

> This is a guaranty of payment and not of collection and the undersigned further waives any right to require that any action be brought against the Borrower or any other person or to require that resort be had to any security. . . .
>
> No delay on the part of the Bank in exercising any rights hereunder or failure to exercise the same shall operate as a waiver of such rights; no notice to or demand on the undersigned shall be deemed to be a waiver of the obligation of the undersigned or of the right of the Bank to take further action without notice or demand as provided herein; nor in any event shall any modification or waiver of the provisions of this guaranty be effective unless in writing, nor shall any such waiver be applicable except in the specific instance for which given.

Thus neither the alleged prior course of conduct nor the alleged promise that it would be continued could modify the obligation of Siegel as guarantor of payment (General Phoenix Corp. v. Cabot, 300 N.Y. 87, 92; General Obligations Law §15-301, subd. 1).

Siegel expressly consented that the

> security at any time held by or available to the Bank . . . may be exchanged, surrendered or released . . . and the undersigned [defendant Siegel] shall remain bound under this guaranty notwithstanding any such . . . release, . . . compromise, . . . inaction, extension of further credit or other dealing.

It is plain that the Bank had the right to release the collateral without discharging the guarantor. If so, the negligence or dishonesty of the Bank's employees in so doing is irrelevant.

As Special Term ruled, the negligence or dishonesty of plaintiff's employees patently would not be deemed within the scope of their authority. Siegel was an unconditional guarantor of payment, not of collection, and the guaranty was not dependent upon any condition precedent other than the non-payment of the indebtedness.

The dissent relies upon Uniform Commercial Code §3-606, which provides in part:

> (1) The holder discharges any party to the instrument to the extent that without such party's consent the holder . . .
>   (b) unjustifiably impairs any collateral for the instrument given by or on behalf of the party or any person against whom he has a right of recourse.

That section applies to commercial paper, negotiable instruments, not to a guaranty such as that here involved (UCC §3-102[1],[e]); Indianapolis Morris Plan Corp. v. Karlen, 28 N.Y.2d 30, 32. Moreover, as that case holds respecting consent to release of collateral:

> Consent may be given in advance, and is commonly incorporated in the instrument, or it may be given afterward. It requires no consideration, and operates as a waiver of the consenting party's right to claim his own discharge. (28 N.Y.2d at p. 34, quoting the Official Comment to UCC §3-606.)

In *Indianapolis Morris Plan Corp.*, supra, the lender consented to the substitution of gas consuming equipment for the mortgaged electrical cooking equipment. The debtor failed and the gas company repossessed the substituted equipment on which it had a seller's lien. The collateral security was dissipated by the substitution and the repossession of the substitute. The consent to release of security provided for in the promissory note operated to prevent the discharge of the sureties although they had no notice of these events and had not consented thereto.

Our case stands on the same footing. The consent to release of security was broad and all encompassing so as to preclude discharge of the guarantor.

Under the terms of this guaranty there was no obligation to preserve and protect the collateral. The dissent's reliance upon Executive Bank [of Fort Lauderdale] v. Tighe (66 A.D.2d 70) is misplaced. That case holds only that pursuant to UCC §3-606, a guarantor's waiver of the obligation not to impair collateral will not excuse the creditor's failure properly to file the security instrument as required by law, unless the waiver expressly so provides. That issue is not here involved. (See Lafayette Bank & Trust Co. of Suffern v. Silver, 58 Misc. 2d 891.)

Similarly, Federal Deposit Insurance Corp. v. Frank L. Marino Corp., 74 A.D.2d 620, relied upon by the dissent, is not applicable. In that case the collateral was in the possession of the creditor who negligently failed to liquidate it upon the guarantor's demand. The guarantor could not be chargeable with the decline in value of the collateral. In our case the collateral was in the possession of the debtor, not the creditor, and Siegel, as guarantor, was afforded the opportunity to liquidate it, which he did.

For the same reason, Sterling Factors Corp. v. Freeman (50 Misc. 2d 715), relied upon by the dissent, is inapposite. In that case the creditor had replevied the collateral and purchased it at a price far less than its worth, without notice to the guarantors. It then proceeded to sell the collateral at a higher price without giving credit to the guarantors. This was a blatant fraud, held to preclude any recovery against the guarantors. This has nothing to do with our case, where the Bank never had possession of the collateral.

Under the express terms of the guaranty here involved, the Bank could release or surrender the collateral without notifying or discharging Siegel. It could also extend further credit to Pic on an unsecured basis without notifying or releasing Siegel. Hence the complained of actions of the Bank's employees are of no aid to Siegel. We must "take the guaranty as we find it as the surest way of determining the rights of these parties." (Corn Exchange Bank Trust Co. v. Gifford, 268 N.Y. 153, 158.)

Nothing in the agreements or in the Uniform Commercial Code provides for the release of Siegel as unconditional guarantor of payment under the circumstances. In the face of the guaranty as written there was no duty upon the creditor to preserve or protect the collateral. Where the collateral is in the possession of the debtor, inaction by the creditor, negligent or otherwise, does not release a guarantor who has executed such a waiver. A surety may waive any obligation upon the part of a creditor, including the obligation of the creditor not to impair the security (Indianapolis Morris Plan Corp. v. Karlen, supra). The parties, by agreement, may determine the standards by which the fulfillment of the rights and duties of the secured party may be measured (UCC §9-501[3]).

Accordingly, the order of the Supreme Court, New York County (Helman, J.), entered on August 12, 1980 granting plaintiff summary judgment against defendant Aaron Siegel in the sum of $189,717.17 should be affirmed with costs.

[All concur except Bloom and Milonas, J., who dissent in an opinion by Milonas, J.]

MILONAS, J. (dissenting). I would reverse and remand for further proceedings. . . .

Under the express terms of the agreement between Siegel and the bank, the undersigned purportedly undertook to remain bound regardless of any compromise to the security. However, where the bank's negligence has, in contravention of UCC §9-207, resulted in a breach of its duty to preserve and protect the collateral, a waiver "will not be enforced so as to bar a viable setoff or counterclaim sounding in fraud . . ." or where "based upon the creditor's negligence in failing to liquidate collateral upon the guarantor's demand . . ." (Federal Deposit Insurance Corp. v. Frank L. Marino Corp., 74 A.D.2d 620, at p. 621). As the court therein explained, to enforce such a waiver provision when there is a triable issue of fact as to the creditor's negligence would enable a creditor to shield itself from its own tortious conduct.

"The holder of security [here the inventory] is not at liberty to do any affirmative act which would impair the security and so deprive the guarantors of the benefit they might derive on a proper liquidation or upon their payment under their guaranty . . ." (Sterling Factors Corporation v. Freeman, 50 Misc. 2d 715, at p. 720). In the instant case, whether the bank can be held liable for the tortious acts of its employees presents a clear issue of fact such as to render summary judgment inappropriate. To maintain that a guarantor will always be bound on the underlying obligation, notwithstanding any negligent, fraudulent or tortious conduct on the part of the creditor, simply by the expedient of the creditor's inserting a clause to that effect in the agreement is to undermine completely the spirit of the UCC and is, in my opinion, contrary to public policy.

Order filed.

PROBLEM 60

George and Martha Washington borrowed $10,000 from the Mt. Vernon Finance Company, both signing a promissory note for the amount borrowed. To secure the note, the bank took a mortgage on Martha's vineyard, but failed to file its mortgage in the proper place. Before the note matured, Martha filed for bankruptcy, and the bankruptcy creditors were able to get the vineyard free and clear of the bank's mortgage. Is George discharged in whole or in part by §3-605(e)? By §3-605(f)? If Martha had not filed for bankruptcy, but the vineyard was still lost when the state seized it because she hadn't paid her taxes, is *she* discharged by the bank's failure to perfect its interest in the vineyard? As to all this, see Official Comment 7 to §3-605.

You will recall that at common law any change in the basic contract discharged the surety unless the surety consented. In addition, a binding agreement by the creditor not to sue the principal or to give the principal extra time to pay released the non-consenting surety unless the creditor "preserved rights" against the surety. These issues are treated very differently in Article 3, which permits certain agreements between the creditor (the current holder of the instrument) and the principal (the accommodated party) without a discharge of the surety/indorser. There is a complication, however, and it is that the 2002 revision of Article 3 substantially rewrote §3-605 to make its rules conform to those of the Restatement (Third) of Suretyship and Guaranty, which is a partial return to the rules of the common law. That 2002 revision has only been adopted in 12 or so states as of this writing, and the other states used the wording of the 1990 version of Article 3. Your instructor will tell you whether to answer the questions in the following Problem by looking at the language of the 1990 version of Article 3 or the newer 2002 version (cited in the Problem by using the letter "R"). The pre-2002 version of this section (which is the law in most states) can be found in the Appendix at the back of the book.

PROBLEM 61

When Jack Point borrowed $75,000 from Yeomen National Bank to start up his carnival business, the bank made him sign a promissory note in its favor and get a surety. Point talked his good friend Wilfred Shadbolt into signing as an accommodation maker. Is Shadbolt discharged by any of the following agreements between Yeoman National and Point?

(a) When the note matured, Point told Yeomen National that his business had gone bust and that he was thinking about filing a bankruptcy petition. Worried that it would get nothing in the bankruptcy distribution, Yeomen National persuaded him to pay all he could, a mere $5,000, and then signed an agreement with Point excusing him from having to pay the rest of the debt. The bank then demanded that Shadbolt pay the amount still due. Does Shadbolt owe it? See §3-605(b); §3R-605(a) and (g). Does the accord and satisfaction agreement between the bank and Point also bind Shadbolt, or may the latter still seek complete reimbursement from Point? See §3-419(e) and Official Comment 3 to §3-605; §3R-605(a) and its Official Comment 4.

(b) Assume instead that when the note matured, Point went to the bank and asked for more time in which to pay. The bank did this, giving Point an extra six months. No one notified Shadbolt of this extension. At the end of the six-month period, Point filed for bankruptcy instead of paying the note. Was Shadbolt discharged by the bank's actions? Would your answer change depending on whether or not Point ever had the money to pay the note at any relevant period? See §3-605(c) and its Official Comment 4; §3R-605(b) and its Official Comment 5. Who has the burden of proof on the issues? See §§3-605(b), 3R-605(h). Could Shadbolt, had he known of the extension agreement, have ignored it, paid the note, and then sued Point for reimbursement? The original statute is silent on this; in the 2002 revision see §3R-605(b)(3).

(c) Assume instead that when the note was signed, the bank also made Point put up 100 shares of stock as collateral for the debt. Before the note matured Point went to the bank and asked to have the stock back, saying he needed to take advantage of a stock split the issuing corporation was offering. The bank returned the stock to him, but made him agree to pay a higher rate of interest. The original note contained a clause by which the surety automatically agreed in advance to any impairment of the collateral. Has Shadbolt nonetheless been discharged? Who has the burden of proof here? See §3-605(d) and its Official Comment 5; §3R-605(c) and (h) and its Official Comment 6.

(d) Is there a simple way that the bank could have avoided all these issues *ab initio*? See §3-605(i) and its Official Comment 2; §3R-605(f).

London Leasing Corp. v. Interfina, Inc.

New York Supreme Court, 1967
53 Misc. 2d 657, 279 N.Y.S.2d 209

CRAWFORD, J.

The fundamental question presented on this motion is whether a corporate officer (president) who makes a note on behalf of his corporation and, also, personally endorses that note is discharged from *personal* liability on the note by an agreement between the payee and the corporate maker, by its said president, which extends the corporate maker's time to pay the note.

This is a motion pursuant to C.P.L.R. 3213 for summary judgment against defendants Interfina, Inc., and its president, Fredrick J. Evans. On May 3, 1966, Interfina made and delivered to plaintiff a promissory note in the sum of $52,000, signed by Fredrick J. Evans, as president of Interfina, and also personally endorsed by Fredrick J. Evans. The note was not paid on its due date, August 2, 1966, and thereafter, on August 3, 15 and 19, Interfina, by its president, entered into letter agreements with the plaintiff extending the time for payment of the note. Fredrick J. Evans signed the agreements, but only in his corporate capacity.

The sum of $19,500 is due on the note and as against defendant Interfina there is no question that summary judgment should be granted.

In opposition to the motion as against him, defendant Evans contends that the extension agreements, which were not signed by him in his personal capacity, as a matter of law discharged him from personal liability on the note because he did not personally consent to the extension.

[The court quoted §3-606, the original version of what is now §3-605 — Eds.] The Code does not explicitly define the meaning of the term "consent." However, the Official Comment to §3-606 states:

> 2. Consent may be given in advance, and is commonly incorporated in the instrument, or it may be given afterward. It requires no consideration, and operates as a waiver of the consenting party's right to claim his own discharge. . . .

In the pre-Code case of National Park Bank v. Koehler (204 N.Y. 174), the court explained the rationale which underlies the rule that an endorser is discharged by the maker's agreement with the payee entered into without the endorser's consent to extend the maker's time to pay a note. The court said at pages 179-180:

> . . . It is a rule, long recognized, that an accommodation indorser, or surety, is entitled to have the engagement of the principal debtor preserved, without variation in its terms, and that his *assent* to any change therein is essential to the continuance of his obligation. The reason of the rule is that his right must not be affected, upon the maturity of the indebtedness, to make payment and, by subrogation to the creditor's place, to, at once, proceed against the principal debtor to enforce repayment. Therefore it is that any agreement of the creditor, which operates to extend the time of payment of the original debt and suspends the right to immediate action, is held to discharge the non-assenting indorser, or surety; as the law will presume injury to him thereby. The creditor may arrange with his debtor, in any way, which does not result in effecting either of these results. He may take, as collateral to the old note, new security, or other notes, and, if time is not given to the debtor, the indorser, or surety, will not be discharged. To prevent such a result, the agreement must expressly reserve all the remedies of the creditor against the indorser, or surety; in which case the latter will be in a position to pay immediately and, then, to proceed against the principal debtor. . . .

In the absence of a clear Code definition of "consent," this court is guided by the statement in Stearns Law of Suretyship (5th ed., §6.13):

> Parties to a contract may always alter it by mutual agreement and this is true of suretyship contract as others. Accordingly, if the creditor and principal modify their contract, and the surety consents thereto, he will not be discharged. Such consent need not be expressly given, *but may be implied from the surrounding circumstances or from his conduct.* [Emphasis supplied.]

The Court in In re Grottola's Estate (124 N.Y.S.2d 85) was also guided by this principle. The court stated, at page 88:

> . . . Thus the voluntary release or surrender of security by the creditor without the consent of the surety will discharge the latter to the extent of the value of the property so released. Stearns Law of Suretyship, Elder's Revision, 5th Edition, §6.46; Cohen v. Rossmoore. If, however, the surety consents to a modification of the contract between the principal debtor and the creditor he will not be discharged. Stearns Law of Suretyship, supra, sec. 6.13. The author states at page 129: "Such consent need not be expressly given, but may be implied from the surrounding circumstances or from his conduct." *Here the deceased endorser was the president and the principal stockholder of Ventura Acres, Inc., the maker of the note. Subsequent to the death of the accommodation endorser the executrix of his will, or her attorney, solicited and secured from the creditor the release of mortgage and satisfaction thereof in question. The court holds that such action on the part of the endorser's legal representative constituted a consent to the satisfaction of the mortgage held by the creditor as security for the loan in question.* Vose v. Florida Railroad Co., Stearns Law of Suretyship, supra. . . . [Emphases supplied.]

The application of this principle to the present question mandates a holding that defendant Evans consented to the extension. As a matter of fact he applied for, negotiated, signed in his corporate capacity, and received the agreements extending the time for payment. While mere knowledge or acquiescence is not, in and of itself, sufficient to prevent discharge, the defendant's conduct here far exceeded these limits and, under the special circumstances here presented, constituted consent.

Accordingly, the motion for summary judgment in the sum of $19,500 is granted as against both defendants. Submit order.

The 2002 revision to §3-605 speaks directly to this point, adding to §3R-605(f) this sentence: "Unless the circumstances indicate otherwise, consent by the principal obligor to an act that would lead to discharge under this section constitutes consent to that act by the secondary obligor if the secondary obligor controls the principal obligor or deals with the person entitled to enforce the instrument on behalf of the principal obligor."

8.   New Notes for Old

PROBLEM 62

In 2018 Rex Lear borrowed $5,000 from the Kent Lending Corporation and gave them his promissory note due June 8, 2021. Rex had his daughter

Cordelia sign as accommodation maker. Early in 2021 Rex defaulted on the installment payments and in return for mercy by the lending company, he signed a new promissory note dated January 11, 2021, payable to the company September 25, 2021, for the same amount but with additional collateral. The Kent Lending Corporation kept the first note as security for the payment of the second. Cordelia never signed the second note. Answer these questions:

(a) Can the payee sue on the *first* note prior to September 25, 2021? See §3-310(b)(2).

(b) If Lear does not pay the second note when it matures, can Kent sue on the *first* note, or has it been paid and discharged by the second note? See §3-310(b)(2).

(c) Assume that Cordelia can prove that the failure of the lender to enforce its rights on the first note caused her major damages in that Lear's financial situation deteriorated drastically between January 11 and September 25, 2021. Is Cordelia still liable on the first note? See §3-605(c); §3R-605(b) and (h).

PROBLEM 63

Sam Selachii was the surety on a promissory note that Marty Make had given to the Dogfish Loan Company along with a pledge of 100 shares of Titanic Telephone stock to secure the loan for $800. Shortly after receiving the loan, Marty asked for the stock back, saying that he wanted to sell it and buy other stock that he would repledge as collateral. Dogfish gave him back the stock, which Marty sold. He used the proceeds to finance a bad day at the races. A week later, Dogfish transferred the note for value to the Hammerhead Loan Company, a bona fide purchaser. Assume that Sam has been discharged under §3-605(e) [§3R-605(d)] (impairment of the collateral). Is he still liable to Hammerhead? See §§3-305(b), 3-601(b), and 3-302(b).

D. The Drawer's Obligation

To make this discussion more relevant, consider that checks are drafts, and the liability described next is the one you incur every time you sign a check and send it out into the world.

The drawer of a draft incurs the obligation specified in §3-414, which you should read now. It is sometimes said that the drawer's liability is *secondary* because the draft must first be presented to the drawee for payment and dishonored by the drawee before the drawer has a legal obligation to pay the instrument (unlike the liability of a maker of a note, which is *primary* since it is not subject to these conditions precedent). Why should the drawer's liability be different from that of a maker? The answer is that, with a draft, it is the understanding of all the parties that the payee will first attempt to secure payment from the drawee (a *presentment*) and only look to the drawer if the drawee refuses to pay (makes a *dishonor*). Consider, for example, that if I, your neighbor, owe you money and give you a check for the amount due, common sense tells you that you must first try to collect the check from my bank. Only if my bank refuses to pay the check can you expect me to make the check good. What are these technical rights of presentment, dishonor, and protest? They are discussed exhaustively in the 3-500 sections of the Code.

1. Presentment and Dishonor

Presentment is the demand for payment made to the maker of the note or, for drafts, to the drawee. Read §3-501 (defining and describing *presentment*). Under the NIL the holder was required to exhibit the instrument at the moment of presentment (NIL 74), but the Code is more flexible — exhibition is required only if the presentee demands it. Read §3-501(b)(2), which sets out other rights of the presentee.

Dishonor is the refusal of the presentee to pay. Read §3-502.

PROBLEM 64

Archibald Grosvenor finally paid off an old debt to Reginald Bunthorne by giving him a check drawn on the Patience National Bank. Bunthorne took the check to the bank and demanded payment. The bank asked him to sign his name on the back, but Bunthorne refused, saying, "I will never put my name on any check Grosvenor has touched." If the bank declines to pay the check, has a technical dishonor occurred? See §§3-501(b)(3)(i), 3-501(b)(2)(iii). This may be important because Grosvenor's §3-414 obligation is conditioned on a dishonor, and he can no longer be sued on the underlying obligation that is suspended until dishonor by §3-310.

PROBLEM 65

When Grosvenor gave Bunthorne a check to pay off an old debt, Bunthorne negligently lost it behind the sofa and didn't find it for eight months. The bank it was drawn on refused to pay it because it was suspiciously old (see §4-404). Is Grosvenor still liable on this check? See §3-414(f). Would he be if the drawee bank had folded five months after the check was written but before it was presented? If Bunthorne had indorsed the check the day after it was issued to him and then cashed it at the corner drugstore and the drugstore mislaid it for five months before the drawee bank dishonored it, is Bunthorne still liable to the drugstore? See §3-415(e).

Messing v. Bank of America, N.A.

Maryland Court of Special Appeals, 2002
143 Md. App. 1, 792 A.2d 312, *aff'd*, 821 A.2d 22

KRAUSER, Judge.

This appeal focuses on one of the most expressive parts of the human body—the thumb: "thumbs up" (approval), "thumbs down" (disapproval), "thumbing one's nose" (defiance), and "thumbing a ride" (requesting transport).[7] Notwithstanding all of the things we ask of this unassuming two-jointed digit, appellee, Bank of America, adds one more task—personal identification. The thumbprint, if Bank of America has its way, will now be one more means by which the identity of a non-account check holder is expressed and confirmed. This idea has of course not met with universal approval, and that is why this matter of first impression is now before us.

Specifically, we are presented with the question of whether Bank of America's practice of requiring non-account check holders to provide a thumbprint signature before it will honor a check is lawful. Appellant, Jeff E. Messing, claims that it is not and filed a complaint for declaratory judgment in the Circuit for Baltimore City, requesting a declaration that the practice is illegal and an order requiring its cessation. In reply, appellee filed a motion for summary judgment. That motion was granted; appellant's complaint was dismissed; and this appeal followed.

In addition to the question of the legality of appellee's thumbprint signature program, appellant also raises questions as to whether appellee "accepted," "dishonored," or "converted" appellant's check upon presentment. . . .

BACKGROUND

On August 3, 2000, appellant attempted to cash a check for $976 at the Light Street branch office of appellee in Baltimore City. That check was made out to appellant and drawn on a Bank of America customer checking account.

Upon entering the bank, appellant handed the check to a teller. The teller then confirmed the availability of the funds on deposit, and placed the check in a computer validation slot. After "validating" the availability of

---

7. Not to mention, we should add: "thumbing through" (perusing a document), "all thumbs" (clumsiness), and "under one's thumb" (dominance and control).

those funds, the computer stamped the time, date, account number, and teller number on the back of the check. It also placed a hold on $976 in the drawer's account.

The teller then gave the check back to appellant to endorse. After he had endorsed the check, the teller asked appellant for identification. In response, appellant presented his driver's license and a major credit card. The identification information on the license and credit card was then transferred by the teller to the back of the check.

During this transaction, the teller asked appellant if he was a Bank of America customer. When he said "no," the teller returned the check to appellant and requested that he place his "thumbprint signature" on the check in accordance with appellee's thumbprint signature policy for "non-account holders." That policy, which is posted at each teller's station, requires a non-account holder, seeking to cash a check drawn on a Bank of America customer account, to provide a thumbprint signature.

The provision of such a signature is neither messy nor time consuming. A thumbprint signature is created by applying one's right thumb to an inkless fingerprinting device that leaves no ink stain or residue. The thumbprint is then placed on the face of the check between the memo and signature line.

After requesting appellant's thumbprint signature, the teller counted out $976 in cash from her drawer anticipating that appellant would comply with that request. When he refused to do so, the teller indicated that the bank would not be able to complete the transaction without his thumbprint. Appellant then asked to see the branch manager, and the teller referred him to a "Mr. Obrigkeit," the branch manager.

Upon entering the branch manager's office, appellant demanded that the check be cashed despite his refusal to place his thumbprint on the check. The branch manager examined the check and returned it to appellant explaining that because appellant was not an account holder, Bank of America would not cash the check without his thumbprint on the instrument. The requirement of a thumbprint signature from non-account holders was in accordance with the deposit agreement that Bank of America has with each of its account holders. That agreement states that Bank of America is permitted "to establish physical and/or documentary requirements" of payees or other holders who seek to cash an item drawn on a Bank of America customer's account.

Appellant then requested that the branch manager provide him with a copy of the Bank's thumbprint policy. The branch manager contacted appellee's regional headquarters and was informed that no such information was available for public distribution. After the branch manager conveyed that information to appellant, appellant left the bank. Moments later, the teller released the hold on the customer's funds, voided the transaction in the computer, and placed the $976 in cash back in her drawer.

Indignant over the bank's policy, appellant filed a complaint. . . . Appellant also requested that the circuit court order appellee to cease and desist from requiring thumbprint signatures in Maryland. . . . [W]e conclude, for the reasons set forth below, that the circuit court was legally correct in granting appellee's motion for summary judgment and dismissing with prejudice appellant's complaint.

DISCUSSION

I.

Appellant contends that the circuit court erred in construing the "reasonable identification" requirement of C.L. §3-501(b)(2) to include a thumbprint signature if demanded by appellee, notwithstanding appellant's proffer of his driver's license and a credit card. C.L. §3-501(b)(2) provides:

> Upon demand of the person to whom presentment is made, the person making presentment must (i) exhibit the instrument, (ii) give *reasonable identification* and, if presentment is made on behalf of another person, reasonable evidence of authority to do so, and (iii) sign a receipt on the instrument for any payment made or surrender the instrument if full payment is made. (Emphasis added). . . .

While the phrase "reasonable identification" under former U.C.C. §3-505(1)(b), now codified in Maryland as C.L. §3-501(b)(2), has been addressed by the other state courts in other contexts, what constitutes "reasonable identification" under C.L. 3-501(b)(2) — particularly whether a "thumbprint signature" does — is a question that has not been addressed by any federal or state court, at least not in any reported opinion.

Appellee's thumbprint requirement is a form of "reasonable identification" for a number of reasons. First, a thumbprint signature has been accepted by the drafters of the Maryland U.C.C. as an effective, reliable, and accurate way to authenticate a writing on a negotiable instrument. "In accord with the systematic presentation of the U.C.C. and its use of consistent terminology," U.C.C. §1-201 sets forth "46 basic terms" to be used throughout the Code to "offer a starting point for the interpretation of many Code sections." 1 William D. Hawkland, Uniform Commercial Code Series, §1-201:1 (1998). The term "signed" is defined in C.L. §1-201(39) (1975, 1997 Repl. Vol.) as "any symbol executed or adopted by a party with present intention to authenticate a writing," and that definition applies throughout the Maryland U.C.C. As to what "signed" means, the Official Comment to C.L. §1-201(39) states:

> The inclusion of authentication in the definition of "signed" is to make clear that as the term is used in this Act a complete signature is not necessary.

> Authentication may be printed, stamped or written; it may be by initials or by *thumbprint*.

C.L. §1-201, Official Comment 39 (1975, 1997 Repl. Vol.) (emphasis added). . . .

Second, the process that a non-account holder goes through to provide a thumbprint signature is not unreasonably inconvenient. As noted, non-account holders seeking to cash a check are asked to apply their right thumb to an inkless fingerprinting device to create a "thumbprint signature." Unlike fingerprinting—which has repeatedly been upheld as an "unobtrusive" form of identification—thumbprint signatures do not require application of ink nor do they require the participation of more than one digit. In fact, appellant's thumbprint signature program uses an inkless fingerprinting device that leaves no ink stains or residue.

And third, this procedure is a reasonable and necessary answer to the growing incidence of check fraud. The American Bankers Association has reported that check fraud losses have grown, between 1995 and 1997, at an average rate of 17.5 percent. Carreker-Antinori, Provide Your Bank with a Shield of Protection against Check Fraud, Thompson Financial Publishing, at http://www.tfp.com/text/Fraudlink.pdf. "Industry estimates based on survey data show that actual losses from check fraud amounted to $512.3 million in 1997, a 5.2 percent increase over the $487.1 million estimated for 1995." Id.

As a result of the rising level of check fraud, thumbprint programs, as appellee notes, "have been endorsed by the American Bankers Association and more than thirty (30) state bankers associations including Arizona, Maryland, Missouri, Oregon, Texas, Utah and Virginia." Testifying before the United States House of Representatives as to the effectiveness of these programs, Charles L. Owens, former Chief of the Financial Crimes Section of the FBI, stated:

> We have supported implementation of inkless fingerprint policies which have been adopted by over 20 State bankers associations for non-bank customers negotiating checks. Where implemented, these procedures have successfully reduced negotiation of stolen and counterfeit checks by as much as 50 percent.

Computer Generated Check Fraud, Subcommittee on Domestic and International Monetary Policy, Committee on Banking and Financial Services, U.S. House of Representatives, May 1, 1997; see also Perkey v. Department of Motor Vehicles, 42 Cal. 3d 185, 228 Cal. Rptr. 169, 721 P.2d 50, 53 (1986) (stating that the fingerprint requirement is one of the few non-invasive reliable means of combating rampant fraud).

Finally, appellant's contention that a thumbprint does not serve the purposes of the Act is unpersuasive. We agree with appellant that a thumbprint cannot be used, in most instances, to confirm the identity of a non-account checkholder at the time that the check is presented for cashing, as his or her thumbprint is usually not on file with the drawee at that time. We disagree, however, with appellant's conclusion that a thumbprint signature is therefore not "reasonable identification" for purposes of C.L. §3-501(b)(2). . . .

III.

Appellant further asserts that the circuit court erred in holding that the appellee did not dishonor the check under C.L. §3-502(d)(1). That section provides that "if the draft is payable on demand, the draft is dishonored if presentment for payment is duly made to the acceptor and the draft is not paid on the day of presentment." Because the check "presented to [appellee] was payable on demand" and because appellee "accepted the check on August 3, 2000, but did not make payment on that date," appellant concludes that appellee "dishonored the check."

C.L. §3-502(d)(1), however, is not relevant to the instant case because the check in question, as we concluded earlier, was never accepted by appellee. In other words, appellant cites the wrong section of the U.C.C. The section that appellant should have cited is C.L. §3-502(b)(2), as it applies to dishonored "unaccepted" checks.

That section provides that if an unaccepted "draft is payable on demand . . . the draft is dishonored if presentment for payment is duly made to the drawee and the draft is not paid on the day of presentment." C.L. §3-502(b)(2). There is no dishonor, however, if presentment fails "to comply with the terms of the instrument, an agreement of the parties, or other applicable law or rule." C.L. §3-501(b)(3). In the words of one authority:

> If the presentment is not proper, payment or acceptance may be refused by the presentee and this refusal does not constitute a dishonoring of the instrument. This provision comes into play if the presentment does not comply "with the terms of the instrument, an agreement of the parties, or other applicable law or rule."

6B Anderson on the Uniform Commercial Code [Rev] §3-501:15 (3d Ed. 1998).

It is undisputed that appellee had the authority to refuse payment in accordance with the deposit agreement it had with each account holder, including with the drawer of the check in question. Pursuant to that agreement, appellee was permitted to set "physical and/or documentary requirements" for all those who seek to cash a check with appellee. And because appellee had the authority to refuse payment by agreement with its customer under C.L. §3-501(b)(2)(ii) unless "reasonable identification" was presented, appellant's failure to provide his thumbprint rendered the presentment ineffective and did not result in a dishonor of the check when appellee returned it to him. . . .

CASE REMANDED TO THE CIRCUIT COURT FOR FURTHER PROCEEDINGS CONSISTENT WITH THIS OPINION.

The Maryland Court of Appeals, the highest court in that state, affirmed, 373 Md. 672, 821 A.2d 22 (2003), noting only that an agreement between the bank and its customer has no effect on the rights of the check's presenter (though it does insulate the bank from a charge of wrongful dishonor). The court quite agreed that a drawee bank may require the presenter to give a thumbprint. Joined by Chief Judge Bell, Judge Eldridge dissented in this short opinion:

> I agree that the Circuit Court erred in failing to render a declaratory judgment. I cannot agree with the majority's holding that, after the petitioner presented his driver's license and a major credit card, it was "reasonable" to require the petitioner's thumbprint as identification.
>
> Today, honest citizens attempting to cope in this world are constantly being required to show or give drivers' licenses, photo identification cards, social security numbers, the last four digits of social security numbers, mothers' "maiden names," 16 digit account numbers, etc. Now, the majority takes the position that it is "reasonable" for banks and other establishments to require, in addition, thumbprints and fingerprints. Enough is enough. The most reasonable thing in this case was petitioner's "irritation with the Bank of America's Thumbprint Signature Program." (Majority opinion at p. 25.)

2. Notice of Dishonor

Indorsers are also entitled to notice of the dishonor after it occurs (but drawers are entitled to notice of dishonor only if a non-bank acceptor refuses payment of the draft; §3-414(d)). *Notice of dishonor* is defined in §3-503, which you should read.[8] Note that subsection (c) of §3-503 requires notice of dishonor to be given very quickly to be effective.

---

8. *Practice Pointer.* A good attorney advises clients to give notice of dishonor to all prior parties immediately on finding out the check is being returned. See §3-503(b).

3. Protest

Protest is a technical ritual in which an official, normally a notary public, makes a formal presentment of a draft to the drawee and, upon dishonor, draws up, signs, and seals an official statement (called a *protest*) of what happened. The protest may also mention to whom notice of dishonor is given. Read §3-505(b). This ritual is no longer required, but is nonetheless sometimes done because it simplifies proof of these matters. See §3-505(a).

4. Excuse

Under some circumstances—spelled out in detail in §3-504, which you should examine carefully—these technical requirements (presentment, dishonor, notice of dishonor) can become either temporarily or completely unnecessary. For the lawyer whose client has failed to take these technical steps, §3-504 can be a bonanza—the treasure chest from which is pulled the excuse that saves the case.

These technical rights must in some situations give way to the exigencies of life. In an early case, Polk v. Spinds, 5 Cold. (45 Tenn.) 431 (1868), the advent of the Civil War made it "difficult" for the Northern holder of a promissory note signed by a Tennessee maker to make a presentment to the maker until the war ended. The Supreme Court of Tennessee held the presentment and delayed notice of dishonor excused, stating a test that is still often quoted:

> Obstacles of the kind which will excuse, need not be of the degree or extent which make travel, intercourse, presentment, impossible. It is enough if they be of the degree and character which deter men of ordinary prudence, energy and courage, from encountering them in prosecution of business, in respect of which they owe an active and earnest duty, and feel an active and earnest interest.

Id. at 433.

In reading §3-504, note that subsection (c) talks about when *delay* in taking one of these steps is excused (but the step must still be taken), and subsections (a) and (b) address themselves to situations in which the step becomes completely unnecessary.

PROBLEM 66

A promissory note contains a clause stating, "All parties to this note hereby waive all rights to presentment, notice of dishonor, and protest. . . ." Is a clause like this buried in the fine print on the front side of a note sufficient to deprive indorsers of their right to notice of dishonor? See §3-504(a)(iv) and (b)(ii).

PROBLEM 67

Frank Fortune was walking along the street, his pockets stuffed with money and checks he had won with a dazzling display of his prowess in the game of poker, when he was stopped by a creditor, one Mr. Holdit. Holdit demanded payment of a long-due $50 obligation, and Fortune was glad to indorse over to him a check for that amount that Fortune had won from Dan Deuces; Fortune was named as payee on the check. After giving the check to Holdit, Fortune thought better of the whole transaction so he contacted Dan Deuces, the drawer, the next day and persuaded him to stop payment on the check. Holdit held onto the check for six weeks and then took it to his bank, the Creditors National, and cashed it. Creditors National presented the check to the drawee bank, which dishonored it, whereupon Creditors National reclaimed its money from Mr. Holdit. Holdit, now very mad, sued Fortune on his indorser's obligation. Was Frank Fortune discharged by the delay in presentment? See §3-415(e). Was the presentment delay excused within the meaning of §3-504(a)(iv)? See Harik v. Harik, 861 F.2d 139 (6th Cir. 1988).

Makel Textiles, Inc. v. Dolly Originals, Inc.

New York Supreme Court, 1967
1967 WL 8938

SPIEGEL, J.

This is an action by the plaintiff to recover $8,000 on promissory notes executed by defendant Dolly Originals, Inc., on certain of which the names of defendants Nathan Goldberg, Richard L. Lewis, and Fred Kushner appear as endorsers.

Dolly Originals, Inc., originally borrowed $40,000; $30,000 was repaid to the plaintiff. Thereafter a promissory note in the sum of $10,000 (Pl. Ex. 1) was made to the order of the plaintiff by Dolly Originals, Inc., by Nathan Goldberg, president, and also bore the purported signature of Richard L. Lewis. The signature of Nathan Goldberg and the purported signature of Richard L. Lewis, as endorsers also appear on the back of said note. This note was not paid. Thereafter two notes each in the sum of $5,000 (Pl. Exs. 2A and 2B) were executed to the order of the plaintiff by Dolly Originals, Inc., through its president, Nathan Goldberg, and purportedly by Richard L. Lewis. The endorsement on the back of these two notes, which were given in lieu of the $10,000 note, bears the signatures of Nathan Goldberg and Fred Kushner. Five checks, each in the sum of $2,000 (Pl. Exs. 3A-3E), to the order of the plaintiff, were executed simultaneously with the two $5,000 notes and bore the signature of Nathan Goldberg, president of Dolly Originals, Inc., and the name of Richard L. Lewis. One of these checks was deposited and returned unpaid (plaintiff's exhibit 4A). None of the other four checks was deposited. No names of any endorsers appear on the back of these checks. Thereafter two other corporate checks for $2,000 were given by Dolly Originals, Inc., to the plaintiff. One of these was paid. The balance of $8,000 is now the subject of this suit.

After the trial of this action the complaint was dismissed as against the defendant Richard L. Lewis after proof that his signature was not genuine, and judgment was rendered against Dolly Originals, Inc., which offered no defense to the action. There remains only the determination of liability of the individual defendants, Nathan Goldberg and Fred Kushner, the endorsers on the notes.

The said defendants moved to dismiss the complaint at the end of the trial on the ground that the promissory notes of the corporation had never been presented for payment and thus the obligation of the endorsers was discharged; further, that subsequent checks given after the endorsement on the previous notes were taken by the plaintiff in payment of this obligation relieved the defendants of any further liability on this debt. The latter contention has no merit. A check given in payment of an obligation is merely a conditional payment and does not relieve the endorser of his liability on the obligation if the check is unpaid (Uniform Commercial Code §3-802 [§3-310(b) in the Revision — EDS.] . . .).

From all the evidence adduced upon the trial of this action, it appears that the defendant Nathan Goldberg was the president and principal officer of the defendant Dolly Originals, Inc. As such president, he executed the promissory notes and signed the corporate checks hereinabove mentioned. The promissory notes were also endorsed by him as an individual. By virtue of his active participation in the affairs of Dolly Originals, Inc., it is obvious that the defendant Nathan Goldberg well knew that the notes could not be and were not paid from corporate funds. Under these circumstances the obligation to serve Goldberg with notice of dishonor and non-payment must be deemed unnecessary, at least impliedly, within the meaning of the Uniform Commercial Code. Plaintiff's failure to present the notes for payment and give the said defendant notice of non-payment could not and did not injure nor prejudice his rights in any way. Formal notice of presentment and dishonor to Mr. Goldberg would be merely a useless gesture of advising him of a fact with which he was most familiar (UCC §§3-507, 3-511 [§3-504 in the Revision — EDS.]; J.W. O'Bannon Co. v. Curran, 129 App. Div. 90;

William S. Chemical Co. v. Root, 152 N.Y.S. 368; Nemser v. Goldman, 145 N.Y.S.2d 841).

The defendant Fred Kushner was an endorser only, on each of two notes for $5,000 (Pl. Exs. 2A and 2B) above mentioned. As to said defendant Kushner, the record is void of any testimony, or proof of notice of presentment and dishonor as required under the Uniform Commercial Code. Nor is there any evidence of any activity or participation in the affairs of the corporation so as to excuse presentment or notice of dishonor.

Accordingly, the defendant Fred Kushner may have judgment against the plaintiff dismissing the complaint, and the plaintiff may have judgment against the defendant Nathan Goldberg in the sum of $8,000 with interest thereon from May 12, 1965. . . .

E. The Drawee's Obligation

PROBLEM 68

After he brought a successful Truth in Lending action against Octopus National Bank (ONB), attorney Sam Ambulance made the mistake of continuing to bank at ONB. At a time when his bank balance greatly exceeded that amount, Sam wrote an alimony check for $3,000 and gave it to his ex-wife, Sue. Because similar checks had bounced in the past, Sue hurriedly walked the check directly into the bank and presented it across the counter. The teller who took the check alerted the bank's manager, who laughed evilly as he threw it back across the counter at Sue, informing her that Sam's business was no longer welcome at ONB and that it refused to pay any more of his checks, even though there was money in the account sufficient to meet the check. You are the attorney who handled Sue's divorce, so she calls you and asks what she should do. See §§3-408, 3-401(a), 3-414, 4-402.

If you worked through all of those citations diligently, you should arrive at this conclusion: the drawee, not having signed the draft, is not liable on it. The drawee, having signed nothing, incurs no contractual obligation (though it may still be liable to the drawer under §4-402 (wrongful dishonor), which we will discuss in a later chapter).

So far, when we have mentioned *drafts*, we have really been talking only about drafts drawn on banks (checks); the drawee we have been discussing is a bank administering a checking account. But the business community makes much use of the non-bank draft in the purchase and sale of goods, particularly when the parties are in different cities.

The seller agrees to ship buyer 10,000 widgets at $20 each, "payment against sight draft." This means that the seller will draw a draft on the buyer payable on "sight" (when the buyer first sees it). Such a procedure permits the seller to discount the draft with the seller's bank, which will indorse the draft over to a collecting bank in the buyer's city. The collecting bank will make a formal presentment to the buyer-drawee. The parties frequently arrange it so that the collecting bank has control over the goods and will turn them over to the buyer at the moment when the latter pays the draft. Thus, at the moment of payment, buyer receives the goods. No one need trust anyone else.

In the hypothetical, the seller is the drawer, and the buyer is the drawee. The payee on the draft could be any of a number of people—the seller itself, the seller's bank, or simply "bearer." The two banks that transfer the draft will presumably sign it, and as soon as they do so, they will become indorsers. If the buyer dishonors the draft on presentment, the collecting bank will send out the required notices of dishonor and then request payment on the basis of the obligations (indorser and drawer) of the prior parties.

1.   The Non-Bank Acceptor

Sometimes in the sales transaction described above, the buyer will ask for time in which to pay the draft after receiving the goods. In such a case, the seller will probably want the buyer to assume liability on the instrument, so the seller will require the buyer to sign the instrument when it is presented and thus become primarily responsible for its payment. The drawee who places a signature on a draft (typically by signing it diagonally across the front) is said to have *accepted* it, and he or she incurs the obligation of an *acceptor*. See §3-413. *Acceptance* is defined in §3-409(a) as the "drawee's signed agreement to pay a draft as presented." Read §3-409.

Norton v. Knapp

Supreme Court of Iowa, 1884
64 Iowa 112, 19 N.W. 867

SEEVERS, J.

Because of the statements contained in an amended abstract, we are required to set out the petition as follows:

That the plaintiffs sold and delivered to the defendant, about February 17, 1882, a certain flaxseed-cleaner mill, at the agreed price of eighty dollars, no part of which had been paid, and that the same was then due.

That on or about April, 1882, plaintiffs drew a sight draft on defendant for the agreed price of said mill, which was in words and figures as follows:

$80   La Crosse, Wis., April 18, 1882.

At sight pay to the order of *Exchange Bank of Nora Springs, Iowa, eighty dollars*, value received, and charge the same to the account of

NORTON & KELLER.

To Miles Knapp, Nora Springs, Ia.

—Which was accepted by said Miles Knapp in written words and figures, on the back thereof, as follows: "Kiss my foot. MILES KNAPP." Also alleging "that said draft was still the property of plaintiff, due and unpaid, and claiming judgment for eighty dollars, interest, and costs." . . .

The amount in controversy being less than $100, the court has certified certain questions upon which the opinion of this court is desired. In substance, two of them are whether the words "kiss my foot," on the back of the draft, signed by the drawee, is a legal and valid acceptance, and whether such acceptance can be introduced in evidence without showing it was the intention to accept the draft. The rule upon this subject is thus stated in 1 Pars. Bills & Notes, 282:

> If a bill is presented to a drawee for the purpose of obtaining his acceptance, and he does anything to or with it which does not distinctly indicate that he will not accept it, he is held to be an acceptor, for he has the power, and it is his duty, to put this question beyond all possibility of doubt. . . .

The rule we understand to be, if the drawee does anything with or to the bill, or writes thereon anything, which does not clearly negative an intention to accept, then he can or will be charged as an acceptor. The question, then, is, what construction should be placed on the words "kiss my foot," written on the bill and signed by him? They cannot be rejected as surplusage. Such language is not ordinarily used in business circles or polite society. But by their use the defendant meant either to accept or refuse to accept the bill. It cannot be he meant the former; therefore, it must be the latter. It seems quite clear to us that the defendant intended by the use of the contemptuous and vulgar words above stated, to give emphasis to his intention not to accept or have anything to do with the bill or with the plaintiff. We understand the words, in common parlance, to mean and express contempt for the person to whom the words are addressed, and when used as a reply to a request, they imply, and are understood to mean, decided, unqualified, and contemptuous refusal to comply with such request. In such sense they were undoubtedly used when the defendant was requested to accept the bill. The question asked upon this point must be answered in the negative. Whether parol evidence is admissible to show the intent of the defendant, we have no occasion to determine, because no such evidence was offered, and our rule is not to determine mere abstract propositions. . . .

If the seller has agreed to give the buyer a credit period prior to payment — say, 60 days — a sight draft similar to this one is drawn:

To Betty Buyer

Sixty (60) days after sight, pay to the order of *Scott Seller $10,000.*

Scott Seller

The seller will then discount the draft with his local bank, indorsing it over to the bank. The bank will forward it to a collecting bank in the buyer's city that will make a "presentment for acceptance" to the buyer and, if she accepts, will see that she gets the goods. When the buyer accepts, she will sign her name, usually diagonally across the face of the instrument, and the instrument will be dated, to start the 60-day period running, and returned to the collecting bank. During the 60-day period the draft (now called a "trade acceptance") may be further negotiated; it is now legally the same as an unmatured promissory note, the acceptor incurring an obligation almost identical to that of a maker. At the end of the 60 days, the holder of the draft will make a second presentment to the drawee (acceptor), this time a "presentment for payment." If the acceptor now dishonors, she can be sued on her §3-413 obligation, or the holder can proceed, after giving notice of dishonor, against the drawer and prior indorsers on their contracts. Note that if the drawee had dishonored the first presentment, the one for acceptance, she would not have been liable on the instrument because at that point she had incurred no §3-413 liability.

When a sight draft gives the drawee time for payment after sight, the holder *must* make a presentment for acceptance in order to start the running of the credit period. Read §3-502(b)(4) and the last paragraph of its Official Comment 4.

2. Checks

When the draft is a *check,* so that the drawee is a bank, the same rules apply. The drawer's writing of the check does not, absent unusual circumstances, create any immediate rights in the checking account funds, and the drawee bank has no liability to the holder of the check until it accepts it. Of course, the drawee bank is bound by the terms of its checking account agreement with its customer, the drawer. This checking account agreement is analogous to the contract of sale in the non-bank drawee situation discussed above. But the checking account agreement is a private contract between the bank and its customers and confers no rights on other parties. Read §3-408.

Galyen Petroleum Co. v. Hixson

Nebraska Supreme Court, 1983
213 Neb. 683, 331 N.W.2d 1

COLWELL, J., Retired.

Plaintiff, Galyen Petroleum Company (Galyen), appeals a summary judgment in favor of the Commercial Bank (Bank) of Bassett, Nebraska, in a suit to recover on three checks personally presented to drawee Bank by payee Galyen, upon which payment was refused, although the drawer had funds on deposit to pay some of the checks.

Galyen was a wholesale supplier of fuels to the defendant, Norman J. Hixson, who had an account in and owed Bank more than $7,000 on promissory notes. On October 1, 1975, Hixson issued check No. 2287, $3,763.25, to Galyen, which was presented through channels to drawee Bank for collection and returned unpaid for insufficient funds. On October 15, 1975, Hixson issued check No. 2304, $2,740.88, to Galyen, which was likewise presented and returned. On November 1, 1975, Hixson issued check No. 2324, $378.94, to Galyen, which was likewise presented and returned. On November 12 and 13, 1975, Galyen personally presented the three checks to Bank during regular banking hours at Bassett, Nebraska; upon each presentment, Bank unconditionally refused payment of all three checks and forthwith returned them to Galyen. Bank's records and the evidence show that at the close of business on November 10, 1975, Hixson's account had a credit balance of $3,048.46. There was no account activity on November 11, 1975. On November 12, three deposits were made to the account, $209.27, $92.90, and $443.17. After Galyen presented the checks for collection on November 12, Bank set off Hixson's account for two items of $1,006.75 and $2,700 that were credited to Hixson's note account, leaving a balance of $87.05. The credited notes were not then due. The printed part of the notes recites in part:

> Payee shall have at all times a security interest in and right of setoff against any deposit balances of the maker(s) . . . and may at the time, without notice, apply the same against payment of this note . . . whether due or not. . . .

Bank had a financing statement and security agreement from Hixson dated March 7, 1975. Hixson did not object to the setoffs. Galyen filed its petition on August 23, 1976. Hixson was discharged as a bankrupt on December 7, 1976, and dismissed as a party defendant.

Galyen claims that summary judgment was not a proper remedy here for the reason there were genuine issues of material fact concerning Bank's transactions on November 12 and 13.

Galyen assigns as error that Bank unlawfully refused payment of the checks on presentment and that it had no authority to make a setoff to credit Hixson's promissory notes where (1) the notes were not due and (2) the setoffs were exercised after presentment.

Neb. UCC §3-409(1) [§3-408 in the Revision — Eds.] (Reissue 1980) provides:

> A check or other draft does not of itself operate as an assignment of any funds in the hands of the drawee available for its payment, and the drawee is not liable on the instrument until he accepts it.

The authorities are agreed . . . that a check, of itself, and in the absence of special circumstances, is neither a legal nor an equitable assignment or appropriation of a corresponding amount of the drawer's funds in the hands of the drawee, and that therefore, in and of itself, it gives the holder of the check no right of action against the drawee and no valid claim to the fund of the drawer in its hands, even though the drawer has on deposit sufficient funds to pay it. It creates no lien on the money which the holder can enforce against the bank. [10 Am. Jur. 2d Banks §563 at 532-533 (1963).]

There are no special circumstances or agreements claimed here. The only evidence was the hearsay statement of Richard W. Galyen that Hixson told him that he had telephoned Bank and that the checks were good.

Summary judgment was a proper procedure here, and Galyen had no standing or cause of action against Bank on account of the dishonor of any of the three checks. It did have a remedy against the drawer. Neb. UCC §3-507(2) (Reissue 1980). We do not get to the question of setoffs. The summary judgment was properly granted.

Affirmed.

Section 3-408 does not mean that under no circumstances can the drawee bank become liable to the holder prior to acceptance. It was the common law rule that by special agreement the drawer could work an immediate assignment of bank-held funds so as to give the holder of the check a claim against the drawee bank prior to acceptance. See Fourth Natl. v. Yardley, 165 U.S. 634 (1897) (special agreement between drawer and payee);

Ballard v. Home Natl. Bank, 91 Kan. 91, 136 P. 935 (1913) (special agreement between drawer and drawee). In Union Bank v. Safanie, 5 Ariz. App. 342, 427 P.2d 146 (1967), an oral statement by a bank officer to the payee that the drawer's check would clear when presented was held to create liability in fraud, and in Trump Taj Mahal Associates v. Bank of New York, 2003 WL 23750688 (N.J. Super. 2003), a bank that told a casino that an altered teller's check was good was held liable in an action for negligence. In a similar situation, the Nebraska Supreme Court used promissory estoppel to defeat the drawee bank; Bigger v. Fremont Natl. Bank, 215 Neb. 580, 340 N.W.2d 142 (1983). In one major UCC case finding such a special contractual liability in the drawee bank, the check was payable out of a special loan fund and was issued by the drawer after consultation with the bank, which immediately marked the account to show that the check was outstanding; this was held to create an immediate right in the payee to reach the funds, so that a stop payment order by the drawer came too late. See MidContinent Cas. Co. v. Jenkins, 2 U.C.C. Rep. Serv. 1164 (Okla. 1965). In Graybar Elec. Co. v. Brookline Trust Co., 39 U.C.C. Rep. Serv. 1721 (Boston Mun. Ct., App. Div. 1984), a bank that issued a personal money order in return for cash was required to pay it even though no signature of the bank appeared thereon; the court reasoned that the fact of issuance was an implied promise to pay the personal money order when it was presented. These causes of action would all be preserved as possibilities by §1-103.

3. Certification

The drawee bank's *acceptance* of a check is called *certification*. All of the Code sections on acceptance apply equally to certification. Read §§3-409(d) and 3-413.

PROBLEM 69

George Generous gave a check for $5,000 to the Grapes of Wrath Church as part of the church's drive to get money for a planned new building. The church did not want to cash any checks it received until it had at least $20,000 worth of pledges. On the other hand, the church didn't want contributors to be able to back out and stop payment either, so the church's lawyer advised the church directors to have all large checks certified. This, the lawyer knew, would have the effect of making the certifying bank primarily liable on the check (§3-413(a)). The church treasurer took George's check down to the drawee bank and asked to have it certified, a presentment for acceptance. The drawee bank refused, saying that its practice was never to certify gift checks.

(a) Is that a dishonor so that the church should give George notice of dishonor? See §3-409(d) and its Official Comment 4.

(b) What should the church's lawyer advise it to do now?

(c) If the bank had certified the check but later refused to pay it, could the church sue George on his drawer's obligation? See §3-414(c). Same result if George had donated a certified check that the bank later dishonored? See Official Comment 3 to §3-414; cf. §3-411.

F. Signature by an Agent

Section 3-402(a) generally defers to the common law governing an agent's signing of a contract on behalf of the principal. Thus, the agent's authority to sign the principal's name may be real (express or implied) or even apparent. See Senate Motors, Inc. v. Industrial Bank of Wash., 1971 WL 17944 (D.C. Super. 1971). The cited section also answers another question the original version of Article 3 had muddied.

PROBLEM 70

When tycoon J.B. Biggley wanted to borrow money for a business venture, he had his agent, J. Pierpont Finch, negotiate the loan from Wickets National Bank. When Finch signed the promissory note payable to the bank, he simply wrote his name as "J. Pierpont Finch, Agent," and failed to mention the name of his principal, J.B. Biggley. Is Biggley bound on this note? See §3-402 and Official Comment 1.

We shall leave the question of the scope of the agent's authority to other courses and instead concentrate on this question: when has the agent signed in so careless a fashion as to become personally liable? For instance, does the signature

Money Corporation, John Smith

make John Smith personally liable on a promissory note? Can he even introduce parol evidence to show that he is the president of the corporation and as such meant to sign only in his official capacity?

The smart way for an authorized agent to sign the instrument so as to avoid personal liability is for the agent to be careful to do two things: name the principal and unambiguously indicate that the agent is signing only in a representative capacity. See §3-402(b)(1). If the agent does one of these two things but not the other, the agent is liable to a holder in due course taking the instrument without notice that the agent was not intended to be liable, but otherwise the agent may prove that the original parties did not intend for the agent to incur liability. Official Comment 2 says that a holder in due course should be able to resolve any ambiguity against the agent.

Look at §3-402, digest the above paragraph, and then test your ability to read and comprehend a statute by resolving the Problems below.

PROBLEM 71

In the last Problem, would Finch himself be liable to a holder in due course? To Wickets National Bank?

Mundaca Investment Corp. v. Febba

New Hampshire Supreme Court, 1999
727 A.2d 990

BROCK, C.J.

The defendants, Doris M. Febba, Thomas G. Scurfield, and Linda L. Kendall, appeal the Superior Court's (Smith, J.) grant of summary judgment in favor of the plaintiff, Mundaca Investment Corporation (Mundaca), holding the defendants personally liable for amounts due on two promissory notes. We reverse and remand. The defendants served as trustees of the L.T.D. Realty Trust (trust). On July 28, 1987, they purchased two condominium units for the trust. To finance this transaction, the defendants executed two promissory notes, secured by two mortgages, payable to the order of Dartmouth Savings Bank (bank). At the end of both notes below the signature line, the name of each defendant was typewritten beside the preprinted term "Borrower." Following their signatures, each of the defendants handwrote the word "Trustee." While both promissory notes state that they are secured by a mortgage, the trust is not identified on the face of the notes. The trust, however, is identified as the "Borrower" in both mortgages.

On August 19, 1993, Mundaca acquired the two notes from the Federal Deposit Insurance Corporation as receiver for the bank. By letters dated October 28, 1994, Mundaca notified defendants Scurfield and Febba that the two promissory notes were in default. Mundaca foreclosed on the condominium units and filed suit against the defendants individually for the remaining amount due on the notes. Both Mundaca and the defendants moved for summary judgment. The defendants' motion for summary judgment was denied. In granting Mundaca's motion for summary judgment, the trial court ruled that the form of the defendants' signatures—"[defendant's signature], Trustee"—did not show unambiguously that the defendants were signing in a representative capacity. See RSA 382-A:3-402(b) comment 2 (1994). The trial court then ruled that the defendants failed to meet their burden of proving that Dart-mouth Savings Bank did not intend to hold them personally liable. See RSA 382-A:3-402(b)(2) (1994). This appeal followed.

On appeal, the defendants argue that reading the notes and mortgages together shows unambiguously that they signed in a representative capacity for the trust as the identified principal, and therefore they are not personally liable under RSA 382-A:3-402(b)(1) (1994). Alternatively, the defendants contend that the trial court erred in granting Mundaca's motion for summary judgment because there was a genuine issue of material fact regarding whether the original parties intended the defendants to be personally liable. See RSA 382-A:3-402(b)(2).

The trial court applied RSA 382-A:3-402 [UCC Revised §3-402 — Eds.] (1994), and the parties do not dispute that this version of the statute governs the defendants' liability. Accordingly, we will assume for purposes of this appeal that this version of the statute applies. But see, e.g., Barnsley v. Empire Mortgage Ltd. Partnership V, 142 N.H. 721, 723, 720 A.2d 63, 64 (1998). RSA 382-A:3-402 (1994) provides in pertinent part:

> (b) If a representative signs the name of the representative to an instrument and the signature is an authorized signature of the represented person, the following rules apply:
> (1) If the form of the signature shows unambiguously that the signature is made on behalf of the represented person who is identified in the instrument, the representative is not liable on the instrument.
> (2) Subject to subsection (c), if (i) the form of the signature does not show unambiguously that the signature is made in a representative capacity or (ii) the represented person is not identified in the instrument, the representative is liable on the instrument to a holder in due course that took the instrument without notice that the representative was not intended to be liable on the instrument. With respect to any other person, the representative is liable on the instrument unless the representative proves that the original parties did not intend the representative to be liable on the instrument.

The defendants argue that under RSA 382-A:3-402(b)(1), the handwritten term "Trustee" appearing next to their signatures on the notes shows unambiguously that the signatures were made in a representative capacity. Further, the defendants argue that while the promissory notes did not explicitly identify the trust, the notes and mortgages read together reveal that the term "Borrower" is identified as the trust. Accordingly, the defendants argue that they are not personally liable.

RSA 382-A:3-402(b)(1) requires that the form of the representative's signature show unambiguously that the signature is made on behalf of the represented person who is identified *in the instrument.* The defendants concede that the instruments in this case are the two promissory notes. The defendants, however, argue that fundamental contract law requires that the notes and mortgages be read together to interpret the contracting parties' intentions. General principles of contract law only apply to negotiable instruments if not displaced by the Uniform Commercial Code. See RSA 382-A:1-103 (1994). Accordingly, we hold that because the represented person, in this case the trust, is not identified in the *instrument* as required by RSA 382-A:3-402(b)(1), this case falls squarely under RSA 382-A:3-402(b)(2).

Pursuant to RSA 382-A:3-402(b)(2), the defendants could be personally liable in two situations: (1) to a holder in due course who takes the instrument without notice that the defendants did not intend to be personally liable; and (2) to any other party unless the defendants prove that the original parties did not intend them to be personally liable. While the trial court did not address the first situation, it ruled that the defendants failed to meet their burden of proving that the original parties did not intend them to be personally liable. The defendants contend, however, that summary judgment was inappropriate because there was a genuine issue of material fact as to the intent of the original parties. We agree. . . .

Our review of the record reveals a disputed issue of material fact as to the intent of the original parties, i.e., Dartmouth Savings Bank and the defendants. While the notes do not explicitly identify the trust as the represented party, the mortgages show that the defendants signed in a representative capacity and identify the trust as the "Borrower." See RSA 382-A:3-402(b)(1). Furthermore, the record contains conflicting affidavits by the defendants and Heidi Postupack, the bank's loan officer who handled this transaction. The defendants' affidavits claim that they intended to sign the notes as representatives of the trust. Conversely, Postupack's affidavit states that she understood that the bank intended the defendants to be personally liable, jointly and severally, on the notes. Considering this evidence in the light most favorable to the defendants, see *Barnsley,* 142 N.H. at 723, 720 A.2d at 64, we conclude that a genuine issue of material fact exists as to the bank's intent regarding the defendants' personal liability on the notes.

As noted earlier, the trial court did not address whether Mundaca was a holder in due course who took without notice that the defendants did not intend to be personally liable on the notes. See RSA 382-A:3-402(b)(2). Because the record before us is silent on this matter, we leave this issue for the trial court on remand.

The defendants also argue that the mortgages act as a defense to their alleged personal liability on the notes. This argument is without merit. The mortgages only provide a defense to the defendants' alleged personal liability on the notes to the extent that the mortgages modify, supplement, or nullify their obligation on the notes. See RSA 382-A:3-117 [UCC Revised §3-117—EDS.] (1994). The defendants argue that it is clear that the mortgages modify and supplement the notes. We disagree. What is clear is that the mortgages were issued as collateral for the notes. What is unclear by reading the notes and the mortgages is the identity of the "Borrower." We have already held that the identity of the "Borrower" is a material issue of fact in dispute.

Accordingly, we reverse the grant of summary judgment and remand this case to the trial court for further proceedings consistent with this opinion.

Reversed and remanded.

All concurred.

PROBLEM 72

The president of Money Corporation was John Smith. He signed three corporate promissory notes as follows:

(1) "John Smith." Money Corporation was not mentioned in the note.
(2) "Money Corporation, John Smith."
(3) "Money Corporation, John Smith, President."

In each case, is he personally liable to a holder in due course of the instrument?

PROBLEM 73

Kit Fielding was the corporate president of Francis Racing Stables. The corporate checks had the words "Francis Racing Stables" printed prominently in the upper left-hand corner of the checks, but when Fielding went to sign the checks on the drawer's line, he simply signed his name and did not sign the name of the company or in any way indicate that he was signing as an agent. If the check is negotiated to a holder in due course and then dishonored by the drawee bank, may the holder in due course successfully impose personal liability on Fielding? See §3-402(c) and its Official Comment 3; Triffin v. Ameripay, LLC, 368 N.J. Super. 587, 847 A.2d 628 (2004).

Nichols v. Seale
Texas Court of Civil Appeals, 1973
493 S.W.2d 589

GUITTARD, J,

In this appeal from a summary judgment on a promissory note, the principal questions are (1) whether as between the original parties extrinsic evidence is admissible to show that the signer acted for a corporation rather than for himself, although the note does not show his representative capacity and contains only an assumed name under which the corporation was doing business, and (2) whether a statement in his affidavit that he was acting on behalf of the corporation rather than for himself is competent summary judgment proof or an inadmissible conclusion. We hold that the evidence is admissible and raises a fact issue.

The note is on a printed form beginning "I, we or either of us," and is signed as follows:

> THE FASHION BEAUTY SALON
> Carl V. Nichols [typewriting]
> *Carl V. Nichols* [handwriting]

The payee sued Carl V. Nichols "individually and doing business as The Fashion Beauty Salon." Nichols filed a sworn answer denying that he signed the note in question in his individual capacity and alleging that he signed on behalf of a corporation, Mr. Carls Fashion, Inc. In response to plaintiff's motion for summary judgment, defendant Nichols filed the following affidavit:

> My name is Carl V. Nichols, and I served as President of Mr. Carls Fashion, Inc., a Texas Corporation, doing business as The Fashion Beauty Salon at 2115 Sherry Lane, Dallas, Texas, from the date of its incorporation, January 14, 1960, and I signed the promissory note attached to Plaintiff's Original Petition and marked Exhibit "A" in the capacity of officer of such corporation and in behalf of such corporation and not in my personal capacity.

The trial court rendered summary judgment against Nichols on the note. We first consider whether we must affirm that judgment on the ground that the form of the signature makes Nichols individually liable as a matter of law under §3-403(2), which provides: [the court quoted the section].

Plaintiff contends that Nichols is personally obligated under subsection (1) because the note neither "names" the corporation nor shows that Nichols "signed in a representative capacity." Admittedly, the note does not show that he "signed in a representative capacity," because it does not describe him as a corporate officer or agent or use any other language, such as "by," indicating that he was acting for someone other than himself. Neither does it "name the person represented" unless "The Fashion Beauty Salon" can be taken as naming the corporation "Mr. Carls Fashion, Inc."

We hold that use of an assumed name does "name the person represented" within the meaning of the code. This section must be read along with §3-401(2), which expressly authorizes use of an assumed name in a negotiable instrument: "A signature is made by use of any name, including any trade or assumed name, upon an instrument. . . ." The official interpretation of this section includes the following comment concerning a signature on commercial paper: "It may be made in any name, including any trade name or assumed name, however false and fictitious, which is adopted for the purpose. Parol evidence is admissible to identify the signer, and when he is identified the signature is effective." This rule applies as well when the person using the assumed name is a corporation, since corporations are expressly permitted to use assumed names by Tex. Bus. Corp. Act Ann. art. 2.05 (1956) VATS, and may sue on contracts made in assumed names. Davis v. Tex-O-Kan Flour Mills Co., 186 F.2d 50 (5th Cir. 1950), W. B. Clarkson & Co. v. Gans S.S. Line, 187 S.W. 1106 (Tex. Civ. App., Galveston 1916, *writ ref'd*). Consequently, extrinsic evidence was admissible to show that "The Fashion Beauty Salon" was an assumed name for "Mr. Carls Fashion, Inc." This conclusion is supported by Weeks v. San Angelo Natl. Bank, 65 S.W.2d 348 (Tex. Civ. App., Austin 1933, *writ ref'd*), in which a note was signed "Weeks Drug Store No. 4 by Jno. A. Weeks." The court held that this signature was ambiguous and that parol evidence was admissible to show the party's intention that the note should be the obligation of "Weeks Drug Store No. 4, Inc.," a corporation not yet organized.

Since, as we have held, a corporation is "named" within §3-403(2) by use of its assumed name, that section does not forbid extrinsic evidence to show further, as between the original parties, that the signer was not personally obligated. Such proof may be admissible, not to vary terms of the instrument or to show a mistake, but rather to explain an ambiguity with respect to the capacity of the signer. An instrument which "names the person represented but does not show that the representative signed in a representative capacity," may be ambiguous with respect to the capacity in which he signed, since, in the absence of explanatory evidence, the signature may be interpreted either as his individual signature, or as a signature on behalf of the person represented. We find the present signature to be ambiguous for that reason. Directly in point here is Canton Provision Co. v. Chaney, 70 N.E.2d 687 (Ohio App. 1945), in which checks signed "Finer Foods, Jack Chaney" were held to be ambiguous so that parol evidence was admissible to show that Chaney signed as agent for another individual doing business as "Finer Foods." See also First State Bank v. Smoot-Curtis Co., 121 S.W.2d 667 (Tex. Civ. App., Fort Worth 1938, *writ dism'd by agr.*) and Norman v. Beling, 33 N.J. 237, 163 A.2d 129 (1960), both holding that a note signed with the name of a corporation and an officer, without showing his representative capacity, is ambiguous so that the representative capacity of the individual may be shown by parol evidence. In our opinion, the ambiguity in the present note is not removed by Nichols' name in typewriting, which, whether above or below his signature, may have been used only to identify the signer in case his handwriting was not legible. Moreover, it seems to us that the conventional printed language, "I, we or either of us" only serves to increase the ambiguity. . . .

Appellant's motion for rehearing is granted, our former opinion is withdrawn, and the cause is reversed and remanded.

NOTE

On appeal, the Texas Supreme Court reversed for a procedural reason:

> Texas law provides that in order for an agent to avoid liability for his signature on a contract, he must *disclose* his intent to sign as a representative to the other contracting party. Uncommunicated intent will not suffice. Heinrichs v. Evins Personnel Consultants, Inc., No. One, 486 S.W.2d 935 (Tex. 1972); Mahoney v. Pitman, 43 S.W.2d 143 (Tex. Civ. App., Amarillo 1931, *writ ref'd*).
>
> Again viewing Nichols' affidavit broadly, it states that he signed the note as president of the corporation, thus clearly indicating his subjective intent to sign as an agent. However, nowhere does Nichols say that he disclosed his intent to Seale. Nor does his statement that ". . . I signed the promissory note . . . in the capacity of officer of such corporation and in behalf of such corporation and not in my personal capacity," intimate that this intended capacity was communicated to Seale. This is his burden in the context of the summary judgment proceedings. Consequently, Nichols has not effectively raised a fact issue upon his alleged affirmative defense of representation and Seale's motion for summary judgment must be granted.

Seale v. Nichols, 505 S.W.2d 251, 255 (Tex. 1974). See also Rotuba Extruders, Inc. v. Ceppos, 46 N.Y.2d 223, 385 N.E.2d 1068, 413 N.Y.S.2d 141 (1978).

III.   *OTHER THEORIES OF LIABILITY*

In commercial paper law, contractual obligations arise from the voluntary act of putting one's signature on a negotiable instrument. But the Code also establishes a host of other theories imposing liability.

Subsequent chapters explore the legal relationship between a bank and its customer, and, as we shall see, these parties may sue each other for violations of the rules arising from that relationship, primarily the "properly payable" rule of §4-401 and the wrongful dishonor rule of §4-402.

In Chapter 8 we will look closely at the legal snarls following forgeries and alterations of negotiable instruments and shall there encounter causes of action based on warranty and conversion.

CHAPTER 5   ASSESSMENT

Multiple Choice Questions

1. Marker borrowed $25,000 from Friendly Finance, signing a negotiable promissory note for that amount plus interest. Marker soon had financial woes and stopped making payments. Marker's sister offered Friendly Finance $5,000 for the note. Friendly Finance accepted the offer gladly. Marker's sister stuck the note in a safe, with no intent to recover from Marker. Several months later, Marker received a big inheritance. Friendly Finance sued Marker for the remaining $20,000 on the debt. Will Friendly Finance succeed?
   a. Yes. Marker is still liable on the portion of the debt that was not paid.
   b. No. Marker's obligation to pay the debt is suspended.
   c. Yes. Friendly Finance may enforce a note that is lost, stolen, or destroyed.
   d. Yes. If Marker's sister does not intend to enforce the note, then Marker would get a windfall if Marker did not have to pay Friendly Finance.

2. Clever Richard was discouraged, because he owed $222,321.42 on his mortgage. Then he wrote "PAYMENT IN FULL FOR ALL MORTGAGE DEBT" conspicuously on the check he sent for his monthly mortgage payment of $1,500. The check was duly paid. Ninety days has passed. Is Clever Richard's entire mortgage debt of $222,321.42 discharged?
   a. Yes, because he tendered a check to pay the debt with PAID IN FULL conspicuously written on the check.
   b. No. "PAID IN FULL" can never be used to unilaterally settle a debt.
   c. No. The amount of the debt was not disputed.
   d. Yes. Clever Richard has simply declared bankruptcy and discharged the debt.

3. Draper sent a check to Praline Produce to pay for a shipment of nuts. Praline indorsed the check over to Careless Shipping to pay off some invoices. Careless Shipping's bookkeeper stuck the check in a file and forgot about it. Eventually, Careless Shipping rediscovered the check and presented it for payment. By this time, Draper had no money in its account and the drawee bank refused to pay the check. Which of the following could make Praline Produce not liable as an indorser?
   a. If the check was not presented or deposited within 30 days of the indorsement.
   b. If Praline Producer was not given timely notice of dishonor.
   c. If Praline Producer had indorsed "Without Recourse."
   d. All of the above.

4. Which of the following could have made Draper not liable as the drawer of the check?
   a. If the check was not presented within 30 days of Draper issuing it.
   b. If Draper was not given timely notice of dishonor.
   c. If Draper had written "Without Recourse" on the memo line of the check.
   d. None of the above.

5. Shaky Shoes issued a check to Flat Feet, a supplier. Flat Feet's manager went quickly to present the check to Shaky Shoe's bank, Wingtip Bank. Wingtip Bank refused to pay. Is Wingtip Bank liable to Flat Feet?
   a. No. Wingtip Bank did not sign the check.
   b. Yes, if there were sufficient funds in Shaky Shoes' account to pay the check.
   c. Yes. A check is an unconditional order to pay.
   d. Yes, otherwise checks would be worthless.

Answers

1. B is the best answer. Under §3-310, when Friendly Finance took the note, that suspended the underlying obligation, the debt of $25,000. That obligation remains suspended until the note is paid (which would discharge the debt) or dishonored. Even if the note were dishonored, Friendly Finance could only enforce the debt if Friendly Finance were in possession of the note. In practical terms, when Friendly Finance sold the note, Friendly Finance gave up its rights to collect the underlying debt—that's exactly how negotiability is supposed to work. So A is incorrect. Marker may still be technically liable on the debt, but Friendly Finance cannot enforce that suspended liability. C is misleading. If Friendly Finance had lost the note, it could still enforce it. But Friendly Finance transferred the note, giving up its right to enforce the note. For the same reason, D is incorrect. It is up to the holder, Marker's sister, whether Marker has to pay the note.

2. C is the best answer. The accord and satisfaction provision of §3-311 is a mechanism to make a good faith offer to settle a dispute. It is not effective where the amount owed is not in dispute. Contrary to A, it cannot simply be used on just any check, where there is no dispute to settle. B misstates the facts. D is simply a fantasy. Discharge of debt in bankruptcy requires filing a case in federal bankruptcy court.

3. D is the best answer. The question illustrates several protections given to indorsers. Indorser liability will be negated if the check is not presented or deposited in timely fashion, §3-415(f) (as in A), or there is not timely

notice of dishonor (per B), §3-415(c). Likewise, an indorser is not liable as an indorser if she indorses "without recourse." §3-415(b), (as in C). The reason for the without-recourse rule is that indorsement may serve different purposes: to negotiate an instrument, to guaranty payment, or to restrict payment. "Without recourse" allows someone to indorse a check in order to negotiate it, while avoiding guarantor liability.

Note the qualification "as an indorser." Someone who indorses without recourse can still be liable on other theories, as we will see. If she deposits a check that is not paid, she would still be liable to her bank for chargeback. If she transferred a check with a forgery or alteration, or subject to a defense, she would still be liable for breach of transfer warranty.

4. D is the best answer, switching from "All of the above" in the last question to "None of the above" here. The drawer of a check is not afforded the same protections as an indorser, because the drawer plays different role. The indorser is indorsing a check issued by someone else. The drawer is the very person who issued the check. So the drawer does not have the same need for the check to be presented in timely fashion, because the drawer should not escape paying the underlying debt (except in the unlikely event that the drawer's bank becomes insolvent in the meantime). The drawer does not need notice of dishonor, because dishonor is usually the one responsible for the check not being paid. The drawer may not have enough money in the account, or the drawer may have stopped payment on the check. Nor should a drawer be able to write a check without recourse, because no one would be liable on the instrument. §3-414(e).

5. A is the best answer. Wingtip Bank simply did not sign the check, so it has not promised to pay the check. If Wingtip Bank signed the check (making it a certified check), then it would be liable. Likewise, when Wingtip Bank issues a cashier's check, it is liable on the cashier's checks. But ordinary checks represent only an obligation of the issuer, something anyone taking a check in payment should be aware of. We will see more about the payment of checks in following chapters. We will see that, although Wing Tip Bank has no liability on the check to the holder, Flat Feet, Wingtip Bank may be liable to its customer, Shaky Shoes, for Wrongful dishonor of the check.

MORTGAGES AND PROMISSORY NOTES[1]

I. INTRODUCTION

Let's begin with what a mortgage actually is. Properly defined, it is a consensual lien placed by the homeowner (called the "mortgagor") on the real estate being financed in order secure the debt incurred by the loan in favor of the lender/mortgagee. The debt is created by the signing of a promissory note; the homeowner will be the maker/issuer of the promissory note and the lending institution will be payee on the note. When someone buying a home attends the closing, three different legal documents will come into being. They are: (1) the contract by which the lender loans the money in return for getting a (2) mortgage deed on the property, and (3) a promissory note signed by the homeowner (the maker) promising to pay the mortgage amount to the lender (the payee on the note).

It is important to appreciate that our law has always considered the promissory note as the primary obligation, with the mortgage contract and

---

1. The text in this chapter is largely adapted from Douglas J. Whaley, Mortgage Foreclosures, Promissory Notes, and the Uniform Commercial Code, 39 W. St. U. L. Rev. 313 (2012), updated periodically in Whaley's blog at http://douglaswhaley.blogspot.com/2013/02/mortgage-foreclosures-missing.html.

deed merely being security (collateral) backing up that obligation. There is a common law maxim that "security follows the debt." This means that it is presumed that whoever is the current holder of the promissory note (the "debt") is entitled to enforce the mortgage lien (the "security"). The United States Supreme Court established the basic rule early in the 1873 case of Carpenter v. Longan:

> The note and mortgage are inseparable; the former as essential, the latter as an incident. An assignment of the note carries the mortgage with it, while an assignment of the latter alone is a nullity. . . . The mortgage can have no separate existence. When the note is paid the mortgage expires. It cannot survive for a moment the debt which the note represents. This dependent and incidental relation is the controlling consideration. . . . A purported assignment of a mortgage to a bank is not proof of a transfer of a promissory note secured by the mortgage, since the mortgage follows the note but not vice versa.

83 U.S. 271, 274 (1872). Almost every state in the country has a similar rule, so that whoever has the note is the proper owner of the property, and the mortgage simply tags along the way a tail follows the dog.

The mortgage is reified as a mortgage deed that the lender should file in the local real property records so that the mortgage properly binds the property not only against the mortgagor but also the rest of the world (this process is called "perfection" of the lien). The "mort" portion of the word mortgage comes from Latin for "death" (as in "mortician," "morgue," "mortal," etc.) because on the payment of the promissory note debt, the mortgage deed dies.

The collapse of the housing market in the middle of the first decade of the twenty-first century was a direct consequence of greedy and unwise business practices. Gullible consumers were encouraged to take out mortgages they could not afford on property that turned out to be worth far less than the mortgage indebtedness. Minority communities were particularly hard hit, often targeted by shady lenders because people of color are more likely to store their wealth in home equity in many U.S. communities. Subprime lenders frequently sold the resulting mortgages (and the promissory notes that, in theory, went with them) to other financial institutions, and these mortgages were then bundled into a mass, placed in a securitization trust, and used as the assets backing the issuance of bonds by the trust. Things went fine until real property stopped appreciating in value and its worth dropped to alarmingly low levels, with a recession that engulfed the country and, indeed, the world. Not just subprime borrowers were affected; the recession reduced the value of almost all property, and perfectly responsible mortgagors (many of whom were also laid off from their jobs) began to struggle to make payments and avoid foreclosure. According to one monitoring agency, a record number of homes received foreclosure filings in 2010 (over 2.9 million).[2] In recent years, the economy has somewhat recovered, but fore-closures are still a major problem.

The combination of subprime lending, securitization of mortgage loans, a housing market that first boomed then busted, rapacious preda-tors who worked hard to take for themselves the equity people had built up in their homes, and foreclosure mills that operated with neither proper paperwork, nor attention to the rules of law, much less common decency, led to an explosion of laws and legal actions designed to deal with these mat-ters. Criminal prosecutions (of which there have so far been none, which is astounding given how venal it all was) from all this will be left to other courses.

What happens to the promissory note in the meantime? In the good old days, the twentieth century, it was kept down at the bank so that when the time for payment arrived, the bank could present it to the maker, and, if the maker didn't pay, could then use legal process (or in some states self-help) to foreclose on the mortgage lien. But during the feeding frenzy that the real estate mortgage community indulged in during the last decade, more bizarre things happened. The mortgages themselves were no longer kept at the originating bank, nor were the notes. Instead, as just explained, they were bundled together with many others and sold as a package to an invest-ment banking firm, which put them in a trust and sold stock in the trust to investors (a process called "securitization"). The bankers all knew the impor-tance of the mortgage, and supposedly kept records as to the identity of the entities to whom the mortgages were assigned. But they were damn careless about the promissory notes, some of which were properly transferred when-ever the mortgage was, some of which were kept at the originating bank, some of which were deliberately destroyed (a really stupid thing to do), and some of which disappeared into the black hole of the financial collapse, never to be seen again.

There was a bright spot in all this for homeowners, however. When they stopped paying the mortgage amounts, and the current owners of the mort-gages/notes tried to foreclose on the property, the rules of Article 3 of the Uniform Commercial Code unexpectedly came to the aid of the debtors.

---

2. RealtyTrac Staff, Record 2.9 Million U.S. Properties Receive Foreclosure Filings in 2010 Despite 30-Month Low in December, RealtyTrac (Jan. 12, 2011), http://www.realtytrac.com/content/press-releases/record-29-million-us-properties-receive-foreclosure-filings-in-2010-despite-30-month-low-in-december-6309. This immediately followed late 2009, where the third quarter saw 937,840 homes receive some sort of foreclosure letter, which at that point was "'the worst three months of all time.'" Les Christie, Foreclosures: "Worst Three Months of All Time," CNN (Oct. 15, 2009, 7:34 A.M.), http://money.cnn.com/2009/10/15/real_estate/foreclosure_crisis_deepens.

UCC §3-301 states that the only entity that is allowed to sue on a promissory note is a "*person entitled to enforce* the instrument" (sometimes called a "PETE"). Read §3-301 and its Official Comment carefully; we will parse out its meaning as we go.

II. THE PERSON ENTITLED TO ENFORCE THE INSTRUMENT

PROBLEM 74

When Harry Potter decided to settle down and buy a house he arranged for a financing loan with Rowling National Bank, which loaned him $200,000 to buy his home and had him sign three documents at the closing: a mortgage contract by which he agreed to repay the mortgage debt to the bank or its assigns, a mortgage deed that the bank would file in the real property records to create a lien on the property in its favor, and a promissory note by which Harry agreed to pay the mortgage amount to the order of Rowling National Bank. Harry, the mortgagor, signed all of these, and the bank kept the promissory note and recorded the mortgage deed.

Three months later the bank sold the mortgage to Muggles Investment Bank (MIB) by a contract assigning the mortgage to MIB. Muggles also took possession of the promissory note. MIB then sold the note and mortgage along with a hundred other mortgages it owned to a securitization trust, which bundled the notes together in the trust corpus and then sold bonds, using the trust assets as collateral for the bonds. As the mortgages matured, they were transferred out of the trust and into the hands of the entity that would seek final payment from the mortgagor and foreclose if he did not make this payment.

All Harry knew about this was that when Rowling National Bank sold his note he was informed that he should make his monthly payment to a mortgage servicing company called the Hogwarts Agency, which he dutifully did until a bad spell of events caused Harry to lose his job. He missed six payments in a row. Harry was then contacted by the Voldemort Financial Company (VFC), which claimed to be the current owner of the mortgage. Assume that VFC can prove a regular chain of mortgage assignment contracts, and that it has a photocopy of the original promissory note. The back of the note is blank, never having been indorsed by the payee Rowling National Bank.

Does Harry's liability as the maker of a promissory note run to VFC? See §§3-412, 3-301? Rephrased, is VFC a "holder" of the note?

The Return of the Allonge. From Chapter 3 on negotiation you may remember that a piece of paper on which indorsements were written, called an allonge, was much used throughout history, with this usage falling off as instruments only infrequently passed through many hands. But the rise of the market in home mortgage promissory notes resulted in many transfers, so allonges came back into fashion and have caused much recent litigation. In Anderson v. Burson, 424 Md. 232, 35 A.3d 452 (2012), there were indorsements on a separate piece of paper that travelled with the note in question, but the court ignored them because, as we saw in Chapter 3, an allonge must be attached to the note in order to be valid. In Shaya v. Karam, 2014 WL 1856392 (Mich. App. 2012), the so-called "allonge" for a $400,000 note itself stated that "It is intended that this Allonge be attached to and made a permanent part of the Note," but the allonge was only folded into an envelope along with the note. The court held it was obviously not attached, and therefore the possessor of the note could not recover the $400,000 due on the note. Given the clear attachment requirement in §3-204(a), why do you suppose that whoever created the supposed allonges in these cases failed to staple them to the notes?

The Shelter Rule. The definition of a person entitled to enforce the note under §3-301 includes "a nonholder in possession of the instrument who has the rights of a holder." This is our old friend the "shelter rule," discussed in prior chapters. That concept reflects the basic idea that if I sell you something you get whatever rights I have in the object sold (you take "shelter" in my rights). This is true of negotiable instruments per §3-203(b), and holder in due course rights could pass in this fashion to someone who clearly was not a holder in due course (see Problem 33 in Chapter 4).

PROBLEM 75

The original promissory note was payable to Octopus National Bank. When ONB sold the note to First State Bank it failed to indorse the note in any way. Is FSB a "holder" of the note without this necessary indorsement? Is it a person entitled to enforce the note under §3-301? See Leyva v. National Default Servicing Corp., 255 P.3d 1275 (Nev. 2011) (to use the shelter rule the transferee must also prove the validity of the transfer from the original owner). What is the reason for giving a nonholder the rights of a holder? See page 117.

In the Harry Potter Problem the entity trying to foreclose only had a *copy* of the original note. In Whaley's article cited in the first footnote to this chapter, he states what he calls the "Golden Rule of Mortgage Foreclosures," which is that such foreclosures cannot proceed without production of the *original promissory note* signed at the closing. The reason for this is that there might be one hundred copies of the original note, but that wouldn't allow one hundred holders to foreclose; see Dickerson v. Regions Bank, 2014 WL 1118076 (Tenn. App. 2014) (copies irrelevant where no explanation of the current location of the original promissory note); In re Veal, 450 B.R. 897 (B.A.P. 9th Cir. 2011) (dueling creditors attempting to foreclose each held only a copy of the note, but not the original, neither successful). The Uniform Commercial Code is clear that if the maker of the note pays the wrong party the maker's liability is not discharged, and the maker must still pay the true holder of the note when it is finally presented; see §3-602.

States following these rules are called "show me the note" jurisdictions (in the language of the cases), but there are other courts that disregard the rules of the UCC and allow foreclosure without production of the original note. The following two cases reflect both possibilities.

Bank of America v. Kabba

Supreme Court of Oklahoma, 2012
276 P.3d 1006

Combs, J.

Factual and Procedural History

¶1 In a petition filed on March 11, 2010, Bank of America, NA, claiming to be the present holder of the note (hereinafter Bank of America) initiated a foreclosure action against Kabba and his wife. Bank of America claimed, at that time, to hold the note and mortgage as Successor by Merger to LaSalle Bank National Association, as Trustee under the Trust agreement for the Structured Asset Investment Loan Trust Series 2004-BNC2. A review of the note shows a blank indorsement. This blank indorsement was filed with the lower court for the first time in the motion for summary judgment. The blank indorsement was not mentioned or referenced in the original petition.

BNC Mortgage, Inc., was the original lender. Bank of America filed with the Court Clerk of Cleveland County, a document entitled "Assignment of Real Estate Mortgage" on January 17, 2011, therein claiming the assignment to be effective as of February 9, 2010. This was nine months after the filing of the petition to foreclose. Additionally, this "Assignment of Mortgage," signed by Mortgage Electronic Registrations Systems, Inc. (hereinafter MERS), as nominee for BNC Mortgage, Inc., and its successors and assigns, merely named Bank of America as Successor by Merger to LaSalle Bank National Association, as Trustee under the Trust agreement for the Structured Asset

Investment Loan Trust Series 2004-BNC2. There was no mention of the note in this "Assignment of Mortgage." On June 13, 2011, Summary judgment was granted and memorialized by a Final Journal Entry of Judgment order in Bank of America's favor, against Kabba and his wife. Kabba appeals this summary judgment asserting Bank of America failed to demonstrate standing. . . .

ANALYSIS

¶3 Appellant argues Appellee does not have standing to bring this foreclosure action. Although Appellee has argued it holds the note, there is nothing in the record that shows when Appellee became the holder. The face of the note indicates it was indorsed in blank. However, this indorsement was not filed with the petition but with the motion for summary judgment. The purported "Assignment of Mortgage" was filed after the filing of the foreclosure proceedings and was signed by MERS, and not BNC Mortgage, Inc. The "Assignment of Mortgage" at no time mentioned the note.

¶4 The issue presented to this Court is standing. This Court has previously held:

> Standing, as a jurisdictional question, may be correctly raised at any level of the judicial process or by the Court on its own motion. This Court has consistently held that standing to raise issues in a proceeding must be predicated on interest that is "direct, immediate and substantial." Standing determines whether the person is the proper party to request adjudication of a certain issue and does not decide the issue itself. The key element is whether the party whose standing is challenged has sufficient interest or stake in the outcome.

Matter of the Estate of Doan, 1986 OK 15, ¶7, 727 P.2d 574, 576. In Hendrick v. Walters, 1993 OK 162, ¶4, 865 P.2d 1232, 1234, this Court also held:

> Respondent challenges Petitioner's *standing* to bring the tendered issue. Standing refers to a person's legal right to seek relief in a judicial forum. *It may be raised as an issue at any stage of the judicial process by any party or by the court sua sponte.* (Emphasis original.)

Furthermore, in Fent v. Contingency Review Board, 2007 OK 27, footnote 19, 163 P.3d 512, 519, this Court stated "[s]tanding may be raised at any stage of the judicial process or by the court on its own motion." Additionally in *Fent*, this Court stated:

> Standing refers to a person's legal right to seek relief in a judicial forum. The three threshold criteria of standing are (1) a legally protected interest which must have been injured in fact — *i.e.,* suffered an injury which is actual, concrete and not conjectural in nature, (2) a causal nexus between the injury

and the complained-of conduct, and (3) a likelihood, as opposed to mere speculation, that the injury is capable of being redressed by a favorable court decision. The doctrine of standing ensures a party has a personal stake in the outcome of a case and the parties are truly adverse.

Fent v. Contingency Review Board, 2007 OK 27, ¶7, 163 P.3d 512, 519-520. In essence, a plaintiff who has not suffered an injury attributable to the defendant lacks standing to bring a suit. And, thus, "standing [must] be determined as of the commencement of suit; . . ." Lujan v. Defenders of Wildlife, 504 U.S. 555, 570, n.5, 112 S. Ct. 2130, 2142 n.5, 119 L. Ed. 2d 351 (1992).

¶5 To commence a foreclosure action in Oklahoma, a plaintiff must demonstrate it has a right to enforce the note and, absent a showing of ownership, the plaintiff lacks standing. Gill v. First Nat. Bank & Trust Co. of Oklahoma City, 1945 OK 181, 159 P.2d 717. An assignment of the mortgage, however, is of no consequence because under Oklahoma law, "[p]roof of ownership of the note carried with it ownership of the mortgage security." Engle v. Federal Nat. Mortg. Ass'n, 1956 OK 176, ¶7, 300 P.2d 997, 999. Therefore, in Oklahoma it is not possible to bifurcate the security interest from the note. BAC Home Loans Servicing, L.P. v. White, 2011 OK CIV APP 35, ¶10, 256 P.3d 1014, 1017. Because the note is a negotiable instrument, it is subject to the requirements of the UCC. A foreclosing entity has the burden of proving it is a "person entitled to enforce an instrument" by showing it was "(i) the holder of the instrument, (ii) a nonholder in possession of the instrument who has the rights of a holder, or (iii) a person not in possession of the instrument who is entitled to enforce the instrument pursuant to Section 12A-3-309 or subsection (d) of Section 12A-3-418 of this title." 12A O.S. 2001 §3-301.

¶6 To demonstrate you are the "holder" of the note you must establish you are in possession of the note and the note is either "payable to bearer" (blank indorsement) or to an identified person that is the person in possession (special indorsement). Therefore, both possession of the note and an indorsement on the note or attached allonge are required in order for one to be a "holder" of the note.

¶7 To be a "nonholder in possession who has the rights of a holder" you must be in possession of a note that has not been indorsed either by special indorsement or blank indorsement. Negotiation is the voluntary or involuntary transfer of an instrument by a person other than the issuer to a person who thereby becomes its holder. 12A O.S. 2001, §3-201. Transfer occurs when the instrument is delivered by a person other than its issuer for the purpose of giving to the person receiving delivery the right to enforce the instrument. 12A O.S. 2001, §3-203. Delivery of the note would still have to occur even though there is no negotiation. Delivery is defined as the voluntary transfer of possession. 12A O.S. 2001, §1-201(b)(15). The transferee would then be vested with any right of the transferor to enforce the note. 12A O.S. 2001, §3-203(b). Some jurisdictions have held, without holder status and therefore the presumption of a right to enforce, the possessor of the note must demonstrate both the fact of the delivery and the purpose of the delivery of the note to the transferee in order to qualify as the person entitled to enforce. In re Veal, 450 B.R. 897, 912 (B.A.P. 9th Cir. 2011). See also, 12A O.S. 2001, §3-203.

¶8 In the present case, Appellee has only presented evidence of an indorsed-in-blank note and an "Assignment of Mortgage." Appellee must prove that it is the holder of the note or the nonholder in possession who has the rights of a holder *prior* to the filing of the foreclosure proceeding. In the present matter the timeliness of the transfer is in question. Since Bank of America did not file the blank indorsement until it filed its motion for summary judgment it is impossible to determine from the record when Bank of America acquired its interest in the underlying note.

¶9 The assignment of a mortgage is not the same as an assignment of the note. If a person is trying to establish they are a nonholder in possession who has the rights of a holder they must bear the burden of establishing their status as a nonholder in possession with the rights of a holder. Appellee must establish delivery of the note as well as the purpose of that delivery. In the present case, it appears Appellee is trying to use the "Assignment of Mortgage" in order to establish the purpose of delivery. The "Assignment of Mortgage" purports to transfer "[f]or value received, the undersigned, Mortgage Electronic Registration Systems, Inc., as nominee for BNC Mortgage, Inc., and its successors and assigns does hereby assign, transfer and set over unto Bank of America, National Association as Successor by Merger to LaSalle Bank National Association, as Trustee under the Trust Agreement for the Structured Asset Investment Loan Trust Series 2004-BNC2, that certain real estate mortgage dated August 30, 2004, granted by Momodu Ahmed Kabba and Humu Hawah Kabba, husband and wife. . . ." This language has been determined by other jurisdictions to not effect an assignment of a note but to be useful only in identifying the mortgage. Therefore, this language is neither proof of transfer of the note nor proof of the purpose of any alleged transfer. See, In re Veal, 450 B.R. 897, 905 (B.A.P. 9th Cir. 2011).

¶10 Appellee must show it became a "person entitled to enforce" *prior* to the filing of the foreclosure proceeding. In the present case, there is a question of fact as to when and if this occurred and summary judgment is not appropriate. Therefore, we reverse the granting of summary judgment by the trial court and remand back for further determinations. If it is determined Bank of America became a person entitled to enforce the note, as either a holder or nonholder in possession who has the rights of a holder after the foreclosure action was filed, then the case may be dismissed *without prejudice* and the action may be re-filed in the name of the proper party.

CONCLUSION

¶11 It is a fundamental precept of the law to expect a foreclosing party to actually be in possession of its claimed interest in the note, and to have the proper supporting documentation in hand when filing suit, showing the history of the note, so that the defendant is duly apprised of the rights of the plaintiff. This is accomplished by showing the party is a holder of the instrument or a nonholder in possession of the instrument who has the rights of a holder, or a person not in possession of the instrument who is entitled to enforce the instrument pursuant to 12A O.S. 2001, §3-309 or 12A O.S. 2001, §3-418. Likewise, for the homeowners, absent adjudication on the underlying indebtedness, the dismissal cannot cancel their obligation arising from an authenticated note, or insulate them from foreclosure proceedings based on proven delinquency and therefore, this Court's decision in no way releases or exonerates the debt owed by the defendants on this home. See, U.S. Bank National Association v. Kimball, 27 A.3d 1087, 2011 VT 81 (VT 2011); and Indymac Bank, F.S.B. v. Yano-Horoski, 78 A.D.3d 895, 912 N.Y.S.2d 239 (2010).

REVERSED AND REMANDED WITH INSTRUCTIONS

GURICH, J., with whom WINCHESTER, J. joins dissenting [omitted since it dealt with technical issues of standing in Oklahoma].

Hogan v. Washington Mutual Bank, N.A.

Supreme Court of Arizona, 2012
230 Ariz. 584, 277 P.3d 781

BERCH, Chief Justice.

¶1 We granted review to decide whether a trustee may foreclose on a deed of trust without the beneficiary first having to show ownership of the note that the deed secures. We hold that Arizona's non-judicial foreclosure statutes do not require the beneficiary to prove its authority or "show the note" before the trustee may commence a non-judicial foreclosure.

I. FACTUAL AND PROCEDURAL BACKGROUND

¶2 These consolidated cases involve two properties in Yavapai County purchased by John F. Hogan in the late 1990s. Each parcel became subject to a deed of trust in 2004 when Hogan took out loans from Long Beach Mortgage Company ("Long Beach"). By 2008, Hogan was delinquent on both loans, which triggered foreclosure proceedings. The trustee recorded a notice of sale for the first parcel, naming Washington Mutual Bank ("WaMu") as the beneficiary. A notice of trustee's sale recorded for the second parcel identified Deutsche Bank as the beneficiary.

¶3 Hogan filed lawsuits seeking to enjoin the trustees' sales unless the beneficiaries, WaMu and Deutsche Bank, proved that they were entitled to collect on the respective notes. The superior court granted the defendants' motions to dismiss and the court of appeals affirmed. Hogan v. Wash. Mut. Bank, N.A., 227 Ariz. 561, 261 P.3d 445 (App. 2011) ("OP"); Hogan v. Wash. Mut. Bank, N.A., 1 CA-CV 10-0385, 2011 WL 1158944 (Ariz. App. Mar. 29, 2011) (mem. Decision) ("MD"). In each case, the court of appeals held that "Arizona's non-judicial foreclosure statute does not require presentation of the original note before commencing foreclosure proceedings." OP at ¶13 (quoting Diessner v. Mortg. Elec. Registration Sys., 618 F. Supp. 2d 1184, 1187 (D. Ariz. 2009), *aff'd mem.*, 384 Fed. Appx. 609 (9th Cir. 2010)); MD at ¶19.

¶4 Hogan petitioned for review. We consolidated the cases and granted review because the cases present a recurring issue of first impression and statewide importance. We have jurisdiction under Article 6, Section 5(3) of the Arizona Constitution and A.R.S. §12-120.24 (2003).

II. Discussion

¶5 In Arizona, non-judicial foreclosure sales, or trustees' sales, are governed by statute. A.R.S. §§33-801 to -821 (2007 & Supp. 2011); *see* In re Vasquez, 228 Ariz. 357, 359 ¶4, 266 P.3d 1053, 1055 (2011). When parties execute a deed of trust and the debtor thereafter defaults, A.R.S. §33-807 empowers the trustee to sell the real property securing the underlying note through a non-judicial sale. Hogan contends that before a trustee may exercise that power of sale, the beneficiary must show possession of, or otherwise document its right to enforce, the underlying note. Nothing in our statutes, however, requires this showing. Section 33-809(C) requires only that, after recording notice of the trustee's sale under §33-808, the trustee must send the trustor notice of the default, signed by the beneficiary or his agent, setting forth the unpaid principal balance. *See also* Transamerica Fin. Servs., Inc. v. Lafferty, 175 Ariz. 310, 313-14, 856 P.2d 1188, 1191-92 (App. 1993) (recognizing that a trustee's obligation is only to mail notice to address provided). Hogan has not alleged that such notice was not given.

¶6 Hogan argues that a deed of trust, like a mortgage, "may be enforced only by, or in behalf of, a person who is entitled to enforce the obligation the mortgage secures." Restatement (Third) of Prop.: Mortgages §5.4(c) (1997); *see* Hill v. Favour, 52 Ariz. 561, 568-69, 84 P.2d 575, 578 (1938). We agree. But Hogan has not alleged that WaMu and Deutsche Bank are not entitled to enforce the underlying note; rather, he alleges that they have the burden of demonstrating their rights before a non-judicial foreclosure may proceed. Nothing in the non-judicial foreclosure statutes, however, imposes such an obligation. *See* Mansour v. Cal-Western Reconveyance Corp., 618 F. Supp. 2d 1178, 1181 (D. Ariz. 2009) (citing A.R.S. §33-807 and observing that "Arizona's [non-]judicial foreclosure statutes . . . do not require presentation of the original note before commencing foreclosure proceedings"); In re Weisband, 427 B.R. 13, 22 (Bankr. D. Ariz. 2010) (stating that non-judicial foreclosures may be conducted under Arizona's deed of trust statutes without presentation of the original note).

¶7 Hogan's complaints do not affirmatively allege that WaMu and Deutsche Bank are not the holders of the notes in question or that they otherwise lack authority to enforce the notes. Although a plaintiff need only set forth a "short and plain statement of the claim showing that [he] is entitled to relief," Ariz. R. Civ. P. 8(a)(2), the truth of which we assume when analyzing a complaint for failure to state a claim under Rule 12(b)(6), Cullen v. Auto-Owners Ins. Co., 218 Ariz. 417, 419 ¶7, 189 P.3d 344, 346 (2008), we will affirm a dismissal when "the plaintiff should be denied relief as a matter of law given the facts alleged," Logan v. Forever Living Products Int'l, Inc., 203 Ariz. 191, 193 ¶7, 52 P.3d 760, 762 (2002).

¶8 Here, assuming the truth of Hogan's factual allegations, Hogan is not entitled to relief because the deed of trust statutes impose no obligation on the beneficiary to "show the note" before the trustee conducts a non-judicial foreclosure. The only proof of authority the trustee's sales statutes require is a statement indicating the basis for the trustee's authority. *See* A.R.S. §33-808(C)(5) (requiring the notice to set forth "the basis for the trustee's qualification pursuant to §33-803, subsection A"); *see also* A.R.S. §33-807(A) (granting the trustee the "power of sale"). Hogan's complaints do not contest that each sale was noticed by a trustee who had recorded an instrument demonstrating that it was a successor in interest to the original trustee.

¶9 Hogan further contends that the trustee, as a party seeking to collect on a note, must demonstrate its authority to do so under §47-3301 of Arizona's Uniform Commercial Code ("UCC"). But the trustees here did not seek to collect on the underlying notes; instead, they noticed these sales pursuant to the trust deeds. The UCC does not govern liens on real property. *See* Rodney v. Ariz. Bank, 172 Ariz. 221, 224-25, 836 P.2d 434, 437-38 (App. 1992). The trust deed statutes do not require compliance with the UCC before a trustee commences a non-judicial foreclosure. *See* In re

Krohn, 203 Ariz. 205, 208 ¶8, 52 P.3d 774, 777 (2002) ("[D]eed of trust sales are conducted on a contract theory under the power of sale authority of the trustee.").

¶10 Hogan also claims that "the note and the trust deed go together" and "must be construed together." *See* A.R.S. §33-817 (providing that a transfer of the underlying contract operates to transfer the security for the contract). Although this is generally true, the note and the deed of trust are nonetheless distinct instruments that serve different purposes. The note is a contract that evidences the loan and the obligor's duty to repay. *See* A.R.S. §33-801(4). The trust deed transfers an interest in real property, securing the repayment of the money owed under the note. *See* A.R.S. §§33-801(4), -801(8), -801(9), -805, -807(A). The dispositive question here is whether the trustee, acting pursuant to its own power of sale or on behalf of the beneficiary, had the statutory right to foreclose on the deeds of trust. *See* Cervantes v. Countrywide Home Loans, Inc., 656 F.3d 1034, 1043-44 (9th Cir. 2011). Hogan does not dispute that he is in default under the deeds of trust and has alleged no reason to dispute the trustee's right.

¶11 Hogan suggests that if we do not require the beneficiary to "show the note," the original noteholder may attempt to later pursue collection despite a foreclosure. But Arizona's anti-deficiency statutes protect against such occurrences by precluding deficiency judgments against debtors whose foreclosed residential property consists of 2.5 acres or less, as is the case here. *See* A.R.S. §33-814(G); Mid Kansas Fed. Sav. & Loan Ass'n of Wichita v. Dynamic Dev. Corp., 167 Ariz. 122, 126, 804 P.2d 1310, 1314 (1991); Emily Gildar, Arizona's Anti-Deficiency Statutes: Ensuring Consumer Protection in a Foreclosure Crisis, 42 Ariz. St. L.J. 1019, 1020 (2010). Moreover, the trustee owes the trustor a duty to comply with the obligations created by the statutes governing trustee sales and the trust deed. *See* Patton v. First Fed. Sav. & Loan Ass'n of Phx., 118 Ariz. 473, 476, 578 P.2d 152, 155 (1978), A.R.S. §33-801(10) (providing that "[t]he trustee's obligations . . . are as specified in this chapter [and] in the trust deed").

¶12 Non-judicial foreclosure sales are meant to operate quickly and efficiently, "outside of the judicial process." *Vasquez*, 228 Ariz. at 359 ¶4 n.1, 266 P.3d at 1055 n.1 (citing Gary E. Lawyer, Note, *The Deed of Trust: Arizona's Alternative to the Real Property Mortgage*, 15 Ariz. L. Rev. 194, 194 (1973)). The legislature balanced the concerns of trustors, trustees, and beneficiaries in arriving at the current statutory process. Requiring the beneficiary to prove ownership of a note to defaulting trustors before instituting non-judicial foreclosure proceedings might again make the "mortgage foreclosure process . . . time-consuming and expensive," *id.* (internal quotation marks omitted), and re-inject litigation, with its attendant cost and delay, into the process, *see* Transamerica Fin. Servs., 175 Ariz. at 313-14, 856 P.2d at 1191-92 (citing I.E. Assocs. v. Safeco Title Ins. Co., 39 Cal. 3d 281, 216 Cal. Rptr. 438, 702 P.2d 596 (1985)).

III. CONCLUSION

¶13 For the reasons set forth above, the superior court's orders dismissing Hogan's complaints are affirmed and, although we agree with the result reached by the court of appeals, its opinion is vacated.

QUESTIONS

1. The Arizona Supreme Court more or less ignores the requirements of the Uniform Commercial Code in this decision, holding that it doesn't apply to real property foreclosures. While it's true that Article 9 [Secured Transactions] does not cover real property mortgages, Article 9 itself states that it does apply to promissory notes given in real property mortgage transactions, and that the foreclosure of the mortgage notes must comply with Article 3; Comment 6 to §9-308 specifically says: "Under this Article, attachment and perfection of a security interest in a secured right to payment do not of themselves affect the obligation to pay. For example, if the obligation is evidenced by a negotiable note, then Article 3 dictates the person to whom the maker must pay to discharge the note and any lien securing it. See Section 3-602."

2. The court holds that in Arizona the foreclosure statute governs who can foreclose and the rules of Article 3 are irrelevant. Hmm. Consider the actual language of Arizona's statute. Arizona Revised Statutes §33-807 permits a foreclosure sale "after a breach or default in performance of the contract or contracts, for which the trust property is conveyed as security, or a breach or default of the trust deed." This statute requires the court to answer the question of whether there has been a breach in the "contract" for which the property is conveyed or the trust deed. That appears to cut out the promissory note as having anything to do with that issue, but is that right? Surely if the maker of the note were current on payments to the holder of the mortgage no one could foreclose on the deed of trust, which would only be available as a cause of action if there were a default on the mortgage obligation. To reach an answer on these matters we need to return to the issue of the merger rule.

III.   THE MERGER RULE

If the plaintiff in the foreclosure suit doesn't possess the original promissory note, it's very tempting to just ignore the note and sue using the breach of the mortgage contract (or, as in Arizona, the deed of trust) as the cause of action. In the frenetic market for real property mortgages that has been with us for years, the banks that bought and sold the mortgages were much better at keeping records of who was the owner of the mortgage than they were at making sure they had possession of the promissory notes. They created a Mortgage Electronic Registration System (MERS), transferred the mortgages to MERS, and then had MERS keep track of which entity was the current assignee of the mortgage. In some cases, the assignee authorized MERS to do the foreclosure on behalf of the assignees of the mortgage (which met with mixed results in the courts as to whether MERS was the real party in interest). When the makers of the notes protested that the assignees of the mortgage and/or MERS had to produce the original promissory note because the UCC said so, there was incredulity. The UCC? Really? That course in law school we all avoided and whose rules we don't understand? Even judges (witness the Arizona Supreme Court) often threw up their hands and said something to the effect of "I'm not going to let the fusty rules of the Code slow down foreclosures in my court and let people get away without paying their mortgages just because the banks missed some technical steps like keeping track of promissory notes."

But the law is the law, and the UCC is statutory law in all U.S. jurisdictions in which foreclosures are going on. The fact that the banks stupidly misplaced the promissory notes and now can't be bothered to use their resources to find them (much less creating forged ones, which, trust us, has happened), ought not be an excuse for ignoring statutes the legislature has enacted.

PROBLEM 76

When the current assignee of the mortgage, Last National Bank, filed a foreclosure suit, the defendant demanded to see the original promissory note the defendant had signed. No one at LNB or its assignor has any idea what happened to the note. You are the attorney for LNB and you tell your client to dig deeper and find that note. The people at LNB reply that investigating this both at LNB and through all the other prior transfers registered at MERS is very expensive, but they'll look around quickly.

(a) One report from LNB's preliminary investigation suggests that the note may possibly have been scanned by a prior holder and the original then burned as part of a "paper reduction effort." Was that a good idea? See §3-604.

(b) If the note can't be found and the court insists on its production, the foreclosure will have to stop. What should LNB now do? See Restatement (Second) of Contracts §333(b), which creates a warranty at the time of assignment that the assignment is valid and there are no defenses to the assignment. What does this rule mean to your client?

(c) The attorney for LSN decides to ignore the note and just sue on the assignment of the mortgage. Can this be done? See §3-310(b)(2), the so-called merger rule, discussed below.

We dealt with the merger rule and its effect on the underlying obligation in the beginning of the last chapter. The rule states that whenever a negotiable instrument is created to pay a debt, the debt obligation is merged into the note until the note is dishonored. Discharge on the note leads to discharge on the underlying obligation. In mortgage situations, as we have seen, the maxim is that "security follows the debt," meaning here that the mortgage (the "security") goes with the "debt" (the promissory note). It is the law in all jurisdictions that the mortgage assignment is a nullity without the valid transfer of the note because the mortgage follows the note (and not the other way around). If the maker pays the note, the mortgage debt is discharged; see §3-310(b)(2). But until the note is dishonored the right to sue on the mortgage contract (the "underlying obligation") is *suspended*; §3-310(b). It cannot be the basis of a lawsuit until the note is dishonored.

In the Arizona foreclosure statute discussed after the last case, foreclosure could only be had "after a breach or default in performance of the contract or contracts, for which the trust property is conveyed as security, or a breach or default of the trust deed." In this statute surely "breach" or "default" means failure to pay the promissory note, because the other obligations are suspended until that happens. The only person who can demand payment of a promissory note is a person entitled to enforce the note, the PETE as defined in §3-301. This means in states that have renounced the "show me the note" defense and counted on the language of the foreclosure statute to authorize this result, a true reading of those statutes will demonstrate they all depend on a "default" of the mortgage obligation. As just explained, that means failure to pay the note when a PETE demands its payment.

The Uniform Commercial Code should make all states "show me the note" states.

IV.   LOST NOTES

PROBLEM 77

Return to the facts of the last Problem where you are the attorney for Last National Bank and no one can find the original promissory note. It comes to your attention that the Code has another possible escape route: §3-309. Read it and decide if it will protect your client. You should know that the 2002 revision of Article 3 (adopted to date in only 12 or so states) is the version of §3-309 in your statute book. The language of the prior version (which is the law in most states) is similar but in that version (b)(1) stated, "the person was in possession of the instrument and entitled to enforce it when loss of possession occurred." That requirement of being in possession when it was lost was dropped in the revision because it was a tough burden to meet, as the following case attests.

State Street Bank and Trust Co. v. Lord

District Court of Appeals of Florida, 2003
851 So. 2d 790

STONE, J.

The issue on appeal is whether a mortgagee by assignment, State Street Bank, may pursue a mortgage foreclosure in the absence of proof that either the mortgagee, or its assignor, ever had possession of the missing promissory note. A summary judgment was entered in favor of the mortgagor, Hartley Lord. We affirm.

State Street sought to establish the promissory note and mortgage under section 71.011, Florida Statutes. State Street alleged that Hartley executed the note and mortgage and that, after multiple assignments, the documents were assigned to State Street by EMC Mortgage Corporation. Although State Street alleged in its pleading that the original documents were received by it, the record established that State Street never had possession of the original note and, further, that its assignor, EMC, never had possession of the note and, thus, was not able to transfer the original note to State Street.

The trial court correctly concluded that as State Street never had actual or constructive possession of the promissory note, State Street could not, as a matter of law, maintain a cause of action to enforce the note or foreclose the mortgage. The right to enforce the lost instrument was not properly assigned where neither State Street nor its predecessor in interest possessed the note and did not otherwise satisfy the requirements of section 673.3091, Florida Statutes, at the time of the assignment. *See* Slizyk v. Smilack, 825 So. 2d 428, 430 (Fla. 4th DCA 2002).

To maintain a mortgage foreclosure, the plaintiff must either present the original promissory note or give a satisfactory explanation for its failure to do so. §90.953(1), Fla. Stat. (2002); W.H. Downing v. First Nat'l Bank of Lake City, 81 So. 2d 486 (Fla. 1955); Nat'l Loan Investors, L.P. v. Joymar Assocs., 767 So. 2d 549, 551 (Fla. 3d DCA 2000). A limited exception applies for lost, destroyed, or stolen instruments, where it is shown that "the person was in possession of the instrument and entitled to enforce it when loss of possession occurred." §673.3091, Fla. Stat. (2002).

Section 673.3091 provides, in part:

(1) A person not in possession of an instrument is entitled to enforce the instrument if:

(a) The person was in possession of the instrument and entitled to enforce it when loss of possession occurred;

(b) The loss of possession was not the result of a transfer by the person or a lawful seizure; and

(c) The person cannot reasonably obtain possession of the instrument because the instrument was destroyed, its whereabouts cannot be determined, or it is the wrongful possession of an unknown person or a person that cannot be found or is not amenable to service of process.

Here, it is unrefuted that State Street was unable to meet the requirement of section 673.3091. The undisputed facts show that the note was lost before the assignment to State Street was made. This court has previously refused to allow a mortgage foreclosure under similar circumstances. In Mason v. Rubin, 727 So. 2d 283 (Fla. 4th DCA 1999), the appellant brought a foreclosure action on a second mortgage, the trial court denied the foreclosure, and this court affirmed on the basis that the appellant had failed to establish the lost note under section 673.3091. Likewise, here, where State Street failed to comply with section 673.3091, the trial court correctly entered summary judgment denying its foreclosure claim.

State Street cannot succeed under an assignment theory. We recognize that this court, and the Third District, have held that the right of enforcement of a lost note can be assigned. *See Slizyk, 825 So. 2d at 430;* Deakter v. Menendez, 830 So. 2d 124 (Fla. 3d DCA 2002); *Nat'l Loan,* 767 So. 2d at 551. Here, however, in contrast to *National Loan, Slizyk,* and *Deakter,* there is no evidence as to who possessed the note when it was lost.

In *Slizyk,* we held that the assignee of a note and mortgage was entitled to foreclose despite his inability to produce the original documents. This court concluded that because the assignor was in possession of the notes, he had the right to enforce them. When the notes were assigned to the appellee, the right to enforce the instruments was assigned to him as well. *Id.* at 430. In contrast, here, the undisputed evidence was that EMC, the assignor, never had possession of the notes and, thus, could not enforce the note under section 673.3091 governing lost notes. Because EMC could not enforce the lost note under section 673.3091, it had no power of enforcement which it could assign to State Street. Were we to allow State Street to enforce the note because some unidentified person further back in the chain may possess the note, it would render the 673.3091 rule meaningless. We do not, and need not, reach any question as to whether *Slizyk* and *National Loan* may be applied where there is proof of an earlier assignor's possession further removed than the most immediate assignor.

We recognize that applying the statute as we do will result in a windfall to the mortgagor and a likely injustice to the mortgagee, unless it is able to obtain new evidence. In Dennis Joslin Company v. Robinson Broadcasting Corp., 977 F. Supp. 491 (D.D.C. 1997), the district court rejected the right to assign the enforcement of a lost note. Apparently, in response to that opinion, the Uniform Commercial Code was amended to delete the requirement that the transferee be in possession at the time the instrument was lost and now provides that the person seeking to enforce the instrument either was entitled to enforce the instrument when loss of possession occurred, or acquired ownership of the instrument from a person who was entitled to enforce the instrument when loss of possession occurred. *See* U.C.C. §3-309(a)(1) (2002). Florida, however, has not similarly amended its code and still requires possession either by the assignor at the time of loss or by the person seeking to enforce the note. Any remedy must, therefore, be left to the legislature.

V.   CONCLUSION

The truth is that the current lending mess is the result of years of sloppy practices, with greed as the fuel; no one paid any attention to details, and increasingly complex transactions led to the loss of a paper trail. But now the orgy has ended with major hangovers for the participants who paid no attention to the basic rules. The borrowers (who also have had to battle this problem at their end, when they can't figure out who is the proper party to negotiate with over repayment issues or settlement discussions) have done nothing wrong. They do owe the debt and the house is still the collateral, so they are not off the hook at all. But the courts won't let someone foreclose just because that someone thinks they are the right entity to do it, or *really, really, really* wants to foreclose. They have to prove they are a PETE by clear evidence. Wishing that they had that evidence is not enough. Indeed, as discussed above, if the buyer pays the wrong person, he/she still owes the debt.

When the consumer agrees to buys a new home and goes to the closing, the lending bank overwhelms the new homeowner with legal paper, after legal paper, after legal paper that the borrower must sign or the loan will not go through. At this end of the transaction, the bank is very careful to make sure everything is in apple pie order and that every "i" is dotted and every "t" is crossed. Perhaps it's not unfair that at the other end of the transaction when banks are attempting to take someone's home, they ought to be required to follow the law then too. As the Third Circuit has commented in a case where the foreclosing bank could not produce the necessary proof, "[f]inancial institutions, noted for insisting on their customers' compliance with numerous ritualistic formalities, are not sympathetic petitioners in urging relaxation of an elementary business practice"; Adams v. Madison Realty & Development, Inc., 853 F.2d 163 (3d Cir. 1988).

CHAPTER 6   ASSESSMENT

Multiple Choice Questions

1. Marley borrowed $100,000 from Securitization Bank, signing a negotiable promissory note and a mortgage deed. Securitization Bank locked the note up in a vault, and a few months later sold the rights to payment to Careless Bank, with a written contract of assignment. Marley meanwhile became unemployed and stopped making monthly payments. Does Careless Bank have the right to enforce the promissory note against Marley?

   a. Yes, because the right to collect was assigned to Careless Bank.

   b. No, because Marley's obligation to pay can run only to the lender, Securitization Bank.

   c. No, because Securitization Bank did not transfer the note to Careless Bank.

   d. No, because Marley did not consent to the assignment of the obligation to pay.

2. Suppose that Marley paid Careless Bank the money owing on the mortgage loan. Then the note showed up in the hands of Titan Bank. Securitization Bank had gotten its records mixed up, and had actually sold the note to Titan Bank before erroneously (and duplicatively) selling the right to collect to Careless Bank, who qualified as a holder in due course. If Titan Bank seeks to collect the note from Marley, would Marley be liable?

   a. No. The double assignment of the note was fraud, a defense that can be raised even against a holder in due course.

   b. Yes. Marley has no defense or discharge that can be raised against a holder in due course.

   c. No. Marley has paid the note, and so is no longer liable on the note.

   d. Yes. A note is collectible until it is stamped PAID.

3. Scrooge Bank sold Fezziwig Bank a negotiable promissory note, from a mortgage loan to Dilbner. Scrooge Bank delivered the note to Fezziwig Bank, but neglected to indorse the note. Does Fezziwig Bank have the right to enforce the note against Dilbner?

    a. No, because the note is still payable to Scrooge Bank, not Fezziwig Bank.

    b. Yes, because Scrooge Bank transferred the note to Fezziwig Bank.

    c. No. Dilbner can be liable only to its lender, Scrooge Bank.

    d. Yes, because the right to collect was assigned to Fezziwig Bank.

4. Careless Bank demanded payment from Homeowner on a mortgage loan assigned to Careless Bank by Shady Lender. Homeowner's attorney notified Careless Bank that Homeowner, if sued, would raise the defense of fraudulent inducement, alleging that Shady Lender had misrepresented the terms of the loan. Preparing for a lawsuit, Careless Bank discovered that Shady Lender not indorsed the promissory note. After some prompting, Shady Lender indorsed the note to Careless Bank. If Careless Bank sues, could Homeowner raise the defense of fraud?

    a. Yes. Fraud can be raised even against a holder in due course.

    b. Yes. Careless Bank is not a holder in due course.

    c. No. Careless Bank is a holder in due course.

    d. No. Careless Bank has the rights of a holder in due course, under the shelter rule.

5. Efficiency Bank sold 300 promissory notes to Trusting Bank, all of which came from mortgage loans made by Efficiency Bank to consumers. Rather than making indorsements on the notes themselves, Efficiency Bank wrote "Pay to the order of Trusting Bank, Efficiency Bank" on 300 pieces of paper, then placed one such paper next to each promissory note in the stack of notes. Trusting Bank paid a good price for the notes, and took them all in good faith, with no notice of any problems or irregularities. Could Trusting Bank be a holder in due course of any of the notes, in a case where the borrower had a defense arising out of Efficiency Bank's handling of the loan?

    a. No, because Trusting Bank is not a holder.

    b. Yes, because Trusting Bank is in possession and took for value, in good faith, and without notice of any problems or irregularities.

    c. Yes, because Trusting Bank is not responsible for Efficiency Bank's behavior.

    d. No, because the holder in due course doctrine does not apply to consumer transactions.

Answers

1. C is the best answer. To be the person entitled to enforce the instrument, Careless Bank must be the holder, a transferee with the rights of a holder, or someone with the right to enforce a lost, stolen, or destroyed

instrument. §3-301. An assignment of the right to collect does not make Careless any of those, so A is incorrect. B misstates the law grievously. The whole point of negotiable instruments is that the right to collect may be transferred by transferring the note. D likewise misstates the law. No consent of the obligor is necessary to transfer an instrument. Rather, in effect, one signing a negotiable instrument authorizes assignment of the right to collect. So a negotiable note may be assigned. But transfer of the note itself is necessary, unless the note has been lost, stolen, or destroyed). So C is the best answer.

2. B is the best answer. Marley did not pay a person who was entitled to enforce the instrument, so he does not get a discharge. See §3-602. This question illustrates why the person entitled to enforce the note must be the holder, a transferee with the rights of a holder, or a person enforcing a lost, stolen, or destroyed note. UCC §3-301. By generally requiring possession of the note to enforce the note, Article 3 protects an obligor against the risk that Marley took on here. To enforce the note, someone has to have possession of the note (be a holder or a transferee with the rights of a holder) or use the §3-309 process for enforcing a lost, stolen, or destroyed note. Under §3-309, such a person can get payment only by providing security against the possibility that a holder in due course will show up with the note and demand payment. In broader terms, this is why courts should enforce the rules of Article 3 and require banks to show the note to enforce mortgage debt: to protect borrowers who pay, against the possibility that the note will show up in the hands of a holder in due course.

3. B is the best answer. This question reminds us that indorsement is not necessary to transfer the note effectively. The note was payable to Scrooge Bank. When Scrooge Bank transferred the note to Fezziwig Bank, even if not indorsing it, that transferred Scrooge Bank's rights to Fezziwig Bank. The note itself is accounted for, and so there is no risk it can show up in the hands of a holder in due course. So the requirement to actually keep track of the note is not too onerous. A transfer without indorsement is sufficient to transfer the right to payment, contrary to A. C is incorrect, because someone signing a *negotiable* promissory note is liable to whoever has the right to enforce the note.

4. B is the best answer. The last question reminded us that indorsement is not necessary to be able to enforce an instrument. But this one reminds us that indorsement may be necessary if one wants to be able to enforce an instrument *as a holder in due course.* To be a holder in due course, Careless Bank must be a holder, which requires being in possession of an instrument payable to Careless Bank. Careless Bank was in possession, but the note was not indorsed to Careless Bank. Shady Bank finally indorsed the

note, but not before Careless Bank had notice of the defense of fraud. Careless Bank never met all four requirements to be a holder in due course (holder, value, good faith, no notice) at the same time. So, contrary to C, Careless Bank is not a holder in due course. Homeowner can raise any defense Homeowner has, such as fraud. A is incorrect, because fraud in the inducement cannot be raised against a holder in due course. Rights of a holder in due course can also be transferred, which does not require an indorsement. But that does not apply here. Shady Lender was not a holder in due course, because Shady Lender would have had notice of any fraud by Shady Lender. So the transfer from Shady Lender did not give Careless Bank the rights of a holder in due course, making D incorrect.

5. A is the best answer. This question also reviews important rules from earlier chapters and applies them in the mortgage context where these issues often arise. An indorsement may be made on an allonge, a separate piece of paper affixed to the instrument. But here the separate pieces of paper were not affixed to the notes, they were simply put next to them. Trusting Bank would therefore not be a holder of the notes, rather, a transferee with the rights of a holder. That would be sufficient for any note where the obligor had no defense to payment. But where an obligor had a defense to raise, Trusting Bank would be unable to establish holder in due course status. Nor could it use the shelter rule. If the defense arose out of Efficiency Bank's handling of the loan, Efficiency Bank would have notice of the defense and so would have no holder in due course rights to transfer to Trusting Bank. So, even though Trusting Bank took the note for value, in good faith, with no notice, it was not a holder and so not a holder in due course, contrary to B. C is incorrect, because a party with a defense may raise it against any non-holder in due course, not just against the party whose conduct gave rise to the defense. D states a common misconception. The holder in due course rule does not apply to promissory notes given by consumers to purchase goods or services. But it does apply to other consumer transactions, such as mortgage loans (or promissory notes given for loans of money, or transactions where payment is by check, as opposed to a promissory note).

CHAPTER 7

BANKS AND THEIR CUSTOMERS

A customer opens a checking account, or acquires a credit card, or uses a debit card to access this new bank account. Both federal and state laws will govern these transactions. Checks must move from one bank to another, a complex system made even more interesting in recent years by electronic conversion of these physical pieces of paper into images that zip in an instant from one bank to another. Centuries of presumptions based on paper must be rethought in the twenty-first century as e-transactions engulf the planet requiring new rules and regulations that become obsolete as they are enacted into law. To the lawyer who must master all of this, the challenge is both exciting and exasperating. How to understand it? Get a grasp on it? Master the new systems as they spring into being?

Twenty-first century casebook authors ask themselves where to begin, and come up with a comforting old answer: with the Uniform Commercial Code, of course. So let's start there and, that tamed, move to on more exotic beasts.

Article 4 of the Uniform Commercial Code covers Bank Deposits and Collections, matters inextricably entwined with the rules of Article 3 on Negotiable Instruments. Section 4-102(a) provides that whenever the provisions of Article 3 conflict with those of Article 4, the latter control. This can be important in warranty actions discussed in the next chapter; §§4-207 and 4-208 will prevail over the similar provisions in §§3-416 and 3-417 if both are arguably applicable. Another matter of concern is terminology. In addition to a general definitions section in §4-104, the complicated nomenclature of Article 4 banks is laid out in §4-105. Under these definitions, a bank can bear more than one label. In §4-105, which you should examine, the Article 3 drawee bank gets a new name and becomes known as the *payor bank* (or, in the federal regulations on check collection, the *paying bank*; 12 C.F.R. §229.2(z)). The depositary bank is the *first* bank to which an item is transferred for collection; it could also be the payor bank in situations where the drawer and the payee happen to do their banking at the same institution. Any bank in the collection process, except the payor bank, can be called a collecting bank; this includes the depositary bank.

I. THE CHECKING ACCOUNT

Whenever anyone opens a checking account with a bank, two legal relationships spring into being: debtor/creditor and principal/agent. The good news is that the depositor is the creditor and the bank the debtor (!); further, the bank is an agent for payment of the principal's drafts and other instructions. We will explore these legal connections shortly.

The opening of the account creates a contract; the force of centuries imbues it with these and other characteristics. Its details may be implied — see §1-303 — or may be the subject of detailed fine print. See, e.g., David v. Manufacturers Hanover Trust Co., 59 Misc. 2d 248, 298 N.Y.S.2d 847 (App. Div. 1969) (waiver of jury trial hidden in fine print of signature card upheld against charge of unconscionability). Read §4-103.

A. *"Properly Payable" Rule*

The basic contract between drawer and drawee, whether detailed or implied, always has at its nucleus this basic understanding: the bank may pay out the customer's money *only* if it follows the customer's orders exactly. If it does not do so, it must recredit the account. Article 4 backs up this understanding in §4-401, wherein it is stated that the bank may charge the account if the item is *properly payable*. What does *properly payable* mean here? Section 4-401(a) tells us that an "item is *properly payable* if it is authorized by the customer and is in accordance with any agreement between the customer and bank." It is easiest to understand this if you think of a check as if it were a letter addressed to the bank telling it what to do with the customer's money. The check is "properly payable" only if the bank follows the instructions of the customer *exactly*. If the bank makes a mistake and pays a check in a manner not instructed by the customer, the item is not properly payable and the bank must put the money back into the account.[1] Read §4-401.

Cincinnati Ins. Co. v. Wachovia Bank, Natl. Assn.

United States District Court, District of Minnesota, 2010
2010 WL 2777478

Opinion by PATRICK J. SCHILTZ.

I. BACKGROUND

Schultz Foods maintained a commercial checking account with Wachovia. Over the course of its relationship with Wachovia Bank, Schultz Foods was the victim of check fraud on four separate occasions. Wachovia and Schultz Foods were able to amicably resolve the first three instances of check fraud. On those three occasions, Schultz Foods closed the compromised account and opened a new account, and Wachovia absorbed the fraud-related loss. The fourth occasion gave rise to this lawsuit.

In late 2005, Schultz Foods issued a check in the amount of $153,856.46 to Amerada Hess Corporation. The check was stolen before it could be deposited by the intended recipient. In what is known as a "washing" scam, thieves removed the name of the original payee from the check and substituted the name of Kenneth Payton—who, as noted, was an unwitting accomplice of the thieves. Payton then endorsed the check and deposited it into his account at TCF Bank. TCF presented the check to Wachovia, and Wachovia transferred $153,856.46 from Schultz Foods's account at Wachovia to Payton's account at TCF. Following the instructions of the thieves, Payton then wired the money to a bank account in Singapore, and the thieves took the money and ran.

When the fraud came to light, Schultz Foods demanded that Wachovia re-credit its account, claiming that Wachovia must bear the loss because it processed the altered check in violation of §4-401(a) of the Uniform Commercial Code ("UCC"). Wachovia disagreed, citing the fact that Schultz Foods had declined to implement "Positive Pay," a check-fraud deterrence

---

1. Of course, there are exceptions, situations where the bank may violate the properly payable rule and live to tell about it. The bank may be able to escape liability by using any one of a number of defenses (customer negligence, subrogation, etc.), to be discussed later.

What should a bank do if the check is ambiguous because, say, the written amount is not the same as the numbers on the dollar sign line? UCC §3-114 states that:

> If an instrument contains contradictory terms, typewritten terms prevail over printed terms, handwritten terms prevail over both, and words prevail over numbers.

program that had been offered by Wachovia and that would have prevented the loss if Schultz Foods had only implemented it. According to Wachovia, under the terms of the deposit agreement between Schultz Foods and Wachovia, the failure of Schultz Foods to implement Positive Pay made Schultz Foods liable for the loss.

A word about Positive Pay: Unless a customer implements a program such as Positive Pay, a bank has little chance of identifying a forged or altered check, because a bank has no way of knowing whether a particular check was actually issued by a customer, whether a particular check was issued to the payee whose name appears on the check, or whether a particular check was issued in the amount that appears on the check. Positive Pay is a software program that enables a customer to transmit to its bank pertinent information about every check that the customer issues. For example, when a customer who uses Positive Pay issues check number 7394 to "Acme, Inc." in the amount of $15,286.25, the customer's bank is promptly *informed* that the customer has issued check number 7394 to "Acme, Inc." in the amount of $15,286.25. When a bearer then presents check number 7394 for payment, the bank's computer can compare the information on the check to the information that was transmitted by the customer. If the information does not match—if, for example, the name of the payee on check number 7394 is "Jane Smith" instead of "Acme, Inc."—the bank can contact the customer before clearing the check. Had Schultz Foods implemented Positive Pay, then, Wachovia would not have paid the "Kenneth Payton" check, and the loss would not have occurred.

Wachovia did pay the check, though, and thus $153,856.46 was deducted from the account of Schultz Foods. After Wachovia refused to re-credit the account, Schultz Foods filed a claim with its insurer, plaintiff Cincinnati Insurance Company ("Cincinnati"). Cincinnati paid the claim and then filed this subrogation action against Wachovia.

Cincinnati contends that, when Wachovia deducted the amount of the altered check from Schultz Foods's account, Wachovia violated §4-401(a) of the UCC. Wachovia responds that, under the terms of the deposit agreement between Schultz Foods and Wachovia, Schultz Foods's failure to implement Positive Pay makes Schultz Foods, and not Wachovia, liable for the loss. Cincinnati disputes Wachovia's interpretation of the deposit agreement. Cincinnati also argues that the risk-shifting provisions on which Wachovia relies are invalid, and Cincinnati contends that Wachovia waived its right to enforce those provisions. . . .

B. THE RELEASES

Bank deposits and collections are governed by Article 4 of the UCC. Section 4-401(a) of the UCC (codified at 13 Pa. Cons. Stat. §4401(a)) provides that "[a] bank may charge against the account of a customer an item that is properly payable from that account. . . . An item is properly payable if it is authorized by the customer and is in accordance with any agreement between the customer and the bank." Ordinarily, if a bank charges a customer's account for a check that is *not* properly payable—for example, a check that has been forged and therefore has not been authorized by the customer—the bank will be liable to the customer for the loss under §4-401(a). But this is merely a default rule. Section 4-103(a) of the UCC (codified at 13 Pa. Cons. Stat. §4103(a)) permits banks and their customers to agree to a different rule, except that an agreement between a bank and a customer "cannot disclaim the responsibility of a bank for its lack of good faith or failure to exercise ordinary care."

Schultz Foods did not issue a check to Kenneth Payton. Wachovia concedes that the altered check, as it was presented to the teller at Payton's bank, was not authorized by Schultz Foods. Thus, the check was not "properly payable" under §4-401(a), and, absent an agreement to the contrary, Wachovia is liable to Schultz Foods for charging the unauthorized check against the company's account.

The problem for Schultz Foods is that there *is* an agreement to the contrary—a deposit agreement signed by Schultz Foods when it opened its commercial checking account at Wachovia. . . . Section 12 of that agreement describes a variety of methods by which a customer can safeguard its account from fraud. These methods fall into two categories:

First, §12 contains a non-exhaustive bullet-pointed list of "precautions" that customers "can and should take to decrease the risk of unauthorized transactions." "Precautions," as that word is used in §12, are actions that any customer of any bank can take on its own to protect the security of its checking account. They include such common-sense measures as protecting the secrecy of passwords, promptly reviewing bank statements for unauthorized activity, and immediately reporting suspicious activity to the bank.

Second, §12 provides that "[i]n addition"—that is, in addition to the "precautions" that customers can take on their own—Wachovia itself may make available to its customers "certain products and services that are designed to detect and/or deter check fraud." Unlike the "precautions," these "products and services" are developed by Wachovia (or purchased from vendors by Wachovia) and offered to customers. Obviously, these "products and services" will do nothing to prevent fraud unless a customer implements them.

After first describing the "precautions" that a customer can take on its own and then mentioning the "products and services" that Wachovia may offer the customer, §12 of the deposit agreement concludes with a conditional release of Wachovia's liability:

> You agree that if you fail to implement any of these products or services, or you fail to follow these and other precautions reasonable for your

particular circumstances, you will be precluded from asserting any claims against [Wachovia] for paying any unauthorized, altered, counterfeit or other fraudulent item that such product, service, or precaution was designed to detect or deter, and we will not be required to re-credit your account or otherwise have any liability for paying such items. . . .

C. VALIDITY OF THE RELEASES

Cincinnati argues that even if the releases purport to bar Schultz Foods (or its subrogee) from seeking to recover $153,856.46 from Wachovia in this action, Wachovia cannot rely on the releases because the releases are invalid for a variety of reasons. The Court addresses Cincinnati's arguments in turn.

1. *Generally*

Cincinnati first argues that banks are strictly liable under §4-401(a) of the UCC for charging against the account of a customer an item that is not properly payable. Cincinnati further argues that a bank and a customer may not enter an agreement that absolves the bank of this strict liability. In support of its argument, Cincinnati relies almost entirely on Cumis Insurance Society v. Girard Bank, 522 F. Supp. 414 (E.D. Pa. 1981).

Cincinnati is right on the first point, but wrong on the second. It is indeed true that, under §4-401(a), "ordinarily a bank is strictly liable for charging a customer's account with an amount that the customer had not authorized the bank to pay." Travelers Cas. & Sur. Co. of Am. v. Wells Fargo Bank N.A., 374 F.3d 521, 525 (7th Cir. 2004). And thus *Cumis* was accurate (or at least accurate enough) in characterizing §4-401 as imposing "strict liability" on a bank for paying an unauthorized check. 522 F. Supp. at 419, 421.

At the same time, "a bank and its customer can contract out of that strict liability." *Travelers*, 374 F.3d at 525. Section 4-103(a) clearly provides that, within certain limits, "[t]he effect of the provisions of this division may be varied by agreement." And *Cumis* itself acknowledged that a bank can contract out of the "strict liability" imposed by §4-401(a); *Cumis* simply held that, under the circumstances of the particular case, the bank had failed to do so. 522 F. Supp. at 422-23. In sum, Cincinnati's contention that a bank cannot contract out of the strict liability imposed under §4-401(a) is contradicted not only by §4-103(a), but by the very decision on which it relies.

Cincinnati next argues that the releases are not valid because they purport to excuse Wachovia from exercising ordinary care. Section 4-103(a) places limits on the ability of parties to use a contract to vary the provisions of Article 4 of the UCC. Under §4-103(a), for example, the parties "cannot disclaim the responsibility of a bank for its lack of good faith or failure to exercise ordinary care." Cincinnati points out that the releases in the deposit agreement between Wachovia and Schultz Foods would, on their face, protect Wachovia from liability for paying an unauthorized check even if Wachovia failed to exercise ordinary care. Therefore, argues Cincinnati, the releases are invalid under §4-103(a).

It is important to emphasize that Cincinnati does not allege that Wachovia in fact failed to exercise ordinary care in paying the unauthorized check to Payton. In other words, Cincinnati does not allege that giving effect to the releases *in this case* would permit Wachovia to evade its nonevadable responsibility to exercise ordinary care. Cincinnati is instead complaining that the releases are overbroad—and thus, in some *other* case, giving effect to the releases would permit Wachovia to evade its responsibility to exercise ordinary care in violation of §4-103(a).

Cincinnati is certainly correct in arguing that the releases are overbroad. But Cincinnati is incorrect in arguing that, because the releases cannot be applied to *some* cases, they cannot be applied to *any* case. Section 46 of the deposit agreement provides:

> If there is any conflict between this Agreement and applicable federal or state law, this Agreement will be considered changed to the extent necessary to comply with the law. If any provision in this Agreement is declared to be invalid, unenforceable or illegal, that part will not affect the validity of other provisions.

This is a severability clause. It provides, in essence, that if some part of the deposit agreement is invalid, the remaining parts of the agreement remain in effect. Some parts of the Wachovia deposit agreement are indeed invalid: the parts of the releases found in §12 and §25E that apply to claims that Wachovia failed to exercise ordinary care in paying unauthorized checks. Under the severability clause in §46, however, the remainder of the deposit agreement remains in effect, including the remainder of the releases found in §12 and §25E. In this action, Wachovia is relying on the valid parts of the releases, and, under §46, those parts are enforceable.

2. Reasonableness of the Releases

Section 4-103 imposes a couple of "reasonableness" requirements on the attempts of parties to use contracts to vary the provisions of Article 4 of the UCC.

First, as discussed above, §4-103(a) forbids the parties to an agreement to "disclaim the responsibility of a bank for its lack of good faith or failure to exercise ordinary care." Section 4-103(a) goes on to clarify that "the parties may determine by agreement the standards by which the responsibility of the bank is to be measured," but only "if those standards are not manifestly unreasonable." Thus, §4-103(a) allows parties to agree to the standards by which a bank's responsibility to exercise ordinary care will be measured, as long as the agreed-upon standards are not "manifestly unreasonable."

Second, §4-103(d) provides generally that "[t]he specification or approval of certain procedures by this division is not disapproval of other procedures that may be reasonable under the circumstances." Section 4-103(d) emphasizes that parties have the freedom to agree to "procedures" that vary from those provided in Article 4, as long as the agreed-upon procedures are "reasonable under the circumstances."

As discussed at length, the deposit agreement between Wachovia and Schultz Foods required Schultz Foods either to implement Positive Pay or to assume responsibility for any fraud losses caused by its failure to implement Positive Pay. Cincinnati and Wachovia agree that these provisions are subject to the "reasonableness" requirements of §4-103, although they disagree about whether the appropriate standard is the "manifestly unreasonable" standard of §4-103(a) or the "reasonable under the circumstances" standard of §4-103(d). The Court need not resolve the dispute because the Court finds that the relevant provisions of the deposit agreement are not "manifestly unreasonable" for purposes of §4-103(a) and are "reasonable under the circumstances" for purposes of §4-103(d).

As the parties agree, reasonableness under either standard is a function of (1) the technical feasibility of implementing Positive Pay and (2) the cost of installing and participating in the program. Cincinnati conceded at oral argument that it was technically feasible for Schultz Foods to implement Positive Pay. *See also* Morrison Decl. PP 13-16. Cincinnati also conceded that Schultz Foods could have configured its existing computer system to work with Positive Pay for less than $500. Although implementing Positive Pay would have required Schultz Foods to pay modest monthly and per-check fees, Wachovia asserts (and Cincinnati does not dispute) that these fees would have been more than offset by credits that Wachovia extends to Pennsylvania customers in lieu of interest. . . . It is clear, then, that Wachovia acted reasonably in requiring Schultz Foods either to implement Positive Pay or to assume responsibility for fraud-related losses that could have been prevented by Positive Pay.

Cincinnati nevertheless insists that requiring Schultz Foods to implement Positive Pay was unreasonable — not because the cost of implementation was *in fact* unreasonable, but because Schultz Foods mistakenly *believed* that the cost of implementation was unreasonable. Cincinnati contends that Schultz Foods wrongly thought that it would cost tens of thousands of dollars to implement Positive Pay. Cincinnati does not allege that Wachovia misled Schultz Foods about the cost of Positive Pay or even that Wachovia knew of Schultz Foods's mistaken belief. Instead, Cincinnati seems to allege that Schultz Foods simply assumed that implementing Positive Pay would be expensive and that its mistake was never corrected — either by Schultz Foods asking Wachovia about the actual costs or by Wachovia volunteering information about the actual costs.

Cincinnati cites no authority suggesting that, under §4-103, the reasonableness of standards or procedures imposed under an agreement is to be judged based on the subjective beliefs of the parties to that agreement. The absence of supporting authority is unsurprising, as a subjective standard would be unworkable. Under an objective standard, a court can look at the face of an agreement and assess the reasonableness of the obligations actually imposed. But under a subjective standard, the validity of any agreement would turn not (or not just) on what was in the agreement, but on what was in the heads of the parties to the agreement. The Wachovia deposit agreement—an agreement that has presumably been signed by countless customers—would be valid in some cases and not valid in others, depending on what the particular customer *believed* about the obligations imposed by the agreement. Just as an agreement that imposes unreasonable obligations should not be valid if a customer mistakenly believes the obligations to be reasonable, an agreement that imposes reasonable obligations should not be invalid if a customer mistakenly believes the obligations to be unreasonable.

In this case, the Positive Pay obligation imposed by the deposit agreement was unquestionably reasonable. Schultz Foods mistakenly reached a contrary conclusion, but there is no evidence that Wachovia misled Schultz Foods about the cost of Positive Pay (indeed, it would have been irrational for Wachovia to do so), and there is no evidence that Wachovia was even aware of Schultz Foods's mistake. Under these circumstances, the Court holds that the relevant provisions of the deposit agreement are not "manifestly unreasonable" for purposes of §4-103(a) and are "reasonable under the circumstances" for purposes of §4-103(d). . . .

ORDER

Based on the foregoing and on all of the files, records, and proceedings herein,

IT IS HEREBY ORDERED THAT:

1. The motion of defendant Wachovia Bank, National Association for summary judgment [Docket No. 33] is GRANTED.
2. Plaintiff's complaint is DISMISSED WITH PREJUDICE AND ON THE MERITS.

LET JUDGMENT BE ENTERED ACCORDINGLY.

Some typical situations in which the bank might violate the "properly payable" rule are explored next.

PROBLEM 78

When Portia Moot paid off a debt she owed to her law school room-mate, she gave her a postdated check, dating it one week later (planning to cover it with the paycheck she would receive before that date). The roommate deposited the check in her own bank immediately, and that bank presented it to the payor bank before the date of the check. Portia's bank paid the check even though this created an overdraft (for which Portia was charged). Was the check properly payable before its date? See §4-401(c). If Portia had phoned the bank and warned it that she had written this postdated check, would it have still been properly payable? See Vincene Verdun, Postdated Checks: An Old Problem with a New Solution in the Revised U.C.C., 14 U. Ark. Little Rock L.J. 37 (1991). Banks hate postdated checks because the electronic information passed through the system does not include the date of the check. Could banks solve this problem by putting a clause in the checking account by which the customer promises not to write postdated checks and agrees that the bank will have no liability for paying a check before the date of the check? See §4-103; Aliaga Medical Center, S.C. v. Harris Bank N.A., 2014 IL App. (1st) 133645-U, 2014 WL 4415328 (Ill. App. 2014).

PROBLEM 79

Jack Point lost his checkbook. A month later his bank, Yeomen National, returned his canceled checks, including one payable to W. Shadbolt for $1,000, to which Jack's name was forged as drawer. He notified Yeoman National Bank promptly. Was this check *properly payable*? See §§3-401, 3-403. If Jack had called Yeomen National immediately on finding out that his checkbook was missing, could the bank have made him stop payment on all those blank checks and also pay a good hefty stop-payment fee on each one? See Official Comment 1 to §4-401.

PROBLEM 80

The Widow Douglas gave a check for $10.00 to Ben Rogers in return for the latter's mowing her lawn. Rogers's friend Joe Harper stole the check from Rogers, raised the amount to $1,000 by erasing the decimal point and cleverly altering the writing, and forged Rogers's signature to the back of the check. Harper presented the check for payment to the drawee bank, Clemens State Bank, which paid Harper $1,000. This reduced the balance in the Widow Douglas's account to zero and caused four other checks she had sent to her creditors to bounce. The Widow Douglas sued her bank, arguing as follows:

> Section 4-401 says that the bank may charge my account only when the item is *properly payable*. On this check I ordered the bank to pay out $10 of my funds to Ben Rogers or his order. But since Ben Rogers never signed it, he never ordered it paid to anyone, and therefore the bank did not pay in accordance with my instructions and must recredit my account. Whatever payment it made was out of the bank's own funds.

Clemens State Bank replied:

> All we are required to do is make sure that the item is apparently *properly payable*, that is, that it *appears* to contain the proper chain of endorsements. We must also, of course, act in good faith, which we have done. Mrs. Douglas paid Rogers, and if Rogers carelessly lost the check, why should that act as a windfall to Mrs. Douglas? If Mrs. Douglas is permitted to win here, she will have gotten a free lawnmowing job, and we will be out $1,000. In the alternative, even if we improperly charged this account with the entire amount, surely §4-401(d)(2) permits us to take $10 out of the account.

Which argument would prevail if you were the judge? As to the bank's "at least $10" argument, notice the word *holder* in §4-401(d). What effect does it have on the resolution of this dispute? If the bank decides to recredit the account, it will be able to recoup its loss by using the warranty theories explored in the next chapter.

Whenever a bank wrongfully takes money out of the account of its customer, it is very tempting for the customer's attorney to sue in conversion because the bank's misappropriation certainly sounds like an act of conversion. Technically, however, conversion will not lie. The reason is that when a customer puts money in the bank, that money is on *loan* to the bank; the bank becomes a *debtor* and the customer is a *creditor*. The bank cannot convert its own property any more than any debtor converts property by failing to repay the debt. Instead, the proper cause of action is for violation of §4-401 (the "properly payable" rule) or is simply an action in contract or quasi-contract (money had and received).

PROBLEM 81

You are the attorney for Octopus National Bank, and the bank has presented you with the following problem: it recently paid a check drawn on a customer's account, and there was no drawer's signature on the check. The payee on the check was a telemarketing firm that had apparently called the bank's customer, sold him some product over the phone, had the customer read off the magnetically encoded numbers at the bottom of the check,[2] and then created the check, including the magnetically encoded line. In lieu of the drawer's signature, the check is stamped "drawer's signature on file." The customer has now called and complained, apparently suffering from "buyer's remorse," and wants the account recredited with the amount of the check. There are a lot of these "pre-authorized drafts" (or "telechecks") now being created. Is the payor bank doing wrong when it honors them?

PROBLEM 82

Lemuel Gulliver opened an account with the Swift State Bank. After using the account for several years, he was away on a sea voyage for a long period of time. When he returned, a check that he had written (and dated) eight years ago was presented and paid against his account, creating an overdraft.[3] Gulliver protested the payment. Will this argument succeed? As to the old

---

2. The information magnetically encoded across the bottom of checks is printed in what are called magnetic ink character recognition (MICR—usually pronounced "mick-er") symbols so that the line can be read by automated check-processing machines. The MICR line reflects a routing number representing the drawee bank, the account number of the drawer, the check number, and certain other routing information. If you look at one of your canceled checks, you will also notice that at some point (normally done at the operations center of the depositary bank) someone put MICR numbers in the lower right-hand corner of the check, reflecting the amount of the check. This is done, of course, so that the check-processing machines can read the amount. Section 4-209 creates a warranty that this information has been correctly encoded. We will have more about the MICR line when we get to check truncation.

3. For consumer accounts, a bank that pays overdrafts and, by contract, charges a greater amount than is charged for returning these checks may accidentally have imposed a finance charge on the transaction. If this is done pursuant to written agreement with the customer, the bank will need to give a Truth in Lending statement to its consumer customers, or it will violate the federal Truth in Lending Act. See Regulation Z, 12 C.F.R. §1026.4(b)(2) and (c)(3). Banks earn an eye-popping amount of money from paying overdrafts and assessing fees—more than $31.6 billion in 2011!—doing this with 30 percent of their customers and therefore making such fees a major source of income. For a detailed discussion of this issue, see Bounce Protection: Payday Lending in Sheep's Clothing?, 8 N.C. Banking Inst. 349 (2004). We will return to this issue in Chapter 9 when we come to debit cards.

check, see §§4-401, 4-404; White & Summers §19-3; compare Granite Equip. Leasing Corp. v. Hempstead Bank, 68 Misc. 2d 350, 326 N.Y.S.2d 881 (Sup. Ct. 1971), with New York Flame-Proofing Co. v. Chemical Bank, 1974 WL 21730 (N.Y. Civ. Ct. 1974), and Charles Ragusa & Son v. Community State Bank, 360 So. 2d 231 (La. App. 1978). Did the creation of an overdraft situation keep the check from being properly payable? See §4-401(a). Does the language of that section mean that a bank must pay overdrafts? See §4-402(a). How quickly must Gulliver file suit? See §4-111; the statute of limitations for actions arising in Article 3 of the Code is found in §3-118.

B.   *Wrongful Dishonor*

Whenever a bank makes an improper payment from an account, this debit may cause other checks written by the customer to be wrongfully dishonored. The customer may recover all actual damages whenever the bank makes a *wrongful* (which includes *mistaken*) dishonor of a check that is properly payable from the account. Read §4-402 and its Official Comment.

Twin City Bank v. Isaacs

Arkansas Supreme Court, 1984
263 Ark. 127, 672 S.W.2d 651

STEELE HAYS, J.

Twin City Bank has appealed from a judgment entered on a jury verdict against it in favor of Kenneth and Vicki Isaacs for damages sustained from the bank's wrongful dishonor of the Isaacs' checks resulting in a hold order against their account for a period of approximately four years.

On Sunday, May 13, 1979, the Isaacs discovered that their checkbook was missing. They reported the loss to Twin City promptly on Monday, May 14, and later learned that two forged checks totalling $2,050 had been written on their account and honored by the bank on May 11 and 12. The sequence of events that followed is disputed, but the end result was a decision by the bank to freeze the Isaacs' checking account which had contained approximately $2,500 before the forgeries occurred. A few checks cleared Monday morning before a hold order was issued leaving the balance at approximately $2,000. Mr. Isaacs had been convicted of burglary and the initial hold on the account was attributable to the bank's concern that the Isaacs were somehow involved with the two forged checks. The individual responsible for the forgeries was charged and convicted soon after the forgeries occurred and on May 30, 1979 the police told the bank there was nothing to connect the Isaacs with the person arrested. Two weeks later the police notified the bank a second time they could not connect the Isaacs to the forgeries. The bank maintains it continued to keep the account frozen on the advice of its attorneys. However that may be, the Isaacs were denied their funds for some four years. The Isaacs filed suit in mid-June of 1979 for wrongful dishonor of their checks and wrongful withholding of their funds.

The jury awarded the Isaacs $18,500 in compensatory damages and $45,000 in punitive damages. The bank made a motion for a new trial pursuant to A.R.C.P. Rule 59, which was denied. From that denial the bank brings this appeal contending error on three grounds: 1) Misconduct of a juror at trial, 2) the trial court's refusal to give two requested instructions, and 3) jury error in assessing excessive damages contrary to the evidence and the law. . . .

On the issue of damages, the bank maintains there was insufficient evidence to support the $18,500 award for mental anguish, for loss of credit and loss of the bargain on a house, that the award of punitive damages should not have been given at all as there was not only insufficient proof of actual damages but insufficient evidence of malice or intent to oppress on the part of the bank. The bank does not challenge the sufficiency of the evidence of its wrongful dishonor, but contends only that there was no evidence to support an award of damages. These arguments cannot be sustained.

The statute upon which this suit was based is Ark. Stat. Ann. §85-4-402. [The court quoted §4-402. — Eds.]

The jury was instructed that if they found the bank liable they were to fix the amount of money which would compensate the Isaacs "for any of the following elements of damage sustained which were proximately caused by the conduct of Twin City Bank: 1) Any amounts of money wrongfully held by the defendant and remaining unpaid, 2) any mental anguish and embarrassment suffered by the plaintiffs, 3) any financial losses sustained by the [Isaacs]." Initially, there can be no serious question as to certain losses, the $2,000 wrongfully withheld by the bank for four years, and the value of two vehicles repossessed because the Isaacs did not have access to their funds, resulting in a loss of approximately $2,200. Additionally, after the account was frozen the bank continued to charge the account a service charge and overdraft fees on checks written before the forgeries but presented after the account was frozen. The bank does not refute these damages but argues there is no showing of any financial deprivation from loss of credit or loss of the bargain on a house the Isaacs wanted to buy, and insufficient proof of mental anguish. We find, however, that in addition to the losses previously mentioned, there was sufficient evidence to sustain damages for mental suffering, loss of credit, and sufficient demonstration of some loss attributable to the inability to pursue the purchase of a home.

Mental suffering under §4-402 of the Uniform Commercial Code is relatively new and has not been frequently addressed by other courts, but of those a majority has allowed recovery. Morse v. Mutual Federal Savings and Loan, 536 F. Supp. 1271 (Mass. 1982); Farmers & Merchants State Bank of Krum v. Ferguson, 617 S.W.2d 918 (Tex. 1981); Northshore Bank v. Palmer, 525 S.W.2d 718 (Tex. 1975); Kendall Yacht Club v. United California Bank, 50 Cal. App. 3d 949, 123 Cal. Rptr. 848 (1975); and see White & Summers, Uniform Commercial Code (1980 2d ed.) §17-4, p. 675. In general, the type of mental anguish suffered under §4-402 does not need to rise to the higher standard of injury for intentional infliction of emotional distress. Wrongful dishonors tend to produce intangible injuries similar to those involved in defamation actions. See State Bank of Siloam Springs v. Marshall, 163 Ark. 566, 260 S.W. 431 (1924). Damages of this kind are more difficult to assess with exactness. In Wasp Oil v. Arkansas Oil and Gas, 280 Ark. 420, 658 S.W.2d 397 (1983) we noted the general rule that damages may not be allowed where they are speculative, resting only upon conjectural evidence, or the opinions of the parties or witnesses, but there are instances where damages cannot be proven with exactness. In *Wasp* we recognized a different rule applies when the cause and existence of damages have been established by the evidence, that recovery will not be denied merely because the damages cannot be determined with exactness. We went on to say the plaintiff in the case at bar was not trying to prove the latter sort of damage such as *mental anguish* as a result of defamation, but loss of income.

Decisions upholding recovery for mental suffering under the code have found injury resulting from circumstances comparable to this case. In *Northshore Bank v. Palmer*, supra, for example, a $275 forged check was paid from Palmer's account. After the bank knew or should have known the check was forged, it charged Palmer with the $275 check and later wrongfully dishonored other checks. Part of the actual damages awarded was attributed to mental suffering for the "embarrassment and humiliation Palmer suffered from having been turned down for credit for the first time in his life."

In *Morse v. Mutual Federal Savings and Loan*, supra, $2,200 was awarded for "false defamatory implications arising from temporary financial embarrassment." And in *Farmers & Merchants State Bank of Krum v. Ferguson*, supra, the plaintiff's account in the amount of $7,000 was frozen for apparently one month for reasons not stated. The plaintiff was awarded $25,000 for mental anguish, $3,000 for loss of credit based on a denial of a loan, $5,000 for loss of time spent making explanations to creditors, and $1,500 for loss of use of his money. The court justified the mental suffering award because the dishonor was found to be with malice — the bank had failed to notify Ferguson that the account was frozen, some checks were honored while others were not, and the bank continued to withdraw loan payments due it during the entire time.

In this case, prior to the forgery incident the Isaacs' credit reputation with Twin City Bank was described by the bank as "impeccable" and the freezing of their funds had a traumatic effect on their lives. They obviously lost their credit standing with Twin City, and were unable to secure credit commercially at other institutions because of their status at Twin City. The Isaacs had to borrow from friends and family, and were left in a precarious position financially. They did not have use of their $2,000 for four years. The allegation relative to the loss of a house resulted from the dishonor of an earnest money check for a home they were planning to buy, ending prospects for the purchase at that time. Though there may have been insufficient proof of loss of the bargain on the house, as the bank argues, nevertheless this evidence was admissible as an element of mental suffering. The denial of credit contributed to some monetary loss as occurred in *Ferguson*, supra, in addition to its being a reasonable element of mental suffering as was found in *Palmer*, supra. There was also testimony that the financial strain contributed to marital difficulties leading at one point to the filing of a divorce suit. The suit was dropped but there was testimony that the difficulties caused by the bank's action caused substantial problems in the marriage. Finally, the Isaacs lost equities in two vehicles repossessed as a result of the withholding of their funds. One of these, a new van, was repossessed by Twin City in June, 1979, before a five-day grace period for a current installment had expired.

We believe there was substantial evidence to support the verdict. The jury heard the evidence of the amount wrongfully withheld, the loss of two vehicles, credit loss through loan denials, loss of the use of their money for four years, the suffering occasioned by marital difficulties, the inability to acquire a home they wanted, and the general anxieties which accompanied the financial strain. We recognize that our holding today presents some conflict with pre-code law by allowing recovery without exactness of proof as to damages. In *State Bank of Siloam Springs v. Marshall*, supra, a suit based on the predecessor to §4-402, we stated that the plaintiff must show the facts and circumstances which occasioned the damage and the amount thereof. However, *Marshall* itself recognized the nature of the damages in this action, and §4-402, although similar to its predecessor, has additional language which impliedly recognizes mental suffering and other intangible injuries of the type noted in *Wasp*, supra, as recoverable under this statute. See White & Summers, supra, §17-4, p. 675. To the extent that exactness in proof is not required, the law as stated in *Marshall* is displaced by §4-402.

The bank's objection to the award of punitive damages is threefold: a) The instruction on punitive damages was in accordance with A.M.I. 2217, which is intended for use in negligence cases and not applicable here; b) there was no evidence that the bank acted intentionally or with malice; and c) the verdict of $45,000 was excessive. However, we address only the question of the excessiveness of the verdict, as the other points were not raised in the trial court by objection to the instruction. Crowder v. Flippo, 263 Ark.

433, 565 S.W.2d 138 (1978); Dodson Creek Inc. v. Walton, 2 Ark. App. 128, 620 S.W.2d 947 (1981); A.R.C.P. Rule 51. . . .

The judgment is affirmed.

PROBLEM 83

Stella and Harry Squabble, after many years of constant fighting, decided to separate and seek a divorce. Stella's attorney filed the proper papers and then, to preserve Harry's financial assets in the status quo, sent a *lis pendens* (notice of litigation) to the bank in which Harry maintained an account for the barber shop he owned. The bank was uncertain what to do about the lis pendens notice, but the bank's attorney was a conservative type and advised the bank to freeze Harry's account until the divorce matter was settled. Fourteen of the barber shop's checks bounced as a result of this decision, and Harry's ulcer acted up and put him in the hospital. Harry filed suit against his bank, asking for $100,000 in damages. At trial he proved only the above facts but offered no evidence as to damages. Should the trial judge grant the defendant's motion for a directed verdict? See White & Summers §19-4.

PROBLEM 84

When Archie Goodwin received his paycheck from Nero Wolfe, his employer, he walked it into New York Metropolitan National Bank, the drawee, and presented it across the counter. The teller asked him if he had an account of his own with the bank. When he replied that he did not, the bank told him that it was the bank's policy not to pay across-the-counter checks drawn on it unless the payee had an account at the bank. Is this a wrongful dishonor? See *Your Style Publications, Inc. v. Mid Town Bank & Trust Co. of Chicago,* 150 Ill. App. 3d 421, 501 N.E.2d 805 (1986); *Buckley v. Trenton Savings Fund Society,* 216 N.J. Super. 705, 524 A.2d 886 (1987). Could the bank solve this problem by putting a clause in the checking account agreement stating that the customer would permit the bank to refuse to pay checks presented across the counter unless the presenter had an account with the bank? See §4-103.

PROBLEM 85

Many of the maintenance workers at Football University had no checking accounts at all (the so-called unbanked). When they received their monthly paychecks, they physically walked them into the bank on which they were drawn and presented them across the counter for payment. The drawee bank informed them that for each check presented, the bank would extract a fee of $10 for honoring an across-the-counter-presentment. The maintenance workers are angry about this. In effect, it is a major cut in pay for many of them. They are in your law office now. Can you suggest any form of relief?

C. Death or Incompetence of Customer

The common law rule that death or incompetence of a principal revokes the authority of an agent to act used to play havoc with checking accounts. It was a sure thing that the drafters of Article 4, among them representatives of the banking industry, would enact a solution to the problem. Read §4-405 and its Official Comment.

PROBLEM 86

Howard Mortus dropped dead while walking back to his house from the corner mailbox in which he had just deposited the month's bill payments. His widow phoned the payor bank the next day and informed the bank of Howard's death. She mentioned the mailed checks and specifically asked the bank manager to keep the account, which was in Howard's name only, open to pay them. The bank manager said that the bank would pay the checks for nine more days. Later that same day, Crazy Nelly, the Mortuses' next-door neighbor, somehow got the idea that Howard had left her all his money (he didn't leave her a cent—he barely knew her) and called up the bank. She explained she was the Mortuses' neighbor and was "sure to be an heir to the estate," so she ordered the bank to stop paying checks on Howard's account. The bank consulted its attorney. Must it stop paying checks, or may it still continue to do so? If it returns checks, will it have made a dishonor? Cf. §3-502. Is it a *wrongful* dishonor so as to subject the bank to §4-402 damages?

D. Bank's Right of Setoff

In the late 1700s, there developed a common law lien by which a bank could unilaterally debit the account of a depositor in order to pay a debt owed to itself. This common law right, which is in existence in virtually all states today, is called the bank's right of *setoff* because one obligation (the customer's to the bank) is offset against another (the bank's to the customer). Prior to the advent of the Fair Credit Billing Act (chapter four of the Truth in Lending Act, 15 U.S.C. §§1601 et seq., effective October 28, 1975), a consumer who had a checking account with the same bank that issued him or her a credit card might be the victim of a non-notification setoff on failing to make a payment. Section 169 of the Fair Credit Billing Act now prohibits this practice in most instances involving customer credit card debts. This section is supplemented by §1026.12(d) of the Consumer Financial Protection Bureau's Regulation Z,[4] 12 C.F.R. part 1026, which explains the rules in more detail. Regulation Z §1026.12(d):

> (1) A card issuer may not take any action, either before or after termination of credit card privileges, to offset a cardholder's indebtedness arising from a consumer credit transaction under the relevant credit card plan against funds of the cardholder held on deposit with the card issuer. . . .

PROBLEM 87

When Portia Moot's financial condition became so moribund that she stopped paying all her debts, Octopus National Bank (ONB), which was annoyed that she currently owed $578 on the credit card it had issued her, simply took this amount from Portia's checking account at ONB. This caused other checks of hers to bounce, and she is furious. The Truth in Lending Act's §130, 15 U.S.C. §1640, allows her to recover actual damages, a small amount of punitive damages, and her attorney's fees for violation of the TILA rules. If she calls you, her attorney cousin, for advice, what do you say to her?[5]

---

4. Authority for Regulation Z was transferred from the Federal Reserve Board to the newly created Consumer Financial Protection Bureau in 2011.

5. The rest of the Regulation Z provision continues like this:

> (2) This paragraph does not alter or affect the right of a card issuer acting under state or federal law to do any of the following with regard to funds of a cardholder held on deposit with the card issuer if the same procedure is constitutionally available to creditors generally: obtain or enforce a consensual security interest in the funds; attach or otherwise levy upon the funds; or obtain or enforce a court order relating to the funds.
>
> (3) This paragraph does not prohibit a plan, if authorized in writing by the cardholder, under which the card issuer may periodically deduct all or part of the cardholder's credit card debt from a deposit account held with the card issuer (subject to the limitations in §1026.13(d)(1)).

It looks like all the bank need do to get around this problem and use its right of setoff is to put a clause in the bank account contract granting itself a security interest in the account to protect credit card extensions, but that won't work either. The official commentary to this Regulation Z section requires that the "consensual security interest" mentioned in subsection (2) be a separately signed writing stating that the account will be used as collateral for the credit card debt, and not merely be a clause in the credit card contract. Further, this commentary requires that the security interest in the consumer's account be open (as a matter of state law) to other creditors or the card issuer cannot claim an interest therein either. Since Article 9 of the UCC will not allow other creditors to take a security interest in consumer bank accounts — see §9-109(d)(13) — the security interest possibility is cut off.

Setoff[6] is recognized in the UCC in several sections that mention it in passing (§§4-201(a), 4-215(e), and 4-303), although the Code neither establishes the right nor regulates its terms. Setoff may be had only against general accounts (such as checking and savings accounts) of the depositor. When the depositor has created a *special* account for a limited purpose, the bank may not set off against it non-related debts of the depositor. See Filosa v. Pecora, 44 Ill. App. 3d 912, 358 N.E.2d 1213 (1976) (setoff not permitted against escrow account). The given reason is that for special accounts the bank is a bailee and not a debtor. See Mid-City Natl. Bank v. Mars Bldg. Corp., 33 Ill. App. 3d 1083, 339 N.E.2d 497 (1975). A bank owes a duty of fair and honorable dealing to its customers. When a bank exercises the right of setoff in an improper fashion, the courts are quick to protect the customer. See Wells v. Washington Heights Fed. Sav. & Loan Assn., 63 Misc. 2d 424, 312 N.Y.S.2d 236 (Cir. Ct. 1970).

Walter v. National City Bank of Cleveland

Ohio Supreme Court, 1975
42 Ohio St. 2d 524, 330 N.E.2d 425

This is an action in civil conversion, involving claims of priority of right to a commercial bank account of Ritzer of Austria, Inc. In the fall of 1969, Ritzer opened a commercial account with The National City Bank of Cleveland, appellant herein. On April 14, 1971, Ritzer executed a 90-day promissory note to appellant in the amount of $3,600, although Ritzer's balance sheet, as of March 31, 1971, showed the company to be insolvent. On May 11, 1971, Robert A. Walter, appellee herein, recovered a judgment against Ritzer in the Euclid Municipal Court for $6,831.95. The following day, the appellant bank was served by mail as garnishee with an order in aid of execution. At the time of service, Ritzer had on deposit with appellant the sum of $3,651.75. The unmatured debt on appellant's promissory note totalled $3,626.25, including interest accrued. On May 24, 1971, appellant sent a letter to the Euclid Municipal Court stating that it was setting off the amount of its loan, leaving a balance of $25.50. Appellant mailed its check for the balance to the Euclid Municipal Court on July 22, 1971.

Appellee brought this action in the Court of Common Pleas of Cuyahoga County. Both parties moved for summary judgment, and judgment was granted for appellee. The Court of Appeals affirmed.

STERN, J. The appellant bank claims a right of equitable setoff of an unmatured indebtedness of its depositor, as against a judgment creditor

---

6. Bankers, perversely, insist on calling setoff *offset*. The bankers may have won this logomachy; the Fair Credit Billing Act calls this subtraction process an *offset*.

seeking to reach the depositor's account by an order in aid of execution. Appellant concedes that it has no statutory right of setoff under R.C. 2309.19.

Setoff, both at law and in equity, is that right which exists between two parties, each of whom under an independent contract owes a definite amount to the other, to set off their respective debts by way of mutual deduction. Witham v. South Side Bldg. & Loan Assn. of Lima (1938), 133 Ohio St. 560, 562, 15 N.E.2d 149.

As a general rule, the courts have held that a bank may set off a bank account against the matured indebtedness of its depositor, although the bank has been garnished at the instance of a creditor of the depositor. Schuler v. Israel (1887), 120 U.S. 506, 7 S. Ct. 648, 30 L. Ed. 707; Bennett v. Campbell (1889), 189 Pa. 647, 42 A. 373; Annotation, 106 A.L.R. 62. In Bank v. Brewing Co. (1893), 50 Ohio St. 151, 33 N.E. 1054, it was held that a bank could set off the amount of an insolvent depositor's checking account against an unpaid and overdue note, without the knowledge or consent of the depositor, and that the bank could refuse payment of a check drawn on the account. The theory of these cases is that a bank stands in the relationship of debtor to its depositor, and has the right to apply the deposit to payment of the depositor's matured debts or obligations held by the bank, in the same way that another debtor might assert setoff as a defense to an action on the debt. Holloway v. First Natl. Bank of Pocatello (1928), 45 Idaho 746, 265 P. 699.

In fact, the exercise of setoff by a bank is often quite different from the case of a usual debtor-creditor relationship. A bank account is a debt, but one which is ordinarily subject to demand withdrawal at any time, and one which imposes clear responsibilities upon the bank depending upon the nature of the account. Historically, the bank's right to setoff derives from the bank lien of the law merchant, and that right still possesses some of the characteristics of a lien, since it permits the bank by self-help to take priority over others claiming a right to the funds on deposit.[7] Whereas, in the case of

---

7. "It is said to be a well-settled rule of the law merchant, that a bank has a general lien on all the funds of a depositor in its possession for any balance due on general account, or other indebtedness contracted in the course of their dealings, and may appropriate the funds to the payment of such indebtedness. The right to make such appropriation, it is held, grows out of the relation of the parties, as debtor and creditor, and rests upon the principle that, 'as the depositor is indebted to the bank upon a demand which is due, the funds in its possession may properly and justly be applied in payment of such debt, and it has therefore a right to retain such funds until payment is actually made.' Falkland v. Bank, 84 N.Y. 145. Though this right is called a 'lien,' strictly it is not, when applied to a general deposit, for, a person cannot have a lien upon his own property, but only on that of another; and, as we have seen, the funds of general deposit in a bank are the property of the bank. Properly speaking, the right, in such case, is that of set-off, arising from the existence of mutual demands. The practical effect, however, is the same. The cross demands are satisfied, so far as they are equal, leaving whatever balance that may be due on either as the true amount of the indebtedness from one party to the other." Bank v. Brewing Co. (1893), 50 Ohio St. 151, 158 n.59, 33 N.E. 1054, 1055 n.59.

an ordinary debtor, setoff is available as an equitable and statutory defense, in the case of a bank, setoff becomes a means by which the bank, because of its position as a commercial middleman, acquires a priority of right whenever it acts as creditor for a depositor.

The courts have generally held that the bank does not have a priority of right in equity where the bank seeks to set off an unmatured indebtedness. United Bank & Trust Co. v. Washburn & Condon (1930), 37 Ariz. 223, 292 P. 1025; Gerseta Corporation v. Equitable Trust Co. of New York (1926), 241 N.Y. 418, 150 N.E. 501; Stockyards Natl. Bank of Presnall (1917), 109 Tex. 32, 194 S.W. 384. Cf. Valley National Bank of Arizona v. Hasper (1967), 6 Ariz. App. 376, 432 P.2d 924. An unmatured debt is not presently due or collectible and is not available for set-off, since set off would alter the contract made by the parties.

An exception to this rule has been made in cases where the depositor is insolvent. In Schuler v. Israel, supra (120 U.S. 506, 7 S. Ct. 648, 30 L. Ed. 708), the court noted that a defense in equity was available to a bank-debtor to prevent an insolvent depositor-creditor from obtaining payment of his debt, where an unmatured obligation was available as setoff and would be lost due to the insolvency.

The same equities do not apply in the case at bar. Here, the negotiation of a 90-day promissory note to Ritzer occurred after the date upon which, the bank itself asserts, Ritzer's balance sheet showed the company to be insolvent. In sum, the bank made a loan for a definite term to an insolvent depositor, and now claims that as a matter of equity it is entitled to priority of right to its depositor's account because of the insolvency. We disagree. The extension of credit to an insolvent was a voluntary act, whether negligent or merely lacking in sound banking practice. In the present case, no equity appears which would require granting priority to the bank's unmatured obligation over the judgment of the appellee.[8]

Lack of maturity is not always permitted to defeat the right of set-off where that right is the only way to prevent clear injustice, and the courts have frequently applied equitable principles in cases of insolvency. "Where insolvency has intervened, a court will not be limited to a strict application

---

8. A banker's right of setoff also raises new equitable questions in situations where the bank may have several types of accounts with a depositor, including savings passbook and checking accounts and long-term certificates of deposit, and may also be a creditor for mortgage loans, installment loans, credit card, and other forms of indebtedness. It has been suggested that the setoff of a customer's indebtedness without notice or regard to his protests is not equitable and in conflict with due process and legislation protecting consumers' rights. Comment, Banking Setoff: A Study in Commercial Obsolescence, 23 Hastings L.J. 1585. See also Olsen, The Appropriation of Deposits for Debt: Levies, Liens, and Setoffs, 90 Banking L.J. 827 (1973).

of statutory set-off but will apply the doctrines of equity." Union Properties
v. Baldwin Brothers Co. (1943), 141 Ohio St. 303, 47 N.E.2d 983 (paragraph
nine of the syllabus). But no equity accrues where insolvency did not "inter-
vene" but occurred prior to the voluntary granting of the loan sought to be
set off.

The bank also claims a contractual right of set-off based upon its rules
and regulations. These rules read, in part, ". . . Bank also reserves the right
to apply any balance in the account to the payment of any indebtedness,
direct or indirect, absolute or contingent, due or to become due and howso-
ever evidenced, of depositor to bank."

The signature card, signed by the corporate officers of Ritzer in 1969,
states that the "depositor acknowledges receipt of a copy of the rules and
regulations . . . relative to commercial accounts and agrees to be bound
thereby and by any amendments and additions thereto hereafter made."
The bank's claim is, in effect, that it could at any time apply any part of the
funds deposited in the commercial account to the payment of the 90-day
promissory note, even before the note was due, and that the garnisheeing
creditor stands in the shoes of the depositor.

The 90-day promissory note executed by Ritzer in favor of the bank
contains no statement that it was made upon the security of the commercial
account, and contains no provision for acceleration, other than for lack of
performance by the debtor. The note was secured by a security agreement
in machinery and equipment,[9] but no security agreement was made with
respect to the commercial account.

If the language of the bank's rules and regulations is taken to mean that
the bank could at any time apply the balance of the commercial account
to the promissory note, those rules are in direct conflict with the contract
embodied in that note. They would have the effect of converting a note
payable at a definite time to one payable on demand. In this case, the later,
specific terms of the promissory note control over the general language of
the rules. The primary intent of the parties in executing the 90-day note
was that it become due in 90 days, not upon demand, and to the extent that
the earlier, general language of the rules conflicts with that intent, it must
be taken to have been superseded. See 3 Corbin on Contracts, 172 n.178,
Section 547; 4 Williston on Contracts (3d ed.), 816, 822, Section 624.

". . . [I]n the construction of any written instrument the primary duty
of the court is to determine and give effect to the intention of the parties."

---

9. That agreement defines "liabilities" in almost the exact terms of the rules and regulations, to include "indebtedness . . . due or to become due. . . ." It is clear that under a security
agreement the rights of a secured party to enforce his security interest do not accrue until
after default by the debtor. UCC §9-501.

United States Fire Ins. Co. v. PhilMar Corporation (1965), 166 Ohio St. 85, 87, 139 N.E.2d 330, 332.

The contract embodied in the promissory note was that the debt would become due and payable in 90 days, and the bank had no contractual right to treat the note as a demand note and set off the commercial account against the debt before maturity.

For the foregoing reasons, the judgment of the Court of Appeals is affirmed.

Judgment affirmed.

Bankruptcy and Setoff. According to §362(a)(7) of the Bankruptcy Code, the filing of a petition in bankruptcy creates an automatic stay against creditor collection activity, specifically including the exercise of the right of setoff. Individuals injured by a violation of the automatic stay may sue under §362(h) of the Bankruptcy Code and recover "actual damages, including costs and attorney fees, and, in appropriate circumstances, may recover punitive damages." Of course, the bank may apply to the bankruptcy court for relief from the stay, §362(d); and, on getting it, may exercise the right of setoff; see §553. In 1995, the U.S. Supreme Court granted some relief to banks by ruling that an *administrative freeze* on a checking account is *not* the same as a setoff and does not violate the automatic stay; Citizens Bank of Maryland v. Strumpf, 516 U.S. 16 (1995). This means that a bank could freeze the account on learning of a bankruptcy, not allowing the customer to reach the funds involved, but not taking the money for itself either, thus preserving the status quo while the bankruptcy court is asked to straighten out what is to become of the monies in the account.

E.   Customer's Right to Stop Payment

1.   Ordinary Checks

The key section on the right to stop payment is §4-403, which you should read. Official Comment 1 states:

> The position taken by this section is that stopping payment or closing an account is a service which depositors expect and are entitled to receive from banks notwithstanding its difficulty, inconvenience and expense. The inevitable occasional losses through failure to stop or close should be borne by the banks as a cost of the business of banking.

Parr v. Security National Bank

Oklahoma Court of Appeals, 1984
680 P.2d 648

REYNOLDS, J.

We are called upon to decide whether Security National Bank had a reasonable opportunity to stop payment on a check when the description received is exact in all respects except for a single digit error in the check amount. This issue has not been decided by an Oklahoma court.

Parr wrote check number 949 to Champlin Oil. She dated and mailed it September 14, 1981. The amount of the check was $972.96. On September 15, 1981, Parr ordered payment stopped by telephone. Parr gave the bank her account number, the check number, the date, the payee and the amount of the check. A 50-cent error was made in identifying the amount of the check. Parr went to the bank on September 16th or 17th and executed a written stop order dated September 15, 1981. The written stop order was also in error. Security National paid check number 949 on September 17, 1981.

Parr brought suit against Security National seeking recovery for the amount of the check, 12-percent interest on that amount, reasonable attorney's fees and costs. Security National defended by showing their computers were programmed to stop payment only if the reported amount of the check were correct. They argued Parr's 50-cent error relieved them of liability. Timeliness of notice was not an issue.

[The court then quoted §4-403(1) and the Official Comment 1 paragraph reprinted prior to the case—EDS.]

Security National contends that whether a stop payment order has been received "in such manner as to afford the bank a reasonable opportunity to act" should be determined *after* examining how the defendant bank handles stop orders. This interpretation has found favor among highly respected legal authorities, but not among the majority of courts that have addressed this issue.

Both groups acknowledge §4-403(1) has not changed the common law rule that a stop payment order must identify the check with "reasonable accuracy." It is from this premise that courts have determined whether the description is reasonably accurate without consideration of the defendant/bank's computer program. In Elsie Rodriguez Fashions, Inc. v. Chase Manhattan Bank, 23 U.C.C. Rep. 133 (N.Y. Sup. Ct. 1978), the customer gave the bank the correct payee, check number and date but made a 10-cent error in the amount of the check. The court determined the check had been described with sufficient accuracy to allow the bank to stop payment. The opinion makes no mention of the bank's computer program. In accord with this approach on similar facts are the New York cases of Pokras v. National

Bank of North America, 30 U.C.C. Rep. 1089 (N.Y. App. Term 1981), and Thomas v. Marine Midland Tinkers National Bank, 86 Misc. 2d 284, 381 N.Y.S.2d 797 (N.Y. Civ. Ct. 1976). A different result was reached by a New York court where the customer was told by the bank the stop order would not be effective unless she provided the exact amount of the check. Poullier v. Nacua Motors, Inc., 108 Misc. 2d 913, 439 N.Y.S.2d 85 (N.Y. Sup. Ct. 1981). Security National does not contend they gave notice to Parr that any discrepancy in the check amount would prevent compliance with her stop payment order.

In Delano v. Putnam Trust Co., 33 U.C.C. Rep. 635 (Conn. Super. Ct. 1981), a single-digit error in the amount of $100.00 did not prevent recovery where customer supplied bank with the correct check number, date, payee, and account number of the check. The bank's computer program required an exact match of check amount before it would stop payment. Court held bank had received sufficient information to allow it a "reasonable opportunity to act" on the stop payment order. Court stated the bank had a duty to inform its customer of the need for precision in reporting the amount before it could rely on customer's error to relieve it of liability.

The Supreme Court of Alabama denied customer's recovery in Sherrill v. Frank Morris Pontiac-Buick-GMC, Inc., 366 So. 2d 251 (Ala. 1979). Customer gave bank three descriptive elements of the check, check amount, payee and date. The check was not numbered. Two of the three pieces of information were incorrect. Court determined the check was not described with reasonable accuracy, therefore the bank was not afforded a "reasonable opportunity to act" on the stop payment order.

In FJS Electronics, Inc. v. Fidelity Bank, 431 A.2d 326 (Pa. Super. Ct. 1981), court allowed customer to prevail even though its 50-cent error in check amount prevented bank's computer from acting on stop payment order. The bank asserted §4-403 "should be read to require compliance with the procedures of a particular bank, regardless of what they are and regardless of whether the customer has been made aware of them." Id. at 328. Court determined that the drafter's policy stated in Comment 2 to §4-403 precluded such an interpretation. They reasoned:

> Fidelity made a choice when it elected to employ a technique which searched for stopped checks by amount alone. It evidently found benefits to this technique which outweighed the risk that an item might be inaccurately described in a stop order. This is precisely the type of inevitable loss which was contemplated by the code drafters and addressed by the comment quoted above. The focus of §4-403 is the service which may be expected by the customer, and a customer may expect a check to be stopped after the bank is given reasonable notice. A bank's decision to reduce operating costs by using a system which increases the risk that checks as to which there is an

outstanding stop payment order will be paid invites liability when such items are paid.

We find this analysis, as well as that in *Delano*, supra, persuasive. We hold Parr described her check with reasonable accuracy, and Security National had a reasonable opportunity to act on the stop payment order.

We are aware of the burden this may place on Oklahoma banks. However, the industry has two alternatives to avoid liability if banking procedures necessitate an exact description of an item: (1) notify the customer at the time a stop order is given, or (2) seek a legislative amendment to §4-403.

We recognize Parr received the benefit of having her debt paid to Champlin Oil and will recover from Security National for failure to stop payment. To avoid this possibility of unjust enrichment, §4-407(b) subrogates the payor bank [Security National] to the rights of the payee [Champlin] against the maker [Parr]. In such a suit, an award of attorney's fees and costs to Security National would be proper under 12 O.S. 1981 §936, as Champlin would have been suing Parr on an open account if Security National had stopped payment on the check.

Trial court is reversed and this cause remanded for award of $972.96 plus reasonable attorney's fees and costs consistent with this opinion.

Reversed and remanded.

PROBLEM 88

Julio Perez, newly arrived in New York from Puerto Rico, was tricked into buying a $50 refrigerator for $280. He paid the seller, Honest Juan, by check and took the appliance home in his truck. His brother saw the refrigerator, told Julio that he had been had, and advised him to call the bank to stop payment on the check. Julio phoned his bank and said, "This is Julio Perez. You must stop—do not give Honest Juan money for my check." The bank clerk who took the call asked, "Which check?" Julio replied, "Today—refrigerator check" and hung up. The bank failed to stop payment on the check, and the next day it was presented by Honest Juan and paid. Julio demanded that the money be replaced in his account, and when the bank refused, Julio retained Juanita Martinez, a lawyer, who filed suit on his behalf, contending that the check was not "properly payable" per §4-401. The complaint set out only the facts of the stop-payment order and the payment in spite of it. As a judge, how would you rule on each of the following issues raised by the bank?

(a) The stop-payment order did not give enough information to be effective. See §4-403(a); Sherrill v. Frank Morris Pontiac-Buick-GMC, Inc., 366 So. 2d 251 (Ala. 1978); White & Summers 19-5; Annot., 35 A.L.R.4th 985; Annot., 29 A.L.R.4th 228. Official Comment 5 to §4-403 says that in "describing the item, the customer, in the absence of a contrary agreement, must meet the standard of what information allows the bank under the technology then existing to identify the item with reasonable certainty."

(b) The contract of deposit that Julio initially signed stated: "Customer agrees that no oral stop-payment order shall be effective; stop-payment orders must be in writing to be effective." The bank argues that fully one-half of its customers are Spanish-speaking Americans and that oral stop-payment orders are a nightmare to try to decode. See §4-103(a); White & Summers 19-2.

(c) The contract of deposit also contained this clause: "Customer agrees that the bank shall not be liable if it mistakenly pays an item on which payment has been stopped." See Official Comment 7 to §4-403.

(d) The bank's rules require that a stop-payment order be accompanied by a $15 stop-payment fee, and Julio failed to tender such a fee. See Official Comment 1 to §4-403. Compare Opinion of Attorney General, 30 U.C.C. Rep. Serv. 1626 (Mich. 1981), with Opinion of Attorney General, 33 U.C.C. Rep. Serv. 1445 (Mich. 1981).

(e) Plaintiff's complaint is defective in that it fails to allege any loss to plaintiff as a result of the bank's alleged wrongful payment, and plaintiff carries this burden under §4-403(c). For all the bank knows, plaintiff has revoked his acceptance of the refrigerator and avoided the sale on grounds of unconscionability. See Cicci v. Lincoln Natl. Bank & Trust Co., 46 Misc. 2d 465, 260 N.Y.S.2d 100 (City Ct. 1965) (which found this argument persuasive); contra Thomas v. Marine Midland Tinkers Natl. Bank, 86 Misc. 2d 284, 381 N.Y.S.2d 797 (Sup. Ct. 1976); see White & Summers 19-6.

If the bank accidentally pays over the stop-payment order and recredits the account, it can use another important section of the Code, §4-407 (the Subrogation Rule), to step into the shoes of its customer and sue any party he or she could have sued (Honest Juan, in the above Problem). Read §4-407(3) carefully. This principle of subrogation also can help out the bank in the following situations where it is resisting the request of a customer to recredit an improper payment.

PROBLEM 89

After he had purchased a new car from Flash Motors, Thomas Crandall got the car home and discovered that it clashed with the color of his garage. He couldn't stand this, of course, so he phoned his bank, Octopus National, and placed an oral stop-payment order on the check he had written for the car. Negligently, the bank paid the check anyway. Must the bank recredit the account? See §4-407(2).

Canty v. Vermont National Bank

Vermont Superior Court, 1994
1994 WL 797862

K ATZ, J.

Plaintiff Joseph Canty had a checking account with Vermont National Bank and a problem with the Internal Revenue Service. When the Internal Revenue asked him for canceled checks to document his payment of certain obligations, he forwarded the checks. The Internal Revenue redeposited those canceled checks, and Vermont National Bank paid them a second time, withdrawing the funds from plaintiff's account. Not surprisingly, plaintiff took the position that he should pay each check once, but not twice. He therefore sues, and now seeks summary judgment, asserting the Bank must recredit his account for the funds improperly withdrawn to make the second payments.

In the words of the Uniform Commercial Code, the payor bank has "paid an item under circumstances giving a basis for objection by the drawer or maker." 9A V.S.A. Sec. 4-407. It is fairly implicit in U.C.C. Sec. 4-401(1) that if an item is not properly payable, the bank may not charge the customer's account, and if it has done so, it must recredit the account. Siegel v. New England Merchants Nat. Bank, 386 Mass. 672, 437 N.E.2d 218, 221 (1982); J. White and R. Summers, Uniform Commercial Code Sec. 17-3 at 657 (2d ed. 1980). Although recrediting may constitute the usually required response, the law does permit a bank to refuse to recredit its customer's account after wrongful payment of an item by subrogating itself to the rights of the presenter of the improperly paid instrument. Id., at 660. . . .

Although a drawer bank can improperly pay on an item in several ways, its right to subrogation is inextricably entwined with its liability to its customer for improper payment. White and Summers, at 683. The customer's realization of his claim may produce unjust enrichment. Even when an item is not properly payable, for any of several reasons, the bank's payment may discharge a legal obligation of the customer, or create a right in the customer's favor against the payee. Siegel v. New England Merchants, 437 N.E.2d at 221. If the customer were permitted to retain such benefits, and recover the amount of the check as well, he would profit at the bank's expense. Id. Although plaintiff here argues that there can be no subrogation until his account is first re-credited, that appears contrary to the provisions of §4-407, which permit a bank to be subrogated to the rights of a payee, against the drawer or maker—its own customer. Manufacturer's Hanover Trust Co. v. Ava Industries, Inc., 414 N.Y.S.2d 425 (Sup. Ct. 1978) (Bank may pursue its own customer upon both subrogation and possible unjust enrichment; 4-407, comments 2 and 3). Siegel v. New England Merchants points out that the subrogation rights of 4-407 refer to those existing prior to the bank's wrongful payment of the item. 437 N.E.2d 221, n.5. Indeed, a bank may invoke subrogation under 4-407 in spite of a settlement agreement between its customer (the drawer) and payee. Swiss Credit Bank v. Balink, 614 F.2d 1269 (10th Cir. 1980). The bank may assert its subrogation rights defensively, when its depositor brings an action for wrongful debit. Siegel, 437 N.E.2d at 222; Chute v. Bank One of Akron, N.A., 460 N.E.2d 720 (Ohio App. 1983).

On the theory that one form of improper payment is functionally no different than another, the *Siegel* court analogizes the customer's right to be recredited to that existing for payment in the face of a proper stop order, which is governed by §4-403. The issue of injust enrichment is common to both. The rule of 4-403(3) is that a depositor bears the burden of proving the fact and amount of any loss. Kupersmith v. Manufacturer's Hanover Trust Co., 15 U.C.C. Rep. 696 (N.Y. Civ. Ct. 1974). Section 4-403(3) simply protects the bank against the need to prove events familiar to the depositor, *Siegel*, 437 N.E.2d 222, in this case his account status with the Internal Revenue.

Clearly there is a difference between a check which has never been paid and one which has already been paid. In the first instance, the drawer has indicated an intent to pay the payee a stated sum, presumably a voluntary and justified decision. In the second, the drawer has already made payment, and thereby satisfied his debt to the amount paid. But among payees, the Internal Revenue must be considered sui generis. One's account with the Internal Revenue is never closed. Even death does not bring immediate finality. Plaintiff argues that he "did not owe any liability to the I.R.S. *for the tax quarters to which his [ill-fated] checks related.*" (Emphasis altered.) But the scope of inquiry, in application of the equitable doctrine of subrogation, is not limited to some particular payment and its due date. Rather, given the purpose of avoiding unjust enrichment, the inquiry must be whether plaintiff depositor actually suffered any loss by the admittedly improper payment. If he did not, he may not recover, for to do so would be to enrich him twice, once on his Internal Revenue account and once on his satisfied judgment.

The purpose of most presumptions is to aid trial by shifting the burden of going forward to the party who has the best access to the facts, or who has the notably less probable side of a common question. Reporter's Notes, Rule 301, V.R. Ev. Lang v. Chase Manhattan Bank, 6 U.C.C. Rep. 1259 (N.Y. App. Div. 1969), reversed a grant of summary judgment against the bank, which was deemed not absolutely liable to its customer for paying in the face of a stop payment order, when the issue of actual loss to the customer "turns upon evidence peculiarly within the knowledge of the customer and her auto dealer. In this unfortunate situation, plaintiff customer has both the best access to the facts of his accounts with the I.R.S. and has the less probable side of the question, namely that a neutral government agency took his money without giving him any credit for it.

Given the difficulty of the bank securing information from the Internal Revenue about the account of another, the presumed regularity of its proceedings, 1 J. Weinstein and M. Berger Weinstein's Evidence, Par. 301 [03] at 301-53 (1994), citing, inter alia, Welch v. Helvering, 290 U.S. 111, 115 (1933), and the fact that we all continue to accrue liability with the Internal Revenue, we conclude that the proper disposition of this most unusual case must require plaintiff actually to prove his loss.

Saratoga Polo Assn., Ltd. v. Adirondack Trust Co., 460 N.Y.S.2d 712 (Sup. Ct. 1983), and Mitchell v. Republic Bank & Trust Co., 239 S.E.2d 867 (N.C. App. 1978), hold that a customer initially establishes a prima facie case by showing that an item was improperly paid. Thereupon the bank, exercising its subrogation rights under §4-407, has the burden of coming forward and presenting evidence of an absence of actual loss to the customer. When the bank meets the burden of coming forward with such evidence, the customer must then sustain the ultimate burden of proof. We hold that when the improperly paid item was paid to the Internal Revenue Service, we will presume an absence of actual loss to the customer; the bank has therefore met its burden of coming forward with such evidence.

We reject plaintiff's contention that the Bank must first re-credit his account, before earning any right to subrogation. Such a rule would tend to see the funds disappear while the case was ongoing. While presumably not so in this case, many of this class of cases—improperly paid checks—arise out of fraud. Requiring subrogated banks to first recredit the funds would tend to put those funds back into the hands of the miscreant, at a time when the court is still in a difficult position to know whether fraud has been practiced in the particular case at hand. Requiring recrediting as a threshold to subrogation would always arise as an interlocutory order, as there is no final judgment until all claims have been resolved. Rule 54, V.R.C.P. The effect would therefore be that the bank would have no appeal, and that the mere filing of a complaint would require the defendant to grant plaintiff the money he seeks, as a price for even litigating an affirmative defense to such recrediting. Requiring threshold recrediting of funds is not supported by *Siegel v. New England Merchants*. Moreover, a bank's §4-407 right of subrogation has been elevated above any duty to adjust its customer's account, Sunshine v. Bankers Trust Co., 34 N.Y.2d 404, 314 N.E.2d 860, 866 (N.Y. 1974), which threshold duty the New York Court of Appeals labeled a "technical mechanical requirement of common-law subrogation." As the right of subrogation has "particular approval" under our law, Lopez v. Concord Genl. Mut. Ins. Group, 155 Vt. 320, 324, 583 A.2d 602 (1990), we conclude that its value should not be diluted by requiring banks to first recredit accounts in order to gain the benefits of this venerable doctrine of equity. This is in accord with the U.C.C's intent that §4-407 was intended to provide a broad, liberal remedy that incorporated and is based upon the common law equitable principles of unjust enrichment and restitution. Swiss Credit Bank v. Balink, 28 U.C.C. Rep. at 482.

We therefore deny plaintiff's motion for summary judgment. Partial summary judgment is accorded to defendant Vermont National Bank; unless plaintiff can show actual loss by the improper second payment of his canceled checks, his claims shall be dismissed. We shall allow plaintiff 60 days to marshall his evidence regarding actual loss, and then expect either a joint status report to the clerk, a request for a pretrial conference, or a further motion for summary judgment, depending on the proof available to plaintiff.

We also grant defendant's motion to dismiss the punitive damage claims. First, we find considerable merit in the defenses raised by the bank. Second, to accept plaintiff's argument would be to telescope into one case both the merits of that case and the "malicious defense" claim inherent in the punitive damage theory. In malicious prosecution, Vermont law has always required a successful outcome in the underlying litigation before supporting punitive damages for the tort of wrongful litigation. Anello v. Vinci, 142 Vt. 583, 587, 458 A.2d 1117 (1983).

PROBLEM 90

Rupert Signer gave his fiancée, Maggie Lee, a check for $1,000 as a birthday gift. She took the check, thanked him politely, and then told him that she was getting ready to marry his best friend Charlie and "this is good-bye." Rupert left in a huff and went straight to his bank, the Careless State Bank, where he filled out a written stop-payment order on the check he had given to Maggie Lee. In the meantime, Maggie Lee indorsed the check over to Computer City in payment for a $1,000 software package she purchased there. When Computer City presented the check to Careless State Bank for payment, the bank paid it without a murmur. Rupert sued when the bank refused to recredit his account, alleging a $1,000 loss because he had tried to revoke a gift promise on which the bank now made him liable. Are either of these defenses by the bank good?

(a) Computer City was a holder in due course of Rupert's check, and he could not have refused to pay Computer City if it had presented the check to him. See Official Comment 7 to §4-403. Under §4-407, the bank is subrogated to the rights of any holder in due course of the check. Does this help the bank? See Official Comment 1 to §4-407.

(b) Same argument that Computer City was a holder in due course and that Rupert would eventually have had to pay Computer City if the bank had been able to remember to stop payment. This being true, Rupert has really suffered no loss by the wrongful payment, so he cannot recover. Cf. §4-403(c); see Seigel v. Merrill Lynch, Pierce, Fenner & Smith, Inc., 745 A.2d 301 (D.C. App. 2000).

PROBLEM 91

Same fact situation, except that Maggie Lee takes the check and deposits it in her checking account with Octopus National Bank. The balance in the checking account prior to the deposit was $.07. Later that same day, Maggie wrote a check for $1,000.07 and cashed it at her bank, thereby withdrawing all the money from her account. Octopus National Bank sent the check to the payor bank, Careless State Bank, which negligently paid the check over the stop-payment order. Can Careless State still use the above two defenses when Rupert sues? See §§4-211, 4-210(a); Universal C.I.T. Credit Corp. v. Guaranty Bank & Trust Co., 161 F. Supp. 790 (D. Mass. 1958).

2.   Cashier's, Teller's, and Certified Checks

At common law and under prior statutes there was much confusion surrounding the question of whether a customer could stop payment on a check that had been certified. The Code now makes it clear that the answer is no. A customer has no right to stop payment on a certified check. See Official Comment 4 to §4-403. The reason is that once the check is certified, the payor bank itself is the primary obligor on the instrument, §3-413(a), and the drawer has no right to require the bank to breach its acceptor's contract.[10] The same thing is true of a cashier's check (a check on which the bank is both drawer and drawee) and of a bank check (a check drawn by one bank on another, also called a *teller's check*); see §3-104(g) and (h).[11]

PROBLEM 92

Harry Flashman agreed to sell his sports car to Tom Brown if the latter paid with a cashier's check (see §3-104(g)) for $15,000, issued by Fraser National Bank. Tom purchased such a cashier's check from the bank; it was payable to the order of Harry Flashman (in such a situation, a person in Tom's position is called a *remitter*; §3-103(a)(15)). After Tom handed the check over to Harry, the latter told him that the car was parked at an address Harry gave him. Tom went

---

10. The so-called Four Legals section, §4-303(a)(1), discussed later in this chapter, states that a customer loses his or her right to stop payment once the bank accepts or certifies an item. In actuality, when a check is certified by the drawee, an amount of money sufficient to pay the check when it is presented is taken from the account and held pending the second presentment; in this way the drawee bank protects itself as it undertakes the primary liability of an acceptor (§3-413).

11. Remember that the giving of an instrument on which a bank is primarily liable is an absolute payment of the underlying obligation and discharges the underlying obligor unless he or she is liable on the instrument. See §3-310(a).

to the address and found it was an automobile dump. The sports car had been wrecked and was worthless. He phoned Fraser National Bank and demanded that the bank not pay the check. Should the bank do this? See §3-411 and its Official Comment; see also §3-305(c). What can Tom do if the bank refuses to help him? See §3-202 and Official Comment 2 to §3-201.

Patriot Bank v. Navy Federal Credit Union

Circuit Court of Virginia, 2002
2002 WL 481129

ROUSH, J.

This case arises under Articles 3A and 4 of the Uniform Commercial Code, Va. Code Ann. §8.1-101, et seq. At issue is whether the defendant Navy Federal Credit Union wrongfully refused to honor a cashier's check it issued.

This matter came on for a bench trial on February 14, 2002 as a de novo appeal from the General District Court. At that time, the Court took the matter under advisement. The Court has now carefully considered the pleadings, the applicable provisions of the Uniform Commercial Code and the arguments of counsel. For the reasons stated below, judgment will be entered in favor of the plaintiff Patriot Bank, N.A. in the amount of $7,000.00, plus interest, costs, and attorney's fees.

FACTS

On April 4, 2001, Thomas Peeso, a member of the Navy Federal Credit Union ("Navy FCU"), obtained a cashier's check from Navy FCU in the amount of $7,000. The check was made payable to Mr. Peeso. Mr. Peeso's account was debited for payment of the check. Mr. Peeso delivered the check to Nation's Auto Loan Center ("Nation's Auto"), a used car dealership. Mr. Peeso intended to use the check to purchase a used car for his daughter. He indorsed the check as follows:

[Peeso's Signature]
Payable to Nation's Auto Loan Center

Beneath that indorsement, was written by hand "# 180180021301"—Nation's Auto's account number at Patriot Bank.

Later on April 4, 2001, Nation's Auto deposited the check in its account at the plaintiff Patriot Bank, N.A. ("Patriot Bank"). Patriot Bank credited Nation's Auto's account in the amount of $7,000. Patriot Bank then submitted the check to Navy FCU for payment through the Federal Reserve System.

Navy FCU received the check on April 9, 2001. Navy FCU's policy requires all checks for $5,000 or more personally to be examined for regularity of indorsements before payment. A bank official examined the check and questioned the indorsements. Navy FCU returned the check to Patriot Bank on April 11, 2001 for the stated reason that "absence of endorsement guarantee required." Mr. William Oeters, the vice president of Patriot Bank, testified that Patriot Bank wanted Navy FCU to guarantee the missing indorsement of its customer, Nation's Auto.

Several days later, on about April 18, 2001, Mr. Peeso received a telephone call from Nation's Auto. After that conversation, it was his understanding that the cashier's check was somehow "no good" and "not negotiable." Without retrieving the original cashier's check, Mr. Peeso returned to Navy FCU and asked the credit union to stop payment on the original cashier's check and issue a new cashier's check in the amount of $7,000 made payable to Nation's Auto. Although Navy FCU knew by that time that the first cashier's check had been deposited for collection at Patriot Bank and was in the collection system, Navy FCU agreed to stop payment. Navy FCU required Mr. Peeso to agree to indemnify Navy FCU for "all claims and demands that may be made upon the said credit union on account of refusing payment" of the original cashier's check. A second cashier's check was issued for $7,000, made payable to Nation's Auto.

Nation's Auto deposited the second cashier's check in a financial institution not involved in this litigation and was credited for the amount of the second cashier's check.

Shortly after April 11, 2001, Patriot Bank received the first cashier's check back from Navy FCU. Although Navy FCU returned the check for the stated reason that "absence of endorsement guarantee required" (emphasis added), Patriot Bank was uncertain what Navy FCU wanted guaranteed. Because Patriot Bank had no relationship with Mr. Peeso, who was not its customer, it was reluctant to guarantee his signature. Patriot Bank returned the check to Nation's Auto. When Patriot Bank attempted to reverse the credit it had given to its customer for the first check, however, it discovered that the account was overdrawn. All attempts to contact the customer failed. Nation's Auto had apparently ceased doing business.

Patriot Bank filed suit against Navy FCU in the General District Court on July 5, 2001. In the course of the litigation, Patriot Bank learned that Navy FCU wanted the absence of the indorsement of Nation's Auto guaranteed when it returned the first check to Patriot in April. Patriot Bank then stamped the cashier's check:

CREDIT TO THE ACCOUNT OF THE WITHIN NAMED PAYEE IN ACCORDANCE WITH PAYEE'S INSTRUCTIONS ABSENCE OF ENDORSEMENT GUARANTEED and resubmitted the first check to Navy FCU in August 2001. Navy FCU refused to honor the first cashier's check when Navy FCU received it with the "absence of endorsement guaranteed." By that time, payment had been stopped on the first check, the second check had been issued and paid, and Navy FCU knew that Nation's Auto was out of business. Navy FCU stamped the first check as "refer to maker" and returned it to Patriot Bank.

Patriot Bank's Position

Patriot Bank argues that Navy FCU wrongfully refused to honor the first cashier's check on presentment. First, Patriot Bank maintains that Nation's Auto properly indorsed the check when it wrote its account number beneath "Payable to Nation's Auto Loan Center." Second, if the account number was not an "indorsement," Patriot Bank can supply the missing indorsement of its customer. No "absence of indorsement guaranteed" is required. Third, even if Navy FCU could require Patriot to guarantee the absence of indorsement, Navy FCU had no right to refuse to honor the first cashier's check when it was resubmitted in August 2001 with the requested "absence of indorsement guaranteed" language. In short, Patriot Bank argues that Navy FCU could not refuse to honor the cashier's check under the facts of this case.

Navy FCU's Position

Navy FCU contends that it acted properly when it returned the cashier's check to Patriot Bank in order for Patriot Bank to guarantee the missing indorsement of its customer, Nation's Auto. According to Navy FCU, it was observing prudent banking practices when it asked that Patriot Bank guarantee the absence of the indorsement of Nation's Auto. Navy FCU acknowledges that an issuer may not stop payment on a cashier's check. Navy FCU explains that it stopped payment on the first check as an accommodation to its customer, Mr. Peeso. Navy FCU maintains that, as between Mr. Peeso and Patriot Bank, Patriot Bank should suffer the loss.

Discussion of Authority

I.   WAS THE CASHIER'S CHECK PROPERLY INDORSED BY NATION'S AUTO LOAN CENTER?

Code §8.3A-204 defines "indorsement" in part as a "signature, other than that of a signer as a maker, drawer, or acceptor, that alone or accompanied by other words is made on an instrument." A "signature" is defined as "a name, . . . word, mark or symbol executed or adopted by a person with the present intent to authenticate a writing." Code 8.3A-401(b). Similarly, "signed" is defined as including "any symbol executed or adopted by a party with the present intention to authenticate a writing." Code §8.1-201(39). The official comment to Code §8.1-201(39) explains that "signed" is to be construed broadly:

> The inclusion of authentication in the definition of "signed" is to make clear that . . . a complete signature is not necessary. Authentication may be printed, stamped or written; it may be by initials or by thumbprint. . . . No catalog of possible authentications can be complete and the court must use common sense and commercial experience in passing upon these matters. The question always is whether the symbol was executed or adopted by the party with a present intention to authenticate the writing.

Code §8.1-201, Official Comment 39.

It is a reasonable inference from the evidence in this case that Nation's Auto wrote its account number at Patriot Bank on the cashier's check in order to authenticate the check for the purposes of deposit. As such, the Court concludes that the account number constitutes an indorsement as that term is defined in the Uniform Commercial Code.

The Court concludes that the cashier's check was properly indorsed when first presented to Navy FCU. Navy FCU should not have returned the check to Patriot Bank because of a missing indorsement.

II. WAS PATRIOT BANK REQUIRED TO GUARANTEE THE ABSENCE OF THE INDORSEMENT OF ITS CUSTOMER?

Even if Nation's Auto's account number did not amount to an indorsement, Navy FCU should not have returned the cashier's check to Patriot Bank for Patriot Bank to guarantee the missing indorsement of its customer.

Under Code §8.4-205.1, when a customer delivers an item to a depository bank for collection, the bank becomes a holder of the item if the customer was a holder, whether or not its customer indorses the item. The depository bank warrants to collecting banks, the payor bank or other payor, and to the drawer that the amount of the item was paid to the customer or deposited to the customer's account. The official comment to that section makes clear that "[w]hether it [the depository bank] supplies the customer's endorsement is immaterial." Code §8.4-205.1, Official Comment.

In light of Code §8.4-205.1, there was no need for Navy FCU to return the cashier's check to Patriot Bank in order for Patriot Bank to guarantee the missing endorsement of its customer, Nation's Auto. Simply by submitting the check to Navy FCU for payment, Patriot Bank warranted to Navy FCU that the item was paid to Nation's Auto or deposited into Nation's Auto's account. That warranty is the functional equivalent of supplying the missing endorsement of its customer. Therefore, Navy FCU should have honored the cashier's check when it was first presented to it for payment on April 9, 2001, before Mr. Peeso made any stop payment request.

III.   COULD NAVY FCU STOP PAYMENT ON THE CASHIER'S CHECK?

The check at issue in this case is a "cashier's check" as that term is defined in the UCC. It is a "draft with respect to which the drawer and the drawee are the same bank or branches of the same bank." Code §8.3A-104(g). A customer may stop payment only on an item drawn on the customer's account. Code §8.4-403(a). The official comments to Code §8.4-403 make clear that a customer has no right to stop payment on a cashier's check: A cashier's check or teller's check purchased by a customer whose account is debited in payment for the check is not a check drawn on the customer's account within the meaning of subsection (a); hence, a customer purchasing a cashier's check or teller's check has no right to stop payment of such a check under subsection (a). Code §8.4-403, Official Comment 4.

If a bank chooses not to honor a cashier's check as an accommodation for its customer, the bank's liability is governed by Code §8.3A-411. That section provides, in pertinent part:

> If the obligated bank wrongfully (i) refuses to pay a cashier's check or certified check, (ii) stops payment of a teller's check, or (iii) refuses to pay a dishonored teller's check, the person asserting the right to enforce the check is entitled to compensation for expenses and loss of interest resulting from the nonpayment and may recover consequential damages if the obligated bank refuses to pay after receiving notice of particular circumstances giving rise to the damages.

Code §8.3A-411(b). The statute is intended to discourage the practice of banks refusing to honor a cashier's check as an accommodation to their customers. Code §8.3A-411, Official Comment 1. Attorney's fees may be awarded as part of the "expenses . . . resulting from nonpayment." Code §8.3A-411, Official Comment 2.

The issue thus becomes whether Navy FCU "wrongfully" refused to honor the cashier's check. "If the bank is not obligated to pay there is no recovery." Code §8.3A-411. Official Comment 3.

When a bank issues a cashier's check it is in essence assuming the liabilities of a maker of a promissory note. Under Code §8.3A-412, "[t]he issuer of a note or cashier's check or other draft drawn on the drawer is obliged to pay the instrument . . . according to its terms at the time it was issued." The bank is obligated to pay the check in the same way a maker is obligated to pay a promissory note. Code §8.3A-412, Official Comment 1. A bank may refuse to pay a cashier's check based on any defenses that the bank itself may have, such as if the bank was not paid by its customer for the check, unless the check is in the hands of a holder in due course. The bank may not, however, refuse to pay a cashier's check based on any defenses that the remitter[12] may have. Code §8.3A-411. Official Comment 2.

In this case, Navy FCU had no defenses to the payment of the cashier's check. Navy FCU received full payment for the check when it debited Mr. Peeso's account for $7,000 upon the issuance of the check. James Marshall, the treasurer of Navy FCU, testified that Navy FCU refused to honor the check when presented in August 2001 with the absence of Nation's Auto's indorsement guaranteed because, by that time, payment had been stopped on the first check, Nation's Auto was out of business, and the second cashier's check had been issued and paid. As discussed above, Navy FCU could not properly "stop payment" on the cashier's check. Navy FCU's other reasons for not honoring the check were defenses that properly belonged to Mr. Peeso, the remitter. A bank that issues a cashier's check may not refuse to honor the check based on defenses of the remitter.

The parties devote much argument to whether Patriot Bank was a holder in due course of the cashier's check when it submitted it for payment in August. Patriot Bank's status as a holder in due course would be relevant only if Navy FCU were asserting its own defenses to payment of the check. Because Navy FCU is asserting only the remitter's defenses, the holder in due course analysis is irrelevant.

Navy FCU conceded at trial that a bank cannot stop payment on a check under the circumstances of this case and that Navy FCU refused to honor the check as an accommodation to Mr. Peeso. Therefore, this case falls squarely within the provisions of Code §8.3A-411.

CONCLUSION

The Court concludes that Navy FCU wrongfully refused to honor the cashier's check. Navy FCU is therefore liable to Patriot Bank for the amount of the wrongfully dishonored check, as well as Patriot Bank's "expenses . . . resulting from the nonpayment." Patriot Bank introduced evidence of its attorney's fees expended in pursuing payment of the check. The Court will enter judgment in favor of Patriot Bank, N.A. against Navy Federal Credit Union, in the principal amount of $7,000, plus interest on the principal amount at the legal rate beginning April 10, 2001 until paid, plus attorney's fees of $5,700 and costs of $182.26. . . .

---

12. The "remitter" is the person who purchases the cashier's check. Code §8.3A-103(a)(11). In this case, the remitter is Mr. Peeso.

In 1991, the drafters of the Uniform Commercial Code proposed an addition to Article 3, §3-312, which provides an elegant solution to the problem of stopping payment on lost, destroyed, or stolen cashier's checks, teller's checks, or certified checks. In this procedure, the person who lost possession files with the issuing bank a *declaration of loss,* and for 90 days after the date of the check the issuing bank must pay it if it is presented by a person entitled to enforce it, but after the 90-day period has passed, the issuing bank should pay the amount of the check to the person filing the declaration of loss.

PROBLEM 93

Portia Moot agreed to buy a car from her uncle who lived in another state, but the uncle demanded a cashier's check in payment. Portia obtained such a check for the correct amount from Octopus National Bank (ONB), which took a corresponding amount from her bank account, making the check payable to the order of Portia Moot. Portia signed her name to the back of the check and mailed it to her uncle. The uncle denied receiving the check (a lie), and Portia went down to ONB and filled out a declaration of loss on March 1. Having heard nothing during the next 90 days, on June 1, the bank refunded the money to Portia. In the meantime, the uncle cashed the check at his local bank on May 25th. Assume that the local bank qualifies as a holder in due course. What should ONB do when the local bank presents the check on June 2 and demands payment? See §3-312(b)(2) and Official Comment 3 (second paragraph). If ONB won't pay, what should the local bank do? See §§3-312(c); 3-415; Willis v. Wells Fargo Bank, N.A., 2012 WL 112942 (E.D. Va. 2012).

Losing a negotiable instrument of whatever kind is always unfortunate. Section 3-309 provides a mechanism whereby the true owner of the check can go to court and, in effect, judicially re-create it, having to post bond or give other adequate protection for the entity that will then pay the instrument. In states adopting §3-312, explored above, the two procedures are alternative possibilities; see §3-312(d) and Official Comment 1 to §3-312.

F. *Bank Statements*

The original version of §4-406, the Bank Statement Rule, presumed that banks were always returning canceled checks with the monthly bank statement, and this presumption proved awkward once banks moved to automation. As the next part of this chapter discusses, banks have instituted a range of measures to speed up check collection, including *check truncation* systems, in which the check itself is photographed shortly after deposit and then destroyed. In place of the check, an electronic signal describing it is forwarded through the system to the payor bank. Since the payor bank never receives the check, it can hardly return it to the customer along with the bank statement, as the original §4-406 arguably required.

Subsection (a) of the new version requires only that the bank return "sufficient information" about the check in the bank statement but does not mandate return of the check. *Sufficient information* is then defined in §4-406(a)'s last sentence as "item number, amount, and date of payment" (these being things either in the payor bank's records or magnetically encoded on the check and hence readable by computers and check-processing equipment). Official Comment 1 opines that with this much information customers (at least those with accurate records) will have enough to be able to locate the check in their records and figure out the missing matters (payee, date, etc.). Of course, nothing forbids the bank from returning the check itself if available, but the three terms required by (a) — item number, amount, and date of payment—provide what Official Comment 1 calls a "safe harbor rule," the absolute minimum the bank can provide and escape liability. Under (b) for seven years the payor bank must be able to furnish its customer with either the check itself or a legible copy thereof.

PROBLEM 94

When she got the ominous letter from the IRS telling her that she was scheduled for an audit, Portia Moot phoned her bank and told the employee with whom she spoke that she needed copies of the 172 checks she had written during the last calendar year. The bank employee replied that the bank would gladly furnish her with these copies but that the charge was $25.00 per copy. Can they do this to her? See Official Comment 3 to §4-406. How quickly must the bank come up with the copies? See §4-406(b). What is Portia's remedy if the bank neglects to produce the promised copies?

After the customer gets the bank statement, the law imposes a duty of examination for unauthorized signatures of the drawer or any alterations on the check (such as changing the amount), and requires prompt reporting of these matters. If the customer does not receive the actual check or a photo thereof but instead is furnished only the information required by the safe harbor rule, how can the customer discover forgeries or alterations? There is no discussion of this in the Comments, but §4-406(c) imposes a customer reporting duty only if "the customer should reasonably have discovered the unauthorized payment."

PROBLEM 95

When Joe Armstrong opened a checking account with Last National Bank, he signed an account agreement authorizing the bank to destroy the checks and return to him only a list of checks paid from the account identified only by check number, amount, and date of payment. The first time he received a statement it reflected the following:

Check Number	Date Paid	Amount
101	6-1-16	$ 132.45
102	6-1-16	$ 84.00
103	6-2-16	$1,204.00
104	6-3-16	$ 50.00
105	6-4-16	$2,000.00

Two things bothered Joe about this: (1) his records show that check 103 was written for $204.00 only, and (2) he has written no more than four checks on this account since he opened it. Looking in his checkbook, he discovered that check 105 was missing. Does §4-406(c) require Joe to report all this to his bank?

The *Check 21* rules, yet to be discussed, should largely solve these issues. As a result of this 2004 federal statute, most banks will be sending their customers either computer files or printouts thereof that will exactly show the fronts and backs of all checks written, allowing the customer all the information needed to reconcile the entries in the bank account.

The rest of §4-406 is so related to the forgery and alteration rules addressed in the next chapter that further discussion of the Bank Statement Rule awaits you there in Chapter 8.

II. BANK COLLECTION

The transfer of an item (*check*) from the depositary bank to the payor bank and the remittance of the proceeds inevitably lead to legal difficulties. To facilitate the handling of the huge number of checks passed around each year, there exists a sophisticated network of banks, federal agencies, and local clearinghouses that generally make up the bank collection system. In addition to Article 4's statutory regulation, the system is governed by a federal statute on point, plus Federal Reserve regulations and clearinghouse contractual agreements, all of which are permitted to vary the rules of Article 4. See §4-103(b).

For decades, the law on this subject was contained in two enactments: Article 4 of the Uniform Commercial Code and the Federal Reserve Board Regulation J on Collection of Checks and Other Items and Wire Transfer of Funds by Federal Reserve Banks, 12 C.F.R. Part 210 (which applies only if the check clears through the Federal Reserve System). But, effective September 1, 1988, a federal statute—the Expedited Funds Availability Act, 12 U.S.C. §§4001-4010, 248a [hereinafter EFAA]—superseded many of the UCC rules and resulted in an amendment to Regulation J as well. The federal statute is also supplemented by a Federal Reserve Board regulation having the force of law, Regulation CC, 12 C.F.R. 229, which will also be explained in the materials that follow (indeed, any reference to a section beginning with the numerals "229" is a reference to Regulation CC). Regulation CC is elaborated on in an official Federal Reserve Board Commentary, which is contained in Appendix E to the Regulation itself; the Commentary also has the force of law. Regulation CC should be in your statute book, likely identified as "Availability of Funds and Collection of Checks."

Thus, a lawyer wanting to understand the rules of check collection must compare the rules of the EFAA (which is almost impenetrable—it reads as if it were badly translated from German), Regulation CC (which, being drafted by the Federal Reserve, is much more readable, if soporific), and the Official Commentary in Appendix E to the regulation (which is very user-friendly, with helpful examples included).

The EFAA and Regulation CC do not completely do away with the Uniform Commercial Code rules on check collection, which still apply in any situation not covered by federal rules, and, of course, those rules were written with the UCC as a back-drop. So we begin our coverage of check collection with the Uniform Commercial Code and then look at the variations worked thereon by the EFAA and Regulation CC.

A. Funds Availability

It is important to appreciate that the rules that follow, both state and federal, set outside time limits on the period that banks can hold deposited funds, but they do not prohibit the depositary bank from allowing the customer *earlier* access to those funds, should the bank so decide. Earlier access is a business decision. The discussion below looks at the question of when as a *matter of legal right* the customer is entitled to the funds.

We begin with the issue of how quickly the depositor can get money back from the bank in which items are deposited. It is easiest to understand the whole process if approached from a personal point of view. So, presuming that you have had some experience with a checking account, let's use the Code to answer the basic questions.

1. Cash

If you deposit cash in your account, how quickly can you take it out again? Answer: on the next banking day. See §4-215(f).[13] The "subject to any right of the bank" language in §4-215(f) refers to the bank's right of setoff.

Banking day is defined in §4-104(a)(3) as that part of the day when the bank is "open to the public for carrying on substantially all of its banking functions."[14] As to this, see §4-108, which further refines *banking day* so as to permit a bank to establish a cutoff hour in the early afternoon and to pretend that items received after that hour were received on the next banking day. Thus, if that bank's banking day ends at 2:30 P.M., a check received at 2:31 P.M. on Friday is treated as if it were received early Monday morning (assuming neither is a holiday and the bank is not open on Saturday and Sunday). The purpose of such a rule is stated in §4-108(a).[15]

2. Checks

a. Across the Counter Presentments. If someone gives you a check and you (the payee) walk into the drawee bank and present it across the counter, how quickly must the bank pay or dishonor it? Answer: before the close of business. When an over-the-counter presentment for payment is made, §3-502(b)(2) requires the bank to make a decision that same day.

b. "On Us" Items. If someone gives you a check and you deposit it in your own account, how quickly may you take it out? Answer: as soon as your bank will let you, though, as discussed below, for certain kinds of checks federal law regulates this issue. If the amount is not great and you are a good customer, your bank may permit you to write checks on the deposited

---

13. Section 603(a)(1), 12 U.S.C. §4002(a)(1), of the EFAA has the same requirement. The Federal Reserve Board has stated that UCC §4-215(f) is *not* preempted by the adoption of Regulation CC. 53 Fed. Reg. 32,354 (Aug. 24, 1988).

14. If a bank has a teller window open on Saturday, is this a banking day? Probably not, since the bank is not open for carrying on "substantially all of its banking functions," the statutory test. See Merrill Lynch, Pierce, Fenner & Smith, Inc. v. Devon Bank, 832 F.2d 1005 (7th Cir. 1987) (where main lobby closed, Saturday not a banking day).

15. The same rule for a cutoff hour is found in Regulation CC, except that for automated teller machines (ATMs) a bank may establish 12:00 noon as the cutoff hour for the receipt of deposits (§229.19(a)). However, Regulation CC draws a distinction not in the UCC between "business day," meaning days other than Saturdays, Sundays, and federal holidays, and "banking day," meaning business days on which a bank is open for carrying on substantially all of its banking functions. Saturday could never be a "banking day" for Regulation CC purposes under these definitions, though it might be a "banking day" under the UCC if the bank were open for business on Saturdays. 12 C.F.R. §229.2(f) and (g).

amount immediately, particularly if the drawer is well known and solvent (e.g., a large corporation). The real question is this: When do you have a legal *right* to draw checks on the deposited amount?

If, by coincidence, you (the payee) and the drawer each maintain an account at the same bank (that is, the depositary and payor banks are one and the same—the bankers call this an "On Us" item), §4-215(e)(2) permits you to remove the money at the opening of the *second banking day* following receipt of the item, unless, of course, in the meantime the check is dishonored, in which case you will be so notified (§§4-202(a)(2) and 3-503(c)). In this period of time, the bank, acting as the drawee-payor, will sort the check into a stack of "On Us" items and then examine the drawer's account and decide whether to pay the check.

The EFAA here makes its first major change. It speeds things up one day by requiring the depositary bank to make same-bank checks available for withdrawal on *the business day after the business day of deposit* (this is commonly referred to as "next day availability"). EFAA §603(a)(2)(E), 12 U.S.C. §4002(a)(2)(E); Regulation CC §229.10(c)(1)(vi). For "On Us" items, the bank must now make its decision to pay or dishonor overnight.

   c. "Transit" Items. If the depositary bank and the payor (drawee) bank are *not* the same, then the check is a "transit" item and must go through some sort of multi-bank collection machinery. This can be as simple as exchanging checks with the bank across the street or as complicated as sending the check to the payor bank in Japan, so of course the rules are more complicated. As soon as your bank (the depositary bank) begins this process, it is called a *collecting bank*. During the process it acts as your agent (§4-201(a)).

PROBLEM 96

   When his son was in Japan as an exchange student, Professor Chalk decided to give him a $1,000 check as a birthday present. He mailed the check to his son, who in turn mailed it, unindorsed, to his own bank back in the United States for deposit. This bank stamped its own indorsement on the back of the check in the spot where depositary banks are supposed to indorse and then forwarded the check for collection. Two things happened before the check was presented: (1) Professor Chalk and his son had a phone conversation that ended so angrily that Chalk stopped payment on the check, and (2) the depositary bank offset against all of the son's bank account to pay a debt the son owed it. When the check was returned to the depositary bank, it threatened to sue Chalk unless he made the check good; see §3-414(b). He responded that the bank did not take pursuant to a valid negotiation (no payee's signature) and was not a "person entitled to enforce the instrument"; see

§3-301. In any event, Chalk added, he had a defense based on the fact that he received no consideration for his drawer's obligation. How does this come out? See §4-205 and its Official Comment.

If the depositary bank and the payor bank are in the same small town, they will typically arrange to exchange checks drawn on each other once each day. At the appointed time, they will present checks to one another in a bundle. Must the banks decide which checks to pay and which to dishonor before the close of the business day, as in §3-502 above? No, because Article 4 has a special rule for interbank collection presentments, and Article 4 overrides Article 3 where they conflict; §4-102(a).

The two banks will probably maintain accounts with each other and, by contract, will agree to permit the depositary bank to debit the account of the payor bank for the amount of the deposited check, subject to the right of the payor bank to dishonor the check later and have the account recredited. Such a contract results in a *provisional settlement* (*provisional* because the so-called settlement is subject to revocation). Thus, at the time the banks exchange the checks each day, they will have already debited each other's accounts with the amounts of the presented checks. If, after receiving the checks drawn on it, the payor bank decides to dishonor one or more, it simply returns the check, and the provisional settlement for that check is wiped out (technically, *charged back*).

Suppose that Mary Depositor deposits a check on which she is the payee in her bank, which we shall call Depositary Bank. Depositary Bank will mark her account with a *provisional settlement* for the amount of the item—in effect a bookkeeping entry reflecting the hope that the check will be paid by the payor/drawee bank. During the time that the check is traveling (called the "float period" by bankers), Depositary Bank may or may not allow Mary access to the money (more about that below), but even if it lets her withdraw it, if the check is later properly returned, she will have to repay any amounts provisionally withdrawn; §4-214 (Charge Back, also discussed in detail in this chapter).

The check collection system works through computers, so the check must be magnetically *encoded* so that all the computers it will pass through can read it. The little fractional number in the upper right-hand corner of the check is the routing symbol of the drawee bank. This routing symbol, along with the drawer's account number, is already encoded across the bottom of the check on the left-hand side. The amount of the check will be encoded on the bottom right-hand side.[16]

---

16. The Code provides for a warranty of proper encoding; §4-209. The courts have had no problem finding liability for mis-encoding checks; see Troy Bank and Trust Co. v. Citizens Bank, 2014 WL 4851511 (Ala. 2014). Regulation CC has a similar encoding warranty in §229.34(c)(3).

If Depositary Bank and the payor bank are located in the same large city, they will probably make the provisional settlements and check exchanges through a central *clearinghouse*, which can be loosely defined as an association of local banks that has drawn up regulations and procedures to effectuate the exchange of checks. Clearinghouse rules are allowed to change the rules of the Uniform Commercial Code, including all the deadlines discussed in this chapter. That means a lawyer for a bank which is a member of a clearinghouse would be well advised to read the clearinghouse rules, with thoughts of malpractice providing the incentive to wade through them carefully.

If Depositary Bank and the payor bank are not located close to one another, Depositary Bank will send the check to the first intermediary bank, typically a Federal Reserve Bank, established by the federal government. The United States is divided into 12 Federal Reserve districts, and in the center of each district sits a Federal Reserve Bank. These Superbanks have only banks as customers (a bank for banks) and permit member banks to open accounts therein and use the efficient cross-country check collection machinery operated by the Federal Reserve Banks. In return, member banks must observe Federal Reserve Board regulations. The Federal Reserve Banks each maintain accounts with one another, which they will debit or credit as they receive checks or payment (*remittances*) from member banks.

As the check passes from one bank to another, the presenting bank will give itself a provisional settlement for the amount of the check in the account it carries with the bank to which it forwards the check (the Federal Reserve Banks do this too). Each bank has two banking days in which to pass the item on to the next bank; §4-202(b). If the payor bank pays the check, all the provisional settlements (those bookkeeping entries) along the check collection route are said to "firm up," and *now final settlement* occurs. When this happens, Mary has a legal right to the money at her end.

The Uniform Commercial Code reaches this result in a section that is difficult to read—§4-215(e). In that subsection, the beginning two small-case roman numerals refer, respectively, to (i) the superior command of federal law (i.e., the EFAA and Regulation CC), and (ii) the bank's own right of setoff. Subsection (2) discusses the rule for "On Us" items (see above), leaving subsection (1) as the relevant part covering the transit item rules described in the last few paragraphs. Read §4-215(e) carefully, remembering that provisional settlements become final settlements when the payor bank pays the check at issue.

d.   The Federal Availability Rules.   Customers objected to holds for long float periods, pointing out that of the billions of checks written every year, 99 percent are honored on first presentment, and that most of the rest are honored on second presentment (or are made good by the depositor).

Customers also highlighted the facts that the banks have the use of the funds during the float period (because the bank has been given a provisional credit during collection), and that the banks were estimated to earn approximately $290 million each year from this practice.

A number of states responded to this problem by passing statutes regulating the hold on deposited funds or, at least, requiring clear disclosure of the bank's policies on the issue. New York, Illinois, California, and Massachusetts, for example, required immediate credit for small checks and for those issued by the government or banks, and specified the float periods for checks that travel various distances from the depositary bank. In 1987, the federal government got into the act, passing the EFAA and Regulation CC and preempting the state laws (except to the extent they are better for depositors than the federal rules, see Appendix F to Regulation CC).

The federal rules in most cases completely displace §4-215(e)(1), which you have just read, and have concrete answers to how long the hold for the float period can be. You should know that it can take depositary banks several days to learn that a check is bad, and that banks annually lose about $1 billion on unpaid checks. Thus the depositary bank has a strong incentive not to release the deposited amount unless it is sure the check will not come bounding back.

(i) **Next Day Availability of Special Items.** The EFAA availability rules are designed to strike a balance between the customer's need for the funds and the risks of non-collection faced by the banks in which these funds are deposited. Congress decided that there should be *next banking day* availability[17] for items that are not likely to be dishonored, and the EFAA (§602, 12 U.S.C. §4001) and Regulation CC (see §229.10) have a list of such items:

(1) Government checks: checks issued by any branch of government, federal, state, or local;
(2) Bank checks: checks on which a bank is primarily liable (cashier, teller, and certified checks); and
(3) Wire transfers: electronically sent payment orders of the sort covered by Article 4A of the Uniform Commercial Code, and covered by Chapter 9 of this book.

---

17. If these items are deposited in an automated teller machine (ATM), the bank is given an extra day, and the items must be available for withdrawal on the second day after deposit; see Regulation CC §229.10(a)(2) and(c)(2).

There is one more addition to this list: the *$200 Availability Rule*, EFAA §603(a)(2)(D), 12 U.S.C. §4002(a)(2)(d).[18] The rule is based on the idea that even for riskier checks we ought to allow the customer access to a small amount immediately. Thus federal law requires the bank to make the following computation: take the aggregate of the day's deposits, from that amount subtract items already requiring next day availability, and give the customer $200 of the amount remaining.

(ii) Availability of Ordinary Checks. The following rules, from Regulation CC §229.12, may have more interest for you if you remember that they govern how fast you are allowed to make withdrawals based on checks that you deposit in your own account that are drawn on other banks. You should understand, however, that even if these rules require your bank to give you access to the deposited funds, if a check is properly returned after you have taken out the money, you will still be required to repay your own bank for the amount withdrawn (under the *charge-back* rules yet to be discussed). The rules vary depending on whether the depositor wants to take out *cash* or simply write *checks* against the deposited amounts, since checks by their very nature have a built-in float period for collection, but cash is cash and gone immediately.[19]

First of all, the $200 availability rule allows you next day access to the first $200 deposited in any one day, whether you want it in cash or by check.

Second, the entire amount above $200 (up to $5,000 in deposits per day) must be available for check-writing purposes on the second banking day following the date of deposit. However, if the customer wants to take out cash, he/she can only get up to $400 of the amount of the check by 5 P.M. on the second banking day (with the rest of the amount available for cash withdrawal on start of business the day following).

---

18. The amount was raised from $100 to $200 by §1086(e) of the Dodd-Frank Wall Street Reform and Consumer Protection Act (Dodd-Frank Act) of 2010. Regulation CC is subject to the statute.

19. These rules used to give banks more time to make funds available from "non-local" checks. In order to process checks, the Federal Reserve had drawn lines across the map of the United States to create 18 different check processing regions. Banks were said to be "local" to one another if they are physically located in the same Federal check processing region. But, as most checks are now processed electronically, the Federal Reserve in 2010 consolidated its check processing (for the minority of checks that still physically travel from bank to bank) in the Federal Reserve Bank of Cleveland. So there are no longer any non-local checks. See Stephen C. Veltri & Greg Cavanagh, Survey: Uniform Commercial Code, Payments, 65 Bus. Law. 1241 (Aug. 2010).

Funds Availability Rules: Ordinary Checks Deposited on Day 0

Noncash use	Day 1	$200		
	Day 2	Remainder (up to $5,000 deposits per day)		
Cash	Day 1	$200		
	Day 2	$400		
	Day 3	Remainder (up to $5,000)		

Congress, ever alert, recognized that the early availability schedules described above could be misused by some bank customers, so it gave the banks a few escape valves in EFAA §604, 12 U.S.C. §4003:

(1) New Accounts. During the first 30 days of the existence of a new account, there must be next day availability for cash or wire deposits, for government checks, and for bank-generated checks (cashier's checks, etc.). If the government check or the bank-generated check exceeds $5,000, the depositary bank may put a hold on the amount that exceeds the $5,000 for up to nine business days. There are no rules that describe the time period for the availability of ordinary checks, so the usual UCC rules would apply—see UCC §4-215(e)(1). See EFAA §604(a), 12 U.S.C. §4003(a), and Regulation CC §229.13(a). There is no requirement of $200 next day availability for new accounts; Regulation CC §229.13(a)(iii).

(2) Large Deposits. According to Regulation CC §229.13(b) and (h), only the first $5,000 of a day's deposit is subject to the normal availability rules. The excess may be held for an *additional reasonable period of time* (and five business days is presumed to be reasonable for ordinary checks; for longer periods the bank must carry the burden of establishing the period is reasonable). Deposits by cash or electronic payment are not subject to this exception for large deposits.

(3) Redeposited Checks. The normal availability rules are extended by an extra reasonable period of time (with the same five/six business days presumption) in the case of redeposited checks, unless the announced reason for the return was a missing indorsement or because the check was postdated, and these problems have been cleared up at the time of redeposit; Regulation CC §229.13(c) and (h).

(4) Repeated Overdrafts. The normal availability rules are extended by an extra reasonable period of time (with the same five/six business days presumption) for six months after the account or any combination of a customer's accounts has been repeatedly overdrawn. As to whether an account is considered to be repeatedly overdrawn, there is a two-prong test and if either prong is met, the bank may hold deposited checks for the extra period of time. Under these tests, the account is considered repeatedly overdrawn if the account balance is negative (or would have been negative if all checks or other charges to the account had been paid) on six or more banking days within the preceding six months, *or* if on two or more banking days within the preceding six months the account balance is negative (or would have been negative if all checks or other charges to the account had been paid) in the amount of $5,000 or more. See Regulation CC §229.13(d) and (h).

(5) The "Reasonable Cause" Exception. Under EFAA §604(c), 12 U.S.C. §4003(c), if the bank has "reasonable cause" to believe that a check is uncollectible, then it may ignore the usual rules if it gives the notice to the customer, described below, telling him/her when the funds will be made available. A bank has "reasonable cause," according to the statutory language, whenever there exist "facts which would cause a well-grounded belief in the mind of a reasonable person." Such reasons must be included in the notice. The Board has elected not to expand upon the statutory language, though the Commentary does give examples of proper use of the exception. These include the fact that the bank has received a notice that the check is being returned, the fact that the check is stale (more than six months old when deposited), or that check kiting is suspected. If the bank is going to invoke this "reasonable cause" exception for cashier's, teller's, or certified checks or those drawn on a Federal Reserve Bank or those deposited at an ATM, it must use the usual times periods plus a later reasonable time (presumed to be five/six days, as above). See Regulation CC §229.13(e) and (h).

(6) Emergency Conditions. Regulation CC §229.13(f) has a rule modeled on UCC §4-109 (described at the end of this chapter in the section called "Delays") that excuses compliance with the normal availability rules due to emergencies beyond the bank's control.

(7) The Notice. Except in the "new accounts" situation, where a bank plans to take advantage of either the "large check," "redeposited check," "repeated overdrafts," or "reasonable cause" exceptions, the depositor must be notified as soon as possible of the date the funds will be made available. Appendix C to the Regulation contains model forms, including a model form of Notice of Exception to the usual availability rules. Since reliance on this form insulates the bank from any civil liability, its use is the better part

of wisdom. The Federal Reserve is very insistent that banks follow whatever availability policy they disclose and not deviate from it unless the right to do so has also been disclosed.

(8) Civil Liability. Under §611 of the Act, 12 U.S.C. §4010, the bank that does not follow the statute or the regulations promulgated thereunder by the Federal Reserve Board can be sued by the injured customer for his/her actual damages, punitive damages (not greater than $1,000, nor less than $100, though in a class action the upper figure is the lesser of $500,000 or 1 percent of the net worth of the bank), plus costs of suit and attorney's fee. The suit may be brought in federal or state court within one year after the occurrence of the violation.

Variation by agreement from the rules of Regulation CC is permitted only for the check return rules of Subpart C, and such agreements only bind the specific parties to the agreement. No variation is permitted from the funds availability and disclosure requirements.

B.   *Check Truncation*

1.   Introduction

Consider that for the last century and the beginning of this one, banks had to daily exchange mountains of paper checks, a very inefficient system. In the last few decades, banks had experimented with a process called "check truncation" (or sometimes "check retention") in which the depositary bank simply keeps the deposited check and forwards only a description of it through the bank collection process. Specific provision is made for electronic presentment and warranties connected with same; see §§4-110 and 4-209(b).[20] In such a system, the customer never gets the check back, although it is reflected on the bank statement. In the 1990s, the bank statement rule, §4-406, was amended to require banks to send certain information back to the customer and to give the customer the right to demand a legible copy of the check for seven years after the statement was sent out.

The idea of creating an "image" of the check and sending it through bank channels instead of the original paper check had been urged for over a decade, but it was expensive to get such a system up and running, and there was a lot of resistance to the suggestion. Some banks did agree to do electronic presentment with each other. But many banks were reluctant to invest in the necessary technology—especially where it might be outdated if

---

20. Federal Reserve Regulation CC has a similar encoding warranty provision in §229.34(c)(3).

other banks adopted different standards. However, the September 11, 2001, attacks gave new life to this idea. Planes were grounded for five or more days that September, and many checks could not move at all from bank to bank, resulting in chaos. Check imaging was an attractive solution.

Congress passed the "Check Clearing for the 21st Century Act" or the "Check 21 Act," effective October 28, 2004.[21] The Federal Reserve created amendments to Regulations CC and J to implement the Act, and the bulk of these new regulations are found in Subpart D to Regulation CC. Check 21 permits banks to do electronic processing, without requiring banks to accept electronic presentment. Rather, a bank may make an electronic image of a check, transmit the image across the country, and either present the image or print out a substitute check, and present it for payment. Check 21 has been very successful in encouraging the use of substitute checks (and also electronic presentment, by agreement between banks). So few checks now travel around the country physically that the Federal Reserve, as noted above, has closed most of its check-processing centers and now sends the remaining checks through a single center in Cleveland.

2. Creating the Image and the Substitute Check

a. Remote Deposit Capture. Many banks engage in a practice called "remote deposit capture" (RDC), which allows their customers to use an app to photograph a check's front and back, and deposit the check image instantly through the app. The customer is often also instructed to write "void" across the original. Customers love the convenience and speed of this, and more than 40 percent of banks now offer this service to their customers. The legal ramifications are less clear.

PROBLEM 97

MegaBank decided to speed up check processing by having its customer sign a remote deposit capture agreement by which the customer would use a cell phone and an app thereon to photograph both sides of any check the customer wished to deposit. The customer was instructed to then send the images to the bank, write "VOID" on the front of the check, and/or destroy the check. A customer named Walter White was one of the bank's customers, and when he received a $50,000 check on which he was the payee he created the required images and sent them via the app to MegaBank. Instead of following the rest of the instructions, White then indorsed the paper check and deposited it in

---

21. The text of the statute is at *http://www.bankersonline.com/check21/check21act.pdf.*

an account he had at Heisenberg State Bank, which allowed him to withdraw $50,000 before the check cleared through the bank on which it was drawn. In the meantime, the image of the check was sent to the same bank, and White also withdrew the same amount from his account at MegaBank. Both the image and the paper versions of the check were presented to the payor bank on which they were drawn, and the image version of the check arrived there first, so the payor bank paid it. When the paper check arrived shortly thereafter the payor bank dishonored it, giving as its reason that this check had already been presented and paid. You are the attorney for Heisenberg State Bank, which has received the return of the paper check. Walter White has left town and can't be found. Your client wants to know who else it can sue and under what theory. As you examine the paper check strange questions begin to form in your mind like "Is my client a holder in due course?" "How can I pass this liability on to other entities in the mess?"

b.   Check Truncation by Banks.   Under the statute, depositary banks or other banks in the collection chain have the option (not duty) to create an image of the original check and pass it on if the receiving bank agrees to accept it in that form; Regulation CC §229.2(ddd). A bank creating such an image is called a "*truncating* bank" in Regulation CC §229.2(ddd).

After truncation, the imaged check is passed along as a computer file until someone (a later bank, the bank's customer, or whoever) refuses to take the imaged version and insists on getting paper. In that case the bank (now named a "*reconverting* bank")[22] will print out a paper version of the check. The paper version is called a "substitute check." To understand the definition of a "substitute check" in the Regulation, you should know what a "MICR line" (usually, but not always, pronounced "mick-er") is. The initials stand for "magnetic character ink recognition" and refer to the line at the bottom of all checks with the strange printing, identifying the routing information so the check can be sent to the payor bank and charged against the correct account. The depositary bank will also encode the amount of the check to the MICR line, below the drawer's signature (and our laws have long had warranties that this encoding is correct).[23] Now read the definition of "substitute check" in Regulation CC §229.2(zz).[24] If the paper reproduction of the image does not meet these standards, it will not technically qualify as a "substitute check," with important consequences as we shall see.

The reconverting bank must also add to the substituted checks all the indorsements that would have been placed on the original check had it

----

22. See Regulation CC §229.2(yy).
23. UCC §4-209(a); Regulation CC §229.34(c)(3).
24. In the statute, see §3(16).

traveled the same route as the image. Regulation CC §229.51(b) creates a duty in the reconverting check to ensure that the substitute check:

(1) Bears all indorsements applied by parties that previously handled the check in any form (including the original check, a substitute check, or another paper or electronic representation of such original check or substitute check) for forward collection or return;

(2) Identifies the reconverting bank in a manner that preserves any previous reconverting bank identifications, in accordance with generally applicable industry standards for substitute checks and appendix D of this part; and

(3) Identifies the bank that truncated the original check in accordance with generally applicable industry standards for substitute checks and appendix D of this part.

3.   Legal Equivalence

No one can refuse to take the substitute check, which is legally the same (for all purposes, including criminal prosecution), as the original. Customers cannot insist on getting the original back. If the parties agree to imaging without a paper copy being created, the image also has the same legal effect as the original. These rules will greatly speed up check collection, though there are some downsides to loss of the original (no fingerprints, for example, which can be important in criminal prosecutions). Section 4(b) of the statute provides:

A substitute check shall be the legal equivalent of the original check for all purposes, including any provision of any Federal or State law, and for all persons if the substitute check—

(1) accurately represents all of the information on the front and back of the original check as of the time the original check was truncated; and

(2) bears the legend: "This is a legal copy of your check. You can use it the same way you would use the original check."[25]

PROBLEM 98

Sharon Bardus paid her state income taxes in full with a check, and was considerably annoyed when the State sent her a letter informing her that the taxes were still due and she would be assessed penalties. When she protested, the State demanded to see the check she had allegedly sent in. Sharon had received that check only as an image returned as part of her monthly bank statement, but she contacted her bank, and the bank printed out a copy of the

25. See the similar language in Reg. CC §229.51.

check and sent it to her. She mailed this copy to the State, but received back a letter informing her that it was State policy to only accept the original cancelled check as proof of payment, so they refused to consider what was clearly a mere copy. Now what should Sharon do?

4. Warranty Liability

Parties passing on the substitute check make both transfer and presentment warranties that everything is on the up and up. Section 5 of the statute states the warranties made by reconverting banks that create the substitute check and transfer it to others:

> A bank that transfers, presents, or returns a substitute check and receives consideration for the check warrants, as a matter of law, to the transferee, any subsequent collecting or returning bank, the depositary bank, the drawee, the drawer, the payee, the depositor, and any endorser (regardless of whether the warrantee receives the substitute check or another paper or electronic form of the substitute check or original check) that—
>
> (1) the substitute check meets all the requirements for legal equivalence under section 4(b); and
>
> (2) no depositary bank, drawee, drawer, or endorser will receive presentment or return of the substitute check, the original check, or a copy or other paper or electronic version of the substitute check or original check such that the bank, drawee, drawer, or endorser will be asked to make a payment based on a check that the bank, drawee, drawer, or endorser has already paid.

PROBLEM 99

When the check was truncated by the depositary bank and turned into an electronic image, the image was blurry. When the reconverting bank printed out the substitute check the account number was incorrectly listed as starting with an "8" when the original started with a "3." As a consequence the wrong account was debited for the amount of this check, causing other checks to bounce. The customer complained and the payor bank recredited the account, and calls you, the bank's attorney. Now what? See Regulation CC §229.52.

The answer is that the account holder could sue for breach of the above warranty of legal equivalence. Liability would flow back to the reconverting bank. That bank could not use the above warranty to pass the loss back to the truncating bank because that bank did not transfer a "substitute check" (a piece of paper). However, the Federal Reserve has created similar warranties for the transfer of electronic images in Regulation J §210.5(a)(3) and (4), and these warranties would operate in the same fashion. Moreover the wise attorney will make sure there is a contractual agreement in place between banks transferring and accepting images that they correctly reflect the terms of the original check, and this contractual agreement would also create liability in the truncating bank.

5. Indemnity Liability

In addition to this warranty liability, §6 of the statute creates *indemnity* liability against banks transferring either the image or the substitute check if doing so causes *damages that could have been prevented by use of the original check*; in the Regulation see §229.53. In the above Problem, the truncating bank would have to respond to an indemnity claim because of its blurry image of the original check; if the original had been transferred, the right amount would have been debited from the correct account. It is unclear what this indemnity liability will mean in many situations, though the Official Commentary to Regulation CC gives this example:

> A drawer received a substitute check that met all the legal equivalence requirements and that was only charged once to the drawer's account, but the drawer believed that the underlying original check was a forgery. If the drawer suffered a loss because it could not prove the forgery based on the substitute check, for example because proving the forgery required analysis of pen pressure that could be determined only from the original check, the drawer would have an indemnity claim. However, the drawer would not have a substitute check warranty claim because the substitute check was the legal equivalent of the original and no person was asked to pay the substitute check more than once. In that case, the amount of the drawer's indemnity would be limited to the amount of the substitute check, plus interest and expenses, although the drawer could attempt to recover additional losses, if any, under other law.[26]

As a practical matter this means that the original check must be preserved so that it can be found in the event of trouble and produced to help resolve the difficulty. All claims must be made within 120 days after the transaction that gives rise to the claim—see Regulation CC §299.55(b)(1)—so that is the relevant period for preserving the original check. Lawsuits under Check 21 must be brought within one year after the transaction,[27] and the prudent bank may wish to hold the original checks until that statute of limitations has passed. Bankers will tell you that these periods are unrealistic and that they routinely destroy most checks after 45 days or fewer. Hmm. The lawyer advises one thing to comply with the law and the bankers do another

---

26. This is the Official Commentary to Regulation CC §229.53(b).
27. Regulation CC §229.56(c).

for economic reasons and also because all the other banks are doing the same ("usage of trade"). Shocking.

First Financial Bank, N.A v. Citibank, N.A.

United States District Court for the Southern District of Indiana, 2012
2012 WL 3065546

WILLIAM T. LAWRENCE, District Judge.

This cause is before the Court on the motion filed by Plaintiff First Financial Bank, N.A. ("First Financial") seeking summary judgment with regard to its claims against Defendant Citibank, N.A. ("Citibank") (dkt. no. 82). The motion is fully briefed and the Court, being duly advised, GRANTS IN PART AND DENIES IN PART the motion as set forth below. . . .

II. BACKGROUND FACTS

The facts relevant to the instant motion, viewed in the light most favorable to Defendant Citibank, the non-moving party, are as follow.

Defendant Misty McDonald, an attorney in Terre Haute, Indiana, deposited a check at her local First Financial bank on July 7, 2010. The check purported to be Citibank Official Check[28] No. 260356932, dated July 2, 2010, in the amount of $298,750.00; the remitter was listed as Accurate Manufactured Products Group, Inc. ("AMPG"), and the check was made payable to "Misty Y. McDonald, Attorney at Law" (the "Check"). McDonald believed the Check to be partial payment of money owed by AMPG to a company that had recently engaged her services to try to collect from AMPG.

First Financial has banking relationships with other institutions that are established by contracts. These relationships are referred to in the banking industry as correspondent banking relationships. First Financial has a correspondent banking relationship with J.P. Morgan Chase, N.A. ("Chase"), for the forward processing of checks. As relevant to this case, "forward processing" means the movement of a check that is deposited at a First Financial bank to the "paying bank" of that check. First Financial does not have a correspondent banking arrangement with Chase for the downstream processing of checks—that is, the movement of checks from paying banks back to First Financial for, among other things, providing notice of nonpayment. Instead, the Federal Reserve Bank is First Financial's correspondent bank for downstream processing.

As is customary in the banking industry, First Financial created an electronic image of the Check for use in the forward and downstream processing

---

28. [Bankers call cashier's checks "official checks." —EDS.]

of the Check. Pursuant to its agreement with Chase, First Financial sent the Check to Chase for forward processing. This was accomplished by including the imaged Check in a cash letter[29] to Chase dated July 7, 2010.

The following day, July 8, 2010, Chase sent an electronic image of the Check to Citibank. Citibank determined that the account number on the Check did not exist and marked it "invalid account number, account unknown." Citibank also determined that the endorsement of the depository bank (First Financial) was illegible. However, the Check contained a "Sending R/T" number on it that indicated that it had come to Citibank from Chase. Citibank therefore returned the Check for nonpayment to Chase. In order to accomplish this, Citibank sent a notice to Chase through the Electronic Advanced Return Notification System ("EARNS") at 8:34 P.M. on July 8, 2010, that indicated that the Check was being returned for an invalid account number. Citibank then sent the Check and its accompanying cash letter to the Federal Reserve Bank.

At 7:10 A.M. on July 9, 2010, Chase opened the EARNS notice that advised it that Citibank was returning the Check because it bore an invalid account number. Chase notified First Financial that the Check had been returned by sending two letters by regular U.S. mail, one dated July 9th and the other dated July 13th. First Financial did not receive either letter until at least July 14th. Chase also sent First Financial a fax bearing the image of the Check with the notice of nonpayment from Citibank on July 14th. First Financial received an EARNS notice of nonpayment on July 15th.

In the meantime, on July 9, 2010, at 12:56 P.M., First Financial completed a wire transfer for McDonald of 90% of the amount of the Check—$268,825.00—to the Bank of China in Beijing, China. When it learned that the check had been returned by Citibank, First Financial attempted to recall McDonald's wire transfer, but was notified by the Bank of China on July 19th that it had paid the beneficiary of McDonald's wire transfer on July 12th and the request to return the wire transfer would not be honored. First Financial set off funds on deposit in McDonald's accounts at First Financial in the total amount of $26,172.21, but has been unable to recover the remaining $272,577.79.

III. DISCUSSION

First Financial argues that "[t]he undisputed material facts of this case demonstrate that Citibank failed to provide timely and proper notice of nonpayment and return of a check, thereby breaching warranty obligations to

29. A cash letter is a compilation of numerous checks that is created by a bank for the purpose of packaging items for distribution to their correspondent banks in the forward or downstream processing of checks.

First Financial and causing damages in the amount of the check's face value, plus interest and expenses, less those amounts mitigated by First Financial's actions." First Financial Brief at 1. First Financial therefore seeks summary judgment on all of its claims against Citibank. . . .

B.   CITIBANK'S DUTIES REGARDING RETURNING THE CHECK

Citibank's obligations with regard to the Check once it decided to dishonor it were governed by what is referred to as "Regulation CC"—a set of implementing regulations promulgated pursuant to the Expedited Funds Availability Act, 12 U.S.C. §4010 et seq. Subpart C of Regulation CC, which is found at 12 C.F.R. §229.30 et seq., sets forth a paying bank's responsibility for the return of a check; First Financial argues that Citibank violated several of Regulation CC's requirements. The Court will address each of First Financial's arguments in turn.

1.   *Failure to Return the Check Expeditiously*

A paying bank that has decided not to pay a check must return the check "expeditiously." 12 C.F.R. §229.30(a). In order to do so, it "may send [the] returned check to the depositary bank, or to any other bank agreeing to handle the returned check expeditiously under §229.31(a)." 12 C.F.R. §229.30(a). Citibank failed to comply with this requirement when it returned the Check to Chase because Chase had no agreement with First Financial to handle returned checks expeditiously on First Financial's behalf. Citibank argues that it nonetheless complied with Regulation CC because it was unable to identify the depositary bank with respect to the Check and therefore was permitted to return the Check to Chase pursuant to 12 C.F.R. §229.30(b), which provides:

> A paying bank that is unable to identify the depositary bank with respect to a check may send the returned check to any bank that handled the check for forward collection even if that bank does not agree to handle the check expeditiously under §229.31(a).

The problem with Citibank's argument is that the evidence of record does not support its assertion that it was unable to identify the depositary bank from the information on the back of the Check. Citibank points to testimony by witnesses who say that the endorsement by First Financial was "not clear." However, Citibank also states that "[t]he image of the Check received by Citibank on July 8, 2010 is depicted in CB 00020," and the Court finds, as a matter of law, that no reasonable jury could examine CB 00020 and conclude that Citibank was unable to decipher First Financial's endorsement. Therefore 12 C.F.R. §229.30(b) did not apply to Citibank's return of the Check.

So Citibank was required to expeditiously return the Check to First Financial, and it failed to do so. The next question is what, if any, liability flows from that failure. Regulation CC provides:

A bank shall exercise ordinary care and act in good faith in complying with the requirements of this subpart. A bank that fails to exercise ordinary care or act in good faith under this subpart may be liable to the depositary bank, the depositary bank's customer, the owner of a check, or another party to the check. *The measure of damages for failure to exercise ordinary care is the amount of the loss incurred, up to the amount of the check, reduced by the amount of the loss that party would have incurred even if the bank had exercised ordinary care.* A bank that fails to act in good faith under this subpart may be liable for other damages, if any, suffered by the party as a proximate consequence. Subject to a bank's duty to exercise ordinary care or act in good faith in choosing the means of return or notice of nonpayment, the bank is not liable for the insolvency, neglect, misconduct, mistake, or default of another bank or person, or for loss or destruction of a check or notice of nonpayment in transit or in the possession of others. This section does not affect a paying bank's liability to its customer under the U.C.C. or other law.

12 C.F.R. §229.38(b) (emphasis added). The Court has no trouble finding, as a matter of law based upon the evidence of record, that Citibank failed to exercise ordinary care when it failed to identify First Financial as the depositary bank. The inquiry, then, is the amount of First Financial's loss, if any, that would have occurred even if Citibank had exercised ordinary care and returned the Check to First Financial expeditiously.

Regulation CC provides two ways in which a paying bank can satisfy the expediency requirement. The first is the "two-day test," which provides, in relevant part:

A paying bank returns a check in an expeditious manner if it sends the returned check in a manner such that the check would normally be received by the depositary bank not later than 4:00 P.M. (local time of the depositary bank) of . . . [t]he second business day following the banking day on which the check was presented to the paying bank.

12 C.F.R. §229.30(a)(1). Pursuant to this test, Citibank unquestionably would have satisfied its obligation to return the Check expeditiously if First Financial had received the Check by 4:00 P.M. on Monday, July 12, 2010, which was the second business day following Thursday, July 8, the day the Check was presented to Citibank. By that time most, if not all, of the damage was already done, as McDonald wired $268,825.00 to the Bank of China on July 9. While it is certainly possible that First Financial could demonstrate that it was damaged by Citibank's failure to expeditiously return the check—if,

for example, it can show that it would have been able to reverse the wire transfer had the check been returned by 4:00 P.M. on July 12—it does not point to any evidence to support such a finding. Accordingly, First Financial has not demonstrated that it is entitled to summary judgment on this claim. However, First Financial is entitled to summary judgment as to the following parts of its claim: (1) Citibank failed to comply with the requirement of 12 C.F.R. §229.30(a) that it return the Check expeditiously; and (2) Citibank failed to exercise reasonable care in complying with its obligation under 12 C.F.R. §229.30(a). Therefore, the only issue remaining for trial with regard to this claim is whether any damages were caused by Citibank's failure to return the Check expeditiously.

2. Failure to Provide Timely Notice of Dishonor

In addition to the obligation to return a dishonored check expeditiously, when the check at issue is for $2500.00 or more, a payor bank is required to "provide notice of nonpayment such that the notice is received by the depositary bank by 4:00 P.M. (local time) on the second business day following the banking day on which the check was presented to the paying bank." 12 C.F.R. §229.33(a). Citibank failed to satisfy this requirement, as it did not provide notice to First Financial that it was not going to pay the Check.

Again, however, Citibank's failure does not translate into liability to First Financial unless that failure proximately caused a loss by First Financial. And again, First Financial has not presented any evidence that this is the case, inasmuch as the wire transfer occurred prior to 4:00 P.M. on July 12, the second business day following the banking day on which the Check was presented to Citibank. So while First Financial is entitled to summary judgment on the issue of whether Citibank failed to comply with 12 C.F.R. §229.33—it did—the question of whether Citibank has any liability for that failure remains for trial.

3. Incorrect Routing of the Check

First Financial also asserts that Citibank incorrectly encoded the Check to indicate that Chase was the bank of first deposit. This, First Financial argues, constituted a breach of the warranty set forth in 12 C.F.R. §229.34(c)(3):

> Each bank that presents or transfers a check or returned check warrants to any bank that subsequently handles it that, at the time of presentment or transfer, the information encoded after issue in magnetic ink on the check or returned check is correct. For purposes of this paragraph, the information encoded after issue on the check or returned check includes any information placed in the MICR line of a substitute check that represents that check or returned check.

The Court is unable to discern from the evidence cited by First Financial that Citibank's actions breached this warranty. The warranty applies to "the information encoded after issue in magnetic ink" on the Check. The testimony cited by First Financial indicates that the Check was prepared for return by Citibank manually — that is, that a Citibank employee, Mr. Gandhi, manually placed information on the Check. Perhaps it is obvious to one in the banking industry, but, unfortunately, the Court is unaware whether the information Mr. Gandhi manually put on the Check was "encoded . . . in magnetic ink." Accordingly, the Court cannot determine whether Citibank breached this warranty, and First Financial is not entitled to summary judgment on this claim.

Even assuming that a breach of the encoding warranty occurred, First Financial has not presented evidence from which the Court could determine whether it suffered injury as a result of that breach. First Financial seems to assert that the EARNS notice that was sent to Chase was subject to the encoding warranty; in other words, First Financial argues that if *the Check* had been encoded properly then *the EARNS notice* would have been sent to First Financial instead of Chase and First Financial would have received the notice as quickly as Chase received it.

There are two problems with this argument. First, there is no evidence regarding when First Financial would have received an EARNS notice sent by Citibank; perhaps Citibank has a faster means of sending notices to Chase than it does to First Financial. More fundamentally, however, the plain language of 12 C.F.R. §§229.34(c)(3) appears to apply only to information encoded on a check, not to an EARNS notice. While perhaps this is incorrect (and, again, that fact might be obvious to someone in the banking industry), all the Court has to go on is the evidence to which the parties have cited, and they have cited to nothing that would contradict the plain language of the regulation. In this case, while the EARNS notice was sent to Chase, the Check itself was sent by Citibank to the Federal Reserve Bank. First Financial has submitted no evidence regarding when it would have received the Check from the Federal Reserve Bank if it had been encoded properly. All the Court knows is that the Federal Reserve Bank had agreed to return checks to First Financial expeditiously, which means that pursuant to 12 C.F.R. §229.31 it had a duty to send the Check to First Financial in a manner such that it would normally have been received by First Financial no later than 4:00 P.M. on July 12. As discussed above, that would have been too late to prevent the wire transfer.

C.   FAILURE TO COMPLY WITH THE MIDNIGHT DEADLINE

First Financial next argues that Citibank breached the warranty set forth in 12 C.F.R. §229.34(a):

Each paying bank or returning bank that transfers a returned check and receives a settlement or other consideration for it warrants to the transferee returning bank, to any subsequent returning bank, to the depositary bank, and to the owner of the check, that—

(1) The paying bank, or in the case of a check payable by a bank and payable through another bank, the bank by which the check is payable, returned the check within its deadline under the U.C.C., Regulation J (12 C.F.R. Part 210), or §229.30(c) of this part.

First Financial argues that Citibank breached this warranty by failing to comply with the U.C.C.'s "midnight deadline." The U.C.C.'s midnight deadline is defined in Indiana Code 26-1-4-104(a)(11) as "midnight on its next banking day following the banking day on which it receives the relevant item or notice or from which the time for taking action commences to run, whichever is later." First Financial argues that Citibank failed to "return" the Check prior to its midnight deadline, which was midnight on July 9, 2010. Pursuant to Indiana Code 26-1-3-301(4)(b), "[a]n item is returned . . . when it is sent or delivered to the bank's customer or transferor or pursuant to instructions."

First Financial asserts, without explanation, that Citibank was required to return the Check *to First Financial* by the midnight deadline. The Court does not believe that to be the case. The definition of "return" required Citibank to return the Check to Citibank's "transferor," which was Chase, not First Financial. First Financial does not allege that Citibank failed to return the check to *Chase* before the midnight deadline; accordingly, First Financial is not entitled to summary judgment on this issue. . . .

D.   CITIBANK'S DUTY TO EXERCISE ORDINARY CARE

First Financial makes several arguments under the subheading "Citibank failed to exercise ordinary care and good faith in handling the Check." First, First Financial argues that had it received notice of nonpayment on July 8 when Chase received notice from Citibank, then it would have been able to stop the wire transfer. That may be true, but it is irrelevant. Citibank had no duty under Regulation CC to provide notice until July 12, and Citibank cannot be held liable under Regulation CC for failing to act as quickly as possible, but rather only for failing to comply with its obligations under Regulation CC. Therefore the relevant inquiry is not whether Citibank could have prevented First Financial's loss, but rather whether Citibank was required by Regulation CC to act in such a way that First Financial's loss would have been prevented. As set forth above, the record as it stands does not compel the conclusion that First Financial's loss would have been avoided, in whole or in part, if Citibank had complied with Regulation CC. . . .

IV.   Conclusion

For the reasons set forth above, First Financial's motion for summary judgment is GRANTED IN PART in that the Court finds the following as a matter of law: (1) Citibank failed to comply with the requirement of 12 C.F.R. §229.30(a) that it return the Check expeditiously; (2) Citibank failed to exercise reasonable care in complying with its obligation under 12 C.F.R. §229.30(a); and (3) Citibank failed to comply with the notice requirement set forth in 12 C.F.R. §229.33. First Financial's motion is DENIED in all other respects, including whether Citibank's failures to comply with Regulation CC as just enumerated caused any injury to First Financial.

6.   Expedited Recredit for Consumer

Section 7 of the Act allows *consumers* (but not *non*-consumer customers) to get an expedited recredit to their account in certain circumstances when the consumer disputes the validity of the charge to the account. Section 7(a) of the statute provides:

> (a) Recredit Claims—
> (1) In General—A consumer may make a claim for expedited recredit from the bank that holds the account of the consumer with respect to a substitute check, if the consumer asserts in good faith that—
> (A) the bank charged the consumer's account for a substitute check that was provided to the consumer;
> (B) either—
> (i) the check was not properly charged to the consumer's account; or
> (ii) the consumer has a warranty claim with respect to such substitute check;
> (C) the consumer suffered a resulting loss; and
> (D) the production of the original check or a better copy of the original check is necessary to determine the validity of any claim described in subparagraph (B). . . .[32]

Suppose, for example, that the consumer cannot read the substitute check because the image is not clear. In that case, the consumer must report the problem within 40 days, and may demand an immediate recredit. The bank may investigate for ten business days, or if it recredits the account while it investigates, for 45 calendar days. Section 7(a)(2) contains these time limits, which are copied from the Electronic Fund Transfer Act (the federal debit card statute we will discuss in Chapter 9):

---

32. Regulation CC §229.54 expands upon the statutory language.

(2) Timing of Recredit.—

(A) In General—The bank shall recredit the consumer's account for the amount described in paragraph (1) no later than the end of the business day following the business day on which the bank determines the consumer's claim is valid.

(B) Recredit Pending Investigation.—If the bank has not yet determined that the consumer's claim is valid before the end of the 10th business day after the business day on which the consumer submitted the claim, the bank shall recredit the consumer's account for—

(i) the lesser of the amount of the substitute check that was charged against the consumer account, or $2,500, together with interest if the account is an interest-bearing account, no later than the end of such 10th business day; and

(ii) the remaining amount of the substitute check that was charged against the consumer account, if any, together with interest if the account is an interest bearing account, not later than the 45th calendar day following the business day on which the consumer submits the claim.

Section 7(d) of the statute has "Safeguard Exceptions" (copied almost word for word from the same safeguard exceptions to funds availability in Regulation CC, discussed earlier in this chapter at pages 283-294), describing situations where the bank need not recredit the account in accordance with the usual time limits.

7. Expedited Recredit for Banks

A bank that is forced to recredit a consumer's account may seek indemnity from the bank that presented the check to it. The indemnity rules are discussed above, and the procedure for an expedited recredit is given in detail in Regulation CC §229.55. It contains a requirement that all claims be made within 120 days of the original transaction giving rise to the claim, and must describe the reasons for the recredit clearly. If the claiming bank includes a copy of any substitute check as part of its claim it must take reasonable steps to make sure that copy will not get into circulation and be mistaken for the legal equivalent of the original check. Within ten business days of the recredit claim, the indemnifying bank must recredit the amount of the check, return the original check, or provide information as to why it will not do so.

8. Lawsuits and Miscellaneous Provisions

Section 10 allows a civil action for violations of the statute with an award of actual damages (up to the amount of the check), plus costs and attorney's fees. Notice of claims must be given within 30 days after a claimant discovers the grounds for the claim or the amount of any recovery is reduced by the amount that such prompt notice would have provided; Regulation CC §229.56(d). Suit may be brought in either federal or state courts, and there is a one year statute of limitations. The rules of Check 21 may not be varied by agreement, except for the expedited recredit provisions between banks in §229.55.

PROBLEM 100

When Jeanie Griffin went to pay for her groceries at the counter of the store, she gave the clerk a check for the relevant amount. The clerk scanned the check, turning it into an electronic file, and then returned the check to her, telling her that the amount would be debited from her checking account. Is this an Article 4 matter? A Check 21 situation?

The answer is no to both questions. Where the check is converted by a non-bank, as here, the transaction (called an "electronic check conversion" and mysteriously given the initials "ECK"[33]) is governed by the same rules we will see in Chapter 9 for debit card use. The relevant regulations for this situation require the merchant who has scanned the check at the point of sale ("POS") to return the original paper check to the consumer (or, if the merchant has received the check through the mail—an "accounts receivable conversion" or "ARC"—to destroy it); see Electronic Fund Transfer Regulation E, 12 C.F.R. §1005.3(b)(2), and the rules of the National Automated Clearinghouse Association.

C. *Final Payment*

A signal legal moment in the check collection rules of both Article 4 of the Uniform Commercial Code and the EFAA is the moment that a payor bank engages in *final payment* of a check. This moment is important because it fixes many of the legal rights arising under Articles 3 and 4. Following final payment, the payor bank is "accountable" for the amount of the check according to the language of §4-302(a), which means that it has lost the right to dishonor the check and must pay it to the person entitled to enforce it. If the check is properly payable (§4-401) from the drawer's account, well and good. If not, the payor bank is in a spot. The only legal theories in its favor that survive final

---

33. This process is also called "back office conversion" or "BRC."

payment are breach of presentment warranties (these have to do with forgeries and alterations, rarely at issue, discussed in the next chapter) and common law restitution, codified in §3-418, against villainous parties (who are hard to find or are often judgment-proof). Hence, this rule: Following final payment, the payor bank bears the risk of any mistaken payment not covered by one of these theories, which almost never help. Read §4-302(b).

When does final payment occur? The key section is §4-215. This section, which you should read carefully, states the events that make a payor bank "accountable" (§4-302(a)) for the item, whether it means to be or not. See Annot., 23 A.L.R.4th 203. The final payment of a check destroys the check as a cause of action. All of the Article 3 implied obligations (§§3-414, 3-415, 3-419, etc.) are at an end because the check has been paid and these obligations, being secondary, are conditioned on *dishonor* by the drawee. Once the drawee makes final payment, dishonor is no longer possible, and the drawer and indorsers are off the hook.

PROBLEM 101

Harold Sure walked into Octopus National Bank and made a presentment of a $12,000 check drawn on the bank to the head cashier, Christopher Coin, who was staffing one of the teller's windows. Coin asked Sure (who was the check's payee) to indorse the check on the back and then tapped the computer's memory bank to check on the state of the drawer's account. The computer replied that the account contained "one thousand dollars," but Coin misread the display and thought it said "one hundred thousand dollars." He went back to the teller's window and counted out the money thoughtfully. When he was done, a nagging doubt about his vision overcame him, and—passing the money to Sure—he said, "Excuse me a minute," and rechecked the computer. This time he read the amount correctly and rushed back to his window to discover Sure still standing there, slowly recounting the money in front of him. Coin snatched the money out of Sure's hands, saying, "I'm sorry, we must dishonor the check." Sure protested, but in vain. If Sure sues, will he win? Had the bank made *final payment*? See §4-215(a)(1).

The above is an elaboration of the fact situation in a famous case, Chambers v. Miller, 13 C.B. (N.S.) 125, 143 Eng. Rep. 50 (1862). (Judge Byles, writing in this case, said, "I think it would be extremely dangerous, and would create a great sensation in the city of London, if it were held in Westminster Hall, that after a check had been regularly handed over the banker's counter and the money received for it, and in the act of being counted, the banker might treat the check as unpaid because he had subsequently ascertained that the state of the customer's account was unfavorable.")

PROBLEM 102

Sally Phillips was the payee on a $1,000 check given to her by Joseph Armstrong. She and Joe both banked at the same bank, Octopus National Bank. Sally took Joe's check to the bank and filled out a deposit slip for her checking account, putting $800 of the check in her account and taking the other $200 in cash across the counter (this is called a *split deposit*). Two hours later, while posting the check, the bank clerk discovered that Joe's account was overdrawn. Can the bank now dishonor the whole check? $800 worth? Does §4-215(a)(1) apply here? See Kirby v. First & Merchants Natl. Bank, 210 Va. 88, 168 S.E.2d 273 (1969).

PROBLEM 103

Sally Phillips was the payee on a $1,000 check given to her by Joseph Armstrong. She walked it into Octopus National Bank, on which the check was drawn, and presented it across the counter, asking for a $1,000 cashier's check payable to her order as the method of payment. The bank gave her such a check; see §§3-104(g) and 3-412. She indorsed the check over to one of her creditors, but when Octopus National Bank failed and closed its doors before the check could be presented and paid, the creditor returned the cashier's check to her and demanded payment. Must she repay the creditor? See 3-310(a). If she does repay the creditor, may she sue Joseph Armstrong either as drawer of the check, §3-414, or on the original obligation, §3-310(b)(1)? See §§4-215(a)(2) and 4-213(c).

The second method of making final payment is settling for a check and not having the legal right to revoke the settlement; §4-215(a)(2). "Settle" is defined in §4-104(a)(11) as meaning "to pay in cash, by clearing-house settlement, in a charge or credit or by remittance, or otherwise as agreed. A settlement may be either provisional or final." If there exists a right to revoke the settlement, §4-215(a)(2) does not apply. Section 4-215(a)(2) is deliberately worded vaguely since the drafters wanted to encompass all possible methods of making payment that a bank might employ: wire transfer, netting of outstanding accounts, tapping of an account, etc. As long as the bank uses one of these methods and does not reserve the right to change its mind, final payment has occurred and the payor bank is accountable for the amount of the check.

The final (and most common) method of making final payment is contained in §4-215(a)(3). Almost all checks are not presented over the counter, but come into the payor bank when presented by another bank, which will have already made a provisional settlement in its own favor for the item.

In that case, final payment is made by simply holding onto the check past the deadline for returning it. Read §4-215(a)(3). What is this deadline? The answer depends on what arrangements the payor bank has made with the presenting bank. If their agreement is that presented items must be returned by 4:00 P.M. on the day following the day of presentment, then that agreement prevails. If the check is presented through a local clearinghouse, the clearing-house rules will govern the required time of return. Absent such agreements, the "statute" mentioned in §4-215(a)(3) is the Uniform Commercial Code itself, which requires return before expiration of the midnight deadline. The "midnight deadline" referred to is not midnight of the date of presentment, as it sounds, but instead is defined thusly in UCC §4-104(a)(10):

> (10) Midnight deadline: with respect to a bank is midnight on its next bank-ing day following the banking day on which it receives the relevant item or notice or from which the time for taking action commences to run, which-ever is later.

PROBLEM 104

What is the latest the payor bank can return a check before expiration of its midnight deadline, assuming: the bank has established a cut-off hour[34] of 2:00 P.M., it is not open on Saturdays (nor, of course, on Sundays), Monday is a holiday, and the Federal Reserve Bank presents a check for $1 million on Friday at 4:00 P.M.?

Bankers must be ever alert to the possible expiration of the midnight deadline because once it has passed for a check, the check may not be dishonored and returned. When the customer of the bank is pleading for more time to cover a check overdrawing the account, the midnight deadline should be uppermost in the thoughts of a banker who is making decisions. The following is the lead-ing case on the legal meaning of missing this deadline.

Rock Island Auction Sales, Inc. v. Empire Packing Co.
Illinois Supreme Court, 1965
32 Ill. 2d 269, 204 N.E.2d 721

SCHAFFER, J., delivered the opinion of the court: This case presents issues concerning the construction and validity of section 4-302 of the Uniform Commercial Code.

---

34. See §4-108.

The facts were admitted or stipulated. On Monday, September 24, 1962, the plaintiff, Rock Island Auction Sales, Inc., sold 61 head of cattle to Empire Packing Co., Inc. and received therefor Empire's check in the sum of $14,706.90. The check was dated September 24, 1962, and on that day the plaintiff deposited it in the First Bank and Trust Company of Davenport, Iowa. It was received by the payor bank, Illinois National Bank and Trust Company of Rockford, Illinois, on Thursday, September 27, 1962. Empire's balance was inadequate to pay the check, but the payor bank, relying upon Empire's assurances that additional funds would be deposited, held the check until Tuesday morning, October 2, 1962. It then marked the check "not sufficient funds," placed it in the mail for return to the Federal Reserve Bank of Chicago and sent notice of dishonor by telegram to the Federal Reserve Bank. The depositary bank, the First Trust and Savings Bank of Davenport, received the check on October 4, 1962. The check was never paid. On November 7, 1962, bankruptcy proceedings were instituted against Empire and on December 13, 1962, it was adjudicated a bankrupt.

On February 15, 1963, the plaintiff instituted this action against Illinois National Bank and Trust Company of Rockford, Empire Packing Co., Inc., and Peter Cacciatori, the officer of Empire who had signed the check. Cacciatori was not served with process, and no further action was taken against Empire after a stay order was issued by the United States District Court in the Bankruptcy proceeding. The plaintiff's case against Illinois National Bank and Trust Company of Rockford (hereafter defendant) rests squarely on the ground that as the payor bank it became liable for the amount of the check because it held the check without payment, return or notice of dishonor, beyond the time limit fixed in section 4-302 of the Uniform Commercial Code. . . .

[The court quoted §§4-302 and 4-104(a)(10).—Eds.]

The important issues in the case involve the construction and validity of section 4-302. The defendant argues that the amount for which it is liable because of its undented retention of the check beyond the time permitted by section 4-302 is not to be determined by that section, but rather under section 4-103(5) which provides that "[t]he measure of damages for failure to exercise ordinary care in handling an item is the amount of the item reduced by an amount which could not have been realized by the use of ordinary care. . . ." To support this argument it points out that other provisions of Article 4 use the words "liable," "must pay," and "may recover." Its position is that the word "accountable" in section 4-302 means that "the defendant must account for what it actually had (which is zero because there were no funds on deposit sufficient to pay the check) plus the damages (as measured by section 4-103(5)) sustained by the plaintiff as the result of the failure to meet the deadline, but for no more."

But the statute provides that the bank is accountable for the amount of the item, and not for something else. "Accountable" is synonymous with "liable" (Webster's New Twentieth Century Dictionary Unabridged, Second Edition, Webster's Dictionary of Synonyms), and section 4-302 uses the word in that sense. The word "accountable" appears to have been used instead of its synonym "liable" in order to accommodate other sections of Article 4 of the Code which relate to provisional and final settlements between banks in the collection process, and to bar the possibility that a payor bank might be thought to be liable both to the owner of the item and to another bank. The circuit court correctly held that the statute imposes liability for the amount of the item.

This construction does not create an irrational classification and so cause the statute to violate constitutional limitations. Defendant's contention to the contrary is based upon the proposition that section 4-302 is invalid because it imposes a liability upon a payor bank for failing to act prior to its midnight deadline that is more severe than the liability which section 4-103(5) imposes upon a depositary bank or a collecting bank for the same default. Of course there are no such separate institutions as depositary, collecting and payor banks. All banks perform all three functions. The argument thus comes down to the proposition that the failure of a bank to meet its deadline must always carry the same consequence, regardless of the function that it is performing.

But the legislature may legitimately have concluded that there are differences in function and in circumstance that justify different consequences. Depositary and collecting banks act primarily as conduits. The steps that they take can only indirectly affect the determination of whether or not a check is to be paid, which is the focal point in the collection process. The legislature could have concluded that the failure of such a bank to meet its deadline would most frequently be the result of negligence, and fixed liability accordingly. The role of a payor bank in the collection process, on the other hand, is crucial. It knows whether or not the drawer has funds available to pay the item. The legislature could have considered that the failure of such a bank to meet its deadline is likely to be due to factors other than negligence, and that the relationship between a payor bank and its customer may so influence its conduct as to cause a conscious disregard of its statutory duty. The present case is illustrative. The defendant, in its position as a payor bank, deliberately aligned itself with its customer in order to protect that customer's credit and consciously disregard the duty imposed upon it. The statutory scheme emphasizes the importance of speed in the collection process. A legislative sanction designed to prevent conscious disregard of deadlines cannot be characterized as arbitrary or unreasonable, nor can it be said to constitute a legislative encroachment on the functions of the judiciary. . . .

Judgment affirmed.

———————————

A payor bank that misses its midnight deadline is *strictly liable* for the amount of the check involved. It is no defense that other parties, such as the depositary bank, were negligent or did not suffer a provable loss. See First Natl. Bank in Harvey v. Colonial Bank, 898 F. Supp. 1220 (N.D. Ill. 1995); Los Angeles National Bank v. Bank of Canton, 280 Cal. Rptr. 831 (Cal. App. 1991); Hanna v. First Natl. Bank of Rochester, 87 N.Y.2d 107, 637 N.Y.S.2d 953 (N.Y. 1995). A payor bank that tries to return a check on which it has already made final payment is said to be making a "late return," which, of course, is not allowed. Regulation CC creates a *warranty of timely return* for checks, so that if a bank is guilty of making a late return it has to respond in damages; Regulation CC §229.34.

When the Federal Reserve was drafting Regulation CC, it decided to make a major alteration to the midnight deadline rule to stop the following practice. Under the Uniform Commercial Code a payor bank was required to "send" the check back before the expiration of the midnight deadline. Suppose that late in the second banking day, shortly before midnight, a payor bank made a last-minute decision to dishonor a check. The fastest way to get the check back to the presenting bank would be to wait until the armored courier could take it back the next day, but the statute did not allow that delay. "Send," as it happens, is defined in the Uniform Commercial Code to include "deposit in the mail" (see §1-201(b)(36)), and the Federal Reserve discovered that that is what the banks were doing with the checks: putting them in an envelope and then into a mailbox before midnight. Who knew when the check would actually get back to the presenting bank, but the payor bank had nonetheless complied with the law. To change this awkward procedure, Regulation CC now provides that a payor bank is permitted to miss its midnight deadline as long as it is able nonetheless to return a check to the collecting bank "on or before the receiving bank's next banking day following the otherwise applicable deadline by the earlier of the close of that banking day or a cutoff hour of 2 P.M. or later set by the receiving bank under U.C.C. 4-108"; Regulation CC §229.30(c)(1). This, in effect, gives the payor bank an extra day to return the check after the expiration of the usual midnight deadline.

Regulation CC §229.30(c)(1) also creates another situation where the bank may miss its midnight deadline: "[T]he deadline is extended further if a paying bank uses a highly expeditious means of transportation." For example, says the Commentary, "a west coast bank may use this further extension to ship a returned check by air courier directly to an east coast depositary bank even if the check arrives after the close of the depositary bank's banking day." Regulation CC has detailed rules concerning the return of checks, discussed in the next section.

First National Bank of Chicago v. Standard Bank & Trust

United States Court of Appeals, Seventh Circuit, 1999
172 F.3d 472

FLAUM, Circuit Judge.

First National Bank of Chicago, known at the time relevant to this suit as NBD Bank ("NBD"), brought an action for declaratory judgment alleging that Standard Bank & Trust ("Standard Bank" or "Standard") failed to return certain checks to NBD in a timely fashion under the Expedited Funds Availability Act, 12 U.S.C. §4010(d) & (f) ("EFAA"). Finding that the checks were returned in a timely fashion, the district court granted summary judgment to the defendant Standard Bank, and awarded it pre-judgment interest on the returned checks. Standard claimed it was entitled to the average prime rate for the relevant time period. However, the district court used the three-month Treasury Bill rate—4.9241%—compounded quarterly. Both sides appeal. For the reasons set out below, we affirm the district court's decision that the checks were properly returned, but vacate the award of interest, and remand for entry of the proper measure of prejudgment interest.

BACKGROUND

This litigation revolves around which party—Standard or NBD—should absorb the losses resulting from a check-kiting scheme perpetrated against both of these banks in November, 1993. On November 18, 1993, an individual presented to NBD checks with an aggregate value of $3,997,406.75, drawn on customer accounts maintained at Standard Bank, which NBD initially accepted. That day, the same person deposited $4,025,000.00 in checks at Standard, drawn on NBD customer accounts.

The following day, Friday, November 19, 1993, NBD presented the checks it received to Standard, and vice versa. LaSalle Bank, in its capacity as the collecting bank, charged both banks' accounts for the checks drawn on them, and provisionally credited each bank for the amount presented to them. On the next business day (Monday, November 22, 1993), NBD opted not to honor the checks, and returned all of the checks, totaling $4,025,000.00, to Standard Bank. Standard received notice of NBD's decision on Tuesday morning, November 23. That afternoon, Standard attempted to dishonor the checks it had received. Three of its bank officers dashed off to NBD's Operations Processing Center carrying checks totaling $3,785,441.35. The checks were received by NBD at 3:58 P.M. that day, but NBD did not credit Standard's account for that sum. On November 30, 1993, NBD filed suit, seeking a declaration that Standard Bank's return of the checks was not timely, because it neither met the "midnight deadline," nor any of the deadline's exceptions laid out in Federal Reserve Board ("the

Board") Regulations appurtenant to EFAA. Standard Bank defended by arguing that its return was proper, and it counterclaimed for prejudgment interest.

On a motion for judgment on the pleadings, the district court originally found for NBD, but reversed its decision in light of a clarifying amendment[35] to the relevant Federal Reserve Regulations. The district court also decided that prejudgment interest was appropriate, but did not award the prime rate. Instead it chose a lower rate (the average T-bill rate) because of the absence of bad faith on NBD's part, and because this was a "close case." Each side appealed portions of the decision below.

I.

NBD's appeal from the district court's order granting Standard Bank's motion for judgment on the pleadings is reviewed by this court de novo. Rooding v. Peters, 92 F.3d 578, 579-80 (7th Cir. 1996).

A.

The legal question at issue is whether Standard Bank's return of the checks comports with Federal Reserve Board Regulation CC sec. 229.30(c)(1), 12 C.F.R. Part 229 ("Regulation CC"). Regulation CC's language states:

> (c) Extension of deadline. The deadline for return or notice of non-payment under the U.C.C. or Regulation sec. 229.36(f)(2) of this part is extended:
> (1) If a paying bank, in an effort to expedite delivery of a returned check to a bank, uses a means of delivery that would ordinarily result in the returned check being received by the bank to which it is sent on or before the receiving bank's next business day following the otherwise applicable deadline; this deadline is extended further if a paying bank uses a highly expeditious means of transportation, even if this means of transportation would ordinarily result in delivery after the receiving bank's next banking day.

As the text notes, Regulation CC extends the UCC's deadline, known in the vernacular as the "midnight deadline." Under the UCC, a paying bank may dishonor or revoke its provisional settlement of a check before midnight on the next business day after it received the check. UCC sec. 4-301(a)(1); Hanna v. First Nat'l Bank of Rochester, 87 N.Y.S.2d 107, 637 N.Y.S.2d 953, 661 N.E.2d 683, 686 n.2 (N.Y. 1995). While the Board favored the UCC's emphasis on expeditiously dealing with dishonored checks, it was concerned that the midnight deadline might unintentionally retard the return

---

35. When we refer to Regulation CC, we refer to the pre-clarification version of that rule. The amended version is referred to as "postclarifying amendment Regulation CC."

of checks. It noted "[b]ecause the return process must begin by midnight, many paying banks return checks by mail when a courier leaving after midnight would be faster." 52 Fed. Reg. 47119, 47123 (Dec. 11, 1987). Thus, the Board enacted the extension to the midnight deadline.

NBD argues that the Board's extension of the midnight deadline does not apply here. It primarily points to a number of statements in Regulation CC's legislative history indicating that use of the extension is limited to banks which regularly use couriers services to return checks. However, NBD is putting the cart before the horse — before we delve into the Board's commentary on Regulation CC, we must first examine its language's plain meaning.

Administrative rules are subject to the same well-known maxims of construction as legislative statutes. Alabama Tissue Ctr. v. Sullivan, 975 F.2d 373, 379 (7th Cir. 1992). As we recently noted, in statutory construction cases, "the beginning point must be the language of the statute, and when a statute speaks with clarity to an issue, judicial inquiry into the statute's meaning, in all but the most extraordinary circumstances, is finished." United States v. Kirschenbaum, 156 F.3d 784, 789 (7th Cir. 1998) (quoting Estate of Cowart v. Nicklos Drilling Co., 505 U.S. 469, 475, 112 S. Ct. 2589, 120 L. Ed. 2d 379 (1992)). If we can decipher Regulation CC's meaning on its face, there is no need to examine legislative history absent extraordinary circumstances. United States v. Hudspeth, 42 F.3d 1015, 1022 (7th Cir. 1994).

There is little in the text of the statute that supports NBD's argument that the extension is only available to banks which regularly or ordinarily use expedited delivery. Regulation CC extends the deadline when a paying bank "expedite[s] delivery of a returned check . . . " and we note the singular "a returned check" rather than the plural "returned checks." See Metropolitan Stevedore Co. v. Rambo, 515 U.S. 291, 295, 115 S. Ct. 2144, 132 L. Ed. 2d 226 (1995). Although it is not dispositive, this use of the singular suggests that Regulation CC may apply to one-time single check transactions. Far more conclusive is the structure of the second clause, which allows a bank to extend the deadline when it "uses a means of delivery that would ordinarily result in the returned check being received by the bank to which it is sent on or before the receiving bank's next business day following the otherwise applicable deadline." NBD argues, implausibly, that this mandates that a bank ordinarily or routinely use a means of expedited delivery in order to avail itself of the extension. For "ordinarily" to have such meaning, however, it would have to modify the verb "uses," causing the sentence to read: "a bank may extend the deadline if it ordinarily uses a means of delivery that would result in the returned check being received. . . ." Of course, in the actual regulation, "ordinarily" modifies the verb "would result," denoting that the bank's means of delivery must ordinarily result in return by the applicable deadline. Any other reading, including the one NBD proposes, is contrary to the clear import of the second clause.

NBD also points to Regulation CC's first clause, which allows banks to use the extension "in an effort to expedite delivery of a returned check to a bank." It argues that Standard Bank's efforts were not in "an effort to expedite delivery" of the dishonored checks. We disagree. There is no doubt that Standard Bank's executives drove the checks to NBD's processing center in order to speed up delivery.

This interpretation squares with a leading commentary on the UCC by Professors White and Summers. Analyzing the plain language of Regulation CC (before the clarifying amendment) White and Summers posed—and answered—the following hypothetical:

> Assume that the payor bank received a $100,000 check on Monday morning and that it discovers on Wednesday morning that it failed to send the check back by Tuesday midnight (the midnight deadline), but it now wishes to dishonor the check. Under the UCC the midnight deadline would have passed, and unless it had an unusual defense, payor would be liable for the $100,000. *Regulation CC* changes that. If the bank can somehow get the check back to the depositary bank before that bank's close of business on Wednesday, it escapes liability under the UCC. That appears to be the meaning of the first sentence of [Regulation CC sec. 229.30(c)].

James J. White & Robert F. Summers, Uniform Commercial Code, at 325 (4th ed. 1995) (emphasis added). Although NBD brings other scholarly points of view to our attention, those positions appear less faithful to Regulation CC's actual text than White & Summers.

We only look past the express language of a regulation when it is ambiguous or where a literal interpretation would lead to an "absurd result or thwart the purpose of the overall statutory scheme." United States v. Hayward, 6 F.3d 1241, 1245 (7th Cir. 1993). We see no ambiguity in Regulation CC which admits of the meaning NBD presses upon us. Also, a literal interpretation does not lead to an "absurd result"—there is nothing absurd about extending the midnight deadline irrespective of whether a bank avails itself of the extension once or repeatedly. Moreover, the reading we adopt does not thwart the purpose of the rule, which promoted the speedy return of dishonored checks over the postmark conscious "midnight deadline." See 52 Fed. Reg. 47112, 47140 (Dec. 11, 1987) (noting that Regulation CC "removes the constraint of the midnight deadline if the check reaches either the depositary bank or the returning bank to which it is sent on the banking day following the expiration of the midnight deadline or other applicable time for return.").

We briefly examine the rule's regulatory history for any signs that our decision would thwart the Board's intent. United States v. Mueller, 112 F.3d 277, 281 (7th Cir. 1997) (where statute is clear, examining legislative history useful to "determine if it reflects a clearly expressed legislative intention" contrary to plain meaning) (citation omitted). Regulation CC's regulatory history is not quite as clear as the text. Both sides present evidence from the available sources to support their statutory interpretations. Among other references, NBD points to Regulation CC's Official Commentary, which lists two circumstances in which the midnight deadline may be extended, one not relevant here. The putatively relevant circumstance is where "a West Coast paying bank . . . ship[s] a returned check by air courier directly to an East Coast depositary bank even if the check arrives after the close of the depositary bank's banking day." Official Commentary sec. 229.30, 12 C.F.R. Part 22, App. E (1997). This does suggest that the intent of the regulation may not have been as broad as its wording indicates. On the other hand, the commentary notes that the West Coast/East Coast bank scenario is an "example" of a highly expeditious means of delivery. 12 C.F.R. part 229, App. E. The history also states that Regulation CC "pertains primarily to air courier arrangements from West Coast banks to East Coast banks." 53 Fed. Reg. 19372, 19418 (May 27, 1988). "Pertains primarily" suggests that other exceptions exist too, and that an overly constricted reading of when the extension applies would be inappropriate. After examining the relative regulatory history, we believe it is a wash. This works to NBD's detriment, because its inability to coax strong support from the regulatory history means that it cannot overcome the clear import of Regulation CC's words. Oneida Tribe v. Wisconsin, 951 F.2d 757, 761 (7th Cir. 1991).

B.

Although our reading of Regulation CC finds little ambiguity, the Board issued a self titled "Clarifying Amendment" in 1997 to remove any doubt as to whether the midnight deadline applies to checks returned to avoid a kite. Assuming that our interpretation of the pre-clarification rule was incorrect—an assumption without which this analysis is superfluous—Standard argues that the Clarifying Amendment has retroactive effect. It was on this ground that the district court found for Standard Bank. NBD argues that the "Clarifying Amendment" was actually a legislative rule, and as such has no retroactive effect under Bowen v. Georgetown University Hospital, 488 U.S. 204, 208, 109 S. Ct. 468, 102 L. Ed. 2d 493 (1988).

The Clarifying Amendment expunged the words "in an effort to expedite delivery of a returned check to a bank" from Regulation CC sec. 229.30(c)(1). 62 Fed. Reg. 13801, 13805 (March 24, 1997). This was done to remove any doubt as to whether an inquiry into the returning bank's motives was appropriate. Id. . . .

Based on our analysis, even if the original Regulation CC did not allow Standard Bank to return the checks, we find that the 1997 Clarifying Amendment retroactively permitted the extension of the midnight deadline.

Thus, the district court's finding that NBD should have honored the checks Standard delivered in the amount of $3,785,441.35 was correct. . . .

CONCLUSION

While we Affirm the judgment on the pleadings in favor of Standard Bank, the district court's grant of prejudgment interest is Vacated and we Remand with instructions to enter an award of prejudgment interest consistent with the average prime rate for the appropriate time period.

PROBLEM 105

Octopus National Bank, which has branches throughout the state, has one central processing center where it makes all decisions about whether to pay checks drawn on the branches. The canceled checks are returned to the branches two days after the processing center decides to pay them. Is the moment of presentment to the payer bank the moment of presentment to the processing center or the moment when the check is returned to the individual branch? See Regulation CC §229.36(b)(4).

D.   Check Return

The major thrust of the EFAA is to require depositary banks to give customers quick access to funds represented by deposited checks. This has the effect, however, of putting the depositary banks at risk. The customer might withdraw the funds under the EFAA rules, and then the check, for whatever reason, might still be returned. The customer is required to repay the money after the check is charged back to the account (§4-214, explored later in this chapter), but all too often the money is gone and cannot be retrieved. Regulation CC therefore has a number of provisions designed to make the check collection machinery operate very quickly to forward checks for collection and return them if they are dishonored.

The Federal Notice for Large Check Return. On checks of $2,500 or more, depositary banks take the biggest risks unless they are alerted to the fact that the check is being dishonored by the payor bank. Section 229.33 of Regulation CC therefore requires the payor bank to send a direct notice to the depositary bank any time it decides not to pay a check in the amount of $2,500 or more. The notice must include the name and routing number of the paying bank, the name of the payee, the amount, the reason for return, the date of the indorsement of the depositary bank, the account number of the depositor, the branch where the item was first deposited, and the trace number on the item of the depositary bank, unless these matters cannot be reasonably determined from an examination of the item itself. Failure of the payor bank to send the required notice makes it liable for actual damages caused (up to the amount of the item) and, if the payor bank failed to act in good faith, for other consequential damages.

How quickly must the notice be given? Regulation CC §229.33(a), in relevant part, states: "If a paying bank determines not to pay a check in the amount of $2,500 or more, it shall provide notice of nonpayment such that the notice is received by the depositary bank by 4:00 P.M. (local time) on the second business day following the banking day on which the check was presented to the paying bank. . . ." Notice may be provided by any reasonable means, including physical return of the check, a writing (which includes a copy of the check), telephone, Fedwire, telex, or other form of telegraph.

Historically, returned checks had not been handled with any great speed, and had taken far longer to get back to the depositary bank than checks being forwarded for collection traveling the same route. Regulation CC, Subpart C, has a number of provisions designed to speed up check returns, requiring what the Regulation calls "expeditious return." Section 229.30 requires the payor bank to return checks in a manner that is as fast or faster than that which would be used to dispatch forward collection were the depositary and payor banks reversed in function, or in lieu of using this "forward collection" test, the payor bank is deemed to act expeditiously if it returns the check in such a manner that it would normally be received by the depositary bank not later than 4:00 P.M. on the second business day following the original presentment to the payor bank.

Regulation CC allows returns directly to the depositary bank (thus skipping over any collecting banks), use of a route different from the one the check traveled originally, and the sending of the check through the Federal Reserve System. The reason for the return of the check must be stamped on the check itself.

E.   Charge Back

These rules about final payment apply only to the actions of the payor (drawee) bank. If that bank dishonors the check and returns it to the depositary bank, the latter will expect reimbursement from its depositor no matter how many days elapsed since the check was first deposited. The bank has three ways to justify its demand for repayment: the initial contract agreement signed when the account was opened, the indorser's obligation (§3-415), and the statutory right of charge back.

Read §4-214.

PROBLEM 106

Damon owed $500 to his friend Pythias and in payment gave him a check for that amount drawn on the Bulfinch National Bank, which Pythias deposited in his account with the Dionysius State Bank on Monday, July 8. On July 11, not having heard anything, Pythias assumed that final payment had occurred and wrote checks against the augmented balance. On July 10, the check reached the Bulfinch National Bank and was marked "NSF" and returned to Dionysius State Bank the next day. Dionysius State Bank took $500 out of Pythias' account without notice, causing several other checks of his to bounce on July 15.

(a) Can Pythias sue Dionysius State Bank under §4-402 for wrongful dishonor of these later checks? See §§4-215(d), 4-215(e)(1), 4-214; Salem Natl. Bank v. Chapman, 64 Ill. App. 3d 625, 381 N.E.2d 741 (1978).

(b) Since Dionysius State Bank has failed to give a proper charge-back notice, is it liable for the amount of the item? See §4-214(a)'s second sentence.

(c) If it had given Pythias notice of dishonor, could Dionysius State Bank have recovered the $500 even if it had let Pythias withdraw all the money from his account prior to the return of the check from the payer bank? See §4-214(d)(1).

(d) Would your answer to the first question be the same if Dionysius State were both the depositary and the payor bank? See §§4-215(e)(2), 4-302; and Regulation CC §229.10(c)(vi).

(e) If the check had been returned by Bulfinch National Bank to Dionysius State Bank on September 25, could Dionysius have still charged back? See §4-214(a)'s final sentence.[36]

(f) Assume that when the check is first returned to Dionysius, the bank does not charge it back against Pythias' account, but instead again sends the check through for re-presentment, hoping this time there will be money in the drawer's account and the check will be paid. If this hope proves fruitless and the check is returned by Bulfinch a second time, does §4-214 allow Dionysius to charge back, assuming that it does so immediately on learning of the second return? See also Leibson, Handling Re-Presented Checks — Risky Business

---

36. The rule here is actually simpler than it looks. Charge back is allowed only for provisional settlements. If the payor bank made final payment on a check, all the provisional settlements "firmed up" and became final. Charge back is not allowed to undo final settlements, and §4-214(a)'s final sentence states such a rule. When the payor bank tries to undo final payment by making a late return, the depositary bank should not accept the check back, since it has lost its right of charge back. How does the depositary bank (or any collecting bank) know whether the payor bank has made timely return? It doesn't, and in all but the rarest situation will assume that the payor bank has acted properly so that the depositary bank's right of charge back still exists. If that assumption is wrong — the payor bank did make a late return — Regulation CC §229.34 creates a warranty of timely return by the payor bank, which, having been breached, provides the needed remedy to the depositary bank.

for Collecting and Payer Banks, 72 Ky. L.J. 549 (1983-1984). Charging back when the bank has no right to do so is indeed risky business. The courts in some states have shown a willingness to impose punitive damages for wrongful charge back. See Gordon v. Planters & Merchants Bancshares, Inc., 326 Ark. 1046, 935 S.W.2d 544 (1996).

PROBLEM 107

Lewis Rakocy sold his vintage motorcycle on eBay for $6,000, and the buyer sent him a cashier's check for $10,000 (payable to his order), asking Lew to refund him a check for the extra $4,000. Lew did this promptly, sending the buyer a $4,000 personal check, and depositing the larger cashier's check in his bank account with Bergen National Bank. The bank gave him next day availability for the amount of the cashier's check. However, two days after that the cashier's check was returned NSF by the bank on which it was drawn. Apparently the cashier's check is a forgery. Is it too late for Bergen National Bank to charge back the amount of the check to Lew's account? See Drew v. Commerce Bank, N.A., 2007 WL 1468683 (N.J. Super. 2007).

Valley Bank of Ronan v. Hughes
Supreme Court of Montana, 2006
334 Mont. 335, 147 P.3d 185

Justice JIM RICE delivered the Opinion of the Court.

¶1 Charles R. Hughes (Hughes) appeals the orders entered in the Twentieth Judicial District Court, Lake County, granting summary judgment to Valley Bank of Ronan (Valley Bank) and granting Valley Bank's motion in limine to exclude the testimony of Hughes' expert witness. We affirm in part, reverse in part, and remand for further proceedings.

¶2 The following issues are dispositive on appeal:

¶3 Did the District Court err by granting summary judgment against Hughes on his counterclaims?

¶4 Did the District Court err by granting summary judgment to Valley Bank on Hughes' promissory note?

¶5 Did the District Court abuse its discretion by excluding the testimony of Hughes' banking expert, Cynthia Shea? . . .

BACKGROUND

¶7 Lured by the promise of quick wealth, Hughes was conned by a "Nigerian scam." The swindlers promised Hughes a $3 million to $4.5 million commission for his aid in procuring agricultural equipment for import into Africa and then proceeded to bilk him for hundreds of thousands of dollars in advanced fees. At least some of the funds Hughes advanced were wired via the services of Valley Bank, resulting in a dispute over which party should bear the loss from the flimflam.

¶8 On Friday, March 22, 2002, Hughes received four checks from one of the con-artists and deposited them into accounts Hughes held at Valley Bank. Two of them were "official" checks, and the other two were personal checks. One official check, for $1 million, was drawn on Colonial Bank. The other official check, for $500,000, was drawn on Firstar. The personal checks were for $62,000—drawn on the account of Maximilian H. Miltzlaff—and for $70,000—drawn on a Capital One credit card account held by Sarah Briscoe and Mary Bullard.

¶9 Prior to depositing the checks, Hughes requested that Nancy Smith, a cashier and officer of Valley Bank, verify the validity of the official checks. In his deposition, Hughes described his conversation with Smith:

> Well, my question was, how long do you have to hold money to have—how long do you have to hold these checks before they're sufficient funds; I think the bank calls them collected funds. And she said, these are official checks, Chuck. These two big ones are official checks. You will be transferring these? And I said I will be transferring a large sum. We'll have to determine next week what it will be. And she says, official checks, same as cash. You can do whatever you want to do.

Smith also assured Hughes that official checks were "just like" cashier's checks. Milanna Shear, another bank employee, told Hughes to believe whatever Smith said regarding the validity of the checks. According to the deposition testimony of Hughes' wife, Barbara, Hughes had told her that "everybody at the bank assured him that the checks would be good."

¶10 On Tuesday, March 26, 2002, Hughes delivered a written request to Valley Bank to wire $800,000 to Ali dh. Abbas, an accountholder at the Housing Bank for Trade and Finance in Amman, Jordan. Valley Bank executed the transfer no later than 1:51 P.M. on the same day. The transfer proceeded through two intermediary banks, Wells Fargo, near Denver, Colorado, and Citibank in New York, before being sent to Amman. Upon receipt in Amman, the funds were promptly withdrawn, never to be seen again.

¶11 At about 2:00 P.M.—approximately ten minutes after initiation of the transfer—Valley Bank and Hughes learned that one of the personal checks was being returned marked "nonsufficient funds." Hughes immediately requested the wire to be stopped. No later than 3:26 P.M. Valley Bank requested that Wells Fargo reverse the wire transfer. The record is unclear about what happened during the interim between Hughes' request for cancellation and Valley Bank's attempts to comply with the request. The efforts of the several banks involved in the transfer to reverse the transaction were unsuccessful, and the later discovery that the two official checks were counterfeit resulted in Hughes' account being overdrawn by $800,000.

¶12 Valley Bank subsequently exercised its right to charge back the account and collect the $800,000 from Hughes. Allen Buhr (Buhr), Valley Bank's president, met with Hughes on March 29, 2002, to discuss Hughes' liability and suggested at that time that Hughes could be involved in a criminal prosecution for fraud. On April 11, 2002, Hughes deposited $607,838, which he had withdrawn from his retirement account, into the Valley Bank account. Also, on April 30, 2002, Hughes executed a promissory note to Valley Bank on behalf of his trust in the amount of $400,000, secured by mortgaged property. Of the $400,000 in proceeds generated by the secured note, $202,751.21 was used to pay off a previous loan against the mortgaged property, and the balance, $197,248.79, was applied to satisfy the charge-back liability in Hughes' account. Hughes was under the impression, given by Buhr, that the bank needed the note and loan agreement because it expected to be the subject of a government audit in the near future, and though Hughes thought that a new agreement might be reached after resolution of the "fraud situation," he understood that the loan may not be forgiven. The trust subsequently made the first interest payment on the note on August 1, 2002, though it was one month late. The trust made no other payments on the note, and Valley Bank sent a notice of default and acceleration on October 15, 2002. Hughes requested that the bank forebear foreclosure until the end of the year, and the bank complied. However, when Hughes failed to make any more payments on the note, Valley Bank initiated an action for judicial foreclosure. Hughes asserted counterclaims of negligence, negligent misrepresentation, constructive fraud, unjust enrichment, breach of contract, breach of the implied covenant of good faith and fair dealing, promissory estoppel, and intentional infliction of emotional distress (which was later abandoned).

¶13 On April 15, 2005, the District Court granted Valley Bank's motion in limine to exclude Cynthia Shea as an expert witness for Hughes. In an order dated April 20, 2005, the District Court granted Valley Bank summary judgment on Hughes' counterclaims. On the same day, the District Court granted Valley Bank summary judgment on its claims regarding the promissory note. From these orders Hughes appeals. . . .

DISCUSSION

¶17 A short introduction to the check settlement process will give context to our following legal analysis. When a customer deposits a check at a bank, the bank will sometimes (but not always) credit the customer's account immediately with the face amount of the check and permit the customer to draw on the deposited funds. This practice is known in Uniform Commercial Code parlance as "provisional settlement" because the bank has not yet presented the check to the drawee bank and received payment from the check maker's account (which would constitute "final settlement"). The depositary bank, however, may "charge back" the depositor's account in the event the check is subsequently dishonored by the drawee bank. Thus, the UCC encourages the provisional settlement process by protecting a depositary bank from fraudulent or otherwise unenforceable check deposits. With this overview of the check settlement process in mind, we turn now to the specifics of the case before us.

¶18 Did the District Court err by granting summary judgment against Hughes on his counterclaims?

UCC Preemption and Ordinary Care

¶19 Hughes argues that the District Court erroneously concluded that the UCC preempts Hughes' equitable and common law claims. Hughes asserts that preemption does not occur because "[t]here are no regulations or UCC provisions which expressly regulate . . . promises and representations that bank personnel make to their customers." Further, Hughes contends that the "practical effect of the District Court's interpretation affords banks absolute immunity for negligence, fraud, misrepresentation and other acts which are not expressly addressed in the UCC. . . ."

¶20 The District Court rested its conclusion on its interpretation of §30-1-103, MCA, which reads as follows:

> Unless displaced by the particular provisions of this code, the principles of law and equity, including the law merchant and the law relative to capacity to contract, principal and agent, estoppel, fraud, misrepresentation, duress, coercion, mistake, bankruptcy, or other validating or invalidating cause shall supplement its provisions.

The District Court stated that the "official comments to UCC §1-103 show that preemption of common law and equitable claims is one purpose of the . . . statute. . . ." The official comment to which the District Court referred clarifies that

> while principles of common law and equity may supplement provisions of the Uniform Commercial Code, they may not be used to supplant its provisions, or the purposes and policies those provisions reflect, unless a specific provision of the Uniform Commercial Code provides otherwise. In the absence of such a provision, the Uniform Commercial Code preempts principles of

common law and equity that are inconsistent with either its provisions or its purposes and policies.

The language of subsection (b) is intended to reflect both the concept of supplementation and the concept of preemption.

UCC §1-103, cmt. 2. The District Court also concluded that three cases from other jurisdictions, Chase v. Morgan Guarantee Trust Co., 590 F. Supp. 1137 (S.D.N.Y. 1984), Allen v. Carver Federal Sav. and Loan Ass'n, 123 Misc. 2d 704, 477 N.Y.S.2d 537 (N.Y. App. Div. 1984), and Call v. Ellenville Nat. Bank, 5 A.D.3d 521, 774 N.Y.S.2d 76 (N.Y. App. Div. 2004), "support preemption of equitable and common law claims under the applicable UCC provisions and facts of this case."

¶21 We disagree with the District Court's interpretation of §30-1-103, MCA, and of *Chase, Allen,* and *Call.* A bank receiving checks from depositors must use "ordinary care"—as that term is defined and used in the UCC—in settling those checks. See §§30-4-103(3), 30-4-103(5), and 30-4-212, MCA. FN3 Section 30-3-102(1)(g), MCA, defines "ordinary care" as follows:

> "Ordinary care" in the case of a person engaged in business means observance of reasonable commercial standards, prevailing in the area in which that person is located, with respect to the business in which that person is engaged. In the case of a bank that takes an instrument for processing for collection or payment by automated means, reasonable commercial standards do not require the bank to examine the instrument if the failure to examine does not violate the bank's prescribed procedures and the bank's procedures do not vary unreasonably from general banking usage not disapproved by this chapter or chapter 4.

In its order, the District Court examined the meaning of "ordinary care" but did not distinguish the term's application to the two different actions at issue here: the settlement of the deposited checks and the alleged representations about the check settlement process. The second sentence of the definition of ordinary care specifically states that, subject to certain exceptions, a bank does not have a duty to examine instruments, in this case, checks. Pursuant to §30-1-103, MCA, and UCC §1-103, cmt. 2, such specificity preempts any common law concepts that might otherwise supplement the UCC. Thus, to the extent that Hughes' common law claims relate to Valley Bank's processing of the checks, they are preempted by the UCC.

¶22 Indeed, Hughes presents a claim directed toward the UCC-defined standard of ordinary care with respect to check processing. Hughes asserts that, by failing to comply with its own policies and the applicable federal regulations, Valley Bank inappropriately charged back his account after the dishonor of the deposited checks. However, §4-214(d), MCA, states, "[t]he right to charge back is not affected by . . . failure by any bank to exercise ordinary care with respect to the item but any bank so failing remains lia-ble." Official Comment 5 to §30-4-214(d), MCA, expounds on this point, stating that "charge-back is permitted *even where nonpayment results from the depositary bank's own negligence.*" (Emphasis added.) Accordingly, in evaluat-ing the propriety of Valley Bank's actions with regard to check processing, it is irrelevant whether Valley Bank exercised ordinary care in exercising its charge back rights, and the claims are preempted.

¶23 However, Hughes' claims encompass not only Valley Bank's pro-cessing of the checks but also the bank's communications to Hughes about that process. Because such communications are not addressed with spec-ificity by the UCC, common law and equitable principles supplement the UCC and govern the legal rights and responsibilities that apply to Valley Bank's representations to Hughes, upon which Hughes allegedly relied. See §30-1-103, MCA; First Georgia Bank v. Webster, 168 Ga. App. 307, 308 S.E.2d 579, 581 (1983) (UCC does not provide relief from common law neg-ligence; thus, common law actions are permissible.); see also Henry J. Bailey & Richard B. Hagedorn, Brady on Bank Checks ¶24.05, n.84 (8th ed., 1999). Thus, the District Court erred by concluding that the UCC preempted com-mon law and equitable principles with respect to the alleged misrepresenta-tions. Therefore, while Hughes bore the obligation to repay Valley Bank to satisfy the bank's right of charge-back under §30-4-214, MCA, it neverthe-less is possible for Hughes to obtain a judgment to compensate him for the charge-back debt, though we express no opinion on the ultimate merits of these common law claims in this case. . . .

¶24 Although holding in favor the bank in each case, *Chase, Allen,* and *Call* do not support preemption with regard to Valley Bank's alleged misrep-resentations. Rather, there is support within these decisions for this Court's determination that common law principles apply to bank communications to a depositor inquiring about the processing of checks. In each of these cases, the bank exercised its right of charge-back under UCC §4-214 and the plaintiff depositor alleged either that the bank had informed him that the deposited check had "cleared" or that the bank had led him to believe that it would clear in a certain amount of time.

¶25 The *Chase* court expressly acknowledged the possibility that com-mon law principles could apply to the type of communications at issue here:

[B]anks have nothing to gain by misleading customers into believing that uncleared items have cleared. Indeed, banks are usually overly cautious in giving provisional credit precisely because of the uncertainty of uncollected items. A bank could be liable for a misstatement in these general circum-stances if the misstatement were part of a scheme to defraud a customer in Chase's position by, for example, a conspiracy between the bank and the party to whom Chase transferred the funds. This of course is merely one example.

As discussed supra, however, [UCC] §4-214(d) simply does not hold liable for charge-back a bank whose employee inadvertently in some remark misleads a customer as to the precise likelihood that an item will clear.

The outcome might be different if a bank expressly informed a customer that it had made a final settlement on the account, but that is not the case here.

Chase, 590 F. Supp. at 1139 n.3 (emphasis added).

¶26 The court in *Allen* also acknowledged the potential for common law liability in this context:

We are dubious that the mere statement of a depositor that an unidentified teller told her (mistakenly) that a check had "cleared," when in fact it had not, constitutes that quantum of proof of negligence which will enable a customer to prevail against the bank under the circumstances disclosed here.

Allen, 477 N.Y.S.2d at 538. Though the *Allen* court did not distinguish the bank's duties in processing the check at issue from its duties in its communications to its depositor about that process, the language employed in the opinion suggests that some "quantum of proof" would be sufficient "to prevail against the bank" on common law claims in different circumstances.

¶27 Similarly, in *Call*, the court indicated that the "term 'cleared' . . . is not the equivalent of 'final settlement'"[37] and that, "although Mr. Call apparently assumed such, *he did not allege that this was a result of any inquiry with or representation to that effect by the defendant bank.*" *Call*, 774 N.Y.S.2d at 79 (emphasis added). Thus, the court, though not squarely addressing the issue, left open the possibility that a bank's misrepresentation of the status of the check settlement process could lead to liability for the bank.

¶28 In each of the above cases, the defendant bank was granted summary judgment because the plaintiff depositor failed to allege facts sufficient to impute liability to the bank. However, though the bank prevailed in each case, the analyses do not support the proposition that common law and equitable principles have been preempted by the UCC. Instead, they intimate that, in certain circumstances, common law and equitable principles may supplement the UCC where the bank—though not

---

37. Though it does not affect our analysis here, we pause to express bewilderment at this statement of the *Call* court. If the term "cleared" means anything in common banking usage, it is that final settlement has occurred. See Black's Law Dictionary (7th ed., 1999) (defining "clear" as "to pay (a check or draft) out of funds held on behalf of the maker 'the bank cleared the employee's check'"); see also §30-4-104(1)(j), MCA (defining "settle"), and Southside Nat. Bank v. Hepp, 739 S.W.2d 720, 723 (Mo. 1987) (final settlement occurs when "the payor bank has paid the item.").

violating its UCC-defined duty of ordinary care with respect to processing checks—breaches a duty to its depositor by misrepresenting the status of the check settlement process.

¶29 In summary, the District Court correctly determined that Valley Bank did not violate the UCC-defined duty of ordinary care in processing the checks. However, the District Court erred by failing to consider whether common law and equitable principles supplement the UCC-defined duty of ordinary care with respect to the representations about the check settlement process. Therefore, we reverse the District Court's order and remand for further proceedings on the matter. . . .

¶49 Affirmed in part, reversed in part, and remanded for further proceedings.

In a similar case, but with a law firm as the depositor (and thus less sympathetic?), the New York Court of Appeals (in a 6-1 opinion) ruled in favor of the depositary bank. It held that a statement that a check had "cleared" was ambiguous, and therefore it did not lead to an estoppel. See Greenberg, Trager & Herbst, LLP v. HSBC Bank USA, 17 N.Y.3d 565, 958 N.E.2d 77 (2011).

PROBLEM 108

When landlord Simon Mustache received a $5,400 check from his shady tenant John Weeks, who was always behind on the rent but finally produced this large check to make up his arrears, Simon deposited it immediately in his account at Last National Bank (LNB), which gave him a provisional credit for the amount. Two days later, fearful that the check would bounce, Simon phoned LNB and was told that the check had cleared, at which point Simon withdrew the money. Later that same day, the check was returned by the payor bank marked "NSF" ("Not Sufficient Funds"). The payor bank had returned the check within all required deadlines, so LNB demanded that Simon refund the amount of the check, claiming a right to charge back the amount of the check per §4-214. Simon refused, saying that the bank had assured him the check had cleared, a statement that he had relied upon, and that the bank's failure to exercise ordinary care in this regard made it liable for his damages per §4-103(e). LNB replied that since the check was worthless at all moments, Simon has *no* damages at all. How does this come out? See Wells Fargo Bank, N.A. v. FSI, Financial Solutions, Inc., 196 Cal. App. 4th 1559, 127 Cal. Rptr. 3d 589 (2011).

F. *Undoing Final Payment*

While UCC rights *off* the instrument (such as the right to sue for breach of the presentment warranties) survive final payment, the instrument itself is canceled by final payment, thus ending all Article 3 suits on the implied obligations created there, and the payor bank, now itself *accountable* for the check, must pay over the check's amount to the presenter. One issue that refuses to go away is whether the payor bank may resist payment, using common law theories such as mistake.

PROBLEM 109

Sandra Shirker and Frank Foxholer, two evil commercial law students, learned about the Midnight Deadline Statutes and decided to see if they could use them to create money out of thin air. Shirker, who had a checking account at the Busy National Bank, withdrew all the money in the account and, by agreement with the bank, closed it. She then wrote a $5,000 check on the account payable to Foxholer, who deposited the check in his own bank account with a different bank. At the same time, Shirker called up her old bank and talked to the vice president in charge of check payment. Shirker told him that a $5,000 check would be presented against the closed-out account but that there was "something funny" about it and Shirker would appreciate it if the vice president would call her when it came in. The vice president did so when the check came in late in the banking day, and Shirker told him that it was important that they meet. Shirker promised to come down to the bank the next day.

The following morning Shirker called the bank and said that she was delayed but was still coming and the vice president should wait. Shirker never showed up and eventually the vice president went home. On the second banking day following receipt, the Busy National Bank marked the check "Account closed" and returned it to the depositary-presenting bank, which passed it on to Foxholer, the payee. Foxholer sued the payer bank, claiming final payment had been made under §4-215(a)(3) in that the provisional settlement had not been revoked within the time allowed by §4-301, so the bank was accountable for the check under §4-302(a). Assume that Foxholer has not breached one of the §4-208 presentment warranties. All right-thinking people would agree that Foxholer should lose this suit; the only question is as to what defense the Code permits. Read §§4-302(b) and 3-418; cf. §1-304.

PROBLEM 110

When the police department of Rome, Wisconsin, opened the box of new police radios it had ordered, it was dismayed to learn that the radios were not the correct size specified in the contract. Since the police department had already sent a check, in payment to Voice of Japan, Inc., the seller, it immediately stopped payment on the check by so notifying its bank, Kelly National Bank. Negligently, Kelly National paid the check, and, when the police department complained that the check was not properly payable, recredited the account. You are the counsel for the bank, and the head of Checking Services calls you wanting to know whether the bank can recover the amount of the check from Voice of Japan. Look at §3-418 and its Official Comment, and give your answer.

If the bank is successful in its restitution action against Voice of Japan, the latter is entitled to get the check back for use in its dispute with the police department. Even if the check is unavailable (it has been destroyed en route by a check truncation system or was returned to the drawer, who refuses to surrender it), §§3-418(d) and 3-301(iii) give Voice of Japan the status of a "person entitled to enforce the instrument" so as to enable Voice of Japan to sue the police department on the §3-414(b) obligation of the drawer of a draft (which runs to a "person entitled to enforce the draft"). Of course, when the §3-414(b) suit is brought, the police department may raise its breach of warranty defense (Voice of Japan is not a holder in due course), which, if valid, would enable it to prevail.

G. Delays

Back to bank collection—and the following true story.

PROBLEM 111

In the early 1970s, a Boise, Idaho, bank's janitor mistakenly placed a box full of 8,000 unprocessed checks on a table reserved for trash. The operator of the bank's paper shredder dutifully fed the checks into his machine, turning them into quarter-inch strips. About $840,000 worth of checks underwent this ordeal. The next morning the error was discovered, and the bank hired 50 temporary employees to work six hours a day for two months to paste the checks back together (puzzle lovers were particularly welcome). At the moment of the shredding, many of the checks involved were bound to be in the process of collection. For some of the checks, the bank would be a depositary or collecting bank, and for others it would be the payer-drawee. Collecting banks are required to take action before their midnight deadline following receipt, §4-202(b), and, of course, the payor bank becomes absolutely accountable for a check not returned before the expiration of the midnight deadline. §§4-215(a)(3), 4-301, 4-302. Should the Boise bank just close down, or is there hope in §4-109(b) (delays)? See *Port City State Bank v. American Natl. Bank*, 486 F.2d 196 (10th Cir. 1973) (computer breakdown); *Sun River Cattle Co. v. Miners Bank*, 164 Mont. 237, 521 P.2d 679 (1974) (armored car broke down). Regulation CC §229.13(f) has a similar exemption for emergency conditions.

H. Restrictive Indorsements and Banks

Section 4-203 establishes the rule that only the collecting bank's transferor can give it binding instructions and the collecting bank need not examine the item to see whether other instructions or restrictions are contained in it. This is the *chain of command* theory of bank collection. See the Official Comment to §4-203.

PROBLEM 112

Nina Needy received her state welfare check and immediately made the following indorsement:

> For deposit only
> */s/Nina Needy*

On her way to the bank, her purse was snatched by Max Runner, who escaped and then examined the purse's contents.

He found the check and wrote his own name below that of Nina. Max then took the check to his bank, Pursesnatchers National, and had the bank cash it. Pursesnatchers National stamped its indorsement on the check and forwarded it to the Innocent State Bank, which also indorsed the check and presented it to the drawee, the Welfare Payor Bank, which held the check past its midnight deadline. In the meantime, Nina Needy reported her loss to the state (the check's drawer), but by the time the state investigated the matter, the check had been paid. Nina consulted a lawyer. Can she sue the depositary, collecting, and drawee banks in conversion, arguing that by paying in violation of her express instruction (the restrictive indorsement "for deposit only"), the banks converted her check? Or can the banks use the chain of command sections cited above to escape liability? See §3-206(c).

People sometimes place restrictive language above their signatures, and the effect of this is to create a *restrictive indorsement*. Read §3-206. A famous case, similar in its facts to the above Problem, *Soma v. Handrulis*, 277 N.Y.

233, 14 N.E.2d 46 (1938), held that all three banks (depositary, intermediary, and payor) had *converted* the check by paying it in obvious violation of a restrictive indorsement. The country's bankers were horrified by the decision; they knew that, as a practical matter, it is impossible for the banks involved in the check collection process to take the time to read and investigate all the restrictive indorsements on the backs of instruments. The Code's solution is stated first in §3-206(c): Of the banks involved, *only the depositary bank* faces liability for non-compliance with the terms of a restrictive indorsement. Only at the depositary bank is the check likely to be examined by a human being (the teller). The computers that process the check thereafter cannot even read the restrictive indorsements. Read §3-206; see C & L Const. Co., Inc. v. BB & T Corp., 2005 WL 2792401 (S.D. W. Va. 2005).

I. Priorities in the Bank Account: The Four Legals

The final bank collection problem we have left is the question of priority: What gets paid first? Bankers must constantly deal with four events — notice (for instance, of a depositor's death), stop-payment orders, service of legal process (garnishment, etc.), and the bank's right of setoff — and decide whether the happening of one of these events, which bankers call *the four legals*, has priority over the payment of a check. The issue is now resolved by §4-303(a), which states in essence that the four legal events come too late, as to any given check, if that check has either been certified or the bank has taken the steps that lead to final payment of the check. Further, the four legal events are too late if they arrive after the time periods described in (a)(5). Read §4-303(a) and consider these matters.

PROBLEM 113

Joseph Armstrong had $4,000 in his checking account with the Antitrust National Bank on the afternoon of October 5 at the moment when he filed a voluntary petition in bankruptcy with the local federal district court. Early in the morning of October 6, the bank received three checks drawn on the account. One for $1,000 was presented in person by the payee and paid over the counter. Another for $500, which had been presented by another bank, was posted against the account, marked "Paid," and placed in the drawer's statement file. A third, which had also been presented by another bank on October 6, was for $3,000, and the bank was unsure what to do with it, so it placed it in a "hold pending consultation with drawer" file. At noon, Armstrong ran into Vivian Visor, the bank's head teller, while eating in the same restaurant, and since they were friends, Armstrong told Visor that the day before he had filed the bankruptcy petition. Visor expressed sympathy. At 1 P.M., just as Visor walked back into the bank, another teller made an over-the-counter payment of $500 on a fourth check. At 2 P.M., the bankruptcy trustee phoned the bank and made a formal demand that the bank freeze the account. On receiving this notice, Robert Startup, a bank vice president, checked the bank's records, found that Armstrong owed the bank $75 on a home improvement loan, and told the bank clerk to deduct this amount from Armstrong's account. Subsequently, the bank reported to the trustee that the account contained $1,925, as follows:

Oct. 5	$4,000
Oct. 6	
First Check	−1,000
	3,000
Second Check	−500
	2,500
Fourth Check	−500
	2,000
Home Improvement Loan	−75
	$1,925

The third check was marked "Not Sufficient Funds" and was returned to the presenting bank on the morning of October 10.

Consider these issues:

(a) Can the trustee in bankruptcy claim that the filing of a voluntary petition in bankruptcy on October 5 automatically froze the account of $4,000 so that the bank owes the bankruptcy estate that amount? Per §542(c) of the Bankruptcy Code the answer is no. The bank is protected as to all transfers made from the account until it had notice of the bankruptcy proceeding, although the trustee can usually recover the money from the payee per Bankruptcy Code §549(a).

(b) At what moment did the bank have notice of the bankruptcy: When Armstrong told Visor, when Visor returned to the bank, or when the phone call was received? The answer to this question will determine the validity of the payment of the fourth check. See UCC §1-202.

(c) Was the home improvement loan payment effective against the trustee? See Bankruptcy Code §553 (setoff permitted on getting relief from the automatic stay of §362(a)(7)).

(d) If you are the attorney representing the bank that presented the third check, what legal theory, if any, might attract your attention?

PROBLEM 114

The newly established Embryo State Bank hires you as counsel to the bank. After a month's operations, the bank calls you up with the following dilemma. One of its customers is Thomas Crandall, whose account currently contains $5,000. This morning, at 9:00 A.M., the bank received a bundle of checks from the bank across the street, and the bundle contained five checks drawn against Crandall's account payable to different payees and totaling $1,258. At 9:05 A.M., the bank received a bundle of checks from the nearest Federal Reserve Bank, and this bundle contained one check drawn on Crandall's account for $4,986. The dilemma: Should the bank dishonor the one big check or the five little ones? Three of the little checks are dated prior to the big check and two after. The bank is afraid that if it dishonors the big one, Crandall will quickly be sued by a major creditor. On the other hand, if it dishonors the little ones, five creditors, not just one, will think Crandall is a bum. The bank is afraid it will face §4-402 damages for wrongful dishonor. Without looking at the Code, what would you advise the bank to do? Now look at §4-303(b) and its Official Comment 7. Almost all courts considering the issue have looked at this same Comment and concluded that banks have clear authority to do as they like here, even if it results in high overdraft fees for customers; see Northampton Restaurant Group, Inc. v. FirstMerit Bank, N.A., 2012 WL 2608807 (6th Cir. 2012). There have been a number of cases attacking "high-to-low" payments in *debit card* transactions (ATMs), arguing unconscionability, to which the courts seem receptive; see, e.g., In re Checking Account Overdraft Litigation, 694 F. Supp. 2d 1302 (S.D. Fla. 2010). The Consumer Financial Protection Bureau, created by Congress in 2010, has contemplated issuing a regulation forbidding the practice, perhaps disallowing "high-to-low" payments for both check processing as well as ATM transactions, but at this writing no such regulation has been promulgated.

CHAPTER 7   ASSESSMENT

Multiple Choice Questions

1. Okonkwo Technology issued a check to a supplier, Nwoye Semiconductor, for six-month's supply of computer chips. There was plenty of money in Okonkwo Technology's account at Careful Bank to cover the check. Careful Bank was a little nervous, however, because Okonkwo Technology owed a lot on its line of credit with the bank and was facing difficult market conditions. When Nwoye Semiconductor presented the check

for payment, Careful Bank refused to pay, to conserve the money in the account. For the lack of these funds, Nwoye Semiconductor missed its monthly equipment loan payment, resulting in repossession of some key fabrication machines and loss of revenue. Is Careful Bank liable to Nwoye Semiconductor?

a. No. Careful Bank had no obligation to Nwoye Semiconductor to pay the check, because Careful Bank did not sign the check.

b. No. Careful Bank had no obligation to anyone to pay the check.

c. Yes. Careful Bank is liable to Nwoye Semiconductor for all losses proximately caused by its wrongful dishonor.

d. Yes. Careful Bank is liable to Nwoye Semiconductor for the amount of the check.

2. On the facts of the last question, is Careful Bank liable to Okonkwo Technology?

a. Yes. Careful Bank is liable to Okonkwo Technology for the amount of the check.

b. No. Careful Bank held on to Okonkwo Technology's money, so it could not have caused any loss.

c. Yes. Careful Bank is liable to Okonkwo Technology for Okonkwo's damages, if any, proximately caused by the wrongful dishonor.

d. No. Careful Bank had no obligation to pay the check, because it did not sign the check.

3. Coyote wrote a check to Loman, happily receiving the motorcycle the two agreed upon. Coyote still tried to wriggle out of payment by issuing a stop order payment to his bank, Careless Bank, specifically identifying the check. Careless Bank absent-mindedly paid the check when presented. Is Coyote liable to Careless Bank?

a. No. The check was not properly payable, because a stop payment order was in effect.

b. No. Careless Bank is not entitled to payment, Loman is.

c. Yes. A bank that pays a check is always entitled to reimbursement from its customer.

d. Yes. The check was not properly payable, but Careless Bank may use subrogation to collect from Coyote.

4. Careless Bank's accounting books stated that Leachman has not paid her last year's mortgage payments. When Careless Bank sued Leachman, she defended by bringing her last year's bank statements from her account at Accurate Bank, which had copies of all the checks. The copies meet the requirements of Check 21. Careless Bank argued that the judge should not accept the copies, because only the original checks would be reliable evidence of payment. Should the judge accept copies of checks as evidence of payment?

a. No. Anyone could Photoshop a plausible image of a check.

b. No. As with promissory notes, a copy is no substitute for the original.

c. Yes. A substitute check under Check 21 is the legal equivalent of the original check.

d. Yes. Banks should afford each other professional courtesy.

5. Nyong'o decided to sell her acting trophy on Craigslist. She received an offer of $1,000 from one Maximilian. The next day, she received a letter from Maximilian with a cashier's check apparently issued by Reputable Bank, payable to Maximilian, for $3,000. She soon got a message from Maximilian: "Please cash the check, keep $1,000, wire me the other $2,000 and send the trophy. I trust you." She took the check to her bank, Careless Bank, who gave her $3,000 cash over the counter. She wired $2,000 to Maximilian, sent the trophy, and spent some of the $1,000 to treat her family to dinner. Ten days later, she saw that her bank had subtracted $3,000 from her account, leaving an overdraft. Checking her account online, she saw a notation that the cashier's check was not paid and her bank had taken back the $3,000 it gave her. Did Careless Bank have the right to do that?

a. No. Careless Bank paid the check over the counter and is bound.

b. No. Careless Bank should not have given her the funds until there was assurance that the cashier's check would be paid.

c. Yes. Careless Bank, as a depositary bank, has a right of charge back, if an item deposited is subsequently not paid.

d. Yes. Careless Bank made a mistaken payment, but may use subrogation to recover from Nyong'o.

Answers

1. A is the best answer, stating quite correctly that Careful Bank had no obligation to Nwoye Semiconductor to pay the check, because Careful Bank did not sign the check. Careful Bank did have an obligation to pay a properly payable check. But that obligation does not run to the holder of the check, who has rights only against those who have signed the check or those who have made warranties by transferring the check. Rather, Careful Bank was obliged to its customer, Okonkwo Technology, to pay checks written on the account that were properly payable, making B incorrect. C and D are incorrect, because Careful Bank, for reasons stated, has no liability to Nwoye Semiconductor.

2. C is the best answer. As discussed above, Careful Bank is obliged to its customer, Okonkwo Technology, to pay checks that are properly payable. Where Careful Bank breached that obligation, it is liable for wrongful dishonor. The measure of liability is, unlike most negotiable instrument actions, not the amount of the check, contrary to A. The check was not paid, so we are not arguing about who is responsible for the amount of the check. Rather, liability is measured by the extent to which the wrongful dishonor proximately caused damages to Okonkwo Technology, as B correctly states. The facts given do not show any damages to Okonkwo. There could be such damages: perhaps the bounced check will cause Nwoye Semiconductor to stop dealing with Okonkwo Technology, or cause harm to Okonkwo Technology's credit rating, or even trigger a default with one of its creditors. But unless there is a showing of harm to Okonkwo Technology, there is no liability. In most cases, there is no harm; the customer simply writes another check or pays by other means.

3. D is the best answer. An effective stop payment makes the check not properly payable, so Careless Bank would normally not be entitled to reimbursement. Contrary to C, a bank is generally entitled to reimbursement only if it pays checks that are properly payable. But a bank that pays a check by mistake may use subrogation, if it can identify another party that is receiving unjust enrichment due to the bank's mistake. Here, Coyote, who tried to stop payment on his debt he owed, would receive a motorcycle for free if Careless Bank took the loss for mistakenly paying the seller. So Careless Bank may use subrogation, in effect, stepping into the shoes of the seller to collect the agreed-upon price from Coyote.

4. C is the best answer. When collecting a promissory note, a copy is indeed no substitute for the original (although it may at least be evidence that at one time the person had possession of the original note). But Check 21, in order to facilitate electronic processing, permits a bank to create a substitute check, which is the legal equivalent of the original check. So the judge should accept the substitute check just as readily as the original check.

5. C is the best answer. This question gives an example of a common scam, one that has fooled many sophisticated people, including a fair number of lawyers. When Nyong'o handed the check to Careless Bank's teller and received cash, Careless Bank was not paying the check, contrary to A. Rather, they were taking the check as an item for deposit, to collect on Nyong'o's behalf from the drawee bank. The cash was not payment of the check; rather, it was an advance against the proceeds of the check. When an item taken for collection is not paid, the depositary bank has a right of charge back, the right to collect any amounts that have been advanced

against the item. Unscrupulous people who know this, like Maximilian, are sometimes able to take advantage of those who do not, like Nyong'o.

B has things backward. Depositary banks are under no duty to hold on to funds until an item has been paid. To the contrary, they may (and often must, under funds availability rules) make the funds available to their customers before receiving payment themselves.

D is a red herring, put here to remind us that subrogation may sometimes be used by a drawee bank when it has paid by mistake. Such subrogation may not be used by a depositary bank.

WRONGDOING AND ERROR

Negotiable instruments represent money, and money attracts thieves. Many an employer checks the books one day to discover that mysterious checks have been written on the corporate account that no one seems to remember authorizing, or that a promissory note, supposedly in the vault, is missing. Criminals look at bank accounts and plot ways to tap them, and in this ingenious century those schemes are magnificent in their clever evilness.

When all goes wrong and the venality is uncovered those caught in the criminal's plot line must figure out who owes what to whom. There are many legal theories that are provided by the Uniform Commercial Code. The lawyer who understands these and how they fit together possesses valuable knowledge.

This course does not get involved with the substance of the crimes one might possibly commit using a negotiable instrument. Suffice it to say that it is a crime in all jurisdictions to write a check against an account known to be insufficient (or non-existent), to forge a signature to a check, or to pass (*utter*) an instrument known to be forged. It is also illegal to try to use the delay period of bank collection, the float, to create money on empty accounts. This process, known as *check kiting*, in its simplest form involves opening two bank accounts in distant locations and writing and depositing checks on the other account in each bank, increasing the amount and using the slowness of the bank collection process to create the false appearance of assets.[1] Ignoring the commercial paper crimes, this section of the book explores the legal tangles that follow in the wake of such nefarious activity.

I.   FORGERY OF THE PAYEE'S NAME

A.   Some Basic Ideas

It is important that you go back and review two concepts that we have already covered and make sure that they are still part of your repertoire.

The first of these was the principle explored at the end of Chapter 3 (Negotiation): the forgery of the payee's name (or of a special indorsee's name) means that no valid negotiation takes place, and therefore no one taking the instrument thereafter can qualify as a *holder*.

PROBLEM 115

When she graduated from law school, Portia Moot received a $500 check signed by her grandmother. She put it in her personal papers when she packed up to move to a new city where she planned on using it to open a checking account there. When her car containing all her belongings was stolen en route, the check went with it. The thief, Harry Villain, forged Portia's name to the back of the check and then signed his own name below hers. He deposited the check in the account he carried with Careless State Bank. Before the check was presented, Portia had her grandmother stop payment on the check, so it was dishonored and returned to Careless State Bank. By this time Harry had withdrawn the money and fled the jurisdiction. Careless State phoned its attorney. Since it gave value for the check, isn't it a holder in due course and, as such, can't it enforce the check against the grandmother per §3-414(b)? See §3-201.

---

1. We hesitate, for some reason, to elaborate on the how-to's of check kiting; let us note that bankers have devised methods of detecting many check-kiting schemes in their early stages. The adoption of the federal Check 21 rules eliminates much of the float period for checks and makes life harder for check kiters. For more on check kiting, see A. Brooke Overby, Allocation of Check Kiting Losses Under the UCC, Regulation CC, and the Bankruptcy Code: Reconciling the Standards, 44 Wake Forest L. Rev. 59, 63 (2009), and Thomas E. McCurnin & Peter A. Frandsen, Grounding Check Kiting with Check 21: The Civil and Criminal Ramifications of Check Kiting in the 21st Century, 125 Banking L.J. 295, 297 (2008).

As we saw at the end of Chapter 3, if a check is payable to the order of a named individual, only that person can be a holder, a status postponed until the payee acquires possession; see §1-201(b)(21). Without a valid indorsement by the payee, no later person can qualify as a holder (much less a holder in due course), and this is true no matter how many times the instrument is thereafter transferred, no matter how good the forgery appears to be, no matter how innocent the later takers, or how much value they paid. Indeed, the check is still the property of the payee whose name was forged and that person could replevy it from the current transferee.

We would get a completely different result if this check were either made out to bearer or if the payee had indorsed it in blank before the check was stolen. In that case, anyone in possession of the check would be a holder and, if otherwise qualifying, a holder in due course.

The second concept to review is the meaning of the phrase "a person entitled to enforce the instrument." Section 3-301 defines the phrase, and you should reread it now. The primary definition is that of *holder* (i.e., someone who takes pursuant to a valid negotiation), but the phrase also includes some others the law thinks worthy of protection. Subsection (ii) speaks of "a non-holder in possession of the instrument who has the rights of a holder." What does this mean? It is our old friend "the shelter rule." Consider the following.

PROBLEM 116

Assume from the last Problem that when Portia was leaving the city she owed $500 to her former roommate, Helen Midlaw, so she gave her the graduation check but forgot to indorse it. Is Helen a "holder"? When she discovers that Portia forgot to indorse the check, could she force Portia to do so? See §3-203.

Helen qualifies as a non-holder with the rights of a holder pursuant to the shelter rule of §3-203(b) and is therefore a person entitled to enforce the instrument. Another example of such a person is a depositary bank. Suppose that Portia took the check from her grandmother and deposited it, unindorsed, in the bank account she opened in the new city to which she moved. Section 4-205 gives the depositary bank Portia's holder rights and makes it a person entitled to enforce the instrument in spite of the lack of payee indorsement.

Return to the definition of "person entitled to enforce the instrument" in §3-301. There are two other possible entities that qualify per subsection (iii). The first of these is someone who has lost the instrument but who has the right to go to court to recreate it pursuant to §3-309. Consider this possibility:

Portia's cat chews up the check while stuck in the car when Portia is driving across country. Portia no longer is a holder—there is nothing to hold. But she has the right to use the mechanism of §3-309 and is therefore still a person entitled to enforce the instrument. The final person so qualifying is the person described in §3-418(d); see the text following Problem 110.

B. Warranty Liability

After the forgers ply their trade, other parties dealing with the check must adjust their responsibilities vis-à-vis each other. There are three primary theories: the properly payable rule of §4-401, the warranties rules discussed next, and the ability of certain parties to sue in conversion (covered later in the chapter).

PROBLEM 117

Portia Moot owed $400 to her landlord, John Clark, so she handed him a check on the first of the month when they met in the lobby. John thought he had put it in his pocket, but in reality it had fluttered to the floor, where it was discovered by Harry Villain, another tenant of the building. Harry took the check down to No Questions Checks Store and asked the manager to cash it for him, pretending to be John Clark, whose name he had forged to the back of the check. The manager then gave Harry $400, stamped "No Questions Check Store" under the forgery, and deposited the check in the account the store carried at Merchants Bank. Merchants Bank presented the check to Octopus National Bank, the drawee bank, and was paid. A week later John Clark searched everywhere for the check. Finally he went back to Portia and told her he had lost it. By this time the check had been returned to Portia by Octopus National Bank as part of her monthly bank statement. Portia showed it to John, and he positively declared that his signature on the back of the check was a forgery. Portia, a law student with a good grasp of the forgery rules of the Uniform Commercial Code, knew just what to do. She wrote him another check and then went down to Octopus National Bank.

(a) Can she make Octopus National Bank recredit her account? What is her theory? See §4-401.

(b) Octopus National Bank has made final payment on this check, and, as we saw in the last chapter, that ends its ability to dishonor the check. However, §4-302(b) provides that final payment does not prevent warranty liability from giving relief to the bank, specifically referring to §4-208. Read that section and answer these two questions: (1) which warranty described therein was breached, and (2) who breached it?

(c) Is it a defense to a transfer warranty lawsuit that the transferor was free of negligence and had no knowledge of a forgery, or is it strict liability? See Huntington Natl. Bank v. Guishard, Wilburn & Shorts, LLC, 2014 WL 6982566 (S.D. Ohio 2014).

Both Articles 3 and 4 contain warranty sections and they are virtually identical as a matter of substance. Sections 3-417 and 4-208 each describe *presentment* warranties and §§3-416 and 4-207 cover *transfer* warranties. The Article 3 warranties control until the check is taken for deposit, at which point the Article 4 warranties take over. This usually has no practical significance, given that the warranty liability is the same in both articles, but if an attorney needs to file a complaint, it is important that the correct article be cited.

What is the difference between *presentment* and *transfer*? The answer is easiest to understand if you think of a negotiable instrument as having three stages in its life: issuance, transfer, and presentment. Issuance (§3-105) is the creation of the instrument and its handing over to the first taker. There are no warranties made on issuance. Skipping for a moment the middle stage (transfer), the final stage in the life of the instrument is presentment: its surrender to the drawee for either acceptance or payment.[2] At that moment presentment warranties are made by not only the entity physically making presentment but also all prior transferors (this giving the drawee a choice of defendants). Every other movement of the instrument for consideration between issuance and presentment is a *transfer* of the instrument and gives rise to the transfer warranties. Warranty suits are said to be suits "off the instrument" because they do not require possession of the instrument as a prerequisite to suit.

PROBLEM 118

Return to the facts of the last Problem. Assume that Octopus National Bank successfully recaptured its money from Merchants Bank under a theory of breach of a presentment warranty. Now Merchants Bank calls in its attorney and asks for legal advice. Can it sue the drugstore using §4-208(a) (note the word *drawee* in subsection (a))? How does it get legal relief? See §4-207(a). What warranties have been breached? Must it give notice to the drugstore within any given period of time? See §4-207(d). If the drugstore refuses to pay, how quickly must suit be commenced? See §4-111; cf. §3-118.

---

2. If the instrument is a promissory note, presentment is made to the maker of the note, in which case the only presentment warranty is that described in §3-417(d).

PROBLEM 119

Still using the facts of the above Problems, now assume that you are the attorney for the check cashing store. To what relief is it entitled, assuming it can find Harry Villain in a solvent condition?

When a forgery of a payee's name occurs, it is the policy of our law to use warranty theories, first presentment and then transfer, to pass the loss back to the wrongdoer (or the first person to trust the wrongdoer). Note that the drugstore was always in the best position to discover the forgery by making Harry produce identification when he tried to cash the check.

As for damages for breach of warranty, the relevant sections in both Articles 3 and 4 are identical with, for example, §3-416(b) providing for a recovery of "the loss suffered as a result of the breach, but not more than the amount of the instrument plus expenses and loss of interest incurred as a result of the breach."

C.   Conversion Liability

Conversion is the civil action for misappropriation of another's property. There are many ways a negotiable instrument can be converted.

PROBLEM 120

Your employer gives you your paycheck, drawn on the employer's bank, Octopus National. You take the check down to the bank and present it across the counter. The teller takes it, walks away from the window and comes back a few minutes later empty-handed. "Yes?" she asks, looking at you blankly. "The check?" you ask. "Sorry," she says, "we are not going to pay it." "Then I want it back," you reply, planning to use it to pursue your employer on the drawer's obligation (§3-414(b)). "Sorry," she says, "we are also keeping the check." Do they have the right to do that?

PROBLEM 121

Mr. Aristotle Wellborn was walking along the street when he was surreptitiously relieved of his wallet by Art Dodger. In the wallet was a check made out to Wellborn, who had already indorsed it. Is Dodger guilty of conversion?

The original language of the conversion section in the first version of Article 3 was so poorly written that it did not appear to cover all the situations where a conversion action should lie, and the courts were forced to fill in the gaps. The 1990 Revision handles this difficulty by simply incorporating the common law of conversion as applicable to negotiable instruments (see the first sentence of §3-420(a)), and that should permit the courts to find conversion liability in both of the last Problems.

Only the person whose property rights are adversely affected may sue for conversion. For negotiable instruments the *holder* is the owner of the instrument and is the person with the property rights therein. Since at the outset only the payee can be the holder of an order instrument, only the payee has a sufficient property interest to become the plaintiff (or if the payee has negotiated the instrument to another, only that person can be the *holder* having a property interest in the instrument). Since the instrument, once delivered, gives the payee these property rights, the payee can take a number of different possible courses of action whenever the check is stolen, his or her name is forged thereon, and the instrument is paid by the drawee bank:

(1) *Conversion.* The payee can sue the drawee bank, or anyone taking the check after the forgery, in conversion. If the drawee is forced to pay the payee, the drawee will sue the check's presenter for breach of the presentment warranty that he or she was a "person entitled to enforce the instrument"; §4-208(a)(1). That person can then sue the transferee for breach of transfer warranties; §3-416(a)(1), (2), and (4). Thus the loss will pass back up the chain until it reaches the forger or, if the forger has departed for parts unknown, the first person to trust the forger. The cases are collected in Annot., 23 A.L.R.4th 855.

(2) *Drawer's Obligation.* Since the check is still the property of the payee, he or she can replevy it from its current possessor (probably the drawer, who will have it among the canceled checks), cross off the forged indorsement, sign it, and present it to the drawee bank for payment. If the drawee pays it, well and good. If not, a dishonor will have occurred, and the payee may then sue the drawer on the drawer's obligation, §3-414(b), or, certainly now, the underlying obligation.

(3) *Quasi-Contract.* Some courts considering the issue will permit the quasi-contractual action by the payee for money had and received, a cause of action that typically has a longer statute of limitations than does conversion. See Peerless Ins. Co. v. Texas Commerce Bank, 791 F.2d 1177(5th Cir. 1986); but see AMX Enterprises, Inc. v. Bank One, N.A., 196 S.W.3d 202 (Tex. App. 2006).

(4) *Negligence.* Most courts considering the issue have not allowed a common law negligence claim against banks handling forged checks, finding that the statutory scheme of Article 3 of the Uniform Commercial Code

preempts all common law theories; see Olympic Title Ins. Co. v. Fifth Third Bank of Western Ohio, 2004 WL 2009285 (Ohio App. 2004). There are a minority of decisions allowing the common law to supplement the Code; Chicago Title Ins. Co. v. Allfirst Bank, 394 Md. 270, 905 A.2d 366 (2006).

The common law had always provided that payment on a forged indorsement was conversion, see Restatement (Second) of Torts §241A, but that statement leaves a lot of substantive law to be explored. The original conversion section did not answer a host of questions that §3-420 now settles. These matters are explored by the following Problems.

PROBLEM 122

When Portia Moot learned that the check she had given to her landlord had been stolen from him, his name forged as payee, and that the check had been paid by her bank, she sued her bank in conversion. Is she the proper plaintiff in this lawsuit? If not, (1) who is, and (2) what relief does the law give her? See §§3-420(a) and 4-401(a). If the landlord (the payee) decides to bring a §3-420 action, who is liable in such a suit?

PROBLEM 123

After he won the lottery, Tim Isle decided to pay off the mortgage on his home. He mailed a check for $80,000 to Octopus National Bank (ONB), the mortgagee, but it was stolen from the mail by an unknown person, who forged "Octopus National Bank" on the back and cashed the check at Sleepy Hollow State Bank, which then collected it from the drawee bank. Since ONB, the payee, never received possession of the check, does it have sufficient property rights therein to succeed in a conversion action against Sleepy Hollow State Bank or the drawee? See §3-420(a). What can the bank do? See §3-310(b).

Leeds v. Chase Manhattan Bank, N.A.

New Jersey Superior Court, Appellate Division, 2000
752 A.2d 332

WECKER, J.A.D.
Plaintiffs William Leeds and Carol Leeds, a mother and son, (collectively "plaintiff" or "Leeds"), hired Louis Egnasko, Esq.[3] to represent them

---

3. Egnasko has since been disbarred by both New York and New Jersey. Matter of Egnasko, 151 N.J. 506, 701 A.2d 701 (1997); Matter of Egnasko, 223 A.D.2d 317, 646 N.Y.S.2d 698 (App. Div. 1996).

in connection with a mortgage foreclosure action, as well as the purchase and resale of the property in East Orange, New Jersey on which they held the mortgage. After plaintiff bought the property at the foreclosure sale, they entered into a contract to sell the property. Egnasko closed the sale and accepted a settlement check for $87,293.56 on plaintiff's behalf. The settlement check payable to William Leeds, Carol Leeds, and Isabel Gibbs,[4] was a United Jersey Bank teller's check drawn at that bank's Hackensack, New Jersey branch. Summit Bank is the successor-in-interest to United Jersey Bank (hereinafter "Summit").

Following the closing, and unknown to Leeds, Egnasko altered the settlement check by typing "* * *Louis Egnasko, as attorney for* * *" above the payee line, so that the check then read:

* * *LOUIS EGNASKO AS ATTORNEY FOR* * *
* * *WILLIAM LEEDS, CAROL LEEDS, ISABEL GIBBS* * *

Egnasko alone endorsed the check "for deposit only, 067003443" and deposited the check into his attorney trust account at Chemical Bank. Chemical Bank stamped the back of the check "Endorsement guaranteed." Defendant Chase Manhattan Bank is the successor-in-interest to Chemical Bank (hereinafter "Chase"). Chase presented the check for collection in the ordinary course, and Summit honored its own teller's check. The check was negotiated between May 8 and May 16, 1996.

On June 6, 1996, Egnasko drew a check for $92,050 payable to William and Carol Leeds from an attorney trust account he held at the Trust Company of New Jersey (Trustco). This check apparently covered the proceeds of the sale of the home. Trustco honored the check drawn to Leeds, and Leeds received payment on that check. However, Egnasko's Trustco account also contained funds that Egnasko had obtained by similarly altering and depositing a check payable to Shrewsbury State Bank ("Shrewsbury"), which was intended to pay off a mortgage loan in an unrelated real estate transaction. Instead of delivering that check to Shrewsbury, Egnasko again inserted his own name, "Louis Egnasko as attorney," above the payee's name and deposited the check into his Trustco attorney trust account. Egnasko thus used funds that belonged to Shrewsbury to pay Leeds.

Facing a claim for conversion by Shrewsbury, Trustco filed suit against Egnasko and Leeds in New York, seeking repayment of monies traceable

---

4. Gibbs had been a record owner with the right of survivorship of an undivided one-third share of the East Orange property along with Grace Livingston and Louise Bevans, to whom Leeds made a mortgage loan. Gibbs apparently died intestate. Although Leeds alone received a deed from the Sheriff, the buyer required that Gibbs be named as a contract seller, and issued the check payable to Leeds and Gibbs, as described. The record reveals no claim by Gibbs' estate to the proceeds of the sale, and the estate is not involved in this appeal.

to Egnasko's fraud. Leeds filed an answer and crossclaim in the New York action on December 5, 1997, admitting receipt of the Trustco check from Egnasko, but denying that "William and Carol Leeds owe [Trustco] the traceable converted proceeds of the check delivered to William Leeds with interest. . . ."

On December 24, 1997, Leeds filed this action alleging strict liability for payment on the altered settlement check against both Chase, the depository bank, and Summit, the drawer/drawee/payor bank. In support of their motion for summary judgment, defendants argued that (1) Leeds had been paid and therefore suffered no damages; (2) Leeds would only be ordered to return that payment in the Trustco action if Leeds were found to have accepted payment with knowledge that the funds were stolen; and (3) if Leeds knowingly accepted stolen monies, the equitable doctrine of unclean hands would bar recovery against the banks. . . .

Leeds argued in opposition to summary judgment and in support of his cross-motion that Chase, as the depository bank, is strictly liable for conversion under N.J.S.A. 12A:3-420, including damages related to the cost of defending the New York suit. The motion judge granted summary judgment in favor of both Chase and Summit dismissing plaintiff's complaint. . . .

We first address Leeds' cause of action in conversion against Chase. The applicable provision of the Uniform Commercial Code (UCC), N.J.S.A. 12A:3-420a, states:

> The law applicable to conversion of personal property applies to instruments. *An instrument is also converted if it* is taken by transfer, other than a negotiation, from a person not entitled to enforce the instrument *or a bank makes or obtains payment with respect to the instrument for a person not entitled to enforce the instrument or receive payment.* An action for conversion of an instrument may not be brought by the issuer or acceptor of the instrument or a payee or indorsee who did not receive delivery of the instrument either directly or through delivery to an agent or a co-payee. [Emphasis added.]

Although the check was not actually delivered to Leeds, it was delivered to Egnasko as Leeds' attorney, with intent that title be transferred to Leeds, the payee. Thus Leeds is entitled to bring this action for conversion as one who "receive[d] delivery of the instrument . . . through delivery to an agent. . . ." N.J.S.A. 12A:3-420a. . . . It is undisputed that Egnasko was not authorized by Leeds to indorse the check and had no right to receive or enforce payment on that check.

Section 3-420a does not explicitly refer to "forgery" or "alteration," but instead addresses a class of persons who are "not entitled to enforce the instrument or receive payment." However, there can be no question that because the Summit teller's check payable to Leeds was altered by Egnasko, he was not "entitled" to payment on the instrument. Such an alteration constitutes a forgery under the Code and the common law. See N.J.S.A. 12A:3-407a. . . . By crediting Egnasko's trust account with the face amount of the check, Chase paid the check to "a person not entitled to . . . receive payment." N.J.S.A. 12A:3-420a.

As a depository bank under the Uniform Commercial Code, see N.J.S.A. 12A:4-105b, Chase is strictly liable for conversion on a forged or stolen instrument. See N.J.S.A. 12A:3-420, comment 1. Therefore, Chase is strictly liable on Leeds' claim for conversion under N.J.S.A. 12A:3-420a, because Chase "[made or obtained] payment with respect to the instrument for a person not entitled to enforce the instrument or receive payment." See New Jersey Lawyers' Fund, 303 N.J. Super, at 224, 696 A.2d 728.

The justification for strict liability upon the depository bank is that "the loss should normally come to rest upon the first solvent party in the stream after the one who forged the indorsement. . . ." 2 James J. White & Robert S. Summers, Uniform Commercial Code §18-4 at 209-10 (4th ed. 1995). See also Uniform Commercial Code, comment 3 to N.J.S.A. 12A:3-420:

> The depositary bank is ultimately liable in the case of a forged indorsement check because of its warranty to the payor bank under Section 4-208(a)(1) and it is usually the most convenient defendant in cases involving multiple checks drawn on different banks. There is no basis for requiring the owner of the check to bring multiple actions against the various payor banks and to require those banks to assert warranty rights against the depositary bank.

We are therefore convinced that the motion court improperly entered summary judgment against Leeds and in favor of Chase. We are also convinced that Chase is not entitled to summary judgment based upon the defense of payment, in light of Leeds' continuing exposure to the New York action, until that action has been resolved. If Leeds is not required in that action to disgorge the payment received from Egnasko, Chase will be entitled to set off that payment against its liability for conversion. Cf. County Concrete Corp. v. Smith, 317 N.J. Super. 50, 61-62, 721 A.2d 34 (App. Div. 1998). Leeds cannot be allowed a double recovery. If Leeds is required to disgorge, we will then address Chase's "unclean hands" defense on a complete record. That Leeds' damage claim may be limited (or even dismissed) in the future does not affect our determination of Chase's liability here and now.

We next address Leeds' cause of action in conversion against Summit. Summit is the drawer, the drawee, and the payor bank on the altered check under the Code definitions. A drawee bank is also strictly liable for conversion when it pays on a forged endorsement. . . . In Gast v. American Cas. Co. of Reading, Pa., 99 N.J. Super. 538, 541, 240 A.2d 682 (1968), we said:

As both drawer and drawee defendant had the responsibility to make payment to the named payees on the instrument. . . . The statute [the former UCC §3-419] created an absolute right to recover in favor of plaintiffs . . . upon proof that the draft was paid on the forged indorsements. Plaintiffs' indorsements were concededly forged. It follows that defendant, having paid the draft, was rendered liable for the conversion in the face amount.

However, N.J.S.A. 12A:3-420c limits damages for conversion against

[a] representative, other than a depository bank, who has in good faith dealt with an instrument or its proceeds on behalf of one who was not the person entitled to enforce the instrument . . . [for any more than] the amount of any proceeds that it has not paid out.

Summit is not a depositary bank in this case. Summit has paid out the entire face amount of the forged check and is not alleged to have acted other than in good faith; it therefore cannot be liable to Leeds for conversion under §3-420. Whether Summit could have been found liable for negligence, as a result of its failure to detect the alteration on its own teller's check, is not before us. Plaintiff has not pled or argued a negligence cause of action against Summit. Summary judgment is therefore affirmed in favor of Summit. . . .

We affirm summary judgment dismissing the complaint against Summit, reverse summary judgment in favor of Chase, and remand for entry of partial summary judgment on liability against Chase. A determination of damages must abide the outcome of the New York action.

The court's conclusion that §3-420(c) excuses the drawee bank from liability as a "representative" is wrong. The Official Comments to §3-420 clearly refer the conversion liability of the drawee bank, and there is general agreement that only intermediary banks qualify as the sorts of "representatives" who are protected by subsection (c). See White & Summers §16-4.

PROBLEM 124

The drawer made the check out to "John and Mary Doe" in order to pay a debt owed to them both. John got the check first, signed his name alone as indorser, and deposited the check in his individual checking account. His bank presented the check to the drawee bank and was paid. The issue: Is a missing signature treated the same as a forged one? Has the presenting bank breached the warranty that it is a person entitled to enforce the check? Could Mary Doe sue the banks in conversion? See §§3-110(d) and 3-420(a); Tri-County Natl. Bank v. GreenPoint Credit, LLC, 190 S.W.3d 360 (Ky. App. 2006).

Finally, you should remember that payment in violation of the terms of a restrictive indorsement ("For Deposit Only," for example) also gives rise to a cause of action in conversion; see §3-206(c) (a matter discussed in Subsection II.H of Chapter 7).

II. FORGERY OF THE DRAWER'S SIGNATURE

When a forger forges the *drawer's* signature (as opposed to that of the payee), the law reaches a completely different result than that we saw in the last section. The basic rule, the rule of Price v. Neal (below), coming to us from 1762, is that the drawee who pays or accepts a draft takes the risk of a forged drawer's signature. Later cases, however, then established the rule that the drawee does not take the risk of a forged *indorser's* signature. Canal Bank v. Bank of Albany, 1 Hill 287 (N.Y. 1841). This dichotomy still exists in our law.

Vital to an understanding of the Code's position on forgery is a grasp of the famous English case of Price v. Neal, reprinted below. Students have been telling me for years that the fact situation is too complicated to follow and, as a consequence, Lord Mansfield's opinion is meaningless. The reason for this confusion is that several key facts are unreported in the decision and have to be guessed at before the decision makes sense. To aid you in this endeavor, I have prepared my own interpretation of the facts, which you may compare with those reported in the decision.

The Facts of Price v. Neal. John Price had agreed with one Benjamin Sutton to accept and pay any drafts that Sutton drew on Price; the drafts were called *bills of exchange.* Sutton became involved in business dealings with two other men, Rogers Ruding and Thomas Ploughfor, the upshot of which was that Sutton apparently drew up two drafts on Price payable to Ruding. Both drafts were indorsed by several people before coming into the hands of Edward Neale.[5] The first draft (bill of exchange), for 40 pounds, Neale presented to Price (the drawee) for payment, and Price, via his servant, paid the draft. The second draft, also for 40 pounds, was presented

---

5. We worry about the "e" at the end of Neale's name—it doesn't appear in the case style, and the defendant's name is written both with and without the "e" in the opinion itself.

for acceptance, and Price wrote on it: "Accepted, John Price," adding an order on the back to his bankers, Messieurs Freame and Barclay, telling them to pay the draft for him when it was presented for payment. We are not told who made the presentment of the second draft for acceptance, but after Price had accepted it, the draft was returned to the presenter, who indorsed it over to Neale. The latter obtained payment from Price's bankers. Subsequently, Price learned that Sutton had not really signed the drafts; his name as drawer had been forged to the instruments by a man named Lee. Price brought suit against Neale for "money had and received," demanding a return of the mistaken payments.

Price v. Neal

King's Bench, 1762
3 Burr. 1354, 97 Eng. Rep. 871

This was a special case reserved at the sittings of Guildhall after Trinity term 1762, before Lord Mansfield.

It was an action upon the case brought by Price against Neal; wherein Price declares that the defendant Edward Neale was indebted to him in 80£ for money had and received to his the plaintiff's use: and damages were laid to 100£. The general issue was pleaded; and issue joined thereon.

It was proved at the trial, that a bill was drawn as follows "Leicester, 22d November 1760. Sir, six weeks after date pay Mr. Rogers Ruding or order forty pounds, value received for Mr. Thomas Ploughfor, as advised by, sir, your humble servant Benjamin Sutton. To Mr. John Price in Bush-Lane Cannon-Street, London"; indorsed "R. Ruding, Antony Topham, Hammond and Laroche. Received the contents, James Watson and Son, witness Edward Neale."

That this bill was indorsed to the defendant for a valuable consideration; and notice of the bill left at the plaintiff's house, on the day it became due. Whereupon the plaintiff sent his servant to call on the defendant, to pay him the said sum of 40£, and to take up the said bill: which was done accordingly.

That another bill was drawn as follows—"Leicester, 1st February 1761. Sir, six weeks after date pay Mr. Rogers Ruding or order forty pounds, value received for Mr. Thomas Ploughfor; as advised by, sir, your humble servant Benjamin Sutton. To Mr. John Price in Bush-Lane, Cannon-Street, London." That this bill was indorsed, "R. Ruding, Thomas Watson and Son. Witness for Smith, Right and Co." That the plaintiff accepted this bill, by writing on it, "Accepted John Price:" and that the plaintiff wrote on the back of it—"Messieurs Freame and Barclay, pray pay forty pounds for John Price."

That this bill being so accepted was indorsed to the defendant for a valuable consideration, and left at his bankers for payment; and was paid by order of the plaintiff, and taken up.

Both these bills were forged by one Lee, who has been since hanged for forgery.

The defendant Neale acted innocently and bona fide, without the least privity or suspicion of the said forgeries or of either of them; and paid the whole value of those bills.

The jury found a verdict for the plaintiff; and assessed damages 80£ and costs 40s. subject to the opinion of the Court upon this question—

Whether the plaintiff under the circumstances of the case, can recover back, from the defendant, the money he paid on the said bills, or either of them.

Mr. Stowe, for the plaintiff, argued that he ought to recover back the money, in this action; as it was paid by him by mistake only, on supposition "that these were true genuine bills"; and as he could never recover it against the drawer, because in fact no drawer exists; nor against the forger, because he is hanged.

He owned that in a case at Guild-Hall, of Jenys v. Fawler et al. (an action by an indorsee of a bill of exchange brought against the acceptor), Lord Raymond would not admit the defendants to prove it a forged bill, by calling persons acquainted with the hand of the drawer, to swear "that they believed it not to be so"; and he even strongly inclined, "that actual proof of forgery would not excuse the defendants against their own acceptance, which had given the bill a credit to the indorsee."

But he urged, that in the case now before the Court, the forgery of the bill does not rest in belief and opinion only; but has been actually proved, and the forger executed for it.

Thus it stands even upon the accepted bill. But the plaintiff's case is much stronger upon the other bill which was not accepted. It is not stated "that this bill was accepted before it was negotiated"; on the contrary, the consideration for it was paid by the defendant, before the plaintiff had seen it. So that the defendant took it upon the credit of the indorsers, not upon the credit of the plaintiff; and therefore the reason, upon which Lord Raymond grounds his inclination to be of opinion "that actual proof of forgery would be no excuse," will not hold here.

Mr. Yates, for the defendant, argued that the plaintiff was not entitled to recover back this money from the defendant.

He denied it to be a payment by mistake: and insisted that it was rather owing to the negligence of the plaintiff; who should have inquired and satisfied himself "whether the bill was really drawn upon him by Sutton, or not."

Here is no fraud in the defendant; who is stated "to have acted innocently and bona fide, without the least privity or suspicion of the forgerys and to have paid the whole value for the bills."

Lord Mansfield stopt him from going on; saying that this was one of those cases that could never be made plainer by argument.

It is an action upon the case, for money had and received to the plaintiff's use. In which action, the plaintiff can not recover the money, unless it be against conscience in the defendant, to retain it; and great liberality is always allowed, in this sort of action.

But it can never be thought unconscientious in the defendant to retain this money, when he has once received it upon a bill of exchange indorsed to him for a fair and valuable consideration, which he had bona fide paid, without the least privity or suspicion of any forgery.

Here was no fraud: no wrong. It was incumbent upon the plaintiff, to be satisfied "that the bill drawn upon him was the drawer's hand," before he accepted or paid it: but it was not incumbent upon the defendant, to inquire into it. Here was notice given by the defendant to the plaintiff of a bill drawn upon him: and he sends his servant to pay it and take it up. The other bill, he actually accepts; after which acceptance the defendant innocently and bona fide discounts it. The plaintiff lies by, for a considerable time after he has paid these bills; and then found out "that they were forged" and the forger comes to be hanged. He made no objection to them, at the time of paying them. Whatever neglect there was, was on his side. The defendant had actual encouragement from the plaintiff himself, for negotiating the second bill, from the plaintiff's having without any scruple or hesitation paid the first: and he paid the whole value, bona fide. It is a misfortune which has happened without the defendant's fault or neglect. If there was no neglect in the plaintiff, yet there is no reason to throw off the loss from one innocent man upon another innocent man: but, in this case, if there was any fault or negligence in any one, it certainly was in the plaintiff, and not in the defendant.

Per Cur'. Rule—That the postea be delivered to the defendant.

This, then, is the rule of Price v. Neal: if the drawee pays or accepts the draft, it cannot pass the risk of the drawer's signature being forged off onto prior good faith parties. Moreover, the rule has been expanded by judicial application to place on the drawee the risk of *any* mistaken payment not covered by a presentment warranty, so that, for example, the bank's payment of a check drawn against insufficient funds is a legal fait accompli (but see §4-401(a)). It is interesting to note that the finality rule of Price v. Neal has been unpopular in the courts. See, e.g., Citizens Bank v. Blach & Sons,

228 Ala. 246, 153 So. 404 (1934). It has also been criticized by lawyers such as John R.H. Kimball, an attorney for the Federal Reserve Bank of Boston, *viz*: "The rule of Price v. Neal has, I believe, outlived its rationalizations, particularly with respect to large dollar checks," Check Collection for the 21st Century, 32 U.C.C. L.J. 3, 10 (1998), and by legal commentators, both recent, White & Summers §16-7, at 770 ("We suppose it would have been too much to ask the drafters of revised Article 3 to repeal the ancient doctrine of Price v. Neal and to leave us with but one rule concerning forged signatures"), and in earlier times, Morse, Banks & Banking §464 (6th ed. 1928) ("This doctrine is fading fast into the misty past, where it belongs. It is almost dead, the funeral notices are ready, and no tears will be shed, for it was founded in misconception of the fundamental principles of law and common sense."). Morse's prediction proved too hasty; Price v. Neal is firmly imbedded in the UCC and is apparently alive and well for decades yet to come. The rule is reflected in Article 4's *final payment* statute, §4-302, which makes the payor bank *accountable* for an item that has been finally paid. In Article 3 the key section is §3-418, *a finality* rule, which is said to be a codification of Price v. Neal. Read carefully §3-418 and its Official Comments. Note that §3-418(b) also applies the finality rule to the analogous situation of makers who have paid notes on which their own signatures have been forged.

Ordinarily, the rules of the Uniform Commercial Code do not control the federal government, since the UCC is a state statute. However, as a matter of federal common law, the federal courts, including the United States Supreme Court, have applied the rule of Price v. Neal to checks drawn on the Federal Treasury and paid through the Federal Reserve System. If the government subsequently discovers that the checks are forgeries and not truly signed by the appropriate federal official, the government cannot recover its money from the banks that presented the checks. See extended discussion in ABN Amro Bank v. United States, 34 Fed. Cl. 126, 1995 WL 539779 (1995). For more on the relationship of federal law and check forgery, see pages 395-396.

The policy reasons for the finality rule are unclear. Lord Mansfield at one point in his decision said that the drawee was guilty of "neglect" if he failed by "fault or negligence" to recognize the drawer's signature. But surely if the forgery is very skillful, the "fault," if any, is minimal. Another reason often given is that at some point it is highly desirable to *end* the transaction and have the liabilities of the parties defined and not subject to change. Professor James Rogers has argued that the proper explanation is that the drawee bank is what economists call the "cheapest cost avoider," and that, having created the system the customer must use, the drawee bank must bear its limitations. See James Steven Rogers, The Basic Principle of Loss Allocation for Unauthorized Checks, 39 Wake Forest L. Rev. 453 (2004).

Decibel Credit Union v. Pueblo Bank & Trust Co.

Colorado Court of Appeals, 2000
996 P.2d 784

Opinion by Judge Ruland.

This case requires us to address which party must bear the loss for amounts paid on forged checks. Defendant, Pueblo Bank & Trust Company, appeals from the summary judgment awarded to plaintiff, Decibel Credit Union. We reverse and remand the case for further proceedings.

A thief stole blank checks furnished by Decibel to one of its checking account customers. During a period of approximately 40 days, the thief forged the signature of the customer on a series of 14 checks totaling $2,350. Each of the checks was cashed at Pueblo Bank where the thief had a bank account.

On some of the days during the 40-day period, the thief cashed more than one check per day. At no time during this period did either the thief's checking account or his ready reserve account have sufficient funds to cover the checks that were being cashed.

Pueblo Bank processed all 14 checks through the Federal Reserve System to Decibel, and Decibel timely paid the checks. Decibel's customer discovered the forgeries when he received his bank statement. The customer immediately notified Decibel. Decibel then made demand upon Pueblo Bank for reimbursement. Pueblo Bank declined, and this litigation followed.

After the complaint was filed, both parties filed motions for summary judgment. Based upon those submissions, the trial court entered judgment for Decibel.

First, the trial court concluded that Decibel had given timely notice to Pueblo Bank as soon as the forgery was discovered by its account holder. Next, the trial court determined that in submitting the checks to Decibel for payment, Pueblo Bank had triggered its responsibility under the Colorado version of the Uniform Commercial Code for both presentment and transfer warranties. The court finally determined that a breach of these warranties had occurred and that Decibel was entitled to reimbursement. This appeal followed.

I.

For purposes of the Colorado Uniform Commercial Code, Decibel was the "drawee" bank in these transactions. See §4-3-103(2), C.R.S. 1999. Pueblo Bank was the "presenting bank." See §4-4-105(6). . . .

The parties also agree on most of the legal principles from the Uniform Commercial Code that apply. Generally, a drawee bank is liable to its checking account customer for payment of a check on which the customer's signature has been forged. See §4-3-418, C.R.S. 1999; Travelers Indemnity Company v. Stedman, 895 F. Supp. 742 (E.D. Pa. 1995). Further, when the drawee bank honors the forged instrument, the payment is deemed final for a person who or an entity which takes the instrument in good faith and for value. See Bank of Glen Burnie v. Loyola Federal Savings Bank, 336 Md. 331, 648 A.2d 453 (1994); North Carolina National Bank v. Hammond, 298 N.C. 703, 709, 260 S.E.2d 617, 622 n.1 (1979). . . .

II.

Pueblo Bank asserts that under the circumstances of this case, there were no presentment or transfer warranties made to Decibel and that the trial court erred in ruling to the contrary. We agree.

A.

Presentment warranties in the Colorado version of the Uniform Commercial Code appear in §4-4-208(a), C.R.S. 1999, as follows: [The court quoted §4-208(a).].

As noted in the Official Comment to a similar section, §4-3-417, C.R.S. 1999, the warranty in subsection (a)(1) is only a warranty that there are no unauthorized or missing endorsements on the checks. Further, subsection (a)(2) does not apply because there was no alteration to the checks. Finally, there is no claim that Pueblo Bank had actual knowledge of the forged signatures, and thus subsection (a)(3) does not apply.

Indeed, as the court noted in Payroll Check Cashing v. New Palestine Bank, 401 N.E.2d 752 (Ind. App. 1980), if the warranty that all signatures were genuine applied to a bank in the position of Pueblo Bank, the final payment doctrine contained in §4-3-418 would be meaningless. This doctrine is of great importance in banking commerce because it creates certainty relative to which institution must bear the loss and thus avoids time consuming and expensive litigation. See Travelers Indemnity Company v. Stedman, supra, at 747 n.9.

Accordingly, we hold that Pueblo Bank did not extend any presentment warranty to Decibel by returning the checks to it through the Federal Reserve System. Hence, the trial court erred in concluding that presentment warranties applied for the benefit of Decibel under the circumstances of this case.

B.

The term "transfer" is defined in §4-3-203(a), C.R.S. 1999, as delivery by a party other than the maker of an instrument for the purpose of giving that party the right to enforce the check. And, §4-4-207, C.R.S. 1999, contains

Colorado's version of the transfer warranties of the Uniform Commercial Code. That section provides:

> (a) A customer or collecting bank that transfers an item and receives a settlement or other consideration warrants to the transferee . . . that:
>
> (1) The warrantor is a person entitled to enforce the item;
> (2) All signatures on the item are authentic and authorized;
> (3) The item has not been altered;
> (4) The item is not subject to a defense or claim in recoupment . . . ;
> (5) The warrantor has no knowledge of any insolvency proceeding commenced with respect to the . . . drawer.

Even if we assume that a transfer is involved here, it is well established that a transfer warranty as to the genuineness of the drawer's signature does not apply for the benefit of the drawee bank. See Bank of Glen Burnie v. Loyola Federal Savings Bank, supra, 336 Md. at 344, 648 A.2d at 459 n.6; see also 5 W. Hawkland, J.F. Leary & R. Alderman, Uniform Commercial Code Series §4-207:1 n.6 (1999). Hence, the trial court erred in relying on this section to enter judgment for Decibel.

To the extent that Decibel relies upon Vectra Bank v. Bank Western, 890 P.2d 259 (Colo. App. 1995) as support for the judgment, we conclude that this case does not apply. Consistent with prior interpretations of the Uniform Commercial Code in other jurisdictions, the division in *Vectra* correctly applied the transfer warranties in a case involving forged endorsements. Here, however, the signatures of the maker have been forged. . . .

The judgment is reversed, and the cause is remanded for further proceedings consistent with the views expressed in this opinion.

Judge CASEBOLT and Judge ROY concur.

PROBLEM 125

Harry Villain climbed into the window of Portia Moot's house when she was not home and stole her checkbook. When he was alone in the quiet of his own apartment, Harry wrote out one of her checks to himself and signed her name to the drawer's line. He then cashed the check at the local drugstore, which passed it on to Merchants Bank. Merchants then presented the check to and was paid by Octopus National Bank, the drawee. When Portia got this check back in her next monthly statement, she was very upset. She immediately demanded that the bank replace the money in her account, saying the check was not properly payable without her valid signature; §4-401(a). The bank recredited her account and then called you, its attorney. Who can it sue and under what theory? See §§4-208(a) and 3-418; Bank of America, N.A. v. Amarillo Natl. Bank, 156 S.W.3d 108 (Tex. App. 2004)

Wachovia Bank, N.A. v. Foster Bancshares, Inc.

United States Court of Appeals, Seventh Circuit, 2006
457 F.3d 619

POSNER, Circuit Judge.

This diversity suit pits two banks (for unexplained reasons, the defendant bank's parent was also joined as a defendant) against each other in a quarrel over liability for a forged or altered check.

A customer of Foster Bank named Choi deposited in her account a check for $133,026 that listed her as the payee. The check had been drawn on Wachovia Bank by a company called MediaEdge that had an account with that bank. Foster presented the check to Wachovia for payment. Wachovia paid Foster and debited MediaEdge's account. Now as it happened the actual payee of the check as originally issued had not been Choi; it had been a company called CMP Media. When CMP Media told MediaEdge that it had not received the check, an investigation ensued and revealed that Choi had somehow gotten her name substituted for CMP Media on the check she'd deposited with Foster. By the time this was discovered, Choi had withdrawn the money from her account and vanished, while Wachovia had destroyed the paper check that Foster had presented to it for payment. It had done this pursuant to its normal practice, the lawfulness of which is not questioned. It had retained a computer image of the check, but whether the image is of the original check drawn on Wachovia, with an alteration, or a forged check, cannot be determined.

MediaEdge sued Wachovia in New York for the amount of the check. That suit has been stayed pending the outcome of the present suit, in which Wachovia seeks a declaratory judgment that Foster must indemnify it in the event that MediaEdge obtains a favorable judgment in the New York suit. Wachovia's suit is based on the Uniform Commercial Code's "presentment warranty": when a depositary bank, Foster in this case, presents a check for payment by the bank that issued the check, it warrants that the check "has not been altered." UCC §§3-417(a) 1-2, 4-208(a) 1-2; Clean World Engineering, Ltd. v. MidAmerica Bank, FSB, 341 Ill. App. 3d 992, 275 Ill. Dec. 630, 793 N.E.2d 110, 117-18 (2003); Wachovia Bank, N.A. v. FRB, 338 F.3d 318, 321-22 (4th Cir. 2003). The district court granted summary judgment for Wachovia. Foster had impleaded Choi as a third-party defendant but could not serve her because of her disappearance, so the district court dismissed the third-party claim. Foster does not challenge that ruling. . . .

The bank argues that Wachovia, because it cannot produce the paper check, cannot prove that the check was altered. For all we know, rather than the check being "altered" in the usual sense, Choi used sophisticated copying technology to produce a copy that was identical in every respect to the original check (including the authorized signature by MediaEdge's chief financial officer) except for an undetectable change of the payee's name. Had the original paper check not been destroyed, it could be examined and the examination might reveal whether the check had been forged as just described or the payee's name had been changed by chemical washing of the check or by some other method that utilized rather than replaced the original check.

The bank on which a check is drawn (Wachovia in this case) warrants to the presenting bank that the check is genuine, UCC §3-418(c); id., Official Comment 1; Henry J. Bailey & Richard B. Hagedorn, Brady on Bank Checks §28.11[1] (2006), hence not forged,[6] while as we know the presenting bank warrants that the check hasn't been altered since its issuance. When checks were inspected by hand, when copying technology was primitive, and when cancelled checks were stored rather than digitized copies alone retained, this allocation of liability was consistent with the sensible economic principle that the duty to avoid a loss should be placed on the party that can prevent the loss at lower cost. Holtz v. J.J.B. Hilliard W.L. Lyons, Inc., 185 F.3d 732, 743 (7th Cir. 1999); Edwards v. Honeywell, Inc., 50 F.3d 484, 490 (7th Cir. 1995); National Union Fire Ins. Co. v. Riggs Nat'l Bank, 5 F.3d 554, 557 (D.C. Cir. 1993) (concurring opinion). Having no dealings with MediaEdge, Foster could not determine at reasonable cost whether, for example, the drawer's signature had been forged. Wachovia might be able to determine this by comparing the signature on the check presented to it for payment with the authorized signature in its files. But Wachovia would have no idea who the intended payee was, while Foster might have reason to suspect that the person who deposited the check with it was not the intended payee. And it would be in as good a position as Wachovia to spot an alteration on the check.

But this last point assumes that a payee's name would be altered in the old-fashioned way, by whiting out or otherwise physically effacing the name on the paper check. If Choi created a new check, there would be no physical alteration to alert Foster when she deposited the check with the bank. That is why Foster complains that Wachovia's failure to retain the paper check prevents determining how the "alteration" was effected—more precisely,

---

6. [This is badly phrased by the court. There is no warranty involved. What the court means is that once a drawee bank has paid a check on which the drawer's name is forged, it cannot return it. That is the rule of Price v. Neal, of course, and as to that the court is correct.—EDS.]

whether it is a case of alteration or of forgery. The fact that MediaEdge acknowledges having issued a check to CMP Media is not conclusive on the question because Choi might have destroyed that check, rather than altering it, and substituted a copy that seemed perfectly genuine, with her name in place of CMP Media.

So the case comes down to whether, in cases of doubt, forgery should be assumed or alteration should be assumed. If the former, Foster wins, and if the latter, Wachovia. It seems to us that the tie should go to the drawee bank, Wachovia. Changing the payee's name is the classic alteration. It can with modern technology be effected by forging a check rather than by altering an original check, but since this is a novel method, the presenting bank must do more than merely assert the possibility of it. Granted, it is the duty of the drawee bank to take reasonable measures to prevent the forging of its checks, as by marking them in a way that a forger could not discover and therefore duplicate. But Foster has made no effort to show that retention of mountains of paper checks—which would be necessary to determine whether the original check had such a marking—would be a reasonable method of determining whether the drawee bank or the presenting bank should be liable for the loss.

Nor did Foster make any effort to show—as it might have been able to do, see Henry Bailey & Richard Hagedorn, supra, §28.3—that duplication of the entire check (that is, forgery of the check deposited with the presenting bank), rather than just physical alteration of the payee's name on the original check, has become a common method of bank fraud. Nor did it try to show that banks have, as they are allowed to do, been contracting around the provisions of the UCC relating to the warranties of drawee and presenting banks in cases such as this. Nor did it try to show what Choi's modus operandi was, assuming that she had stolen money in this way on other occasions, though such evidence may of course have been unobtainable.

Even if Foster had shown that forgery of the entire check has become a routine method of altering the payee's name, we would not adopt the rule for which it contends, which is that the drawee bank cannot enforce the presentment warranty unless it retains the paper check. The question of which bank was, in the language of economic analysis of law, the "cheaper cost avoider" would still be open. (Maybe neither bank is—which would hardly be a persuasive ground for changing a long-settled rule of law.) A depositary bank can sometimes discover an alteration of the payee's name even when there is no physical alteration in the check presented to the bank for deposit. The size of the check may be a warning flag that induces the bank to delay making funds deposited by the check available for withdrawal. E.g., Bank of America, "Frequently Asked Questions," http://www.bankofamerica.com/deposits/checksave/index.cfm?template=lc_faq_acct_info (visited July 5, 2006); Kennebunk Savings Bank, "Deposit Account Agreement,"

http://www.kennebunksavings.com/depositagreement.html, (visited July 5, 2006). The check that Choi deposited with Foster was for a hefty $133,000, and there is no evidence that Choi had previously deposited large checks. We do not suggest that Foster was careless in deciding to make the money available for withdrawal when it did. But the uncertainties that the bank has made no effort to dispel counsel against adopting the legal change that it urges. Reform if needed in the light of modern copying technology should be left to the Uniform State Commissioners rather than engineered by a federal court in a diversity case. The judgment for Wachovia is therefore
Affirmed.

QUESTION

The court seems to think that the only problem with this check was the possible "alteration" of the payee's name, so that if there had been no "alteration," the drawee bank would have lost the case. What happened to the presentment warranty in §4-208(a)(1), and why wasn't it discussed by Judge Posner?

For years one of your authors (Whaley) wandered around the country lecturing bankers on the law of checking accounts. It amazed him that banking usage of trade ignores the rule of Price v. Neal. Over and over he was told by bankers that when the payor bank, having made final payment and then discovering the drawer's name was forged, demands repayment from the depositary bank, the latter simply coughs up the money. "We always do it that way," the banks explained. "Stop that!" Whaley would reply. "You have no right to give away your customer's money without authority, and the next time a payor bank demands its money back, ask it to specify the legal theory for its recovery." That will end that.

PROBLEM 126

In the last Problem, ONB, unhappy with being told that the depositary bank did not violate §4-208(a)(3), now asks you if the depositary bank violated §4-208(a)(1). Did it?

The answer is no, but it is a rather complicated no. Start by reading §3-403. Subsection (a) contains the basic idea that the forgery acts as if the forger had signed his or her *own* name instead of the name forged. Were that true in the above Problems, Harry Villain would be the true drawer of this check. In that case, we would have a check drawn by Harry Villain, payable to the order of Harry Villain, properly indorsed by the payee, and then properly negotiated by the drugstore and the depositary bank. The depository bank *was* a "person entitled to enforce the draft" of Harry Villain. In effect, the payor bank here paid the draft of a non-customer payee. That isn't the draft they thought they were paying, but the rule of Price v. Neal puts that risk squarely on the drawee; there was nothing wrong with the negotiation. The age-old saying is that "the drawee must know the drawer's signature as a mother must know her child," and making a mistake on this cannot pass the loss back to innocent parties.

PROBLEM 127

In Problem 81 of the last chapter a drawee bank paid a check with no drawer's signature at all because the check had been created over the telephone by the telemarketing payee. When we did this Problem the last time, the relevant question was whether the check was properly payable from the drawer's bank account under §4-401 (the "properly payable" rule), and the answer (as yet unaddressed by the courts) is highly likely to be "no." Thus the drawee bank must replace the money in the drawer's account (unless the subrogation rule of §4-407 can be brought into play to protect the bank). Having done so, the bank now calls you, its attorney. It wants to pass the liability back to the depository bank. Can this be done, and, if so, under what theory?

The answer to this question is complicated by that fact that the original rules of law would place the liability here on the drawee bank as an extension of the rule of Price v. Neal: the bank has made a mistaken payment from its customer's account and must eat the loss unless the telemarketing payee can be found and made to cough up the money; see §3-418 for the cause of action against the payee here. The trouble with this result is that it is contrary to banking practices. Unaware of the rules of law, the drawee banks in this situation routinely return the preauthorized draft to the depository bank, which debits the account of the telemarketing payee. The drafters of the UCC in 2002 proposed amendments to the presentment warranty sections that would allow the drawee bank to return what the Code now calls a "remotely-created consumer item" to the depository bank — see §4-208(a)(4) — but these amendments have only been adopted in about 12 states as of this writing.

The Federal Reserve has now solved the problem in all U.S. jurisdictions. Effective July 1, 2006, the Fed adopted amendments to Regulation CC, 12 C.F.R. Part 229. The Regulation calls these items "remotely created checks" [Reg. CC §229.2(fff)], and creates both presentment and transfer warranties that these checks were authorized by the person on whose account they are drawn in the amount specified. This allows the return of the check to the depository bank, which is thought to be in a better position to monitor the activities of the payee than is the payor bank. See Reg. CC §229.34(d).[7]

Federal Government.   The Uniform Commercial Code is a state statute and does not, of course, bind the federal government. However, as a matter of federal common law (inherited from Great Britain) the federal courts, including the United States Supreme Court, have applied the rule of Price v. Neal to checks drawn on the Federal Treasury and thereafter paid. If the government subsequently discovers that the checks are forgeries and not truly signed by the appropriate federal official, the government cannot recover its money from the banks that presented the checks. See extended discussion in ABN Amro Bank v. United States, 34 Fed. Cl. 126, 1995 WL 539779 (1995).

What steps do banks take to protect themselves from the vicious bite of Price v. Neal? In an era of check truncation and electronic presentment, many payor banks don't recapture their drawers' checks and have no opportunity to compare drawers' signatures with the signature cards (though as Check 21 imaging becomes more prevalent, the banks would be able to check the customer's signature, though most will not for economic reasons). Most banks engage in a practice called "bulk filing," in which the banks don't physically examine the checks at all if they are below a certain amount but simply file them away in bulk. If a check proves forged and the forger cannot be found, these banks recredit the drawers' accounts and look to their forgery insurance.

QUESTION

If the drawer's signature is forged, but the bank pays the check anyway, the rule of Price v. Neal puts the loss on the payor bank. However, if the payee's name is forged, the loss tends to fall on the depositary bank. Are these results merely whimsical, or is there a rational reason for the two different placements of liability? In his book The End of Negotiable Instruments (2011), Professor James Rogers concludes that forgery rules placing responsibility on the banks themselves offer the optimum solution. Banks are best able to guard against or absorb the loss (if not able to pass it off to the wrongdoer), as opposed to innocent parties outside the banking system, such as the person whose name was forged.

---

7. It should also be noted that the Federal Trade Commission's Telemarketing Sales Rule, 16 C.F.R. §310.3(a)(3) already requires telemarketers to obtain the customer's "express verifiable authorization" before issuing the check. One can speculate how often this is actually done.

III. VALIDATION OF THE FORGERY

Both Price v. Neal and the rule that the forged indorsement is ineffective to negotiate the instrument put a heavy burden on the drawee bank, which must frequently bear the forgery loss (or insure against it). To militate against the harshness of these rules, the basic forgery rule, §3-403(a), has an escape clause in the words "Unless otherwise provided in this Article or Article 4" and "an unauthorized signature may be ratified." This means that under some circumstances the forged signature will be treated as genuine. What are these circumstances that validate a forgery?

Ratification, a doctrine coming to us from agency law, for negotiable instrument purposes occurs when the party in question, with full knowledge of the forgery or alteration, accepts the benefits thereof or actively assents to the wrongful activity. See Rakestraw v. Rodrigues, 8 Cal. 3d 67, 500 P.2d 1401, 104 Cal. Rptr. 57 (1972); cf. Salsman v. National Community Bank, 102 N.J. Super. 482, 246 A.2d 162 (1968), *aff'd*, 105 N.J. Super. 164, 251 A.2d 460 (1969); Bank of Hoven v. Rausch, 382 N.W.2d 39 (S.D. 1986).

PROBLEM 128

George learned that his wife, Martha, had been forging his name to business checks received in his business on which he was the named payee. Except for this peccadillo, she was a model wife, and it was a good marriage, so he said nothing rather than embarrass her. Two years later his extramarital affair caused a divorce, so he decided to recover the money by bringing a conversion action against the banks that had paid money on the forged indorsements. Will his suit succeed? See Johnson v. Johnson, 2005 WL 3276177 (N.J. Super. 2005).

Ratification of supposed agency status can also occur, as where the non-agent has apparent authority due to the alleged principal's actions or inactions. See §3-402(a) and its Official Comment 1; Fulka v. Florida Commercial Banks, Inc., 371 So. 2d 521 (Fla. Dist. App. 1979) (payee estopped to bring conversion action where she knew a business associate was forging her name to checks, but kept silent); Annot., 82 A.L.R.3d 625. The major UCC case is Senate Motors, Inc. v. Industrial Bank of Washington, 1971 WL 17944 (D.C. Super. 1971). For pre-Code cases finding apparent authority in an agent to cash the alleged principal's checks, see Corbett v. Kleinsmith, 112 F.2d 511 (6th Cir. 1940); Commercial Cas. Ins. Co. v. Isabell Natl. Bank, 223 Ala. 48, 134 So. 810 (1931); Arcade Realty Co. v. Bank of Commerce, 180 Cal. 318, 181 P. 66 (1919); Rosser-Moon Furn. Co. v. Oklahoma State Bank, 192 Okla.

169, 135 P.2d 336 (1943). It is important to appreciate that the courts are slow to presume such authority. See, e.g., Taylor v. Equitable Trust Co., 269 Md. 149, 304 A.2d 838 (1973).

A.   Common Law Validation

Hutzler v. Hertz Corp.

Court of Appeals of New York, 1976
39 N.Y.2d 209, 347 N.E.2d 627, 383 N.Y.S.2d 266

JASEN, J.

In this action against defendant tortfeasor arising out of the compromise of a personal injury and wrongful death claim made with the tortfeasor by plaintiff's attorney with the consent of the plaintiff, we are asked to decide whether defendant tortfeasor was discharged from liability where its settlement draft, naming plaintiff and her attorney as payees, was negotiated by the attorney on plaintiff's forged indorsement and the proceeds of the draft appropriated. For the reasons which follow, we hold that the tortfeasor's liability was discharged upon payment of the settlement draft by the drawee bank, the forgery notwithstanding, and that the claimant may not thereafter recover against the tortfeasor.

The parties are in agreement as to the basic facts. On June 1, 1966, Christina Hutzler was granted limited letters of administration by the Surrogate of Queens County on the estate of her husband who had perished on October 4, 1965, in an automobile accident. Through her attorney, Daniel D. Yudow, she commenced an action against Hertz Corporation to recover damages for the personal injuries and wrongful death of her husband. After some time Yudow succeeded in settling the action with Hertz and on November 23, 1970, in consideration of that settlement, Mrs. Hutzler, after obtaining permission of the Surrogate's Court to compromise the action, executed a general release in Hertz' favor. On December 11, 1970, Hertz issued and mailed to Yudow two checks totalling $11,500, the amount of the settlement, both of which were drawn on the Manufacturers Hanover Trust Company. One of these with which we are not concerned, was in the sum of $571, made payable to "The State Insurance Fund c/o Daniel D. Yudow." The second check was for $10,929, the balance of the settlement, and was payable to "Christina Hutzler Individually And As Administratrix of the Estate of Michael E. Hutzler and Daniel D. Yudow as attorney." On December 14, 1970, Yudow, having indorsed this check with his own signature and with the forged signature of Mrs. Hutzler, deposited it in an account in his name at Manufacturers Hanover. Four months later, in April 1971, he closed the account. In the meantime, Mrs. Hutzler attempted to obtain her share of the proceeds of the settlement, but was unsuccessful in locating Yudow until June, 1973. In the interim she learned that he had closed his office and was no longer in practice.[8] Thereafter she retained her present counsel who made oral and written demand for payment on Hertz in June, 1973. Hertz produced a copy of its settlement draft and refused payment. Upon examination of the indorsements, the forgery was at once apparent to Mrs. Hutzler, and both Hertz and Manufacturers Hanover were immediately apprised of this fact. Since no satisfactory resolution could be made, Mrs. Hutzler, a short time later, commenced this action against Hertz and Manufacturers Hanover to recover the amount of the settlement check. She alleged one cause of action against Hertz for negligence in not comparing the forged signature with her signature on the settlement agreement, and two causes of action against Manufacturers Hanover, one for conversion of the check and its proceeds and the other for breach of warranty.

On cross-motions for summary judgment, Special Term granted Mrs. Hutzler judgment against Hertz for the amount of the check, and denied Hertz' motion for summary judgment. Summary judgment was also granted to the defendant bank on which the check was drawn, but no appeal was taken by the plaintiff from this part of the judgment and order. On Hertz' appeal, a divided Appellate Division modified the judgment and order "by adding to each of them a provision that the amount of plaintiff's recovery against defendant The Hertz Corporation be reduced by the amount of the lien that attorney Yudow, had he not engaged in misconduct with respect to the settlement check, and not converted the proceeds thereof, would have been entitled to for professional services," and remitted the case for a determination of the amount of that lien. (47 A.D.2d 839.) Special Term thereupon determined the amount of the lien, and amended its earlier judgment accordingly. Hertz now appeals directly, as of right, from this amended judgment, bringing up for review with it the prior non-final order of the Appellate Division. (C.P.L.R. 5601, subd. [d].) Mrs. Hutzler cross appeals, also as of right (C.P.L.R. 5601, subd. [a], par. [iii]), claiming that the Appellate Division erred in reducing the amount of her judgment by the amount of her former attorney's lien for services rendered.

At the outset, we note that the courts of other jurisdictions have divided on the question now before us and it seems as though no majority rule can

---

8. We are informed that the records of the First Department indicate that Yudow's name was stricken from the Roll of Attorneys and Counselors-at-Law, on consent, on March 22, 1972.

be stated. (See generally Annot., Forgery by Debtor's Agent Discharge, 49 A.L.R.3d 843, 846.) Indeed, the cases of this state have been characterized as representing in microcosm this division of authority, with no definitive statement of our rule possible. (Id., at pp.847, 859.)

As we view this case, we are concerned with two separate sets of legal relationships. The first involves a plaintiff and a tortfeasor, and the tortfeasor's payment to the plaintiff's attorney in settlement of the tort action. Reference must be made to principles of agency law in analyzing the rights and duties which arise from this set of relationships. The second concerns the relationships created when payment is made by a negotiable instrument. The rights and duties growing out of this set of relationships evolve from the law of negotiable instruments embodied principally in the Uniform Commercial Code. Only by keeping in mind that we are dealing with two separate bodies of law can we properly resolve this controversy.

We start with agency considerations. An attorney retained to collect a debt, or as here, to recover damages for personal injuries and wrongful death, normally also has at least apparent authority to receive payment from the debtor or tortfeasor once a settlement has been reached or a judgment entered. (McCoy v. Barclay, 250 App. Div. 682, 684; Moss v. Standard Brands, 68 Misc. 2d 625, 627; 2 Mechem, Agency 2180, p.1762.) This is clearly the rule, at least where payment is in cash. (See 7 Am. Jur. 2d, Attorneys at Law 102; 7 C.J.S., Attorney and Client 106, subd. c.) Having made such a payment to the creditor's or claimant's attorney, the debtor or tortfeasor can be assured that he has been discharged from liability. If the attorney absconds with the cash without paying it over to his client, the client may not thereafter compel the debtor or tortfeasor to pay a second time. (See Morrison v. Chapman, 155 App. Div. 509, 514; Burstein v. Sullivan, 134 App. Div. 623, 625.) He must instead look to the defalcating attorney.

An analogous situation develops where payment is made to the attorney for a claimant by means of a check made payable solely to the attorney. Payment by check, sometimes referred to as "conditional payment," is not, by itself, payment of the underlying obligation. (Chatham Securities Corp. v. Williston & Beane, 41 Misc. 2d 817, 821, *aff'd*, 22 A.D.2d 260, *aff'd without op.*, 16 N.Y.2d 1016; Mansion Carpets v. Marinoff, 24 A.D.2d 947; Uniform Commercial Code §3-802, Official Comment 3 [now §3-310(b) — Ed.].) Only when the drawee bank pays on the check is payment actually effected. Thus, once the drawee bank has paid on the check the debtor or tortfeasor is discharged from the underlying obligation as fully as though he had paid the attorney cash. As where payment is in cash, if the agent appropriates the proceeds of a check for himself, the claimant may not seek repayment from the debtor or tortfeasor.

The situation becomes somewhat more complicated where the check is made payable only to the creditor or claimant, or, as here, to the claimant and attorney jointly. It is at this juncture that the agency principles just described and certain principles of the law of negotiable instruments would seem to come into conflict. Indeed, Mrs. Hutzler argues that the forged indorsement by Yudow was "wholly inoperative as that of the person [Mrs. Hutzler] whose name is signed" (Uniform Commercial Code §3-404 subd. (1)) and that Hertz' liability was therefore not discharged by its settlement draft. This argument, if accepted, would require Hertz to pay a second time.

Long ago the rule developed in this state that debtor's liability is discharged when a check payable to the creditor is wrongfully indorsed by the creditor's agent and is paid by the drawee bank, and the proceeds converted by the agent. (Sage v. Burton, 84 Hun. 267; Allen v. Tarrant & Co., 7 App. Div. 172; Morris v. Hofferberth, 81 App. Div. 512, *aff'd*, 180 N.Y. 545.) The basis for this rule is that the drawer's only obligation to the payee, upon issuance of the check, is to "see that funds are in the bank." (Sage v. Burton, supra, at p. 270.) The drawer thereafter has no obligation to examine the check for forged indorsements. (See National Surety Co. v. Manhattan Co., 252 N.Y. 247, 254.) Since checks and drafts are the usual and ordinary means of transferring money in the transaction of business, a contrary rule would add an unnecessary element of risk and uncertainty where payment is made by check to an authorized agent. Because of the time factors involved in processing a check through the depositary bank, intermediate collecting banks and the drawee bank, the discovery of the forgery by the drawer, even if possible, would often be of little practical value to the payee. Moreover, as indicated above, if a check is payable solely to the agent, there is no question that the obligation would be discharged upon payment by the drawee bank. By making the check payable to the creditor, the drawer has given the creditor a measure of protection by requiring the agent to expose himself to criminal prosecution by forging an indorsement before converting the proceeds. (See Burstein v. Sullivan, 134 App. Div. 623, 625, supra.) Therefore, as between the creditor and the drawer of the check, the party who should be required to bear the loss under such circumstances is the creditor. It is the creditor, after all, who selected a dishonest person to represent him, and he, not the drawer, should bear the risk of his unauthorized acts, having placed him in a position to perpetrate the wrong. (Sage v. Burton, 84 Hun. 267, 270, supra, Morrison v. Chapman, 155 App. Div. 509, 512, 514, supra.) The fact that the agent acted in excess of his authority in forging the indorsement is, of course, no more helpful to the creditor than is the fact that the agent who absconds with a cash payment also acts in excess of his authority. (Morrison v. Chapman, supra, at p. 514.) . . .

We note that this resolution squares with the position taken by the American Law Institute in the Restatement Second of Agency.[9] We expressly approve of that provision and hold that it correctly states the law of this state.

Returning to considerations of the law of negotiable instruments, we conclude that our holding today, in the context of the kind of relationship involved, is consistent with §3-404 of the Uniform Commercial Code [now §3-403(a) — Eds.], despite the apparent conflict noted earlier. Subdivision (1) of that section provides in part that "[a]ny unauthorized signature is wholly inoperative as that of the person whose name is signed unless he ratifies it or is precluded from denying it. . . ." Since our resolution of the issue before us is based primarily upon the principles of agency, we would hold that a person whose name is forged on an instrument by his agent is, by his unwise selection of this agent, estopped or "precluded from denying" the unauthorized signature.

Finally, we note that this rule is not unduly harsh on a person who has been defrauded in this manner by a dishonest agent. To be sure, the unfaithful agent is an unpromising defendant, and often there is little likelihood of recovering from him. However, generally the creditor could pursue an action for conversion against the drawee bank. (Henderson v. Lincoln Rochester Trust Co., 303 N.Y. 27, 31; Spaulding v. First Natl. Bank, 210 App. Div. 216, 217, *aff'd without op.,* 239 N.Y. 586; Uniform Commercial Code §3-419, subd. [1], par. [c] [now §3-420(a) — Eds.].) Unfortunately, that rule does little for the plaintiff in this case as no appeal was taken from the order dismissing her conversion action against Manufacturers Hanover. Our compassion for the plaintiff cannot, however, serve as a basis for granting her relief against Hertz.

Accordingly, the amended judgment should be reversed and Hertz' motion for summary judgment granted and the complaint dismissed.

---

9. The relevant section is as follows

§178. Agent Authorized to Collect a Debt . . .
(2) If an agent who is authorized to receive a check payable to the principal as conditional payment forges the principal's endorsement to such a check, the maker is relieved of liability to the principal if the drawee bank pays the check and charges the amount to the maker.

This subsection is discussed in Comment c:

If a debtor, having an account at a solvent bank sufficient to pay a check, gives to an authorized agent a check payable to the principal in accordance with business customs as conditional payment, he has performed his obligation, and any loss caused by delay because of the conduct of the agent is at the creditor's risk. Thus, if the drawee bank cashes the check after a forgery and embezzlement by the agent and charges the amount to the debtor, the latter is relieved of his debt. The creditor then would be subrogated to the right of the debtor against the bank. If, in the meantime, the bank becomes insolvent, it is the creditor and not the debtor who loses.

Judgment reversed, without costs, the motion by defendant The Hertz Corporation for summary judgment granted and the complaint dismissed. All concur.

QUESTION

Could the plaintiff sue the drawee bank? What would be her cause of action? See §3-420(a); Florida Bar v. Allstate Ins. Co., 391 So. 2d 238 (Fla. Dist. App. 1980).

PROBLEM 129

Donna Drawer gave her check to Paul Payee, who lost it before he indorsed it. The finder was an evil person, identity unknown, who forged "Paul Payee" to the back of the check and received payment from the drawee, Octopus National Bank (ONB). Is ONB liable to Paul Payee? See §3-420(a). If ONB pays Paul, is it also liable to Donna? See §§4-401, 4-407.

The common law handled this double liability problem by saying that it is always a defense to a negotiable instruments action to show that the money got where it was supposed to go, and, thus, the plaintiff has no damages. See Ambassador Fin. Serv., Inc. v. Indiana National Bank, 605 N.E.2d 746 (Ind. 1992); Tonelli v. Chase Manhattan Bank, N.A., 41 N.Y.2d 667, 363 N.E.2d 564, 394 N.Y.S.2d 858 (1977); Middle States Leasing Corp. v. Manufacturers Hanover Trust Co., 62 A.D.2d 273, 404 N.Y.S.2d 846 (1978). Whether approached under this idea or under §4-407's subrogation rule, the result is the same: a successful conversion action by the payee destroys the drawer's §4-401 not *properly payable* suit against the drawee.

The four Uniform Commercial Code sections that validate the wrongdoing in certain circumstances are §3-404 (the Impostor Rule), §3-405 (the Employee Forgery Rule), §3-406 (the Negligence Rule), and §4-406 (the Bank Statement Rule). They come up next, one by one.

B.   *The Impostor Rule*

An "impostor"[10] is someone pretending to be someone else. The Impostor Rule in the Uniform Commercial Code validates the forgery of

---

10. The word *impostor* is undergoing a spelling change. Originally, it was almost always spelled with an "or" at the end, but in recent years "er" seems to have won the day. Either spelling is now considered correct.

the *payee's* name (and only the payee's name) in the situations described in §3-404. In each of these situations, the drawer or maker has been duped by either an outsider or a trusted employee into creating an instrument on which the name of the payee is highly likely to be forged, and it is proper to put the resulting liability on the drawer/maker rather than on non-negligent parties, such as the indorsers or banks involved in collecting or paying the checks.

PROBLEM 130

Old and rich Amy Altruism was well known for her charitable contributions. One day, she answered her door to find Sandra Sting, a woman whose photograph was at that moment decorating the post offices of the country, standing on the front stoop. Sandra told Amy that she was Hilda Humane, the founder of Humane's Home for Homeless Dogs, Inc., and that she wished to solicit a contribution for this worthy cause, which she described in much detail. Amy was taken in by this story, and while weeping copiously over the plight of the canine element of the world, she wrote a check for $5,000 payable to "Hilda Humane." Sandra pocketed the check, thanked her warmly, and left her quickly. She went straight to the drawee bank where, after signing "Hilda Humane" to the back of the check, she received payment. If Amy discovers that there is no such thing as Humane's Home for Homeless Dogs, Inc., can she successfully demand that her account be recredited on the theory that the check was cashed on an improper signature (not "properly payable")? See §3-404(a).

PROBLEM 131

Mrs. Walter Heartstrong wrote the Methuselah Life Insurance Company telling them, "I want to discontinue my life insurance policy. Please cancel it and mail me the cash surrender value. I hereby certify that I have lost the policy (#112-011Z) itself or misplaced it somewhere, (signed) Walter Heartstrong." The company mailed a check to the order of "Walter Heartstrong." Mrs. Heartstrong got to the mailbox before her husband did, obtained the check, forged her husband's name on the back, and deposited the check at the Smalltown State Bank. The latter presented it to the drawee, Octopus National, which cashed it without a murmur. When Walter sues the insurance company and they call you, what would you advise? See Hicks v. Northwestern Mut. Life Ins. Co., 166 Iowa 532, 147 N.W. 883 (1914); cf. Franklin Natl. Bank v. Shapiro, 1970 WL 12588 (N.Y. Sup. Ct. 1970).

To understand §3-404(b) you need to conquer the concept of the "person whose intent determines to whom an instrument is payable" in §3-110(a) and (b). Generally, it means the person who signed the instrument, though for check-writing machines it means the person who supplied the name of the payee, whether or not authorized to do so. Apply §3-404(b) to the following Problem.

PROBLEM 132

One day it occurred to the corporate treasurer of the Business Corporation that his personal situation would be easier if he started adding fictitious employees to the payroll and took their checks each month for deposit into accounts opened under the phony names. Are such checks properly payable from the account Business Corporation has with its bank? See §3-404(b). Would the result be different if the treasurer padded the payroll with the names of real former employees and then did the same thing with these checks? If the depositary banks that took these checks were negligent in allowing the treasurer to open the accounts, would that change the result? See §3-404(d).[11]

State Sec. Check Cashing, Inc. v. American General Financial

Court of Appeals of Maryland, 2009
409 Md. 81, 972 A.2d 882

HARRELL, Judge.

In this case we are asked to determine which party, as between the issuer of a check and the check cashing business that cashed it, is liable under Md. Code, Commercial Law Art. §3-404 (2002 Repl. Vol. & Supp. 2008) for the face amount of the check, when an imposter, posing successfully as another individual in securing a loan (the proceeds of which were represented by the check) from the issuer, subsequently negotiated the check at the check cashing business. We shall hold that, under the circumstances presented in this case, the issuer of the check is liable for the amount of the check.

I. FACTUAL AND PROCEDURAL BACKGROUND

On 20 June 2007, American General Financial Services, Inc., ("American General") was contacted by telephone by a man, later revealed to be an imposter posing as Ronald E. Wilder (we shall refer to this person as the

---

11. There are similar comparative fault sections in each of the validation sections; see §§3-405(b), 3-406(b), and 4-406(e).

"imposter," though he was not known to be so at most relevant times in this case). The imposter sought a $20,000.00 loan. Based on the information supplied by him over the telephone, American General ran a credit check on Ronald E. Wilder, finding his credit to be excellent. American General informed the imposter that it would need personal tax returns for the prior two years, and asked him what he intended to do with the proceeds of the desired loan. The imposter sent by electronic facsimile to American General the requested tax returns of Mr. Wilder and explained that he wanted the loan to renovate a property he owned. On Friday, 22 June 2007, American General's District Manager received the completed loan application and tax returns, performed a cash flow analysis, and obtained approval from senior management for an $18,000.00 loan.

On that same morning, American General informed the imposter that the loan was approved. The imposter appeared at noon at American General's Security Boulevard office in Baltimore County. He proffered an apparent Maryland driver's license bearing Mr. Wilder's personal information and the imposter's photograph. He remained in the loan office for approximately thirty minutes, meeting with the branch manager and a customer account specialist during the loan closing. After all the loan documents were signed, American General issued to the imposter a loan check for $18,000.00, drawn on Wachovia Bank, N.A., and payable to Ronald E. Wilder.

Later that afternoon, the imposter presented the check to State Security Check Cashing, Inc. ("State Security"), a check cashing business. At the time the imposter appeared in State Security's office, also on Security Boulevard in Baltimore County, only one employee was on duty, Wanda Decker. Decker considered the same driver's license that the imposter presented to American General, and reviewed the American General loan documents related to the check. She also compared the check to other checks issued by American General which had been cashed previously by State Security. Deeming the amount of the check relatively "large," Decker called Joel Deutsch, State Security's compliance officer, to confirm that she had taken the proper steps in verifying the check. Deutsch directed Decker to verify the date of the check, the name of the payee on the check, the address of the licensee, the supporting loan paperwork, and whether the check matched other checks in State Security's system from the issuer. Decker confirmed the results of all of these steps, and, upon Deutsch's approval, cashed the check, on behalf of State Security, for the imposter for a fee of 3-5% of the face value of the check.

On Monday, 25 June, the next business day after the imposter negotiated the check at State Security, the real Ronald E. Wilder appeared at the offices of American General indicating that he had been notified by the U.S.

Secret Service that a person applied for a loan in his name. At that time, the true Ronald E. Wilder completed an Affidavit of Forgery. As a result of the Affidavit, Thurman Toland, the Branch Manager of American General's Security Boulevard branch, called Wachovia Bank to determine whether the $18,000.00 check had been presented for payment. Learning that the check had not been presented yet, Toland placed a "stop payment" on the check.

State Security filed a civil claim in the District Court of Maryland, sitting in Baltimore County, against American General for the face value of the check, plus interest, asserting that it was a holder in due course of American General's check, that it received the check in good faith, without knowledge of fraud, and that it gave value for the check. On 3 December 2007, the District Court conducted a bench trial. During the trial, the testimonies of Deutsch and Toland revealed three additional, potentially important points: (a) had State Security personnel called American General on 22 June 2007 to verify that American General issued a check to Ronald E. Wilder for $18,000.00, Toland would have confirmed that to be the case; (b) State Security employed a thumb print identification system for its check-cashing business, but, at the time the imposter cashed the check, it was unclear whether it was functional; and (c) although, as part of the loan application process, American General obtained names and telephone numbers of personal references from the imposter, it did not call any of the references before delivering the check.

On 19 December 2007, the District Court held in favor of American General, explaining:

> What was the one action that either party could have taken "to prevent the loss"? In the Court's view Security could have withheld payment, to the imposter, until the check cleared on the Defendant's "out of town" bank. But Security is in the business of cashing checks and charges a fee of between 3% and 5% for the check cashing service; and with a check of this amount, it probably earned a fee of approximately nine hundred ($900.00) dollars. If one is charging that type of a fee, a customer cashing a check on Friday is not going to wait until the following Monday to receive the proceeds. That is a risk of doing the type of business[ ] the Plaintiff chooses to do.

The District Court concluded that, under Md. Code, Commercial Law Art. §3-404(d), State Security had not exercised ordinary care in paying the imposter's check, and that its failure to exercise ordinary care contributed substantially to the loss.

State Security appealed to the Circuit Court for Baltimore County. A hearing was held on 24 July 2008, based on the record made in the District Court. On 8 August 2008, the Circuit Court issued its Memorandum Opinion and Order affirming the judgment of the District Court. . . .

State Security pressed on. It filed a petition for writ of certiorari with this Court, pursuant to Md. Code, Courts and Judicial Proceedings Art. §§12-305 and 12-307 (2006 Repl. Vol. & Supp. 2008), seeking review of the Circuit Court's judgment. We issued the writ. State Sec. v. Am. Gen., 406 Md. 443, 959 A.2d 793 (2008).

II. DISCUSSION

[In a controversial portion of the opinion, the court first concluded that State Security qualified as a holder in due course and so American General could not raise its defense of fraud by the payee. The court then turned to the Impostor Rule.]

B. COMMERCIAL LAW ART. §3-404

Commercial Law Art. §3-404 addresses the circumstances, among other situations, of imposters. Md. Code, Com. Law Art. §3-404. Regarding our imposter in the present case, the District Court ruled, under §3-404(d), that State Security did not exercise ordinary care in paying the check presented by him, and that the failure to exercise such care contributed substantially to the loss. The Circuit Court, in affirming that judgment, concluded that there was substantial evidence to support the District Court's finding, and therefore the District Court's finding was not clearly erroneous. . . .

The District Court determined initially and correctly that the imposter rule applies in this case because all of the pertinent requirements of Commercial Law Art. §3-404(a) were present. As noted, *supra*, §3-404(a) provides:

> (a) If an impostor, by use of the mails or otherwise, induces the issuer of an instrument to issue the instrument to the impostor, or to a person acting in concert with the impostor, by impersonating the payee of the instrument or a person authorized to act for the payee, an indorsement of the instrument by any person in the name of the payee is effective as the indorsement of the payee in favor of a person who, in good faith, pays the instrument or takes it for value or for collection.

Md. Code, Com. Law Art. §3-404(a). Although "imposter" is not defined in the Commercial Law Article, in Bank of Glen Burnie v. Elkridge Bank, 120 Md. App. 402, 707 A.2d 438 (1998), the Court of Special Appeals concluded that "'[i]mposter' is defined as 'one who poses as another to obtain benefits under a negotiable instrument.'" *Bank of Glen Burnie*, 120 Md. App. at 408-09, 707 A.2d at 441 (citing Black's Law Dictionary 756 (6th ed. 1991)). There is no doubt that, by appearing in person at both American General and State Security to conduct transactions, which included the presentation of a forged driver's license with the imposter's picture, but the name and personal identification information of Ronald E. Wilder, the individual in this case was a person who posed as another to obtain the benefits of the check issued by American General. There also is no doubt that, by posing as Mr. Wilder, the imposter induced American General to issue the check to him. When the imposter negotiated the check at State Security, he indorsed the check in the name of the check's payee, Ronald E. Wilder. As we have concluded already, *supra*, State Security took the instrument in good faith. Thus, our reversal of the judgments below turns on the interpretation of the remaining pertinent subsection, subsection (d), of §3-404.

As quoted, *supra*, §3-404(d) provides:

> (d) With respect to an instrument to which subsection (a) or (b) applies, if a person paying the instrument or taking it for value or for collection fails to exercise ordinary care in paying or taking the instrument and that failure substantially contributes to loss resulting from payment of the instrument, the person bearing the loss may recover from the person failing to exercise ordinary care to the extent the failure to exercise ordinary care contributed to the loss.

Md. Code, Com. Law Art. §3-404(d). "Ordinary care" is defined in §3-103(a)(7):

> (7) "Ordinary care" in the case of a person engaged in business means observance of reasonable commercial standards, prevailing in the area in which the person is located, with respect to the business in which the person is engaged. In the case of a bank that takes an instrument for processing for collection or payment by automated means, reasonable commercial standards do not require the bank to examine the instrument if the failure to examine does not violate the bank's prescribed procedures and the bank's procedures do not vary unreasonably from general banking usage not disapproved by this title or Title 4.

Md. Code, Com. Law Art. §3-103(a)(7).

Official Comment 3 to §3-404 addresses expressly the default allocation of loss in circumstances such as the present one. Comment 3 provides:

> 3. In cases governed by subsection (a) the dispute will normally be between the drawer of the check that was obtained by the impostor and the drawee bank that paid it. The drawer is precluded from obtaining recredit of the drawer's account by arguing that the check was paid on a forged indorsement so long as the drawee bank acted in good faith in paying the check. Cases governed by subsection (d) are illustrated by Cases #1 through #5 in Comment 2. *In Cases #1, #2, and #3 there is no forgery of the check, thus the drawer of the check takes the loss if there is no lack of good faith by the banks involved.* Cases #4 and #5 are forged check cases. Depositary Bank is entitled to retain

the proceeds of the check if it didn't know about the forgery. Under Section 3-418 the drawee bank is not entitled to recover from Depositary Bank on the basis of payment by mistake because Depositary Bank took the check in good faith and gave value for the check when the credit given for the check was withdrawn. And there is no breach of warranty under Section 3-417(a)(1) or (3) or 4-208(a)(1) or (3). Unless Section 3-406 applies the loss is taken by the drawee bank if a forged check is paid, and that is the result in Case #5. In Case #4 the loss is taken by Corporation, the drawer, because an agreement between Corporation and the drawee bank allowed the bank to debit Corporation's account despite the unauthorized use of the check-writing machine.

If a check payable to an impostor, fictitious payee, or payee not intended to have an interest in the check is paid, the effect of subsections (a) and (b) is to place the loss on the drawer of the check rather than on the drawee or the Depositary Bank that took the check for collection. Cases governed by subsection (a) always involve fraud, and fraud is almost always involved in cases governed by subsection (b). The drawer is in the best position to avoid the fraud and thus should take the loss. This is true in Case #1, Case #2, and Case #3. But in some cases the person taking the check might have detected the fraud and thus have prevented the loss by the exercise of ordinary care. In those cases, if that person failed to exercise ordinary care, it is reasonable that that person bear loss to the extent the failure contributed to the loss. Subsection (d) is intended to reach that result. It allows the person who suffers loss as a result of payment of the check to recover from the person who failed to exercise ordinary care. In Case #1, Case #2, and Case #3, the person suffering the loss is Corporation, the drawer of the check. In each case the most likely defendant is the depositary bank that took the check and failed to exercise ordinary care. In those cases, the drawer has a cause of action against the offending bank to recover a portion of the loss. The amount of loss to be allocated to each party is left to the trier of fact. Ordinary care is defined in Section 3-103(a)(7). An example of the type of conduct by a depositary bank that could give rise to recovery under subsection (d) is discussed in Comment 4 to Section 3-405. That comment addresses the last sentence of Section 3-405(b) which is similar to Section 3-404(d).

In Case #1, Case #2, and Case #3, there was no forgery of the drawer's signature. But cases involving checks payable to a fictitious payee or a payee not intended to have an interest in the check are often forged check cases as well. Examples are Case #4 and Case #5. Normally, the loss in forged check cases is on the drawee bank that paid the check. Case #5 is an example. In Case #4 the risk with respect to the forgery is shifted to the drawer because of the agreement between the drawer and the drawee bank. The doctrine that prevents a drawee bank from recovering payment with respect to a forged check if the payment was made to a person who took the check for value and in good faith is incorporated into Section 3-418 and Sections 3-417(a)(3) and 4-208(a)(3). This doctrine is based on the assumption that the depositary bank normally has no way of detecting the forgery because the drawer is not that bank's customer. On the other hand, the drawee bank, at least in some cases, may be able to detect the forgery by comparing the signature on the check with the specimen signature that the drawee has on file. But in some forged check cases the depositary bank is in a position to detect the fraud. Those cases typically involve a check payable to a fictitious payee or a payee not intended to have an interest in the check. Subsection (d) applies to those cases. If the depositary bank failed to exercise ordinary care and the failure substantially contributed to the loss, the drawer in Case #4 or the drawee bank in Case #5 has a cause of action against the depositary bank under subsection (d). Comment 4 to Section 3-405 can be used as a guide to the type of conduct that could give rise to recovery under Section 3-404(d).

Md. Code, Com. Law Art. §3-404 cmt. 3 (emphasis added). As Official Comment 3 indicates, the default loss in cases involving imposters lies with the drawer because the drawer is the party that dealt directly with the imposter and thus was in the best position to detect the fraud. *Cf.* Dominion Bank, N.A. v. Household Bank, F.S.B., 827 F. Supp. 463, 466-67 (S.D. Ohio 1993) ("The loss is shifted to the drawer, because the drawer is presumed to have been in the best position to have prevented the fraud. The rationale supporting the impostor rule is essentially the same as that supporting the general rule: the party with the closest contact with the forger ought to bear the responsibility for the loss occasioned by the forgery."); N. Side State Bank v. Bd. of County Comm'rs, 894 P.2d 1046, 1053 (Okla. 1994) ("Known as the 'impostor rule,' §3-405(1)(a) creates an exception to the general notions that govern forged documents. This is so because this section places the loss on the drawer when one who impersonates a third person fraudulently induces the drawer to issue a check and places him in possession. The drawer in that scenario is in the best position to prevent forgery by exercising reasonable care in identifying the party for whom the check is to be issued.") (footnotes omitted); Fair Park Nat'l Bank v. Sw. Inv. Co., 541 S.W.2d 266, 269-70 (Tex. Civ. App. 1976) ("This interpretation is consistent with the policy of the impostor rule, which is to throw the loss resulting from dealing with an impostor on the person who dealt with the impostor, and, presumably, had the best opportunity to take precautions that would have detected the fraud, rather than on a subsequent holder, who had no similar opportunity.") (citations omitted). In certain situations, a drawer may reduce its loss by recovering damages from a person who failed to exercise ordinary care in paying the instrument or taking it for value or collection, if that failure contributed substantially to loss resulting from payment of the instrument, to the extent the failure to exercise care contributed to the loss. Md. Code, Com. Law Art. §3-404(d).

The District Court's ruling in favor of American General erred in two respects: a) the ruling is not in accord with the statutory definition of "ordinary care," in light of the uncontradicted testimony of Deutsch, State Security's compliance officer, and b) the ruling erred by shifting the default burden of loss in an imposter case to the subsequent holder, State Security, rather than the party who was in the best position to detect the fraud, the drawer, American General.

With regard to the interpretation of "ordinary care," the statutory definition of "ordinary care" contains three elements: 1) observance of reasonable commercial standards, 2) which prevail in the area in which the person is located, 3) with respect to the business in which the person is engaged. Md. Code, Com. Law Art. §3-103(a)(7). In the proceedings before the District Court, the testimony of Deutsch, the manager who "run[s] State Security Check Cashing," bore directly upon State Security's conduct on the day in question and, more generally, upon State Security's general business procedures in the check cashing business. Deutsch testified that he has been involved in the check cashing business for twenty-two years and that he had occasion to cash "large" checks in the past. American General did not challenge Deutsch's testimony on cross-examination, nor did American General offer any countervailing testimony reflecting upon State Security's conduct in light of its business practices or the location of its branch office. The only testimony American General elicited on point was through cross-examination of Wanda Decker, State Security's clerk, who testified that State Security, before disbursing, does not hold a check (regardless of the amount) to ascertain whether the funds are available. That testimony alone, however, does not diminish State Security's conduct in the matter in question. Thus, American General did not present sufficient evidence at trial to establish that State Security's conduct lacked "ordinary care" under the statutory definition.

With regard to the burden of loss, the District Court imagined that the one action either party could have taken to prevent the loss was for State Security to have withheld payment until American General's check cleared. The trial court concluded that State Security chose not to delay the payment because it earned a fee from cashing the check, and that in so doing, it ran the risk that the check may be dishonored.

Simply put, the conclusion the trial court reached does not comport with sustainable "ordinary care" analysis. That a business charges a fee for the utilization of its services, albeit here a check cashing business, for cashing the check, is not determinative of whether the conduct of that business on the occasion in question lacked "ordinary care." Under the circumstances of this case, the trial court's reasoning seems directed more towards the "good faith," rather than the "ordinary care," requirement. As Judge Easterbrook stated succinctly in State Bank of the Lakes v. Kansas Bankers Surety Co., 328 F.3d 906 (7th Cir. 2003):

> "[G]ood faith" is in a different phylum from "due care." . . . Article 3 of the UCC, which contains a definition of "good faith[,]" . . . links commercial

reasonableness to "fair dealing." Avoidance of advantage-taking, which this section is getting at, differs from due care.

Id. at 909. The trial court seemed persuaded that by cashing the check for a percentage fee, State Security took unfair advantage of the situation. We have already rejected, *supra*, however, American General's claim that State Security's taking the check from the imposter in the circumstances noted above lacked "good faith."

More significantly, the trial court's ruling in favor of American General is contrary to the position emphasized in Official Comment 3 of §3-404 that "[i]f a check payable to an impostor . . . is paid, the effect of subsections (a) and (b) is to place the loss on the drawer of the check rather than on the drawee or the Depositary Bank that took the check for collection." Md. Code, Com. Law Art. §3-404 cmt. 3. This is due to the recognition that the "drawer is in the best position to avoid the fraud and thus should take the loss." Md. Code, Com. Law Art. §3-404 cmt. 3. We found no evidence in the record of this case to suggest the application of this default rule would be inappropriate. Of either party involved here, American General had the best means available by which to protect itself against the fraud, the least of which included contacting the personal references the imposter listed on the credit application, which may have helped protect American General against the fraud. We reject American General's attempt to shift the burden of the loss here to State Security on so tenuous a basis as State Security's failure to ask the imposter for his thumbprint before cashing the check, where State Security examined the same driver's license and the loan documents American General created and found satisfactory in issuing the check. *See supra* notes 14 and 18.

JUDGMENT OF THE CIRCUIT COURT FOR BALTIMORE COUNTY REVERSED; CASE REMANDED TO THAT COURT WITH DIRECTIONS TO REVERSE THE JUDGMENT OF THE DISTRICT COURT AND REMAND THE CASE TO THE DISTRICT COURT WITH DIRECTIONS TO ENTER JUDGMENT IN FAVOR OF APPELLANT; COSTS TO BE PAID BY APPELLEE.

Would the "fictitious payee" portion of §3-404(b) be applicable to Problem 132?

PROBLEM 133

Lawyer Sam Ambulance was sitting in his office when his secretary brought him his checkbook. The secretary informed him that he owed $1,500.00 to John Creditor on a debt, so he wrote out a check for that amount to John. As it turned out, Sam really didn't owe any money to John Creditor, and the secretary forged John's name to the check and pocketed the proceeds. Is this check properly payable from Sam Ambulance's account? See §3-110(a). Does it make any difference whether or not John Creditor is a real or fictitious person?

C.   The Employee Forgery Rule

In the last Problem, §3-404(b) offers no relief because it is Sam Ambulance's intent that controls under §3-110(a), since he is the drawer of the check. Now do the Problem again, this time looking at §3-405.

Official Comment 1 to this section explains the policy here:

> Section 3-405 is based on the belief that the employer is in a far better position to avoid the loss by care in choosing employees, in supervising them, and in adopting other measures to prevent forged indorsements on instruments payable to the employer or fraud in issuance of instruments in the name of the employer. If the bank failed to exercise ordinary care, subsection (b) allows the employer to shift loss to the bank to the extent the bank's failure to exercise ordinary care contributed to the loss. "Ordinary care" is defined in Section 3-103(a)(7). The provision applies regardless of whether the employer is negligent.

PROBLEM 134

When a check for $800,000 came into Business Corporation to pay a bill owed to it by one of its buyers, the amount dazzled Lucille Larceny, the head of the bookkeeping department. She promptly forged the indorsement "Business Corporation" as payee on the back of the check, and then negotiated it through an account she opened in that name at a bank. Lucille had no authority to indorse the company name, though she was generally in charge of the handling of checks. Does §3-405 make the employer responsible for employees' forgeries where the employer is itself the *payee* (as opposed to the issuer) of the instrument? See Official Comment 1 to §3-405. See Hantz Financial Services, Inc. v. Chemical Bank, 2014 WL 5500383 (Mich. App. 2014). Would that section reach a different result if the forgeries were done by Brad Byte, who had found a check payable to his employer behind the computer he was repairing as part of his job as an in-house computer maintenance specialist?

The Official Comments to both §§3-404 and 3-405 have a number of "case" studies giving examples of fact patterns in which these rules either apply or don't, and you should read these case studies to make sure you appreciate what the drafters intended.

Auto-Owners Ins. Co. v. Bank One

Supreme Court of Indiana, 2008
879 N.E.2d 1086

SULLIVAN, Justice.

Kenneth B. Wulf stole more than $500,000 from his employer, Auto-Owners Insurance Company, by depositing checks payable to Auto-Owners into a personal account he opened at Bank One in the name of "Auto-Owners, Kenneth B. Wulf." Auto-Owners contends that Bank One violated §405 of the Indiana Uniform Commercial Code by not exercising ordinary care when it opened Wulf's account. However, we hold that §405 applies to opening new accounts only in circumstances not present here.

BACKGROUND

Kenneth Wulf worked in the Claims Division of Auto-Owners Insurance from May 1988 until he was terminated in July 1998. Wulf started out as a claims representative, and then became a resident adjustor. In his capacity as a resident adjustor, Wulf handled various kinds of insurance claims for Auto-Owners. One of Wulf's responsibilities was to pursue subrogation and salvage claims on behalf of the insurance company. In the context of this responsibility, Wulf (like other adjustors) handled the file for each case and the checks that Auto-Owners received for subrogation and salvage. When a check arrived, clerical staff would open it and attach it to the relevant file before passing the check and file on to the adjustor. No other record was kept of such checks. It was the adjustor's responsibility to forward the checks back to clerical staff, who would then send the checks to Auto-Owners's main office in Michigan. It was Auto-Owners's policy for all files to be reviewed by a manager every six months.

In 1991, Wulf opened an account at Bank One in the name of "Auto-Owners, Kenneth B. Wulf." (App. at 396.) Wulf used a post office box as the address for the account. Bank One did not request, nor did Wulf provide, any documents to confirm his authorization to open and use the account on behalf of Auto-Owners. Wulf used a stamp that said "Auto Owners Insurance Deposit Only" to endorse checks made out to Auto-Owners and deposit them into his account. (App. at 392.) Wulf deposited a total of $546,000 meant for Auto-Owners into his account over the course of almost eight years. Another Auto-Owners employee discovered Wulf's conduct in 1998, while Wulf was on vacation, during an examination of the file of one of the claims Wulf had handled. Until that time, Auto-Owners did not suspect any untoward activity.

In the trial court, Auto-Owners alleged that Bank One had failed to exercise ordinary care in its opening of Wulf's account, that this failure substantially contributed to Auto-Owners's losses, and that Bank One was liable for Auto-Owners's losses up to the moment of discovery, regardless of any statute of limitations. Bank One denied that it had failed to exercise ordinary care at any time and contended that the three-year statute of limitations, Ind. Code §26-1-3.1-118(g), precluded recovery for any checks paid before October 30, 1995. The trial court granted Bank One's motion for summary judgment and denied Auto-Owners's motion for partial summary judgment (on the statute of limitations issue only) on October 15, 2005. The Court of Appeals affirmed. . . .

DISCUSSION

I

Much of the disagreement in this case revolves around, and our decision rests upon, Indiana's version of §3-405 of the Uniform Commercial Code ("UCC"). [The court quoted §3-405(b).]

Auto-Owners asserts in its Petition for Transfer that Bank One failed to "exercise ordinary care" in opening a bank account in Auto-Owners's name for Wulf, and that this failure "substantially contributed" to Auto-Owners's loss. (Appellant's Pet. to Trans. at ii.)

We begin with the question of whether Bank One exercised ordinary care. Auto-Owners's reading of §405(b) on this point fails to take into account both the language of and the purpose behind the statute. Auto-Owners claims that Bank One should have invested more energy in confirming Wulf's legitimacy when Wulf opened a bank account in Auto-Owners's name in 1991. However, §3-405(b) makes no mention of a bank's responsibilities when opening an account for a new customer. Rather, subsection (b) requires ordinary care from a bank in the "paying" or "taking" of an instrument. Indeed, Bank One pointed out during oral argument that the procedures in place to be applied during the opening of an account are often there for the protection of the bank, not a particular customer. *See also* 2 James J. White & Robert S. Summers, *Uniform Commercial Code* §19-4(h) (4th ed. 1995) (implying that bank account-opening procedures may be self protection). Such an approach, which is not incompatible with the requirements of §405(b), would suggest that often a bank hurts no one but itself if it fails to follow its own procedures when opening a new account.

As to the purpose behind the statute, the first comment to §405 reveals, and the Court of Appeals also pointed out, that in the absence of a bank's negligence, §3-405 shifts the responsibility for monitoring possibly wayward employees away from a bank and onto the employer. The rationale for this responsibility shift is that an employer is in a better position to select and supervise its employees than an outside bank. More relevant to the situation at hand, an employer is also better able to put in place measures to prevent fraud among its employees. *Auto-Owners Ins. Co.*, 852 N.E.2d at 612-13 (*citing* I.C. §26-1-3.1-405 cmt. 1). *Accord* White & Summers, *supra*, §19-4.

This is not to say that the circumstances of opening an account could never play a role in whether a bank has used ordinary care in paying or taking a check. Auto-Owners calls attention to the fourth comment to §3-405, which outlines a scenario in which an employee might open an account in the name of a prominent corporation and use the account to deposit instruments payable to the corporation. I.C. §26-1-3.1-405 cmt. 4. By Auto-Owners's interpretation, comment four supports liability for Bank One because the comment countenances an employee doing what Wulf did—opening a bank account in his employer's name. However, the comment states that "[f]ailure to exercise ordinary care is to be determined in the context of all the facts *relating to the bank's conduct with respect to the bank's collection of the check.*" *Id.* (emphasis added). This emphasis is consistent with the language of §3-405(b), which stresses "ordinary care in paying or taking the instrument." Thus, while the manner of opening an account might be considered in the context of all the facts surrounding the paying or taking of a check, the manner of opening an account, by itself, is not a focus of the rule.

In this case, the facts differ materially from the relevant behavior in the comment's example. In the comment, the employee opens an account for a "well-known national corporation" and deposits a check for a "very large amount of money." After the account is credited, the money is transferred out of the account. I.C. §26-1-3.1-405 cmt. 4. While we may quibble about whether Auto-Owners is a sufficiently well-known national corporation, the vast majority of the checks Wulf deposited were worth well under $10,000 and deposited over a period of almost eight years. Many checks had been deposited by the time Auto-Owners noticed a problem. Because "[a]ny cause of action Auto-Owners may have had accrued at the time each check was negotiated by Wulf," *Auto-Owners Ins. Co.*, 852 N.E.2d at 612, a connection between the individual checks currently at issue (those not excluded by the statute of limitations) and the manner of the opening of the account five years before is minimal. Under these circumstances, Auto-Owners may not argue that the opening of the account in 1991 is included in the "context of all the facts relating to . . . the bank's collection of the check[s]," I.C. §26-1-3.1-405 cmt. 4, after October 30, 1995.

The Court of Appeals has correctly analyzed whether Bank One exercised ordinary care in taking and paying the checks proffered by Wulf after October 30, 1995, in Auto-Owners's name, and found that it did. The language of the statute does not contemplate a general requirement that banks use ordinary care when opening accounts, and Auto-Owners does not raise this question again in the context of the paying and taking of instruments in its Petition for Transfer. *Auto-Owners Ins. Co.*, 852 N.E.2d at 616-18.

II

Even if Bank One did not demonstrate ordinary care in its acceptance of the checks proffered by Wulf, Auto-Owners must still show that such a lack of ordinary care "substantially contributed" to its losses. The comments to I.C. §26-1-3.1-406 explain the test:

> The "substantially contributes" test of former Section 3-406 is continued in this section in preference to a "direct and proximate cause" test. The "substantially contributes" test is meant to be less stringent than a "direct and proximate cause" test. Under the less stringent test the preclusion should be easier to establish. Conduct "substantially contributes" to a material alteration or forged signature if it is a contributing cause of the alteration or signature and a substantial factor in bringing it about. The analysis of "substantially contributes" in former Section 3-406 by the court in Thompson Maple Products v. Citizens National Bank of Corry, 211 Pa. Super. 42, 234 A.2d 32 (1967), states what is intended by the use of the same words in revised Section 3-406(b). Since Section 3-404(d) and Section 3-405(b) also use the words "substantially contributes" the analysis of these words also applies to those provisions.

I.C. §26-1-3.1-406 cmt. 2. White & Summers defines the "substantially contributes" standard expansively: "The acts sufficient to 'substantially contribute' to a material alteration or to the making of an unauthorized signature are limited only by man's capacity for slovenly business transactions." White & Summers, *supra*, §19-3(b). We do not interpret the standard quite as broadly as White & Summers does in the examples that follow this summary, though we agree that those examples may contribute to a party's meeting the "substantially contributes" test. Rather, we look to *Thompson Maple Products*, which is cited in the second comment to §406. There, the court followed a chain of company practices that allowed forgery to flourish, and then held:

> While none of these practices, in isolation, might be sufficient to charge the plaintiff with negligence within the meaning of §3-406, the company's course of conduct, *viewed in its entirety*, is surely sufficient to support the trial judge's determination that it substantially contributed to the making of the unauthorized signatures.

Thompson Maple Products, Inc., 211 Pa. Super. 42, 234 A.2d 32, 36 (1967) (emphasis added).

Thus, to determine whether conduct has substantially contributed to a loss, we follow the second comment to §3-406 and ask whether the opening of the bank account was (1) a contributing factor to Auto-Owners's loss *and* (2) whether the opening of the bank account was a substantial factor in bringing the loss about. I.C. §26-1-3.1-406 cmt. 2. Like the court in *Thompson*

Maple Products, we will view the conduct of Bank One "in its entirety." 234 A.2d at 36.

Wulf opened an account with Bank One in 1991 and began depositing checks meant for Auto-Owners. Wulf's deception was not discovered for almost eight years. Other than the lack of procedure used in opening the bank account in 1991, Bank One appears to have followed required protocol in depositing checks from Wulf. *See Auto-Owners Ins. Co., 852 N.E.2d at 612-16*. Even if we assume that Bank One's conduct in opening the account was a contributing factor to Auto-Owners's loss, and meets the first part of the "substantially contributed" test, we agree with the trial court and the Court of Appeals that Bank One's conduct was not a substantial factor in bringing that loss about under the second part of the test. In other words, when viewed in its entirety Bank One's conduct does not meet the "substantially contributed" test. *See Thompson Maple Products, 234 A.2d at 36*. Indeed, it appears that Auto Owners was the substantial contributor to its own losses, particularly those at issue here, with its less than rigorous monitoring of its files and incoming checks.

For the reasons addressed above, we affirm the trial court's determination that summary judgment for Bank One was appropriate in this case. There is no disagreement between the parties as to the material facts of the case. We agree with the trial court's determination that Bank One was entitled to summary judgment and that Auto-Owners is not entitled to a trial under §405. We express no opinion as to whether Auto-Owners might have been able to demonstrate Bank One's negligence under another law, regulation, or the common law.

CONCLUSION

For the foregoing reasons, we affirm the trial court. The issues not addressed in this opinion, but addressed by the Court of Appeals, are summarily affirmed pursuant to App. R. 58(A).

SHEPARD, C.J., and RUCKER, J., concur.

BOEHM, Justice, dissenting in part.

I believe the facts relevant to the bank's exercise of ordinary care are easily stated, and present an issue for trial. Wulf, an employee of Auto-Owners, opened an account in the name of Auto-Owners Insurance. The designated evidence does not include any documentation of the opening of the account, and the exact nature of the account is not clear from this record. But under any view of this evidence, the account was not owned by an insurance company. The tax identification number obtained for the account was Wulf's social security number, rather than a number appropriate for a business entity.

More importantly, opening a bank account for a legal entity, such as a business corporation or insurance company, ordinarily requires proof of identity and authority in the form of tax identification numbers and corporate resolutions. *See* 2 James J. White & Robert S. Summers, *Uniform Commercial Code* §19-4(h) (4th ed. 1995). Auto-Owners provided an affidavit from an experienced bank officer to the effect that the prevailing standard for opening a business checking account requires proof of identity and authority. Given the lack of corporate documentation, from Bank One's point of view, the only owner the account could have was Wulf himself, as an individual perhaps using "Auto-Owners Insurance" as his assumed business name. I assume such a name could be used by an insurance agency operated as a sole proprietorship. Ind. Code §27-1-15.6-10 (2004) (permitting use of assumed names by licensed sellers of insurance if the Commissioner is notified). If so, Auto-Owners designated evidence that it was Bank One's practice, and the practice throughout the industry, to obtain an assumed business name certificate to open such an account. All of this adds up to a genuine issue of material fact as to the bank's exercise of ordinary care in opening the account.

I disagree with the majority's conclusion that the bank's failure to exercise ordinary care can be confined to opening the account. When it came time to deposit checks into this account, Wulf showed up with checks payable to "Auto-Owners Insurance Company" and similar names. That payee would ordinarily be taken to be an insurance company, most of which are organized as corporations. Thus, it seems to me to present at least a jury question whether acceptance of such a check deposited into an individual's account with no authorizing documentation whatever constitutes failure to exercise "ordinary care" as that term is used in section 3-405(b). The majority suggests that actions in opening the account cannot support recovery under section 3-405 because that section applies only to "paying" or "taking" an instrument (in this case the checks). But the two cannot be separated. In simple terms, after the account was opened, the bank accepted checks payable to Auto-Owners for deposit into Wulf's personal account, which permitted Wulf to write checks on the account. The initial alleged oversight was in opening an account for an individual under the "Auto-Owners Insurance" name, without either corporate authorization or an assumed business name certificate. But the bank then proceeded to accept checks payable to an insurance company—a corporate entity—for deposit into an account that was established for an individual under a similar but different name.[3]

___

3. Auto-Owners supplied an affidavit from an experienced bank officer stating that the existing commercial practice for sole proprietorship accounts was to list first the name of the individual, in this case, Wulf. In this case, the first name on the account was "Auto-Owners Insurance." The affidavit also states that existing commercial practices prohibit the deposit of a corporate check into a noncorporate account.

Whether acceptance of some or all of these deposits also constituted failure to exercise ordinary care is not resolvable on the evidence in this record.

The majority points out that comment 4 to section 405 describes a deposit into an individual account of a large check payable to a well-known corporation as a possible failure of ordinary care. First, it seems clear that this comment recognizes that the circumstances of opening an account may be relevant to whether ordinary care is exercised in subsequently accepting deposits into the account. Moreover, I think the majority reads comment 4 far too restrictively. It is an example, not an attempt to set the bounds of section 3-405. The point of the example is that discrepancies between the payee, the endorsement, and the type of account can create an ordinary care question. For example, anyone reading the name of the payee on a check payable to General Motors Corporation and endorsed by "General Motors" would wonder why it is being deposited in an individual account. This does not depend on the amount of the check, though I assume the $10,000 checks Wulf deposited were "large" in the context of most individual accounts. Nor does it depend on the prominence of the payee. If the check in any amount were payable to "General Widget Corporation" and endorsed by "General Widget," I would think a jury could find failure to exercise ordinary care if a bank concluded without further investigation that the account was owned by a military officer whose surname was Widget. Here we have acceptance of checks payable to an insurance company, endorsed by a variant of the company's name, and deposited into an individual account created with none of the paperwork associated with a corporate account or an assumed business name.

The majority suggests that any requirements for opening an account in a corporate name are for the benefit of the bank, not the general public. But it is plain that section 3-405 contemplates liability of the bank for "failure to exercise ordinary care" in accepting an endorsement. I.C. §26-1-3.1-405 cmt. 1 ("If the bank failed to exercise ordinary care, subsection (b) allows the employer to shift loss to the bank to the extent the bank's failure to exercise ordinary care contributed to the loss."); White & Summers, *supra*, §19-3(f) (describing possible failures to exercise ordinary care in accepting an endorsement). I see no reason why ordinary banking procedures are not evidence relevant to that determination. As White and Summers explain

> Comment 4 deals with cases in which the prevailing standard is to investigate or at least to get some evidence from the person seeking to open the account that the principal exists and that the person opening the account is an authorized agent. If the bank fails to comply with the prevailing standard, failure to collect the necessary information may itself be held to be negligence that contributes to the loss.

Id. §19-4(h).

I disagree with the majority's view of the "substantial contribution" issue in two respects. First, the majority cites Auto-Owners's substantial contribution to its own losses as a ground for granting summary judgment to the bank. Slip op. at 7-8. Assuming the majority is correct that the designated evidence establishes that Auto-Owners contributed substantially to the loss, that does not warrant summary judgment for the bank. Section 405 sets up a "pure" comparative negligence exercise. In such a regime, the plaintiff's negligence proportionally reduces, but does not eliminate, the right to recover, even if the plaintiff's negligence is greater than the defendant's. Arthur Best, Impediments to Reasonable Tort Reform: Lessons from the Adoption of Comparative Negligence, 40 Ind. L. Rev. 1-2 nn. 4-5 (2007) (citing Restatement (Third) of Torts: Apportionment of Liability §7 cmt. a (2000)). . . . It seems clear to me that the bank's acceptance of these many checks over a period of years substantially contributed to Auto-Owners's loss. The "extent" of that contribution compared to the lack of oversight attributable to Auto-Owners is a jury question not resolvable on summary judgment. *See* White & Summers, *supra*, §19-3(d) (describing the comparative fault provisions as "an invitation for a plaintiff to roll the dice with the jury").

DICKSON, J., concurs.

———————

Not all courts would agree with the Indiana Supreme Court's analysis in this case. In YF Trust v. JP Morgan Chase Bank, N.A., 2008 WL 4277902 (D. Ariz. Sept. 18, 2008), the court, following White & Summers and specifically declining to follow *Auto-Owners*, held that negligence in opening an account can be used to apportion loss where one of the validation rules applies. This case involved not just negligence in opening the account, but negligence in the "formation, maintenance and use" of the account; see also Miller v. Bennett, 2014 WL 2567925 (Ohio App. 2014).

NOTE ON FEDERAL COMMERCIAL PAPER LAW

As mentioned before, the Uniform Commercial Code is a *state* statute, and the federal government does not feel bound thereby. In an actual case, you may discover that, for example, the Midnight Deadline statutes and other rules of bank collection are much altered when a check is drawn on the Treasury of the United States. So it is with the padded payroll part of the Impostor Rule. While the U.S. Supreme Court decisions to date preclude the use of §§3-404(b) and 3-405, the part of these sections that deals with a true *impostor*, §3-404(a), *has* been adopted as a federal rule by lower federal courts, the Supreme Court having expressed no opinion on the issue; see Bank of Am. Natl. Trust & Sav. Assn. v. United States, 552 F.2d 302 (9th Cir. 1977); see also Comment, Federal Commercial Paper and the Common Law, 14 Tulsa L.J. 208 (1978). In United States v. Kimbell Foods, 440 U.S. 715 (1979), the Supreme Court adopted Article 9 of the Uniform Commercial Code as a matter of federal common law. This has given hope of the Court's possible federal incorporation of Articles 3 and 4 the next time the issue arises. See Official Comment 4 to §3-102 and Official Comment 1 to §4-102.

PROBLEM 135

Peter Shopper left his checkbook laying on a department store counter, and it was picked up by "Fingers" McGee. McGee wrote out a check for $100 payable to the order of "John Doe," a name he rather imaginatively made up; then he forged Shopper's name to the drawer's line. He indorsed the check "John Doe" and "Fingers McGee" and deposited the check in his own account with the Fence State Bank. The latter was paid $100 by the drawee, the Antitrust National Bank. Shopper complained to the drawee about the forgery, and the bank reluctantly recredited his account. It now wants to pass the loss on to the presenting bank, claiming that it breached the warranty that it was a person entitled to enforce the draft because of the forged indorsement of "John Doe." Has that warranty been breached, or did Fence State somehow become a *holder*? See §3-404(b), and remember the rule of Price v. Neal.

D. The Negligence Rule

Another situation in which a party may be estopped to complain about a forgery occurs when the person's own negligence substantially contributed to the creation of the forgery. (The same rule applies to the creation of alterations of the instrument.) The leading case establishing this negligence-as-estoppel principle is the 1827 English case, Young v. Grote, 4 Bing. 253 (Common Pleas). The Problem below is based on the facts in that case.

PROBLEM 136

Young decided to go abroad for a while, so he signed five checks and left them with his wife. After he had been gone a week, one of Young's employees, Worcester, a clerk, showed Mrs. Young how to fill out the check so as to pay employees' wages for 50 pounds. She filled out the check as directed and gave it to Worcester to cash. He inserted the numeral 3 on the check in the blank he had had Mrs. Young leave in writing the amount and cashed the check for 350 pounds with the drawee, Grote & Co. When Young returned, he sued Grote & Co. for wrongly paying that amount. In the actual case, the court gave a sexist explanation for its result, deciding that Young's negligence was in trusting a woman with a business matter (remember this was 1827): "If Young, instead of leaving the check with a female, had left it with a man of business, he would have guarded against fraud in the mode of filling it up. . . ." In our century, is it enough negligence that a space was left on the amount line to which a numeral could be added? See Official Comment 1 to §3-406.

Note that the language of §3-406 uses the doctrine of negligence only as a defense, not as a separate affirmative cause of action. The Code does not authorize an affirmative cause of action based on negligence. Read Official Comment 1, last paragraph, to §3-406, which explains why not. Affirmative negligence actions must be brought outside the Code (see §1-103) and judged by common law standards. See, e.g., Faulkner v. Hillside Bank & Trust Co., 526 S.W.2d 274 (Tex. Civ. App. 1975) (bank telling an inquirer that a stolen cashier's check was good held liable in negligence).

PROBLEM 137

Arena Auto Auction (AAA) by coincidence dealt with two customers named Plunkett Auto Sales, one in Illinois and the other in Alabama. AAA sold a car for the Alabama customer, but AAA's secretary mistakenly mailed a check to Plunkett Auto Sales in Illinois. The surprised owner of the Illinois Plunkett operation promptly cashed the check with his own bank, Park State, which forwarded the check to the drawee bank. The latter dishonored the check at AAA's request—AAA had stopped payment when it learned about its secretary's error. The Illinois Plunkett skipped the state, and the Park State Bank was left holding the check. Park State sued AAA on its drawer's obligation, §3-414(b), and the latter tried to raise the defense of mistake. Does §3-406 apply? See Official Comment 3, Case No. 2. The actual case is Park State Bank v. Arena Auto Auction, Inc., 59 Ill. App. 2d 235, 207 N.E.2d 158 (1965).

The Bank/First Citizens Bank v. Citizens and Associates

The Supreme Court of Tennessee, 2002
82 S.W.3d 259

WILLIAM M. BARKER

This case involves the application of Tennessee Code Annotated section 47-3-406 to determine who bears the loss of a bank's acceptance of forged instruments. The drawer issued three checks payable to a mortgage company and delivered these checks to a branch manager of that company for transfer to the main office. The manager, however, forged the endorsement of the company and deposited these checks into her personal bank account. In a suit to recover the funds, the trial court applied section 47-3-406 and found that both the drawer and the depository bank failed to exercise ordinary care. It then allocated the loss between the parties as eighty percent to the drawer and twenty percent to the bank. A majority of the Court of Appeals affirmed. On appeal to this Court, we hold that the bank may not assert that the drawer is precluded from asserting the forgery against it under section 47-3-406, because it did not show that any failure by the drawer to exercise ordinary care substantially contributed to the making of the forged endorsements. The judgment of the Court of Appeals is reversed.

FACTUAL BACKGROUND

In January 1997, Allied Mortgage Capital Company ("Allied Mortgage") opened a branch office in Cleveland, Tennessee, and shortly thereafter, it hired Ms. Frieda Gray as its branch manager for this office. In this capacity, Ms. Gray possessed the authority to conduct the day-to-day operations of the branch and to make loans. Ms. Gray was also authorized to receive, hold, and forward monies and documents to Allied Mortgage at its principal place of business in Texas.

The next month, Ms. Gray, representing herself as a branch manager of Allied Mortgage, contacted a land-development partnership, Citizens and Associates, about opening a branch office of Allied Mortgage in upper-east Tennessee. Ms. Gray hosted a seminar in Knoxville for about fifteen or twenty people to show how profitable investing in Allied Mortgage could be. Following this seminar, Citizens and Associates agreed to invest in the mortgage company in order to compl[e]ment its other land development interests. Ms. Gray stated that she would handle the transaction, and she obtained information from Citizens and Associates which she said was necessary for the main office to approve the investment.

Over the next thirty days, Citizens and Associates issued three checks to Allied Mortgage, in the total amount of $50,000.02, and it gave these checks to Ms. Gray for delivery to Allied Mortgage's main office in Texas. However, Ms. Gray did not forward the checks to the main office. Instead, she endorsed each in the name of the corporation and deposited the instruments in her personal account at The Bank/First Citizens Bank ("First Citizens Bank") in Cleveland. First Citizens Bank, as the depository bank, presented these checks to the drawee bank in Knoxville, which paid the checks and deducted the amounts paid from Citizens and Associates' account.

Citizens and Associates soon discovered that a fraud had taken place. It contacted Allied Mortgage's main office and confirmed that Allied Mortgage does not license franchises and that Ms. Gray was not authorized to negotiate franchise agreements. Citizens and Associates then contacted First Citizens Bank and demanded repayment of the face amounts of the checks, but First Citizens Bank denied any liability on the instruments. The bank then filed suit in the Bradley County Circuit Court, seeking a declaration that it possessed no liability on the three checks. Citizens and Associates filed a counterclaim against First Citizens Bank alleging that the bank failed to exercise ordinary care in taking the instruments.

Following a bench trial, the court applied Tennessee Code Annotated section 47-3-406 and found that First Citizens Bank failed to exercise ordinary care in taking the checks. More specifically, the court concluded that the bank was negligent in permitting the deposit of checks made payable to a corporation into a personal account, especially when the corporation itself did not have an account with the bank. The court also found that Citizens and Associates was negligent in delivering the instruments to Ms. Gray without first confirming the transaction with Allied Mortgage. It then allocated the loss of the instruments, as required by section 47-3-406(c), as eighty percent to Citizens and Associates and twenty percent to First Citizens Bank. A final order confirming this ruling was entered on July 11, 2000.

Citizens and Associates appealed to the Court of Appeals, and a majority of that court affirmed the judgment of the trial court. The intermediate court found that the evidence supported the trial court's findings regarding the failure of both parties to exercise ordinary care. The majority also affirmed the trial court's allocation of the loss as supported by the evidence. However, in dissent, Judge Susano concluded that First Citizens Bank should be responsible for the entire loss. He found that because Ms. Gray was "without question an employee of Allied [Mortgage] and was authorized to receive documents and checks for her employer," Citizens and Associates did not fail to exercise the ordinary care contemplated by section 47-3-406(a).

We granted permission to appeal to Citizens and Associates to resolve the proper application of Tennessee Code Annotated section 47-3-406 in this case. We now hold that First Citizens Bank may not assert the defense provided by section 47-3-406. Although we conclude that the record supports a finding that First Citizens Bank took the instruments in good faith, the bank did not show that the failure of Citizens and Associates to exercise ordinary care substantially contributed to the actual making of the forged endorsements. . . .

[The court quoted §3-406.]

Thus, viewing the statute in terms of this case, First Citizens Bank may assert that Citizens and Associates is precluded from asserting the forgery against the bank by showing (1) that it took the instruments in good faith;

(2) that Citizens and Associates failed to exercise ordinary care; and (3) that this failure by Citizens and Associates "substantially contributed" to making of Ms. Gray's forged signatures. Tenn. Code Ann. §47-3-406(a). However, even if Citizens and Associates is found to be precluded from asserting the entire loss against First Citizens Bank, it may nevertheless seek to shift the burden of the loss to the bank by showing (1) that First Citizens Bank failed to exercise ordinary care in taking the instrument; and (2) that this failure substantially contributed to the loss. *See* Tenn. Code Ann. §47-3-406(b). The court may then apportion the loss to the extent "that the failure of each to exercise ordinary care contributed to the loss." Tenn. Code Ann. §47-3-406(c).

"Each of these steps in section [47-3-406] presents a question of fact, ordinarily to be resolved by the fact finder." San Tan Irrigation Dist. v. Wells Fargo Bank, 197 Ariz. 193, 3 P.3d 1113, 1118 (2000). Importantly, however, if First Citizens Bank cannot meet its initial burden of showing that Citizens and Associates is precluded from asserting the forgery against it, then the entire loss must be borne by the bank itself. *Cf.* John Hancock Fin. Servs. v. Old Kent Bank, 185 F. Supp. 2d 771, 779 (E.D. Mich. 2002) (denying preclusion under UCC section 3-406 because the bank did not show good faith in paying the instrument). We examine each of these elements in turn.

First Citizen's Bank's Good Faith Payment of the Instruments

The first issue is whether First Citizens Bank took the instruments in good faith. Citing the general code definition of "good faith" in Tennessee Code Annotated section 47-1-201(19), First Citizens Bank asserts that it has met this standard because it acted with "honesty in fact" in taking the checks. A majority of the Court of Appeals agreed, noting that the record contains no evidence that "there was any dishonesty or collusion involved in the transaction." However, although the Court of Appeals ultimately appears to have applied the correct definition of "good faith" in this context, it did not specifically examine the proper definition of this term as it applies to TUCC Article 3. Consequently, to clarify the law in this area, we undertake a more detailed analysis of this issue.

In 1990, the American Law Institute and the National Conference of Commissioners on Uniform State Laws revised Articles 3 and 4 of the Uniform Commercial Code dealing with negotiable instruments, bank deposits, and collections. Prior to these revisions, the term "good faith" was defined in these articles by the general subjective standard of "honesty in fact." However, one of the more significant revisions to Article 3 was to redefine the term "good faith" to require a party to show that it acted with "honesty in fact" in the transaction *and* that it adhered to "reasonable commercial standards of fair dealing." *See* UCC §3-103(a)(4).

In 1995, the Tennessee General Assembly substantially adopted Revised Articles 3 and 4, although, interestingly, it did not include the definition of "good faith" contained in UCC section 3-103(a)(4). Admittedly, there is some evidence that the legislature omitted the definition of this term inadvertently. For example, the legislature retained Official Comment [3] to section 47-3-103, which specifically refers to the definition of "good faith" as requiring "not only honesty in fact, but also 'observance of reasonable commercial standards of fair dealing.'" This comment is quite detailed, and it elaborates on the difference between the exercise of "ordinary care" and the observance of "reasonable commercial standards of fair dealing." One could also suppose that the inclusion of this Official Comment here is more than a mere anomaly, as comments in *three* other sections of Title 47 specifically refer to the definition of "good faith" as purportedly set forth in section 47-3-103(a)(4).

Nevertheless, "[t]his court does not lightly assume drafting error by the Legislature." *See* People v. Robles, 23 Cal. 4th 1106, 99 Cal. Rptr. 2d 120, 5 P.3d 176, 182 (2000). To the contrary, we presume that where the legislature departs from the language of a model act, it usually does so to express an intention different from the model act. *See* Heirs of Ellis v. Estate of Ellis, 71 S.W.3d 705, 713-14 (Tenn. 2002); Kradel v. Piper Indus., Inc., 60 S.W.3d 744 (Tenn. 2001). We note that the presence of the unedited comments may not be as curious as first appears, especially considering that the General Assembly has, on at least one other occasion, adopted the official UCC comments verbatim even while otherwise departing from the uniform language of the statute itself. *See* Tenn. Code Ann. §47-2-318 cmt. 3 (referring to all three alternative versions proposed by UCC section 2-318, even though the General Assembly ultimately adopted only Alternative *A*). Further, the Compilers Notes to section 47-3-103 specifically observe that the UCC's Article 3 definition of "good faith" has been omitted from the Tennessee statutes, and these Notes permit the General Assembly to correct any unintended oversight should it so desire. Consequently, we must conclude that the General Assembly intentionally omitted the UCC definition of "good faith" as it applies in Chapters 3 and 4 of Title 47, and we construe this term in accord with the general code definition to mean "honesty in fact in the conduct or transaction involved." *See* Tenn. Code Ann. §47-1-201(19).

Applying the general code definitions in this context, we agree with the lower court that the record supports a finding that First Citizens Bank took the instruments in good faith. This Court has defined the "honesty in fact" standard to mean an absence of a "knowing or reckless disregard of a customer's rights." Glazer v. First Am. Nat'l Bank, 930 S.W.2d 546, 549 (Tenn. 1996) (defining "good faith" in section 47-1-102(19)). Our review of the record reveals that while First Citizens Bank was certainly negligent in permitting the deposit of a check made payable to a corporation into an individual account, no evidence shows that it knowingly disregarded the rights of anyone. Nor does a preponderance of the evidence support a finding that the bank acted recklessly in this regard. Therefore, we conclude that the record supports the conclusions of the lower courts that First Citizens Bank took the instruments in good faith.

CITIZEN'S AND ASSOCIATE'S FAILURE TO EXERCISE ORDINARY CARE AND ITS SUBSTANTIAL CONTRIBUTION TO THE FORGERY

Although the record supports a finding that First Citizens Bank took the instruments in good faith, section 47-3-406 also requires the bank to show that the drawer's failure to exercise ordinary care substantially contributed to the forgery of the instrument. Although the Court of Appeals reached a contrary conclusion, we cannot conclude that the bank has met its burden in this regard.

No reported case in this state has discussed the requirements of "ordinary care" or "substantial contribution" as they relate to the conduct of the drawer. However, the official comments shed some light on what was intended by these standards. For instance, Comment 2 to section 47-3-406 states that conduct is a substantial contribution to a forged signature if the conduct is a "contributing cause" of the signature and is "a substantial factor in bringing it about." The comment also notes that the "substantial contribution" standard "is meant to be less stringent than a 'direct and proximate cause' test" that prevailed prior to the UCC's adoption, thereby making the preclusion generally easier to establish.

Relying upon this comment, the Court of Appeals held that a drawer can be precluded under this section if the drawer negligently issues an instrument to a third party for delivery to the payee. Though the intermediate court's analysis is not without some support, several other courts have held that "only negligence which proximately relates or contributes to the forgery, *and not merely to the issuance of the checks*, would relieve a collecting bank of liability for improper payment of a fraudulently endorsed check." *See, e.g.,* Vectra Bank v. Bank W., 890 P.2d 259, 263 (Colo. Ct. App. 1995) (emphasis added).[12] Indeed, at least one court has held, as a matter of law,

---

12. *See also* Bagby v. Merrill Lynch, Pierce, Fenner & Smith, Inc., 491 F.2d 192, 197 (8th Cir. 1974) ("In the final analysis, we are convinced that the meaning of §3-406 is best reflected by precluding a drawer from recovery under these or similar circumstances only where his negligent conduct contributes to the forgery, not merely to the unwarranted issuance of the checks, such as in the situation before us."); First Nat'l Bank v. MidAmerica Fed. Sav. Bank, 303 Ill. App. 3d 176, 236 Ill. Dec. 546, 707 N.E.2d 673, 678 (1999) ("The meaning of section 3-406 is best reflected by precluding a drawer from recovery under these or similar circumstances only where his negligent conduct contributes to the forgery, not merely to the unwarranted issuance of the checks." (citation and quotation marks omitted)); Twellman v.

that the drawer's negligence in issuing the instrument, without more, cannot substantially contribute to the forgery within the contemplation of UCC section 3-406. *See* Guaranty Bank & Trust Co. v. Federal Reserve Bank, 454 F. Supp. 488, 490-91 (W.D. Okla. 1977) (addressing factual scenario in which a loan was negotiated and an instrument was delivered to a party not named as the payee).

This latter position certainly comports more closely with the plain language of section 47-3-406, which speaks only of the drawer's negligence being a substantial contribution "to the *making* of a forged signature." (emphasis added). Consequently, we agree with those cases holding that a drawer's negligence leading to the unwarranted issuance of checks will not generally suffice to establish a defense under section 47-3-406. Rather, the party asserting the preclusion must show some causal relationship between the lack of ordinary care and the actual making of the forged signature, such that the drawer's negligence can be said to have substantially contributed to the ability of the unauthorized person to forge the payee's name and to pose as the intended payee. *See* Fidelity Bank v. United Nat'l Bank, 630 F. Supp. 16, 20 (D.D.C. 1985) (citing Dominion Constr., Inc. v. First Nat'l Bank, 271 Md. 154, 315 A.2d 69, 73 (1974)).

Whatever negligence Citizens and Associates may have been guilty of in issuing the three checks payable to Allied Mortgage, we cannot say that it increased the possibility that Ms. Gray would forge the endorsement of Allied Mortgage and pose as the payee of the instruments to her bank. Citizens and Associates, for example, did not leave blank the name of the payees in the various checks or make the checks payable to Ms. Gray as an agent of Allied Mortgage. *See Fidelity Bank,* 630 F. Supp. at 20. Rather, Citizens and Associates only delivered these checks to an acknowledged agent of the payee that, according to testimony by an employee of Allied Mortgage, possessed the actual authority to receive checks on behalf of the payee. Without something more, this conduct alone simply cannot be said to have substantially contributed to the making of the forged endorsements.

Lindell Trust Co., 534 S.W.2d 83, 90-91 (Mo. Ct. App. 1976) ("The U.C.C. seems to foresee a more direct type of contribution to a forgery. . . . We do not think that plaintiff's actions in trusting Londe and giving Londe a check which plaintiff had made payable to International Harvester could be said to have substantially contributed to Londe's forgery."); Maddox v. First Westroads Bank, 199 Neb. 81, 256 N.W.2d 647, 655 (1977) (quoting and approving *Bagby*); *Society Nat'l Bank,* 281 N.E.2d at 566 ("Even if [the drawer] had been lax in the conduct of his business affairs, mere laxity is not sufficient to prevent him from recovering against the drawee bank for the amount charged against his account and paid by the drawee over a forged indorsement, unless the lax conduct was the proximate cause of the loss.").

Consequently, while the record supports the trial court's conclusion that Citizens and Associates was negligent in issuing the checks payable to Allied Mortgage, the record does not show that this negligence substantially contributed to the ability of Ms. Gray to forge the endorsements and pose as the actual payee. Accordingly, we hold that even if First Citizens Bank took the instruments in good faith, the bank cannot assert the negligent drawer defense of section 47-3-406 because it has not shown that any failure by Citizens and Associates to exercise ordinary care substantially contributed to the making of the forged endorsements. . . . Accordingly, the judgment of the Court of Appeals is reversed.

The 1974 case of Bagby v. Merrill Lynch, Pierce, Fenner & Smith, Inc., 491 F.2d 192, 197 (8th Cir. 1974), cited in the above case's footnote, resurrected the tort doctrine of "proximate cause" (even though Official Comment 2 to §3-406 disclaims it), and one of your authors wrote a law review article attacking the court for dragging the messy "proximate cause" imbroglio into §3-406; see Douglas J. Whaley, Negligence and Negotiable Instruments, 53 N.C. L. Rev. 1 (1974). White and Summers cited the article with approval in earlier editions of their treatise, but when the issue died out, they dropped any discussion of "proximate cause," and now simply state that "where there are multiple causes of loss (not the least of which may be a deficiency in the thief's morality), one person's act could be a substantial cause even though other events might be more direct and powerful causes"; White & Summers §17-3. The subsequent rewrite of Article 3 has commanded the courts to use comparative negligence in all these forgery situations, thus recognizing there can be more than one cause of a forgery. You'd think therefore that "proximate cause" would be dead in Article 3 case law, but as the above case indicates that horror is apparently still with us.

PROBLEM 138

Lucille Larceny, corporate treasurer of Business Corporation, had the authority to indorse the corporate name to checks coming into the corporation. Over a period of months she took a number of such checks, stamped the corporate name as payee, then indorsed her own name below the corporate stamp and deposited the checks in her personal account at Busy National Bank. Is it negligent for the depositary bank to allow her to do this? See §3-307(b)(2); Al Sarena Mines, Inc. v. Southtrust Bank, 548 So. 2d 1356 (Ala. 1989); In re Lou Levy & Sons Fashions, Inc., 785 F. Supp. 1163 (S.D.N.Y. 1992), aff'd, 988 F.2d 311 (2d Cir. 1993).

PROBLEM 139

It was the practice of Octopus National Bank to treat checks payable to the bank as if they were payable to bearer. It did this because many check drawers made the same assumption. Whenever Business Corporation wanted to put money into a special account reserved for the payment of taxes, it wrote a check for the requisite amount, payable to the order of "Octopus National Bank," and, by use of a deposit slip with the tax account number on it, made the deposit. Lucille Larceny, the corporate treasurer of Business Corporation, wrote out a check for $250,000, payable to the order of "Octopus National Bank," cooking the books so that it appeared this amount was going into the tax account but in reality putting it into her own personal account, using a deposit slip with her account number on it. When the check cleared, Lucille disappeared with the money. Business Corporation protested to the bank and, when the bank refused to recredit its account, sued, arguing that these checks were not "properly payable" under §4-401 of the UCC. Was the bank negligent? See Olean Area Camp Fire Council, Inc. v. Olean Dresser Clark Fed. Credit Union, 142 Misc. 2d 1049, 538 N.Y.S.2d 905 (Sup. Ct. 1989) ("In charity we will withhold characterizing such conduct as 'abject stupidity' and call it merely negligence of the grossest kind"); Govoni & Sons Const. Co. v. Mechanics Bank, 51 Mass. App. 35, 742 N.E.2d 1094 (2001); Master Chemical Corp. v. Inkrott, 55 Ohio St. 3d 23, 563 N.E.2d 26 (1990); but see Trail Leasing, Inc. v. Drovers First American Bank, 447 N.W.2d 190 (Minn. 1989) (bank is a holder in due course and takes free of the defenses of the drawer).[13] For an Annotation on the subject, see 69 A.L.R.4th 778. If the corporation were also found to be negligent in not better supervising Lucille, how does that affect the result?

PROBLEM 140

When Edwin Dennis died, he left all of his property in trust to his minor son, Patrick, whose guardianship was given over to Edwin's sister, Mame, who was named as trustee. One of the assets thus transferred was a $10,000 certificate of deposit, changed after Edwin's death so that it was payable to "Mame Dennis, as guardian and trustee for Patrick Dennis, a minor." When Mame decided to open her own catering business, she took the CD down to Babcock

---

13. This decision seems terribly wrong to us. What possible value does the bank give? It is merely releasing the customer's money and parting with none of its own. Furthermore, the bank is hardly in good faith and without notice (requirements to become a holder in due course) when it is behaving this carelessly. For a case saying that the bank cannot be a holder in due course in this situation, see Mutual Service Cas. Ins. Co. v. Elizabeth State Bank, 265 F.3d 601 (7th Cir. 2001).

National Bank and pledged it as collateral for an $8,000 loan to her personally, and the bank took possession of the CD and put it in its vault. When Patrick came of age he consulted you, a former schoolmate and newly licensed attorney, and asked if he can get the CD back from the bank without having to repay the loan. See §3-307.

If Mame had used the Patrick Dennis Trust Account carried at Babcock National Bank, on which she was the named trustee, to write herself a check to pay her salary as trustee, would that be a suspicious circumstance giving rise to a claim in Patrick's favor to recover the money? See §3-307(b)(3) and its Official Comment 4.

E. The Bank Statement Rule

In the earlier discussion of the bank and its customer, we covered §4-406, which establishes the rule that the customer must examine the bank statement or be estopped from asserting unauthorized signatures or material alterations that could have been discovered. That section, which you should read again, is nothing more than an extension of §3-406, the Negligence Rule; it establishes a specific act of negligence, failure to examine bank statements, which leads to an estoppel.

PROBLEM 141

While repairing a furnace in Rhonda Rivers' home, John Burly took advantage of her absence to sneak to her desk and tear out a blank check from the back of her checkbook. On March 25, this check cleared through Rhonda's checking account with her name forged thereto; the amount was $500. This check was returned to Rhonda on April 1. She failed to balance her checkbook until August 1 of that year, when she discovered and reported the forgery. Must the bank recredit her account? See §4-406(d)(1). Would it help or hurt the bank's position if John Burly had also had an account at the bank and had had $500 or more in this account at all times up until the end of July?

PROBLEM 142

Lucille Larceny was secretary to Howard Head, CEO of Business Corporation. Over a period of three years she stole 87 blank corporate checks from Head's checkbook, made the checks out to her brother, forged Head's name as drawer, and (with the help of her equally wicked brother) managed to take $378,000 out of the corporate account before she was caught and she and her brother, both penniless, went to jail. You are the corporate counsel for Business Corporation. How much, if anything, can it make its bank recredit? See §4-406(c), (d), (e), and (f); Spacemakers of America, Inc. v. SunTrust Bank, 271 Ga. App. 335, 609 S.E.2d 683 (2005).

Peters v. Riggs Natl. Bank, N.A.

District of Columbia Court of Appeals, 2008
942 A.2d 1163

WASHINGTON, Chief Judge:

Appellant Winston D. Peters, the personal representative of the Estate of Rhona Graves, appeals from the trial court's grant of summary judgment against his claims of breach of contract, negligence, and violations of the Electronic Funds Transfer Act ("EFTA"). Appellant claimed that appellee Riggs Bank permitted unauthorized withdrawals in the amount of $131,278.61 from his mother's account despite the fact that she had been incapacitated and later died while most of the transactions occurred. Riggs Bank denied liability, but further asserted that appellant's claims were untimely. We agree that appellant's claims are time-barred. Thus, we affirm.

I.

On October 31, 1980, Rhona Graves opened a checking account at Riggs Bank. Graves entered into a customer agreement with Riggs, which included adoption of Riggs's Rules and Regulations that covered the checking account, and executed a signature card. Graves later opened a savings account with Riggs on October 3, 1986. This account was also governed by Riggs's Rules and Regulations.[14]

At some point prior to June of 2002, Ms. Graves won a substantial amount of money in the lottery. She deposited her lump sum payment into her accounts at Riggs Bank. However, on June 8, 2002, Ms. Graves suffered a serious stroke and was hospitalized. She lost the ability to communicate. She was later transferred to a nursing home where she remained in a seriously ill condition until she died on November 9, 2002.

Between May and December of 2002, someone withdrew money from Ms. Graves's accounts through the writing of checks, phone transfers, and

---

14. Relevant to this appeal is the following provision:

Your statement is considered correct, and we [Riggs Bank] will not be liable for payments made and charged to your account . . . unless you notify us of an error, including . . . unauthorized payment or other irregularity within (a) sixty (60) calendar days . . . of the mailing date of the earliest statement describing the charge or deposit to your account.

ATM withdrawals. Although uncertain, appellant suspects that Ms. Graves's sister, who lived with and assisted Ms. Graves for about three years between Ms. Graves's first stroke (in 2000) and her death, took the money. Appellant concedes that he does not know that his mother did not want her sister to have access to the funds, nor can he be sure that Ms. Graves did not sign the checks. However, while Ms. Graves was in the hospital, appellant told his aunt that he would bring her money to pay the household bills. Appellant claims he told his aunt not to use money from his mother's accounts.

During the 153-day period from Ms. Graves's stroke until her death, there were 73 ATM withdrawals from her account, including 72 of them at the $500.00 daily limit for withdrawals. Then, 21 additional withdrawals were made during the 41 days after Ms. Graves died, including 19 at the $500 maximum. All together, $46,547.00 was withdrawn from the account, including $10,159.50 after her death. Also, during this time, 128 checks were written, resulting in her account being debited $84,731.61. According to appellant, the signature on checks provided back to him does not match his mother's authorized signature on file with the bank. Six of the checks (totaling $62,000) were made out to his mother's sister, and another check was written to her daughter. Appellant asserts that during the time period of Ms. Graves's critical illness, she did not have the capacity to review bank statements, and that in any event, there is no evidence that she received any bank statements at the hospital.

After Ms. Graves died in November of 2002, appellant petitioned for letters of administration in January 2003 and received authority to open Ms. Graves's safety deposit box. In January 2003, appellant inspected the safety deposit box and discovered that his mother had won the lottery. At that time, her accounts showed balances of $2,174.18 and $159.81. On March 10, 2003, Riggs issued a check to appellant, payable to the Estate of Rhona Graves, in the amount of $2,301.12-the remaining account balance.

Appellant tried to track down the amount and location of the proceeds of Mrs. Graves's lottery winnings. He was finally appointed personal representative of the estate on April 2, 2003. Also in April, appellant discovered a Riggs bank statement from August 13, 2002 through September 12, 2002, showing that Ms. Graves's account had held $92,187.45, but closed at the end of the period with only $58,935.98. On April 16, 2003, appellant (through counsel) wrote Riggs Bank requesting more information about Ms. Graves's account. Appellant claims he had no basis for asserting that Riggs Bank had done anything improper at that time. On May 28, 2003, Riggs responded by providing appellant's counsel with copies of some account statements and other records and informed him that Riggs was still in the process of gathering further information. Riggs provided more documents on June 4, 2003.

Appellant apparently believed Riggs was investigating the withdrawals up until a November 12, 2003 meeting. By that point, Riggs had not provided results of an investigation. On November 7, 2003, appellant (through counsel) indicated to Riggs Bank that Riggs may have improperly permitted the payment on unauthorized checks and allowed unauthorized ATM cash withdrawals, but stated that appellant was awaiting the results of Riggs Bank's investigation before asserting a formal claim. According to appellant, Riggs failed to provide any further information. On August 4, 2004, appellant filed a complaint with the Superior Court, alleging breach of contract, negligence, and violations of EFTA. Appellee moved for summary judgment against appellant, claiming that appellant's claims were time-barred, as well as asserting that appellant had conceded that he could not say for certain that the checks and withdrawals had been unauthorized.

On Friday, October 14, 2005, the Honorable Michael L. Rankin held a hearing on the summary judgment motion. At the hearing, Judge Rankin, in the absence of evidence to the contrary, accepted the representations of Riggs Bank that it had sent monthly account statements to Ms. Graves, and that neither she nor appellant had notified the Bank of any unauthorized transactions in a timely manner. Judge Rankin ruled:

> In my view the defendant has the better of this argument and that it would be against the Uniform Commercial Code as applied in this case to hold the bank responsible for the loss of this money when they were sending notices of the monthly transactions, as they were required to do under their contract, to the only address that they had.
>
> In light of my view that that is the correct application of the law in this case, I'm going to enter summary judgment in favor of the defendant.

The court subsequently issued a one-page order, granting defendant's motion for summary judgment on all claims. This appeal followed.

A.   UNAUTHORIZED CHECKS

Articles 3 and 4 of D.C. Code, Commercial Law and Transactions ("U.C.C.") apply to negotiable instruments, including checks. *See* D.C. Code §28:3-102(a) (2001); D.C. Code §28:3-104 (2001). Thus, the U.C.C. governs the disposition of the unauthorized checks in this case. Under the U.C.C., a person is not liable for a negotiable instrument unless he or she signed it. *See* D.C. Code §28:3-401 (2001). However, D.C. Code §28:4-406 imposes upon bank customers a duty to discover and report unauthorized signatures or alterations to the bank.[15] D.C. Code § 28:4-406(f) establishes an absolute

---

15. The rationale for this U.C.C. provision is to allocate the burden of discovering forgeries to the party best able to detect the forgery: customers are more familiar with their own signatures and transactions than a financial institution that may process thousands of transactions. *See* American Airlines Employees Fed. Credit Union v. Martin, 29 S.W.3d 86, 92 (Tex. 2000).

notice requirement for customers as a pre-requisite to bringing any claim against the bank: [The court quoted §4-406(f).].

Other jurisdictions have consistently characterized this U.C.C. provision as a statute of repose, as opposed to a statute of limitations. *See* Jensen v. Essexbank, 396 Mass. 65, 483 N.E.2d 821, 822 (1985) ("The one-year period in §4-406(4) [precursor to §4-406(f)] is not a statute of limitations. . . . It is a statutory prerequisite of notice"); Indiana Nat'l Corp. v. FACO, Inc., 400 N.E.2d 202, 205 (Ind. Ct. App. 1980) (calling the provision "substantive law"). Other courts have noted that the provision constitutes a condition precedent to the customer's right to file claims against a bank. *See* National Title Insur. Corp. Agency v. First Union Nat'l Bank, 263 Va. 355, 559 S.E.2d 668, 671 (2002). According to this court, "[a] statute of repose . . . establishes an absolute time period within which legal proceedings must be initiated, regardless of when a cause of action accrues." Sandoe v. Lefta Assoc., 559 A.2d 732, 736 n.5 (D.C. 1989). Based on the clear statutory language of D.C. Code §28:4-406(f) — "[A] customer who does not . . . discover and report . . . is precluded from asserting against the bank the unauthorized signature or alteration" — we hold that D.C. Code §28:4-406(f) is a statute of repose.

We must next determine whether Riggs Bank permissibly shortened the length of the statute of repose from D.C. Code §28:4-406(f)'s provision of one-year to a period of sixty days. The U.C.C. establishes that contracting parties may vary U.C.C. terms by contract:

> The effect of the provisions of this article may be varied by agreement, but the parties to the agreement cannot disclaim a bank's responsibility for its lack of good faith or failure to exercise ordinary care or limit the measure of damages for the lack or failure. However, the parties may determine by agreement the standards by which the bank's responsibility is to be measured if those standards are not manifestly unreasonable.

D.C. Code §28:4-103(a) (2001). Further, this court has noted that "'[t]he relationship between a bank and a depositor is a contractual relationship that is governed by the written agreement between the parties.'" Geiger v. Crestar Bank, 778 A.2d 1085, 1090 (D.C. 2001) (quoting Isaac v. First Nat'l Bank of Maryland, D.C., 647 A.2d 1159, 1161 (D.C. 1994)). Here, Riggs Bank and Ms. Graves entered into a contractual agreement providing, *inter alia*:

> Your statement is considered correct, and we [Riggs Bank] will not be liable for payments made and charged to your account . . . unless you notify us of an error, including . . . unauthorized payment or other irregularity within (a) sixty (60) calendar days . . . of the mailing date of the earliest statement describing the charge or deposit to your account.

Thus, following the terms of the contract, Ms. Graves had sixty days from the mailing of her account statements to discover and report unauthorized transactions.

Appellant contends that Riggs's shortening of the period to sixty days is invalid as it provides too short a period of time for a person to discover and report problems in their account, or alternatively, it effectively excuses the bank from exercising due care. However, a review of other jurisdictions reveals that courts have consistently upheld the contractual shortening of the notice provision to periods of sixty days or shorter. *See, e.g., National Title Ins. Corp. Agency, supra,* 559 S.E.2d at 672 (upholding a sixty-day notice provision); *American Airlines Employees Fed. Credit Union, supra,* 29 S.W.3d at 96 (same); Jamison v. First Georgia Bank, 193 Ga. App. 219, 387 S.E.2d 375, 376-77 (1989) (same). The contractual shortening does not alter the bank's duty to exercise ordinary care or good faith; it "merely varies" the U.C.C.'s contractual notice provision. *See* National Title Ins. Corp. Agency, *supra,* 559 S.E.2d at 671. Neither has appellant shown the sixty day time period to be unconscionable, as he has not demonstrated both that Ms. Graves lacked a meaningful choice in entering the contract and that the contract terms unreasonably favor Riggs Bank. *See* Riggs Nat'l Bank of Washington, D.C. v. District of Columbia, 581 A.2d 1229, 1251 (D.C. 1990) (citing Williams v. Walker-Thomas Furniture Co., 121 U.S. App. D.C. 315, 319, 350 F.2d 445, 449 (1965)). Because the U.C.C. provision allocates the duty of discovering forgeries or unauthorized transactions to the customer, a reasonable contraction of the discovery and notice period encourages due diligence by the customer in inspecting account statements; it also promotes the U.C.C.'s goal of finality. *See* Silvia v. Indus. Nat'l Bank of Rhode Island, 121 R.I. 810, 403 A.2d 1075, 1077 (1979) (discussing the policy underlying the U.C.C. statutory notice provision as one that promotes finality of transactions). Accordingly, we agree that contracting parties may permissibly shorten the notice period to sixty days.

Appellant, however, contends that the statutory notice provision should be tolled in this case because of Ms. Graves's incapacitation and subsequent death and because appellant did not discover the unauthorized transactions until months after his mother's death. In essence, appellant asks this court to read a discovery rule into D.C. Code §28:4-406(f) that would permit equitable tolling of the provision. Appellant's position is untenable: equitable tolling cannot apply to statutes of repose. "Under the discovery rule, a particular cause of action accrues when the plaintiff knows or through the exercise of due diligence should have known of the injury." Ehrenhaft v. Malcolm Price, Inc., 483 A.2d 1192, 1201 (D.C. 1984) (internal quotation omitted). However, "[a] statute of repose . . . establishes an absolute time period within which legal proceedings must be initiated, *regardless of when a cause of action accrues.*" *Sandoe, supra,* 559 A.2d at 736 n.5 (emphasis added).

Therefore, if a statute of repose applies regardless of when the cause of action accrues, and the discovery rule merely alters when the cause of action accrues, then the discovery rule cannot apply to a statute of repose.[16] This logic is consistent with holdings from other jurisdictions. *See, e.g.,* Estate of Decker v. Farm Credit Servs. of Mid-America, ACA, 684 N.E.2d 1137, 1139 (Ind. 1997) ("While equitable principles may extend the time for commencing an action under statutes of limitation, nonclaim statutes impose a condition precedent to the enforcement of a right of action and are not subject to equitable exceptions."); Brighton, Inc. v. Colonial First Nat'l Bank, 176 N.J. Super. 101, 422 A.2d 433, 437 (App. Div. 1980) ("The one-year period limitation in §4-406(4) is not merely a statute of limitations, but a rule of substantive law barring absolutely a customer's untimely asserted right to make such a claim against the bank.").

Courts have applied this statutory bar even in cases where the result is harsh. In Siecinski v. First State Bank of East Detroit, 209 Mich. App. 459, 531 N.W.2d 768, 769 (1995), an account holder suffered a head injury, fell into a coma, and died around a month later. Prior to her death, someone presented the incapacitated woman's bank with a forged power of attorney and ultimately withdrew everything in the account (around $175,000, most of it *after* the woman had died). *Id.* The appellant in the case had been appointed personal representative and had eventually discovered the wrongful withdrawals. *Id.* The Michigan Court of Appeals concluded that its version of §4-406(4) [the predecessor to §4-406(f)] barred the action despite the fact that no one was in a position to discover the forgery. *See id. at 770.* The court concluded that the statutory language created an absolute bar and that actual receipt of customer bank statements was not required:

> Courts of other jurisdictions have held that the subsection is not a limitation statute subject to tolling under compelling circumstances but is a statutory prerequisite of notice that absolutely bars a customer's right to make a claim against the bank after one year without regard to the care or lack of care of either the customer or the bank.

Id. The court further concluded that the statutory provision barred all causes of action-thus, appellant's negligence claim failed as well. *Id.* at 770-71.

---

16. This reasoning is also reflected in Black's Law Dictionary: "'statutes of limitations' extinguish, after [a] period of time, [the] right to prosecute accrued cause[s] of action; [a] 'statute of repose,' by contrast, limits potential liability by limiting [the] time during which cause of action can arise. It is distinguishable from [a] statute of limitations, in that [a] statute of repose cuts off right of action after [a] specified time measured from delivery of product or completion of work, regardless of time of accrual of cause of action or of notice of legal rights." Black's Law Dictionary 1411 (6th ed. 1990).

Courts have applied this reasoning against mentally incompetent plaintiffs as well. In Brown v. Cash Mgmt. Trust of Am., 963 F. Supp. 504, 504-05 (D. Md. 1997) (applying N.Y. law), the U.S. District Court in Maryland barred the plaintiff's claim in a case where a woman had opened a checking account as a co-signor with plaintiff, a mentally incompetent woman, before forging the incompetent plaintiff's signature and looting the account. Further, the bank sent statements to either the co-signor or the plaintiff's agent, but never to the plaintiff. *Id.* at 505. Nevertheless, the court held that the provision was "an unalterable condition precedent to suit" and declined to make an exception due to the plaintiff's mental state: "The certainty which the Uniform Commercial Code seeks to achieve in respect to commercial transactions would quickly dissipate if *ad hoc* exceptions to its commands were too eagerly crafted to accommodate the occasional 'hard case.'" *Id.* at 506. The North Carolina Court of Appeals reached the same conclusion. *See* Union v. Branch Banking & Trust Co., 176 N.C. App. 711, 627 S.E.2d 276, 279 (2006) ("[F]ailure of a customer or his representative to report his unauthorized signature within one year after the bank makes account statements available precludes a claim against the bank, even if the customer is incompetent (whether adjudicated or unadjudicated) during the one-year period for providing notice.").

These principles have also been applied in a number of fraud cases where the party forging checks intercepted bank statements — thus preventing the account holder from actually receiving the statements and reporting any errors. In Stowell v. Cloquet Co-op Credit Union, 557 N.W.2d 567, 569-70 (Minn. 1997), a man forged his neighbor's signature on fifty checks, misappropriated a total amount of $22,000, and stole his neighbor's credit union statements every month. In concluding that §4-406(f) applied to bar the plaintiff's claims, the court explained that the U.C.C. provision assigns the risk of non-receipt to the bank customer:

> The modern U.C.C. case law of other jurisdictions is virtually unanimous in holding that, once account statements are mailed to the account holder's proper address, the risk of nonreceipt falls on the account holder and interception of the statements by a wrongdoer does not relieve the account holder of the duty to examine the statements and report unauthorized items to the bank.

Id. at 571-72; *see also id. at 568-69* (pointing out that the credit union processed roughly one million transactions a day, and thus provided monthly account statements, rather than manually checking individual signature cards). The court further noted that requiring actual receipt of the statements (which would be the result of placing the risk of non-receipt on the bank) "would place unreasonable financial burdens on banks and other financial institutions by forcing them to prove receipt either through the use of certified mail or by individually contacting each account holder to confirm that they had, in fact, received their account statement." *Id.* at 572. Other courts have reached the same conclusion. *See, e.g.,* Borowski v. Firstar Bank Milwaukee, N.A., 217 Wis. 2d 565, 579 N.W.2d 247, 252-53 (Ct. App. 1998) (concluding that notice provision still barred claims even where plaintiff's girlfriend forged checks (totaling around $150,000) and intercepted bank statements); PTA, Pub. Sch. 72 v. Mfrs. Hanover Trust Co., 138 Misc. 2d 289, 295, 524 N.Y.S.2d 336, 340 (N.Y. City Civ. Ct. 1988) (upholding bar of claim despite fact that forger intercepted statements, meaning that account holder had no actual receipt).

These courts based their decisions on the underlying policies of the Uniform Commercial Code: encouraging the efficiency and finality of transactions through a uniform and predictable application of the law. *See, e.g., Brown, supra,* 963 F. Supp. at 506 n.4 ("[T]he U.C.C. has the objective of promoting certainty and predictability in commercial transactions.") (internal quotation omitted); Fundacion Museo de Arte Contemporaneo de Caracas-Sofia Imber v. CBI-TDB Union Bancaire Privee, 996 F. Supp. 277, 291 (S.D.N.Y. 1998) (declining to impose actual receipt requirement because it would require banks to send account statements by certified mail); *Silvia, supra,* 403 A.2d at 1077 (discussing the policy underlying §4-406(4) as one that promotes finality of transactions). According to the U.C.C. itself, U.C.C. provisions "shall be liberally construed and applied to promote its underlying purposes and policies," including a policy "to make uniform the law among the various jurisdictions." D.C. Code §28:1-102 (2001).

Appellant urges the court to accept an exception carved out by a California appellate court. In Mac v. Bank of Am., 76 Cal. App. 4th 562, 567-68, 90 Cal. Rptr. 2d 476 (Cal. Ct. App. 1999), the court found that §4-406(f) did not apply and did not bar the claim of a personal representative to recover for unauthorized transactions that cleared after the account holder's death because §4-406(a) requires that statements be "made available to the customer," and in that case, there was no customer because the customer had died. We decline to adopt *Mac*; it functionally imposes a discovery rule inconsistent with the principles underlying statutes of repose, as well as the policies of uniformity and predictability espoused by the U.C.C. Its application to other cases would create the type of *ad hoc* exception that other jurisdictions have avoided. Further, it would impose upon banks the duty of ensuring actual receipt—a logistical problem whose extra costs would undoubtedly be passed on to the consumer. Therefore, consistent with other jurisdictions and in promotion of the underlying policies of the U.C.C., we hold that D.C. Code §28:4-406(f) is not subject to equitable tolling. Because it is undisputed that neither Ms. Graves nor appellant timely notified Riggs Bank of the unauthorized transactions, appellant's claims are barred. . . .

Accordingly, the decision of the trial court is

Affirmed.

PROBLEM 143

Original National Bank engaged in the practice of "bulk filing," meaning that the bank did not examine checks for forgeries if they were written for amounts less than $5,000. The bank justified this practice as necessary for economic reasons. It therefore paid a series of $3,500 checks on which a customer's signature as drawer was forged and sent them over a period of months to its customer as part of his monthly statement. The customer negligently failed to report the forgeries of his name until seven months after the first one was returned to him. When he did complain, the bank pointed to §4-406(c) and (d). The customer replied that §4-406(e) requires the bank to share the loss since it did not observe ordinary care. As to the meaning of *ordinary care*, see §4-103(c) and a definition of the term in §3-103(a)(9) that should prove very interesting to the bank's attorney. Who prevails here?

Clemente Bros. Contracting Corp. v. Hafner-Milazzo

Court of Appeals of New York, 2014
23 N.Y.3d 277, 14 N.E.3d 367, 991 N.Y.S.2d 14

Chief Judge LIPPMAN.

The primary issue presented is whether a bank and its customer may agree to shorten from one year to 14 days the statutory time period under UCC 4-406(4) within which a customer must notify its bank of an improperly paid item in order to recover the payment thereon. In two opinions issued over 20 years ago, this Court declined to decide this issue because it was not presented directly, but questioned whether a 14-day period could be reasonable and observed that the question "raise[d] policy considerations" (Putnam Rolling Ladder Co. v. Manufacturers Hanover Trust Co., 74 N.Y.2d 340, 349 n.2, 547 N.Y.S.2d 611, 546 N.E.2d 904 [1989]; SOS Oil Corp. v. Norstar Bank of Long Is., 76 N.Y.2d 561, 568, 561 N.Y.S.2d 887, 563 N.E.2d 258 [1990]). We now hold that, at least in this case, the parties' agreement to shorten the period was permissible.

I

In April 2007, plaintiff Clemente Brothers Contracting Corp. opened three corporate operating accounts at North Fork Bank (which subsequently merged with defendant Capital One, N.A. [collectively Capital One]) and took out a loan and a line of credit, each backed by a promissory note. Clemente Brothers could draw money on the line of credit by sending a signed drawdown request to Capital One. As a condition precedent to opening the accounts at Capital One, plaintiff Jeffrey Clemente, the company's principal, executed a personal guaranty with respect to the loan and line of credit, and Clemente Brothers passed a corporate resolution, which provided that Jeffrey Clemente was the only authorized signatory on the accounts and the only one authorized to sign drawdown requests on the line of credit.

The corporate resolution also provided,

> That unless [Clemente Brothers] shall notify the Bank in writing *within fourteen calendar days* of the delivery or mailing of any statement of account and cancelled check, draft or other instrument for the payment of money (hereinafter referred to as "Instrument") of any claimed errors in such statement, or that [Clemente Brothers'] signature upon any such returned Instrument was forged, or that any such Instrument was made or drawn without the authority of [Clemente Brothers] . . . or that it was raised or otherwise altered . . . said statement of account shall be considered correct for all purposes and said Bank shall not be liable for any payments made and charged to the account of [Clemente Brothers] or for any other errors in the statement of account as rendered to it.

Capital One mailed statements of account for all three of the operating accounts to the business address provided by Clemente Brothers. The monthly statements included copies of cancelled checks drawn on that account.

As for the line of credit, Capital One mailed a statement to Clemente Brothers each month showing the principal balance and the monthly interest payment, which was automatically debited from the primary operating account. Capital One has not offered any evidence that it included copies of the drawdown requests on the line of credit with the monthly statements. But the drawdowns appeared as credits on the operating account statements.

Defendant Aprile Hafner-Milazzo worked as a secretary and bookkeeper for Clemente Brothers until it was discovered that she had been forging Clemente's signature on certain Capital One bank documents, including drawdown requests on the line of credit and checks paid from one of Clemente Brothers' accounts. According to plaintiffs, Hafner-Milazzo embezzled approximately $386,000 over the course of approximately two years, from January 2008 through December 2009.

In February 2010, Clemente Brothers notified Capital One of Hafner-Milazzo's thefts. Thereafter, Capital One determined that an event had occurred that adversely affected Clemente Brothers' ability to repay its debts and, pursuant to a clause in the two promissory notes, declared all amounts due and payable.

Plaintiffs subsequently commenced this action against Hafner-Milazzo and Capital One to recover damages resulting from Hafner-Milazzo's forgeries and to prevent Capital One from forcing repayment on the loans. In its answer, Capital One interposed several counterclaims to recover amounts due under the loans and Clemente's personal guaranty.

Capital One moved for summary judgment dismissing the complaint insofar as asserted against it and on its counterclaims. Supreme Court granted Capital One's motion in its entirety and awarded it the principal sum of $1,146,262.90 on its counterclaims (Clemente Bros. Contr. Corp. v. Hafner-Milazzo, 2011 N.Y. Slip Op. 30384[U] [Sup. Ct., N.Y. County 2011]). According to the court, Capital One was "entitled to the protection afforded by UCC 4-406(4)," which precludes liability for a bank to its customer when it pays a check on a forged signature but makes statements of the account and the allegedly forged items available to the customer, and the customer fails to report the alleged forgery to the bank within one year (*id.* at *4). Here, the court observed, Clemente Brothers and Capital One, by agreement, properly abbreviated the one-year period to 14 days, within which plaintiffs failed to report each of the alleged forgeries.

The Appellate Division affirmed (Clemente Bros. Contr. Corp. v. Hafner-Milazzo, 100 A.D.3d 677, 954 N.Y.S.2d 156 [2d Dept. 2012]). This Court granted plaintiffs leave to appeal (21 N.Y.3d 856, 2013 WL 2395327 [2013]).

II

New York's version of the Uniform Commercial Code (hereinafter UCC) imposes strict liability upon a bank that charges against its customer's account any "item" that is not "properly payable" (UCC 4-401[1]; Monreal v. Fleet Bank, 95 N.Y.2d 204, 207, 713 N.Y.S.2d 301, 735 N.E.2d 880 [2000]). An "item" is "any instrument for the payment of money even though it is not negotiable but does not include money" (UCC 4-104[1][g]). Black's Law Dictionary defines "instrument" as a "written legal document that defines rights, duties, entitlements, or liabilities" (Black's Law Dictionary 869 [9th ed. 2009]). Put another way, a bank may not charge a check, or other written document defining a right to or liability for payment, bearing a forged signature against its customer's account (*Monreal*, 95 N.Y.2d at 207, 713 N.Y.S.2d 301, 735 N.E.2d 880).

The UCC nevertheless limits banks' exposure by imposing obligations on customers that, if unfulfilled, may preclude a customer's suit against the bank. When a bank sends to its customer statements of account and copies of the items paid, the customer must review those documents promptly and notify the bank of any irregularities:

> "When a bank sends to its customer a statement of account accompanied by items paid in good faith in support of the debit entries or holds the statement and items pursuant to a request or instructions of its customer or otherwise in a reasonable manner makes the statement and items available to the customer, the customer must exercise reasonable care and promptness to examine the statement and items to discover his unauthorized signature or any alteration on an item and must notify the bank promptly after discovery thereof" (UCC 4-406 [1]; *see also Monreal*, 95 N.Y.2d at 207, 713 N.Y.S.2d 301, 735 N.E.2d 880).

If the customer fails to fulfill its obligation, then the customer is precluded from asserting against the bank (1) "his unauthorized signature or any alteration on the item if the bank also establishes that it suffered a loss by reason of such failure" and (2) "an unauthorized signature or alteration by the same wrongdoer on any other item paid in good faith by the bank after the first item and statement was available to the customer for a reasonable period not exceeding fourteen calendar days" (UCC 4-406[2][a], [b]). These bars to recovery do not apply "if the customer establishes lack of ordinary care on the part of the bank in paying the item(s)" (UCC 4-406[3]).

An additional limitation, pertinent here, is found in UCC 4-406(4), which creates something akin to a statute of repose that bars a customer's claim for recovery on a wrongfully paid item when the customer fails to report the irregularity within one year after the bank provides the statement and item, regardless of either party's failure to exercise reasonable care:

> "Without regard to care or lack of care of either the customer or the bank a customer who does not within one year from the time the statement and items are made available to the customer (subsection (1)) discover and report his unauthorized signature . . . is precluded from asserting against the bank such unauthorized signature or indorsement or such alteration" (UCC 4-406 [4]).

Here, the parties shortened the one-year period to 14 days by agreement.

A

Capital One argues that UCC 4-406(4) defeats plaintiffs' claims with respect to both the operating accounts and the line of credit. But the application of UCC 4-406(4) is contingent upon the bank providing the customer with account statements and copies of the items paid under UCC 4-406(1).

The parties do not seriously dispute that Capital One complied with UCC 4-406(1) with respect to the operating accounts by providing monthly statements and copies of cancelled checks. But they do dispute whether the line of credit is subject to UCC article 4 at all, and, if it is, whether Capital One complied with UCC 4-406(1).

Plaintiffs argue that the drawdown requests on the line of credit do not qualify as "items" within the meaning of UCC article 4. We disagree. The requests are written instruments formally exercising a contractual right to the payment of money from the line of credit. We do agree with plaintiffs, however, that, at least on this motion for summary judgment, Capital One cannot avail itself of UCC 4-406(4). Capital One argues that the drawdown requests should be treated as items and that it is entitled to the protections of UCC 4-406(4), but it conspicuously has not offered evidence showing that it complied with the threshold requirements of UCC 4-406(1) quoted above.

The language of the New York statute tracks the language of the original model Uniform Commercial Code (Model UCC), and has not been amended by the legislature since adoption in 1962. Section 4-406 of the Model UCC was amended in 1991 to require that the bank must provide a statement of account and "shall either return or make available to the customer the items paid *or* provide information in the statement of account sufficient to allow the customer reasonably to identify the items paid" (Model UCC [2002] §4-406[a] [maintaining 1991 language] [emphasis added]).

The Model UCC's official commentary explains that under the new language:

> "[i]f the bank supplies its customer with an image of the paid item, it complies with this standard. But a safe harbor rule is provided. The bank complies with the standard of providing 'sufficient information' if 'the item is described by item number, amount, and date of payment.' This means that the customer's duties under [what was Model UCC 4-406(4)] are triggered if the bank sends a statement of account complying with the safe harbor rule without returning the paid items" (Model UCC 4-406, Comment 1).

Many states have adopted some form of the revised Model UCC 4-406. Ohio and Illinois, for example, require only that a bank provide an account statement with information sufficient to identify an item paid (*see* Ohio Rev. Code Ann. §1304.35[A]; 810 Ill. Comp. Stat. §5/4–406 [a]). But New York has not adopted the revised Model UCC.

Banks in New York, as elsewhere, must comply in good faith with UCC 4-406(1) to seek the protections of UCC 4-406(4) (*see* Elden v. Merrill Lynch, Pierce, Fenner & Smith Inc., 2011 WL 1236141, *7, 2011 U.S. Dist. LEXIS 35886, *21-22 [S.D.N.Y., Mar. 30, 2011, No. 08-Civ-8738 (RJS)] [holding that bank did not send copies of the items and did not otherwise reasonably make them available, thus precluding relief under UCC 4-406(4)]). Again, they may do this in one of three ways: supply the items to the customer with the statement of account, hold the items for the customer, or "otherwise in a reasonable manner make[] the statement and items available" (UCC 4-406 [1]). The official commentary explains that this third option is to be used only in "unusual situations" (UCC 4-406, Comment 2). But one treatise author has noted that "literal compliance with this triggering event seem[s] impossible," and argues that the bank practice of sending or posting simple account statements should be sufficient to satisfy the requirements of section 4-406(1) (*see* 5 Hawkland et al., Uniform Commercial Code Series §4-406:2 at Art. 4-988, 4-992; *accord* Barkley Clark & Barbara Clark, 1 Bank Deposits, Collections and Credit Cards ¶10.05[1][a] at 10-39-10-40 [2013]).

Here, the record does not show that the drawdown requests were provided to Clemente Brothers. Absent any record evidence or discussion in the briefs about relevant banking practice or applicable regulations on this point, we do not hold that Capital One failed to comply with section 4-406(1) as a matter of law. But neither has the bank demonstrated its compliance with the statute. Consequently, Capital One is not entitled to summary judgment on the line-of-credit claims under UCC 4-406(4), and, on remittal, the judgment in its favor must be amended accordingly pending further proceedings on these claims.

Capital One argues in the alternative, and the lower courts also reasoned, that the wrongfully paid drawdown requests did not harm plaintiff. Capital One contends that paying the drawdown requests merely effectuated a transfer of funds from one of plaintiffs' accounts to another. But this is not an accurate description of the transactions; the funds did not come from plaintiffs' account, but from the bank itself.

The line of credit was, in effect, a pre-approved loan upon which plaintiffs could draw at will. Plaintiffs did not possess any borrowed funds or owe anything in repayment in the absence of a drawdown request. Upon such a request, Capital One would transfer funds to one of plaintiffs' accounts, interest immediately would begin to accrue and plaintiffs would be liable to repay the principal. Therefore, when Capital One wrongfully paid the drawdown requests at issue in this case, plaintiffs suffered financial harm.

B

Turning to the application of UCC 4-406(4), the UCC permits parties to alter the provisions of article 4 by agreement (*see* UCC 4-103[1]). The Official Comments go so far as to say that there exists a "blanket power to vary all provisions of the Article" (*id.*, Comment 2). But that power is not boundless:

> "[N]o agreement can disclaim a bank's responsibility for its own lack of good faith or failure to exercise ordinary care or can limit the measure of damages

for such lack or failure; but the parties may by agreement determine the standards by which such responsibility is to be measured if such standards are not manifestly unreasonable" (UCC 4-103[1]).

The application of these limitations raises two issues: first, whether parties can vary the one-year period by agreement; we hold that they can; and second, whether shortening the one-year period to 14 days is manifestly unreasonable; we hold that it is not, at least under these facts.

The argument that modification is not allowed is that by shortening the period, the bank is "disclaiming" its obligation to act with care or that it is limiting the measure of damages for a failure to act with care in violation of UCC 4-403(1). This argument finds some slender support in our decision in Regatos v. North Fork Bank, 5 N.Y.3d 395, 804 N.Y.S.2d 713, 838 N.E.2d 629 (2005).

Regatos involved the funds transfers provisions of UCC article 4-A. Banks are liable under article 4-A for improper funds transfers, similar to how they are liable under article 4 for improperly paid items. As for funds transfers, UCC 4-A-204 (2) provides that "the obligation of a receiving bank to refund payment . . . may not otherwise be varied by agreement."

UCC 4-A-505 contains a one-year notice period similar to that found in UCC 4-406(4). This Court held that parties could not shorten the one-year period in UCC 4-A-505 by agreement (*Regatos*, 5 N.Y.3d at 398-399, 804 N.Y.S.2d 713, 838 N.E.2d 629). The Court reasoned that shortening the one-year period effectively would "var[y]" the bank's "obligation . . . to refund payment" in violation of the plain language of UCC 4-A-204 (2) (*id.* at 402-403, 804 N.Y.S.2d 713, 838 N.E.2d 629).

Plaintiffs would have us apply *Regatos* to this case. They rely on two Appellate Division decisions that could be read as extending the logic of *Regatos* to UCC 4-406 (*see* Aikens Constr. of Rome v. Simons, 284 A.D.2d 946, 947, 727 N.Y.S.2d 213 [4th Dept. 2001]; Herzog, Engstrom & Koplovitz v. Union Natl. Bank, 226 A.D.2d 1004, 1004-1005, 640 N.Y.S.2d 703 [3d Dept. 1996]). But this result neither follows from the provisions of article 4 nor is it desirable as a policy matter.

Unlike UCC 4-A-204, UCC 4-103(1) does not prohibit a bank from altering its obligation to refund payments made in good faith. And shortening the one-year period does not violate any of the prohibitions in UCC 4-103(1). Capital One did not disclaim its responsibility to act with care by requiring its customer to notify it of an improperly paid item within 14 days of receiving the account statement. While shortening the period certainly affected Capital One's liability for improperly paid items, whether paid in good faith or not, it did not exclude all liability for negligence. Nor did the modification affect the measure of damages; it merely limited the time within which plaintiffs must provide notice of the improper charge.

Courts around the country have permitted parties to shorten the one year to various periods, from as short as 14 days to more than 60 days (*see e.g.* Gluck v. JPMorgan Chase Bank, 12 A.D.3d 305, 306, 785 N.Y.S.2d 77 [1st Dept. 2004] [60 days]; Peters v. Riggs Natl. Bank, N.A., 942 A.2d 1163, 1168 [D.C. 2008] [60 days]; Borowski v. Firstar Bank Milwaukee, N.A., 217 Wis. 2d 565, 576-580, 579 N.W.2d 247, 252-253 [1998] [14 days]). And the record and case law suggest that most banks do shorten the period.

To apply *Regatos*'s logic to this case would be to hold not only the 14-day period impermissible, but every other longer period used in the industry, be it 30 days or nine months. We perceive no good reason for creating such an inconsistency in the banking laws of the various states. We therefore hold that parties may modify by agreement the one-year period in UCC 4-406(4), as long as the modification is not manifestly unreasonable.

The modification in this case is not manifestly unreasonable. Clemente Brothers had numerous employees, regularly moved hundreds of thousands of dollars in and out of its operating accounts, and had the resources to make an informed decision about opening accounts at Capital One. Critically, Clemente was fully aware of the terms of the agreements with Capital One because Clemente Brothers passed a corporate resolution acknowledging its obligation to notify Capital One of any irregularities within 14 days of each statement of account.

It is not manifestly unreasonable to expect a company with numerous employees and hundreds of thousands of dollars under its control to monitor its accounts once a month, within 14 days of each statement, particularly where it has acknowledged its responsibility to do so in a corporate resolution. That expectation is all the more reasonable in this age, when customers can monitor their account transactions minute by minute online from around the world.

We stress, however, that our holding is limited to the case of a corporate entity that either is financially sophisticated or has the resources to acquire professional guidance. It could well be unreasonable for banks to use contracts of adhesion to impose an exacting 14-day limit on unsophisticated customers, small family businesses, or individual consumers, including, for example, the elderly, people suffering from certain disabilities, or others for whom the 14-day rule could be too unforgiving. These customers may lack the time, technology, or other resources to check their account statements within such a limited period every month. They are more susceptible to unforeseen events disrupting their routines or normal business operations. And it may be that banks need less protection on these accounts because the total assets held may be less than those of larger companies. But whether it would be *manifestly* unreasonable for these customers to be subject to a 14-day notice period, as opposed to a 30- or 60-day period, is a question for a later day.

The order of the Appellate Division should be modified, without costs, by remitting to Supreme Court for further proceedings in accordance with this opinion, and, as so modified, affirmed.

PIGOTT, J. (dissenting in part).

Uniform Commercial Code §4-406, titled "Customer's Duty to Discover and Report Unauthorized Signature or Alteration," sets forth a customer's and bank's respective duties concerning a customer's statement of account. When the bank sends the customer such a statement accompanied by items paid in good faith, the customer must "exercise reasonable care and promptness to examine the statement and items to discover his unauthorized signature . . . and . . . notify the bank promptly after discovery thereof" (UCC 4-406[1]). If the customer does not comply with that provision he or she is precluded from asserting against the bank: A customer is not precluded from asserting against a bank an unauthorized signature under subsection (2), however, "if the customer establishes lack of ordinary care on the part of the bank in paying the item(s)" (UCC 4-406[3]). UCC 4-406(4) prescribes a one-year time limit on a customer to make a claim against a bank for its payment of an altered or forged paper irrespective of whether the bank exercised ordinary care.

> "(a) his unauthorized signature or any alteration on the item if the bank also establishes that it suffered a loss by reason of such failure; and
>
> "(b) an unauthorized signature or alteration by the same wrong-doer on any other item paid in good faith by the bank after the first item and statement was available to the customer for a reasonable period not exceeding fourteen calendar days and before the bank receives notification from the customer of any such unauthorized signature or alteration" (UCC 4-406[2][a], [b]).

Plaintiff claims that Capital One had notice of defendant Hafner-Milazzo's predisposition to commit illegal acts and failed to exercise ordinary care. By boilerplate resolution, however, the bank claims to have reduced the time under which the plaintiff could assert such a lack of ordinary care from one year to the same 14-day time period as set forth in section 4-406(2), effectively repealing section 4-406(4) as it applies to its customers. The majority finds this reasonable, relying on UCC 4-103(1), which provides, as relevant here, that UCC article 4's provisions "may be varied by agreement" with the caveat "that no agreement can disclaim a bank's responsibility *for its own lack of good faith or failure to exercise ordinary care* or can limit the measure of damages for such lack or failure; but the parties may by agreement determine the *standards* by which such responsibility is to be measured if such standards are not manifestly unreasonable" (emphasis supplied).

In my view, because section 4-406(4) clearly imposes a one-year limitation on claims involving a bank's "failure to exercise ordinary care," the time period cannot be changed by agreement. To be sure, there may be a variation in standards by which a bank's responsibility is to be measured (so long as such standards are not manifestly unreasonable), but the one-year limitation remains.

The majority claims that the shortening of the period resulted in a limitation of liability, and reduced only plaintiff's time to provide notice of the improper charge (majority op. at 288, 991 N.Y.S.2d at 19, 14 N.E.3d at 372). That is mere semantics, however, because the overall effect of the time reduction is to eliminate plaintiff's opportunity to assert, after the 14-day period had passed (but before the one-year time period had elapsed) that Capital One had failed to exercise ordinary care and, consequently, recover damages as a result of that negligence. The shortening of the time period works a de facto disclaimer of liability, which is prohibited under section 4-103(1).

It is my view that just as the customer and bank in Regatos v. North Fork Bank, 5 N.Y.3d 395, 804 N.Y.S.2d 713, 838 N.E.2d 629 (2005), were prohibited from modifying by contract the one-year statute of repose set forth in UCC 4-A-505 —which grants a customer one year to notify the bank of an unauthorized wire transfer—plaintiff and Capital One were prohibited from contractually shortening section 4-406(4)'s one-year time limitation. In *Regatos*, the bank received two unauthorized funds transfers totaling $600,000 and, in violation of the agreed security procedures, transferred the funds from the customer's account. When the customer notified the bank of the unauthorized transfers five months later, the bank refused to refund the money, relying on the account agreement's provision that the customer was to notify the bank of "any unauthorized signature or alteration" within 15 days (*see Regatos*, 5 N.Y.3d at 399-400, 804 N.Y.S.2d 713, 838 N.E.2d 629). Relying on UCC 4-A-204 (*l*)'s language that a "bank is not entitled to any recovery from the customer on account of a failure by the customer to give notification as stated in this section," we concluded that the bank had an obligation to refund the principal so long as notice was given within one year as required by section 4-A-505 (*id.* at 402-403, 804 N.Y.S.2d 713, 838 N.E.2d 629). We explained that the policy behind UCC article 4-A was to encourage financial institutions "to adopt appropriate security procedures," and that allowing them "to vary the notice period by agreement would reduce the effectiveness of the statute's one-year period of repose as an incentive for banks to create and follow security procedures" (*id.* at 402, 804 N.Y.S.2d 713, 838 N.E.2d 629).

Likewise, UCC article 4 imposes upon a bank the obligation to act with ordinary care, which required Capital One to follow commercially reasonable security procedures to ensure it was not making payments on unauthorized checks. A reduction in the one-year period to 14 days provides little, if any, incentive for a bank to act with ordinary care. And, of course, a bank's obligation to exercise ordinary care may not be varied by agreement (*see* Aikens Constr. of Rome v. Simons, 284 A.D.2d 946, 947, 727 N.Y.S.2d 213 [4th Dept. 2001]; Herzog, Engstrom & Koplovitz v. Union Natl. Bank, 226 A.D.2d 1004, 1005, 640 N.Y.S.2d 703 [3d Dept. 1996]). But that is precisely what the corporate resolution does in this case. Prior to today, our courts have never sanctioned such a practice.

The majority approach has at least two significant drawbacks. First, it impairs the incentive the authors of UCC article 4 created for banks to exercise ordinary care in the payment of items. Second, it seems to make the outcome of cases depend upon whether the customer is a Fortune 500 company, a medium-sized one (this plaintiff is no corporate giant), a small one, or an individual. It would be better to interpret the statute in a way that obviates the need for a court to analyze whether the customer was "financially sophisticated," possessed "the resources to acquire professional guidance," was a "small family business" or an "elderly" individual (majority op. at 289, 991 N.Y.S.2d at 20, 14 N.E.3d at 373) because the rule would apply to every type of consumer. The rule proposed by the majority provides less certainty and will create more litigation because it doesn't apply to everyone in like fashion. The fact that the majority is concerned that financial institutions will "use contracts of adhesion to impose" what it acknowledges is "an *exacting 14-day limit* on unsophisticated consumers" (majority op. at 289, 991 N.Y.S.2d at 20, 14 N.E.3d at 373 [emphasis supplied]) only underscores why customers and banks should not be permitted to contractually reduce section 4-406(4)'s one-year limitation period.

Accordingly, I respectfully dissent from that part of the majority holding that a customer and bank may contractually reduce section 4-406(4)'s one-year limitations period.

Judges GRAFFEO, READ, RIVERA and ABDUS-SALAAM concur with Chief Judge LIPPMAN; Judge PIGOTT dissents in part in an opinion in which Judge SMITH concurs.

Order modified, without costs, by remitting to Supreme Court, Suffolk County, for further proceedings in accordance with the opinion herein and, as so modified, affirmed.

PROBLEM 144

When the law firm of Factory, Factory & Money (F.F. & M.) opened a checking account with Octopus National Bank (ONB), the firm members signed a deposit contract, stating that they would report all irregularities in their bank statements within 10 days of their receipt. Failure to do so resulted in a waiver of any problems with the statement. Two years later LeNore Ledger, F.F. & M.'s bookkeeper, wrote three checks to herself, each for $5,000, and forged the necessary F.F. & M. signatures to the drawer's line. The first check cleared through the bank in time to be returned with the bank statement that arrived at the law office on December 10. Ledger burned the statement and then took off for parts unknown. On January 23, Amos Factory, a senior partner, notified ONB that he could not find the December statement. When a duplicate was furnished to F.F. & M., they pointed out the first $5,000 check. By this time the other two checks had cleared through F.F. & M.'s account and were ready to be sent out in the February statement. The bank declined to recredit F.F. & M.'s account with any of the $15,000, pointing to the 10-day notice requirement in the deposit contract and to §4-406(d). F.F. & M. sued under §4-401's *properly payable* rule and argued that §4-103 invalidated the 10-day notice provision. How should this come out? See the preceding case and White & Summers 19-2, at 891-894. Would it make a difference if Ledger's forgeries were very badly done? See §4-406(e).

Another issue that has split courts is whether the one-year bar in §4-406(f) applies when the bank has acted in bad faith. Compare Falk v. Northern Trust Co., 763 N.E.2d 380 (Ill. App. 2001) (holding one-year bar effective even where bank acts in bad faith); and Pinigis v. Regions Bank, 977 So. 2d 446 (Ala. 2007) (*contra*). We have received phone calls and emails from a number of attorneys litigating similar issues in other states. They want to know which position is right. What do you think?

PROBLEM 145

When Octopus National Bank found out about the rule of Price v. Neal (making the drawee liable for forgeries of the drawer's name unless the wrongdoer could be found), it asked its attorney what could be done to avoid this liability. The bank's attorney had the bank add a clause to the checking account agreement as follows: "Customer understands and agrees that the bank is no longer examining checks written for amounts less than $5,000, and also agrees that if the drawer's signature on such checks shall be unauthorized, the checks shall nonetheless be properly payable from the bank account, with the customer having the sole duty to pursue legal remedies against others." Is this clause valid? See §§4-103, 4-401(a), and 3-103(a)(9); James Steven Rogers, The Basic Principle of Loss Allocation for Unauthorized Checks, 39 Wake Forest L. Rev. 453 (2004); cf. Lor-Mar/Toto, Inc. v. 1st Constitution Bank, 376 N.J. Super. 520, 871 A.2d 110 (2005).

PROBLEM 146

Maximilian Money was not only very rich but also very lazy. He let the Investors National Bank handle all his affairs, the least of which was to act as drawee of his checking account. So as to save time, he signed all of his checks with a little rubber signature stamp when he first received his checkbook. Though the bank regularly sent him monthly statements, he never even opened them. At income tax time his tax lawyer discovered that his bank account was $4,000 short due to a check that had been stolen from Max and filled in to "Cash" for $4,000 over two years ago. The lawyer, as Max's agent, demanded that the account be replenished with this amount. The bank, to which $4,000 was a small matter in comparison to its income as trustee of Max's affairs, instantly complied. The $4,000 was not, however, so small a matter that it could be forgotten, so the Investors National Bank demanded repayment from the presenting bank, the Fallguy State Bank, charging breach of the §4-208(a)(2) warranty of no alteration. What result if Fallguy State refuses and suit is brought? See §4-406(f)'s last sentence and §4-208(c).

PROBLEM 147

Bertrand Balance was the payroll clerk for Tentacles Corporation, and one day in a moment of weakness he drew up 107 extra paychecks payable to phony names. He signed the payees' names to the back of every check and cashed each of the checks at various local depositary banks over the period of one month. As soon as the last one had been cashed, Balance hurriedly left the state, leaving behind only an apologetic letter explaining what he had done. The corporation immediately demanded that the money be recredited to its payroll account. The bank comes to you for advice. Tentacles Corporation is one of the bank's largest depositors, and the bank doesn't want to lose it. If it recredits the account, can it sue the depositary banks for breach of presentment warranties?

Note that (c) of §4-208 (and the corresponding (c) in Article 3's presentment warranty section, §3-417) permits the entity making presentment warranties to raise the various validation rules to avoid warranty liability. This is as it should be. If the payor bank did make proper payment in spite of the forgery/alteration because these irregularities are validated by one of the sections we have studied, then the payor bank should not be permitted to ignore the validation and pass the loss on to innocent parties such as the presenting bank. Of course, the payor bank may be reluctant to offend its wealthy depositors, as in the above Problems, and, as a business matter, may elect to eat the loss itself rather than lose their trade, but if it is going to be this nice to its customers, any damages caused thereby are self-inflicted. Any time anyone has a valid defense and fails to raise it, that person has shot himself in the foot. The proximate cause of this loss is the unwillingness to raise the defense, not the technical breach of a presentment warranty.

IV. ALTERATIONS

PROBLEM 148

Earnest Innocent went into the Mafia Loan Company and asked to borrow $100 to finance the repair of a broken tooth. The loan company advanced him the money after he signed a promissory note for this amount plus 8 percent interest per annum, payable to the order of the Mafia Loan Company on demand. After Innocent left the office, the loan officer took out his special chemicals and used them to erase the original typewritten amount ($100). In its place he typed in $9,500. The Mafia Loan Company discounted the paper for $100 to Michael Schmidt, a self-employed commercial factor, who always bought the company's altered paper. Schmidt presented the note to Innocent for payment, and when Innocent protested, Schmidt's "collectors" broke both his arms. They said they would return the following month and would expect him to have the money ready then. Assuming Innocent can get police protection against Schmidt's "self-help" collection procedures, what legal defenses does he have? Read §3-407 carefully.

Note that §3-407(b) states that a fraudulent alteration completely *discharges* any non-negligent person whose negotiable instruments contract is changed by the alteration. The alteration in the above Problem is technically said to be a *raising* of the amount.

PROBLEM 149

George Johnson owed around $50 to Marmaduke Brown and, while making out checks to his creditors, decided to write out a check to Brown. Unfortunately, he couldn't remember how to spell Brown's name or the exact amount owed, so he simply signed his name to the drawer's line while making a mental note to fill in the rest later. He put the check in his wallet, and it was stolen along with the wallet when he was mugged the following night. The check, made out to "Cash" for $150, cleared through his checking account the next week. Johnson brought suit against his bank, demanding that the bank recredit his account since the amount was not *properly payable*. He argues that this was an alteration under §3-407 and that he was discharged by the alteration. What reply should the bank's attorney make? See §§3-115, 3-407, 3-406, and 4-401(d).

PROBLEM 150

Joseph Goodheart was the owner and manager of the Goodheart Home for the Aged. He was also the payee of a promissory note for $1,000 given him by Nick Nephew to pay for three months' care Goodheart had given to Nephew's elderly aunt, Strange Molly. One day Strange Molly, who was not responsible for her actions, sneaked into Goodheart's empty office and ransacked his files. She found her nephew's promissory note and took a pen and deftly changed the amount to $1,000,000. Does this operate, under §3-407, to discharge Nephew from his maker's obligation? What would be the result if Strange Molly had torn up and eaten the note? See §3-309 and its Official Comment.

PROBLEM 151

Lloyd Smith mailed a check for $5.00 to his friend, David Rouge, as a birthday gift. Rouge cleverly raised the amount to $500.00 and cashed it at his own bank, Octopus National Bank, which then obtained payment from Last National Bank, the drawee. When Smith received his bank statement, he immediately complained to ONB about the alteration of the check. Assuming he was not negligent in writing the check, can Smith make the bank recredit the account for $500.00, or only $495.00? See §§3-407, 4-401(d). Is the bank without a remedy? See §4-208(a).

CHAPTER 8   ASSESSMENT

Multiple Choice Questions

1. Seward issued a check to Konstantin to purchase some land. Gorchakov stole the check, forged Konstantin's indorsement, and sold the check to Check Casher. Check Casher deposited it in its account at Crown Bank. Crown Bank presented the check to Sitka Bank, which paid the check and took the money from Seward's account. When Seward saw the statement,

he notified Sitka Bank of the improperly paid check. Gorchakov is long gone. Of the innocents, who is liable to whom?

   a. Crown Bank is liable to Sitka Bank for breach of presentment warranty.

   b. Check Casher is liable to Crown Bank for breach of transfer warranty.

   c. Check Casher, Crown Bank, and Sitka Bank are liable to Konstantin for conversion.

   d. Seward is liable to Konstantin on the check.

   e. All of the above.

2. Who would be liable if Konstantin had indorsed the check himself before Gorchakov stole it?

   a. Crown Bank is liable to Sitka Bank for breach of presentment warranty.

   b. Check Casher is liable to Crown Bank for breach of transfer warranty.

   c. Check Casher, Crown Bank, and Sitka Bank are liable to Konstantin for conversion.

   d. Seward is liable to Konstantin on the check.

   e. None of the above.

3. Bering paid Steller for some livestock with a check. Steller then used software to create and print another check on Bering's account, forged Bering's signature, and deposited the check at Malaspina Bank. Steller withdrew the money and disappeared. Malaspina Bank presented the check for payment to Kotzebue Bank, who paid the check. Bering soon objected and Kotzebue recredited Bering's account. Is Malaspina Bank liable to Kotzebue Bank?

   a. Yes. Malaspina Bank is liable for breach of transfer warranty.

   b. Yes. Malaspina Bank is liable for breach of presentment warranty.

   c. No. The forged drawer's signature does not breach the presentment warranty.

   d. No. Malaspina Bank was only an intermediary, collecting the check for its customer, so makes no warranty.

4. Stevens, the bookkeeper at Mala Films, stole five checks to suppliers that Mala Films had signed and prepared for mailing. Stevens forged Mala Film's indorsement and deposited the checks in his account at Soapy Bank. Mala Film's bank, Palin Bank, paid the checks when presented. Is Palin Bank entitled to the money from Mala Films for the checks?

   a. No. The checks were not properly payable, because Palin Bank paid the wrong person.

   b. No, but Palin Bank can recover from Soapy Bank for breach of presentment warranty.

   c. Yes. The forged indorsements are validated because they were made by an employee with responsibility for checks.

   d. Yes, because Palin Bank is not expected to be able to determine whether the indorsements are authentic.

5. One fine week in May, despite good security measures, the bookkeeper at Peratovich Consulting forged a dozen checks to himself on the company account, deposited them, and absconded with the proceeds. Upon receiving its monthly statement, Peratovich Consulting immediately cried foul. Can the drawee bank, which paid the checks, recover from its customer, Peratovich Consulting?

   a. Yes. Under the bank statement rule, Peratovich Consulting takes the loss for multiple acts of wrongdoing by the same person.

   b. Yes. Under the employee forgery rule, Peratovich Consulting takes the loss for its employee's malefaction.

   c. No. The checks were not properly payable.

   d. No. Banks take the loss for all forged checks, in order to spread the loss among all customers.

   e. No. Customers take the loss for all forged checks, to encourage them to combat forgery.

Answers

1. E is the best answer. A simple diagram helps to keep the characters straight in these multi-party cases:

Seward $\to$ Konstantin $\to$ Gorchakov $\to$ Casher $\to$ Crown $\to$ Sitka
issues   steals   transfers   transfers presents pays

This question shows the typical allocation of loss for stolen checks bearing forged indorsements. The check was not properly payable, so Sitka Bank must recredit Seward's account, as in A. Sitka Bank, however, can turn around and recover from Crown Bank, as stated in B, because the forged indorsement meant Crown Bank was not the person entitled to enforce the instrument. Crown Bank in turn can turn around and recover from Check Casher for breach of the transfer warranty, due to the forged indorsement. Check Casher has no one to collect from, and so would take the loss, as the person who took a stolen check from the thief over a forged indorsement by the thief.

C states another way to reach the same result: Konstantin could simply recover from Check Casher for conversion, because Check Casher took a check from someone who was not the person entitled to enforce it (or Konstantin could recover in conversion from Crown Bank or Sitka Bank, who would again use warranty liability to put the loss on Check Casher).

Indeed, if we wanted, we could add, as in D, that Konstantin could recover from Seward, because Konstantin is still the PETE, under §3-301 and §3-309. So the answer is "E. All of the Above." No doubt you could come up with more possibilities.

2. E is the best answer. This question illustrates the risk of bearer paper. Remember the Laura Lawyer Problems from Chapter 3. Konstantin made the check into bearer paper by indorsing it in blank. When the check was presented, it was properly payable, contrary to A, because it was bearer paper payable to whomever was in possession. Likewise, there was no breach of presentment warranty, because Crown Bank was the holder, so B is incorrect. Check Casher would qualify as a holder in due course, so there would be no breach of the transfer warranty (no forged signature and no claim or defense that would be good against Check Casher). C is incorrect. Everyone took the check from a holder, so no one is liable for conversion, making D incorrect. Konstantin could not recover from Seward on the check under §3-309, because Seward has already paid once on the check.

No one is liable — meaning the loss will effectively fall on Konstantin, who created the risk by making the check into bearer paper.

3. C is the best answer. The drawee bank typically bears the risk of loss for checks paid over a forged drawer's signature. Malaspina Bank made a presentment warranty, by presenting a check that was paid. But, contrary to B, a forged drawer's signature (unlike a forged indorsement) does not breach the presentment warranty (unless the warrantor knows of the forgery). The drawee bank does not get the broader transfer warranty, so A is incorrect. D is inaccurate. Depositary banks do indeed make warranties on the checks they present.

4. C is the best answer. This question illustrates how a validation rule can shift the loss. Normally, where a check is paid over a forged indorsement, the loss will fall on the party who took the check from the thief/forger, as in Question 1. But one of the validation rules may apply to change that result. The most frequently applied validation rule is the employee forgery rule. Where an indorsement is made by an employee with responsibility for instruments, as in this question, the employee forgery rule makes the indorsement effective. So the result is similar to Question 2 — it is as if the check is bearer paper, because the forged indorsement is effective. The check is properly payable, contrary to A. There is no breach of presentment warranty, contrary to B. Note that D misstates the law. Drawee banks are generally not entitled to reimbursement if they pay over forged indorsements. But, as here, a rule may change that result in particular cases. Note also how helpful the employee forgery rule is to banks, because it puts the loss on employers rather than banks for embezzlement, which is a substantial portion of check fraud.

5. C is the best answer. The checks were not authorized by the customer, so were not properly payable. The bank statement rule may put the loss on the customer for multiple wrongdoing, but only where loss is caused by the customer's failure to make a timely report of the wrongdoing. Here, Peratovich Consulting gave timely notice. This is not a case where a forged check appeared on the statement, the customer did not give notice, and that enabled the forger to do it again. Here, the multiple checks were written close together in time. A is incorrect. The employee forgery rule does not apply, because that rule (like the impostor rule), only applies to forged indorsement, contrary to B. D and E misstate the law; sometimes banks take the loss, sometimes customers do.

ELECTRONIC BANKING

Some law schools have eliminated the course called "Commercial Paper" in recent years and in the survey course of "Commercial Law" many instructors skip over Articles 3 and 4 as irrelevant to modern life, as if there were no more checks or promissory notes out there causing no end of legal difficulties. But the number of cases involving these instruments has not lessened, and, indeed, in the case of promissory notes connected with mortgage foreclosures has dramatically increased. Clients with Articles 3 and 4 problems will still appear in law offices. Try to imagine how difficult it would be to teach yourself the rules we have studied so far in this course if you had a client with a case that forced you to figure them out for the first time in your career.

It is true that many payments are made electronically these days, and this chapter explores the legal issues that arise from credit cards, debit cards, wire transfers, and other electronic forms of banking. Be warned that these matter change as bankers think up new and quicker means of moving money around, so the alert attorney who practices in this field must be careful to remain up-to-date.

Elimination of the tons of checks that daily must be carted around the world is of obvious benefit to the banks involved. (Similar concerns in connection with investment securities led to the redrafting of Article 8 of the Code so as to permit corporations to issue securities that are recorded in a computer and are not evidenced by pieces of paper, a matter we will explore in the next chapter.) The benefits to some of the banks' customers are more questionable. As electronic fund transfers (EFTs) replace checks, the consumer drawer at least faces loss of control over the account and the evidentiary nightmare of proving that computers are in error.

Our study in this chapter is divided into two parts. The first concerns the rights and duties of the parties when a consumer is permitted (or required) to use electronic fund transfers to move monies in and out of the consumer's bank account. The second looks at the wire transfers of funds between banking institutions. Both areas of EFT law are changing fast (faster than pleases casebook writers).

I. CONSUMERS AND ELECTRONIC FUND TRANSFERS

In 1968, after a decade of attempts, Congress passed the comprehensive Consumer Credit Protection Act, 15 U.S.C. §§1600 et seq. (1976). This much-amended statute is divided into titles: Title I is the Truth in Lending (TILA) Act, Title VII is the Equal Credit Opportunity Act, etc. Most of these titles authorize a federal agency, typically the Federal Reserve Board (FRB), to issue regulations having the force of law. These regulations then implement and supplement the statute and are "explained" in frequent pronouncements, official and unofficial, by the agency involved. Thus the Truth in Lending Act's statutory provisions are the bare bones on which the FRB hung its Regulation Z, now 12 C.F.R. §1026, which is the primary reference for resolving TILA disputes. In 2010, authority for Regulation Z was transferred to the newly created Consumer Financial Protection Bureau. The Truth in Lending Act and Regulation Z are relevant to our discussion because they cover three related matters: credit card liability, available defenses to credit card bills, and procedures for resolving billing disputes. Detailed exploration of these provisions awaits you in a consumer law course, but a brief look at each follows.

A. Credit Cards

1. Basic Liability

PROBLEM 152

When his sister Alice went off to California to "find herself," Clark Consumer loaned her his bank charge card. She promised to charge no more than $200 worth of purchases. Now Clark, who lives in Ohio, hasn't heard from her in months, but she has so far run up $1,800 in charges, and the charge slips mount each day. Octopus National, the bank that issued the card, says Clark is liable for all her charges until he can find her and reclaim his card. Is he? See Martin v. American Express, Inc., 361 So. 2d 597 (Ala. Civ. App. 1978); Walker Bank & Trust Co. v. Jones, 672 P.2d 73 (Utah 1983). If this were a debit card, the Electronic Fund Transfer Act would apply. What result under the implementing Regulation E, 12 C.F.R. §1005.2(m)?

In the above Problem, the use of the card was *authorized*, at least at its inception, and the consumer usually must pay the resulting bills. Where, however, the use is *unauthorized* (because, for instance, the credit card was stolen), §1026.12 of Regulation Z limits the cardholder's liability to $50 (or whatever lesser amount has been charged before the cardholder notifies the issuer of the loss), and the cardholder is not even liable for this amount unless the card issuer has notified the cardholder of the rights, the card identifies the user, and the card issuer has provided the cardholder with a means of notifying the card issuer of the loss (a telephone number, for example). Currently, by contract, many major credit card companies are waiving the right to collect the $50 maximum, and thus give their cardholders a free ride for completely unauthorized use.

Azur v. Chase Bank, USA

United States Court of Appeals for the Third Circuit, 2010
601 F.3d 212

FISHER, Circuit Judge.

Francis H. Azur filed suit against Chase Bank, USA, alleging violations of 15 U.S.C. §§1643 and 1666 of the Truth in Lending Act (TILA) and a common law negligence claim after Azur's personal assistant, Michele Vanek, misappropriated over $1 million from Azur through the fraudulent use of a Chase credit card over the course of seven years. The District Court granted Chase's motion for summary judgment, and Azur appealed. We are presented here with three discrete issues for our review. First, we must determine whether §1643 of the TILA provides the cardholder with a right to reimbursement. Second, we must evaluate whether Azur's §§1643 and 1666 claims are precluded because Azur vested Vanek with apparent authority to use the Chase credit card. Third and finally, we must decide whether Azur's negligence claim is barred by Pennsylvania's "economic loss doctrine." For the reasons stated herein, we will affirm, on partly different grounds, the District Court's order granting Chase's motion for summary judgment.

I.

ATM Corporation of America, Inc. (ATM) manages settlement services for large national lenders. Azur, the founder of ATM, served as its president and chief executive officer from 1993 until September 2007, when ATM was sold. In July 1997, ATM hired Vanek to be Azur's personal assistant. Vanek's responsibilities consisted of picking up Azur's personal bills, including his credit card bills, from a Post Office Box in Coraopolis, Pennsylvania; opening the bills; preparing and presenting checks for Azur to sign; mailing the payments; and balancing Azur's checking and savings accounts at Dollar Bank. According to Azur, it was Vanek's job alone to review Azur's credit card and bank statements and contact the credit card company to discuss any odd charges. Azur also provided Vanek with access to his credit card number to enable her to make purchases at his request.

From around November 1999 to March 2006, Vanek withdrew without authorization cash advances of between $200 and $700, typically twice a day, from a Chase credit card account in Azur's name. Azur was the sole cardholder and only authorized user on the account. Although Azur recalls opening a credit card account in or around 1987 with First USA, Chase's predecessor, Azur was unaware that he had a Chase credit card.

Each fraudulent transaction included a fee of approximately $2.00 and a finance charge that corresponded to the amount withdrawn, ranging from $4.00 for a $100 advance, to $21.06 for a $700 advance. The fraudulent charges were reflected on at least 65 monthly billing statements sent by Chase to Azur, and Vanek paid the bills by either writing checks or making on-line payments from Azur's Dollar Bank checking account. When writing checks, Vanek forged Azur's signature. Over the course of seven years, Vanek misappropriated over $1 million from Azur.

The transactions occasionally triggered Chase's fraud strategies. On April 16, 2004, Chase detected its first potentially fraudulent transaction, made outbound calls to the account's home telephone number, and left an automated message on the number's answering machine. Chase received no response. On April 23, 2004, one week later, Chase detected a second potential problem and left another automated message at the same telephone number. Three days later, Chase received a call from someone that was able to verify the account's security questions and validate the card activity. Although Chase's records indicate that the caller was female, Chase did not use voice recognition or gender identification as a means of security verification. Finally, on May 14, 2005, approximately one year later, Chase detected a third potentially fraudulent transaction and called the home telephone number. As before, five days later, a return caller once again verified the account activity. The account was paid in full without protest after each incident.

On or about March 7, 2006, Azur discovered a suspicious letter requesting a transfer of funds from his checking account. After investigating, Azur and ATM discovered Vanek's fraudulent scheme and terminated her employment. On March 8, 2006, Azur notified Chase by telephone of the fraudulent use of the Chase account and closed the account. Thereafter, Azur sent Chase three pieces of correspondence relevant to this appeal: (1) a letter dated April 7, 2006; (2) an executed Affirmation of Unauthorized Use dated April 21, 2006; and (3) a letter dated May 17, 2006.

In the letter dated April 7, 2006, Azur notified Chase of the fraudulent use of the card, stated that he "is formally disputing that he is responsible for the payment of any unpaid charges and accompanying finance charges on [the] account" (App. at 48A), and requested statements, correspondence, and other documents regarding the account.

The Affirmation of Unauthorized Use, which Chase drafted and sent to Azur for execution, stated, "Any transaction(s) occurring on or after 10/09/2001 is/are also unauthorized." (*Id.* at 50A.) The Affirmation listed three credits, titled "unauthorized transactions," to Azur's account: (1) a "returned payment" in the amount of $10,000; (2) a "returned payment" in the amount of $20,000; and (3) a "fraudulent transaction" in the amount of $28,717.38. (*Id.*) Azur executed the document and returned it to Chase on April 21, 2006.

Finally, in the letter dated May 17, 2006, Azur once again notified Chase that he "continues to dispute any and all unpaid charges stemming from the [Chase account], as well as all prior fraudulent transactions on that account, which have been the subject of prior communications between you and Mr. Azur and/or his representatives." (*Id.* at 52A.)

Because Azur closed the account on March 8, 2006, the account's final billing period ended on March 6, 2006. Chase has a "policy and practice" of mailing billing statements within two days of the close of each billing cycle. . . .

A. RIGHT TO REIMBURSEMENT

Chase argues that Azur cannot recover the money already paid to Chase under §1643 of the TILA. We agree. Section 1643 does not provide the cardholder with a right to reimbursement. This is clear from the statute's language: "A cardholder shall be liable for the unauthorized use of a credit card only if. . . ." 15 U.S.C. §1643(a). "Liable" means "[r]esponsible or answerable in law" or "legally obligated." *Black's Law Dictionary* 998 (9th ed. 2009). *See also Webster's Third New Int'l Dictionary* 1302 (1993) (defining "liable" as "bound or obliged according to law or equity"). Accordingly, the statute's plain meaning places a ceiling on a cardholder's obligations under the law and thus limits a card issuer's ability to sue a cardholder to recover fraudulent purchases. The language of §1643 does not, however, enlarge a card issuer's liability or give the cardholder a right to reimbursement.

We already reached this conclusion in *Sovereign Bank*, 533 F.3d 162. *Sovereign Bank* concerned, among other things, an indemnification action by Sovereign Bank, a card "Issuer," against Fifth Third Bank, an "Acquirer," and BJ's Wholesale Club, Inc., a "Merchant," based on Sovereign Bank's assertion that it had a duty under §1643 to reimburse a cardholder's account for all fraudulent charges in excess of $50. *Id.* at 164, 174. We disagreed:

> "TILA §1643 does not impose any obligation on issuers of credit cards to pay the costs associated with unauthorized or fraudulent use of credit cards. It simply limits the liability of cardholders, under certain circumstances, to a maximum of $50 for unauthorized charges. Indeed, §1643 does not address, nor is it even concerned with, the liability of an Issuer or any party other than the cardholder for unauthorized charges on a credit card. Section 1643 imposes liability only upon the cardholder."

Id. at 175. Faced here with the same issue in a new context, we arrive at the same outcome: §1643 of the TILA does not provide the cardholder with a right to reimbursement.[1] Accordingly, to the extent that Azur requests reimbursement under §1643 for money already paid to Chase, his claim fails.

B.   APPARENT AUTHORITY

Vanek's alleged apparent authority is a more difficult issue. Relying on three cases, Minskoff v. American Express Travel Related Services. Co., Inc., 98 F.3d 703 (2d Cir. 1996), DBI Architects, P.C. v. American Express Travel-Related Services. Co., Inc., 388 F.3d 886, 363 U.S. App. D.C. 365 (D.C. Cir.

---

1. Although other federal courts of appeals have assumed that a right to reimbursement exists, they have done so without analysis. See Minskoff v. Am. Exp. Travel Related Servs. Co., Inc., 98 F.3d 703, 707, 710 (2d Cir. 1996) (holding that the "appropriate resolution" on remand of a cardholder's §1643 reimbursement claim is that "[the card issuer] is liable for [the user's] fraudulent purchases . . . from the time the credit card was issued until [the cardholder] received the first statement from [the card issuer] containing [the user's] fraudulent charges plus a reasonable time to examine that statement."); DBI Architects, P.C. v. Am. Express Travel-Related Servs. Co., Inc., 388 F.3d 886, 888, 894 (D.C. Cir. 2004) (remanding a cardholder's §1643 reimbursement claim to determine at what point the cardholder created apparent authority in the fraudulent user). See also Asher v. Chase Bank USA, N.A., 310 Fed. Appx. 912, 919 (7th Cir. 2009) (stating, for statute of limitations purposes, that "a violation [of §1643] occurs when the card issuer notifies the cardholder that despite the cardholder's claim of fraud, the card issuer will not reimburse the cardholder for the disputed amount" in a nonprecedential opinion, which we cite solely due to Azur's reliance on the case at oral argument and in a subsequent Rule 28(j) letter) and Carrier v. Citibank (S.D.), N.A., 383 F. Supp. 2d 334, 338, 341 (D. Conn. 2005) (assuming a right to reimbursement under a card issuer's policy of "$0 liability for unauthorized use" but holding that the fraudulent user had apparent authority).

2004), and Carrier v. Citibank (S.D.), N.A., 383 F. Supp. 2d 334 (D. Conn. 2005), the Magistrate Judge recommended that Azur's §1643 claim be dismissed because Azur vested Vanek with apparent authority to make charges to the Chase account as a matter of law:

> "[T]he plaintiff vested Michele Vanek with apparent authority to use the account, as the repeated payment of billed charges led Chase to reasonably believe the charges were authorized. Furthermore, the plaintiff's failure to review his account statements and his lax supervision of Vanek, in whom he delegated authority to review his statements, prepare checks on the account, and discuss routine questions with the card issuer, constituted a negligent omission that created apparent authority in Vanek to incur the charges."

(App. at 17A.) The District Court agreed and dismissed Azur's §1643 claim. On appeal, Azur argues that whether he clothed Vanek with apparent authority is an issue of fact to be decided by a jury.

The application of both §§1643 and 1666 of the TILA depend, in part, on whether the fraudulent user had apparent authority to use the credit card. As stated above, §1643 provides that "[a] cardholder shall be liable for the unauthorized use of a credit card" in certain circumstances. 15 U.S.C. §1643(a). The term "unauthorized use" is defined as the "use of a credit card by a person other than the cardholder who does not have actual, implied, or apparent authority for such use and from which the cardholder receives no benefit." 15 U.S.C. §1602(o). Relatedly, §1666(a) sets forth the procedures a creditor must follow to resolve alleged billing errors. 15 U.S.C. §1666(a). Like the phrase "unauthorized use," the phrase "billing error" includes "[a] reflection on or with a periodic statement of an extension of credit that is not made to the consumer or to a person who has actual, implied, or apparent authority to use the consumer's credit card or open-end credit plan." 12 C.F.R. § 226.13(a)(1) [now 12 C.F.R. §1026.13(a)(1) —EDS.].

To determine whether apparent authority exists, we turn to applicable state agency law. *See* 12 C.F.R. Pt. 226, Supp. I ("Whether such [apparent] authority exists must be determined under state or other applicable law."); *Minskoff*, 98 F.3d at 708 ("'Congress apparently contemplated, and courts have accepted, primary reliance on background principles of agency law in determining the' liability of cardholders for charges incurred by third-party card bearers.'" (quoting Towers World Airways v. PHH Aviation Sys., 933 F.2d 174, 176-77 (2d Cir. 1991))). In this case, the parties do not refute the application of Pennsylvania law. Citing the Restatement (Second) of Agency, the Pennsylvania Supreme Court has explained as follows:

> "Apparent authority is power to bind a principal which the principal has not actually granted but which he leads persons with whom his agent deals to

believe that he has granted. Persons with whom the agent deals can reason-ably believe that the agent has power to bind his principal if, for instance, the principal knowingly permits the agent to exercise such power or if the principal holds the agent out as possessing such power."

Revere Press, Inc. v. Blumberg, 431 Pa. 370, 246 A.2d 407, 410 (Pa. 1968). Similarly, we have stated that under Pennsylvania law "[t]he test for deter-mining whether an agent possesses apparent authority is whether a man of ordinary prudence, diligence and discretion would have a right to believe and would actually believe that the agent possessed the authority he pur-ported to exercise." In re Mushroom Transp. Co., Inc., 382 F.3d 325, 345 (3d Cir. 2004) (quotations and citations omitted).

Although the articulation of the proper agency law standard is fairly easy, the application of that standard is difficult. Two decisions of the Second and D.C. Circuits, respectively, are instructive. In both cases, the Second and D.C. Circuits held that a cardholder's negligent omissions clothed the fraud-ulent card user with apparent authority under facts similar to those present in the instant case.

The Second Circuit in *Minskoff* was the first court of appeals to address this issue. Minskoff served as the president and chief executive officer of a real estate firm. 98 F.3d at 706. In 1988, the firm opened an American Express corporate credit card account and issued one card in Minskoff's name. *Id.* In 1992, Minskoff's assistant, whom the firm had recently hired, applied for and obtained an additional card to the account in her own name without Minskoff's or the firm's knowledge. *Id.* From April 1992 to March 1993, the assistant charged a total of $28,213.88 on the corporate card. *Id.* During this period, American Express sent twelve monthly billing statements to the firm's address; each statement listed both Minskoff and the assistant as cardholders and separately itemized their charges. *Id.* At the same time, American Express was paid in full by a total of twelve forged checks drawn on bank accounts maintained by either Minskoff or the firm at Manufacturers Hanover Trust (MHT), which also periodically mailed statements to the firm showing that the payments had been made. *Id.* at 706-07, 710. The assistant used the same system to misappropriate another $300,000 after applying for a platinum account. *Id.* at 707, 710. After discovering the fraud, Minskoff filed suit against American Express under the TILA. *Id.* at 707.

In determining whether or not the assistant had apparent authority to use the credit card, the Second Circuit began by differentiating between the acquisition and use of a credit card obtained through fraud or theft: "[W]hile we accept the proposition that the *acquisition* of a credit card through fraud or theft cannot be said to occur under the apparent authority of the cardholder, [that] should not . . . preclude a finding of apparent authority for the subsequent *use* of a credit card so obtained." *Id.* at 709. Then, noting that "[n]othing in the TILA suggests that Congress intended to sanction intentional or negligent conduct by the cardholder that furthers the fraud or theft of an unauthorized card user," the court held that "the negligent acts or omissions of a cardholder may create apparent authority to use the card in a person who obtained the card through theft or fraud." *Id.* Applying that reasoning to the facts before it, the Second Circuit found that Minskoff's and the firm's failure to examine any of the credit card or bank statements created, as a matter of law, "apparent authority for [the assistant's] continuing use of the cards, especially because it enabled [the assistant] to pay all of the American Express statements with forged checks, thereby fortifying American Express' continuing impression that nothing was amiss with the Corporate and Platinum Accounts." *Id.* at 710.

In *DBI Architects*, the D.C. Circuit took a narrower approach. DBI was a corporation with an AMEX credit card account. 388 F.3d at 888. In 2001, DBI appointed a new account manager of its D.C. and Virginia offices. Soon thereafter, the new manager requested that AMEX add her as a cardholder on DBI's corporate account without DBI's knowledge, although AMEX sent DBI an account statement reflecting the change. *Id.* From August 2001 to May 2002, the manager charged a total of $134,810.40 to the credit card. *Id.* As in *Minskoff*, AMEX sent DBI ten monthly billing statements—each listing the manager as a cardholder and itemizing her charges—and the manager paid AMEX with thirteen DBI checks. *Id.* Most of the checks were signed or stamped in the name of DBI's president; none were signed in the manager's own name. *Id.* Like Minskoff, DBI eventually filed suit against AMEX under the TILA. *Id.* at 888.

Acquainted with the Second Circuit's decision in *Minskoff*, the D.C. Circuit decided its case on narrower grounds. Rather than fault the cardholder for merely failing to inspect monthly credit card statements, the court focused on the cardholder's continuous payment of the fraudulent charges without complaint:

> "DBI is correct that its failure to inspect its monthly billing statements did not clothe [the manager] with apparent authority to use its corporate AMEX account. [However,] AMEX is correct that DBI clothed [the manager] with apparent authority to use its corporate AMEX account by repeatedly paying without protest all of [the manager's] charges on the account after receiving notice of them from AMEX."

Id. at 891. The court later explained its reasoning as follows:

> "By identifying apparent authority as a limit on the cardholder's protection under §1643, Congress recognized that a cardholder has certain obligations to prevent fraudulent use of its card. DBI's troubles stemmed from its failure

to separate the approval and payment functions within its cash disbursement process. [The manager] had actual authority both to receive the billing statements and to issue DBI checks for payment to AMEX. While DBI did not voluntarily relinquish its corporate card to [the manager], it did mislead AMEX into reasonably believing that [the manager] had authority to use the corporate card by paying her charges on the corporate account after receiving AMEX's monthly statements identifying her as a cardholder and itemizing her charges."

Id. at 893. Although the court acknowledged that payment might not always create apparent authority, it held that such authority existed as a matter of law in that case:

"[T]his is not a case involving an occasional transgression buried in a welter of financial detail. [] Nor is this a case involving payment without notice, as might occur when a cardholder authorizes its bank to pay its credit card bills automatically each month. Where, as here, the cardholder repeatedly paid thousands of dollars in fraudulent charges for almost a year after monthly billing statements identifying the fraudulent user and itemizing the fraudulent charges were sent to its corporate address, no reasonable juror could disagree that at some point the cardholder led the card issuer reasonably to believe that the fraudulent user had authority to use its card."

Id. at 893-94 (quotations and citation omitted). Ultimately, the court remanded the case to determine at what point the manager's apparent authority began. *Id.* at 894.

We agree with the D.C. Circuit's more nuanced analysis. "Apparent authority is power to bind a principal which the principal has not actually granted but which he leads persons with whom his agent deals to believe that he has granted." *Revere Press*, 246 A.2d at 410. A cardholder may, in certain circumstances, vest a fraudulent user with the apparent authority to use a credit card by enabling the continuous payment of the credit card charges over a period of time. As the D.C. Circuit reasoned, by identifying apparent authority as a limitation on the cardholder's protections under §1643, Congress recognized that the cardholder is oftentimes in the best position to identify fraud committed by its employees.

Here, Azur's negligent omissions led Chase to reasonably believe that the fraudulent charges were authorized. Although Azur may not have been aware that Vanek was using the Chase credit card, or even that the Chase credit card account existed, Azur knew that he had a Dollar Bank checking account, and he did not review his Dollar Bank statements or exercise any other oversight over Vanek, his employee. Instead, Azur did exactly what the D.C. Circuit in *DBI Architects* cautioned against: he "fail[ed] to separate the approval and payment functions within [his] cash disbursement process." 388 F.3d at 893. Had Azur occasionally reviewed his statements, Azur would have likely noticed that checks had been written to Chase. Because Chase reasonably believed that a prudent business person would oversee his employees in such a manner, Chase reasonably relied on the continuous payment of the fraudulent charges.

Many of Azur's counter-arguments are beside the point. Azur asserts that *Minskoff* and *DBI Architects* are distinguishable because the fraudulent users in those cases were cardholders on the accounts. This distinction is irrelevant: Chase's belief that the fraudulent charges were authorized did not depend on whether the fraudulent charges were made by a second cardholder; Chase's belief was contingent upon the continuous payment of the fraudulent charges—regardless of which card they were on—without objection. Azur also focuses on Chase's failure to identify the fraud. The issue, however, is whether Azur led Chase to believe that Vanek had authority to make the charges, not whether Chase's fraud-detecting tools were effective. Moreover, Vanek's ability to answer the account security questions over the telephone and the fact that Chase's fraud-detecting tools identified relatively few problems reinforce the conclusion that Chase was reasonable in believing, and did in fact believe, that the charges were authorized. In short, none of the arguments Azur has advanced persuade us to disturb the District Court's apparent authority determination.

Accordingly, we hold that Azur vested Vanek with apparent authority to use the Chase credit card, thus barring his §§1643 and 1666 claims.

[The court also held that Azur's negligence claim was barred by the "economic loss doctrine."]

NOTE

The *Azur* court first holds that a cardholder is not entitled to reimbursement from the issuer if the cardholder has paid for charges that were unauthorized. As the *Azur* court notes, other courts have assumed the contrary. Was it necessary for the court to address the issue where it next held the charges in this case were not unauthorized? Do you agree with the *Azur* court's holding on reimbursement? Where Congress wanted to state that cardholder rights did not include reimbursement, it said so. As we will see below, a cardholder's right to raise defenses against the issuer in authorized transactions is explicitly limited to amounts not yet paid. See TILA §170(b), 15 U.S.C. §1666i(b). By contrast, it seems unlikely that Congress intended a cardholder to be liable for unauthorized charges, simply because the cardholder had unknowingly paid the relevant bill. Otherwise, the $50 cap on liability for fraudulent charges offers only thin protection.

2.   Asserting Defenses Against the Credit Card Issuer

PROBLEM 153

Linda Liable lived in Newark, New Jersey. One year she took a trip to San Francisco. While there, she charged her hotel bill using her bank credit card issued by Octopus National Bank in Newark, but she protested to the hotel manager that the bill was twice the amount it should have been. The hotel manager refused to listen. On her return to Newark, Linda refused to pay ONB's credit card bill for this charge; she also refused to pay for other charges: an $80 suitcase she had purchased in New York City that fell apart on the trip (the New York seller is now bankrupt) and a $25 art print ordered from Florida that had never arrived (ONB had included promotional literature on these Florida artworks in its last credit card billing). Is she liable to ONB?

To resolve this issue, see Regulation Z §1026.12(c) (implementing TILA §170, 15 U.S.C. §1666i):

(c) *Right of cardholder to assert claims or defenses against card issuer.*

(1) *General rule.* When a person who honors a credit card fails to resolve satisfactorily a dispute as to property or services purchased with the credit card in a consumer credit transaction, the cardholder may assert against the card issuer all claims (other than tort claims) and defenses arising out of the transaction and relating to the failure to resolve the dispute. The cardholder may withhold payment up to the amount of credit outstanding for the property or services that gave rise to the dispute and any finance or other charges imposed on that amount.

(2) *Adverse credit reports prohibited.* If, in accordance with paragraph (c)(1) of this section, the cardholder withholds payment of the amount of credit outstanding for the disputed transaction, the card issuer shall not report that amount as delinquent until the dispute is settled or judgment is rendered.

(3) *Limitations.*

(i) *General.* The rights stated in paragraphs (c)(1) and (c)(2) of this section apply only if:

(A) The cardholder has made a good faith attempt to resolve the dispute with the person honoring the credit card; and

(B) The amount of credit extended to obtain the property or services that result in the assertion of the claim or defense by the cardholder exceeds $50, and the disputed transaction occurred in the same state as the cardholder's current designated address or, if not within the same state, within 100 miles from that address.

(ii) *Exclusion.* The limitations stated in paragraph (c)(3)(i)(B) of this section shall not apply when the person honoring the credit card:

(A) Is the same person as the card issuer;

(B) Is controlled by the card issuer directly or indirectly;

(C) Is under the direct or indirect control of a third person that also directly or indirectly controls the card issuer;

(D) Controls the card issuer directly or indirectly;

(E) Is a franchised dealer in the card issuer's products or services; or

(F) Has obtained the order for the disputed transaction through a mail solicitation made or participated in by the card issuer.

3. Billing Errors

Under §1026.13 of Regulation Z, if the cardholder complains to the issuer of a billing error, the card issuer must acknowledge the complaint within 30 days, conduct a good faith investigation of the problem, and resolve the difficulty one way or the other within 90 days of the complaint (or within two billing cycles, whichever is less). During the interim the issuer must not treat the disputed amount as overdue or report it adversely to credit reporting agencies. Failure to honor the consumer's rights under this provision leads to the card issuer's forfeiture of up to $50 of the disputed amount and to additional liability, including attorney's fees, under §130 of the Truth in Lending Act. These penalties can be collected even if the consumer was in error and the bank was right all along.

B. Debit Cards and Other Consumer Electronic Funds Transfers

The applicability of Regulation Z to debit cards and other electronic fund transfers involving consumers was unclear until 1978 when Congress solved the problem by passing the Electronic Fund Transfer Act, 15 U.S.C. §§1693 et seq., making it the new Title IX of the Consumer Credit Protection Act of 1968. Section 904 of the Act, 15 U.S.C. §1693b, authorized the FRB to prescribe regulations to carry out the purposes of the Act, and the Federal Reserve Board responded with Regulation E, now 12 C.F.R. 1005 (authority for which has been transferred to the Consumer Financial Protection Bureau). Both can be found in your statute book. You should also know that the Federal Reserve Board published an Official Interpretation for the rules of Regulation E, 12 C.F.R. part 1005, which explains the rules in detail and gives examples. These Interpretations (which are not likely to be in your statute book but are easily found online) are appended to the Regulation's sections and have the force of law, and should therefore be consulted when difficult questions arise in practice.

PROBLEM 154

Electra Smith was employed as a clerk for the Business Corporation. One day it informed her that henceforth all her paychecks would automatically be deposited in the local bank of her choice. She chose Octopus National Bank (ONB), her usual bank. Could she have demanded a check and refused the EFT?[2]

ONB informed Electra that she could pay all her bills online and that many creditors would be willing to set up an automatic monthly payment plan whereby ONB would pay routine bills unless she instructed otherwise. Electra signed such a contract with her landlord, to whom ONB agreed to transfer $300 on the first day of each month as rent. What details does ONB have to explain to her? See Regulation E §1005.7. (The government promulgated model forms for this purpose, and the bank is well advised to use them since such use shields the bank from arguments about disclosure errors. See §916(d)(2) of the Act, 15 U.S.C. §1693(l-1)(d)(2).) Consider these issues:

(a) One day ONB's computer malfunctioned and for no apparent reason deducted $1,000 from Electra's checking account and credited it to an account designated "Computer Maintenance." Several of her checks bounced as a result. Is the computer's deduction an "electronic fund transfer" under Regulation E §1005.3(b)? If so, is it also an "unauthorized electronic fund transfer" under §1005.2(m)? Is the bank liable under §910? Under UCC §4-401(a)? (Note UCC §4-104(a)(9).) Are there common law theories that she might use? As to the bounced checks, see UCC §4-402 (Wrongful Dishonor).

(b) ONB failed to pay Electra's rent on the first of January because the computer got backlogged with the huge Christmas volume. Can her landlord evict her? See §912, 15 U.S.C. §1693j. When she is evicted and sues ONB over §910, 15 U.S.C. §1693h, can the bank defend using §910(b)(1), 15 U.S.C. §1693h(b)(1)? Cf. Blake v. Woodford Bank & Trust Co., 555 S.W.2d 589 (Ky. Ct. App. 1977) (a case deciding a similar issue under UCC §4-109).

(c) One month Electra had a dispute with her landlord, so she phoned ONB and told them not to pay the next month's rent due to be transferred four days later. Is oral notice sufficient? Is her notice timely? See §907(a), 15 U.S.C.

---

2. This issue is resolved by §913 of the EFTA, 15 U.S.C. §1693k, reprinted below:

Section 913. Compulsory Use of Electronic Fund Transfers
No person may—
(1) condition the extension of credit to a consumer on such consumer's repayment by means of preauthorized electronic fund transfers; or
(2) require a consumer to establish an account for receipt of electronic fund transfers with a particular financial institution as a condition of employment or receipt of a government benefit.

§1693e(a); Regulation E §1005.10(c). If the bank fails to stop payment, what remedy does she have? See §910, 15 U.S.C. §1693h. What damages does she have? Can she recover her attorney's fees? Compare §910(c) and §916(a) (15 U.S.C. §§1693h(c) and 1693l-1(a)).

(d) If Linda Liable in the last Problem had made purchases with point of sale (POS) EFTs, would she be able to assert her defenses against her bank under the EFTA?

PROBLEM 155

Jane Austen owned a bookstore and handled the store's financial affairs through a checking account with Octopus National Bank (ONB). If ONB grants the store an ability to pay its debts by EFTs, does the EFTA apply? See §903(2), 15 U.S.C. §1693a(2); Regulation E §1005.2(b).

PROBLEM 156

The first time Arthur Greenbaum used his access card at an all-night auto-mated teller machine, he told the machine to give him $50 from his checking account, and it promptly did so. At the same time the ATM deducted $500 from Arthur's account and reported that Arthur had withdrawn this amount. It gave Arthur no written statement.

(a) At the end of the month Arthur's bank sent him a statement showing the status of his checking account. Should it reflect this transaction? How? See §906, 15 U.S.C. §1693d; Regulation E §1005.9(b). May it be combined with the statement required by UCC §4-406? See §906(c), 15 U.S.C. §1693d(c).

(b) If Arthur does not examine this statement for one year, does the EFTA cause him problems? Note §§909(a), 903(11), and 916(g)(15 U.S.C. §§1693g(a), 1693a(11), and 1693l-1(g),. Does UCC §4-406(f) cause problems?

(c) If Arthur examines the statement promptly and discovers the error, what should he do? See Regulation E §1005.11(b). The bank received Arthur's notice on May 1. By what date need it act? Need it put the money back in his account during its investigation? See §908(a), (c), 15 U.S.C. §1693f; Regulation E §1005.11(c).[3]

---

3. The time periods for recrediting the account that are explored here are incorpo-rated with only small changes into the similar issue that arises under the federal Check 21 Act, discussed in Chapter 7. The fact pattern there is that a bank wrongly debits a consumer's account in connection with a substitute check or computer image of a check, and the con-sumer demands the amount be promptly recredited to the account.

(d) Who bears the burden of proof as to whether the ATM gave Arthur $50 or $500? See §909(b); cf. Gramore Stores, Inc. v. Bankers Trust Co., 93 Misc. 2d 112, 402 N.Y.S.2d 326 (Sup. Ct. 1978) (dispute over deposit made in a bank's night depository).

(e) What liability does the bank have simply because it never programmed the ATM to hand out written statements? See §§906(a), 916, §§1693d(a), 1693l-1; Regulation E §1005.9(a). If the ATM had been so programmed but failed to give the statement to Arthur due to mechanical failure, is this a defense? See §916(c), §1693l-1(c). Is it a defense that the ATM growled at Arthur when he walked up to it, so that he should have known it wasn't working, and thus he assumed the risk of the resulting error? Cf. §910(b)(2), 15 U.S.C. §1693h(b)(2).

(f) After receiving Arthur's complaint (and also the complaint of every single person using that particular ATM), the bank's investigation consisted solely of having a computer printout made of the transaction and mailing it to Arthur. Similar documentation was sent to each complainant. Does this satisfy §908, 15 U.S.C. §1693f? Note particularly §908(e), 15 U.S.C. §1693f(e).

Consumers use debit cards to make almost 80 percent of their small purchases nowadays, typically by the use of a secret number (a *personal identification number* or PIN). As with credit cards, this access card and/or the PIN must be guarded by the customer, or life can become difficult even should the customer prevail in the resulting legal dispute. Read §909 and Regulation E §1005.6, which follows.

§1005.6 Liability of Consumer for Unauthorized Transfers

(a) *Conditions for liability.* A consumer may be held liable, within the limitations described in paragraph (b) of this section, for an unauthorized electronic fund transfer involving the consumer's account only if the financial institution has provided the disclosures required by §1005.7(b)(1), (2), and (3). If the unauthorized transfer involved an access device, it must be an accepted access device and the financial institution must have provided a means to identify the consumer to whom it was issued.

(b) *Limitations on amount of liability.* A consumer's liability for an unauthorized electronic fund transfer or a series of related unauthorized transfers shall be determined as follows:

(1) Timely notice given. If the consumer notifies the financial institution within two business days after learning of the loss or theft of the access device, the consumer's liability shall not exceed the lesser of $50 or the amount of unauthorized transfers that occur before notice to the financial institution.

(2) Timely notice not given. If the consumer fails to notify the financial institution within two business days after learning of the loss or theft of the access device, the consumer's liability shall not exceed the lesser of $500 or the sum of:

(i) $50 or the amount of unauthorized transfers that occur within the two business days, whichever is less; and

(ii) The amount of unauthorized transfers that occur after the close of two business days and before notice to the institution, provided the institution establishes that these transfers would not have occurred had the consumer notified the institution within the two-day period.

(3) *Periodic statement; timely notice not given.* A consumer must report an unauthorized electronic fund transfer that appears on a periodic statement within 60 days of the financial institution's transmittal of the statement to avoid liability for subsequent transfers. If the consumer fails to do so, the consumer's liability shall not exceed the amount of the unauthorized transfers that occur after the close of the 60 days and before notice to the institution, and that the institution establishes would not have occurred had the consumer notified the institution within the 60-day period. When an access device is involved in the unauthorized transfer, the consumer may be liable for other amounts set forth in paragraphs (b)(1) or (b)(2) of this section, as applicable.

(4) *Extensions of time limits.* If the consumer's delay in notifying the financial institution was due to extenuating circumstances, the institution shall extend the times specified above to a reasonable period.

(5) *Notice to financial institution.*

(i) Notice to a financial institution is given when a consumer takes steps reasonably necessary to provide the institution with the pertinent information, whether or not a particular employee or agent of the institution actually receives the information.

(ii) The consumer may notify the institution in person, by telephone, or in writing.

(iii) Written notice is considered given at the time the consumer mails the notice or delivers it for transmission to the institution by any other usual means. Notice may be considered constructively given when the institution becomes aware of circumstances leading to the reasonable belief that an unauthorized transfer to or from the consumer's account has been or may be made.

(6) *Liability under state law or agreement.* If state law or an agreement between the consumer and the financial institution imposes less liability than is provided by this section, the consumer's liability shall not exceed the amount imposed under the state law or agreement.

PROBLEM 157

Ebenezer Scrooge owned a bank credit card issued by Dickens National Bank, the same bank with whom he maintained a checking account. One day the mail contained a letter assigning Scrooge a PIN and explaining to him that by inserting his credit card in an ATM and punching in the PIN, he could receive immediate cash withdrawals from his checking account.

(a) Has Dickens National violated the EFTA? See §911, §1693i; Regulation E §1005.5.

(b) Scrooge threw the PIN letter in the wastebasket, from which it was removed by his employee Bob Cratchit, who stole Scrooge's card and extracted $100 from the ATM in order to buy crutches for his crippled son. Is Scrooge liable for this withdrawal? See §§909(a), 903(1), §§1693g(a), 1693a(1); Regulation E §1005.6.

PROBLEM 158

While Carl Consumer was asleep one day, his sister Nancy sneaked into his bedroom and stole his bank card. She knew his PIN because he had once loaned her the card and authorized her to make a small series of withdrawals, but this time it was an out and out theft.[4] She took the card on April 30 and used it to take $500 from his account with Original National Bank on that same day. He missed the card when he woke up, and he rightly guessed that Nancy had taken it. Rather than notify the bank, he tried to track her down and retrieve the card. On May 5, she used the card to remove $800 from his bank account, and then she left the state. Heartsick at her perfidy, Carl slumped into a depression so severe that he could not leave his bed. On May 31, the bank sent Carl the usual bank statement; it reflected all of these transactions. On June 10, Nancy returned to the state and used the card to take $3,000 from Carl's account. A lawsuit followed. Resolve it, using §1005.6 of Regulation E, reproduced above.

PROBLEM 159

When Joseph Armstrong first received his debit card he was afraid he would forget the PIN, so he wrote it right on the card itself. If Armstrong subsequently lost his wallet, would his liability for unauthorized use increase due to his stupidity? See the Official Interpretation to §1005.6(b).

Many major debit card issuers now waive the right to collect for unauthorized charges. But the potentially unlimited liability for unauthorized charges still applies to other consumer electronic funds transfers, such as online funds transfers (as some careless individuals have learned the hard way). See The Bank Account That Sprang a Leak, N.Y. Times (Aug. 29,

---

4. For a case saying that disclosure of the PIN for one authorized use does not make subsequent uses authorized as well, see Vaughan v. United States National Bank, 79 Or. App. 172, 718 P.2d 769 (1986).

2008) (where persons unknown "siphoned nearly $300,000 from his personal account at the private bank through many small electronic transfers over a 15-month period," a wealthy individual took loss for transfers made after the 60-day reporting deadline).

The Dodd-Frank Act gave some relief to debit card users as of 2010 when it prohibited overdraft fees from being taken from the consumer's bank account unless the consumer had opted in to such overdraft protection; see Regulation E §1005.17. Most consumers would rather the debit card be declined in the situations where the debit is small but the overdraft fee is large, but don't understand that overdraft protection is far too expensive. One study found that 77 percent of consumers are opting in to overdraft protection. In 2013, banks earned $40 billion in overdraft fees!

One real burden facing the bank's customer in an EFT world is uncertainty as to the daily bank balance. This problem is sure to arise unless the customer keeps accurate account of all checks, charges, ATM and POS transactions, preauthorized EFTs, bank service fees, and telephonic EFTs. Furthermore, when the monthly statement arrives, the customer must be very organized to do an accurate reconciliation within the EFTA's 60-day period. The lack of documentation that is one of the benefits of EFTs for banks is making the customer's life more difficult. Some banks are experimenting with the so-called *smart card,* a debit card that has an internal memory of each transaction for which it has been used so that the card itself can do all of the consumer's recordkeeping, and some cell phones (also used for EFTs) have similar recording functions. O brave new world, that has such machines in it!

C. Foreign Remittances

Since 2010, the EFTA contains provisions dealing with remittances sent to foreign countries, and the Regulation E provisions are in Subpart B, §§1005.30 to 1005.36. Use those sections to resolve the next Problem.

PROBLEM 160

Fatima Ramon, who had moved to the United States from Guatemala when she married an American citizen, decided to send her mother in Guatemala $30.00 every month out of the paycheck she received from her employer. She went to Speedy International Money Service, a business that made such transfers to foreign countries, and signed an agreement to send the first $30.00 to her mother. Ramon's English is not good and she was confused about much of what happened, none of which was conducted in Spanish. When her mother later informed Ramon that the money had not arrived, Ramon went back to Speedy, where she was told that $17.00 was sent to the mother on the day after Ramon had given it to Speedy. When Ramon asked why only $17.00 had been sent, she was told that the transfer fee was $13.00. Ramon, unhappy, then disputed that even this lower amount had made it to Guatemala. Speedy denied any responsibility for whatever had happened. Fatima Ramon, confused and disgusted, contacts you, the only lawyer she knows. What can be done?

D.   Other Payment Systems

The Internet now offers payment methods of various kinds, and so far these so-called alternative payment services are unregulated or their status is unclear. PayPal, for example, claims to offer more protection than is required by the Electronic Fund Transfer Act, and, while there is an argument that the EFTA already covers PayPal and similar entities, the resolution of this is murky and must await court decisions. For a student article urging the Consumer Financial Protection Bureau to issue regulations clearing this up, see Eric Pacifici, Making PayPal Pay: Regulation E and Its Application to Alternative Payment Services, 13 Duke L. & Tech. Rev. 89 (2015).

II.   WIRE TRANSFERS

The safe and efficient movement of money is now accomplished electronically through a host of systems devised by bankers and implemented by government action (the Federal Reserve System) or private agreement. Consider the advantage to the federal government of electronic payment of Social Security debts: mountains of paper (paper that can be lost or stolen) need not move clumsily through the mails. Instead, electronic signals do all the work quickly and with fewer errors. Similarly, imagine the benefits to a national retailer if the movement of money to and from its thousands of outlets can be accomplished efficiently at the end of every business day by the mere electronic adjustment of funds.

Until 1990 there was no organized body of law to deal with such transfers, though the Federal Reserve had promulgated its Regulation J, 12 C.F.R. §210, to resolve disputes internal to transfers through the Federal Reserve System.[5] But there was no guidance to resolve a host of disputes likely to

---

5. In 1991, the Federal Reserve Board amended Regulation J so that its rules are in accordance with those of Article 4A.

occur: bank failure, computer hackers mugging the system to steal electronic dollars, glitches whereby the computer sent out duplicate order after duplicate order, etc. Nor is this a small matter; each day's wire transfers in the United States averaged $3,000,000,000,000 (that's $3 trillion; yes, *trillion*). This number is, of course, growing.

The Federal Reserve System's wire transfer mechanism is called *Fedwire*. It electronically moves funds from one Federal Reserve bank to another at the instruction of the sending institution to the receiving institution, both of which will maintain accounts at Federal Reserve banks. These wholesale wire transactions are enormous in scale. The average Fedwire transfer is $2 million (compared with a $600 average for checks). In 2014, Fedwire handled 1,380,000 electronic transfers with a total value of $663,837,575 million; see http://www.federalreserve.gov/paymentsystems/fedfunds__ann.htm.

The international transfer of money is accomplished through a New York-based system called CHIPS (for "Clearinghouse Interbank Payments System," run by the New York Clearinghouse Association). Its transfers are made in U.S. dollar amounts converted from foreign currencies. The sender instructs its bank to make the wire transfer to a designated payee's account at a different receiving bank. The sending bank informs the CHIPS computer to make the transfer and then sends a verification of the proposed transfer. At the end of the banking day, settlement must occur when CHIPS informs all banks involved of their net position for the day. At this point wire transfers through the New York Federal Reserve Bank are made to adjust the accounts of all participants. CHIPS transfers are also of fantastic amounts, averaging $1,606,968,294 a day, for a total of $403,349,041,732 in 2011.

The advantages of wire transfers are their speed and safety. Typically, a receiving bank allows its non-bank customer immediate access to the funds even though settlement (and thus the actual transfer of the money) will not occur until the end of the day. If, for one reason or another (bank failure, for example), settlement never happens, the receiving bank faces the very real risk of being unable to recapture the funds.

Since many wire transfers occur in the computers before the funds are actually exchanged, all participating banks at some point during the banking day face exposures often greater than the bank's assets. If settlement is made at the end of the day, fine, but in the meantime there is a situation called *daylight overdraft*, and the rules of the various wire transfer systems may limit the amount of exposure by imposing a *debit cap*—a limit on the daylight overdraft that a participating bank may incur.[6]

An *automated clearinghouse*, or ACH, is, as its name suggests, a mechanism for the electronic transfer of recurring debits and credits between

---

6. Sometimes called the *bilateral net credit limit*.

participants, typically for low-dollar/high-volume batched messages such as payrolls. There are a number of such privately created ACHs in the United States, typically linking the transfers through a Federal Reserve bank.[7] ACH networks cleared 22 billion payments in 2014, totaling $39 trillion, with the bulk being transfers by the federal government to pay its routine debts (social security, veteran's benefits, employee paychecks, etc.). Transfers through the ACH are accomplished by telephone, electronic communication, or manual delivery to the ACH of a computer program containing all the relevant payment or debit instructions. The actual transfer of funds typically occurs on the day *after* the ACH receives the sender's instructions (or, by agreement, even later).

With new systems and private associations being created constantly (and old ones dropping by the wayside, their usefulness spent), the law is sorely pressed to keep up with the technology. Many of the legal disputes are resolved by contract between the participants, though a body of electronic fund transfer law is developing. We have already considered the Electronic Fund Transfer Act, which protects consumers. Non-consumer wire transfers are regulated in part by Regulation J, promulgated by the Federal Reserve Board to govern transfers using the federal system, and in part by the Uniform Commercial Code's Article 4A, "Funds Transfers." This article has now been adopted by all the states, and Regulation J has been amended so that its rules are virtually identical, thus producing one area in which we have a happy coincidence of both state and federal law.

A. Scope of Article 4A

While Article 4A is largely concerned with wholesale wire transfers, it is not limited to transfers by wire alone. It includes any *payment order*, whether the instruction is to be transmitted orally, electronically, or in writing; §4A-103(a)(1). A payment order *pushes* funds of the person giving the order (the *sender*) out of his or her bank account and into the bank account of the payee (the *beneficiary*). Article 4A does not cover payment instructions, such as checks, that involve the efforts of the payee to *pull* funds from the payor's

---

7. The National Automated Clearing House Association (NACHA) is an organization of such clearinghouses that regulates ACH activities through a comprehensive set of rules, now amended to incorporate Article 4A for electronic credit transfers. For example, NACHA Rule §2.2.1.1 allows fraudulent checks that are electronically processed at point of sale transactions (the grocery store that creates an image of the check, hands the original back to the drawer, and then sends the check through as an image only) to be returned to the depositary bank, and from there to the merchant, by the creation of a transfer warranty of proper authorization.

bank account into the bank account of the payee. A payment order requires an electronic *credit*, not an electronic *debit*.

PROBLEM 161

Big Department Store was a national operation, the largest retailer of goods in the United States. Every month it paid its employees by electronic transfer of funds (through an ACH) to their bank accounts throughout the country. Every Friday it received the weekly receipts from its thousands of retail stores by instructing Big Department Store's bank to transfer to itself all the monies the retail outlets had deposited in their *Friday Receipts* accounts. Are the payroll ACH transfers *payment orders*? Are the Friday remittances? See §4A-103(a)(1); Official Comment 4 to §4A-104; Brannon v. BankTrust, Inc., 2009 WL 2343702 (Ala. 2009).

The courts have consistently held that Article 4 of the Uniform Commercial Code does not govern purely electronic capture of payment.[8] If electronic debits are not within the scope of Article 4A, what body of law covers them? Until a comprehensive law is enacted, the matter will likely be covered by Operating Letters of the Federal Reserve Banks or private agreements such as those reflected in the rules of the National Automated Clearing House Association.

PROBLEM 162

When Sheridan Whiteside, a resident of New York, agreed to buy the Mesalia Journal, a newspaper in Mesalia, Ohio from Bert Jefferson, its current owner, he instructed his bank, New York Metropolitan National Bank (NYMNB), to wire $1 million to Jefferson's bank, the Mesalia County Bank (MCB). The bank did so through Fedwire, having the Federal Reserve Bank of New York (N.Y. Fed) debit this amount from NYMNB's account with it and crediting the same amount to itself. The N.Y. Fed used Fedwire to transfer the $1 million to the account it carried with the Federal Reserve Bank of Cincinnati (Cincy Fed). Since the Mesalia County Bank did not have an account with Cincy Fed, Cincy Fed transferred the money to the account of the Lake Erie

---

8. NACHA rules have been used by the courts to fill in the blanks; Sinclair Oil Corp. v. Sylvan State Bank, 254 Kan. 836, 869 P.2d 675 (1994). However, Article 4 does govern an electronic presentment if the item began as a check and then a truncation system stopped its physical movement and simply presented its relevant information by electronic means (called a *presentment notice*); see §4-110.

State Bank (LESB), which did, and LESB credited the $1 million into the account that MCB carried with it. MCB, in turn, placed the money into Bert Jefferson's account. All this happened in one day.

(a) Look at §§4A-103, 4A-104, and 4A-105, and put the appropriate labels on the parties: *originator, originator's bank, sender, intermediary bank, receiving bank, beneficiary,* and *beneficiary's bank.* Which of these parties gave a *payment order* as that phrase is defined in §4A-103?

(b) At what exact moment does Bert Jefferson have a legal right to the money? See §4A-404(a). Must MCB notify Jefferson that the money is in his account? See §4A-404(b). Can MCB impose a charge against Jefferson for its actions in accepting the funds transfer? See §4A-406(c) and Official Comment 5.

(c) MCB believed that Jefferson owed it $40,000 on a loan it made to him last year, so it told him that it was allowing him access to only $960,000. He protested, telling the bank that he had repaid the entire loan two weeks ago (this was true) and that he needed the $40,000 to pay off the newspaper's creditors so that the sale to Whiteside could go through. Does the bank have a right of setoff for legitimate debts that its customer owes it? See §4A-502(c)(1). If the newspaper sale collapses because Jefferson failed to pay off the creditors, what damages can he recover from MCB? See §4A-404(a).

Most funds transfers are completed on the day that the sender gives the originating payment order to his or her bank. However, in ACH transfers, as mentioned above, the usual arrangement is that the funds become available to the beneficiary on the day *after* the transfer is completed. You should also remember that the Expedited Funds Availability Act (see page 210) requires next business day availability for wire transfers. EFAA §603(a), 12 U.S.C. §4002(a); Regulation CC §229.10(b).

B. Acceptance of Payment Orders

A key concept in Article 4A is *acceptance* of a payment order. If a receiving bank makes a technical acceptance of such an order, it cannot change its mind and reverse the acceptance; there is no right of *charge back* simply because a bank fails to receive payment.[9] If the receiving bank does not want to make an acceptance, it must *reject* the payment order.

It is important to appreciate this: Article 4A itself *never* requires any bank to make an acceptance of a payment order. A bank, therefore, is always

---

9. However, for ACH transfers, §4A-405(d) does permit provisional payment, revocable if the beneficiary's bank does not receive full payment from the sender. In such a case the beneficiary must be warned of this possibility and agree to it. If so, any acceptance of the payment order by the beneficiary's bank can be nullified.

free to reject the payment order unless it has made a separate agreement otherwise. If the bank does make an agreement to accept a payment order and then wrongfully refuses to do so, the law of contracts, not Article 4A, governs its liability. See §4A-212.

If the payment order specifies a payment date,[10] no *acceptance* can occur until that date, even if the banks have made provisional settlements with each other prior to that time; §4A-209(d). A receiving bank (other than the beneficiary's bank) makes acceptance by *executing* the payment order (passing it on). The beneficiary's bank makes acceptance in one of four ways, whichever occurs first: (1) payment of the amount of the order to the beneficiary, (2) notification to the beneficiary that the amount is available for withdrawal, (3) receipt itself of full payment of the order, or (4) failure of the beneficiary's bank to reject the payment order within the time limits set forth in §4A-209(b)(3).[11] Following acceptance of the payment order, the beneficiary's bank must notify the beneficiary of the receipt of the order before midnight of the next funds-transfer business day following the payment date.[12]

Before acceptance, any credit in the beneficiary's account is provisional only (see Official Comment 2 to §4A-502). The way that a beneficiary's bank avoids liability to the beneficiary is by delaying *acceptance* of the payment order in one of the ways specified above (typically saying nothing to the beneficiary until payment is received). Once acceptance occurs, the beneficiary has a right to the funds and the debt between the originator and the beneficiary is paid. If the beneficiary's bank accepts the payment order and then, for whatever reason, fails to make payment to the beneficiary, it is liable to the beneficiary for the amount of the payment (plus interest thereon) and for any consequential damages (say, for example, the failure of the beneficiary's business) of which it was made aware, unless the beneficiary's bank

---

10. Some do, some don't. If none is specified, the payment date is the date of receipt by the beneficiary's bank; §4A-401.

11. These time limits are as follows: the opening of the next funds-transfer business day following the order's payment date if the beneficiary's bank has received payment or the sender's account is fully covered by a withdrawable credit balance, unless the beneficiary's bank rejects the order before that time, or within one hour of that time, or within one hour after the opening of the sender's next business day if the sender was not immediately available to receive rejection.

Funds-transfer business day is defined in §4A-105(a)(4) as "the part of a day during which the receiving bank is open for the receipt, processing, and transmittal of payment orders and cancellations and amendments of payment orders." Section 4A-106(a) permits the bank to establish a cut-off time for the funds-transfer business day, and treat payment orders and other Article 4A communications received after the cut-off time as if received on the next funds-transfer business day.

12. "Funds-transfer business day" is defined in the previous footnote.

proves it did not pay because of a reasonable doubt concerning the right of the beneficiary to payment; §4A-404(a).

First Place Bank v. Olympia Logistics & Services, Inc.

United States District Court, Eastern District of Michigan, 2013
2013 WL 1122559

Victoria A. Roberts, District Judge.

I. Introduction

First Place Bank settled its interpleader action against one defendant, Greis Jewelers, Inc. First Place now stands in Greis's shoes to assert claims Greis has against co-defendant Olympia Logistics & Services, Inc. First Place claims it is entitled to $47,000.00 which was wired to its bank account by Olympia in a fraud perpetrated by Jay Ritz who is nowhere to be found. Ritz arranged to purchase watches online from Greis. The price of $47,000.00 was agreed upon, and Ritz got Greis's account number to wire funds. Ritz had no intention of wiring his own funds to pay for the watches. Instead, he intended to sell a car which he did not own—online—to Olympia, for $47,000.00, and get Olympia to wire its $47,000 to Greis's account. The fraud was uncovered, but not before Ritz made off with Greis's watches, Olympia was out both $47,000.00 and the car, and Greis was out of the watches with First Place holding the $47,000.00.

Oral argument was held on March 18, 2013. For the reasons stated, Greis is entitled to the wire transfer funds, and Olympia is estopped from any equitable arguments for restitution. First Place's motions are GRANTED; Olympia's motion is DENIED.

II. Background and Procedural History

A. The Underlying Transactions

The pertinent facts in this case are undisputed. Greis and Olympia were victims of fraud perpetrated by a third-party—Jay Ritz. In July 2011, Ritz conjured a scheme to gain valuable property from Greis at Olympia's expense.

Greis is a jewelry store located in Farmington Hills, Michigan. Greis does business in its store as well as over the internet. Beginning in July 2011, Greis posted a rare Audemars Piguet watch for online sale at a price of $41,000.00. Greis did not own the watch, but was selling it on consignment for another party. On July 27, 2011, Ritz contacted Greis about buying the watch. According to Greis, it is normal practice for online customers to contact the store directly to finalize a sale. In addition to the Audemars

Piguet, Ritz also wanted to purchase a ladies' watch. Greis did not have the ladies' watch in stock, but Ritz agreed that Greis would purchase the parts and assemble it in-house for a reduced price. In all, the two watches cost $47,000.00.

Ritz and Greis agreed to a wire transfer. On July 28, 2011, after exchanging emails, Greis provided Ritz with wiring information to its bank account at First Place. Greis instructed that the funds were to be transferred to its First Place account, held in the name "Greis Jewelers, Inc.," account number ending in 7140.

At the same time Ritz negotiated with Greis, he was negotiating a transaction with Olympia. Olympia is an export business based in Miami, Florida. In July 2011, Hakan Sayin, Olympia's owner, found a 2009 BMW X6 for sale online. Sayin called the listed seller, Motor Tran, and spoke with its owner — Jason Ritz, also known as "Jay" Ritz. Sayin asked his friend, Levent Bozkurt, to help him negotiate the purchase of the BMW. After exchanging emails in July 2011, Sayin, Bozkurt, and Ritz negotiated the sale of the car, which, according to Ritz, was located outside Portland, Oregon. Eventually, Ritz and Sayin settled on a purchase price of $47,000.00. They agreed on a wire transfer payment.

B. THE TRANSFER DATE

Both transactions were set to take place on July 29, 2011. After Greis provided Ritz with Greis' wiring information for its First Place account, Ritz gave that information to Olympia, representing that it was his personal account. On July 29th, Ritz emailed Olympia his wiring information — the Greis account ending in 7140. Ritz also told Olympia to earmark the recipient as "Greis JEW, Inc." Later that day, Olympia instructed its bank, Regions Bank, to wire $47,000.00 to "Greis JEW, Inc," account ending in 7140, located at First Place. Sayin's wife, an authorized signer of Olympia's accounts, signed the Wire Transfer/Request Authorization form at Regions.

As Olympia was in the process of wiring the funds, Ritz and Greis exchanged emails about shipping the watches after the funds were received. Ritz informed Greis that the wire transfer was sent and Greis verified the transaction with First Place.

According to Jaime Lowther, Manager of Electronic Banking at First Place's Warren, Ohio branch, wire transfers sent to First Place use the Fedwire funds transfer system. It works like this. Incoming wire transfers sent to First Place are processed through the FedLine Advantage Program. When the wire is received, an electronic message confirms the transfer. A First Place "Processing Employee" prints the message and saves it to a file. The Processing Employee then reviews the beneficiary's bank account to confirm that the bank account and the wire transfer beneficiary are the same person or entity. Only if there is a complete disconnect between the name and the account number, does First Place returns the wire transfer.

Lowther says Greis's account was credited because "Greis JEW, Inc," was an abbreviation of the listed account holder "Greis Jewelers, Inc." This was consistent with First Place's internal policies.

Later on July 29th, Greis received verification over the phone that the funds were received and its account was credited. Greis emailed Ritz confirming that it received the money. Greis verified the shipping address and shipped the Audemars Piguet to Ritz.

The same day, Greis paid the consignor $35,000.00 for the Audemars Piguet. Greis also paid a vendor $3,000.00 for the parts to assemble Ritz's ladies' watch, and used some of its own inventory. Overall, Greis spent roughly $5,000.00 assembling the ladies' watch. On August 3, 2011, Greis shipped the ladies' watch to Ritz.

C. DISCOVERING THE FRAUD

Between July 30 and August 3, 2011, Olympia tried to arrange to get the car from Ritz. On August 3rd, Ritz gave Olympia a location. However, when Olympia's trucking company went to the place, neither Ritz, nor the BMW was there. Sayin never heard from Ritz again.

On August 4, 2011, Sayin, after realizing that Ritz had defrauded him, obtained a CARFAX report using the VIN-number for the BMW provided by Ritz. The report disclosed that neither Ritz, nor Motor Tran was the registered owners of the car; it was actually registered to another party located in Colorado. Sayin contacted Regions and asked that it rescind the wire transfer. Regions made that request to First Place.

First Place began an internal investigation, placed a temporary hold on Greis's account, and contacted Greis about its transaction with Olympia. When First Place realized that both Greis and Olympia claimed ownership of the $47,000.00, it initiated this interpleader action.

D. PROCEDURAL HISTORY

Greis filed a counter-claim against First Place alleging conversion of the disputed funds. Additionally, Olympia filed an unjust enrichment cross-claim against Greis seeking restitution.

First Place and Greis settled Greis's counter-claim and it was dismissed. Under the settlement, Greis assigned all of its rights, title, and interest in the disputed funds to First Place—as well as any claims or defenses. By virtue of this assignment, whatever rights or liabilities Greis incurs regarding the disputed funds and Olympia's cross-claim, become First Place's.

In its motion for summary judgment, First Place says that no genuine issues of fact exist regarding its entitlement to the wired funds and that Olympia has no claim to the funds in either law or equity. Olympia claims interest in the same funds and also moves for summary judgment on its cross-claim. . . .

III. ANALYSIS

* * *

C. UNDER THE UCC, FIRST PLACE HAS TITLE TO THE DISPUTED FUNDS

The "[r]ights and liabilities for payment orders, or wire transfers," fall under Article 4A of the Uniform Commercial Code ("UCC"). First Sec. Bank of N.M. v. Pan American Bank, 215 F.3d 1147, 1152 (10th Cir. 2000). "Article 4A was crafted with the express purpose of creating—in an age of increasing automation—inflexible rules of liability for wire transfer disputes." Id. But, in statutory interpleader cases, "in which jurisdiction is founded on the diversity of the parties' citizenship," the court applies the "rules of the forum state." Republican Nat. Committee v. Taylor, 299 F.3d 887, 890 (D.C. Cir. 2002) (citing Klaxon Co. v. Stentor Elc. Mfg. Co., 313 U.S. 487, 496 (1941)). In Michigan, Article 4A of the UCC is codified under Mich. Comp. Laws §440.4601 *et seq.*

Given the UCC's complexity in wire transfer cases, it is important to clarify who the immediate parties are under Article 4A.

i. The Parties Under Article 4A of the UCC

Under Michigan's codification of the UCC, a "payment order" is "an instruction of a sender to a receiving bank, transmitted orally, electronically, or in writing, to pay, or to cause another bank to pay, a fixed or determinable amount of money to a beneficiary. . . ." M.C.L. §440.4603(a) (West 2012). A "beneficiary" is "the person to be paid by the beneficiary's bank." *Id.* §4603(b). The "beneficiary bank" is "the bank identified in a payment order in which an account of the beneficiary is to be credited" according to the payment order. *Id.* §4603(c). A "receiving bank" is "the bank to which the sender's instruction is addressed." *Id.* §4603(d). And, a "sender" is "the person giving the instruction to the receiving bank." *Id.* §4603(d).

Additionally, a "funds transfer" is "the series of transactions, beginning with the originator's payment order, made for the purpose of making payment to the beneficiary of the order." *Id.* §4604(a). "The term includes any payment order issued by the originator's bank . . . intended to carry out the originator's payment order." *Id.* The "originator" is "the sender of the first payment order in a funds transfer." *Id.* §4604(c). Finally, because the originator here is not a bank, the "originator's bank" is "the receiving bank to which the payment order of the originator is issued. . . ." *Id.* §4604(d)(i).

Under Article 4A, Olympia is the sender and originator; Greis is the beneficiary; Regions Bank is the receiving bank and the originator's bank;

First Place is the beneficiary bank (Greis's bank); and, the wire transfer is both the payment order and the funds transfer.

ii. First Place Accepted the Wire Transfer Entitling Greis to the Funds Transfer

"Acceptance within the meaning of Article 4A is the key[ ]" to entitlement to disputed funds "because title to funds in a wire transfer passes upon acceptance of a payment order." U.S. v. BCCI Holdings (Luxembourg), S.A., 980 F. Supp. 21, 27 (D.D.C. 1997). According to Article 4A, "a funds transfer is complete when the beneficiary's bank accepts the payment order." *Id.*; M.C.L. §440.4604(a). In most cases, acceptance occurs "[w]hen the bank pays the beneficiary[,]" according to M.C.L. §440.4905, "or notifies the beneficiary of receipt of the order or that the account of the beneficiary has been credited" concerning that order. M.C.L §440.4709(2)(a).

Under §4905, if the beneficiary bank credits the beneficiary's account with the payment order, "payment of the bank's obligation . . . occurs when . . . the beneficiary is notified of the right to withdraw the credit." *Id.* §4905(1). Additionally, "[n]otice (and thus knowledge of the credit on the part of the beneficiary) is not required to effectuate payment . . . if the funds otherwise are made available to the beneficiary." *First Sec. Bank of N.M.*, 215 F.3d at 1158.

Furthermore, "an accepted transfer cannot be revoked without the consent of the beneficiary." *BCCI Holdings*, 980 F. Supp. at 27 (citing Middle East Banking Co. v. State Street Bank Int'l, 821 F.2d 897, 901-02 (2d Cir. 1987)). The beneficiary bank is obligated to pay the beneficiary after accepting the payment order. *Id.*; M.C.L. §440.4904(1). Thus, "the ownership interest in those funds must pass from the originator" after the funds transfer is completed. *Id.*

Greis and Olympia acknowledge that on July 29, 2011, Ritz informed Greis that the disputed funds were to be wired that day. On that same day, Olympia ordered Regions Bank to wire funds to First Place. After Ritz informed Greis that the funds had been wired, Greis confirmed receipt of the funds with First Place, which sent a response to Greis acknowledging that the funds transfer was complete. Not only was Greis' account credited with the wired funds, but notification of receipt of the funds was accomplished as well. Therefore, on July 29, 2011, First Place accepted the funds and ownership of those funds vested in Greis.

iii. No Exception Under the UCC Disentitles Greis to the Wired Funds

But, "there are important exceptions to the rules regarding acceptance under" Article 4A. *BCCI Holdings*, 980 F. Supp. at 27. Olympia cites to an exception under M.C.L. §440.4707(2):

(1) . . .

(2) If a payment order received by the beneficiary's bank identifies the beneficiary both by name and by an identifying or bank account number and the name and number identify different persons, the following rules apply:

(a) Except as otherwise provided in subsection (3), if the beneficiary's bank does not know that the name and number refer to different persons, it may rely on the number as the proper identification of the beneficiary of the order. The beneficiary's bank need not determine whether the name and number refer to the same person.

(b) If the beneficiary's bank pays the person identified by name or knows that the name and number identify different persons, no person has rights as beneficiary except the person paid by the beneficiary's bank if that person was entitled to receive payment from the originator of the funds transfer. If no person has rights as beneficiary, acceptance of the order cannot occur.

It is not clear that §4707(2) applies here, since "Greis JEW, Inc" and "Greis Jewelers, Inc.," do not identify different persons; one is just an abbreviated version of the correct name. However, a second condition must be met: Knowledge. The beneficiary bank must have knowledge of the conflict before acceptance under the UCC can be nullified. "'Knowledge' means actual knowledge, not constructive knowledge, and is determined at the time of payment." *First Sec. Bank of N.M.*, 215 F.3d at 1153 (citing UCC 4A-207 (M.C.L. §440.4707), Official Comment 2).

If the beneficiary's bank "did not know about the conflict between the name and number," then acceptance was proper. M.C.L. §440.4707, Official Comment 2. The reason is that the beneficiary's bank "has no duty to determine whether there is a conflict and it may rely on the number as the proper identification of the beneficiary." *Id.* "Thus, the drafters of [§4707] clarified that although it is possible for the beneficiary's bank to determine whether the name and number refer to the same person," the beneficiary's bank has no affirmative duty to clarify a conflict. *First Sec. Bank of N.M.*, 215 F.3d at 1152. Finally, "the statute 'is not limited to cases in which processing is done by automated means . . . [a] bank that processes by semi-automated means or even manually may rely on'" the account number. *Id.* (citing 4A-207 (M.C.L. §440.4707), Official Comment 2).

Although First Place and Olympia genuinely disagree as to whether "Greis JEW, Inc," and "Greis Jewelers, Inc." refer to "different persons," that disagreement is immaterial. Two requirements must be met for the exception to apply: (1) the name and the account number must identify different persons; and (2) the beneficiary bank, or First Place, must have had actual knowledge of the conflict at the time it credited Greis's account. Olympia's argument focuses on the difference between the names; it does not adequately address whether First Place had actual knowledge.

Olympia argues that based on the longtime bank-customer relationship between First Place and Greis, the Court should presume that First Place should have known that the two names were different. However, it could also be argued that the long-term relationship may have given First Place all the more reason to know "Greis JEW Inc" and "Greis Jeweler, Inc." were, indeed, the same person. But, constructive knowledge is not the standard. Olympia must allege sufficient facts to create a genuine issue of material fact that First Place had actual knowledge at the time it credited Greis's account, that there was a conflict between the beneficiary's name and the account number. There are no facts presented which support a finding that First Place had actual knowledge of any conflict. Moreover, there was not a complete disconnect between the account name and the account number. The designated name and account number bore a sufficient resemblance to one another such that the exception in §4707(2) is not triggered.

Because Olympia cannot meet the requirements under §4707(2), the exception does not apply. Acceptance was proper and Greis is entitled to the wired funds.

[The court then concluded that Olympia could not prevail under either of its equitable claims for unjust enrichment or mistake.]

First Place's motion for summary judgment on the interpleader and Olympia's cross-claim are GRANTED. Olympia's cross-motion for summary judgment is DENIED. Judgment will enter in favor of First Place Bank.

IT IS ORDERED.

PROBLEM 163

During the great bank collapse of 2020, wire transfer completion became a major concern. You are the chief counsel for Octopus National Bank. If it receives a payment order from a bank whose financial status is either shaky or unknown, how can it protect itself from liability to its customers in the event that the sender fails to forward the funds (or settle at the end of the business day)? See §§4A-403, 4A-405(e) (the "doomsday" rule), 4A-209 (and its Official Comment 8).

PROBLEM 164

Octopus National Bank (ONB) made its customers sign an agreement providing that even though the bank had informed them that they were the beneficiaries of a wire transfer, no acceptance was final unless the bank itself actually received the funds. Any withdrawal of the funds prior to the bank's receipt was merely a loan by ONB to its customers, to be repaid either by receipt of the funds or, failing that, by customer repayment. Is this agreement enforceable? See §§4A-209(b)(1) (and its Official Comment 5), 4A-405(c).

C. Transmission Errors

Mistakes will happen, of course, and there are many kinds: wrong dollar amount, duplicate orders, misidentified beneficiary, etc. Fraud might also be at work: some crook might send an unauthorized payment order to sender's bank telling it to make payment to the account of the crook at another bank. Who bears the loss in these situations?

Grain Traders, Inc. v. Citibank, N.A.

United States District Court, Southern District of New York, 1997
960 F. Supp. 784

CHIN, District Judge.

Plaintiff Grain Traders, Inc. ("Grain Traders") brings this diversity action under Article 4-A of New York's Uniform Commercial Code (the "U.C.C.") and principles of common law seeking the refund of money it alleges it lost in the process of an electronic funds transfer. The funds transfer—which was to "pass" through several banks—was not completed, allegedly because defendant Citibank, N.A. ("Citibank") froze an account of one of the banks in question. Grain Traders claims that Citibank acted improperly by accepting $310,000 for a funds transfer and then failing to forward the funds in accordance with instructions, and contends that Citibank instead took the funds as a set-off against a debt owed to Citibank by one of the intermediary banks.

On the record before the court, however, no reasonable fact-finder could conclude that Citibank engaged in any conduct that would form the basis for liability under the U.C.C. or the common law. Rather, Citibank did all that it was required to do: it debited one account $310,000, credited another account $310,000, and forwarded payment instructions to the bank whose account it credited. That bank was supposed to carry out the next step in the funds transfer, but it was unable to do so because of apparent financial problems that eventually caused it to cease doing business. Likewise, the final bank in the chain also was suffering from financial problems that forced it to go out of business. Both banks were chosen by Grain Traders, not Citibank, and it was those choices—rather than any wrongdoing by Citibank—that led to the apparent loss of the $310,000.

Grain Traders's principal argument is that Citibank should not have accepted the payment order. Rather, Grain Traders argues that because

Citibank knew or should have known that the next bank in the chain was experiencing financial problems, Citibank should have exercised its judgment to reject the payment order. Grain Traders's arguments, however, do not make sense and they are inconsistent with the concept of funds transfers as well as the letter and spirit of Article 4-A.

Funds transfers are high-speed means of moving large sums of money at a low cost. As the Prefatory Note to Article 4-A observes:

> There are a number of characteristics of funds transfers covered by Article [4-A] that have influenced the drafting of the statute. The typical funds transfer involves a large sum of money. Multimillion dollar transactions are commonplace. The originator of the transfer and the beneficiary are typically sophisticated business or financial organizations. High speed is another predominant characteristic. Most funds transfers are completed on the same day, even in complex transactions in which there are several intermediary banks in the transmission chain. A funds transfer is a highly efficient substitute for payments made by the delivery of paper instruments. Another characteristic is extremely low cost. A transfer that involves many millions of dollars can be made for a price of a few dollars. Price does not normally vary very much or at all with the amount of the transfer. This system of pricing may not be feasible if the bank is exposed to very large liabilities in connection with the transaction. . . .

U.C.C. Art. 4-A, Prefatory Note, p. 38 (McKinney Supp. 1997). Because of these characteristics—high speed and low cost—one could not expect an intermediary bank in the funds transfer to engage in due diligence to verify the creditworthiness of subsequent banks in the chain, particularly when those banks were designated by the originator itself. Indeed, in such circumstances, the risk of loss must be borne by the originator, for it was the originator's choice of an intermediary bank that led to the loss.

Grain Traders's motion for summary judgment on its claims under Article 4-A of the U.C.C. is denied and Citibank's cross-motion for summary judgment dismissing Grain Traders's claims is granted. The complaint is dismissed.

BACKGROUND

A. THE FACTS

On December 22, 1994, Grain Traders initiated a funds transfer (the "Funds Transfer") to effectuate the payment of $310,000 to Claudio Goidanich Kraemer ("Kraemer"). (Pl. Rule 3(g) Statement ¶3). The Funds Transfer was designed to move money from Grain Traders to Kraemer in one day. The payment order issued by Grain Traders to its bank, Banco de Credito Nacional ("BCN"), stated as follows:

> WE HEREBY AUTHORIZE YOU DEBIT OUR ACCOUNT NR 509364 FOR THE AMOUNT OF US $310,000.00 AND TRANSFER TO: BANQUE DU CREDIT ET INVESTISSEMENT LTD ACCOUNT 36013997 AT CITIBANK NEW YORK IN FAVOUR OF BANCO EXTRADER S.A. ACCOUNT NR 30114 BENEFICIARY CLAUDIO GOIDANICH KRAEMER UNDER FAX ADVISE TO BANCO EXTRADER NR 00541-312 0057/318-0124 AT. DISTEFANO/M. FLIGUEIRA.

(Pargana Aff. ¶3 & Ex. C). Thus, the funds transfer was to proceed as follows: (1) Grain Traders's account at BCN was to be debited $310,000; (2) the $310,000 was then to be "transferred" to Banque Du Credit Et Investissement Ltd.'s ("BCI") at Citibank by way of a debit to BCN's Citibank account and a corresponding credit in that amount to BCI's Citibank account; (3) the $310,000 was in turn to be "transferred" from BCI to Banco Extrader, S.A. ("Extrader") by way of an unspecified transaction between BCI and Extrader; and (4) the $310,000 was finally to be transferred to Kraemer by way of a credit to his account at Extrader.

After the payment order was issued by Grain Traders to BCN, the Funds Transfer initially proceeded as expected. BCN's account at Citibank was debited $310,000 and BCI's account at Citibank was credited $310,000. At the same time, BCN sent instructions to Citibank, directing Citibank to instruct BCI to instruct Extrader to credit $310,000 to Kraemer. (Patrickakos Aff. ¶6 & Ex. 1). Citibank in turn sent instructions to BCI on the same day, notifying BCI that Citibank had credited its account with $310,000 and instructing BCI to instruct Extrader to credit this amount to Kraemer. (Patrickakos Aff. ¶7 & Ex. 2).

Either just before or just after BCI's account at Citibank was credited with the $310,000, however, the BCI account was placed by Citibank on "hold for funds" status. (Pl. Rule 3(g) Statement ¶19). The "hold for funds" status, which was put into place because BCI's account with Citi-bank was overdrawn by more than $12 million, prevented BCI from making any further withdrawals from the account. (Id. ¶¶19, 22).

Kraemer apparently never received a credit to his Extrader account for the $310,000. Kraemer's affidavit, submitted by Grain Traders, states that on December 28, 1994, just six days after the attempted Funds Transfer, the government of Argentina ordered Extrader to suspend payments and that Extrader became insolvent "[s]ometime later." (Kraemer Aff. ¶5). Likewise, BCI, a Bahamian bank, ceased making payments in January 1995; it was closed by supervisory authorities in the Bahamas on July 31, 1995. (Def. Rule 3(g) Statement ¶10-12).

B. PRIOR PROCEEDINGS

Grain Traders commenced this action against Citibank in November 1995. The complaint asserts four causes of action: (1) for a refund under

U.C.C. §4-A-402; (2) for a refund as well as reasonable expenses and attorneys' fees under U.C.C. §§4-A-209, 4-A-301, and 4-A-305; (3) for breach of the obligation to deal in good faith under U.C.C. §1-203; and (4) for conversion and money had and received under common law.

These motions followed. . . .

DISCUSSION

B.   FUNDS TRANSFERS AND ARTICLE 4-A

Funds transfers, also commonly referred to as wire transfers, are a specialized "method of payment in which the person making the payment (the 'originator') directly transmits an instruction to a bank," generally through electronic means, "to make payment to the person receiving payment (the 'beneficiary') or to instruct some other bank to make payment to the beneficiary." §4-A-104, Official Comment 1. A funds transfer consists of one or more payment orders each instructing the next party in line as to the steps it must follow to carry out the funds transfer. Id. Hence, funds are "transferred" through a series of debits and credits to a series of bank accounts. Most often, funds transfers are used as an inexpensive and efficient method of discharging an "underlying payment obligation which arose through earlier commercial dealings between the originator . . . and the beneficiary." Sheerbonnet, Ltd. v. American Express Bank, Ltd., 905 F. Supp. 127, 130 (S.D.N.Y. 1995).

In the present case, Grain Traders was the originator of a funds transfer intended to pay $310,000 to Kraemer, the beneficiary. Grain Traders requested a series of payment orders that would "transfer" the funds from its bank, BCN, through two "intermediary" banks, Citibank and BCI and, finally into Kraemer's account at his bank, Extrader. Grain Traders asserts that Citibank did not carry out the Funds Transfer as directed and instead improperly used the funds it received as a set-off against debt owed to Citibank by BCI.

1.   §4-A-402

In its first cause of action, Grain Traders claims that it is entitled to a refund of the $310,000 from Citibank under the "money back guarantee" of §4-A-402. Section 4-A-402 states:

> (3) . . . With respect to a payment order issued to a receiving bank other than the beneficiary's bank, acceptance of the order by the receiving bank obliges the sender to pay the bank the amount of the sender's order. . . . The obligation of that sender to pay its payment order is excused if the funds transfer is not completed. . . .
>
> (4) If the sender of a payment order pays the order and was not obliged to pay all or part of the amount paid [because the funds transfer was not

completed], the bank receiving payment is obliged to refund payment to the extent the sender was not obliged to pay.

§4-A-402(3), (4).

Grain Traders argues that its obligation to pay BCN, and BCN's obligation to pay Citibank, was excused because the Funds Transfer was not completed. Grain Traders therefore asserts that it is entitled to a refund of its payment—pursuant to §4-A-402—from Citibank. Citibank, however, argues that Grain Traders has sued the wrong party. Citibank claims that §4-A-402 only allows a party to a funds transfer to obtain a refund from the next party or bank in line. Hence, Grain Traders may only seek a refund—if at all—from BCN. For at least four reasons, I agree with Citibank's interpretation of §4-A-402.

(i) Plain Language of §4-A-402. First, the plain language of §4-A-402 and other provisions of Article 4-A make it clear that a party to a funds transfer is only entitled to a refund from the specific party to which it made payment. Article 4-A treats a funds transfer as a series of individual transactions, each of which involve two parties dealing directly with each other. This notion is embodied in the very definition of a "funds transfer" as set forth in §4-A-104(1):

> "Funds transfer" means the series of transactions, beginning with the originator's payment order, made for the purpose of making payment to the beneficiary of the order. The term includes *any* payment order issued by the originator's bank or an intermediary bank intended to carry out the originator's payment order.

§4-A-104(1) (*emphasis added*). Thus, Article 4-A approaches each funds transfer not as a single payment order, but rather as a series of transactions each of which involves only the parties to the individual payment order.

After establishing this structure, Article 4-A proceeds to define the rights and duties of each bank involved in a funds transfer. First, §4-A-402(3) states that the bank that sent the payment order must pay the bank that received the payment order when the payment order is accepted. §4-A-402(3). Thus, the obligation of payment runs only from the sender bank—the bank that sent the payment order—to the bank that received the payment order. Id. This subsection further provides that the sending bank's obligation to pay the receiving bank is excused if the funds transfer is not completed. Id.

Then, §4-A-402(4) provides that when a sending bank that is not required to pay—because the funds transfer has not been completed—has already paid, the sending bank is entitled to a "refund" from the receiving bank. §4-A-402(4). Thus, these sections do not create an obligation to pay or refund a payment with respect to all the parties to a fund transfer, but instead only create an obligation between the sending bank and the receiving bank pursuant to each individual payment order making up the funds transfer. This conclusion is supported by the fact that the singular form of "bank," as opposed to the plural "banks," is used when §4-A-402 provides that "the *bank* receiving payment is obliged to refund" the payment. §4-A-402 (*emphasis added*). Thus, the plain language of §4-A-402 makes it clear that a right of refund lies only with respect to parties to a specific payment order and not as to all the parties to a funds transfer.

(ii) Official Comment to §4-A-402. Second, the Official Comment to §4-A-402 further underscores the intent of Article 4-A's drafters to limit the right of refund under §4-A-402 to the parties to a specific payment order. The Comment states as follows:

> The money-back guarantee [of §4-A-402(4)] is particularly important to Originator if noncompletion of the funds transfer is due to the fault of an intermediary bank rather than Bank A [the Originator's bank]. In that case Bank A must refund payment to Originator, and Bank A has the burden of obtaining refund from the intermediary bank that it paid.

§4-A-402, Official Comment 2. Thus, as the Comment explains, the originator is entitled to a refund from the bank to which it issued its payment order, and the originator's bank must then look to the intermediary bank—the bank to which it issued a payment order—to get a refund.

Accordingly, the Comment shows that Article 4-A's drafters intended the "money back guarantee" to apply only as between the parties to a payment order and not the parties to the funds transfer as a whole. Applied to the facts of this case, the originator—Grain Traders—would be entitled to a refund under §4-A-402(4) from its bank, BCN, but not from Citibank.

(iii) Right of Subrogation. Third, the subrogation language of §4-A-402(5) demonstrates that the originator does not, as a general matter, have a right to sue all the parties to a funds transfer. Subsection (5) deals with a situation where an intermediary-receiving bank cannot give a refund to its sending bank because the intermediary bank "suspends payment." In that case, §4-A-402(5) relieves the sending bank of its obligation to refund the payment it received. Instead, §4-A-402(5) provides that:

> [t]he first sender in the funds transfer that issued an instruction requiring routing through that intermediary bank [i.e., the one that "suspends payment"] is subrogated to the right of the bank that paid the intermediary bank to [a] refund.

Hence, the first sender to designate the defaulting bank (the bank that suspended payments) is the one that, by virtue of the subrogation, has the burden of seeking recovery.

What subsection (5) makes clear is that under §4-A-402(4) no right to a refund otherwise exists between the originator and an intermediary bank. This is evident because there would be no need for the subrogation language of subsection (5) if the originator (as the first sender) already had a right to assert a refund claim directly against all intermediary banks.

The Official Comments to §4-A-402 confirm that when it is the originator who chooses an intermediary bank that is unable, for financial reasons, to complete its part of the funds transfer, it is the originator, and not any other bank in the funds transfer, who bears the risk of loss. Comment 2 gives the following example:

> Suppose Originator instructs Bank A to pay to Beneficiary's account in Bank B and to use Bank C as an intermediary bank. Bank A executes Originator's order by issuing a payment order to Bank C. Bank A pays Bank C. Bank C fails to execute the order of Bank A and suspends payments. Under subsections [(3) and (4)], Originator is not obliged to pay Bank A and is entitled to a refund from Bank A of any payments that it may have made. Bank A is entitled to a refund from Bank C, but Bank C is insolvent. Subsection [(5)] deals with this case. *Bank A was required to issue its payment order to Bank C because Bank C was designated as an intermediary bank by Originator.* Section [4-A-302(1)(a)]. *In this case Originator takes the risk of insolvency of Bank C.* Under subsection [(5)], Bank A is entitled to payment from Originator and Originator is subrogated to the right of Bank A under [subsection (4)] to refund of payment from Bank C.

§4-A-402, Official Comment 2 (emphasis added).

Subsection (5) may not be precisely applicable here because it applies to a situation where an intermediary bank suspends payments and it is unclear from the record when BCI suspended payments. Nonetheless, the reasoning of subsection (5) supports the conclusion that in the present case Grain Traders must bear the risk of loss, for it was Grain Traders that chose BCI and Extrader to carry out the funds transfer. Grain Traders thus may not turn to Citibank to recover the loss suffered as a result of Grain Traders's choice of BCI and Extrader to complete the transfer.

(iv) Creation of Explicit Cause of Action by Originator Against Intermediary Bank. Finally, Citibank's argument that it owes no refund to Grain Traders finds support from the working of §4-A-305. Section 4-A-305 (2) provides that a "receiving bank" is liable to the "originator" for interest and expenses under certain circumstances. §4-A-305(2). Grain Traders points to this section as proof that all intermediary-receiving banks are liable directly to the originator for a refund. However, this section shows just the opposite. Section 4-A-305(2), which has no relationship to the refund provisions of §4-A-402, demonstrates that when the drafters of Article 4-A wanted to give

the originator the right to bring a cause of action against any bank in the funds transfer chain, they knew how to make that clear. Thus, had the drafters of Article 4-A intended to allow the originator to seek a refund from any bank in the funds transfer chain, they could have made that clear also.

Accordingly, I hold that Grain Traders may not, as a matter of law, assert a claim against Citibank under §4-A-402 and hence summary judgment is granted in favor of Citibank on Grain Traders's first claim for relief.

2.   §§4-A-209 and 4-A-301

Grain Traders's second claim for relief is premised on §§4-A-209 and 4-A-301, which govern "acceptance" and "execution" of a payment order, respectively. Grain Traders alleges that because Citibank intended to use the $310,000 as a set-off to the debt owed to Citibank by BCI, Citibank did not intend to carry out the payment order received from BCN. Grain Traders argues that because of Citibank's misplaced intent, the payment order issued by Citibank of BCI did not constitute the "execution" or "acceptance" of BCN's payment order under §4-A-209 or §4-A-301. See §4-A-301 ("A payment order is 'executed' by the receiving bank when it issues a payment order intended to carry out the payment order received by the bank.") (emphasis [sic] added). Grain Traders thus concludes that Citibank is liable for its failure to properly execute BCN's payment order. I disagree.

As a threshold matter, the record shows unequivocally that Citibank properly executed the payment order that it received. It debited BCN's account $310,000; it credited BCFs account $310,000; and it forwarded instructions to BCI to instruct Extrader to credit Kraemer with $310,000. That was all that it was required to do. As §4-A-302 makes clear, an intermediary bank that accepts a payment order "is obliged to issue . . . a payment order complying with the sender's order and follow the sender's instructions concerning . . . any intermediary bank. . . ." Here, Citibank accepted a payment order from BCN that instructed it to instruct BCI to instruct Extrader to credit $310,000 to Kraemer. Citibank followed these instructions, thereby meeting its obligations, as it relayed the appropriate instructions to the next intermediary bank, BCI.

Moreover, even if Grain Traders were able to prove that Citibank failed to execute or accept BCN's payment order, it would nevertheless not be entitled to prevail on its second claim for relief. This is because neither §4-A-209 nor §4-A-301 provides a remedy for the failure to carry out a payment order. Rather, these two sections simply define the terms "acceptance" and "execution" as those terms are used in the rest of Article 4-A. If a funds transfer is not completed because one of the parties involved in the funds transfer fails to either "accept" or "execute" a payment order, the only remedy to which the originator is entitled is a refund—pursuant to §4-A-402—of any payment it made. Thus, Grain Traders's second claim for relief simply leads us back to the same place as its first claim — i.e., a claim for a refund under the "money back guarantee" of §4-A-402. Accordingly, Grain Traders's second claim for relief is dismissed for the same reasons as its first claim for relief.

c. u.c.c. §1-203[13]

In its third claim for relief, Grain Traders asserts that Citibank's actions violated §1-203. Section 1-203 imposes an obligation of good faith and fair dealing on a party's performance or enforcement of any contract or duty within the ambit of the Uniform Commercial Code. N.Y.U.C.C. §1-203. Grain Traders alleges that it is entitled to damages because Citi-bank violated this section. For two reasons, I disagree.

First, §1-203 only imposes an obligation of good faith and fair dealing on the performance of a "contract or duty." Id. In this case, Grain Traders has not alleged that any contract existed between Citibank and itself. Thus, Grain Traders must be relying on a statutory duty as the predicate for its third claim for relief. The only statutory duty that applied in this case, however, is Article 4-A and, for the reasons I have already discussed, Grain Traders has failed to state a claim under that Article. Thus, there is no contract or statutory duty to which Grain Traders can argue that its good faith claim under §1-203 applies.

Second, to the extent that Grain Traders is asserting that a violation of §1-203 gives rise to an independent cause of action, its assertion is without merit, for §1-203 does not give rise to an independent cause of action. See, e.g., Super Glue Corp. v. Avis Rent A Car System, Inc., 132 A.D.2d 604, 517 N.Y.S.2d 764, 766 (2d Dep't 1987) ("the Code does not permit recovery of money damages for not acting in good faith where no other basis of recovery is present"). The Official Comment to §1-203 supports this conclusion:

> This section does not support an independent cause of action for failure to perform or enforce in good faith. . . . [T]he doctrine of good faith merely directs a court towards interpreting contracts within *the* commercial context in which they are created, performed, and enforced, and does not create a separate duty of fairness and reasonableness which can be independently breached.

§1-203, Official Comment, at Supp. p. 13. Accordingly, Grain Traders's third claim for relief is dismissed.

d. common law claims

Grain Traders's fourth claim for relief relies on the common law torts of "conversion" and "money had and received." Grain Traders's tort claims,

---

13. [Now §1-304 — Eds.]

however, must be dismissed because Grain Traders has failed to present evidence to support either of those claims.

To prevail on either of its common law claims, Grain Traders must prove that at the time it alleges Citibank improperly kept the $310,000, Grain Traders still had a possessory interest in the funds. Lind v. Vanguard Offset Printers, Inc., 857 F. Supp. 1060, 1066 (S.D.N.Y. 1994) (under New York law, conversion "requires a showing . . . that the plaintiff had an ownership interest or an 'immediate superior right to possession of property'"); Aaron Ferer & Sons Ltd. v. Chase Manhattan Bank, 731 F.2d 112, 125 (2d Cir. 1984) (to state a claim for money *had and received* under New York Law, the plaintiff must show that "defendant received money belonging to plaintiff") (*emphasis added*). Grain Traders, however, did not have possession of the funds at the time Citibank credited them to BCFs account. This is because a depositor loses title to money deposited in a general account at the moment those funds are deposited. . . .

Rather, it debited one account $310,000 and credited another account $310,000, and it forwarded the appropriate payment instructions. That was all it was required to do. BCI should have carried out those instructions, but it was unwilling or unable to do so.

CONCLUSION

For the foregoing reasons, Grain Traders's motion for summary judgment is denied and Citibank's cross-motion for summary judgment is granted. Accordingly, the Clerk of the Court shall enter judgment in favor of Citibank dismissing the complaint with prejudice and without costs.

So ordered.

———————————

Most courts considering the issue have ruled that common law theories are preempted in wire transfer cases by the statutory scheme of Article 4A (except as to matters the Article does not cover). ADS Associates Group, Inc. v. Oritani Sav. Bank, 219 N.J. 496, 99 A.3d 345 (2014), has a good discussion of this.

PROBLEM 165

Saul Sender agreed to buy Betty Beneficiary's business from her for the amount of $1 million, the deal to be off unless he made payment of this amount to her account (12345) at Merchants Bank on September 25. On September 24, Saul ordered his bank, Original National Bank (ONB), to wire $1 million from his account with ONB to Betty Beneficiary, Account #12345, at Merchants

Bank, with a payment date of the next day. ONB executed this payment order by issuing an identical payment order to Merchants Bank, but unfortunately, it mistakenly gave the account number as 12346, though it correctly identified Betty by name. Merchants Bank notified Harry Innocent, the holder of Account #12346, that $1 million had been deposited in his account and was available for withdrawal as of September 25. Harry, delighted, withdrew the money and lit out for parts unknown. When Betty didn't receive the money, she phoned Saul on September 26 and told him that the deal was off and that she was selling the business to her brother. Saul, furious, sued his bank. Who bears what liability here?

The drafters of Article 4A discovered that the usage of trade in wire transfers was for all banks involved to look only at the account number and ignore the actual name of the beneficiary and rather than trying to change the practice, they decided to give it statutory blessing. Thus §4A-207 deals with misdescription of the beneficiary and provides that the beneficiary's bank may ignore the name specified in the payment order and deal only on the basis of the given account number (unless it was actually aware of the discrepancy, in which case it is responsible for seeing that the correct beneficiary gets the funds—see TME Enterprises, Inc. v. Norwest Corp., 124 Cal. App. 4th 1021, 22 Cal. Rptr. 3d 146 (2004)). Thus Merchants Bank is off the hook in this situation even though it put the money in the wrong account. Under what is called the "money-back guarantee" (see Official Comment 2 to §4A-402), Original National Bank must refund the money to its customer because it made the mistake, and then go after Harry Innocent in order to recover the money.[14] ONB is liable to its customer, Saul, though he has a duty to discover and report the problem within 90 days after his bank sends him notification of the payment or be responsible for whatever loss the bank can prove it suffered because of his delay in reporting; §4A-304. Any time a bank does not properly execute the payment order, the originator must be made whole, including interest per §4A-204(a). Official Comment 2 to §4A-402 calls this the "money-back guarantee." ONB is liable for Saul's expenses, the $1 million and interest thereon, but the bank is not liable for any consequential damages (for example, the loss of the chance to buy Betty's business) unless a written agreement between Saul and ONB provides that the bank will bear this greater loss; §4A-305 (which also provides that in certain circumstances the bank may have to pay Saul's attorney's fees—see (e)).

---

14. Its cause of action is common law restitution ("money had and received"); §4A-207(d); HSBC Bank USA, N.A. v. A.T.A. Const. Corp., 2009 WL 1456529 (E.D.N.Y. 2009).

Corfan Banco Asuncion Paraguay v. Ocean Bank

Florida District Court of Appeal, 1998
715 So. 2d 967

SORONDO, J.

Corfan Banco Asuncion Paraguay, a foreign banking corporation (Corfan Bank), appeals the lower court's entry of a Final Summary Judgment in favor of Ocean Bank, a Florida bank.

On March 22, 1995, Corfan Bank originated a wire transfer of $72,972 via its intermediary Swiss Bank to the account of its customer, Jorge Alberto Dos Santos Silva (Silva), in Ocean Bank. The transfer order bore Silva's name as the recipient and indicated that his account number was 01007*0*21*040*0 (in fact, this was a nonexistent account). Upon receipt of the wire transfer, Ocean Bank noticed a discrepancy in this number and before depositing the money, confirmed with Silva that his correct account number was 01007*6*21*640*6.[15] Ocean Bank did not, however, inform Corfan Bank or Swiss Bank of the error. Once the correct number was confirmed by Silva, Ocean Bank accepted the wire transfer and credited Silva's account.

The next day, Corfan Bank became aware of the account number discrepancy and, without first checking with either Silva or Ocean Bank, sent a second wire transfer of $72,972 to Silva's correct account number at Ocean Bank. The second transfer order did not indicate that it was a correction, replacement or amendment of the March 22nd transfer. Because the information of the transfer was correct, it was automatically processed at Ocean Bank and was credited to Silva's account. Several days later, Corfan Bank inquired of Ocean Bank regarding the two transfers, maintaining that only one transfer was intended. By that time, Silva had withdrawn the proceeds of both wire transfers. When Ocean Bank refused to repay $72,972 to Corfan Bank, this litigation ensued. Corfan Bank proceeded on two claims, one based on the §670.207, Florida Statutes (1995), which codifies as Florida law §4A-207 of the Uniform Commercial Code (UCC), and one based on common law negligence. Ocean Bank answered denying liability under the statute and also contending that the negligence claim was precluded by the preemptive statutory scheme.

The trial court, emphasizing that Florida's adoption of the UCC sections concerning wire transfers did not abrogate the basic tenets of commercial law, found that Ocean Bank had not contravened §670.207 by crediting the erroneous March 22nd wire transfer to Silva's account. Finding that Corfan Bank was the party best situated to have avoided this loss, the court held that Corfan Bank must bear that loss and, therefore, the court granted

---

15. As indicated by the italicized numbers, the three sixes in the account number had been replaced with zeros on the transfer order.

Ocean Bank's motion for summary judgment as to count one (the UCC count). Additionally, the court dismissed count two (the negligence count).

We begin with a review of the exact language of §670.207(1), Florida Statutes:

> (1) Subject to subsection (2), if, in a payment order received by the beneficiary's bank, the name, bank account number, or other identification of the beneficiary refers to a nonexistent or unidentifiable person or account, no person has rights as a beneficiary of the order and acceptance of the order cannot occur.

Corfan Bank argues that this language is clear and unambiguous, where a name *or* bank account number, *or* other identification refers either to a nonexistent or unidentified person or a nonexistent account, the order *cannot* be accepted. Ocean Bank responds that such a "highly technical" reading of the statute is "contrary to commercial and practical considerations and common sense." It suggests that we look to the legislative intent and conclude that the "or" in the statute should be given conjunctive rather than disjunctive effect. We respectfully decline Ocean Bank's invitation to look behind the plain language of the statute and conclude that given its clarity it must be read as written.

In Capers v. State, 678 So. 2d 330 (Fla. 1996), the Florida Supreme Court stated:

> [T]he plain meaning of statutory language is the first consideration of statutory construction. St. Petersburg Bank & Trust Co. v. Hamm, 414 So. 2d 1071, 1073 (Fla. 1982). Only when a statute is of doubtful meaning should matters extrinsic to the statute be considered in construing the language employed by the legislature. Florida State Racing Comm'n v. McLaughlin, 102 So. 2d 574, 576 (Fla. 1958). . . .

In the present case, although the payment order correctly identified the beneficiary, it referred to a nonexistent account number. Under the clear and unambiguous terms of the statute, acceptance of the order could not have occurred. As the Florida Supreme Court stated in [State v. Jett, 626 So. 2d 691 (Fla. 1993)]:

> We trust that if the legislature did not intend the result mandated by the statute's plain language, the legislature itself will amend the statute at the next opportunity.

Jett, 626 So. 2d at 693.

As indicated above, the trial court dismissed count two of the complaint which sounded in negligence. The court concluded that the statutory scheme preempts the common law remedy of negligence. It is not clear whether the adoption of Article 4A of the UCC abrogated the common law cause of action for negligence relating to a wire transfer, as raised in count two of the complaint. The Uniform Commercial Code Comment following §670.102, Florida Statutes (1995), which delineates the subject matter for chapter 670, provides in part:

> In the drafting of Article 4A, a deliberate decision was made to write on a clean slate and to treat a funds transfer as a unique method of payment to be governed by unique rules that address the particular issues raised in this method of payment. A deliberate decision was also made to use precise and detailed rules to assign responsibility, define behavioral norms, allocate risks and establish limits on liability, rather than to rely on broadly stated, flexible principles. In the drafting of these rules, a critical consideration was that the various parties to funds transfers need to be able to predict risk with certainty, to insure against risk, to adjust operational and security procedures, and to price funds transfer services appropriately. This consideration is particularly important given the very large amounts of money that are involved in funds transfers.
>
> Funds transfers involve competing interests — those of the banks that provide funds transfer services and the commercial and financial organizations that use the services, as well as the public interest. These competing interests were represented in the drafting process and they were thoroughly considered. *The rules that emerged represent a careful and delicate balancing of those interests and are intended to be the exclusive means of determining the rights, duties and liabilities of the affected parties in any situation covered by particular provisions of the Article.* Consequently, resort to principles of law or equity outside of Article 4A is not appropriate to create rights, duties and liabilities inconsistent with those stated in this Article.

(Emphasis added). See U.C.C. §4A-102 cmt. (1977); see also, 19A Fla. Stat. Ann. 15 (U.C.C. cmt. 1995) (emphasis added). This comment suggests the exclusivity of Article 4A as a remedy. Although the commentary to the UCC is not controlling authority, see Solitron Devices, Inc. v. Veeco Instruments, Inc., 492 So. 2d 1357, 1359 (Fla. 4th DCA 1986); 1 Ronald A. Anderson, Anderson on the Uniform Commercial Code, §1-102:34-:37 (1995 Revision), we are persuaded by the expressed intent of the drafters.

In addressing this issue we restrict our analysis to the pleadings and facts of this case. In pertinent part, count two reads as follows:

> Ocean Bank owed Corfan Bank a duty of care to follow the accepted banking practice of the community, and to return the funds from the first transfer to Corfan Bank upon receipt due to the reference in the first transfer to a non-existent account number.

The duty claimed to have been breached by Ocean Bank in its negligence count is exactly the same duty established and now governed by the statute. Under such circumstances we agree with the trial judge that the statutory scheme preempts the negligence claim in this case and affirm the dismissal of count two.[16] We do not reach the issue of whether the adoption of Article 4A of the UCC preempts negligence claims in all cases.

We reverse the Final Summary Judgment entered by the trial court in favor of Ocean Bank as to count one of the complaint and affirm the dismissal of count two. We remand this case for further proceedings consistent with this opinion.

LEVY, J., concurs.

NESBITT, J., dissenting. I respectfully dissent. I would affirm final summary judgment for Ocean Bank. In my view, the trial court's well-reasoned and pragmatic approach to the interpretation of §670.207, Florida Statutes (1995), was the best solution to the disagreement between these parties. Corfan Bank itself was negligent in handling the wire transfer in question. Corfan Bank incorrectly listed Silva's account number on the first wire transfer order and, compounding that error, Corfan sent the second wire transfer order with no indication that it was a correction of the first. These errors caused Corfan's loss.

More important, the language of §670.207 does not proscribe the actions taken by Ocean Bank. Section 670.207 precludes acceptance of a wire transfer order only if "the name, account number, or other identification of the beneficiary refers to a nonexistent or unidentifiable person or account." Considering this section in its entirety as statutory construction requires, see Fleischman v. Department of Professional Regulation, 441 So. 2d 1121, 1123 (Fla. 3d DCA 1983), it seems apparent that the part of the statute that permits the receiving bank to look to "other identification" surely allows more flexibility than the majority here would permit.

---

16. We note that allowing a negligence claim in this case would "create rights, duties and liabilities inconsistent" with those set forth in §670.207. In a negligence cause of action, Ocean Bank would be entitled to defend on a theory of comparative negligence because Corfan Bank provided the erroneous account number which created the problem at issue and then initiated the second transfer without communicating with Ocean Bank. Section 670.207 does not contemplate such a defense. (Oddly enough, allowing Corfan Bank's negligence claim in this case might actually inure to Ocean Bank's benefit). As explained in the comment, one of the primary purposes of the section is to enable the parties to wire funds transfers to predict risk with certainty and to insure against risk. The uniformity and certainty sought by the statute for these transactions could not possibly exist if parties could opt to sue by way of pre-Code remedies where the statute has specifically defined the duties, rights and liabilities of the parties.

In my view, the statute question should neither be construed in the disjunctive or the conjunctive. As stated above, the construction of a statute that will reject part of it should be avoided. See Snively Groves, Inc. v. Mayo, 135 Fla. 300, 184 So. 839 (1938); or, as sometimes stated, "A court should avoid reading the statute so that it will render part of the statute meaningless." Unruh v. State, 669 So. 2d 242, 245 (Fla. 1996). There are segments of this statute that plainly permit a receiving bank to look at other identification, thus affording the receiving bank more flexibility in making the correct identification than the court recognizes today.

Ocean Bank's actions seem to better comport with the overall statutory scheme relating to funds transfers than the avenue supported by the court. The primary purpose of using a wire transfer of funds is to enable the beneficiary to get the funds quickly. Indeed, commercial or contract deadlines may be adversely impacted if the wire transfer does not go through quickly, as anticipated. We should recognize that the importance of speed in a wire transfer becomes even more critical in transactions involving different countries with, perhaps, different time zones. For example, if transmitting back Corfan was closed by the time the funds were received by Ocean Bank, Ocean Bank would not have been in a position to rectify the error until the next business day—which might well render the entire reason for the transfer moot.

Ocean Bank chose to use the beneficiary's name (which was properly included on the first wire transfer order) and "other identification of the beneficiary"—the fact that the account number given was similar to that of the beneficiary, as well as verification that the beneficiary was expecting the transfer in order to accept the wire transfer and properly credit the beneficiary's account. Ocean Bank decided that there was enough information in the first wire transfer order for it, after verification, to credit the transfer to the beneficiary's account. The order contained the beneficiary's name and account number, with a few zeros replacing the correct "6"s. This information referred not to a "nonexistent or unidentifiable person or account" but rather to an existing customer—the intended beneficiary—and to an identifiable (through "other identification") account.

I can find no common sense reason to prohibit Ocean Bank or other banks from accepting the responsibility that goes with choosing to use "other identification" in order to deposit funds into a customer's account. Basically, by verifying with Silva that he was the intended beneficiary, Ocean Bank was correcting Corfan Bank's error. Ocean Bank was seeking to aid its customer, the intended beneficiary of the funds, in getting the funds in an expeditious manner. Had Ocean Bank erroneously deposited the funds into the wrong account, it would have to face the liability associated with that decision. However, it should not face liability because it deposited the funds into the correct account—the intended beneficiary's account. Indeed, it was only because of Ocean Bank's actions that the intended beneficiary, Mr. Silva, received the funds from the first transfer.

Moreover, as the trial court emphasized, Florida's enactment of the U.C.C. did not abrogate other common law principles applicable to commercial transactions. A longstanding equitable tenet of Florida law is that, as between two innocent parties, the party best suited to prevent the loss caused by a third party wrongdoer must bear that loss. See Exchange Bank of St. Augustine v. Florida Nat'l Bank of Jacksonville, 292 So. 2d 361, 363 (Fla. 1974) ("[I]f one of two innocent parties is to suffer a loss, it should be borne by the one whose negligence put in motion the flow of circumstances causing the loss.") . . .

Here, Corfan put in issue the question of the correlative negligence of its and Ocean's actions. It is undisputed that Corfan was initially negligent in transmittal of the first wire transfer. It realized its mistake the following business day, and sent a second wire transfer with no indication it was a correction of the former. It was entirely unnecessary to transmit additional funds merely to correct the previous day's error. If it had not sent the additional funds, it is unlikely there would ever have been a dispute bringing the matter before us. Simply, Corfan Bank was in a better position to prevent the loss and, indeed, Corfan's negligence played a "substantial role" in that loss. These facts should prevent its recovery from Ocean Bank. . . .

For the above-mentioned reasons, I would affirm.

PROBLEM 166

Same facts as the last Problem, except that Saul is the one that gave his bank the incorrect account number, though he correctly listed the beneficiary's name. What result? See §4A-207(c) (and its Official Comment 3). What practical step does this section suggest to the bank?

Bank of America N.T.S.A. v. Sanati

California Court of Appeal, 1992
14 Cal. Rptr. 2d 615

JOHNSON, J.

In an action for unjust enrichment, money had and received, conversion, and declaratory relief, the trial court granted plaintiff's motion for summary judgment, finding that defendants had no defense to plaintiff's request for restitution for an erroneous fund transfer. Defendants appeal from the adverse judgment, claiming the trial court erroneously applied the common law pertaining to checks and negotiable instruments instead of the law specifically pertaining to funds transfers. We affirm.

FACTS AND PROCEEDINGS BELOW

In 1963 Hassan and Fatane Sanati were married in Tehran, Iran. They lived in Iran until Mrs. Fatane Sanati moved with their two children to Los Angeles in 1983. Between 1983 and 1987 Mr. Sanati spent nearly half his time living in Los Angeles. In 1987 Mr. Sanati permanently left the United States.

When Mr. Sanati left, he arranged for payments to be made to Mrs. Sanati in Los Angeles. He instructed Bank of America in London to send interest, as it accrued monthly from an account held in his name only, to an account he held jointly at Bank of America with Mrs. Sanati in Tarzana, California.

The amount of each interest payment was between $2,000 and $3,000.

On April 30, 1990, Bank of America in London erroneously sent the principal of Mr. Sanati's bank account as well as the accrued interest to the joint Sanati account in Tarzana, California. The amount of the errone-ous fund transfer was $203,750. The next day Mrs. Sanati authorized her children to withdraw $200,000 from this account. These funds were then deposited into various bank accounts under Mrs. Sanati's and her children's names.

Bank of America (bank) immediately realized its error and requested reimbursement for the erroneous payment. Mrs. Sanati and her children, Babek and Haleh Sanati (collectively Sanatis or defendants) refused the bank's requests.

In July 1990, the bank filed a complaint against the Sanatis seeking res-titution for the amount of the erroneous payment. Eventually Mr. Sanati's bank account in London was re-credited the amount of the principal trans-ferred without his authority and he was dismissed as a defendant in the action. The remaining parties stipulated the funds from the erroneous transfer would be placed in a blocked account at Bank of America pending resolution of the litigation. . . .

The trial court granted the bank's motion [for summary judgment] and this appeal followed.

DISCUSSION

I.   REVIEW OF THE COMMON LAW GOVERNING ERRONEOUS FUND TRANSFERS

At the time of the fund transfer in this case the law controlling the risks and liabilities of banks, beneficiaries and originators was general common law and equitable principles. Courts often borrowed concepts from Articles 3 and 4 of the Uniform Commercial Code governing commercial paper and negotiable instruments as well. This sometimes resulted in inconsistent decisions and was generally determined to be an unsatisfactory method of allocating risks and responsibilities in these widely used transactions generally involving large sums of money. Ultimately the American Law Institute developed section 4A of the Uniform Commercial Code to specifically deal with fund transfers. In 1990 the California Legislature adopted Article 4A of the Uniform Commercial Code as Division 11 of the California Uniform Commercial Code.

However, as stated, under the law in effect at the time of the fund transfer in this case, the general common law and equitable principles controlled. Under the law as it then existed, the bank was entitled to restitution from the beneficiaries for the amount of the unauthorized transfer despite its negligence under general legal principles of mistake and unjust enrichment. (Rest., Restitution, Sec. 59, com. a, p. 232; American Oil Service, Inc. v. Hope Oil Co. (1965) 233 Cal. App. 2d 822, 830; Frontier Refining Co. v. Home Bank (1969) 272 Cal. App. 2d 630, 634; Aebli v. Board of Education (1944) 62 Cal. App. 2d 706, 724-725; see also Annot., Recovery by Bank of Money Paid Out to Customer by Mistake (1981) 10 A.L.R.4th 524 Secs. 6-7 and cases collected.)

This rule, however, was subject to certain defenses. The most widely acknowledged defense to a claim for restitution for an erroneous transfer of funds was detrimental reliance by an innocent beneficiary. (Rest., Restitution Sec. 142, com. c; 1 Witkin Summary of Cal. Law (9th ed. 1987) Contracts, Sec. 94, pp.124-125; Doyle v. Matheron (1957) 148 Cal. App. 2d 521, 522.)

A less widely acknowledged defense to a claim for restitution was the "discharge for value" rule. (Rest., Restitution, Sec. 14.) This defense arises where there is a preexisting liquidated debt or lien owed to the beneficiary by the originator of the payment. If the originator or some third party erroneously gives the beneficiary funds at the originator's request, and the beneficiary in good faith believes the funds have been submitted in full or partial payment of that preexisting debt or lien and is unaware of the originator's or third party's mistake, the originator or third party will not be entitled to seek repayment from the beneficiary of the erroneously submitted funds. (1 Witkin (9th ed. 1987) Contracts, Secs, 94, 100, 102, pp.124, 129-130.) . . .

. . . Thus, under existing law the bank was entitled to seek restitution for the overpayment to defendants despite its negligence, unless defendants had detrimentally relied on the additional payment without notice of the mistake or unless the defendants had applied in good faith the additional erroneous payment to a preexisting debt or lien owed to them from Mr. Sanati.

II.   THE BANK WAS ENTITLED TO JUDGMENT EVEN IF THE STATUTORY PROVISIONS
      GOVERNING ERRONEOUS FUND TRANSFERS CONTROLLED

On appeal defendants vigorously argue the trial court erred in applying to a fund transfer case the general common law pertaining to commercial paper and negotiable instruments.

They argue the court should have applied Division 11 of the California Uniform Commercial Code [UCC Article 4A] which governs the consequences of an erroneous execution of a payment order. Defendants also suggest that had the court applied the new law, summary judgment would have been inappropriate because there would have been a triable issue of material fact whether defendants believed in good faith the additional erroneous payment was sent in satisfaction or discharge of a preexisting debt or lien from Mr. Sanati.

Defendants' argument fails for two reasons. First, the trial court did not err in failing to apply the new fund transfer provisions of Division 11 of the California Uniform Commercial Code [UCC Article 4A]. The Legislature expressly stated that division only applied to fund transfers in which the originator's payment order was transmitted on or after January 1, 1991. (Stats. 1990, c. 125, Sec. 3.) The payment order in the present case was transmitted in April of 1990. Thus, by its terms the new fund transfer provisions of the California Uniform Commercial Code did not apply to the transfer in this case.

Secondly, even if the new fund transfer provisions were applied to this case, we conclude defendants have failed to create a triable issue of material fact whether Mr. Sanati owed them a preexisting debt or lien even assuming their good faith.

Section 11303 of the California Uniform Commercial Code [UCC §4A-303] discusses the effect of an erroneous transfer. That section merely restates existing law governing such errors and provides in pertinent part:

> (a) A receiving bank that (i) executes the payment order of the sender by issuing a payment order in an amount greater than the amount of the sender's order, . . . is entitled to payment of the amount of the sender's order. . . . The bank is entitled to recover from the beneficiary of the erroneous order the excess payment received to the extent allowed by the law governing mistake and restitution.

The comment to the Uniform Commercial Code which was incorporated into the comments in the California Uniform Commercial Code provides examples illustrating how this section should operate. The effect of the comment explicating this section is to expressly adopt the "discharge for value" rule found in §14 of the Restatement of Restitution.

The relevant comment [2] provides:

> Subsections (a) and (b) deal with cases in which the receiving bank executes by issuing a payment order in the wrong amount. If Originator ordered Originator's Bank to pay $1,000,000 to the account of Beneficiary in Beneficiary's Bank, but Originator's Bank erroneously instructed Beneficiary's Bank to pay $2,000,000 to Beneficiary's account, subsection (a) applies. If

Beneficiary's Bank accepts the order of Originator's Bank, Beneficiary's Bank is entitled to receive $2,000,000 from Originator's Bank, but Originator's Bank is entitled to receive only $1,000,000 from Originator. Originator's Bank is entitled to recover the overpayment from Beneficiary to the extent allowed by the law governing mistake and restitution. Originator's Bank would normally have a right to recover the overpayment from Beneficiary, but in unusual cases the law of restitution might allow Beneficiary to keep all or part of the overpayment. For example, if Originator owed $2,000,000 to Beneficiary and Beneficiary received the extra $1,000,000 in good faith in discharge of the debt, Beneficiary may be allowed to keep it. In this case Originator's Bank has paid an obligation of Originator and under the law of restitution, which applies through section 1-103, Originator's Bank would be subrogated to Beneficiary's rights against Originator on the obligation paid by Originator's Bank.

Thus, under this section defendants would be entitled to retain the erroneously sent funds if in good faith they believed the funds were sent to them in satisfaction of or in discharge of a valid preexisting debt or lien.

Toward this end, Fatane Sanati asserted she had a quasi community property interest in Mr. Sanati's London bank account as well as in all other property accumulated during their marriage. In an affidavit offered in opposition to the bank's motion for summary judgment Mrs. Sanati declared:

> . . . 3. I was married to Hassan Sanati, ("husband") on September 7, 1963 in Tehran, Iran where we resided until I came to Los Angeles with our two children.
>
> 4. My husband and I lived with our children, also defendants in this action, in Los Angeles since 1983. My husband was travelling in and out of the United States and until November of 1987, he had collectively spent 22 months in California during that period.
>
> 5. During our marriage we accumulated a substantial amount of money and real property, most of which was located in Iran and England.
>
> 6. My husband has always kept all of the bank accounts and most of the real property, wherever situated, in his own name.
>
> 7. Since he left in November, 1987, my children and I have been receiving interest monthly from our bank account in London, England to our account . . . at Bank of America, Tarzana branch. The account in London was opened by my husband with funds derived from our bank accounts and real property in Iran.
>
> 8. I had asked my husband on numerous occasions to transfer the London account to me in Los Angeles. Although he had agreed to do so on several occasions he had never done it.
>
> 9. My children and I have been virtual prisoners here and completely at my husband's mercy with regard to financial matters. For the last twenty-five years, my husband has always exercised complete control over all of our marital community assets worldwide.

. . . 11. In May, 1990, the Bank of America in London transferred the monthly interest and the entire principal of the account to my and my husband's account in Bank of America in Tarzana.

12. I used some of these funds for the family and I removed the remainder to accounts under my control.

. . . 17. Since the London account was transferred to our joint account in California, I have spoken to my husband via telephone. On several occasions, he agreed to keep the transferred money in our joint account under both our names. However, to this date, he has not done so.

. . . 19. I have filed a petition for Dissolution of Marriage at the Los Angeles Superior Court on July 2, 1990. . . . The Summons and Complaint were personally served upon my husband, in Tehran, Iran, by Rosy Shahbodaghi, on September 24, 1990. I have instructed my counsel to enter his default therein. . . .

Thus, Mrs. Sanati's declaration raises a reasonable inference of a potential quasi community property interest in the funds in the London bank account held in Mr. Sanati's name alone. However, this evidence does not raise a reasonable inference of a preexisting debt or lien at the time of the transfer of the type recognized in those decisions applying the "discharge for value" rule.

For example, in Banque Worms v. Bank America International (S.D.N.Y. 1989) 726 F. Supp. 940, *aff'd*, (2d Cir. 1991) 928 F.2d 538, the case upon which defendants primarily rely, the debt was a bank loan. In that case the originator had an outstanding loan for $2,000,000 from Banque Worms. On the day before the erroneous transfer, Banque Worms notified the originator it was calling the loan. The next day Banque Worms received a wire transfer for $2,000,000 from Security Pacific International Bank (SPIB), the originator's bank, and applied it to the originator's outstanding loan balance.

Shortly thereafter Banque Worms received a second wire transfer from the originator's bank for $1,974,267.97 which was the amount the originator actually requested to be sent. Because it only had instructions for the latter payment, SPIB could not debit the originator's bank account for the first erroneous payment. Because Banque Worms received the payment in the good faith belief it was in response to their demand for repayment of the loan, the court held SPIB had to suffer the loss for the mistaken payment under the "discharge for value" rule.

Examples in the Restatement of Restitution describing the "discharge for value" rule describe debts that are liquidated, concrete and preexisting, not merely probable and undetermined. (E.g., Rest., Restitution, Sec. 14, com. b, illus. facts 1 [no restitution for proceeds erroneously used to pay existing mortgage on real estate]; illus. 2 [no restitution from city for property taxes paid on property not actually owned]; illus. 3 [no restitution where bank erroneously cashes customer's check given to payee in payment for services rendered]; illus. 4 [no restitution from judgment creditor for execution of judgment of wrong person's property].) No decision we are aware of has applied the discharge for value rule where the debt or lien in question was anything less than an objectively verifiable, preexisting, liquidated obligation. (See Rest., Restitution (append.), Sec. 14 and cases collected.) Indeed, allowing the rule to apply to debts or obligations any less substantial would risk destroying the certainty of the rule and allow the exception to control its application.

Consequently, it does not appear the "discharge for value" rule can be properly invoked in a case such as this where the alleged preexisting debt or lien is at best a probable yet undetermined interest in a portion of the funds in Mr. Sanati's bank account in London.[17]

The defendants do not contend they changed their position to their detriment in reliance on the erroneously transmitted funds. Nor do the defendants' opposition papers raise any other potential defense to the bank's action for restitution. Thus, in the absence of any viable defense, the bank was entitled to restitution from the beneficiaries for the erroneously transmitted funds. We therefore conclude the trial court did not err in finding the bank was entitled to judgment as a matter of law.

DISPOSITION

The judgment is affirmed. Each side to bear its costs of appeal.

D.   Unauthorized Funds Transfers

Every payment system has a rule allocating loss in the event of unauthorized payments. A customer is not liable for unauthorized checks written on an account, unless the customer was negligent or failed to check bank statements, thus permitting multiple fraudulent checks to be written. A credit card holder is liable only for $50 of unauthorized use. A consumer is not liable for most debit transfers beyond $50, as long as the customer gives timely notice to her bank. For commercial funds transfers, UCC 4A places somewhat more risk on customers. As the following materials discuss, if the bank and the customer have agreed to use a commercially reasonable security procedure, the customer takes the loss for unauthorized transfers as long

---

17. This case would raise entirely different issues if, for example, there was a preexisting judgment dividing the parties' marital assets decreeing a sum certain of $200,000 or more in cash to be transferred to Mrs. Sanati as part of the settlement and that this amount was due and owing to her at the time of the erroneous wire transfer. But those are not the facts of this case. In fact, Mrs. Sanati did not file for dissolution of marriage until several months after the erroneous fund transfer.

as the bank has followed the procedure in good faith. That is a significant risk for customers in a time where criminals use increasingly sophisticated means to hack into bank accounts with both technical tricks and social engineering. Many customers may not realize the risk to their bank accounts, thinking that they are only liable for actually authorized transfers.

Choice Escrow and Land Title, LLC v. BancorpSouth Bank

United States Court of Appeals for the Eighth Circuit, 2014
754 F.3d 611

WOLLMAN, Circuit Judge.

Internet fraudsters stole $440,000 from a bank account that Choice Escrow and Land Title, LLC (Choice), maintained at BancorpSouth Bank (BancorpSouth). Choice sued BancorpSouth for the lost funds, and BancorpSouth counterclaimed for attorney's fees. The questions presented in this case are thus (1) who should bear the loss of the funds from Choice's account, and (2) who should pay BancorpSouth's attorney's fees. The district court, interpreting Article 4A of the Uniform Commercial Code (U.C.C.), held that Choice should bear the loss of the funds from its account and that BancorpSouth should pay its own attorney's fees. We affirm the district court's loss-of-funds ruling, reverse its dismissal of BancorpSouth's counterclaim, and remand for further proceedings.

I.

This litigation began after an unknown third party accessed Choice's online bank account at BancorpSouth and instructed BancorpSouth to "wire" a large sum of money from Choice's account to a bank account in the Republic of Cypress. To wire money is to transfer it electronically, so named because it was once done via telegram. In a typical wire transfer, a bank's customer transmits instructions to the bank to transfer money from the customer's account to the account of a beneficiary; these instructions are called a payment order. Because the customer is not physically present at the bank, the bank uses security procedures, such as passwords and electronic tokens, to verify that the person sending the payment order is actually the customer. In this case, we confront what happens when those security procedures fail.

Choice is a Missouri company that provides real estate escrow services. When parties to a real estate transaction need a third party to hold money in escrow until closing, they give it to Choice for safekeeping. In 2009, Choice opened a trust account at BancorpSouth for this purpose: when a buyer entrusted funds to Choice, Choice deposited the funds in its account at BancorpSouth and then wired the money to the seller at closing. Choice's employees performed these tasks over the Internet using an online banking platform called InView. BancorpSouth provided Choice with four security measures designed to ensure that Choice's employees, and only Choice's employees, would be able to access Choice's account.

First, BancorpSouth required each InView user to register a unique user id and password. Whenever an employee of one of BancorpSouth's institutional customers wished to access the customer's online bank account, the employee would be prompted to enter this information. Without it, access to the account was impossible.

Second, BancorpSouth installed device authentication software called PassMark. When a customer's employee first registered for InView, PassMark recorded the IP address[18] of the employee's computer as well as information about the computer itself—information relating to, for instance, the computer's operating system, central processing unit, browser, screen, time zone settings, and language settings. Whenever any subsequent user attempted to access InView using that employee's user id and password, PassMark verified that the characteristics of that user's computer were consistent with the information PassMark had recorded about the employee's computer. In this way, PassMark verified that each InView user was accessing InView from a recognized computer. If a user attempted to access InView from an unrecognized computer, the user would be prompted to answer "challenge questions" to verify the user's identity. If the user answered these questions correctly, the new computer would be added to the list of recognized computers, and the user would be able to access InView.

Third, BancorpSouth allowed its customers to place dollar limits on the daily volume of wire transfer activity from their accounts. For instance, a customer could limit the daily volume of wire transfers to $10,000 per day, in which case any attempt to transfer more than $10,000 in a single day would be automatically denied. Choice declined to place daily transfer limits on its account.

Fourth, BancorpSouth offered its customers a security measure called "dual control." Under this system, when an InView user submitted a payment order, InView would not send the order to the bank immediately; rather, the request would create a "pending" payment order that would appear in a separate queue in InView. To send a pending payment order to the bank, a second authorized user, using a unique user id and password, would have to log in to InView and separately approve the pending payment order. If a customer declined the use of dual control, BancorpSouth required that customer to sign a waiver acknowledging that it was waiving dual control

18. IP stands for Internet Protocol. An IP address is a series of numbers that identifies a computer or other device on a network.

and that it understood the risks associated with using a single-control (i.e., single-user) security system.

Choice declined the use of dual control and signed the requisite waiver. Thus, Choice's account at BancorpSouth was protected only by (1) the user id's and passwords of its employees, and (2) PassMark. Choice authorized two of its employees, Cara Thulin and Brooke Black, to use InView, and it issued each employee a unique user id and password for this purpose.

With these security measures in place, Choice could issue a payment order by taking the following steps: First, either Thulin or Black would access BancorpSouth's website and log in to InView using her user id and password. Second, PassMark would verify that Thulin or Black was accessing InView from a recognized computer by checking the IP address and other specifications of the computer. If the user was accessing InView from an unrecognized computer, she would be prompted to answer challenge questions. Once the user cleared PassMark, either by using a recognized computer or by correctly answering the challenge questions, she would gain access to Choice's bank account via InView. From there, the user could issue payment orders to BancorpSouth and, as long as Choice had enough funds in its account, those orders would be sent to one of six BancorpSouth employees responsible for routing Choice's payment orders. That employee would then execute the payment order based on the information contained therein, and BancorpSouth would debit the funds from Choice's account and send Choice a fax confirmation of the wire transfer.

In November 2009, Choice received an e-mail from one of its underwriters describing a "phishing" scam in which an unscrupulous person tricks an unsuspecting Internet user into downloading a computer virus, uses the virus to collect the victim's user id's and passwords, and then uses that information to issue fraudulent payment orders to the victim's bank, transferring money from the victim's account to overseas banks beyond the reach of U.S. authorities.[19] Jim Payne, the Director of Business Development at Choice, forwarded the e-mail to BancorpSouth on November 11, 2009, with the following note:

---

19. As another court has explained:

Phishing involves an attempt to acquire information such as usernames, passwords, or financial data by a perpetrator masquerading as a legitimate enterprise. Typically, the perpetrator will provide an e-mail or link that directs the victim to enter or update personal information at a phony website that mimics an established, legitimate website which the victim either has used before or perceives to be a safe place to enter information.

Patco Constr. Co. v. People's United Bank, 684 F.3d 197, 204 (1st Cir. 2012).

Please read the email forwarded from one of our underwriters. They suggest a plan of action that included limiting wires to foreign banks. Can we implement this and to what extent would our liability be if fraudulent wire transfers were to occur?

Ashley Kester of BancorpSouth responded two days later:

Hi Jim, sorry to just now be responding. I had to do some research to find out if this was possible. We are unable to stop just foreign wires, the solution is dual control. We always recommend dual control on wires. We discussed this when we setup InView and you decided to waive the dual control. Would you like to consider adding it now? This is the best solution, that way if someone in the company is compromised then the hacker would not be able to initiate a wire with just the one user's information.

After Kester described the mechanics of dual control to Payne, Payne e-mailed Kester once again declining the use of dual control:

Actually I don't think that would be a good procedure for us—lots of times Paige [Payne] is here by herself and that would be really tough unless we all shared pass words.

Sometime after this exchange, a Choice employee fell prey to a phishing attack and contracted a computer virus. This virus gave an unknown third party access to the employee's username and password and allowed the third party to mimic the computer's IP address and other characteristics, rendering InView's password prompts and PassMark's device authentication procedures ineffectual. On March 17, 2010, this third party accessed Choice's online bank account and issued a payment order instructing BancorpSouth to transfer $440,000 from Choice's account to a banking institution in the Republic of Cypress. BancorpSouth accepted and executed the payment order. After attempts to recover the funds failed, Choice sued BancorpSouth for the lost funds, and BancorpSouth counterclaimed for attorney's fees based on an indemnification agreement that it had executed with Choice.

The district court granted summary judgment to BancorpSouth after concluding that Article 4A of the U.C.C. allocated the risk of loss from the fraudulent payment order to Choice. The court then dismissed BancorpSouth's counterclaim for attorney's fees on the pleadings after concluding that the indemnification agreement at issue conflicted with the provisions of Article 4A and was thus unenforceable.

II.

We review the district court's grant of summary judgment to BancorpSouth *de novo*, viewing the evidence in the light most favorable to

Choice. Hill v. Walker, 737 F.3d 1209, 1216 (8th Cir. 2013). Summary judgment is appropriate when there is "no genuine dispute as to any material fact and the movant is entitled to judgment as a matter of law." Fed. R. Civ. P. 56(a). The parties agree that Article 4A, which Mississippi enacted in its entirety in 1991, *see* Miss. Code Ann. §75-4A-101 *et seq.*, governs this dispute.

Article 4A was drafted in 1989 to account for a dramatic increase in wire transfers between financial institutions and other commercial entities, commonly called wholesale wire transfers to differentiate them from wire transfers by consumers, which are governed by a separate federal statute, *see* 15 U.S.C. §1693. At the time Article 4A was drafted, the total volume of these wholesale transfers exceeded one trillion dollars per day, *see* U.C.C. Art. 4A Refs. & Annos. prefatory note, yet "there was no comprehensive body of law—statutory or judicial—that defined the juridical nature of a funds transfer or the rights and obligations flowing from payment orders[,]" Miss. Code Ann. §75-4A-102 cmt. The drafters of Article 4A sought to create a legal framework that balanced these rights and obligations between the bank and its institutional customer. As the Official Comments note:

> Funds transfers involve competing interests—those of the banks that provide funds transfer services and the commercial and financial organizations that use the services, as well as the public interest. These competing interests were represented in the drafting process and they were thoroughly considered. The rules that emerged represent a careful and delicate balancing of those interests and are intended to be the exclusive means of determining the rights, duties and liabilities of the affected parties in any situation covered by particular provisions of the Article.

Id.

One of the liabilities balanced by Article 4A is the risk that a third party will steal a customer's identity and issue a fraudulent payment order to the bank. Generally, the bank bears this risk. Miss. Code Ann. §75-4A-204. In two circumstances, however, the bank may shift the risk of a fraudulent payment order to the customer. The first is the rare circumstance in which the bank can prove that the customer "authorized the order or is otherwise bound by it under the law of agency." Miss. Code Ann. §75-4A-202(a). This circumstance is rare because ordinarily the bank has "no way of determining the identity or the authority of the person who caused the message to be sent," and thus "[c]ommon law concepts of authority of agent to bind principal are not helpful" in determining whether a customer is bound by a payment order issued in its name. Miss. Code Ann. §75-4A-203 cmt. 1.

Because of this inadequacy, Article 4A contemplates a second circumstance in which a customer will bear the risk of a fraudulent payment order. If a bank and its customer agree to implement a security procedure designed to protect themselves against fraud, then the customer will bear the risk of a fraudulent payment order if:

> (i) the security procedure is a commercially reasonable method of providing security against unauthorized payment orders, and
> (ii) the bank proves that it accepted the payment order in good faith and in compliance with the security procedure and any written agreement or instruction of the customer restricting acceptance of payment orders issued in the name of the customer.

Miss. Code Ann. §75-4A-202(b). Article 4A thus permits the bank to take steps to protect itself from liability by implementing commercially reasonable security procedures. If the bank complies with these procedures in good faith and in accordance with the customer's instructions, the customer will bear the risk of loss from a fraudulent payment order. Choice concedes that BancorpSouth complied with its security procedures in accepting the March 17 payment order. Thus, BancorpSouth is entitled to summary judgment if the undisputed facts show (1) that BancorpSouth's security procedures were commercially reasonable, (2) that BancorpSouth accepted the payment order in good faith, and (3) that BancorpSouth accepted the payment order in compliance with Choice's written instructions.

A.

We first consider whether BancorpSouth's security procedures were commercially reasonable. We conclude that they were.

1.

A "security procedure" is a "procedure established by agreement of a customer and a receiving bank for the purpose of . . . verifying that a payment order . . . is that of the customer." Miss. Code Ann. §75-4A-201. As this definition makes clear, only security measures "established by agreement" are considered "security procedures" for purposes of Article 4A; security measures implemented unilaterally by the bank are irrelevant. *See* Miss. Code Ann. §75-4A-201 cmt.

There is one exception to the "established by agreement" rule. If a bank offers its customer a security procedure, and the customer declines to use that procedure and agrees in writing to be bound by payment orders issued in its name and accepted by the bank in accordance with another security procedure, then the customer will bear the risk of loss from a fraudulent payment order if the *declined* procedure was commercially reasonable. Miss. Code Ann. §75-4A-202(c). To synthesize the rule and its exception: in assessing commercial reasonableness, courts consider (1) security measures that the bank and customer agree to implement, and (2) security measures that the bank offers to the customer but the customer declines, as long as the customer agrees in writing to be bound by payment orders issued in its name in and accepted by the bank in accordance with another procedure.

Our first task is determining which of BancorpSouth's security measures fit this definition. Choice does not dispute that BancorpSouth's password prompts, daily transfer limits, and dual control system are security procedures that we may consider under Article 4A, but it asserts that PassMark does not qualify as a security procedure because BancorpSouth did not mention PassMark in any of its written contracts with Choice or formally offer Choice the option to use the software.

Notwithstanding the absence of any explicit reference to PassMark in the parties' written contracts, however, there is ample evidence that the parties agreed to implement PassMark. An agreement under the U.C.C. need not be a written contract; rather, an "'[a]greement,' as distinguished from 'contract,' means the bargain of the parties in fact, as found in their language or inferred from other circumstances[.]" Miss. Code Ann. §75-1-201. All BancorpSouth customers were required to register for PassMark when they signed up for InView. It was thus impossible for any InView user not to know that they were also using PassMark, and any customer that declined to register for PassMark would be unable to use InView. Additionally, the addendum to the Business Services Agreement between Choice and BancorpSouth states that Choice "assumes full responsibility and risk of loss for all transactions made by BancorpSouth . . . in accordance with . . . the procedures set forth in the InView User Manual(s) and Help screens." BancorpSouth posted a digital manual entitled "PassMark Login Security" on the InView portal, so PassMark was incorporated at least implicitly into the parties' written contracts. In light of these facts, we are satisfied that PassMark was "established by agreement" between Choice and BancorpSouth. We thus consider all four of BancorpSouth's security measures—password protection, daily transfer limits, PassMark, and dual control—in determining whether BancorpSouth's security procedures were commercially reasonable.

2.

In making this determination, we consider:

> the wishes of the customer expressed to the bank, the circumstances of the customer known to the bank, including the size, type, and frequency of payment orders normally issued by the customer to the bank, alternative security procedures offered to the customer, and security procedures in general use by customers and receiving banks similarly situated.

Miss. Code Ann. §75-4A-202. The commercial reasonableness standard is designed "to encourage banks to institute reasonable safeguards against fraud but not to make them insurers against fraud." Miss. Code Ann. §75-4A-203 cmt. 4. Thus, "[t]he standard is not whether the security procedure is the best available. Rather it is whether the procedure is reasonable for the particular customer and the particular bank, which is a lower standard." *Id.*

At the threshold, we reject Choice's argument that a commercially reasonable security procedure must include a process whereby a human being manually reviews every payment order submitted to the bank to ensure that no irregularities exist—what Choice calls "transactional analysis." Article 4A never mentions transactional analysis, but Choice argues that because commercial reasonableness depends on the "size, type, and frequency" of a customer's payment orders, a commercially reasonable security procedure must differentiate between payment orders based on these factors. Choice further asserts that transactional analysis is the only way to achieve this differentiation.

This argument misunderstands Article 4A's intended audience. Article 4A does not instruct the bank to consider the "size, type, and frequency" of each payment order it receives in determining if those payment orders are potentially fraudulent; it instructs the court to consider these factors in determining if a bank's security procedure is commercially reasonable—in other words, that the commercial reasonableness of a bank's security procedure depends on whether that procedure is adequate to screen payment orders of the size, type, and frequency normally issued to the bank. Such a procedure might involve "algorithms or other codes, identifying words or numbers, encryption, callback procedures, or similar security devices," Miss. Code Ann. §75-4A-201, none of which differentiate between payment orders based on their "size, type, [or] frequency." Yet notwithstanding that "[t]he concept of what is commercially reasonable in each case is flexible," Miss. Code Ann. §75-4A-203 cmt. 4, Choice argues that even all of these procedures combined would be commercially unreasonable, as none of them involve transactional analysis. This attempt to graft a rigid, foreign standard onto the commercial reasonableness inquiry is at odds with essentially all of Article 4A, and we reject it.

Nor does the record evidence establish that BancorpSouth was required to perform transactional analysis under these specific circumstances. The only person who mentioned transactional analysis was Choice's expert, who stated in his report that transactional analysis "could be a very effective aid in deterring fraudulent payment order transactions" and "would . . . be in line with Article 4A202(c)." Neither statement indicates that BancorpSouth's failure to use transactional analysis was commercially unreasonable, and at any rate Choice's expert admitted in his deposition that, under the circumstances of this case, dual control could be a commercially reasonable security procedure. BancorpSouth's Senior Vice President further testified that BancorpSouth conducts tens of thousands of wire transfers on behalf of its roughly 400,000 checking account customers and that reviewing each one of these transactions would be impracticable. Choice has presented no evidence to contradict this testimony and, indeed, has failed to present any evidence tending to show that a genuine question of fact exists as to whether BancorpSouth was required to perform transactional analysis.

Having determined that BancorpSouth was not required to perform transactional analysis, we turn to what it was required to do. We begin at the broadest level of generality, by considering "security procedures in general use by customers and receiving banks similarly situated[,]" Miss. Code Ann. §75-4A-202. Our primary authority in this endeavor is a 2005 report published by the Federal Financial Institutions Examination Council (FFIEC) called "Authentication in an Internet Banking Environment," (the Guidance), *see* Fed. Fin. Insts. Examination Council, Authentication in an Internet Banking Environment (Oct. 12, 2005), *available at* https://www.ffiec. gov/pdf/authentication_guidance.pdf. The parties agree that the Guidance provides applicable standards of commercial reasonableness in this case.

The Guidance draws a basic distinction between single-factor and multifactor authentication. As the Guidance explains, most modern security procedures involve one or more of the following three factors:

(1) Something the user knows, like a password or PIN;
(2) Something the user has, like an ATM card or smart card; and
(3) Something the user is, like a person with a unique fingerprint or biometric characteristic.

Id. at 3. Security procedures that involve only one of the above three factors, according to the Guidance, are inadequate to safeguard against modern Internet fraud. Accordingly, the Guidance recommends that financial institutions implement security procedures that use two or more of the above factors in combination. An ATM, for instance, uses a multifactor security procedure that requires the user to provide something the user has (an ATM card) as well as something the user knows (a PIN) to use the machine. BancorpSouth's security procedures also used multifactor authentication: to access InView, a BancorpSouth customer had to enter the correct password (something the user knows) and use a recognized computer (something the user has).

Of course, cyber-crime evolves rapidly, and guidance issued in 2005 may become obsolete in subsequent years. The Guidance thus states that banks should "[a]djust, as appropriate, their information security program[s] in light of any relevant changes in technology, the sensitivity of its customer information, and internal or external threats to information." *Id.*

As BancorpSouth's expert acknowledged, during 2009 and 2010, cyber-criminals began using more sophisticated software that could "take on the identity and internet configuration of the victim organization's personnel that were involved in the wire transfer process," emulating the computer's IP address and using the employee's passwords to bypass even multifactor security procedures. This testimony suggests that multifactor authentication alone may have been an inadequate safeguard against Internet fraud perpetrated in 2010.

BancorpSouth responded to this new threat by offering its customers dual control, which dramatically reduces the possibility of such a breach. With dual control in place, a customer's account remains secure even if a third party manages to obtain an employee's password and IP address; to issue a payment order, that third party would have to obtain a second, wholly independent set of identifying information. Phishing scams work because one out of every few thousand recipients of a malicious e-mail will click on a link containing a virus, and the probability that two employees at the same company would fall for the same scam is quite low. Moreover, without a second user's information, any attempt by a third party to issue a payment order would alert the customer to the security breach by creating a pending payment order that no one at the company had authorized.

Accordingly, because BancorpSouth comported with the 2005 Guidance and expanded its security procedures to address security threats that arose after 2005, we conclude that BancorpSouth's security procedures comported with the standards set by "security procedures in general use by customers and receiving banks similarly situated."

This does not end the inquiry, however: we must also consider whether BancorpSouth's security procedures were suitable for Choice given "the wishes of the customer expressed to the bank" and "the circumstances of the customer known to the bank, including the size, type, and frequency of payment orders normally issued by the customer to the bank." Miss. Code Ann. §75-4A-202.

Contrary to Choice's assertion, this does not mean that a bank must always use a different security procedure for each customer. The Official Comment to §75-4A-203 states that "[a] receiving bank *might* have several security procedures that are designed to meet the varying needs of different customers" (emphasis added), but it does not make this a requirement. If a bank develops a single effective and versatile security procedure, it is not commercially unreasonable for the bank to use that security procedure for the majority of its customers and depart from the procedure only when necessary.

Choice asserts that such a departure was necessary in this case because Choice did not have enough employees on hand to use dual control effectively—in other words, that dual control was commercially unreasonable given the "circumstances of the customer known to the bank" and the "wishes of the customer expressed to the bank." As set forth above, when BancorpSouth offered Choice dual control for the second time, on November 13, 2009, Jim Payne of Choice responded, "Actually, I don't think that would be a good procedure for us — lots of times Paige [Payne] is here by herself and that would be really tough unless we all shared pass words."

Assuming that this statement is true, it does not mean that dual control was any less suitable for Choice than the single-control option Choice ultimately chose to implement. Paige Payne was not an authorized InView user, and if she was in the office by herself, she would have been unable to issue payment orders regardless of whether Choice had implemented single or dual control.

Perhaps Jim Payne intended in his e-mail to refer to either Thulin or Black, the two Choice employees authorized to use InView, instead of Paige Payne. But both Thulin and Black were full-time employees who were typically in the office during normal business hours. To the extent that Choice needed to issue payment orders outside of these hours, dual control would have been no less suitable for Choice than single control, since neither Black nor Thulin would have been in the office at that time.

Even if only one authorized InView user was in the office at certain times, dual control would not have been a major hindrance on Choice's ability to issue payment orders. Simultaneous approval of a payment order is not required under dual control; one employee may create a pending payment order in the morning, and a second employee may come into the office in the afternoon and confirm the pending payment order. Choice has not argued that it needed to be able to wire money at a moment's notice; indeed, the nature of its business suggests that Choice generally knew beforehand when it needed to wire money to beneficiaries (namely, the date of a real estate closing) and that it could plan accordingly. And even if a quick response time was necessary in some circumstances, Choice could have solved this problem by authorizing employees besides Black and Thulin to use InView.

In short, no genuine dispute of fact exists as to whether BancorpSouth's security procedures were commercially reasonable. Rather, this appears to be a case where "an informed customer refuses a security procedure that is commercially reasonable and suitable for that customer and insists on using a higher-risk procedure because it is more convenient or cheaper[,]" in which case "the customer has voluntarily assumed the risk of failure of the procedure and cannot shift the loss to the bank." *See* Miss. Code Ann. §75-4A-203 cmt. 4. Choice knew that dual control provided a reliable safeguard against Internet fraud, and it explicitly assumed the risks of a lesser procedure notwithstanding the relative ease with which it could have implemented dual control. Accordingly, we conclude that BancorpSouth's security procedures, which included password protection, daily transfer limits, device authentication, and dual control, were commercially reasonable.

B.

The risk of a fraudulent payment order remains with BancorpSouth, however, unless BancorpSouth also "proves that it accepted the [March 17] payment order in good faith and in compliance with the security procedure and any written agreement or instruction of the customer restricting acceptance of payment orders issued in the name of the customer." Miss. Code Ann. §75-4A-202(b). Choice asserts that BancorpSouth did not accept the payment order in good faith and that it violated Choice's written instructions in doing so. We disagree.

1.

Good faith "means honesty in fact and the observance of reasonable commercial standards of fair dealing." Miss. Code Ann. §75-1-201(b)(20). This two-pronged definition has both a subjective component—honesty in fact—and an objective component—the observance of reasonable commercial standards of fair dealing. In re Nieves, 648 F.3d 232, 239 (3d Cir. 2011). We are concerned with the latter prong in this case: Choice concedes that BancorpSouth accepted the payment order honestly, but it asserts that BancorpSouth did not observe reasonable commercial standards of fair dealing in doing so.

The U.C.C.'s requirement that parties to a contract abide by reasonable commercial standards of fair dealing—and the good faith doctrine generally—is designed to ensure that each party to the contract performs its contractual duties in a way that reflects the reasonable expectations of the other party. As the Permanent Editorial Board Commentary explains:

> The principal author of the Code, Karl Llewellyn, recognized that parties develop expectations over time against the background of commercial practices and that if commercial law fails to account for those practices, it will cut against the parties' actual expectations. . . . [T]he doctrine of good faith . . . [thus] serves as a directive to protect the reasonable expectations of the contracting parties.

U.C.C. App. II Commentary 10; *see also* Restatement (Second) of Contracts §205 cmt. a ("Good faith performance or enforcement of a contract emphasizes faithfulness to an agreed common purpose and consistency with the justified expectations of the other party."). One of the challenges in applying the good faith doctrine in the Article 4A context is the apparent overlap between a bank's compliance with "commercial standards of fair dealing" and its compliance with "commercially reasonable" security procedures. It may appear at first glance that these inquiries are redundant, and some courts have suggested (although not in the Article 4A context) that this is indeed the case. *See* Watson Coatings, Inc. v. Am. Exp. Travel Related Servs., Inc., 436 F.3d 1036, 1042 (8th Cir. 2006); DBI Architects, P.C. v. Am. Express Travel-Related Servs. Co., 388 F.3d 886, 895 (D.C. Cir. 2004).

But while there may be some evidentiary overlap between the commercial reasonableness of a bank's security procedures and its compliance with reasonable commercial standards of fair dealing, we do not believe that the two inquiries are coextensive. While the commercial reasonableness inquiry concerns the adequacy of a bank's security procedures, the objective good faith inquiry concerns a bank's acceptance of payment orders in accordance with those security procedures. In other words, technical compliance with a security procedure is not enough under Article 4A; instead, as the above-quoted materials indicate, the bank must abide by its procedures in a way that reflects the parties' reasonable expectations as to how those procedures will operate.

Thus, the focus of our good faith inquiry is on the aspects of wire transfer that are left to the bank's discretion. *See* Milford-Bennington R. Co., Inc. v. Pan Am Railways, Inc., 695 F.3d 175, 179 (1st Cir. 2012) ("The good-faith obligation limits the parties' discretion in contractual performance."). Where, as here, a bank's security procedures do not depend on the judgment or discretion of its employees, the scope of the good-faith inquiry under Article 4A is correspondingly narrow. The automation of agreed-upon procedures generally ensures that those procedures will operate in a way that is consistent with the customer's expectations, as long as the procedures do not "unreasonably vary from general banking usage"—in other words, as long as they are commercially reasonable. *Watson Coatings*, 436 F.3d at 1042. We have already determined that BancorpSouth's security procedures were commercially reasonable, and we need not revisit that determination here. Rather, to establish that it acted in good faith, BancorpSouth must establish that its employees accepted and executed the March 17 payment order in a way that comported with Choice's reasonable expectations, as established by reasonable commercial standards of fair dealing.

We are satisfied that BancorpSouth has met this burden. Choice was well aware that the only time BancorpSouth employees saw its payment orders was after those orders had already cleared BancorpSouth's security procedures. Choice was also aware that the role of those employees was not to check for any irregularities but to route these payment orders to the correct beneficiaries. Jeff Jaggers, a senior vice president at BancorpSouth, testified that in his thirty years of banking experience it was "normal banking practice" for a bank's employees to route payment orders submitted in compliance with a security procedure without conducting any further review to determine if those payment orders were somehow suspicious. And even if BancorpSouth's employees should have been expected to conduct some commonsense manual review of payment orders—for instance, by flagging a payment order for $10,000,000 from a customer with only $10,000 in its account—the March 17 payment order was not so unusual that it should have raised eyebrows. BancorpSouth provided evidence that the March 17 payment order was not the largest order that Choice had ever submitted and that Choice's wire transfers followed no general pattern and varied in size from a few thousand dollars to a few hundred thousand dollars. In response, Choice asserts that the memo line of the March 17 payment order, which read "invoice: equipment," was inconsistent with Choice's business and with its past practice in issuing payment orders. Choice, of course, is a real estate escrow company with little use for equipment, and the memo line had been filled out in only 13% of Choice's previous payment orders. But the memo line's two-word description does not make the March 17 payment order so suspicious that BancorpSouth acted in bad faith by failing to notice it; if BancorpSouth's employees had to remember the business of each of BancorpSouth's 400,000 clients to ensure that the memo line of each payment order made sense, BancorpSouth would not be in business long. This is not a case where a bank "allow[ed] overdrafts totaling *$5 million* from a single account that usually ha[d] a zero balance." Experi-Metal, Inc. v. Comerica Bank, 2011 WL 2433383, at *14 (E.D. Mich. June 13, 2011). This is a case where a bank promptly executed a payment order that had cleared the bank's commercially reasonable security procedures and that the bank had no independent reason to suspect was fraudulent. Accordingly, we conclude that BancorpSouth has met its burden of establishing beyond genuine factual dispute that it accepted the March 17 payment order in good faith.

2.

The last element BancorpSouth must prove to shift the loss from the March 17 payment order to Choice is that BancorpSouth accepted the payment order in compliance with Choice's instructions. Choice attempts to shortcut the issue by arguing that BancorpSouth admitted in its answer that it had violated Choice's instructions by "Admit[ting]" the following allegation in Choice's complaint:

> 61. Choice by email on or about November 11, 2009, from Jim Payne to Ashley Kester, expressed to BancorpSouth its wish, requirement and/or instruction that BancorpSouth limit transfers to foreign banks.

According to Choice, BancorpSouth's response of "Admit" to this paragraph amounts to an admission that BancorpSouth violated Choice's "wish, requirement, and/or instruction" to limit foreign wire transfers. The merit of this argument depends on how one interprets "and/or." Choice asserts that "and/or" means "and," which is incorrect: "and/or" is an ambiguous phrase that usually means "one or the other or both." *See* Bryan A. Garner, Garner's Modern American Usage 45 (3d ed. 2009). The natural reading of BancorpSouth's admission is thus that Choice had expressed to BancorpSouth its "wish, requirement, or instruction, or some combination of the three" that BancorpSouth stop foreign wires. A judicial admission must be deliberate, clear, and unambiguous, *see* MacDonald v. Gen. Motors Corp., 110 F.3d 337, 340 (6th Cir. 1997); Rowe Int'l, Inc. v. J-B Enterprises, Inc., 647 F.2d 830, 836 (8th Cir. 1981), and Choice's use of the phrase "and/or" in its complaint renders BancorpSouth's subsequent concession anything but.

Turning to the substance of this dispute, we conclude that BancorpSouth did not violate any of Choice's instructions by accepting the March 17 payment order. The only evidence of an instruction is the November 11 e-mail from Jim Payne to Ashley Kester asking if it would be possible to stop foreign wire transfers. Payne himself agreed in his deposition that the e-mail was properly characterized as an "inquir[y]," and when BancorpSouth replied that it was "unable to stop just foreign wires," Choice did not press the issue further. This exchange does not constitute an instruction.

In sum, because BancorpSouth's security procedures were commercially reasonable, because BancorpSouth complied with its security procedures and with Choice's instructions, and because BancorpSouth accepted the March 17 payment order in good faith, the loss of funds from Choice's account falls on Choice.

III.

Finally, we turn to whether BancorpSouth is entitled to attorney's fees based on an indemnification agreement it executed with Choice. The district court dismissed BancorpSouth's counterclaim for attorney's fees on the pleadings after concluding that the indemnification provision in question conflicted with the provisions of Article 4A and was thus unenforceable. We review the dismissal of this counterclaim *de novo*. Levy v. Ohl, 477 F.3d 988, 991 (8th Cir. 2007).

The indemnification provision states as follows:

> As long as BancorpSouth has performed as provided in Section 8 above, the Customer shall indemnify and hold BancorpSouth harmless from any and all claims, damages, losses, liabilities, and costs and expenses, including reasonable attorney's fees, which relate in any manner to the Services performed under this Agreement.

"Unless displaced by the particular provisions of the Uniform Commercial Code, the principles of law and equity . . . supplement" the provisions of Article 4A. Miss. Code Ann. §75-1-103. But Article 4A preempts common law causes of action "in two specific areas: (1) where the common law claims would create rights, duties, or liability inconsistent with [Article 4A]; and (2) where the circumstances giving rise to the common law claims are specifically covered by [Article 4A]." Zengen, Inc. v. Comerica Bank, 41 Cal. 4th 239, 59 Cal. Rptr. 3d 240, 158 P.3d 800, 808 (2007). The district court, acknowledging that the issue was a "close call," held that the above-quoted indemnification provision would create rights and liabilities that were inconsistent with Article 4A because the provision "could effectively require Choice to pay back to [BancorpSouth] those amounts that [BancorpSouth] might owe to Choice under [Article 4A]." D. Ct. Order of Aug. 30, 2012, at 3. In other words, by requiring Choice to indemnify BancorpSouth for all "damages, losses, [and] liabilities" stemming from a fraudulent payment order, the indemnification provision would frustrate Article 4A's attempts to balance this risk between the bank and its customer.

But the section of the indemnification provision dealing with "damages, losses, [and] liabilities" is not at issue in BancorpSouth's counterclaim. BancorpSouth's counterclaim seeks attorney's fees, not damages stemming from the fraudulent payment order, and Article 4A contains no provision allocating attorney's fees between the bank and its customer in the event of litigation. Although awarding attorney's fees to a bank under an indemnification agreement might reduce a customer's overall recovery against that bank, it would do so for reasons extrinsic to Article 4A's attempts to balance the risk of loss due to a fraudulent payment order. We thus conclude that the portion of the indemnification provision relating to attorney's fees is not inconsistent with Article 4A and that BancorpSouth may seek attorney's fees from Choice under this provision.

IV.

We affirm the district court's grant of summary judgment to BancorpSouth, reverse the district court's dismissal of BancorpSouth's counterclaim on the pleadings, and remand for further proceedings consistent with this opinion.

PROBLEM 167

Business Corporation paid all of its bills by funds transfers through its bank, Original National Bank (ONB). These two entities signed an agreement providing that funds transfers could be made only if the originator included in the payment order a secret code number, which would change daily according to the number assigned by a computer program accessed by both the corporation and the bank. The Business Corporation employee in charge of approving its payment orders was John Smith and he was so proud of his new job that he described it in detail (including how to access the secret code) to his wife, Mary. Mary, who was the owner of her own computer repair business, became curious whether, from the safety of her own home, her skills as a computer hacker would permit her to access Business Corporation's files, issue phony payment orders, and have ONB execute them. She was amazed how easy it all was, and by the end of the day, she had ordered ONB to transfer $830,756 to the account of her business at another bank. The next morning she withdrew the money from that account, left her husband a "Dear John" letter, and has not been heard from since. Can Business Corporation demand that ONB recredit its account for the amount she stole? See §§4A-201, 4A-202(b), and 4A-203. How long does Business Corporation have in which to demand a recredit of its account? See §4A-505; Regatos v. North Fork Bank, 5 N.Y.3d 395, 838 N.E.2d 629 (2005).

Official Comment 5 to §4A-203:

Breach of a commercially reasonable security procedure requires that the person committing the fraud have knowledge of how the procedure works and knowledge of codes, identifying devices, and the like. That person may also need access to transmitting facilities through an access device or other software in order to breach the security procedure. This confidential information must be obtained either from a source controlled by the customer or from a source controlled by the receiving bank. If the customer can prove that the person committing the fraud did not obtain the confidential information from an agent or former agent of the customer or from a source controlled by the customer, the loss is shifted to the bank.

PROBLEM 168

Suppose, in the last Problem, the security procedure between the parties had one other wrinkle: if the amount transferred was above $500,000, the secret code had to begin with the letter "A," but the secret code itself did not tell senders this. Mary didn't know about it either (John had forgotten to mention this extra step), so when she transferred the $830,756 to her bank account, she failed to put the "A" in front of the secret code. ONB accepted the payment order anyway when it made the funds transfer to Mary's bank. Now what? See §4A-205(a)(1).

PROBLEM 169

Backwater Builders used funds transfers from its account at Schadenfreude Bank to pay suppliers, sending about seven transfers a month to local contractors, none more than $7,000. One afternoon, Schadenfreude Bank received 19 payment orders on Backwater Builders' account, ordering the transfer of a total of $450,000 to various accounts in foreign countries, most of which happen to lack extradition treaties with the United States. The staff at Schadenfreude Bank's wire transfer department recognized that the orders were likely the result of a phishing expedition, and checked that the orders all complied with the security procedure that Backwater Builders agreed to, including usernames, passwords and answers to automated challenge questions. The wire department chief smiled wryly and said, "Not my problem. Orders are in order." The staff then wired the funds abroad, never to be seen again. It turns out that Backwater Builders' trusting bookkeeper had been tricked by a phony email into submitting his username, password, and challenge question answer to some nefarious hacker. Is Backwater Builders obliged to reimburse Schadenfreude Bank? Cf. Experi-Metal, Inc. v. Comerica Bank, 2011 WL 2433383 (E.D. Mich. 2011).

E. Conclusion

Section 4A-501(a) contains an important rule for banks: "Except as otherwise provided in this Article, the rights and obligations of a party to a funds transfer may be varied by agreement of the affected party." If you, as counsel for the bank, don't like the results explained above, negotiate a contract with those involved that reaches a happier conclusion. Be warned, however, that in various places throughout Article 4A, the sections do restrict the right of the parties to change the Code's rules by agreement. For example, §4A-404(c) provides: "The right of a beneficiary to receive payment and damages as stated in subsection (a) may not be varied by agreement or a funds-transfer system rule." Thus, the contract negotiated by the bank must be checked against Article 4A carefully to ensure that it does not attempt impermissible variations.[20] Banks do not charge much for the execution and acceptance of payment orders, and the system would collapse if the banks faced enormous exposure for wire transfer mishaps. Article 4A recognizes this and is animated by a spirit of bank protection. See, e.g., Official Comment 2 to §4A-305. In the event of bank insolvency, banks that have accepted payment orders but not received payment must bear the loss unless a funds-transfer system (such as CHIPS) has adopted a plan for loss-sharing and the plan fails, in which case §4A-405(e) (the "doomsday" rule) provides that the payment is undone even though acceptance had occurred. Many funds-transfer systems have loss-sharing plans (typically providing for

---

20. There is a strong presumption in favor of the effectiveness of a rule adopted by a funds-transfer system; §4A-501(b). Such systems are particularly encouraged to adopt rules making payments provisional, and plans for the sharing of losses in the event of bank insolvency; see §4A-405(d) and (e).

the creation of a "settlement kitty"), and they should help ease the problem of bank exposure.

CHAPTER 9   ASSESSMENT

Multiple Choice Questions

1. Miranda forgot her credit card on a table at the Hamilton Tavern. Nadal found it there two days later. Over the next two months, Nadal used the card to run up thousands of dollars of charges at restaurants and retail stores. Miranda, meanwhile, ignored the matter. Is Miranda liable for any of the charges?
   a. Yes, for $50.
   b. Yes, for all the charges, for failure to give notice of the loss of the card.
   c. Yes, for any charges made after she received the statement on which any fraudulent charges appeared.
   d. Yes, for all charges made more than 48 hours after she lost her card.

2. Spalding ran a music talent agency. Her bookkeeper, Jones, had no permission from Spalding to write checks or use the agency credit card. Nevertheless, Jones used the card extravagantly for over a year on vacations, jewelry, and fine dining. Jones prepared a check each month to pay the credit card bill. Spalding signed the check without a glance at the bill. Spalding eventually caught on to the embezzlement. Is the credit card issuer liable to Spalding for the payments for unauthorized charges?
   a. Only for $50.
   b. Yes, for all charges made after Spalding received statements listing unauthorized charges and had a reasonable time to give notice.
   c. Yes, for all charges for which more than 60 days has passed since the statement was made available to Spalding.
   d. No. Unauthorized charges cannot be contested after the charges have been paid by the cardholder.

3. Korins purchased some antique furniture with Korins's personal credit card at Jefferson Furniture, located in Cairo, Illinois, some 400 miles from Korins's home in Lake Forest, Illinois. Korins soon realized the furniture was quite new, treated to look old. Korins had no success when requesting a refund from Jefferson Furniture. Can Korins raise the breach as a defense against paying the charge on the credit card?
   a. Yes, because the purchase was in Korins's state of residence.
   b. No, because Korins made the purchase more than 100 miles from his residence.

  c. No. Purchases with a credit card may be contested with the merchant, but not with the card issuer. Banks do not warranty furniture.

  d. Yes. Consumers always may raise defenses to payment.

4. Hughes Aircraft had a typical wire transfer agreement with Imperial Bank. Hughes Aircraft sent a payment order to its bank, Imperial Bank, instructing the bank to transfer $1,977,000 to Maximilian H. Miltzlaff Manufacturing, Inc., Account No. 9031 9801 at Aeronautical Bank, as payment for some fuselages. Hughes Aircraft was careful to correctly state the name of the bank and, especially, the unusual name of the beneficiary. However, Hughes Aircraft made one minor error: the correct bank account was 9081 9801. Aeronautical Bank processed the order quickly, looking only at the account number, and put the money in account no. 9031 9801. The account owner, Harry Spludd, quickly took the money and disappeared. Is Hughes Aircraft liable for $1,977,000?

  a. No. Aeronautical Bank cannot recover, because it could not distinguish Maximilian H. Miltzlaff Manufacturing, Inc. from Harry Spludd.

  b. No. A bank that gets the account number wrong takes the loss, but customers are not charged to follow such banking practices.

  c. Yes. Aeronautical Bank is entitled to rely on the account number, and is entitled to reimbursement from Imperial Bank, who in turn is entitled to reimbursement from Hughes Aircraft.

  d. No. Aeronautical Bank did not process the order with due care, because it processed a transfer of $1,977,000 without checking carefully.

5. Dismayed by reports of breaches of bank account security, Belt & Suspenders Bank radically ratcheted up the security on wire transfer orders. Rather than issuing "challenge questions" (questions such as "What was your first pet's name?", for which users supply answers when setting up an account) only for payment orders that did not fit usual patterns of use or that were for large amounts, its software generated challenge questions for every payment order. The bank also lowered the threshold for reporting suspicious payment orders to its fraud team. This extra security, unfortunately, greatly increased the risk of fraud. Because challenge questions were so frequent, they were more likely to be revealed to fraudsters. Because suspicious payment warnings became so numerous, the fraud team was unable to investigate them all. As one result, phishers were able to infiltrate Patsy Architecture's account and send over $500,000 to accounts unknown. Patsy Architecture had signed an account agreement, including agreement to use of the enhanced security measures. Is Patsy Architecture required to reimburse Belt & Suspenders Bank?

    a. Yes, because it had agreed to the security procedure.

    b. No. Customers are only liable for funds transfers they actually authorize.

    c. No, because the security procedure was not commercially reasonable.

    d. No, provided that Patsy Architecture notifies Belt & Suspender Bank within 60 days of receiving its account statement.

Answers

1. A is the best answer. The Truth in Lending Act caps liability for unauthorized use at $50. The limit is not dependent on whether the cardholder was negligent with the card or failed to give timely notice of loss of the card or notice of the unauthorized charges upon receiving the statement, making B, C, and D incorrect.

2. B is the best answer. As set out in the *Azur* case, courts have imported notions of negligence, in a limited manner, to credit card law's $50 cap on liability. Where an employer fails to supervise an employee and fails to monitor account statements in a timely manner, courts have held the employer has given the employee apparent authority to use the card. C is misleading; the 60-day rule is the rule for debit cards, not credit cards. D likewise refers to a different rule. Where the cardholder makes authorized use of the card, but has grounds not pay the merchant, the cardholder may raise defenses against the merchant, but only until the cardholder has paid for that particular charge.

3. A is the best answer. Consumer credit cards, under the TILA, provide buyer protection. If a cardholder has a defense to payment against the merchant, the cardholder may raise that defense against the issuer, contrary to C. Banks do indeed warrant furniture and everything else purchased with consumer credit cards, in effect. There are several conditions: the cardholder must make a good faith effort to resolve the matter with the merchant, the amount of the charge must exceed $50, and the purchase must occur within the state or within 100 miles of the cardholder's residence. That last geographical limitation is met in this case, because the purchase was in Illinois, albeit 400 miles from home. It need not be both in-state and within 100 miles, contrary to B.

4. C is the best answer. UCC 4A has an unusual rule with respect to errors. A bank is entitled to rely on the account number, and may effectively ignore whether that number matches the name on the account. That sounds like a license for banks to be careless, but makes sense in practice. The rule was adopted to match banking practice. It provides a clear rule, and avoids banks' refusing payment orders for failure to correctly state the beneficiary's name. The name on the account often may not

exactly match the name that the originator uses, for many reasons. Banks are charged to know the rule and follow it. Contrary to B, customers are likewise bound by the rule if they agree to it—and every wire transfer contract will contain a clause where the customer agrees to the rule. So, although customers may not always know it, the key part of the payment order to get correct is the account number, not the name of the beneficiary. Banks are not required to check that they match, contrary to A and D.

5. C is the best answer. For commercial wire transfers, a customer is indeed bound by an unauthorized payment order, provided the bank paid the order in good faith, pursuant to a commercially reasonable security procedure accepted by the customer. Customers can be liable for unauthorized payment orders, contrary to B. But the security procedure here was not commercially reasonable. Rather, it was so burdensome that it actually was insecure. The problem is based on an actual case, Patco Constr. Co. v. People's United Bank, 684 F.3d 197 (1st Cir. 2012). Because the security procedure was not commercially reasonable, the customer's agreement did not submit it to liability for unauthorized orders, so A is incorrect. D refers to a rule that does not apply here. For *consumer* funds transfers, under the EFTA, there is no liability for unauthorized transfers as long as notice is given within 60 days of the statement date. But this is a commercial wire transfer, governed by UCC 4A.

INVESTMENT SECURITIES

Article 8 of the Uniform Commercial Code is entitled "Investment Securities," but that fancy description is meant to describe stocks and bonds and the Article regulates their sale, transfer, and use as collateral for loans. Originally, these stocks and bonds were reflected as pieces of paper and their transfer was controlled by rules similar to those in Article 3 for negotiable instruments. But in the twenty-first century, stocks and bonds, like much else, moved into the electronic world, and most of them are now held by brokers and transferred electronically as "security entitlements."

Article 8 is something of a stepchild to the rest of the Uniform Commercial Code. White and Summers do not even cover it in their hornbook, and it is embarrassing how often the issues it addresses are litigated without Article 8 even once being cited. To avoid malpractice in this field, you should know something about its scope and general area of regulation.

The original version of Article 8 was created at a time when all investment securities were evidenced by the issuance of pieces of paper labeled as stocks or bonds (now called *certificated securities*). As corporate and government issuers moved from paper to registration of the investors' interest at the issuer's headquarters or some other central location, Article 8 was rewritten in 1978 to deal with these so-called uncertificated securities. But developments in the world of stocks and bonds made the 1978 version obsolete rather quickly because investors began holding their investments merely as bookkeeping entries on the records of their brokers, and often the brokers themselves did not hold the paper certificates either but instead had similar accounts at clearing corporations.

The 1978 Article 8 did not deal with these investment rights, leaving the law in limbo. In 1994 a new version of Article 8 made its appearance and was rapidly adopted by the various jurisdictions.[1] The 8-100s to the 8-400s deal with certificated and uncertificated securities, doing little to change the prior law, but a new part, the 8-500s, now regulates the rights that investors have in security accounts (calling these rights *security entitlements*). A wonderfully detailed "Prefatory Note" (included in most statute books reprinting Article 8) explains the evolution of the law in this area and examines the business background for investment securities and securities holding systems.

I. TERMINOLOGY

Article 8 of the Code (Investment Securities) deals with the rights and liabilities created by the issuance and transfer of stocks and bonds. These items, called *securities* in the Code, are defined in §8-102(a)(15). Under §8-103(d) all securities are governed by Article 8, not by Article 3, even if the security is technically negotiable under §3-104(a).

Essential to your comprehension of Article 8 is an understanding of the meaning of some of the technical terms, such as *registered owner*. What follows is a brief sketch of the basic business transaction that results in the creation of Article 8 paper.

Corporate securities can be divided into two main classes: *debt* securities (generally bonds or debentures and the interest coupons attached thereto), which represent the obligation of the corporation to pay the holder a specified sum, and *equity* securities (such as preferred or common shares of stock), which represent an ownership interest in the corporate enterprise. A corporation, hereinafter called the *issuer*, will make use of both types of securities to provide financing for its activities.

If the issuer is offering the securities to the public (making a *public offering*), it frequently must register them with the Securities and Exchange Commission pursuant to the Securities Act of 1933, 15 U.S.C. §§77a et seq. When printed, the securities are either signed manually, which is quite a

---

1. Even better, the Department of the Treasury has adopted the Revised Article 8 as a matter of federal law; see 31 C.F.R. §357.

task in the issue of, say, 100,000 shares of stock, or by facsimile (printed) signature. Debt securities are almost always placed under the control of an independent trustee, frequently a bank, called the *authenticating trustee*, who signs the securities manually, thereby expressly certifying that the item signed is one of the securities intended as part of the offering.

Debt securities may be made payable to the *bearer* or to a named person, the *registered owner* (so called because the owner's name is registered on the corporation's books as the record owner). Equity securities in this country are always issued in registered form; the registered owner then has voting rights, rights to dividends, etc. If the security is in registered form, the issuer need recognize these rights only in the registered owner. Section 8-207(a) provides:

> Before due presentment for registration of transfer of a certificated security in registered form or of an instruction requesting registration of transfer of an uncertificated security, the issuer or indenture trustee may treat the registered owner as the person exclusively entitled to vote, receive notifications, and otherwise exercise all the rights and powers of an owner.

If the registered owner sells the security, the purchaser will want to have the corporate records changed to show the purchaser as the new registered owner. To do this, the registered owner (transferor) *indorses* the instrument, by writing either on it or on a separate sheet of paper, over to the new owner, and the instrument is presented to the *transfer agent*, who may be either an employee of the corporation or a separate entity. The registered owner may simply indorse the instrument in blank, naming no transferee. This is frequently done when the registered owner is selling the security through a broker and the name of the eventual purchaser is unknown.

Prior to seeking a new registration, a blank instrument is filled in with the name of the purchaser and then submitted to the transfer agent. Of course, instruments indorsed in blank give rise to a situation that can easily become exciting when the security falls into the hands of an individual whose respect for other people's property is minimal. For this reason it has become common for registered owners who wish to sell their securities on the market to indorse them over to their brokers, who then register the security in the brokers' names.

Securities registered to a broker are said to be *street name* securities (so-called because of the broker's connection with New York's Wall Street). When the selling broker finds a purchaser, the broker submits the security to the transfer agent so that the records can be changed to switch the registered ownership from the broker (the street name) to the purchaser. As mentioned above, in today's world the actual certificate may be held only by a clearing corporation, and rights therein are passed down to lower tiers of owners by bookkeeping entries. In these indirect holding situations, the beneficial owner of the security is said to have a *security entitlement* in a *securities account* held with a *security intermediary,* who one instructs by giving an entitlement order (read §8-102(a)), in which all these terms are defined in more detail (*securities account* is defined in §8-501(a)).

To facilitate a change in the registered ownership of a certificated security, a typical security has printed on the back a transfer form more or less similar to the following language that I copied off a debenture:

> For value received, _____ hereby sell, assign and transfer unto _____ the within registered debenture and do hereby irrevocably constitute and appoint _____ my attorney to transfer the said registered debenture on the books of the within named company with full power of substitution in the premises.
>
> Dated: _____
> Signed: _____
> In the presence of: _____

The filling in of the third blank in the above form gives a power of attorney to the person named (frequently a broker). If no transferee is named, the transfer agent will register the security to whomever the attorney nominates; this procedure is sometimes used in lieu of the additional steps involved in registering the security in the street name. If no attorney is named and only the transferee blank (the second one above) is filled in, then the transfer agent will register the security in the name of the transferee. "Where both the name of a transferee and that of an attorney are filled in, the same person should be designated in both blanks. Otherwise, even registration in the name of the specified transferee will require instructions from, if not further indorsement by, the specified attorney." E. Guttman, Modern Securities Transfers §8-8, pp. 8-13 (4th ed. 2010). You will note that the power of attorney gives the attorney full power to substitute a new transferee. Cf. §8-308.

Another entity sometimes involved in Article 8 problems is the *registrar.* A registrar — normally, though not always, a separate entity from the issuer — has the duty to inspect proposed transfers to determine whether they will result in the issuer's having outstanding more stock than it is authorized to have, a situation called *overissue.* In effect, the registrar is an auditor of the corporate capacity of the transfer. The registrar may also be the transfer agent, the entity keeping the records and performing the physical process involved in the transfer. See Hollywood Natl. Bank v. International Bus. Machs. Corp., 38 Cal. App. 3d 607, 113 Cal. Rptr. 494 (1974); E. Guttman, Modern Securities Transfers, *supra,* ch. 10.

The practice of issuing shares of stock that are registered with the issuing company but that are not represented by a physical piece of paper results in what are called *uncertificated securities*. With uncertificated securities, the owner's interest is registered in the issuer's computer and only an initial *transaction statement* is sent to the purchaser to evidence that purchaser's right to the security. Thereafter, transfers of the uncertificated security are accomplished by the current owner's issuing *instruction* to the issuer, telling it to whom the security now belongs. Read §§8-102(a)(12) and 8-305.

II. OVERISSUE

Read §8-210 carefully.

PROBLEM 170

Colossus Corporation was authorized to issue 100,000 shares of stock at a par value of $1; it had 150,000 printed up, and the extra 50,000 were saved for the purpose of replacing the old pieces of paper as they became worn. The company sold 100,000 shares. The extra 50,000 shares were stolen by a clever thief, who negotiated them to a bona fide purchaser (BFP). Can the BFP require the corporation to recognize the 50,000 shares as valid? What remedy does §8-210 give to the BFP? See Hughes Developers, Inc. v. Montgomery, 903 So. 2d 94 (Ala. 2004).

III. THE ISSUER AND THE HOLDER

Read §§8-201 through 8-206, 8-208, and 8-407, which explain duties of the issuer and its agents.

As for §8-204, the most common restriction on transfer is the following, which is frequently printed on securities:

> The shares represented by this certificate have been exchanged exclusively with the Corporation's shareholders and have not been registered under the Securities Act of 1933. These shares may not be pledged or hypothecated and may not be sold or transferred in the absence of an effective Registration Statement under the Securities Act of 1933 or an opinion of counsel to the Corporation that registration is not required under the said Act.

Another common restriction is that the corporation itself is to be given the right of first refusal when sale of the stock is contemplated.

Sections 8-205, 8-208, and 8-406 deal with the responsibilities of the issuer and its agents. Look at these sections in light of the following quote. Guttman's Modern Securities Transfers, *supra*, states, at §11-5, p. 11-14:

> Where the issuer relies on the manual signatures of its officers, "John Beta," who is an employee of the issuer might sign the name of "Richard Gamma, President," who is in fact the only officer authorized to sign. . . . This security is clearly not genuine under the Code definition and the issuer need not recognize it.

Do you agree? Consider the following case.

First American National Bank v. Christian Foundation Life Insurance Co.

Arkansas Supreme Court, 1967
242 Ark. 678, 420 S.W.2d 912

Smith, J.

This is a suit brought by one of the appellees, Christian Foundation Life Insurance Company, for a declaratory judgment with respect to the validity of certain duplicate bearer bonds ostensibly issued by the First Methodist Church of Mena. That duplicate bonds were outstanding was due to the fraud of the late Lawrence Hayes, former president of Institutional Finance Company, which handled the bond issue as fiscal agent for the church. Parties to the suit include the rival owners of the duplicate bonds, the church and its trustees, the Union Bank of Mena, which acted as paying agent for the bonds, the estate of Hayes, the receiver for Institutional Finance, and the corporate surety upon Institutional Finance's qualifying bond as a securities dealer. . . .

We need state the facts only in broad outline. On January 19, 1964, the church adopted a resolution authorizing a $90,000 bond issue for the construction of a new church and employing Institutional Finance as its fiscal agent to market the bonds. On the same day the church treasurer, Bettie Jean Montgomery, in the presence of the pastor and a trustee of the church, affixed her signature to a blank sheet of paper and delivered it to Joe B. Springfield, executive vice-president of Institutional Finance, for use as a facsimile signature upon the bonds.

Two days later Springfield requested a printing company to print the bonds, which were numbered from 1 to 188 and totaled $94,000. (The record does not explain why an extra $4,000 of bonds was printed.) On January 30 the printer delivered the bonds to Springfield. They bore the facsimile signatures of Springfield and Mrs. Montgomery, with no provision for an authenticating manual signature.

Institutional Finance sold $45,000 of the bonds to members of the church but had trouble in finding buyers for all the rest of the issue. On July 3, 1964, Hayes personally borrowed $25,000 from First American National Bank and pledged as collateral, along with other securities, $27,000 (later increased to $28,800) of the Mena church bonds. There is no sound basis for questioning the bank's standing as a good faith purchaser for value, as those terms are defined in the Uniform Commercial Code. Ark. Stat. Ann. §85-1-201 (Add. 1961). Hayes had borrowed money from the bank on a number of occasions. The bank's president, who handled this loan, understood Hayes to be an employee of a Texas dealer in church bonds and was unaware of his connection with Institutional Finance. Nothing in the transaction warned the bank that Hayes did not own the bonds.

On February 1, 1965, Hayes fraudulently ordered the printer to print $25,000 of numbered bonds that included duplicates of some of those pledged to the bank. Later in the month, Hayes, in order to complete a sale to Christian Foundation Life, had printed additional bonds in certain larger denominations requested by that insurance company. The duplicate bonds now held by Richards and Christian Foundation Life are among those obtained by Hayes in the two supplemental printings.

We find no merit in the appellant's insistence that its adversaries were not purchasers in good faith because they bought the bonds at discounts of 10 and 15 percent. We have held that the price paid for a negotiable instrument may be so grossly inadequate as to support a finding of bad faith, Hogg v. Thurman, 90 Ark. 93, 117 S.W. 1070, 17 Ann. Gas. 383 (1909), but there is no proof in this record to indicate that the discounts offered to the appellees were so great as to arouse suspicion. Nor is there evidence to sustain the appellant's argument that the purchasers of the duplicates should have been put upon inquiry by the church's apparent inability to market the entire bond issue within a period of about a year.

Hayes' dishonesty finally became known when duplicate interest coupons were presented to the Mena bank for payment. The paying agent refused to honor the coupons until their validity had been established. Hence this suit.

We think the chancellor should have found all bonds held by bona fide purchasers to be binding obligations of the church. It is plain enough that the church was careless in entrusting its treasurer's facsimile signature to Institutional Finance and in failing to take the precaution of requiring authentication of the bonds by a manual signature. By contrast, the holders of the bonds acquired them in the ordinary course of business and in circumstances entitling them to the protection afforded to bona fide purchasers.

The case is controlled by the pertinent provisions of the Uniform Commercial Code. Before the adoption of the Code the church might have been held liable by contract to one purchaser and in damages to the other, but the draftsmen of the Code point out in their Comment to our §8-205 that the Code simply validates most defective securities in the hands of innocent purchasers, refusing to prefer one such purchaser over another.

Specifically, this controversy falls within §8-205, which provides that an unauthorized signature is effective in favor of an innocent purchaser when the signing is done either by a person entrusted by the issuer with the signing of the security or by an employee of such a person or of the issuer itself. By resolution the church employed Institutional Finance as its fiscal agent to handle the sale of the bonds. The first line of the printed prospectus for the bond issue identified that concern as the issuer's fiscal agent. There can hardly be any serious contention that Hayes's wrongful use of the treasurer's facsimile signature did not fall within the purview of the Code. . . .

Reversed and remanded.

Jones, J. (dissenting). I do not agree with the conclusion reached by the majority in this case, nor do I agree with the decision of the chancellor.

Our Uniform Commercial Code §8-202(3) [now §8-202(c) — Eds.] is as follows:

> Except as otherwise provided in the case of certain unauthorized signatures on issue (Section 8-205), lack of genuineness of a security is a complete defense even against a purchaser for value and without notice.

Just what constitutes the genuineness of a security is not set out in chapter 8 of the Code on investment securities, but §1-201 contains 46 numbered general definitions, one of which is as follows: "(18) 'Genuine' means free of forgery or counterfeiting." . . .

It is my view that the duplicate bonds printed without authority and certainly with the apparent intent to defraud, were forged counterfeits of the original bonds and lacked the genuineness of the original authorized bonds, and that their lack of genuineness was a complete defense even against Christian Foundation and Reverend C.R. Richards. . . .

Under the majority holding in this case, once authority is given to an unscrupulous agent to print and sell a limited number of bonds over a facsimile signature, the principal or issuer has no further protection from being bound by such individual. A revocation of authority, or even confinement in the penitentiary, would offer no protection. Such agent or ex-agent, would be able to bind his former principal, or the issuer of bonds, for as long as such agent could find innocent purchasers and access to a printing press.

I would reverse the chancellor in this case and hold that the original bonds held by First American are genuine and legal bonds, but that the duplicates sold to Christian Foundation and Reverend Richards are forged counterfeits of the originals and are not genuine but are void as binding obligations of First Methodist.

PROBLEM 171

Titanic Telephone Company (TTC), Inc. called up the Pronto Printing Corporation (PPC) and asked Felix Pronto (founder and president) if PPC would run off 100 more of the $100 TTC bearer bonds PPC had printed in the past. PPC had previously printed 1,000 of these bonds and still had the plates. The bonds had the facsimile signatures of the TTC president, secretary, and authenticating trustee already printed on them. Felix agreed and called up Happy Clatter, the chief printer, and told him to run off 100 more of the bonds and send them by messenger to TTC. Happy ran off 200 of the bonds. He sent 100 by messenger to the offices of TTC, and he sent the other 100 as a Christmas present to his mother in Twin Falls, Idaho. Eventually, the latter bonds turned up as the property of Bing, Bong & Bell Brokerage, a purchaser for value without notice of anything unusual, which presented the bonds to TTC for payment of the interest due that year. Titanic Telephone comes to you for advice. It doesn't know whether it should treat the bonds as valid or not and is afraid that if it pays the interest, TTC's stockholders will bring suit against TTC's officers for misusing corporate funds. Give TTC your opinion as to whether the law requires TTC to honor the bonds, noting carefully §§8-202(c) and 8-205.

IV. TRANSFERS BETWEEN PURCHASERS

The proper transfer of a registered security is a three-step process: indorsement by the owner, delivery to the purchaser, and registration with the corporation in the name of the new owner. The effective transfer of a bearer security requires *only* delivery. Read §§8-304, 8-108(f), and 8-307.

The Article 8 equivalent of Article 3's holder in due course is called a *protected purchaser* (see §8-303), and he or she takes free of adverse claims in both direct and indirect holding systems. Section 8-303(a)(3) requires that the protected purchaser obtain *control* over the security, and while *control* is defined extensively in 8-106, the requirements are nicely summarized in Official Comment 3 to §8-303, which you should now read. It should be noted that *purchase* is defined so broadly in §1-201(b)(32) that, incredibly enough, it includes taking by *gift*. See Rogers v. Rogers, 271 Md. 603, 319 A.2d 119 (1974). *Notice* is defined in §8-105. Read it.

Note that Article 8 has a shelter rule very similar in effect to §3-203(b) in Article 3. See §8-302. Thus, even a person with notice of an adverse claim can get the rights of a protected purchaser by taking from one.

Warranties. On transfer to a purchaser for value, the seller makes the warranties listed in §8-108. A *broker* (defined in §8-102(a)(3)) makes the warranties in §8-108(i). As in Articles 3 and 4, warranty theories are frequently used to pass liability from one person to another.

PROBLEM 172

Lynn Brown was the registered owner of 20 shares of Regional Telephone Company when the stock was stolen from her by a clever thief who forged her indorsement on the shares and sold them to Bing, Bong & Bell (B.B. & B.), stockbrokers, who purchased the shares for the brokerage firm. B.B. & B. then had the stock reregistered by Regional Telephone to its own (street) name and thereafter sold the shares to Barbara Shipek, a wealthy client who was trying to buy up all the shares of Regional Telephone that she could. When Lynn found that the shares were missing, she contacted Barbara and demanded the return of her stock. Must Barbara surrender the shares? Would B.B. & B. have had to surrender the shares if Lynn had made a demand to do so before B.B. & B. had the shares reregistered? After? See §§8-106(b), 8-108 (f) (and its Official Comment 3), 8-303 (and particularly its own Official Comment 3). Who is obviously liable to Lynn here? See §8-404.

V. *REGISTRATION*

When a transfer of a registered security occurs between purchasers, the transfer is *complete* upon delivery to the purchaser (§8-304(c)). But the new owner will want to have the security registered on the company's books in his or her name.[2] The impetus to registration is that until the corporate records are changed, the issuer can send dividend checks, etc., to the record owner (§8-207(a)). The seller must supply the documentation needed to register, §8-307, but does not in any way warrant that the issuer will honor the security, §§8-304(f) and 8-305(b).

---

2. The company, once it decides to change the registration, cancels the old certificate and issues a new one to the new registered owner.

On presenting the security for registration, the presenter makes the warranties stated in §8-108(f). The issuer is under a legal *duty* to register the transfer if the requirements of §8-401, which you should now read, are met; Campbell v. Liberty Transfer Co., 2006 WL 3751529 (E.D.N.Y. 2006). If any of these requirements has not been satisfied, the issuer can refuse the registration.

PROBLEM 173

Professor Chalk was the registered owner of 50 shares of the Beaten Path Mousetrap Corporation, and he wanted to sell. The shares bore a restrictive legend like the one on page 515, stating that no SEC registration had occurred and that no transfer could take place unless a registration was filed with the Securities Exchange Commission (SEC) or the owner could supply the written opinion of counsel that such a registration was unnecessary. Professor Chalk wrote the SEC and received a *No Action* letter, which is a non-binding recommendation by an SEC staff counsel that states that the counsel will not recommend that any action be taken by the Commission in connection with the transfer. He then submitted this letter to Beaten Path Mousetrap's transfer agent along with the stock and requested registration to his buyer. The transfer agent refused, claiming non-compliance with the restriction. While the dispute was going on, Beaten Path Mousetrap Corporation went bankrupt. Professor Chalk sued. Who should win? See §§8-401, 8-407; Kenler v. Canal Natl. Bank, 489 F.2d 482 (1st Cir. 1973).

The Guarantee of Signature.   The transfer blanks on securities frequently contain a place for the signature of a *guarantor.* Consider the following quotations from Guttman, Modern Securities Transfers, *supra,* at §2-5, p. 2-20-2-21, §2-7 p. 2-22-2-23:

> For over a century, the legal responsibility of the transfer office was construed in extremely stringent terms. That office was and remains today fully responsible for the genuineness of the signature of the "member" purporting to transfer his interest. This responsibility is absolute. Good faith, even the highest degree of diligence and care, does not relieve the issuer from liability where the signature is not in fact genuine or, or is authorized. . . .
> . . . To mitigate the issuer's absolute liability in respect of genuineness of a necessary signature, commercial practice developed a working solution, the guarantee of signature. That guarantee remains today the cornerstone of the structure and the essential lubricant of the transfer process.

Read §8-306, ignoring subsections (c) and (d). Do you understand why Professor Israels (one of the drafters of Article 8) once stated that if lawyers discover that their broker clients have rubber stamps reading "Indorsement guaranteed," they should see that the stamps are jettisoned immediately? Israels, How to Handle Transfers, 19 Bus. Law. 90, 98 (1963). Note that an issuer may not *require* a guarantee of an *indorsement*; a guarantee of *signature* is required as a matter of course. Read §8-402 carefully.

Jennie Clarkson Home for Children v. Missouri, Kansas & Texas Railway
Court of Appeals of New York, 1905
182 N.Y. 47, 74 N.E. 571

HAIGHT, J.

This action was brought to recover four registered bonds, of the par value of $1,000 each, payable in gold, in the year 1990, with 4 percent interest coupons attached, numbered respectively 8,872, 8,873, 8,874, and 8,875, issued by the defendant Missouri, Kansas and Texas Railway Company, and secured by first mortgage on the property of the company, or bonds of like amount and value, or, in default thereof, to recover the value of such bonds. The trial resulted in a judgment for the plaintiff substantially for the relief demanded in the complaint, which has been affirmed in the Appellate Division. The facts are without substantial dispute. The plaintiff, the Jennie Clarkson Home for Children, is a domestic corporation organized under the laws of this state for charitable purposes. It was the owner of the bonds in question, which by their terms were not transferable after registration, unless made on the books of the railway company by the registered holder, or by his attorney duly authorized, and noted on the bonds. They were kept in a safe deposit vault in one of the banks in the city, the president and the treasurer of the plaintiff each having a key thereto. On or about the 11th day of March, 1902, George W. Lessels, treasurer of the plaintiff, without the knowledge or consent of any of the officers or directors of the plaintiff corporation, took the bonds in question from the safe deposit vault where they were stored, for the purpose of converting them to his own use, and thereupon he took them to the office of Robert Gibson, who was a member of the stock exchange, doing business as stockbroker under the name of the limited partnership of H. Knickerbacker & Co., and asked that they be sold. The cashier of the defendant Gibson, seeing that the bonds were registered in the name of the plaintiff corporation, informed Lessels that, before the bonds could be sold, the registration must be so altered that they would be payable to bearer. Lessels asked how that could be done and he was then instructed to take them to the transfer office of the defendant railway company, and that there he could find out what was to be done in order to effect the change. Upon application to the railway company he was advised, in substance, that it would be necessary to have a resolution of the board of directors of the plaintiff corporation passed, authorizing a transfer of the bonds, and the furnishing of the company with a copy authenticated by the certificate of the secretary, under the seal of the corporation, to the effect that the copy presented was a true and correct copy of the resolution of the board and that a power of attorney would have to be executed by the corporation, authorizing the transfer of the bonds to bearer, the signature of which must be witnessed by some stock exchange house. Thereupon Lessels returned to the office of H. Knickerbacker and Co., and had the power of attorney drawn, and signed it in the name of the plaintiff, the Jennie Clarkson Home for Children, George W. Lessels, treasurer, and underneath is the statement that it was signed and acknowledged in the presence of John F. Busch, who was the cashier for H. Knickerbacker & Co., and by H. Knickerbacker & Co., which was signed by Gibson. At the same time Lessels presented to H. Knickerbacker & Co. a paper purporting to be a copy of the resolution of the board of directors, authorizing a sale of the bonds, with the certificate of the secretary, under seal, attached. But the resolution was never passed by the board of directors, the certificate of the secretary was never signed by him, and the seal affixed thereto was not the seal of the corporation. All of these papers had been forged. Upon their presentation to defendant Gibson, he caused them to be transmitted to the office of the railway company and there the bonds were changed and made payable to bearer; and then they were returned to the defendant Gibson, who sold them and paid the proceeds over to Lessels, who converted the money to his own use and subsequently absconded.

[The court then quoted Story on Agency to the effect that a principal is not bound by the actions of an agent done beyond the scope of his employment, and concluded that the treasurer was not acting within the scope of his employment while carrying out his defalcation.]

The plaintiff was the owner of the bonds in question. They had been registered by the defendant railway company. That company undertook to keep a registry of such bonds, and not to transfer them, except upon the books of the company by the direction of the owner or by his duly authorized attorney. It is deemed to have undertaken to pay the interest accruing upon these bonds, and the principal, when due, to such registered owner. The purpose of such registration was to save the owner from loss resulting from larceny or destruction of the bonds. Being registered, they could not be sold. If presented to the railway company for payment of the interest or principal by other than the registered owner, payment would be refused. They were only property in the hands of the registered owner. The bonds having been stolen from the plaintiff, it had the right to follow them and recover them wherever found. If they could not be found, it had the right to recover their value from those who had been instrumental in changing them from registered to negotiable bonds. Pollock v. National Bank, 7 N.Y.

274, 57 Am. Dec. 520. The defendant railway company knew that the bonds belonged to the plaintiff, and that it had no right to cancel the registration thereof without the authority of the plaintiff. In cancelling such registry and making them payable to bearer, thus enabling them to be sold in the market, it violated its agreement with the plaintiff, and it cannot be relieved from the effect of such violation by reason of the fact that its transfer agent was deceived by the forgeries of Lessels. So, also, did the defendant Gibson know that the bonds belonged to the plaintiff, and that they were registered, and could not be sold until the registration was changed. To some extent he assisted Lessels in procuring the registration to be changed. He advised Lessels how to obtain the information to make the change. After the requisite information had been obtained, he assisted him in drawing the power of attorney, and took part in its execution, becoming a witness thereto. He had been furnished with copies of what purported to be a resolution of the board of directors, with the false signatures of the president and secretary attached, which he transmitted, with the bonds, to the transfer agent of the railway company, to procure the change in the registry. Even after that change had been made, he still knew that the bonds belonged to the plaintiff, and that he had no right to sell them without its authority. And the fact that he was deceived by the fraudulent misrepresentations of Lessels did not relieve him from the responsibility of his acts with reference to depriving the plaintiff of them. The bonds had been traced into his hands, and the plaintiff had the right to seek them there and recover them if they were still in his possession, or if he had sold them and misappropriated the proceeds, knowing that they were the plaintiff's, to recover the value thereof from him. . . .

After the complaint in this action had been served upon the defendant railway company, it served an answer upon the defendant Gibson, in which it demanded relief as against him to the effect that, in case it was compelled to restore the bonds or pay plaintiff's claim, it should have a judgment for the amount so compelled to be paid over as against Gibson. We thus have an issue raised as between the defendants, in which the plaintiff is not interested. Under the provisions of the bonds, they may be registered in the books of the company, and, if so registered, they will thereafter be transferable only upon the books of the company by the owner in person or by attorney duly authorized. It therefore became necessary, in order to change the registry of the bonds, to have a power of attorney executed by the plaintiff. This power of attorney, as we have seen, was drawn in the office of the defendant Gibson, and executed in his presence and that of his cashier, by Lessels signing the name of the corporation thereto, and underneath his own name with the word "treasurer." It was then witnessed by Gibson and by his cashier. Both Gibson and the transfer agent of the railway company were members of the stock exchange. The trial court found as a fact "that in and by the custom among the members of the New York Stock Exchange and of railway transfer agencies in the city of New York the signature of a stock exchange house or a member thereof upon a power of attorney to transfer securities was, during all the times mentioned in the complaint, a guaranty of the correctness of the signature of the parties purporting to execute it." This finding is based upon the rule of the exchange and the testimony of the witness. The rule is as follows: "An indorsement by a member of the exchange, or a firm represented by the exchange, on a certificate is considered a guaranty of the correctness of the signature of the party in whose name the stock stands. In all cases where powers of substitution are used, the original assignment and power of attorney, and each power of substitution, must be guaranteed by a member, or a firm represented in the exchange, resident or doing business in New York." James L. Carter was sworn as a witness on behalf of the defendant railway company, and testified that he was employed by the banking house of J.P. Morgan & Co., that they were transfer agents for about 150 companies, and that there was an established custom as to the requirements upon the transfer of bonds in the city of New York, and that was to require the guaranty of a stock exchange house, or a member of the stock exchange, on the power of attorney on which the transfer is made.

As we have seen, Gibson not only witnessed the power of attorney authorizing the transfer of the bonds on the books of the railway company, but he also transmitted the bonds accompanied by such power of attorney, and with what purported to be the resolution of the board of directors, to the transfer agent of the defendant railway company to have the change of the registration made. The transfer agent, in making the change in the bonds, acted upon the papers so forwarded from defendant Gibson's house. Gibson was a member of the stock exchange in good standing, acquainted with Lessels, his customer, and he must be deemed to have become a witness to the power of attorney under the custom in force. As we have seen, the bonds stood in the name of the Jennie Clarkson Home for Children. Lessels had no power or authority to sell or transfer the bonds or to sign the plaintiff's name as attorney or agent authorizing the transfer of the bonds. The power of attorney was not, therefore, signed by the genuine or the correct signature of the corporation. Under these circumstances the courts below have held that the defendant Gibson was liable over to the defendant railway company. . . .

This much is conceded. But it is contended on behalf of Gibson that he did not, by becoming a witness, undertake to guaranty that Lessels had authority to sign the name of the corporation. This presents the real question in the case, and it really becomes one of construction as to the meaning of the rule of the stock exchange which is the basis of the custom found by the trial court. Under the rule, an indorsement by a member of the exchange on a certificate is considered "a guaranty of the correctness of the signature of the party in whose name the stock stands." If stock is held by an individual who is executing a power of attorney for its transfer, the member of the exchange who signs as a witness thereto guarantees not only the genuineness of the signature affixed to the power of attorney, but that the person signing is the individual in whose name the stock stands. With reference to stock standing in the name of a corporation, which can only sign a power of attorney through its authorized officers or agents, a different situation is presented. If the witnessing of the signature of the corporation is only that of the signature of a person who signs for the corporation, then the guaranty is of no value, and there is nothing to protect purchasers of the companies who are called upon to issue new stock in the place of that transferred from the frauds of persons who have signed the names of corporations without authority. If such is the only effect of the guaranty, purchasers and transfer agents must first go to the corporation in whose name the stock stands and ascertain whether the individual who signed the power of attorney had authority to so do. This will require time, and in many cases will necessitate the postponement of the completion of the purchase by the payment of the money until the facts can be ascertained. The broker who is acting for the owner has an opportunity to become acquainted with his customer, and may readily before sale ascertain, in case of a corporation, the name of the officer who is authorized to execute the power of attorney. It was therefore, we think, the purpose of the rule to cast upon the broker who witnesses the signature the duty of ascertaining whether the person signing the name of the corporation has authority to so do, and making the witness a guarantor that it is the signature of the corporation in whose name the stock stands. . . .

The judgment should be affirmed, with costs.

Official Comment 2 to §8-306 quotes extensively from this very case, so it still accurately states the law. The New York markets require that the guarantor be either a member of an exchange in New York (individual or corporate) or a commercial bank or trust company either located in New York or having a correspondent in New York. See N.Y.S.E. Rule 209, A.S.E. Rule Sr-47, N.Y.S.T.A. Rule 20. In theory, any person may guarantee a signature. Read Official Comment 2 to §8-402.

PROBLEM 174

Maude Raisin was 80 years old and the registered owner of 100 shares of IBM stock. Her faithful companion of 15 years was Charleyne Rikki, who, one day after being turned down for a raise, took the stock and forged Ms. Raisin's signature to it. She took the stock to Bing, Bong & Bell (B.B. & B.), stockbrokers, and asked them to sell it. B.B. & B. did so, guaranteeing the Raisin signature as part of the registration process. Maude discovered the loss, Charleyne went to jail, and Maude sued B.B. & B. on their signature guarantee. Should she prevail? See §8-306(h). Would a common law suit for conversion prevail? See §8-115 and its Official Comment 3; Decker v. Yorkton Securities, Inc., 106 Cal. App. 4th 1315 (2003). Who should she sue? See §8-404 and its Official Comment; Scott v. Ametek, Inc., 277 A.2d 714 (Del. Ch. 1971).

PROBLEM 175

Assume in the last Problem that Maude Raisin realizes that the stock had been taken and immediately contacts the issuer of the stock and alerts the issuer to the theft. When the stock is presented to the issuer later in the week, what duties does it have? See §§8-403 and 8-404. Does Maude have a duty to notify the issuer promptly? Read §8-406. If the issuer gives her a replacement for her missing stock and then the original shares turn up in the hands of a protected purchaser, what are the issuer's rights? See §8-405(b).[3]

VI. SECURITY ENTITLEMENTS

Part 5 of Article 8 deals with security entitlements in indirect holding systems. The rules of that Part are explored next.

In re Estate of Rider

Supreme Court of South Carolina, 2014
407 S.C. 386, 756 S.E.2d 136

Justice BEATTY.

This Court granted a petition for a writ of certiorari to review the decision of the Court of Appeals in Rider v. Estate of Rider, 394 S.C. 84, 713 S.E.2d 643 (Ct. App. 2011), which applied the common law of agency to

---

3. Under §17(f) of the Securities Act of 1934, 15 U.S.C. §78q(f) (1967), and S.E.C. Rule, 17 C.F.R. §240.17f-1, brokers and others regularly dealing with securities must comply with rigorous notification procedures for lost securities. See Pillero, Ilkson, & Yadley, Does SEC Rule 17f-1 Destroy Bona Fide Purchaser Status Under the UCC?, N.Y. L.J., Dec. 13, 1976, at 46. For a case denying protected purchaser status to a bank that failed to check with the Securities Information Center computer before buying stolen bonds, see First Natl. Bank of Cicero v. Lewco Sec. Corp., 860 F.2d 1407 (7th Cir. 1988).

hold that certain financial assets were part of the decedent's probate estate. The decedent had directed his bank to transfer specified assets in his investment account to a new account for his spouse, but died before all of the assets were credited to her account. At issue in this case of first impression is whether South Carolina's Uniform Commercial Code ("UCC") or the common law of agency controls the transfer. We reverse.

I. FACTS

Charles Galen Rider ("Husband") executed an Investment Agency Agreement/Discretionary Account ("Account Agreement") with First Union National Bank of North Carolina ("First Union"), a predecessor of Wachovia Bank, N.A. ("Wachovia"), on September 27, 1993. The Account Agreement authorized First Union "to open and maintain an Agency Account" for Husband and "to hold therein, as [his] Agent, all cash, stocks, bonds, securities and other property . . . subject to" Husband's current and future written instructions. The Account Agreement stated First Union was "to provide investment review and management of the Account, taking such action as [the bank], in [its] discretion, deem[s] best . . . as though [the bank] were the owner of such property." This discretionary authority permitted First Union to buy, sell, and exercise certain rights regarding the securities in accordance with the overall investment objective selected by Husband. The terms of the Account Agreement called for its termination upon the bank acquiring actual knowledge of Husband's death, but that Husband's death "shall not affect the validity of any prior actions."

On June 8, 2005, Husband called Ruth DiLella in the Capital Management Group of what was then Wachovia and informed her that he had met with his estate attorney, who had advised him to transfer some assets to his spouse, Carolyn S. Rider ("Wife"). Husband was suffering from terminal cancer and reportedly wanted Wife to have sufficient funds to maintain her standard of living during the inevitable time that probate would be going on. Husband instructed DiLella to move $2 million in securities from his account at Wachovia and place them in a new account in Wife's name. DiLella told Husband that Wachovia would send him a list of specific securities to transfer, along with a signature page for him to sign to approve the transfer. The same day, DiLella e-mailed a list of assets totaling $2 million to Wachovia's trust department, along with Husband's instruction, so it could prepare a letter and asset listing for the client's approval.

On June 17, 2005, Husband signed the letter and returned it to the attention of Wachovia's trust administrator. The letter provided: "Please accept this letter as my authority and direction to transfer the assets listed on the following page to a new agency account to be opened for my wife, Carolyn Sue Rider." A total of $2 million in assets were listed, which included specific securities and a small sum of cash.

In response, Wachovia made a series of four transfers from June to October 2005. On June 21, 2005, four days after Husband's signing of the June 17th directive, Wachovia made the first transfer of $733,228.00 in securities (stocks) to Wife's account. On July 8, 2005, Wachovia transferred $39,672.00 in securities (stocks). That afternoon, Husband passed away in Charlotte, North Carolina, and Husband's daughter, respondent Deborah Rider McClure, notified Wachovia the same day. The next business day, Monday, July 11, 2005, Wachovia transferred $935,032.64 in securities (mutual funds) to Wife's account, and on October 20, 2005, Wachovia made a fourth and final transfer of $304,182.46 in securities (mutual funds). The total amount transferred to Wife's account was $2,012,115.00, the excess being due to the appreciation in the value of the securities.

In 2006, Thomas M. Grady, as personal representative of Husband's estate ("PR"), instituted this declaratory judgment action in the probate court for Beaufort County asking the court to determine either (1) that the securities transferred pursuant to Husband's June 17, 2005 letter to Wachovia were completed transfers on June 17, 2005 and, thus, were not includible in Husband's probate estate; or (2) that the securities transferred after Husband's death on July 8, 2005 were incomplete transfers and were includible in Husband's probate estate. The PR did not take a position, but sought guidance as to whether the UCC or the law of agency under the South Carolina common law controlled the outcome.

In its order, the probate court stated much of the argument in this case centered on whether the UCC's provision on Investment Securities applies to the securities transfer directed by Husband on June 17, 2005. The probate court stated Wife argued the UCC applies, Husband's June 17, 2005 directive was an "entitlement order" under the applicable definition in the UCC found in S.C. Code Ann. §36-8-102, the transfer was effectuated on June 17, 2005, and it was unaffected by Husband's death before completion of the transfers. In contrast, Husband's two daughters from his prior marriage, Deborah Rider McClure and Ginger C. McClure, and his two grandsons, Christian McClure and Austin McClure (collectively, "the McClure Respondents") argued, *inter alia*, that the UCC did not apply and, even if it did, it did not supplant the law of agency that governed the parties' Account Agreement. Either way, Wachovia's authority to make the transfers ended when it acquired actual knowledge of Husband's death and the disputed assets belonged to Husband's probate estate.

The probate court found the UCC controlled this securities transaction, that Husband's June 17, 2005 directive was an "entitlement order," and Wachovia was a "securities intermediary." However, it determined an entitlement order's "effective date" is a distinguishable concept from when an entitlement order is "effectuated." The probate court agreed with Wife that Husband's entitlement order was "effective" upon its issuance to Wachovia on June 17, 2005, but reasoned it still had to be carried out by Wachovia, the securities intermediary, to be "effectuated," and the UCC did not supplant the laws of property or agency, nor did it vitiate the terms of the Account Agreement.

The probate court noted Wachovia received actual notice of Husband's death on Friday, July 8th, that the second transfer of $39,672.00 was posted to Wife's account that day, and that the third transfer of $935,032.64 was posted to Wife's account the next business day, Monday, July 11th. The court stated the credible testimony at trial persuaded it that Wachovia took the necessary actions to effectuate the second and third transfers before it knew of Husband's death. The court observed, "In the commercial context of the transactions, it would be unreasonable to conclude otherwise."

The probate court concluded the first three transfers, totaling $1,707,932.64, which were posted to Wife's account on June 21, July 8, and July 11, 2005, respectively, were carried out and effectuated before Husband's death and are not part of his probate estate. However, the securities posted to Wife's account on October 20, 2005 in the amount of $304,082.46 belonged to Husband's probate estate because it was not effectuated until after Husband's death, when Wachovia's authority to act had already terminated.

Wife appealed to the circuit court, which affirmed in an order adopting the probate court's factual findings and legal conclusions. Wife appealed to the Court of Appeals, which found both the third and fourth transfers properly belonged to Husband's probate estate because they occurred after the bank had actual knowledge of Husband's death, but that no error was preserved regarding the third transfer because the McClure Respondents did not cross-appeal, so it too affirmed. Rider v. Estate of Rider, 394 S.C. 84, 713 S.E.2d 643 (Ct. App. 2011). The Court of Appeals also distinguished the "effective date" of Husband's entitlement order from the date it was "effectuated" and found the latter determinative of the question of ownership. This Court granted Wife's petition for a writ of certiorari to review the decision of the Court of Appeals. . . .

III. Law/Analysis

Wife contends the UCC addresses the subject matter at issue in this appeal, arguing only where the UCC is incomplete does the common law provide the applicable rule. *See* S.C. Code Ann. §36-1-103 (2003) ("Unless displaced by the particular provisions of this act [Title 36, the UCC], the principles of law and equity, including . . . the law relative to capacity to contract, principal and agent, estoppel, fraud, . . . or other validating or invalidating cause shall supplement its provisions."); Hitachi Elec. Devices (USA), Inc. v. Platinum Techns., Inc., 366 S.C. 163, 170, 621 S.E.2d 38, 41

(2005) ("Only where the U.C.C. is incomplete does the common law provide applicable rules.").

Chapter 8 of our state's UCC governs "Investment Securities." S.C. Code Ann. §36-8-101 (2003). It is based on the state's adoption of the revised Article 8 contained in the model Uniform Commercial Code prepared by the American Law Institute in collaboration with the National Conference of Commissioners on Uniform State Laws. Its primary purposes are to provide uniformity in the securities industry and to provide an accurate description of the realities of the securities markets, and secondarily to enhance the value-adding factors of liquidity and certainty in securities transactions. S.C. Code Ann. §§36-8-101 to -511 cmt. at 82 (2003 & Supp. 2013) (S.C. Reporter's Introductory Comment to the 2000 Revision). Part 5 of Chapter 8, entitled "Security Entitlements," specifically governs the "indirect holding system," whereby purchasers of securities deal with intermediaries who hold securities for others, as compared to the traditional system whereby purchasers deal directly with the issuers of those securities. *See* cmt. at 83. It is noted in the Introductory Comment that these provisions "supplant a pastiche of common law rules and agreed practices." *Id.*

In the current matter, Wachovia held certain financial assets (securities) for Husband and managed those assets, subject to his oversight, pursuant to the Account Agreement, by which the bank acted as Husband's agent. This relationship thus implicates the indirect holding system set forth in Part 5 as well as general UCC provisions. Under the terms of the UCC, Husband was an "entitlement holder" with a "security entitlement" to the "financial assets" in a "securities account" maintained and managed by Wachovia for Husband's benefit in its capacity as a "securities intermediary." These and related terms are statutorily defined.

A "financial asset" includes "a security" or a share or other interest in property "which is, or is of a type, dealt in or traded on financial markets [.]" S.C. Code Ann. §36-8-102(a)(9) (2003). A "securities account" is "an account to which a financial asset is or may be credited in accordance with an agreement under which the person maintaining the account undertakes to treat the person for whom the account is maintained as entitled to exercise the rights that comprise the financial asset." *Id.* §36-8-501(a).

Wachovia is a "securities intermediary," which is defined to include "a bank . . . that in the ordinary course of its business maintains securities accounts for others and is acting in that capacity." *Id.* §36-8-102(a)(14)(ii).

Husband was the "entitlement holder," which the UCC defines as follows: "A person identified in the records of a security intermediary as the person having a security entitlement against the securities intermediary. If a person acquires a security entitlement by virtue of Section 36-8-501(b)(2) or (3), that person is the entitlement holder." *Id.* §36-8-102(a)(7).

A "security entitlement" consists of "the rights and property interest of an entitlement holder with respect to a financial asset specified in Part 5 [of Title 36]." *Id.* §36-8-102(a)(17). Section 36-8-501(b) of the UCC provides a person generally acquires a security entitlement if a securities intermediary does any of the following three things: "(1) indicates by book entry that a financial asset has been credited to the person's securities account; (2) receives a financial asset from the person or acquires a financial asset for the person and, in either case, accepts it for credit to the person's securities account; or (3) becomes obligated under other law, regulation, or rule to credit a financial asset to the person's securities account." *Id.* §36-8-501(b).

Husband, as the entitlement holder, retained the right to direct Wachovia to make changes in his account by issuing an "entitlement order," i.e., "a notification communicated to a securities intermediary directing transfer or redemption of a financial asset to which the entitlement holder has a security entitlement." *Id.* §36-8-102(a)(8).

Wachovia was statutorily required to respond to an appropriate entitlement order. *See id.* §36-8-506 ("A securities intermediary shall exercise rights with respect to a financial asset if directed to do so by an entitlement holder."); *id.* §36-8-507(a) ("A securities intermediary *shall comply* with an entitlement order if [1] the entitlement order is *originated by the appropriate person*, [2] the securities intermediary has had reasonable opportunity to assure itself that the entitlement order is genuine and authorized, and [3] the securities intermediary has had *reasonable opportunity to comply* with the entitlement order." (emphasis added)).

An "appropriate person" with respect to an entitlement order is the entitlement holder. *Id.* §36-8-107(a)(3). However, if the person "is deceased, the designated person's successor taking under other law or the designated person's personal representative acting for the estate of the decedent" is an appropriate person to initiate an entitlement order. *Id.* §36-8-107(a)(4).

The UCC further provides that "[e]ffectiveness of an . . . entitlement order is determined as of the date the . . . entitlement order *is made*, and an . . . entitlement order *does not become ineffective by reason of any later change in circumstances*." *Id.* §36-8-107(e) (emphasis added). Subsection (e) clarifies the protection from liability of securities intermediaries who rely on appropriate persons, and "[t]his protection reflects the policy of revised Article 8 to enhance liquidity and finality in securities transactions." *Id.* §36-8-107 cmt. at 143 (S.C. Reporter's Comment to 2000 Revision).

In the Court of Appeals, the court first reviewed the terms of the Account Agreement and found the "prior actions" clause therein refers to both Husband's and Wachovia's conduct and that the plain language of the agreement showed Wachovia's authority ended upon actual knowledge of Husband's death. Rider v. Estate of Rider, 394 S.C. 84, 91, 713 S.E.2d 643, 646-47 (Ct. App. 2011). The court stated the determination whether the securities in the fourth transfer were part of Husband's estate was, therefore, determined by whether Husband's and Wachovia's conduct was sufficient to complete the transfers before Wachovia learned of Husband's death. *Id.* at 91, 713 S.E.2d at 647.

Wife argued the general agency rule that an agent lacks authority to act for a principal after a principal's death, relied upon by the McClure Respondents, does not apply to this situation because Husband's June 17, 2005 directive was an effective entitlement order under Article 8 of the UCC. *Id.* Wife contended (1) an effective entitlement order transfers the right to financial assets the date it is made and, (2) even if it does not, an entitlement order *remains effective* pursuant to the UCC provision above, which displaces the agency rule under the common law, so that actions taken to comply with the entitlement order may be completed regardless of later changes in circumstances. *Id.* at 91-92, 713 S.E.2d at 647.

The Court of Appeals rejected both of Wife's contentions and determined "the probate court properly found the [securities in] the fourth transfer are part of [Husband's] estate." *Id.* at 93, 713 S.E.2d at 648. In reaching this conclusion, the Court of Appeals stated the UCC applied, but nevertheless found the UCC's rule as to the effective date of an entitlement order contained in section 36-8-107(e) of the UCC did not fully address the subject, so it did not displace the relevant agency rule. *Id.* at 93-95, 713 S.E.2d at 648-49.

Applying the common law of agency, the Court of Appeals reasoned that an entitlement order does not complete a transfer of financial assets at the time it is made, so like other orders to agents, it is an instruction to act in the manner the principal desires, and the request is terminated by the principal's death, citing Carver v. Morrow, 213 S.C. 199, 204, 48 S.E.2d 814, 817 (1948) (stating as a general rule, an "agency terminates upon the death of the principal") and C.J.S. *Agency* §122 (2003) ("The fact that the agent has performed, as authorized, one or several acts of that which was contemplated as a single transaction does not operate to preserve or keep alive the power until the completion of the transaction."). *Id.* at 93-94, 713 S.E.2d at 648.

The court distinguished the effective date of the entitlement order from the date it was completed by Wachovia, which it defined as when the assets were credited to Wife's account, and it found the fourth transfer at issue was completed by Wachovia in October 2005, citing S.C. Code Ann. §36-8-501(b)(1) (providing a book entry by the securities intermediary to a person's account establishes a security entitlement). *Id.* at 94, 713 S.E.2d at 648. As a result, the court held the securities in the fourth transfer, having been credited after the bank's knowledge of Husband's death, are properly part of Husband's probate estate because the bank's authority under the Account Agreement had ended. *Id.* at 96, 713 S.E.2d at 649.

Several jurisdictions have observed there is a dearth of authority addressing the unique problems arising under Article 8 of the UCC. *See, e.g.,* Meadow Homes Dev. Corp. v. Bowens, 211 P.3d 743, 745 (Colo. App. 2009) (stating the "appeal raises issues of first impression under Revised UCC Article 8 (Investment Securities)" that had not previously been considered in the jurisdiction and that "have received surprisingly little attention elsewhere"); Watson v. Sears, 766 N.E.2d 784, 788 (Ind. Ct. App. 2002) ("Unfortunately, there is no discernible case law anywhere under revised Article 8 of the U.C.C. (Title 8 in Maryland)—and very little commentary—dealing with the question of the effect of an entitlement order that is authorized by only one of the entitlement holders on a joint account.").

As one legal commentator has opined, a significant body of case law has not developed for the indirect holding system, and the reported cases generally have applied whatever principles were necessary to protect an innocent investor, so they did not create well-reasoned legal doctrines to resolve the competing policies unique to the indirect holding system. Russell A. Hakes, *UCC Article 8: Will the Indirect Holding of Securities Survive the Light of Day?*, 35 Loy. L.A. L. Rev. 661, 678 (2002). "The drafters [of UCC Article 8] had the benefit of effectively starting with a clean slate." *Id.* "Troubling precedents could be overruled by the adoption of contrary concepts that matched the perceptions of those most familiar with the operation of the system-securities professionals." *Id.* "The interest and experience of securities professionals were essential to an Article 8 that could successfully govern the indirect holding system." *Id.*

"The securities industry did not want to use principles of bailment, agency, or trust law to describe the basic operations of the indirect holding system, even though agency law governs much in the relationship between the securities industry and its customers." *Id.* at 678-79. "One important goal in revising Article 8 was to simplify transfer rules for the indirect holding system." *Id.* at 679. Moreover, "[t]he drafters also caution courts not to use 'mechanical jurisprudence' but to interpret the definitions based upon the suitability of applying Article 8's substantive rules." *Id.* at 681 (citation omitted).

We agree with the Court of Appeals that the UCC does not invalidate all general principles of agency, but, as noted by the commentator above, those principles must be viewed in light of the unique nature of the indirect holding system. The UCC provisions were created to provide a uniform method of resolving issues in order to promote liquidity and finality, to be supplemented by (not thwarted by) the rules of agency and other applicable laws. *See* S.C. Code Ann. §§36-8-101 to -511 cmt. at 82 (2003 & Supp. 2013) (S.C. Reporter's Introductory Comment to the 2000 Revision) (observing the provisions in Part 5 of the UCC governing Investment Securities "supplant a pastiche of common law rules and agreed practices"); *see also* Psak, Graziano, Piasecki & Whitelaw v. Fleet Nat'l Bank, 390 N.J. Super. 199, 915 A.2d 42, 45

(Ct. App. Div. 2007) ("Indeed, the UCC displaces the common-law where reliance on the common law would thwart the purposes of the UCC." (citing Sebastian v. D & S Express, Inc., 61 F. Supp. 2d 386, 391 (D.N.J. 1999))).

In relying upon agency law to mandate that both Husband's execution of the entitlement order and full compliance by the securities intermediary exist prior to Husband's death, the Court of Appeals has created an additional requirement that does not exist under the UCC and that thwarts the purpose of the language in section 36-8-107(e) establishing a uniform effective date for entitlement orders, regardless of subsequent events. Moreover, it also overlooks the fact that under UCC section 36-8-501(b), the making of a "book entry" is but one of several means by which Wife can acquire an interest in the securities.

Once Husband issued the entitlement order and was the appropriate person, Wachovia was obligated by the UCC and the parties' Account Agreement to obey his directive. Wachovia had set up a new investment account in Wife's name and commenced the transfer of securities within a few days of Husband's request, so at that point, Wife already had a recognizable interest, even though Wachovia had not posted all of the securities to her account. The Court of Appeals, in focusing solely on the date of the "book entry," which it took to mean the date the securities were credited or posted to Wife's account, seemed to view this as the exclusive means for obtaining an interest in the securities. However, a security entitlement is created if a securities intermediary does *any* of the following three things:

(1) indicates by book entry that a financial asset has been credited to the person's securities account;
(2) receives a financial asset from the person or acquires a financial asset for the person and, in either case, accepts it for credit to the person's securities account; or
(3) becomes obligated under other law, regulation, or rule to credit a financial asset to the person's securities account.

S.C. Code Ann. §36-8-501(b).

In this case, while the Court of Appeals relied on book entry under subsection (b)(1), we agree with Wife that under subsection (b)(3), Wachovia had a legal obligation to credit the securities to Wife's account. As noted in the Official Comment to §8-501 of the Uniform Act:

Paragraph (3) of subsection (b) sets out a residual test, *to avoid any implication that the failure of an intermediary to make the appropriate entries* to credit a position to a customer's securities account *would prevent the customer from acquiring the rights* of an entitlement holder under Part 5. As is the case with the paragraph (2) test, the paragraph (3) test *would not be needed for the ordinary cases,* since they are covered by paragraph (1).

Unif. Commercial Code, Official Comment to §8-501, 2C U.L.A. 579, 581 (2005) (emphasis added).

Wachovia's failure to more quickly make the last posting to Wife's account clearly is not the ordinary case, and it falls squarely within the parameters of the residual provision in section 36-8-501(b)(3). Although the Court of Appeals treats the transfers as separate, unrelated events subject to termination under general agency law, we conclude Husband's execution of an entitlement order directing Wachovia to transfer certain specified securities to Wife is a singular act that falls squarely within the "prior act" language of the parties' agreement. Further, Wachovia's obligation to comply with Husband's entitlement order is supported by the UCC provisions examined above and comports with Article 8's goals of liquidity and finality in securities transactions. Consequently, we hold the disputed assets in this case properly belong to Wife and are not includible in Husband's probate estate.

IV. CONCLUSION

For the foregoing reasons, the decision of the Court of Appeals is reversed.

PROBLEM 176

Mr. Goldbury, an investor, told his broker, Bing, Bong & Bell (B.B. & B.), to buy him 100 shares of Utopia, Ltd. stock. The broker placed the order by having this number of shares transferred to the account it carried with Clearing Corporation. B.B. & B. then marked its books to reflect that Mr. Goldbury owned 100 shares of Utopia, Ltd.

(a) Using the definitions in §8-102, who are the *entitlement holder* and the *securities intermediary*, and what is the *security entitlement*? Who has a *securities account* as that phrase is defined in §8-501(a)?

(b) If the former owner of the 100 shares Mr. Goldbury purchased claims that they were stolen from her and somehow traces them to the account B.B. & B. has with Clearing Corporation, will she succeed in reclaiming the stock? See §8-502 and its Official Comment. If Mr. Goldbury decides to sell his stock, can the former owner announce her ownership rights to the world and thereby give such notice that no one could be free from her adverse claim? See §8-510(a) and (b).

(c) B.B. & B. became insolvent. Mr. Goldbury discovered that he was not the only owner of Utopia, Ltd. stock held by B.B. & B. but that Mr. Blushington also supposedly owned 100 shares of the same stock, according to B.B. & B.'s records. However, in violation of §8-504(a), B.B. & B. only had 50 shares of this stock in its account with Clearing Corporation. Mr. Goldbury's transaction with B.B. & B. occurred two days before Mr. Blushington's. Does that mean that he gets the entire 50 shares? See §8-503(b).

Powers v. American Express Financial Advisors, Inc.

United States Court of Appeals, Fourth Circuit, 2000
238 F.3d 414

Per Curiam.

Amy Powers and Michael D'Ambrosia, who lived together, had a joint investment account with American Express Financial Advisors (American Express). On the instructions of D'Ambrosia alone, American Express transferred all of the funds ($86,836.79) in the investment account to a bank account in the couple's joint name. After D'Ambrosia took all of the money, Powers sued American Express, claiming that its transfer to the bank account was ineffective because the signature of both owners of the investment account was required for a transfer of more than $50,000. The district court granted summary judgment to Powers and awarded her damages of $86,836.79, together with prejudgment interest. We affirm.

I.

Powers and D'Ambrosia began living together in 1983. On July 28, 1994, the couple opened an investment account, as joint tenants with right of survivorship, with American Express. The account was initially funded with a $15,000 transfer from the couple's joint bank account. Additions to the account were to come from D'Ambrosia's earnings. D'Ambrosia agreed to the joint account because Powers provided him with "domestic needs" and because she had contributed to improvements made to the couple's residence. To open the American Express account, Powers and D'Ambrosia filled out an investment application. In Section C of the application, Powers and D'Ambrosia checked the box next to the "Joint Tenant" provision, which reads:

> First and second clients have right of Survivorship. This is not the same as tenants-in-common. The first client's home or mailing address will be used for account-related purposes. You understand that only one signature is required for redemption requests up to $50,000.

The couple's application also directed American Express to place their money in four separate mutual funds.

On August 4, 1997, Powers and D'Ambrosia parted ways. By that time their American Express account was valued at over $80,000. Both of them contacted American Express and asked it to freeze the account. Later, in a letter dated September 26, 1997, D'Ambrosia and Powers authorized a release of the freeze and directed American Express to transfer the funds to a Prudential Securities account.

On October 15 and 16, 1997, D'Ambrosia sent American Express two separate faxes. The first, on October 15, contained a memo signed by D'Ambrosia, a copy of D'Ambrosia and Powers's statement of account at American Express, and a copy of the September 26 letter. D'Ambrosia's memo, included in the fax, changed the instructions in the September 26 letter. The memo directed American Express to close the couple's account and to mail the proceeds to D'Ambrosia and Powers's former residence in Columbia, MD. The second fax, dated October 16, also contained a memo from D'Ambrosia, a statement of the couple's account at American Express, and a copy of the September 26 letter. The memo attached to this fax again changed the instructions in the September 26 letter. The memo, signed only by D'Ambrosia, directed American Express to transfer the funds to a joint bank account held by Powers and D'Ambrosia at FCNB Bank. After receiving both faxes, American Express ignored the September 26 letter and followed the instruction in D'Ambrosia's October 16 fax memo. The company wired $86,836.79 to Powers and D'Ambrosia's FCNB joint account, and within a few days, D'Ambrosia absconded with the money.

When Powers discovered what had happened, she filed this action against American Express to recover the money. Both parties moved for summary judgment. Powers claimed that American Express transferred the funds in contravention of section 8-507(b) of Maryland's Commercial Code. See Md. Com. Law (U.C.C.) §8-507(b). Under U.C.C. §8-507(b), a "securities intermediary," like American Express, which transfers funds pursuant to an "ineffective entitlement order," is liable to an "entitlement holder" for any damages caused by the improper transfer. Powers contended that the faxes were ineffective entitlement orders because Section C of the investment application required both signatures for redemption requests over $50,000. Thus, as an entitlement holder, Powers claimed that American Express was liable to her for acting on D'Ambrosia's fax requests of October 15 and 16, 1997, which she did not sign. American Express claimed that Powers's authorization was not necessary. It claimed that D'Ambrosia's faxes constituted an effective entitlement order because, under U.C.C. §8-107(b)(1), D'Ambrosia was an "appropriate person" to order the transfer of the couple's funds.

The district court agreed with Powers that the faxes received by American Express constituted an "ineffective entitlement order." Powers v. American Express Fin. Advisors, Inc., 82 F. Supp. 2d 448, 452 (D. Md. 2000). The court recognized that Powers and D'Ambrosia were "entitlement holders" because as co-owners of the American Express account, "they were identified in the records of the securities intermediary (American Express) as having a security entitlement against the intermediary." Id. at 451. Because D'Ambrosia was an entitlement holder, the court acknowledged American Express's contention that D'Ambrosia was an "appropriate person" to give an entitlement order to American Express under U.C.C. §8-107. Id. at 451-52. The court also noted that when an "appropriate person" issues an entitlement order to a securities intermediary, the intermediary has a duty to execute the order under U.C.C. §8-507(a)(2). Id. at 452. The court decided, however, that section 8-507(a)(2) cannot be read in a vacuum because Section C of the couple's investment application with American Express requires the signatures of both investors for any redemption request above $50,000. The district court held that Section C's joint signature requirement was valid under U.C.C. §1-103. See id. at 453. Section 1-103 states that "the principles of law and equity . . . shall supplement [the U.C.C.]." Thus, "when an intermediary has agreed that the 'appropriate person' to make an order is both owners of a joint account, both owners must make the order." Id. Because Powers did not authorize or otherwise ratify the transfer of the $86,836.79 to an account at FCNB, the district court concluded that the transfer was ineffective. See id. at 452.

The district court also rejected American Express's assertion that the $50,000 threshold only applied to transfers from a single mutual fund account. See id. at 454. Because Powers and D'Ambrosia did not have more than $50,000 in any one of their four mutual funds, American Express asserted that two signatures were not required for the $86,836.79 redemption. The district court held, however, that American Express's interpretation was contrary to the plain language of Section C which states that "only one signature is required for redemption requests up to $50,000." Because the language of Section C refers to redemption requests generally and not to redemption requests out of individual funds, the district court concluded that two signatures were required for any transfer greater than $50,000. See id.

The district court summarily rejected American Express's remaining contentions. American Express claimed that Powers was barred from seeking damages under U.C.C. §8-115. According to U.C.C. §8-115, a securities intermediary is not liable to an individual who has an adverse claim to an asset that a securities intermediary transfers at the direction of a customer. The district court held that Powers was not an adverse claimant for the simple reason that she was one of two entitlement holders with respect to the account. See id. at 453.

Finally, the district court rejected American Express's request that the court impress the funds in the FCNB account with a constructive trust on behalf of D'Ambrosia's former employer, Signal Perfection Limited. See id. D'Ambrosia had been an accountant at Signal Perfection. Around December 1997 or January 1998, Signal Perfection discovered that D'Ambrosia had been embezzling money from the company for some time. In late January of 1998 D'Ambrosia and Signal Perfection signed a settlement agreement disposing of all claims the company had against D'Ambrosia. In exchange for the release D'Ambrosia assigned to Signal Perfection his interest in certain accounts, including the FCNB joint account. American Express argued that the district court should impose a constructive trust on the FCNB account because D'Ambrosia allegedly had deposited the converted American Express funds in that account. The district court denied American Express's request, holding that American Express did not have standing to seek a constructive trust on behalf of Signal Perfection and that, in any event, American Express had failed to demonstrate that it could trace the converted funds. See id.

Based on this reasoning, the district court granted Powers's motion for summary judgment and concluded that she was entitled to damages caused by American Express's improper transfer of the funds from the joint investment account. See id. at 454. The district court subsequently entered judgment against American Express in the amount of $86,836.79, together with prejudgment interest. See id. at 457-58. American Express appeals.

II.

After considering the joint appendix, the briefs, and the oral arguments of counsel, we are persuaded that the district court reached the correct result. We therefore affirm substantially on the reasoning of the district court. See Powers v. American Express Fin. Advisors, Inc., 82 F. Supp. 2d 448 (D. Md. 2000).

Affirmed.

CHAPTER 10   ASSESSMENT

Multiple Choice Questions

1. Careless Corporation had already issued all the stock it had power to issue but carelessly issued and sold an extra 100 shares to Rockefeller. What are Rockefeller's rights against Careless Corporation?
   a. Zero.
   b. Careless Corporation must amend its charter to authorize the additional shares.
   c. Careless Corporation must attempt to purchase substitute shares and if they are not reasonably available, refund to Rockefeller the money paid.
   d. Rockefeller's shares are valid, like any other shares.

2. Oversight Corporation's comptroller was in charge of handling stock certificates, but had not authority to issue or sign them. The comptroller, however, printed up 100 share certificates, forged the signature of the necessary corporate officers on the certificates, and sold them to a good faith purchaser without notice of the wrongdoing. What are the purchaser's rights?

   a. The certificates are effective.

   b. The purchaser takes the loss, for dealing with a forger.

   c. The certificates are ineffective, but the purchaser is entitled to the money from Oversight Corporation.

   d. The purchaser should try to sell them to someone else.

3. Share certificates of Rigid Corporation bear a conspicuous notice that shares may not be sold until the corporation has made an initial public offering, which has not taken place. Happy sold 100 shares to Grumpy, but Rigid Corporation's transfer agent refused to register the transfer. Is the corporation obliged to register the transfer?

   a. Yes. The shares have been sold and now belong to Grumpy.

   b. Yes. Shares are freely transferable and such restrictions are ineffective.

   c. No. The issuer has no obligation to register a transfer that does not comply with a restriction on transfer.

   d. No. The issuer has complete discretion about what to record in its own books.

4. Durant stole Whitney's certificates for shares in Morgan Corporation. Upon request by Durant, along with Whitney's forged signature, Morgan Corporation registered the shares, enabling Durant to sell them to Dow, a bona fide purchaser without notice. What are Whitney's rights?

   a. She can collect from Morgan Corporation for wrongful registration.

   b. She can claim the shares back from Dow.

   c. Both A and B.

   d. She has no rights against Morgan Corporation or Dow, only against Durant. She should have been more careful with the certificates, which are freely negotiable.

5. Paish, a trustee, breached her fiduciary duty by selling the trust's shares in XYZ Corp. and spending the money on a trip to Antarctica. Babson, the trust's beneficiary, somehow traced the shares, which are now held in Keynes' account at Friedman Securities. Can Babson recover the shares from Keynes?

   a. Yes. The shares still belong to the trust.

   b. Yes. The shares would be subject to a constructive trust, due to the wrongful sale.

    c. No. Keynes is protected from all claims, provided Keynes acquired the shares for value and without notice.

    d. Yes, because Keynes would merely have a securities entitlement against Friedman Securities, not a right to those particular shares.

Answers

1. C is the best answer. Under §8-210, in the event of overissue, the issuer must attempt to buy substitute shares. If they are not reasonably available, the issuer is liable for the amount last paid for the shares. The shares are not valid, because the corporation did not have power to issue them, contrary to D. Nor must the corporation amend its charter, so B is incorrect. These last two points are really matters of corporation law.

2. A is the best answer. Unauthorized signatures are normally ineffective, but are effective if made by an "employee entrusted with responsible handling of the security certificate." §8-205(2).

3. C is the best answer. An issuer is obliged to honor a transfer request that complies with §8-401, so D is incorrect. But §8-401 provides that an issuer need not register a transfer that is contrary to a valid restriction under §8-201, contrary to B. This restriction complies with §8-204, because it is noted conspicuously on the certificate. So even if the shares were purportedly sold, Rigid Corporation has no duty to recognize that sale, making A incorrect.

4. A is the best answer. Morgan Corporation is liable for wrongful registration under §8-404, due to the ineffective indorsement. This is quite similar to the rule for negotiable instruments. Whitney does not have rights against Dow, who is protected as a bona fide purchaser of registered shares, making B incorrect.

5. C is the best answer. This question is drawn from the Official Comment to §8-502, which explains that §8-502 precludes any action by Babson against Keynes under any theory, as long as Keynes acquired the security entitlement for value and without notice. Section 8-502 provides "investors in the indirect holding system with protection against adverse claims," as Official Comment 1 puts it. So claims based on ownership or constructive trust will fail, making A and B incorrect. That means Keynes has protection even though Keynes has a securities entitlement, as opposed to owning the security directly. That makes D incorrect.

1990 Version of §3-605

[This is the 1990 version of this section, which is the law in all jurisdictions (as of the summer of 2015) except Arkansas, District of Columbia, Indiana, Kentucky, Michigan, Minnesota, Mississippi, Nevada, New Mexico, Oklahoma, South Carolina, and Texas.]

§3-605. Discharge of Indorsers and Accommodation Parties

(a) In this section, the term "indorser" includes a drawer having the obligation described in Section 3-414(d).

(b) Discharge, under Section 3-604, of the obligation of a party to pay an instrument does not discharge the obligation of an indorser or accommodation party having a right of recourse against the discharged party.

(c) If a person entitled to enforce an instrument agrees, with or without consideration, to an extension of the due date of the obligation of a party to pay the instrument, the extension discharges an indorser or accommodation party having a right of recourse against the party whose obligation is extended to the extent the indorser or accommodation party proves that the extension caused loss to the indorser or accommodation party with respect to the right of recourse.

(d) If a person entitled to enforce an instrument agrees, with or without consideration, to a material modification of the obligation of a party other than an extension of the due date, the modification discharges the obligation of an indorser or accommodation party having a right of recourse against the person whose obligation is modified to the extent the modification causes loss to the indorser or accommodation party with respect to the right of recourse. The loss suffered by the indorser or accommodation party as a result of the modification is equal to the amount of the right of recourse unless the person enforcing the instrument proves that no loss was caused by the modification or that the loss caused by the modification was an amount less than the amount of the right of recourse.

(e) If the obligation of a party to pay an instrument is secured by an interest in collateral and a person entitled to enforce the instrument impairs the value of the interest in collateral, the obligation of an indorser or accommodation party having a right of recourse against the obligor is discharged to the extent of the impairment. The value of an interest in collateral is impaired to the extent (i) the value of the interest is reduced to an amount less than the amount of the right of recourse of the party asserting discharge, or (ii) the reduction in value of the interest causes an increase in the amount by which the amount of the right of recourse exceeds the value of the interest. The burden of proving impairment is on the party asserting discharge.

(f) If the obligation of a party is secured by an interest in collateral not provided by an accommodation party and a person entitled to enforce the instrument impairs the value of the interest in collateral, the obligation of any party who is jointly and severally liable with respect to the secured obligation is discharged to the extent the impairment causes the party asserting discharge to pay more than that party would have been obliged to pay, taking into account rights of contribution, if impairment had not occurred. If the party asserting discharge is an accommodation party not entitled to discharge under subsection (e), the party is deemed to have a right to contribution based on joint and several liability rather than a right to reimbursement. The burden of proving impairment is on the party asserting discharge.

(g) Under subsection (e) or (f), impairing value of an interest in collateral includes (i) failure to obtain or maintain perfection or recordation of the interest in collateral, (ii) release of collateral without substitution of collateral of equal value, (iii) failure to perform a duty to preserve the value of collateral owed, under Article 9 or other law, to a debtor or surety or other person secondarily liable, or (iv) failure to comply with applicable law in disposing of collateral.

(h) An accommodation party is not discharged under subsection (c), (d), or (e) unless the person entitled to enforce the instrument knows of the accommodation or has notice under Section 3-419(c) that the instrument was signed for accommodation.

(i) A party is not discharged under this section if (i) the party asserting discharge consents to the event or conduct that is the basis of the discharge, or (ii) the instrument or a separate agreement of the party provides for waiver of discharge under this section either specifically or by general language indicating that parties waive defenses based on suretyship or impairment of collateral.

OFFICIAL COMMENT

1. Section 3-605, which replaces former Section 3-606, can be illustrated by an example. Bank lends $10,000 to Borrower who signs a note under which Borrower is obliged to pay $10,000 to Bank on a due date stated in the note. Bank insists, however, that Accommodation Party also become liable to pay the note. Accommodation Party can incur this liability by signing the note as a co-maker or by indorsing the note. In either case the note is signed for accommodation and Borrower is the accommodated party. Rights and obligations of Accommodation Party in this case are stated in Section 3-419. Suppose that after the note is signed, Bank agrees to a modification of the rights and obligations between Bank and Borrower. For example, Bank agrees that Borrower may pay the note at some date after the due date, or that Borrower may discharge Borrower's $10,000 obligation to pay the note by paying Bank $3,000, or that Bank releases collateral given by Borrower to secure the note. Under the law of suretyship Borrower is usually referred to as the principal debtor and Accommodation Party is referred to as the surety. Under that law, the surety can be discharged under certain circumstances if changes of this kind are made by Bank, the creditor, without the consent of Accommodation Party, the surety. Rights of the surety to discharge in such cases are commonly referred to as suretyship defenses. Section 3-605 is concerned with this kind of problem in the context of a negotiable instrument to which the principal debtor and the surety are parties. But Section 3-605 has a wider scope. It also applies to indorsers who are not accommodation parties. Unless an indorser signs without recourse, the indorser's liability under Section 3-415(a) is that of a guarantor of payment. If Bank in our

hypothetical case indorsed the note and transferred it to Second Bank, Bank has rights given to an indorser under Section 3-605 if it is Second Bank that modifies rights and obligations of Borrower. Both accommodation parties and indorsers will be referred to in these Comments as sureties. The scope of Section 3-605 is also widened by subsection (e) which deals with rights of a non-accommodation party co-maker when collateral is impaired.

2. The importance of suretyship defenses is greatly diminished by the fact that they can be waived. The waiver is usually made by a provision in the note or other writing that represents the obligation of the principal debtor. It is standard practice to include a waiver of suretyship defenses in notes given to financial institutions or other commercial creditors. Section 3-605(i) allows waiver. Thus, Section 3-605 applies to the occasional case in which the creditor did not include a waiver clause in the instrument or in which the creditor did not obtain the permission of the surety to take the action that triggers the suretyship defense.

3. Subsection (b) addresses the effect of discharge under Section 3-604 of the principal debtor. In the hypothetical case stated in Comment 1, release of Borrower by Bank does not release Accommodation Party. As a practical matter, Bank will not gratuitously release Borrower. Discharge of Borrower normally would be part of a settlement with Borrower if Borrower is insolvent or in financial difficulty. If Borrower is unable to pay all creditors, it may be prudent for Bank to take partial payment, but Borrower will normally insist on a release of the obligation. If Bank takes $3,000 and releases Borrower from the $10,000 debt, Accommodation Party is not injured. To the extent of the payment Accommodation Party's obligation to Bank is reduced. The release of Borrower by Bank does not affect the right of Accommodation Party to obtain reimbursement from Borrower or to enforce the note against Borrower if Accommodation Party pays Bank. Section 3-419(e). Subsection (b) is designed to allow a creditor to settle with the principal debtor without risk of losing rights against sureties. Settlement is in the interest of sureties as well as the creditor. Subsection (b), however, is not intended to apply to a settlement of a disputed claim which discharges the obligation.

Subsection (b) changes the law stated in former Section 3-606 but the change relates largely to formalities rather than substance. Under former Section 3-606, Bank in the hypothetical case stated in Comment 1 could settle with and release Borrower without releasing Accommodation Party, but to accomplish that result Bank had to either obtain the consent of Accommodation Party or make an express reservation of rights against Accommodation Party at the time it released Borrower. The reservation of rights was made in the agreement between Bank and Borrower by which the release of Borrower was made. There was no requirement in former Section 3-606 that any notice be given to Accommodation Party. Section 3-605 elimi-nates the necessity that Bank formally reserve rights against Accommodation

Party in order to retain rights of recourse against Accommodation Party. See PEB Commentary No. 11, dated February 10, 1994 [Appendix II, Vol. 3A Uniform Laws Annotated, Master Edition or ULA Database on Westlaw].

4. Subsection (c) relates to extensions of the due date of the instrument. In most cases an extension of time to pay a note is a benefit to both the principal debtor and sureties having recourse against the principal debtor. In relatively few cases the extension may cause loss if deterioration of the financial condition of the principal debtor reduces the amount that the surety will be able to recover on its right of recourse when default occurs. Former Section 3-606(1)(a) did not take into account the presence or absence of loss to the surety. For example, suppose the instrument is an installment note and the principal debtor is temporarily short of funds to pay a monthly installment. The payee agrees to extend the due date of the installment for a month or two to allow the debtor to pay when funds are available. Under former Section 3-606 surety was discharged if consent was not given unless the payee expressly reserved rights against the surety. It did not matter that the extension of time was a trivial change in the guaranteed obligation and that there was no evidence that the surety suffered any loss because of the extension. Wilmington Trust Co. v. Gesullo, 29 U.C.C. Rep. 144 (Del. Super. Ct. 1980). Under subsection (c) an extension of time results in discharge only to the extent the surety proves that the extension caused loss. For example, if the extension is for a long period the surety might be able to prove that during the period of extension the principal debtor became insolvent, thus reducing the value of the right of recourse of the surety. By putting the burden on the surety to prove loss, subsection (c) more accurately reflects what the parties would have done by agreement, and it facilitates workouts.

Under other provisions of Article 3, what is the effect of an extension agreement between the holder of a note and the maker who is an accommodated party? The question is illustrated by the following case:

Case #1. A borrows money from Lender and issues a note payable on April 1, 1992. B signs the note for accommodation at the request of Lender. B signed the note either as co-maker or as an anomalous indorser. In either case Lender subsequently makes an agreement with A extending the due date of A's obligation to pay the note to July 1, 1992. In either case B did not agree to the extension.

What is the effect of the extension agreement on B? Could Lender enforce the note against B if the note is not paid on April 1, 1992? A's obligation to Lender to pay the note on April 1, 1992 may be modified by the agreement of Lender. If B is an anomalous indorser Lender cannot enforce the note against B unless the note has been dishonored. Section 3-415(a). Under Section 3-502(a)(3) dishonor occurs if it is not paid on the day it becomes payable. Since the agreement between A and Lender extended the due date of A's obligation to July 1, 1992 there is no dishonor because A was not obligated to pay Lender on April 1, 1992. If B is a co-maker the analysis is somewhat different. Lender has no power to amend the terms of the note without the consent of both A and B. By an agreement with A, Lender can extend the due date of A's obligation to Lender to pay the note but B's obligation is to pay the note according to the terms of the note at the time of issue. Section 3-412. However, B's obligation to pay the note is subject to a defense because B is an accommodation party. B is not obliged to pay Lender if A is not obliged to pay Lender. Under Section 3-305(d), B as an accommodation party can assert against Lender any defense of A. A has a defense based on the extension agreement. Thus, the result is that Lender could not enforce the note against B until July 1, 1992. This result is consistent with the right of B if B is an anomalous indorser.

As a practical matter an extension of the due date will normally occur when the accommodated party is unable to pay on the due date. The interest of the accommodation party normally is to defer payment to the holder rather than to pay right away and rely on an action against the accommodated party that may have little or no value. But in unusual cases the accommodation party may prefer to pay the holder on the original due date. In such cases, the accommodation party may do so. This is because the extension agreement between the accommodated party and the holder cannot bind the accommodation party to a change in its obligation without the accommodation party's consent. The effect on the recourse of the accommodation party against the accommodation party of performance by the accommodation party on the original due date is not addressed in §3-419 and is left to the general law of suretyship.

Even though an accommodation party has the option of paying the instrument on the original due date, the accommodation party is not precluded from asserting its rights to discharge under Section 3-605(c) if it does not exercise that option. The critical issue is whether the extension caused the accommodation party a loss by increasing the difference between its cost of performing its obligation on the instrument and the amount recoverable from the accommodated party pursuant to Section 3-419(e). The decision by the accommodation party not to exercise its option to pay on the original due date may, under the circumstances, be a factor to be considered in the determination of that issue. See PEB Commentary No. 11, dated February 10, 1994 [Appendix II Vol. 3A Uniform Laws Annotated, Master Edition or ULA Database on Westlaw].

5. Former Section 3-606 applied to extensions of the due date of a note but not to other modifications of the obligation of the principal debtor. There was no apparent reason why former Section 3-606 did not follow general suretyship law in covering both. Under Section 3-605(d) a material modification of the obligation of the principal debtor, other than an extension

of the due date, will result in discharge of the surety to the extent the modification caused loss to the surety with respect to the right of recourse. The loss caused by the modification is deemed to be the entire amount of the right of recourse unless the person seeking enforcement of the instrument proves that no loss occurred or that the loss was less than the full amount of the right of recourse. In the absence of that proof, the surety is completely discharged. The rationale for having different rules with respect to loss for extensions of the due date and other modifications is that extensions are likely to be beneficial to the surety and they are often made. Other modifications are less common and they may very well be detrimental to the surety. Modification of the obligation of the principal debtor without permission of the surety is unreasonable unless the modification is benign. Subsection (d) puts the burden on the person seeking enforcement of the instrument to prove the extent to which loss was not caused by the modification.

The following is an illustration of the kind of case to which Section 3-605(d) would apply:

Case #2. Corporation borrows money from Lender and issues a note payable to Lender. X signs the note as an accommodation party for Corporation. The loan agreement under which the note was issued states various events of default which allow Lender to accelerate the due date of the note. Among the events of default are breach of covenants not to incur debt beyond specified limits and not to engage in any line of business substantially different from that currently carried on by Corporation. Without consent of X, Lender agrees to modify the covenants to allow Corporation to enter into a new line of business that X considers to be risky, and to incur debt beyond the limits specified in the loan agreement to finance the new venture. This modification releases X unless Lender proves that the modification did not cause loss to X or that the loss caused by the modification was less than X's right of recourse.

Sometimes there is both an extension of the due date and some other modification. In that case both subsections (c) and (d) apply. The following is an example:

Case #3. Corporation was indebted to Lender on a note payable on April 1, 1992 and X signed the note as an accommodation party for Corporation. The interest rate on the note was 12 percent. Lender and Corporation agreed to a six-month extension of the due date of the note to October 1, 1992 and an increase in the interest rate to 14 percent after April 1, 1992. Corporation defaulted on October 1, 1992. Corporation paid no interest during the six-month extension period. Corporation is insolvent and has no assets from which unsecured creditors can be paid. Lender demanded payment from X.

Assume X is an anomalous indorser. First consider Section 3-605(c) alone. If there had been no change in the interest rate, the fact that Lender gave an extension of six months to Corporation would not result in discharge unless X could prove loss with respect to the right of recourse because of the extension. If the financial condition of Corporation on April 1, 1992 would not have allowed any recovery on the right of recourse, X can't show any loss as a result of the extension with respect to the amount due on the note on April 1, 1992. Since the note accrued interest during the six-month extension, is there a loss equal to the accrued interest? Since the interest rate was not raised, only Section 3-605(c) would apply and X probably could not prove any loss. The obligation of X includes interest on the note until the note is paid. To the extent payment was delayed X had the use of the money that X otherwise would have had to pay to Lender. X could have prevented the running of interest by paying the debt. Since X did not do so, X suffered no loss as the result of the extension.

If the interest rate was raised, Section 3-605(d) also must be considered. If X is an anomalous indorser, X's liability is to pay the note according to its terms at the time of indorsement. Section 3-415(a). Thus, X's obligation to pay interest is measured by the terms of the note (12%) rather than by the increased amount of 14 percent. The same analysis applies if X had been a co-maker. Under Section 3-412 the liability of the issuer of a note is to pay the note according to its terms at the time it was issued. Either obligation could be changed by contract and that occurred with respect to Corporation when it agreed to the increase in the interest rate, but X did not join in that agreement and is not bound by it. Thus, the most that X can be required to pay is the amount due on the note plus interest at the rate of 12 percent.

Does the modification discharge X under Section 3-605(d)? Any modification that increases the monetary obligation of X is material. An increase of the interest rate from 12 percent to 14 percent is certainly a material modification. There is a presumption that X is discharged because Section 3-605(d) creates a presumption that the modification caused a loss to X equal to the amount of the right of recourse. Thus, Lender has the burden of proving absence of loss or a loss less than the amount of the right of recourse. Since Corporation paid no interest during the six-month period, the issue is like the issue presented under Section 3-605(c) which we have just discussed. The increase in the interest rate could not have affected the right of recourse because no interest was paid by Corporation. X is in the same position as X would have been in if there had been an extension without an increase in the interest rate.

The analysis with respect to Section 3-605(c) and (d) would have been different if we change the assumptions. Suppose Corporation was not insolvent on April 1, 1992, that Corporation paid interest at the higher rate during the six-month period, and that Corporation was insolvent at the end of the six-month period. In this case it is possible that the extension and the additional burden placed on Corporation by the increased interest rate may have been detrimental to X.

There are difficulties in properly allocating burden of proof when the agreement between Lender and Corporation involves both an extension under Section 3-605(c) and a modification under Section 3-605(d). The agreement may have caused loss to X but it may be difficult to identify the extent to which the loss was caused by the extension or the other modification. If neither Lender nor X introduces evidence on the issue, the result is full discharge because Section 3-605(d) applies. Thus, Lender has the burden of overcoming the presumption in Section 3-605(d). In doing so, Lender should be entitled to a presumption that the extension of time by itself caused no loss. Section 3- 605(c) is based on such a presumption and X should be required to introduce evidence on the effect of the extension on the right of recourse. Lender would have to introduce evidence on the effect of the increased interest rate. Thus, both sides will have to introduce evidence. On the basis of this evidence the court will have to make a determination of the overall effect of the agreement on X's right of recourse. See PEB Commentary No. 11, dated February 10, 1994 [Appendix II Vol. 3A Uniform Laws Annotated, Master Edition or ULA Database on Westlaw].

6. Subsection (e) deals with discharge of sureties by impairment of collateral. It generally conforms to former Section 3-606(1)(b). Subsection (g) states common examples of what is meant by impairment. By using the term "includes," it allows a court to find impairment in other cases as well. There is extensive case law on impairment of collateral. The surety is discharged to the extent the surety proves that impairment was caused by a person entitled to enforce the instrument. For example, suppose the payee of a secured note fails to perfect the security interest. The collateral is owned by the principal debtor who subsequently files in bankruptcy. As a result of the failure to perfect, the security interest is not enforceable in bankruptcy. If the payee obtains payment from the surety, the surety is subrogated to the payee's security interest in the collateral. In this case the value of the security interest is impaired completely because the security interest is unenforceable. If the value of the collateral is as much or more than the amount of the note there is a complete discharge.

In some states a real property grantee who assumes the obligation of the grantor as maker of a note secured by the real property becomes by operation of law a principal debtor and the grantor becomes a surety. The meager case authority was split on whether former Section 3-606 applied to release the grantor if the holder released or extended the obligation of the grantee. Revised Article 3 takes no position on the effect of the release of the grantee in this case. Section 3-605(b) does not apply because the holder has not discharged the obligation of a "party," a term defined in Section

3-103(a)(8) as "party to an instrument." The assuming grantee is not a party to the instrument. The resolution of this question is governed by general principles of law, including the law of suretyship. See PEB Commentary No. 11, dated February 10, 1994 [Appendix II Vol. 3A Uniform Laws Annotated, Master Edition or ULA Database on Westlaw].

7. Subsection (f) is illustrated by the following case. X and Y sign a note for $1,000 as co-makers. Neither is an accommodation party. X grants a security interest in X's property to secure the note. The collateral is worth more than $1,000. Payee fails to perfect the security interest in X's property before X files in bankruptcy. As a result, the security interest is not enforceable in bankruptcy. Had Payee perfected the security interest, Y could have paid the note and gained rights to X's collateral by subrogation. If the security interest had been perfected, Y could have realized on the collateral to the extent of $500 to satisfy its right of contribution against X. Payee's failure to perfect deprived Y of the benefit of the collateral. Subsection (f) discharges Y to the extent of its loss. If there are no assets in the bankruptcy for unsecured claims, the loss is $500, the amount of Y's contribution claim against X which now has a zero value. If some amount is payable on unsecured claims, the loss is reduced by the amount receivable by Y. The same result follows if Y is an accommodation party but Payee has no knowledge of the accommodation or notice under Section 3-419(c). In that event Y is not discharged under subsection (e), but subsection (f) applies because X and Y are jointly and severally liable on the note. Under subsection (f), Y is treated as a co-maker with a right of contribution rather than an accommodation party with a right of reimbursement. Y is discharged to the extent of $500. If Y is the principal debtor and X is the accommodation party subsection (f) doesn't apply. Y, as principal debtor, is not injured by the impairment of collateral because Y would have been obliged to reimburse X for the entire $1,000 even if Payee had obtained payment from sale of the collateral.

8. Subsection (i) is a continuation of former law which allowed suretyship defenses to be waived. As the subsection provides, a party is not discharged under this section if the instrument or a separate agreement of the party waives discharge either specifically or by general language indicating that defenses based on suretyship and impairment of collateral are waived. No particular language or form of agreement is required, and the standards for enforcing such a term are the same as the standards for enforcing any other term in an instrument or agreement.

Subsection (i), however, applies only to a "discharge under this section." The right of an accommodation party to be discharged under Section 3-605(e) because of an impairment of collateral can be waived. But with respect to a note secured by personal property collateral, Article 9 also applies. If an accommodation party is a "debtor" under Section 9-105(1)(d), the accommodation party has rights under Article 9. Under Section

9-501(3)(b) rights of an Article 9 debtor under Section 9-504(3) and Section 9-505(1), which deal with disposition of collateral, cannot be waived except as provided in Article 9. These Article 9 rights are independent of rights under Section 3-605. Since Section 3-605(i) is specifically limited to discharge under Section 3-605, a waiver of rights with respect to Section 3-605 has no effect on rights under Article 9. With respect to Article 9 rights, Section 9-501(3)(b) controls. See PEB Commentary No. 11, dated February 10, 1994 [Appendix II Vol. 3A Uniform Laws Annotated, Master Edition or ULA Database on Westlaw].

TABLE OF STATUTES